Snow
on the Pine

Japan's Quest for
a Leadership Role in Asia

Snow
on the Pine

Japan's Quest for
a Leadership Role in Asia

Kyoko Hatakeyama
Craig F Freedman
Macquarie University, Australia

World Scientific

NEW JERSEY · LONDON · SINGAPORE · BEIJING · SHANGHAI · HONG KONG · TAIPEI · CHENNAI

Published by

World Scientific Publishing Co. Pte. Ltd.

5 Toh Tuck Link, Singapore 596224

USA office: 27 Warren Street, Suite 401-402, Hackensack, NJ 07601

UK office: 57 Shelton Street, Covent Garden, London WC2H 9HE

British Library Cataloguing-in-Publication Data
A catalogue record for this book is available from the British Library.

First published 2010 (Hard cover)
Reprinted 2015 (in paperback edition)
ISBN 978-981-4730-37-2

SNOW ON THE PINE
Japan's Quest for a Leadership Role in Asia

ISBN-13 978-981-4289-99-3
ISBN-10 981-4289-99-X

Typeset by Stallion Press
Email: enquiries@stallionpress.com

For Ayami and Hisaya Uesugi

Foreword

Courageous Pine —
enduring the snow
that is piling up,
color unchanging.
Let people be like this
Emperor Hirohito, as quoted in Dower (1999, p. 318).

It is difficult to convince a trained economist that economic incentives are not the mainspring of all human actions. These narrowly focused academic scribblers are inclined to replace the dramatic heart of darkness dwelling at the center of daily activity with a more comprehensible and pointedly mundane cash register. Naturally then, their immediate impulse when confronted by the measured phrases of the professional diplomat is to begin an extensive search for vested economic interests.

As a result, the initial suggestion by my co-author that economics was only a means of achieving clear-cut foreign policy objectives was met with a good deal of scepticism on my part. As an economist, I implicitly assumed that foreign policy was only economic competition by some other means. This firmly held belief was then further aggravated by a determined insistence that the underlying motivation of post-war policy in Japan was not only innocent of purely economic motivations but entirely consistent with a foreign policy stance that stretched back to the Meiji period. As an analytical position, this was far removed from the received wisdom on this subject and, at least superficially, distinctly detached from more obvious explanations of post-war events. However, when dealing with matters Japanese, a researcher should be well aware that it is often wise to eschew superficial appearances (*tatemae*) and instead dig much deeper in the hope of discovering at least a small chunk of reality (*honne*).

Economic issues have always been a crucial motivating element behind policy measures. Losing the Pacific War did nothing to change that. But economic interests have always composed only one among a number of threads forming foreign policy decisions. What my astute co-author makes clear is that the drive to dominate and influence East Asia has been the consistent determinant motivating Japan's diplomatic maneuvres since the Meiji restoration. Tactics and even strategies over time have changed to meet the ever-evolving economic and political environment, but the overall objective has remained much the same. Thus, foreign policy has not simply been a stripped-down vehicle to assist Japanese economic development. Instead, we have become increasingly convinced that understanding foreign policy is not simply a matter of searching for and assigning the relevant set of economic incentives to each critical event. If it was, then Japan's long-running battle over its insistence on conducting what it has fancifully labeled "scientific whaling" could only be described as downright lunacy. Japan's refusal to budge from this stubbornly held position in recent years has had little, if anything, to do with economic consequences or advantages.

We find a policy that has almost carelessly irritated two of its major trading partners, Australia and the US, both of which must face widespread public displeasure at what is often portrayed as a needless slaughter of whales. Even so, such a policy might begin to make some economic sense if it was clearly a matter of appeasing some key domestic special interest.[1] But not only is whaling a non-viable industry that requires explicit subsidisation to survive; it affects and has the support of no discernable voting group. Instead, we seem to have a distinct instance of diplomatic symbolism. Whaling has been transformed into an issue of Japanese nationalism, namely the right of Japan as a sovereign nation to make its own, independent decisions, even if such decisions seem to be conspicuously devoid of any overt rationality or

---

[1]We have often thought that a campaign which would transform whales into lovably cute cartoon figures would end the whaling issue by mobilizing the Japanese population against destroying such adorable animals.

even intelligence. It is an assertion of self that is more commonly stumbled across in the writing of Dostoevsky than in the more turgid pages of an economics textbook.

In much the same way, reducing post-war diplomacy to a simple effort to foster economic interests misses much of the real purpose behind Japanese diplomacy and other overseas activity. Our modest contribution then seeks to correct such a simple-minded approach. To read this account is to understand the consistency of Japanese foreign policy, instead of viewing such diplomatic efforts as episodic and ever changing. The snow melts, the pine endures.

Kyoko Hatakeyama and Craig Freedman
August 2009

Reference

Dower JW. (1999) *Embracing Defeat*. W.W. Norton & Company, Inc., New York.

Acknowledgments

The authors and publisher would like to acknowledge earlier versions of the following chapters:

Chapter 9 "Intellectual leadership: Japan's relationship with Vietnam" appeared in an earlier version as "Japan's aid to Vietnam: Becoming an intellectual leader?" in *Japanese Studies*, 28(3), 345–364, 2008.

Chapter 11 "*Tatemae* and *Honne*: Understanding the post-war Japanese economy" appeared in an earlier version as "Japan: Myth and reality" in Chowdhury A (ed.), *Handbook of Northeast and Southeast Asian Economies*, pp. 17–42, 2007, Edward Elgar, Cheltenham.

Chapter 12 "The long arm of the Japanese economy: The role of foreign direct investment in post-war Japan" appeared in an earlier version as "The handmaiden's tale: Japan's foreign investment as a reflection of its domestic economy" (written with Alex Blair and Demi Chung), *International Journal of Business and Globalisation*, [forthcoming] 2009.

The first 10 chapters derive largely from the work that Kyoko Hatakeyama developed as a PhD student under the supervision of Craig Freedman. Of course, over the years, this work has been mutually fertilized by numerous discussions between the two authors.

Contents

Chapter 1

Unpacking Japanese Foreign Policy: The Case Against Conventional Wisdom

1.1 Cracking the Code: Discovering the Reality behind Japan's Diplomacy

Japan's post-war economic success created a heated debate over Japan's broader intentions. What would the Japanese do with their newfound wealth? Leading academics, and other commentators on Asian-Pacific trends, questioned whether, buoyed by success, renewed ambitions might lead the Japanese to seek a more dominant regional position. At the peak of their success in the early 1990s, more than 90 percent of business executives and scholars in Indonesia, Thailand and the Philippines, responding to a poll, thought that Japan should lay claim to such a leadership role (Fallows, 1994, p. 251).[1] However, even more fundamental than the issue of whether Japan should actively seize such a position has been the difficulty in discerning what the very nature of that Japanese leadership might be, if it in fact ever came to be wielded. Upon examination, what sort of power or influence the Japanese might care to exert is far from a straightforward matter. In the post-war era, what passes for Japanese leadership tends to be invisible, at least to outsiders. This lack of definition may stem from the societal value placed on consensus and harmony when reaching a decision (Hayao, 1993,

---

[1] It should come as no surprise that a majority of those polled in China and South Korea disagreed.

1

pp. 6–7; Nakane, 1970). This approach tends to bury the process and gloss over the issues at stake. The Japanese typically try to arrive at a behind-the-scenes consensus. The final agreement is meant to encompass all participants, leaving little, if any, room for public conflict or heated argument. As former Prime Minister Noboru Takeshita once insisted, "It is the role of the leader today not to pull people along, it is to get the consensus of the people" (Hayao, 1993, pp. 6–7).

This implicit approach, that is so much a hallmark of domestic politics, also extends to Japan's diplomatic policy. Since it is not an overtly top-down regimen, leadership efforts tend to be largely imperceptible. But a subtle nature does not imply an absence of Japanese ambition. Quite the opposite is the actual case. This tendency has become increasingly explicit over the last few decades. Despite an inherent dislike of overt pretension, the subtitle of the 1999 'Bible' of the Foreign Ministry (Ministry of Foreign Affairs, 1999) bears the caption, "Diplomacy with a Leadership Role." Japan has become steadily more assertive and confident despite moments of confusion and seeming indecision. Though more apparent these last two decades, this drive for recognition, as well as for a leadership position among Asian nations, is nothing new. Japan's power aspirations date back to the opening up of a previously self-enclosed country.

Following the end of 250 years of isolation under the Tokugawa regime, Japan embarked, after the 1868 Meiji Restoration, on a modernization program designed to enrich the country and strengthen its military power. More precisely, the prevailing belief at this time was that a rich country was also a strong country. This status was to be sought after, not merely as a matter of achieving the respect Japan yearned for but rather, to survive as a strong and independent nation. Japan was quite naturally reluctant to travel down the same dismal road that the rest of Asia had. Part of national honor then, as well as pragmatic survival, demanded that Japan become the equal of any of the ruling Western powers.

This modernization period was an era defined and dominated by early 20th-century imperialism. After being forced to end its isolation, Japan faced a bleak reality characterized by an internationally ordained "law of the jungle." In order not to follow the same fate as other colonized nations in the region, Japan had to urgently, and rapidly, "catch up with the West" by "strengthening the army and enriching the nation." Japan had been tossed into what was essentially a "dog-eat-dog" situation with the Japanese not relishing the prospect of becoming lunch. The newly formed Japanese government became convinced that only by evolving into at least a recognized regional power[2] could Japan hope to continue to survive as a truly independent country. To accomplish this goal, the Japanese political leaders of the day realized the necessity of creating a favorable environment to ensure Japan's national identity and survival. They agreed with the prevailing rationale embraced by their Western counterparts. Strategic defense at times required aggressive, if not brutal, action buttressed by a strong and secure economy. Strength was built by creating an environment where a growing economy could support a strong army and navy. Military force was then the best means by which Japan could not only maintain its identity, but flourish and grow even stronger.

However, tactics must change with the times. A defeated and devastated Japan had to forswear all future military aspirations after the misfortune of the Pacific War.[3] In the post-war period, Japan had little choice but to pursue a course of intensive economic rehabilitation. Japan during this new period once again embarked on a national building process, devoting most of its resources and energy not to military strength, but rather to economic revival. National defense, at this time, was deemed a luxury to be avoided, rather than pursued. Being unable to provide for their own security, the Japanese had no other viable choice than to accept protection thrust upon them by their American occupiers.[4]

---

[2]What it might mean for a country to become a powerful nation is less than obvious. For purposes of simplicity, we will use the idea of Japanese power as the simple ability to influence other nations to act in a way that would benefit Japan. Note that this need not be accomplished by exercising overt force.

[3]Japan's industrial production declined to 30 percent and its agricultural production dropped down to about 60 percent of pre-war (1924–1926) levels (Ministry of Foreign Affairs, 1985, p. 55).

[4]The simple rationale for this behavior was the infamous Article 9 in the American conceived constitution. However, this provided a convenient rationale rather than an actual policy-shaping reality. The war weary population had firmly turned its back on the former military state and its values. In addition, Japan's neighbors were quick to interpret any ambiguous, let alone explicit, military gesture as a return of Japan's old, discredited ambitions. A full status military establishment lacked any feasibility at this time with or without constitutional prohibitions.

The result of this turning away from all things military was Japan's well-publicized "economic miracle."[5] In contrast to its pre-war strategy, Japan would try to garner a symmetrical level of influence through foreign assistance rather than by coercion. Driven by its economic growth Japan became, by 1989, the world's largest aid donor, although inevitably after the sluggish growth of the 1990s, slipping once more behind the US in 2001.[6] Japan did succeed in becoming a veritable economic powerhouse whose shadow over the years would loom ever larger. In fact, today, no international organization can operate effectively without a significant contribution from Japan.[7] But whether this economic virility has translated into the leadership role that Japan coveted for so long is a more complex question.

Still, despite its avowed pacifism, Japan has been able to gradually afford and develop a real military capability over the years, though ostensibly restricted to defensive purposes only. It is now a serious force even judged by global standards, let alone restricted to a more parochial basis (Drifte, 1990, p. 35). However, any overt offensive use is still prohibited under Article 9 of the constitution. Japan's armed forces can only constitutionally be maintained exclusively for defense-oriented policies (Ministry of Foreign Affairs, 1992, p. 29).[8] Given

---

[5] The reasons for a basic tripling of Japan's economy, from 1955 to 1970, remain a subject of academic debate both then and now. For example, Chalmers Johnson (1982) argued that Japan is a developmental state. He pointed to the administrative guidance provided by the Ministry of International Trade and Industry (MITI). Johnson insisted that the Ministry exercised overwhelming power to intervene within Japan's economy. According to his reasoning, this intensive oversight consequently brought about quick and miraculous success. It is certainly undeniable that during those decades when Japan focused on economic development without any equivalent attention paid to security matters, MITI managed to have a decisive influence not only on Japan's trade policy but on its foreign policy as well. Daniel Okimoto (1989) also located this causative power as lying within Japan's domestic politics and bureaucracy. On the other hand, Pempel (1978) denied that Japan has been or currently is a neo-mercantilist state and argues that the "definition and implementation of foreign economic policy in Japan rests essentially on the domestic political structures of the country, particularly strength of the state and its network of conservative support" (1978, p. 145).

[6] The then Prime Minister Koizumi made a show of belt-tightening and reform by slashing the Official Development Assistance (ODA) budget. Rumors insisted that this was actually a ploy to undercut his political rivals in the LDP.

[7] Japan contributed $24 billion (20.6 percent of the total fund) to the UN in 2000.

[8] The Self-Defense Forces (SDF) has no offensive weapons such as aircraft carriers, long-range missiles, or bombers.

the US-provided security umbrella, this apparent limitation provided a decided advantage by allowing the Japanese to dodge regional and global security issues during the Cold War. Instead, they were free to concentrate on their own economic recovery and growth.[9]

Given this short sketch of Japan's post-war tactics, the temptation, yielded to by far too many analysts, would be to ascribe Japan's strategic policy to the pursuit of a single-minded mercantilist objective during the Cold War period. Under this understanding, the Japanese sought only to embellish their economic prosperity, while shunning any active role in international affairs that could divert them from this chosen path. However, an alternative and more comprehensive explanation would view Japan's low profile in the security field as the natural result of prevailing international and domestic circumstances. If we examine the environment in which Japan, by necessity, had to operate, we find there were no other viable alternatives available, especially if Japan's focus was aimed at building a low-risk, middle-class society fueled by economic growth. With a divisive international situation controlled largely by two nuclear super powers, Japan did not have the conceivable wherewithal to deal with security issues single-handedly. Some sort of alliance or accommodation was an inevitability. Neither the US nor the Soviet Union would have welcomed a military competitor during this Cold War period. Other Asian nations, still nursing their wounds and grievances left over from the Japanese occupation, remained highly suspicious of any move that could be interpreted as the re-emergence of a militarized Japan.

The international resistance to Japan as a military state was equally matched by a distinct domestic repugnance. The war generation had had enough of the sort of glory and sacrifice that had nearly destroyed their country. Given these barriers erected at every turning, the route to becoming an economic powerhouse was the only legitimate path open during Japan's period of reconstruction. The safest course then was one which portrayed Japan as a peaceful nation with no aspiration to power. With some adroitness, the Japanese government could promote this

---

[9]The US–Japan Security Treaty, concluded in 1951, guaranteed Japan's security.

reformulation of the country without drastically altering its underlying drives and wider objectives. The Japanese would still embrace the dream of becoming once again a dominant major Asian power. They would continue hoping to recover the leadership position so carelessly tossed away during the Pacific War. But Japan would skillfully change tactics to adjust to the fundamental environmental changes that had occurred after that war. Japan was still ruthless enough to employ all means possible (except for the proscribed alternative of military force) in pursuit of its goals, but this time sufficiently wise to employ subtlety by operating in a non-threatening manner.

Carrying out these objectives was hindered by its initial limited wealth and the Cold War stalemate. Movement toward Japan's overarching goals only gathered increasing momentum over the last three decades. Concrete fruition became somewhat more explicit starting in the 1990s. The end of the Cold War provided a clear structural break from the heretofore prevailing international system. Within a world order where armed confrontation dominated, Japan had been left without room to maneuver, or an effective way to manipulate its existing environment. Vanishing Cold War certainties created a new world order. This evolving global regime did not appear to be so completely defined by coercive military power. Instead, the possibility to build international relationships based upon dialog and cooperation seemed imminent (if only fleetingly).[10] Given this opportunity, Japan renewed its determination to achieve a set of long-held objectives. Japan's diplomatic initiatives until this time had been largely based on the ability to create levels of economic leverage through its foreign assistance program. Starting in the 1990s, Japan became more willing to use military personnel, as well as stacks of dollars, to achieve its long-held goals.

Peacekeeping operations under the auspices of the UN implied an expanding military role for the heretofore pacifist Japanese. This seemed to represent a serious break from its post-war diplomatic

---

[10]This idea is enunciated in a key speech by the then Prime Minister Kaifu (1990).

stance.[11] The reality was quite different. A greater role for the Self-Defense Forces in the 1990s was indeed a tactical change. This is hardly surprising given the drastic shifts occurring in the international political arena. What it did not represent is a deviation away from Japan's long-standing pursuit of regional influence.

Unfortunately, just as the Japanese had positioned themselves to take advantage of this rare confluence of events that marked the 1990s, the economic base of their regional leverage began to wobble. Symbolic of their woes in the post-bubble era, Japan experienced the ignominy of having its credit rating downgraded to AA-minus in 2002 (Green, 2002).[12] While the desire remained, the hard won legitimacy of the Japanese drive for recognition lost some credence. Their vaunted development model now seemed vulnerable to criticism as more market-oriented prescriptions gained favor. At least diplomatically, Japan seemed oblivious to its own plight and how others perceived it. The Japanese still pushed their idea of exerting economic strength and influence outside the purely military realm.

> ... while the reality of international politics today is that military force undoubtedly continues to play a certain role ... it is becoming increasingly important for countries to enhance their international influence through a variety of strengths outside the purely military (Ministry of Foreign Affairs, 1999, p. 9).[13]

Maintaining national security through non-military means sounds like a basic contradiction. However, from these vague beginnings in the

---

[11] In terms of military expenditure, no such departure was noticeable. This remained the case even after the government decided to gradually expand its military role, albeit remaining very careful to stay within the framework of the US–Japan alliance.

[12] The rating agency, Standard & Poor's, downgraded Japan's credit rating. Japan became the only country in the G7 (Canada, France, Germany, Italy, Japan, UK and US) with such a low rating. This made headlines though, for a country like Japan that maintained large foreign exchange reserves, the importance of such a step in the foreseeable future was actually negligible. It was more symbolic of a general lack of confidence in the Japanese economy and its political masters. In an even greater collapse of confidence, the Nikkei stock average of the Tokyo Stock Exchange, which had hit a peak of 38,975 in December 1989, plunged below the 8,000 level in 2003.

[13] While Japan may not have entirely succeeded in using economic leverage to further its diplomatic objectives, other countries have adopted their own versions of this approach. It would seem that this Japanese method was not quite so quixotic. No one would of course deny China's military establishment. However, these days it is Chinese economic prowess that provides more conclusive evidence of its growing power. Sunk in a recession, the focal question in 2009 has been the ability of China's economy to perform the locomotive role traditionally reserved for the US.

years immediately after the Pacific conflict, discovering peaceful routes to further its ambition has become Japan's characteristic diplomatic approach. The difference in more recent years has been a growing acceptance of Japan's Self-Defense Forces, once the public's vigilant pacifism began to ebb. Still, the basic policy thrust has continued to be non-combative. These days, Japan's regional approach displays elements of change and consistency. Strictly speaking, what has evolved are the Japanese methods that have been applied. New tactics have allowed the Japanese to maintain their traditional quest for a proverbial place in the sun (or at least a spot in Asia). Prior to World War II, obtaining influence or political power to assure economic and national security seemed feasible only if carried out through military means. Thus, the whole focus of the state apparatus revolved around creating and nurturing a world class army and navy. At a military dead-end after its unconditional surrender, the strategy adopted to further Japan's consistent ambitions had to change, given a very different post-war environment.[14] To understand Japan's diplomatic approach during this period, looking for signs of continuity is more likely to be productive than becoming immersed in all the tactical shifts, which lend a certain incoherence to Japanese policies. In terms of Japan, it is always dangerous to become distracted by the *tatemae* (outside face — appearance) and lose sight of the *honne* (inside face — reality).

This willingness to make its positions known publicly and push other governments to see things China's way "is very different from 10 years ago, when Beijing was much quieter and more low-profile," says Jun Ma, an economist at Deutsche Bank in Hong Kong (Powell, 2009, p. 20).

[14]The September 11 attacks served as a catalyst that made Japan's new found activism explicit. The resulting US-led "war on terrorism" greatly influenced Japan's behavior in the context of devising an appropriate security policy response. This event provided an opportunity for Japan's leadership to legitimately expand the scope of its initiatives under the catch-all banner of "humanitarian and reconstruction assistance." The ramifications of the "war on terrorism" were not confined to Japan's expanding role in the world. Japan's approach to regional issues addressed later in this volume was undoubtedly influenced to some degree by the September 11 attacks. However, whatever constraints such an attack imposed on Japan's foreign policy in the Asia-Pacific will remain outside the purview of this book.

1.2 Other Views, Other Voices: Debating Japan's Foreign Policy

Japan's re-emergence in the post-war era as a potential leading Asiatic power was a unique event. Exercising economic without proportionate military power seems an unrealistic, if not unworkable, ambition. Japan's unanticipated emergence as the world's number two economy was in its own way remarkable and generated reams of explanatory material (some of which were worth reading). But its attempts to carve out a serious leadership role lacked any parallel precedent or existing theory underpinning such a diplomatic approach. The mystique of "exceptionalism" that has so much surrounded Japanese success grew in part because of their long effort over the post-war decades to maximize the country's economic strength while eschewing the attempt to bolster that inherent power with military force.[15] Puzzles, on their own volition, create an expected, if mostly unexceptional, supply of answers. This enigma that defines Japan's foreign policy has yielded no scarcity of perspectives, all of which claim to explain, at least partially, Japan's behavior.

Seizing on the obvious, many analysts have reduced this idiosyncratic foreign policy to a purely economic basis. Given Japan's economic rise during the Cold War period, this equivalent to the 700-pound gorilla sucks the air away from any alternative theory. In this simplistic approach, the entire range of Japan's diplomatic positions and initiatives has aimed solely at enhancing its economic power. Proof of this is said to lay in the mercantilist twist to its trading policies and

---

[15] Japan's economic success created something of a publishing boomlet in the 1980s with academics, business consultants, and journalists trying to explain Japan's economic miracle in terms of cultural values. In this view, Japan had discovered the key to economic success by being able to break all the rules the West was obeying so slavishly. The Japanese, according to this analysis, operated under different principles and norms. This approach became so persuasive that even the Japanese themselves got caught up in this idea of being part of a special race. In other words, success persuaded them to believe their own propaganda. (There was a faint whiff of the 1930s here.) Much of this confidence and the belief in an inherent superiority crashed simultaneously with the economy in an almost manic-depressive sequence. A closer examination of Japan's political economy is reserved for the appendix, which provides a wider context for Japanese foreign policy.

its reduction of any issue to purely monetary terms. This explanation unfortunately confuses the means with the ends. We can observe that all of Japan's energy and resources went into rehabilitating and reinforcing the country's recovery and growth. Moreover, relatively little of this wealth went into building a usable military force. Since diplomacy, at least in some textbook prescriptions, must be ultimately backed up by force, the mundane conclusion of this analysis inevitably has been that Japanese concerns were strictly limited to those which remained narrowly economic. In this view, Japan was able to pursue such a highly specialized course only because of its unique dependency on the US for national security. Safe under the American nuclear umbrella, Japan could avoid deep involvement in the ideological conflicts characterizing West versus East. Even achieving status through its wealth did not seem to tempt Japan away from these purely material concerns. It is understandable then, no matter how inaccurate, that the low profile Japan has found suitable in conducting its diplomatic activities has in turn misled many observers into believing that Japan's national interests could be categorically defined in simple economic terms.

For example, Kenneth B. Pyle has pigeonholed Japan's Cold War posture by claiming that "during the Cold War, Japanese leaders maintained their mercantilist priorities at considerable cost to national pride." Japan's single-minded pursuit of its narrow commercial interests "often seemed more appropriate to an international trading firm than to a nation-state" (Pyle, 2006, p. 9). Reinforcing this limited analysis, Richard Rosecrance had previously argued that jumping to the assumption that a newly wealthy Japan would become a world power with commensurate political and military interests was clearly a misconception. As a trading state, it would not be in Japan's interests to dominate the world, control its sea lanes or guarantee military access to markets in Western countries (Rosecrance, 1986, p. xi). Robert Gilpin proved ready to support this view. Although he pointed out that Japan had sought further political autonomy through its foreign economic policy, he agreed that the Japanese had "identified their national interest primarily in commercial terms" (Gilpin, 1990, pp. 5–21). Expanding on the same theme, Edward Lincoln insisted that Japan's primary concern was advancing its economic strength by expanding trade and investment for the benefit of Japan's business sector (Lincoln, 1993).

However, all these commentators essentially focused on Japan's economic activities and its parallel foreign policy rather than simply on Japanese foreign policy alone. In other words, diplomacy was reduced to just another aspect of Japan's economic destiny. This popular picture of Japan defined as a trading state was also taken up by Richard J. Samuel in his attempt to make sense of Japanese foreign policy. His influential book (1994) carefully examined Japan's history after the Tokugawa seclusion by focusing on the ingrained technological authority behind the conception of "rich nation, strong army." In the years prior to World War II, Japanese leaders regarded this slogan as encapsulating the essential requirement for survival in a world defined by imperialism. Samuels argued that Japan consistently operated under what he terms "techno-nationalism."[16] In this view, Japan's basic approach stays the same though its form changes, as it must, over time. This technological imperative successfully transformed military techno-nationalism (guns) characterizing the pre-war period into the commercial techno-nationalism (butter) that defined the post-war era. Japan throughout has been pursuing technological superiority in the belief that a dominant capability of this sort lies at the core of national security. Ultimately, it is Japan's skills base, its ability to outperform

---

[16]The term techo-nationalism is far from a self-revealing label. In Japan's case, it refers to targeting certain industries for protection and subsidies. This strategy of "picking winners" aims to develop a leading technological edge for selected domestic sectors. In essence, it is an attempt to accelerate the catch-up process of economic development.

> Although no standard definition exists, in common usage, techno-nationalism refers to such public policies that "target" the strategic (usually high-tech) industries and give them various governmental support: government procurements, import restrictions, export subsidies, research and development (R&D) subsidies, R&D tax credits, controls on inward foreign direct investments, protection of intellectual properties, government-funded R&D projects, and others. All support is given only to domestic firms (i.e. firms owned by its own citizens), for their aim is to strengthen the competitiveness of domestic industries against foreign rivals in a growing world market (Yamada, 2000, p. 1).

other countries in whatever relevant realm that makes the country safe. Such thinking has over time become deeply embedded and now forms a key component of Japanese ideology. This approach though seems heavily focused on the process chosen to achieve a given set of goals without sufficiently exploring Japan's more fundamental objectives.

Writing somewhat in the same vein, Samuel P. Huntington concluded that "Japanese strategy is a strategy of economic warfare." Consequently, Huntington contended that Japanese leaders believe that Japan must prevail at all costs in economic competition if it is to prosper. According to Huntington, "Japan has accepted all the assumptions of realism but applied them purely in the economic realm" (Huntington, 1993, pp. 68–83).[17] We will later argue that focusing on the obvious economic aspect of Japan's post-war diplomacy is a misleading, rather than a fruitful approach. It is far more pertinent to see the economic as a transformation of the pre-war military. With the military realm pre-empted, at least temporarily, by post-war reality, the economic sphere acted as a second best (or only viable) option during the extended Cold War period. If one is willing to accept the underlying consistency of Japanese policy, then the real illumination comes from examining the way an array of constraints have shaped the boundaries of activities undertaken to achieve those policy goals.

Despite its limited explanatory power, a consensus of authors continues to stress this purely economic rationale. Remaining within this approach Samuels and Eric Heignbotham explored a new concept that they labeled "mercantile realism" in order to more precisely explicate Japan's behavior. "Mercantile realism" implies that Japan "clearly does not ignore military security issues but its foreign policy is

---

[17] Since the term is used here and in the following paragraphs, it might be useful to provide a short explanation of the realist school of international relations. Quite naturally there are many variants that are included under this label, but they all share some common elements. International relations, according to this view, depend on national interest and security, rather than ideals, social reconstructions, or ethics. Like their cousins in the economics discipline, realists believe that states operate out of their own rational self-interest. For that reason, they focus on national survival and fostering their own security in the face of external threats. Relations between states are determined by their comparative level of power derived primarily from their military and economic capabilities. For that reason, international relations are outside the sphere of ethical behavior. Nation-states can only rely on their own capabilities for their security and survival.

organized around the goal of advancing its techno-economic position" (Heignbotham and Samuels, 1998, pp. 171–203).[18] Such reasoning clearly draws on Samuels' (1994) previous work. In essence, their explanation for Japan's reluctance to carve out a larger international role is simple. Japan is deftly categorized as an economic-centered state. By definition its goals fail to extend beyond furthering a discreet set of material interests. Once classified in this manner, Japan's foreign policy can conveniently be dismissed as uni-dimensional.

No one can, of course, ignore Japan's economic growth and subsequent dominance when analyzing the path its policy has carved. A rise of such startling dimensions was one of the most remarkable events characterizing the Asian-Pacific region. Moreover, Japan's economic strength was critical in spurring regional integration through trade, direct investment, aid, financial services and technology transfers. However, this obvious observation should not lead an analyst to jump to the simplified conclusion that Japan's diplomatic behavior is entirely explicable in terms of its economic interests. As we will demonstrate in the following chapters, it was not the strict pursuit of economic advantage that limited Japanese options and the policies they pursued, but rather the binding constraints they faced in attempting to gain their long-held and quite consistent objectives.

After World War II, Japanese leaders possessed the wisdom to bow to the inevitable. They thought it was the better part of valor, given the prevailing bifurcated environment that swept away other considerations, to portray Japan as a peaceful nation with no political aspirations. Meanwhile, they quietly pursued a leading regional position whenever and wherever opportunities occurred. These dual and dichotomous identities organized around the axis of Japan's alliance with the US confused even many Japanese politicians. Trying to fit together these two irreconcilable characteristics has helped to create a blanketing obscurity over Japan's diplomatic strategies

---

[18] Likewise, Hollerman (1988, pp. 1–31) argues that Japan pursued foreign economic objectives because of its lack of natural resources. On the basis of his reasoning, Japan's foreign economic and industrial policies are both designed to maximize its comparative advantage in the world economy.

and objectives (Soeya, 2005, pp. 16–19).[19] In other words, trying to achieve dominance not by coercion but by stealthily projecting a positive image seems contradictory. However, by the 1990s, the limitations inherent in the more prevalent view that relied purely on reductive economic explanations became evident. By accepting that material viewpoint, the steady expansion of Japan's military stance and options, although still highly constrained, must either be considered an anomaly or taken to signal a policy departure.

The economic-centered model cannot, for example, satisfactorily explain Japan's single-minded, though unsuccessful, pursuit of a permanent seat on the UN Security Council. This doomed attempt, which gathered momentum after 2004, seemed more a reflection of Japan's clear desire to exert greater influence in international affairs than any direct pursuit of a discernible economic advantage. Other diplomatic efforts were less obvious than Japan's UN Security Council bid, though equally unsuccessful. But the traditional emphasis and fixation on Japan's foreign economic policy and activities, which paid scant attention to these quiet but active attempts, misled many analysts into continuing to describe Japan as a "mercantilist state" or the equivalent.[20]

Unfortunately, this view seeks an explanation for Japan's behavior by focusing too narrowly on a single, though most obvious, aspect of post-war Japan. As previously discussed, this uni-dimensional approach reduces all of Japan's foreign policy to only its economic aspects. This simplified explanation of a far more nuanced country begins (and ends) by positing an economic fixation. When economic interests are low or absent, Japan's profile in international affairs will also be low or absent. Following this logic, foreign policy must be consistently subordinated to economic issues. Admittedly, Japan's posture in the security field

---

[19] Soeya (2005) argues that Japan's approach is basically a type of "middle power diplomacy." This label defines a category which allows a state to play a leading role in a given "niche" sanctioned by the hegemonic powers.

[20] To prepare for its expiry date in 2006 as a non-permanent member of the UN Security Council, Japan purchased the right to stand again as a non-permanent member of the Security Council in an upcoming election from Mongolia ("Mongol anporisen jitai," *Yomiuri Shimbun*, 26 January 2007).

had been extremely unbalanced relative to its economic strength. This behavior has misled observers into thinking that Japan's ultimate goal consists only of advancing its economic advantage. However, it is not only unsatisfying but also unjustified to then conclude that since Japan has maintained a low key position in the security field that this must imply Japan's ultimate goal to be purely economic. Looked at another way, Japan pursued the only avenues open to it. Given that the international structure during the Cold War was essentially dominated by two superpowers, little, if any, room remained for Japan to conduct an independent international policy.

Since the US withdrew its occupying forces in 1952,[21] Japan has been heavily dependent on its former occupiers for national security. There had been no pressing need for Japan to build up its military power or to become active as a major player in the security field. Given its devastated economy, Japanese political leaders concluded that the best, perhaps only viable, path to achieving national security lay in an alliance with the US. Due to a set of what was then overwhelming constraints at both the domestic and international level, Japan lacked the opportunity rather than the willingness to pursue an active policy of either national defense or international realpolitik. Japan's low profile in the security field, especially prior to the 1990s, did not reflect indifference, but rather the constraints that it inevitably faced. No viable path existed for it to follow. Looked at realistically, Japan has been trying to achieve its goals given the limitations surrounding any action that the Japanese chose. Simply put, Japan did focus on economic matters, as was imperative, during the Cold War period. It is also undoubtedly true that the Japanese were rather quiet, if not passive, on the international stage. Accepting these two observations, it still remains illegitimate for a careful analyst to leap automatically to the conclusion that Japan was actively shunning power and influence to concentrate instead on an

---

[21] The official end of the occupation brings with it a confusion of dates. The peace treaty was signed in San Francisco on 8 September 1951. However, it went into effect on 29 April 1952. We will use the later date throughout. It is literally inaccurate to talk about the year occupation forces left since 47,000 members of the US armed forces remained after the effective date. Technically on that day they ceased to be occupying troops.

array of relatively narrow economic interests. If instead of being mate-rially based, Japan's actions were the result of heavy constraints rather than derived from its preferred option, then Japan's anomalous behav-ior in international politics becomes much more comprehensible.

This anomaly, of course, has been recognized and attempts have been made to explicate this puzzle. Peter J. Katzenstein tried by focus-ing on specific domestic factors. He argued that Japan's behavior in the security field had been constrained by its anti-militarist norms. Domestically, military issues had long been subordinated to economic considerations as the Japanese tried to rebuild their shattered country. Wartime experiences quite naturally made the Japanese people hyper-sensitive to security issues. Despite the more publicized constitutional limits, prevailing pacifist traits were deeply embedded in Japanese minds during this period. This factor limited the possibility of Japan expanding its role in the realm of national security (Katzenstein, 1996). Working much the same vein, Thomas U. Berger claimed that a "culture of anti-militarism" widely accepted by the Japanese public greatly constrained any activist security policy (Berger, 1998).

Sharing this view, Kenneth B. Pyle's book explained Japan's post-war ideology and culture as a reflection of its historical experience. Japan's ideologically driven choice of a low-profile posture was a product of wartime trauma, unconditional surrender, popular pacifism, nuclear allergy, and restraints of the peace constitution; all of which were peri-odically aggravated by bureaucratic immobility (Pyle, 1996, p. 20). Following this analysis, Hugo Dobson concluded that peacekeeping operations served as an ingenious tool, which allowed Japan to partic-ipate in security matters without forswearing its anti-militarist culture (Dobson, 2003). All of these explanations relied heavily on essen-tially cultural motivations to make sense of Japan's diplomatic policies. Clearly our own analysis adopts many of these same domestic rationales. However, these authors have chosen to focus exclusively on domestic constraints without due consideration placed on their interchange with Japan's underlying motivations.

Kent Calder, on the other hand, has stressed a more "reactive state" model. In his view, Japan basically responds only to foreign pressure (Calder, 1988, pp. 517–541). If this analysis is correct, then

Japan's diplomacy is entirely shaped by external forces. Japan will move diplomatically, when it must, to respond to those demands, but otherwise remain basically inactive. Calder tried to explain this disparity between Japan's economic strength and its minimalist diplomacy as an outgrowth of its political structure. Elected representatives faced a virtual one-party system characterized by strong sectionalism and vested interests. These politicians were in turn underpinned by an inherently fragmented bureaucracy. Given its bureaucratic immobility, Japan has been neither willing nor prepared to take on the essential responsibilities of leadership.

Whatever its applicability, Calder's work displays a flaw common to many similar explanations. They all fall into what might be termed the "blind men and the elephant syndrome."[22] Each analyst (the blind men) tends to fixate on a single characteristic of foreign policy (the elephant) and attempts to generalize from this one particular aspect of the whole. While it is quite true that Calder is successful in accurately differentiating one of the limiting constraints shaping Japanese behavior, his analysis is far from comprehensive. His approach, for instance, does help to explain Japan's slow response to the first Gulf War by focusing on the ingrained bureaucratic stasis that is only aggravated by a prevailing sense of turf protection.[23] As we have stressed, however, this explanation forms only a part of the entire picture.

Akitoshi Miyashita (2003) further extends this reactive state model, but when doing so, seizes on a quite different aspect of the problem. He concluded that the reason for Japan's largely reactive behavior lay

---

[22] Some readers who survived primary school in the US might have been required to recite John Godfrey Saxe's poem about the six blind men of India who feel capable of describing an elephant after examining just one part.

> And so these men of Indostan
> Disputed loud and long,
> Each in his own opinion
> Exceeding stiff and strong,
> Though each was partly in the right,
> And all were in the wrong! (Saxe, 1973, p. 78)

[23] Prime Minister Hashimoto attributed Japan's recurrent slowness in making decisions to bureaucratic immobility caused by "turf consciousness." See Iokibe (2002).

in its asymmetrical relationship with the US. In the post-war period, Japan has been heavily dependent on America for both its national security and its trade. Differing with Miyashita, Dennis Yasutomo (1995) maintains that this approach describes only a specific period of the post-war era. He prefers to support the claim that Japan's foreign economic policy became active once Japan decided to push its developmental model. This displayed Japan's willingness to buck the financial architecture normally dominated by the World Bank and the IMF by attempting to reform these US-dominated institutions. Comfortably straddling these alternatives, Keiko Hirata (2001) argued that Japan was best understood as a hybrid state, one that was active or reactive depending on the circumstances. (This particular depiction would seem to make Japan either similar to any other state or unable to conduct anything resembling mature diplomacy.) Unfortunately, Hirata fails to say anything definitive about Japan's diplomatic efforts. She also implies a certain episodic understanding of Japanese foreign policy that denies, or ignores any underlying consistency to that policy and shows a distinct lack of interest in objectives and goals. In fact, all of these external pressure models fail to make Japan's actions purposive and tend to focus instead on a specific constraint, rather than examining the full array of possibilities. Such models are, by definition, not comprehensive. Incompleteness inevitably leads to questionable, more controversial models.[24] They tend to describe only a fraction of the entire diplomatic landscape. In our estimation, this tendency explains why so much of the debate in this area has been inconclusive up to now. Too many who are party to this discussion seem to be arguing at cross purposes to one another.

Reinhard Drifte adds his own, somewhat different, approach based on the notion of capabilities. His argument focuses more on Japanese willingness to act rather than actual ability to do so. According to Drifte, Japan has "attained such power that it can wield power in many areas"

---

[24] Calder (1993) later re-examined the "reactive model" by taking into account all of the major domestic, as well as, international constraints. He concluded that Japan's behavior was reactive. However, he started with the questionable precondition that Japan's objective could be characterized as advancing its economic interests.

and "become at least regionally a political superpower" but Japan's "leadership by stealth" has not transformed this potential into actual power (Drifte, 1996, pp. 162–168).[25] Thus, Japan has simply refused to sip from the cup of power. His work seems to pose the problem more than it solves the conundrum he raises. Drifte fails to focus sufficiently on the constraints limiting Japan's initiatives and the effect they might have had on Japan's successes and failures. This category of explanation tends to skirt around a problem instead of attacking it with a consistent and systematic approach. On the other hand, Michael J. Green (2001) does attempt to comprehensively explicate Japan's foreign policy. In his approach, Japan's new assertive posture can best be understood as a type of "reluctant realism," which has been shaped by such unstable international situations as the security threat posed by North Korea and subsequently further fueled by Japan's renewed aspirations after power. Green includes some of the reactive aspects of other theorists yet provides an underlying motive or rationale for Japan's specific diplomatic initiatives. In essence, Japan, once firmly shoved into the international arena (responding to an external constraint), now has to play an increasingly active role to achieve its goals. If we follow Green's line of reasoning, the 1990s then appear as a clear break from previous diplomatic patterns while retaining a certain consistency in their motivating goals. Left largely unmet is a rationale for Japan's previous dormancy, as well as the need for an external shock to budge the Japanese away from this former passivity.

In a similar manner, Kenneth B. Pyle (2006) attempts to piece together the puzzle that Japan's rising activism provides. He argues that this shift is no more than an accurate representation of a changing Japan. Pyle goes on to attribute this switch away from an essentially passive or reactive posture to a generational change. It is not difficult to understand his implicit argument. Start with the fact that a consensus of observers agrees that Japan's diplomatic efforts are much more active than they have been previously. Since the collective decisions of individuals create policy stances, a distinct shift must indicate a different cast

[25] Alan Rix (1993) also described Japan's style of leadership as being "leadership from behind."

of decision makers. All that remains to be done is to delineate how this current group differs from the old guard that it has replaced. The logic here seems more definitional than based on fundamental observations. In opposition to Pyle's somewhat ad hoc approach, we will offer a different explanation. If we are in fact correct, this observed change that several analysts have seized upon is more of a necessary tactical shift rather than a significant break with the past. People need not radically change for different outcomes to occur. All that is needed is a changed set of incentives. Therefore, just as constraints determined the shape of former policy, new factors derived from an evolving domestic and international environment defined Japan's current assertiveness. The key then to comprehending Japanese behavior is to realize the basic unchanging contours of Japan's objectives.

There are few works which comprehensively examine Japan's foreign policy by explaining both its objectives and the determinative constraints that direct Japan's decision making. This is the crucial aspect distinguishing our work from that which has preceded it. We will focus instead on the domestic and international factors which have constrained Japan's diplomacy and the way in which they have determined its path.

1.3 A Different View: Has Japan Been Pursuing Leadership?

1.3.1 *What is Leadership and Influence?*

An underlying difficulty in identifying Japan's quest for influence is the atypical path it has taken in the post-war period. Japan's attempts are often dismissed or overlooked by those who insist upon a rather narrow definition of this term. According to those who take a realist slant on these issues, leadership requires political power; a combination of activism and initiatives, which can shape international environments. Political power, which traditionally has been based on military strength, is essential for a state to pursue its national interests. These goals include assuming a leadership role regionally as well as in the world (Morgenthau, 1978, pp. 31–51). However, the definition of political power (sometimes ambiguously condensed to "power") has generated controversies over the years. In part, this is due to a lack of precision in its use and sometimes just outright carelessness by employing the term without properly defining it. The amorphous nature of the concept has resulted in a variety of often inconsistent interpretations and confusion among analysts. As mentioned, writers examining international relations explain "political power" as the ability to influence the actions of others or the ability to shape the international environment. In other words, those who possess this elusive power are able to set "the rules of the games." Although variations flourish, most writing in this field of tends to accept this fundamental definition.

A widely accepted formulation of this idea equates political power with the "ability of an actor to get others to do something they otherwise would not do" (Keohane and Nye, 1977, p. 11; Deutch, 1978, p. 45; Rothgeb, 1993, pp. 17–45). It is a psychological concept defining the relationship between participants. Broadly understood, this is no more than the concrete application of strategic behavior. One party's deliberate actions yield the desired response, or responses, from the other. It allows the former to influence (with a varying degree of control) certain actions of the latter (Morgenthau, 1965, p. 30). However, influence *per se* is not the most interesting issue to consider. The extensiveness and efficiency such modes of control achieve is often more relevant. Given this general understanding of power, physical coercion, or its threatened use, does not provide the only set of effective incentives. Circumstances and objectives are of course fundamental in devising appropriate methods to achieve specific ends.

While other aspects such as economic strength or even ideology have usually been included as constituents of political power, military force has in the past been deemed the primary or most fundamental basis for exercising power in the realm of international relations (Gilpin, 1975, p. 24). Indeed, a widely accepted view of global politics is that international society is at its core basically anarchic. The primary way then for sovereign states to pursue their national interests is by obtaining and exercising power. Since conflicts of interest are considered an integral part of international relations, military force must be an essential instrument for resolving the resulting disputes and conflicts. The panoply of armed forces and destructive weaponry becomes the best way that states can protect and advance their national interests.

What has become known as the realist view of international relations accepts this elemental dependency between political power and military force. Given this stance, the Soviet Union obtained overwhelming power during the Cold War even though it had a less than reliable economy. While coercion may be a starting point in analyzing power, this Cold War-influenced approach is also willing to accept ideology as a contributing factor. For example, the post-war struggle was often reduced by its proponents into a struggle between democracy and communism. This ideological device proved to be a convenient measure for organizing and motivating intrinsically useful blocks of allies. Employing strategy of this type is, of course, nothing new, as demonstrated by the war of values that formed a context for World War II. Or specifically in the case of the Japanese, their World War II attempt to harness anti-colonialism under the banner of breaking free from the West is a clear example. The Japanese supposedly offered this option to the mass of struggling Asians by establishing the "East Asia Greater Co-Prosperity Sphere." As always, by posing as Asia's liberator, Japan hoped to influence the actions taken by other Asian nations. Rallying them behind a Japanese vanguard would successfully substitute ideology for applied military force. The appeal of doing so seems obvious, though it more easily formulated than implemented.

Yet, as the post-war period progressed, a shift in international relations became noticeable. This made more simplistic explanations, previously in vogue, somewhat outmoded. Increasingly, interdependent patterns of economic trade and investment made military strength less dominant in establishing political power. The terms were no longer unarguably synonymous. From then on, economic aspects belonged in any power calculation as well. The "low politics" defined by economics may seem trivial on any given day. Lacking drama, it only sporadically makes for riveting headlines. Rather than having sudden effects, these less dramatic components of power act slowly and are often dismissed or slighted. But cumulatively, the results can be observed not only economically but politically as well. However, skeptics still abound who doubt the long run efficacy of using economic approaches to achieve political ends (Baldwin, 1985, pp. 116–118, 133–136).[26] The case for dismissing the leverage provided by wealth remains nonetheless dubious. A more useful working definition of political power would start by concluding that there are now various elements which constitute this particular form of influence. The exact formula is inevitably difficult to generalize since the importance of any component necessarily reflects changes in international and domestic circumstances and the way in which these elements interact over time.

Thus, measuring influence (political power) is more than a simple accounting task requiring an adding up all available resources. "Possessional power" such as a country's gross domestic product, level of military expenditure, collective natural resource base, or trade surplus does not automatically convert to influence. In fact, a concerted attempt to focus on these figures may only mislead us in comprehending the nature of power or its practical use. What we might term "power assets" does not always translate into usable power that assists a country to achieve its goals. A nation has to be both capable and willing to use its assets, if it is to exercise real power and influence (Rothgeb, 1993, pp. 29, 30).

1.3.2 *What Has Japan Been Pursuing and By Which Routes?*

Using a realist view, Japan's diplomatic presence is best characterized by the absence of the most crucial material factor underlying success, namely, military strength. Prevailing wisdom would insist that armed force inevitably follows economic strength. Creating wealth while eschewing any significant military strength leaves Japan as a clear outlier. Certainly, Japan is not bereft of deployable troops. It has

---

[26]The US success in shaping an increasingly free and open trading system after World War II demonstrates the complexity of this issue. America used its economic power in this case, not only to achieve obvious economic ends, but to forward its political agenda as well. However, it is questionable whether the US would have had quite the same degree of economic success had it lacked overwhelming military power in these early post-war years. Additional cases extend to establishing the dollar as the reserve currency and installing the US public as the global consumer of last resort.

provided itself with a first-ranked defense-oriented military capability. However, Japan labors under a core inability to dispatch those forces overseas. This limitation is the result of a constitutional restriction which then determines the nature of Japan's defense-centered military force. The result is the absence of an offensive capability, which leaves Japan lacking any coercive influence over other countries. But even without the explicit legal limitation, Japan in the past has been seriously hamstrung from pursuing this orthodox path to influence. As previously discussed, reactive pacifism and the very minor degree of maneuverability provided under Cold War structures, made an independent and more traditional route to power largely inaccessible. Successive Japanese governments were in essence forced to choose an alternative path, being completely hemmed in by past and present realities.

Lacking the ability to employ standard force or "hard power," we would suggest that in the absence of any better options, Japan has had to make use of what is often designated as "soft power," an all purpose label seeming to cover anything short of military might. As initially defined by Joseph Nye (1990), "soft power" is what remains after subtracting the "hard power" of the military or the "material power" of economic strength. However, the essential vagueness of this categorization tends to be too simplistic, shallow and even outright misleading. (Economic strength is sometimes considered soft and sometimes hard depending on its use.) The purpose behind this definition is perhaps to contrast influence built on negative incentives (the stick) versus those of a more positive character (the carrot). Certainly, military resources were created for and used extensively to coerce or threaten others. But the potential exists for such assets also to be employed as a more positive force which can encourage peace and stability. There may be something of an underlying coercive threat making its use effective, but the objective remains clearly differentiable. A typical example of this application is the increased use of peacekeeping operations under the auspices of the UN. The threat of force is used to protect an established status quo rather than to enforce the will of one country over another. In the 1990s, Japan incrementally extended the scope of its diplomacy by adapting its Self-Defense Forces to bear a larger level of active responsibility. Japan's participation in non-combative peacekeeping operations, its contribution to nation building and reconstruction, all reflect this expanded strategy.

But to comprehend the full scope of Japan's post-war policy requires more than just employing a label to camouflage a much more complex issue. A deeper understanding starts with the realization that the observed changes in Japan's diplomatic tactics do not reflect a fundamental alteration of its objectives. Constraints certainly have changed, including the international environment in which the Japanese operate. What have not varied are Japanese aspirations. Whenever possible they have used available economic tools to gain regional influence. Doing so required a rather painstaking process of targeting foreign assistance as carefully as possible. But Japan has shown a willingness to use other options, as they have become deployable and effective. The Japanese use power like any other country, if we reasonably accept that power is merely a resource "to achieve one's purpose by affecting the behavior of others" (Nye, 2004, p. 7). What becomes interesting is the context in which a country employs its available power, rather than the exact nature of that power. Using this framework Japan is not wedded to employing only "soft power." Understanding the way in which Japan chooses to use its resources is crucial then for comprehending the purpose behind its diplomatic policy. As pointed out, Japan has been willing, if perhaps reluctantly, to use its military capability to gain non-coercive influence. Like foreign assistance, countries would be likely to welcome such aid for positive reasons rather than induced by fear.

In the past, it has been downright easy to reduce Japan's attempts to carve out a leadership role to purely economic motivations. Yet the ever increasing size of Japan's foreign assistance during the Cold War was not driven by some purely economic rationale. Of course, foreign assistance was often understood as just another aspect of foreign trade and could under the right conditions nurture it. But if more carefully examined, other objectives determined the extent of such aid as well as its targets. The trade aspect of economic power was simply more obvious than the cumulative influence such strength could yield in the long term (Baldwin, 1985, pp. 116–118, 133–136).[27]

Moreover, the influence gained through these alternative routes was perhaps even more unreliable than that achieved through the threat of force. For example, at the 63rd UN General Assembly held in 2008, Vietnam, Indonesia and Malaysia opposed the resolution on the situation of human rights in North Korea. Among other provisions included was a clause demanding that North Korea resolve the Japanese abduction issue as soon as possible. At that time, Japan remained the largest aid donor to these countries. This donor carrot should have been able to tip the balance of voting intentions toward support of (or at least an abstention on) the UN resolution. But aid did not translate automatically into sympathy, let alone obedience. Other factors appeared to weigh more heavily. In this case, possible worries over their own human rights record could have transcended financial considerations. In addition, it is unclear that Japan attempted to apply pressure (whether explicit or implicit) in terms of future aid allotments. In any case, influence cannot be so easily bought, but as the US has demonstrated more recently, military force does not always guarantee success either.

Nor could the Japanese easily transform its growing economic strength into an independent policy during the Cold War. Dependent on the US, Japanese foreign aid was largely limited to playing a subsidiary role within the boundaries set by US policy. Japanese efforts were channeled to support American security initiatives. Stymied from pursuing an independent path, Japanese policies were almost invisible in terms of Japan's fundamental objectives. But though often thwarted, this does not mean that these aspirations were non-functional. Understanding Japan's policy, even during these years, still equates to an ability to focus on Japanese objectives and the operative constraints during the relevant period. The end of the Cold War has made it accordingly

---

[27] The use of economic tools to further long-run foreign policy objectives is thus more subtle and difficult to discern than any immediate short-run economic results. Confused by the obvious, some observers have jumped to the conclusion that Japan had only narrow economic interests driving their policy decisions.

easier to understand this fundamental insight. Under a growing global interdependence characterized by an assumed absence, or certainly weakening, of the hierarchy that defined military and economic issues, it has become increasingly easier for a state to transform its position or influence through economic growth rather than military power (Nye, 1988, p. 240).

In contrast to much of the previous work examining Japan's international relations, we attempt to make the case for the consistency of Japan's post-war policy. Such a claim would seem to be contrary to at least casual observation, which instead presents a jumble of ad hoc tactics for advancing Japan's economic growth. Lacking military punch, the idea that Japan has been pursuing influence, much like any other state, may not seem to be a particularly reasonable interpretation. Reducing Japan to a collection of economic animals inhabiting a state focused solely on material advancement is far easier. But unless analysts want to insist that Japan made a complete break with the past in the 1990s, it makes much more sense to accept the idea that the Japanese have employed either economic or military tools of influence depending upon their relative effectiveness. In all cases, deployment has been consistently non-threatening, promising and assuring, which is in fact what makes the Japanese approach quite distinctive. Out of necessity, as well as experience, the Japanese have come to suspect that in gaining a leadership position, threats can be rather counterproductive and lack any real punch. They would rather make use of promises and assurances to achieve similar goals. When made under the appropriate conditions, this approach can be more effective than open aggression as a tool for garnering influence (Davis, 2000, pp. 146–147).

Naturally, we are not speaking of the same sort of dominant position that Imperial Japan pursued prior to World War II. The nature of leadership that Japan has been seeking is now more quiet or consensual than the visible or hegemonic power that reflected the honor and glory of the emperor. Though Japan is still focused on achieving a central role, it is one based on a reciprocal flow of benefits that is largely built on mutual trust, not fear and coercion. This brand of post-war influence then is distinctly different from the more familiar relationship that is simply a matter of overwhelming domination deliberately imposed upon a weaker country (Keohane and Nye, 1977, p. 26).

Using this type of analytical lens reveals that Japan has made a sharp break from the days when military supremacy formed the backbone of its foreign policy. In that pre-war period, shaped by the dominant colonial powers, the ability to lead depended solely on military capability. Hegemonic leadership required overwhelming force and was aptly represented as an asymmetrical dependence between a powerful state and a weaker client country (Knorr, 1975, p. 25). Even during the Cold War era, though the absolute importance of military power as a prerequisite of influence was lessened, it was still the decisive factor. However, the emergence of "new threats" such as terrorism, the proliferation of weapons of mass destruction, the uncertainties of climate change and the recent financial crisis, make unilateral action difficult without first orchestrating effective international cooperation. The requirement for achieving leadership certainly has changed. Military power still matters, but its use has evolved. This difference creates the possibility that Japan could come close to achieving its much sought after leadership position without resorting to the offensive use of military power.

1.3.3   *Operating in a Bounded Environment: The Role of Constraints on Japan's Diplomatic Behavior*

The central argument of this book is that although forced to transform its methods, Japan continued to pursue regional leadership, even after its devastating defeat in World War II. In which case, Japan's objective has remained consistent throughout the post-war era although its strategies necessarily evolved to reflect changes in its international and domestic environment. For most of that time, despite an increasingly important economic position within the international system, Japan opted for a low-key approach that eschewed either an explicit political role or participating in security issues. A basic misunderstanding of its objectives and strategic approach caused Japan's observed policy to meet with continuous and occasionally harsh criticism. Japan was dismissed for being an economic "giant" but choosing to remain a political "midget." This unprecedented behavior, which seemed to deliberately shy away from "power," appeared inexplicable using the framework of orthodox international relations theory.

However, a closer examination of the internal and external constraints under which Japan labored should help us understand Japan's behavior even when examined within the lens of more orthodox theories. As is often the case, the most comprehensive and consistent explanation is a relatively simple one. Japan's diplomacy has not been erratic or driven by narrow economic objectives. Nor has Japan's policy been characterized by inexplicable shifts or about faces. Japan has been steadily pursuing regional influence. Not unexpectedly, the Japanese have often been blocked from following a more straightforward path to this goal. International and domestic constraints have caused Japan to behave in a manner that appears inconsistent with standard theoretical expectations. This superficial divergence has caused Japan to be viewed as something of a puzzle. But the mystery largely vanishes if we begin to focus on the operative constraints that have determined Japan's policy orientation. The analysis then becomes much less complex and much more comprehensible. During the six decades composing the post-war period, Japan has focused on gaining back a position of influence while necessarily dealing with a roster of constraining limitations as best as it could. This was true in the early years of recovery and it remains true today.

We need then to make a few core assumptions to structure this simple analytical framework. In the following analysis, we assume that the state is responsible for forming and implementing foreign policy. The same state will also be treated as a rational decision maker capable of calculating the cost of its behavior in attempting to maximize the benefits of any given policy. Simply put, policy decisions are formed based on existing incentives and constraints. Rationality removes the possibility of explaining away behavior by falling back on the all inclusive idea of "exceptionality" (Keohane, 1986, pp. 166–167). However, rationality does not imply unconstrained maximization. Policies will differ depending on past histories and the nature of the constraints a state faces.

1.3.3.1   *Outward barriers: Facing external constraints*

International structure

Structural theorists have argued that a country's external environment is the most critical factor determining the behavior and the diplomacy of an individual state. Accepting this view implies that by examining international structural factors, we can then accurately analyze and predict a state's behavior. Since no country operates in a void, it would seem obvious that no country determines its own behavior without first taking into account the international environment surrounding it. Structure inevitably becomes a principle determinant, encouraging certain actions and discouraging others (Waltz, 1979, pp. 104–111).

To analyze a state's behavior, we therefore need to understand the context of its actions in terms of the prevailing international environment. Japan is not an exception to this particular rule. In the pre-war period, the prevailing Western power structure left Imperial Japan with two choices. It could follow the lead of other Asian countries and submit by accepting dependency status. Or, the Japanese could try to compete by maximizing their military power. Given the realities of empire and imperialism, the choice for the Japanese appeared obvious. In a parallel fashion, Japan shunned power politics after World War II, even when it had firmly grasped its share of economic dominance. Again, the choice seemed indisputable. The power structure during those decades was determined by the two Cold War superpowers. This arrangement left little or no room for Japan to pursue a military strategy or even to play any serious role. Even had the Japanese decided to pursue this option, any sign of regional ambition would have been met by a widespread negative and even antagonistic reaction to any initiative that hinted at the restoration of Japan as a military power. Grievances in the wake of World War II were still fresh and largely unforgotten in many Asian nations that had been occupied by Japanese troops.

While it is true that prevailing international structures played an important, determinative role, it is a mistake to confuse this approach with a complete answer. If accepted, this method still fails to explain the length and breadth of Japan's foreign policy. In plain terms, fundamental changes in the world's structural architecture will continue to affect Japanese behavior, but it fails to entirely predict it. Other factors are equally important. For instance, the dominance of military strength, while still remaining essential, became more intertwined with economic issues. Strategic policy became more multi-faceted. Thus, in the aftermath of the Cold War, the obvious restraints on a Japanese military build-up weakened. Yet, Japan still eschewed this option, even while a number of its East Asian neighbors did not. Instead, Japan tried to maintain the same low profile after the end of the Cold War. Japan persisted with this approach, even courting unpopularity with its allies during the First Gulf War. More than the prevailing international environment was at work here. Trying to explain Japan's persistent low profile through just this one factor will inevitably prove to be less than successful. This failure strongly indicates that other decisive factors must have been at work.

Dominant Americans

Starting with the "black ships" that Commodore Perry used to prise open Japan for the benefit of Western countries, the fates of these two countries have been intertwined. In post-war Japan, ignoring the influence that its erstwhile occupiers had and continue to have on the Japanese would provide a distorted analysis at best. America's dominance stems from the asymmetrical relationship which Japan has maintained with the US. The Japanese have leaned heavily on the US for its economic and national security, certainly ever since it concluded the US–Japan Security Treaty in 1951. Export markets relied on American consumers, while the US nuclear umbrella provided Japan with a satisfactory level of national security. Given these linkages, it is hardly remarkable that Japan has proven to be particularly susceptible to US pressure (Miyashita, 2003, pp. 15–30). This uneasy relationship continued, even though Japan became a giant in its own right. Despite these changes, at a fundamental level not much has shifted between the two allies. Even today, Japan still maintains an asymmetrical security relationship with the US. In practical terms, Japan lacks the reciprocal ability to defend the US from attack. Still, many US observers have claimed over the years that the effectiveness of American pressure has been largely illusionary. In their view, the Japanese have only provided the appearance of compliance while doggedly pursuing their own agenda. Though not entirely without foundation, such blanket generalities ignore the obvious. Despite serious differences of opinion, the US clearly has been able to induce Japan to follow its lead in a number of instances.

To some extent, US pressure did help to shape Japan's foreign aid policy. But often American success in doing so, depended less on coercion than on existing political realities. Notice that the effectiveness of these US initiatives was often correlated with objectives that had been nurtured already by the Ministry of Foreign Affairs (MOFA). Pressure created an opportunity to bring these goals to fruition. The ministry could shift at least partial responsibility for the policy onto American shoulders, while simultaneously pursuing its own agenda. This sleight of hand allowed MOFA to use the leverage generated by US insistence to persuade and bring into agreement other key ministries (Orr, 1990, p. 12). Japanese bureaucrats and politicians have never been shy of employing *gaiatsu* (foreign pressure) when it suits their purpose and potentially ignoring it otherwise (Hatakeyama, interview with MOFA Director for Economic Affairs Bureau, 12 April 2004).[28] That American pressure has been used selectively points to the fundamental inter-relationship between external and internal factors. Policies are easier to forward when a number of key factors are all aligned. However, it is not so easy for Japan to simply ignore strongly pursued US objectives. Japan's susceptibility, as pointed out, has been conditioned on its dependence on the US for national security. Japan then continues to face severe limitations in pursuing a purely independent path. Thus, the most direct path for the Japanese often dips and swerves to reach its objective. Almost automatically, the Japanese have needed to avoid policy or diplomatic initiatives that directly clashed with any American agenda. In contrast, when aims are broadly aligned, Japan has had considerably more room to carve out an independent course. The obvious conclusion is that any analysis of Japanese diplomacy begins by examining the American factor.

---

[28] The MOFA Director for Economic Affairs Bureau was quite clear on this point.

1.3.3.2   *Domestic landmines: The politics of internal constraints*

Pacifism

Both Thomas Berger (1998) and Peter Katzenstein (1996) have pointed out the obvious fact that Japanese cultural perceptions and norms are bound to be important factors affecting Japan's behavior as a nation-state. The devastation due to World War II, and the disillusionment in their military class experienced by Japanese people, left them hypersensitive to any resurgence of these discarded traditions.[29] Even without the imposition of explicit constitutional limitations, these post-war cultural norms became so embedded among the general populace, that the possibility of Japan adopting a more aggressive military profile was at best minimal. For decades, a deeply rooted "culture of anti-militarism" effectively shaped Japan's strategic decision making (Berger, 1998, pp. 194–195). At an early stage, even maintaining the prevailing status quo was a sensitive issue. The Japanese public viewed plans to renew the US alliance in 1960 as a stepping stone to re-militarization. The resulting political turmoil subsequently led to the resignation of the Kishi administration. The very ferocity of the tempest that marked the negotiations led the US to have second thoughts about their ally's reliability. At the height of this unrest, the Eisenhower administration even feared that Japan might turn into a socialist state.

A corollary of this deep-bred pacifism was the ambiguous status of the Self-Defense Forces (SDF). This organization, or anything with a whiff of the military attached, remained implicitly taboo for many decades. Anti-militarism was further organized and structured by the politics of post-war Japan. The Japan Socialist Party opposed both the SDF and a security alliance with the US. The party acted as something of a watchdog, sniffing out any attempts to change the prevailing attitudes to, or employment of, the SDF. Public sentiment only began to change in the 1990s. Japan's successful participation in the Cambodian peacekeeping operations created a more favorable impression of the SDF. The population began to see it as a force that could contribute to

---

[29] The hard right element, symbolized by ear-splitting sound trucks, have more to do with politics and borderline criminal activities than displays of nationalism and patriotism.

peace and stability. This positive impression was fortified in 1995 by the assistance that soldiers offered to the victims of the *Hanshin* earthquake and the Tokyo subway Sarin gas attack by the *Aum Shinrikyo* cult. Until then, the Japanese had long been entrapped in what could be described as disregard or even contempt for the Self-Defense Forces.

This strong, domestic anti-military sentiment could not be ignored by any politician even those belonging to the Liberal Democratic Party (LDP). A prevailing mindset of this type created insurmountable obstacles for successive post-war governments, limiting any attempts to broaden the scope of security-related initiatives. As a consequence, playing a significant role in this realm had been virtually ruled out until both the Japanese government and the public heard alarm bells as the result of the First Gulf War in 1990–1991. Previously, this normative consensus had significantly limited Japan's security policy (Katzenstein, 1996, p. 22).

Institutional barriers

The legal status of the SDF has been ambiguous from its foundation. Both the Japanese Communist Party (JCP) and the Japanese Socialist Party (JSP) adamantly insisted that any military force was by definition unconstitutional. This lack of acceptance reduced the SDF and its officers to a subordinate role, one lacking any real respect. As a result, politically astute prime ministers have tended to keep their distance from the SDF. Any appearance of military access to political power would have proven potentially fatal (Funabashi, 1997, pp. 83–133). That the Defense Agency lacked full ministerial status symbolized the disdain in which the armed forces were held. More practically, it indicated a fundamental lack of influence. (The Defense Agency was only upgraded to ministerial status in 2007.) Reflecting the highly institutionalized level of civilian control, the Defense Agency consisted of officials who had been seconded from other, more influential ministries. Given this environment, any attempt to formalize military objectives was actively discouraged (Katzenstein and Okawara, 1993, p. 92). As one might expect, the end result of such ingrained pacifism were policies that explicitly constrained defense initiatives. Public sentiment

reflected in governmental structure meant that military issues continued to be clearly subordinated to economic considerations (Berger,
1998, pp. 194–195).

It is then critical to remember that the more these basic constraints
worked together (both external and internal ones) the more they determined actual policy decisions. The shape of Japanese policy changed
as these constraints themselves either gathered or lost importance. For
instance, the unstable international situation of the 1990s concentrated
attention on security issues quite wonderfully. The changing external environment encouraged the Defense Agency to exert a growing
influence on policy formation. Peacekeeping operations in Cambodia
weakened some of the ingrained internal resistance. These two changes
aligned to boost the position of the Defense Agency. This shift allowed
the Japanese government to strengthen cooperation and political dialog on security matters with the US in the mid-1990s. The same set
of events provided an opportunity for the Defense Agency to play a
more central role in terms of security policy coordination. Thus, the
increasingly uncertain regional security architecture, exemplified by the
Taiwan crisis and the continuing North Korean fiasco, helped to legitimize the Defense Agency (Funabashi, 1997, pp. 112–116). Notice
however that broad Japanese objectives had not changed whatsoever.
A realignment of external and internal constraints shifted incentives and
by doing so created new policy paths for Japan to follow.

Prior to this change, Japan resorted to using economic methods
to further its aims in lieu of a practically taboo use of military troops.
However, even unalloyed economic policy can prove to be inconsistent or ineffective largely due to a basic fragmentation that creates
disjointed initiatives. Analysts allege that this reflects a strong "turf-
consciousness" among the ministries involved in these decisions (Orr,
1990; Calder, 1988, pp. 517–541). Japan's attempts to mobilize Official Development Assistance (ODA) to further its aims exemplify this
problem. Fragmented decision making, rather than confused objectives, long inhibited the government from formulating and implementing an effective Japanese aid policy (Koppel and Orr, 1993, p. 38).

Growing sectionalism and turf protection of this sort reflected a
system of entangled interests encompassing ministries, politicians and

business sectors.[30] Governments (in the guise of the LDP) offered special assistance and favorable regulation to selected industries in exchange for political contributions. (Loveday (1982, p. 208) makes this point for the more general case.) Moreover, interest groups maintained close contact with the bureaucracy. As a result, each ministry tended to voice the competing interests of their clientele. These myopic sub-goals created a strong "territorial consciousness" within the ministerial ranks (Johnson, 1982, p. 74; Muramatsu and Krauss, 1987, p. 533). For example, an official in the Ministry of Foreign Affairs explained Japan's slow response in concluding free trading agreements (FTAs) with other countries by citing the concerted resistance arising from other ministries, an array of interests groups, and politicians aligned with them (Hatakeyama, interview with MOFA Director for Economic Affairs Bureau, 12 April 2004).[31] These concerted forces, by making it difficult to conclude such agreements, could conceivably serve to undermine Japan's broader interests over a longer time span. However, lacking strong leadership, competing ministries, each allied to their own set of embedded vested interests, have constrained the ability of successive governments to form effective foreign policy.[32]

Domestic political structure

The Liberal Democratic Party (the LDP) has dominated Japan's domestic politics since its inception in 1955. For more than 50 years, Japan has been the rough equivalent of a one-party state. Its long post-war rule has only been broken briefly by the Hosokawa coalition

---

[30]On this view, see Tsurutani (1977).

[31]Japan seemed little interested in pursuing free trade agreements until China became active in this area. We can see here how external factors can push policy in one direction while internal constraints (agricultural interests) can push in quite the opposite.

[32]Japan's slow response at the time of the Gulf War indicated both the immobility of Japan's bureaucracy and the strong sense of turf control that characterized the relevant ministries. The then Prime Minister Hashimoto criticized Japan's slow response, which was caused not only by the lack of an effective information gathering network but also by a lack of communication between the concerned ministries, due once again to a strong "turf-consciousness" (Iokibe, 2002, pp. 62–79). The slow and belated response to the First Gulf War, and the decision to make only economic contributions, demonstrated the inherent sectionalism existing between the Ministry of Foreign Affairs and the Ministry of Finance.

government in August 1993.[33] While the domestic political scene has been an LDP stronghold, this did not prevent left-wing parties, such as the JSP, the largest left-wing opposition group, from effectively constraining Japan's post-war security policy. As previously noted, the JSP, which anointed itself the "guardian of the constitution," insisted that the SDF and the alliance with the US were unconstitutional. On that basis, they consistently opposed any expansion of Japan's security role. This deeply embedded pacifist sentiment was not exclusive to members of the JSP. A number of LDP stalwarts also shared this same viewpoint. This widely spread political resistance effectively impeded any expansion of Japan's military role. The same essential reluctance extended to any military aspect including participating in UN-sanctioned peacekeeping operations.

Therefore, the formation of a new coalition government in June 1994 (JSP, LDP, and Sakigake Party), under Prime Minister Tomi-ichii Murayama (JSP), helped break the seemingly immovable log jam in even discussing Japan's security policy.[34] From the government's very inception, Murayama abandoned his party's long-standing position and announced that he would recognize the legitimacy of the SDF

---

[33] For a discussion of Japanese politics during this time, see Inoguchi (2005) and Kusano (1999). A consensus of observers expects the LDP's long domination of Japanese politics to come to an end with the 30 August 2009 elections. Whether this will mean the end of one-party politics remains to be seen. It is even possible that the LDP may go the way of Italy's long-dominant Christian Democrats and fragment into newly formed parties. But up to now, it has never paid to underestimate the resiliency of the LDP.

> If the DPJ [Democratic Party of Japan] does rule through 2013, the LDP may not survive. An LDP without access to the public trough to hand out goodies to its base is like a fish out of water. Some LDPers will defect to the DPJ-led coalition, either as individuals or via the way station of new, smaller parties. If the LDP does survive through 2013 and then loses again, it could easily go the way of the Italian Christian Democrats who disappeared not long after they finally lost power. If so, the fractious DPJ could eventually split. A decisive party turnover this year opens the door to a very fluid interregnum (Katz, 2009, p. 1).

[34] As noted, the return of the LDP to power took less than a year. The LDP was not in fact voted out, but rather lost power due to the desertion of 55 of its members. During the LDP's time in the wilderness, weak coalitions (eight different, fractious parties) seemed to come and go with a sort of heedless speed. For this reason, there was no effective break in the LDP's political domination.

and the US–Japan Security Treaty. Murayama felt confident in doing so, since according to opinion polls taken at the time, 77.9 percent of the Japanese felt that they needed the SDF, while 62 percent of the Japanese were supportive of the American alliance (Sorifu, 1994, p. 519; 1995, p. 498). The JSP was clearly faced with a dilemma when deciding to jettison one of the party's core principles. Public support was swinging in support of the SDF and the alliance. If the party wanted to lead a coalition government the Socialists would have to essentially sell out their long-held principles. Ironically, by grasping for the reins of government, the JSP undermined its own viability. Suffering a large loss in the 1996 House of Representatives election, their short stay in government represented a last hurrah for the Party. It ceased to play a major role in Japanese politics and instead paved the way for a sustained LDP comeback.[35]

However, the coalition period came to represent something of a policy watershed. The major restraint to a Japanese-based security stance started to loosen and eventually would cease to be effective. For the first time, Japan's approach to military matters reached something of a consensus (excluding of course the Japanese Communist Party). All major parties, whether ruling or in opposition, now supported the SDF and the US–Japan Security Treaty. The two major groupings after 2003, the LDP and the Democratic Party of Japan (DPJ), were in broad agreement, although differences continued not only between the parties but within them as well. Since 1994, Japan has featured two or three major parties in broad agreement on key features of what a viable security policy might be (Hughes, 1999, pp. 16–17). Politicians were now willing to debate the details openly. With the taboo a thing of the past, Japanese governments could broaden the scope of future policy initiatives.

Public sentiment

Public opinion has a varying impact on decision making, although the degree of public support is not a particularly reliable indicator of the

---

[35]The Japan Socialist Party relabeled itself as the Socialist Democratic Party (SDP) in 1996. To avoid confusion, the term "JSP" is used throughout.

quality of foreign policy (Morgenthau, 1978, p. 165). For instance, Japan's war-time policy had nearly universal support, yet was intrinsically foolish. Nonetheless, public opinion can form a binding constraint on a government's decisions. Politicians may go against the general sentiment, yet it is never simply ignored. The potential impact is naturally amplified as a government nears an election. For the most part, politicians are tempted to openly cite public opinion only in support of their own arguments. Thus, it is important to separate real effects from attempts to spin public opinion so that it becomes a tool to lobby for or to justify predetermined policy.

Nevertheless, the fact that polling is so frequently done by a diverse array of Japanese institutions (newspaper companies, television production outfits, and the Ministry of Foreign Affairs) indicates something of the importance of public opinion. It must inevitably exert some degree of influence on the thoughts and actions of politicians (Watanabe, 1977, p. 106). For example, public opposition to normalizing relations with South Korea certainly delayed government action, although not ultimately preventing it (Watanabe, 1977, p. 144). Foreign policy then is never conducted in a rarefied atmosphere impervious to public sentiment.

1.4 Mining the Coalface: Foreign Policy Sources

There are numerous works that investigate Japan's foreign policy or its leadership role. However, those works employing private primary source focus mainly on the pre-war or early post-war period. The inaccessibility of these private primary sources inevitably limits the research on more recent decades.

Since 1976, the Japanese Ministry of Foreign Affairs has partly disclosed diplomatic documents that are 30 or more years old. Unfortunately, this applies only when the disclosure will not affect diplomatic relationships with other countries and/or not interfere with Japan's national interests. Although the ministry has published a series of *Documents on Japanese Foreign Policy*, which is similar to the *Foreign Relations of the US*, many documents in the post-war period still have yet to be publicly disclosed.[36] As noted historian John W. Dower pointed out, "response to petitions calling for more open and convenient access has been essentially tokenistic; numerous materials have been made available through microfilm, but most of this is of little or no interest to scholars even on issues in regard to the occupation" (Dower, 1993, p. 197). A government's predilection for secrecy always runs at cross-currents to the aims and spirit of analysis. Therefore, researching areas of Japanese foreign policy ultimately requires an inescapable dependency on foreign primary sources such as those held by the US State Department.

The lack of private primary source material, especially for more recent periods, means that analysis and research are quite limited. This increases the risk of making an incorrect interpretation and assessment due to a lack of sufficient sources. Under these circumstances, analyzing the *Diplomatic Bluebook*, which the government has published every year since 1957, is the only possible way to systematically study the official attitudes of the Japanese government. *ODA Annual Reports* and *ODA White Papers* published by the Ministry of Foreign Affairs since 1989 also serve as valuable primary sources. To supplement this lack of private primary source material, we also employed, for the early postwar period, foreign primary sources such as *Foreign Relations of the US*. Unfortunately, information garnered from these public sources is rather limited. In view of the superficiality of the public primary sources, interviews were conducted with officials in the Ministry of Foreign Affairs, the Japan Bank of International Cooperation, the Japan International Cooperation Agency, the Ministry of Finance, as well as academics and informed journalists during a number of field trips to Japan. Questionnaires were tailored to suit the interviewees' specific expertise. Such interviews added accuracy and detail to the analysis.

---

[36] Since November 2001, diplomatic records and documents can be accessed via a government web site (http://www.jacar.go.jp). However, documents from the National Archives, the Diplomatic Record Office of the Ministry of Foreign Affairs and the National Institute for Defense Studies are limited to 1945 or before. Documents from the Diplomatic Record Office of the Ministry of Foreign Affairs extend no further than matters dealing directly with politics and diplomacy. Still, in comparative terms, the accessibility to all these documents on the web is epoch-making.

References

Baldwin DA. (1985) *Economic Statecraft*. Princeton University Press, New Jersey.
Berger TU. (1998) *Cultures of Anti-Militarism: National Security in Germany and Japan*. Johns Hopkins University Press, London and Baltimore.
Calder KE. (2003) Japan as a post-reactive state? *Orbis*, 47(4), 605–616.
Calder KE. (1988) Japanese foreign economic policy formation: Explaining the reactive state. *World Politics*, 40(4), 517–541.
Davis JW, Jr. (2000) *Threats and Promises: The Pursuit of International Influence*. Johns Hopkins University Press, London and Baltimore.
Deutch KW. (1978) *The Analysis of International Relations*. Prentice Hall, Englewood Cliffs.
Dobson H. (2003) *Japan and United Nations Peacekeeping*. Routledge Curson, London.
Dower JW. (1993) *Japan in War and Peace*. The New York Press, New York.
Drifte R. (1996) *Japan's Foreign Policy in the 1990s*. St. Martin's Press, New York.
Drifte R. (1990) *Japan's Foreign Policy*. Routledge, New York.
Fallows J. (1994) *Looking at the Sun*. Pantheon Books, New York.
Funabashi Y. (1997) *Doumei Hyoryu*. Iwanami, Tokyo.
Gilpin R. (1975) *US Power and the Multinational Corporation*. Basic Books, New York.
Gilpin R. (1990) Where does Japan fit in? In: Newland, K (ed.), *The International Relations of Japan*, pp. 5–21. Macmillan, London.
Green MJ. (2001) *Japan's Reluctant Realism*. Palgrave, New York.
Green S. (2002) S&P rates Japan as the dunce of G7 nations. *Sydney Morning Herald*, 17 April.
Hayao K. (1993) *The Japanese Prime Minister and Public Policy*. University of Pittsburgh Press, Pittsburgh and London.
Heignbotham E, Samuels RJ. (1998) Mercantile realism and Japanese foreign policy. *International Security*, 22(4), 171–203.
Hirata K. (2001) Cautious proactivims and reluctant reactivism. In: Akitoshi M, Sato Y (eds.), *Japanese Foreign Policy in Asia and the Pacific*, pp. 75–100. Palgrave, New York.
Hollerman L. (1988) *Japan's Economic Strategy in Brazil: Challenge for the United States*, Lexington, Massachusetts: Lexington Press.
Hughes CW. (1999) *Japan's Economic Power and Security*. Routledge, London and New York.
Huntington SP. (1993) Why International Primacy Matters. *International Security*, 17(4), 68–83.
Inoguchi T. (2005) *Japanese Politics*. Trans Pacific Press, Melbourne.
Iokibe M. (2002) Interview Series 3, Hashimoto Ryutaro. *Kokusai Mondai*, 504, 62–79.
Johnson C. (1982) *MITI and the Japanese Miracle*. Stanford University Press, Stanford.
Kaifu T. (1990) Policy speech by Prime Minister Kaifu, March 2. *Diplomatic Bluebook 1990*, Ministry of Foreign Affairs, p. 274.

Keohane RO. (1986) Theory of world politics: Structural realism and beyond. In: Kaohane RO (ed.), *Neorealism and Its Critics*, pp. 158–203. Columbia University Press, New York.

Keohane RO, Nye JS. Jr. (1977) *Power and Interdependence*. Little Brown, Boston.

Katz R. (2009) Making history. *The Oriental Economist*, 77(8), 1–3.

Katzenstein PJ. (1996) *Cultural Norms and National Security: Police and Military in Postwar Japan*. Cornell University Press, Ithaca and London.

Katzenstein PJ, Okawara N. (1993) Japan's national security. *International Security*, 17(4), 153–185.

Knorr K. (1975) *The Power of Nations*. Basic Books, Inc, New York.

Koppel BM, Orr RM (eds.) (1993) *Japan's Foreign Aid: Power and Policy in a New Era*. Westview Press, Boulder.

Kusano A. (1999) *Renritsu Seiken: Nihon no Seiji 1993*. Bunshunshinsho, Tokyo.

Lincoln EJ. (1993) *Japan's New Global Role*. Brookings Institution, Washington DC.

Loveday P. (1982) *Promoting Industry*. University of Queensland Press, St. Lucia.

Morgenthau HJ. (1965) *Politics among Nations: the Struggle for Power and Peace*, 3rd ed. A. A. Knopf, New York.

Ministry of Foreign Affairs (1985) *Diplomatic Bluebook 1985*. Okurasho Insatsukyoku, Tokyo.

Ministry of Foreign Affairs (1990) *Diplomatic Bluebook 1990*. Okurasho Insatsukyoku, Tokyo.

Ministry of Foreign Affairs (1992) *Diplomatic Bluebook 1992*. Okurasho Insatsukyoku, Tokyo.

Ministry of Foreign Affairs (1999) *Diplomatic Bluebook 1999*. Okurasho Insatsukyoku, Tokyo.

Miyashita A. (2003) *Limits to Power*. Lexington Books, Lanham.

Muramatsu M, Krauss ES. (1987) The conservative policy line and the development of patterned pluralism. In: Yamamura K, Yasukichi Y (eds.), *The Political Economy of Japan Volume I: The Domestic Transformation (the Political Economy of Japan)*, pp. 516–554. Stanford University Press, Stanford.

Nakane C. (1970) *Japanese Society*. University of California Press, Berkeley and Los Angeles.

Nye JS. (1988) Neorealism and Neoliberalism. *World Politics*, 40(2), 235–251.

Nye JS. (1990) Soft Power. *Foreign Policy*, 80, 153–171.

Nye JS. (2004) *Soft Power*. Public Affairs, New York.

Okimoto DT. (1989) *Between MITI and the Market: Japanese Industrial Policy for High Technology*. Stanford University Press, Stanford.

Orr RM. Jr. (1990) *The Emergence of Japan's Foreign Aid Power*. New York: Colombia University Press.

Pempel TJ. (1978) Japanese foreign economic policy: The domestic basis for international behavior. In: Katzenstein P (ed.), *Between Power and Plenty*, pp. 139–190. The University of Wisconsin Press, Wisconsin.

Powell B. (2009) China Flies High. *Time Magazine*. 10 August. 18–21.

Pyle KB. (2006) Abe Shinzo and Japan's Change of Course. *National Bureau of Asian Research*, 17(4), 5–31.

Pyle KB. (1996) *The Japanese Question: Power and Purpose in a New Era.* AEI Press, Washington, DC.

Rix A. (1993) Managing Japan's Aid: ASEAN. In: Koppel BM, Orr RM (eds.), *Japan's Foreign Aid: Power and Policy in a New Era*, pp. 19–40. Westview Press, Boulder.

Rosecrance R. (1986) *The Rise of the Trading State: Commerce and Conquest in the Modern World.* Basic Books, New York.

Rothgeb JM. (1993) *Defining Power: Influence and Force in the Contemporary International System.* St. Martin's Press, New York.

Samuels RJ. (1994) *Rich Nation, Strong Army: National Security and the Technological Transformation of Japan.* Cornell University Press, Ithaca.

Saxe JG. (1973) The Blind Men and the Elephant. In: *The Poems of John Godfrey Saxe, Complete edition*, pp. 77–78. James R. Osgood and Company, Boston.

Soeya Y. (2005) *Nihon no 'Middle Power' Gaiko.* Chikuma Sobo, Tokyo.

Sorifu (1994) *Yoron chosa nenkan.* Okurasho Insatsukyoku, Tokyo.

Sorifu (1995) *Yoron chosa nenkan.* Okurasho Insatsukyoku, Tokyo.

Tsurutani T. (1977) *Political Change in Japan: Response to Postindustrial Change.* David McKay Company Inc, New York.

Watanabe A. (1977) Japanese Public Opinion. In: Scalapino RA (ed.), *The Foreign Policy of Modern Japan*, pp. 105–146. University of California Press, Berkeley.

Waltz KN. (1979) *Theory of International Politics.* Addison Wesley, Reading, Mass.

Yamado A. (2000) Neo-Techno-Nationalism: How and Why It Grows. Columbia international affairs online [working papers], No. 5/00: 1–5. http://www.ciaonet.org/isa/yaa01/ accessed August 10, 2009.

Yasutomo D. (1995) *The New Multilateralism in Japan's Foreign Policy.* St. Martin's Press, New York.

PART I
A Modern Historical Background

Perhaps in the past, Japan has suffered from having too much history.

"That's the effect of living backwards," the Queen said kindly: "it always makes one a little giddy at first —"

"Living backwards!" Alice repeated in great astonishment. "I never heard of such a thing!"

"— but there's one great advantage in it, that one's memory works both ways."

"I'm sure *mine* only works one way," Alice remarked. "I can't remember things before they happen."

"It's a poor sort of memory that only works backwards," the Queen remarked (Lewis Carroll, *Through the Looking Glass*).

Modernization meant creating the idea of Japan as a nation. To do so required manufacturing new historical traditions and transforming conventions in strategic and convenient ways. With China representing the potential desolation facing Japan if it failed in its task, the Meiji regime sought to bring its fragile experiment to a degree of parity with the Western colonial powers. With a growing economy as the basis for a powerful military potential, Japan persistently attempted to become a dominant regional presence, and by doing so safeguard its security. The failure of this experiment, as revealed by the post-war occupation, did little to blunt Japan's foreign policy ambitions. It still equated its survival with the need to dominate within the East Asian region. That in the post-war period, Japan chose a path other than brute military power was dictated more by the reality of prevailing circumstances, than by any radical reversion of policy objectives. The following overview represents our attempt to acquaint readers with the fundamentals of modern Japanese foreign policy.

Chapter 2

Tumultuous Japan: Regional Diplomacy 1868–1965

2.1 Starting from Scratch: The Rise of Modern-Day Japan

In the history of the Asia–Pacific region, the unanticipated rise of Japan dominated the first half of the twentieth century. Since the start of the Meiji era, Japan had devoted itself to nation building, encapsulated by the formula "catch up with and overtake the West." The result of Japan's relentless ambition was the creation of the first Asian industrial power. Yet, all of Japan's efforts to gain unquestioned pre-eminence within Asia were comprehensively smashed by the folly of precipitating World War II in the Pacific. Though dreams of military dominance were irreparably lost, the hope of gaining respect and Japan's rightful place in the sun was not. After losing the war, Japan redevoted itself to gaining the leading position it had so carelessly squandered, but this time it chose to build an economic, rather than a military, powerhouse. The success of Japan's "miracle economy" achieved not only domestic stability and rising incomes, but also the first use of war reparations, followed by targeted foreign assistance, to pave the way for a smooth re-entry into the Asian community. Ironically, Japan's escape from being a pariah nation was partially engineered by its old enemy. Riding the coattails of a US Cold War alliance enabled the Japanese to regain a measure of respectability. Of course, newfound wealth also largely buried old wrongs and unresolved grievances. Despite ceding all pretences of leadership to the Americans, and seeming to become inwardly focused on rebuilding their economy, the Japanese did not entirely forswear their dreams of becoming the leading nation in the Asian region.

The key then to understanding Japan's post-war diplomacy, its strategies and goals, is to draw out the motivations driving Japan from the Meiji restoration through to World War II. Between 1868 and 1945, Japan's objective can be reduced to the slogan popularized during that period, "strong army, strong nation." To gain the position that Japan thought itself entitled to required a military establishment able to rival that of the then-dominant Western powers. Defeated decisively, the Japanese were forced to change their mode of operation after the war, but not forswear their goals. We might say that post-war Japan operated under the revised motto of "strong economy, strong nation." Japan was wise enough to understand that a flattened country must change its ways, but at the same time realized that there were alternative paths to achieving desired results.

2.2 Japan Tries Its Hand at Regional Dominance: The Road from Samurai to Soldier

The end of the Pacific War (1941–1945) was more than the conclusion of a relatively brief struggle between Japan and the allied Western powers. The smashing of Japan's colonial empire,[1] and its dream of an East Asian Co-prosperity Sphere, was also the end of a form of competition whose roots went back nearly 80 years. Japan, at that time, was forced by the dominant West to play an imposed role on the world stage.[2] In 1868, after almost 250 years of isolation, the Meiji restoration gave birth to the beginnings of a modern Japan. This startling transformation would make Japan the first Asian country not only

---

[1] Unintentionally, and in a way quite unforeseen, the end of World War II not only smashed Japan's hopes of empire but ate away at the underpinnings of Western colonial empires. Old-style imperialism would be a historical relic within two decades of the war's conclusion.

[2] See Beasley (1995) or Irie (1987). For an excellent analysis from the power and cultural perspectives of the binational US–Japan framework, see Irie (1981) or Feis (1950). For primary documents, a rewarding source would be Ministry of Foreign Affairs (1965).

free from Western domination, but able to compete on equal terms with the existing imperial powers. Part of the modernization process required the re-creation of Japan as a single nation rather than one composed of disparate fiefdoms. The feudal system, which underpinned the Tokugawa shogunate, needed to be replaced with a powerful, centralized government. Carried out in the name of the Meiji emperor, the restructuring of an entire country gained, by this convenient device, a needed dollop of legitimacy.

Shifting from feudal arrangements to those of a modern capitalist country was a journey that all Western nations had made prior to the Japanese.[3] Inspired, as well as frightened, by the methods of the major imperialist nations (Britain, France and Russia), who were expanding their influence and empires in Asia, Japan reacted by creating a strategy of nation building and rapid industrialization. The aim was not only to elude the grasp of the Western powers, but to meet them as equals on a level plane. To succeed against obvious odds, a backbone of "nation builders" within Japan urged putting in place a policy that would "enrich the country; strengthen the military" by adopting the methods, as well as the appearance, of Western civilization. Modernization was not to be a limited or half-hearted endeavor. Reform would extend not only to the obvious fields of politics and military matters, but also encompass law, education, economics and much else. As the policy played out over the years, it in fact ended up touching almost every surface of Japanese society (Beasley, 1963, p. 137). But as far as determining the direction and goals of this newly formulated country of Japan, the embrace of the modern reached out not only to the European model of economic development. Perhaps even more important in shaping a turbulent future, Japan's initiatives increasingly imitated Europe's continuing cultivation of colonialism and its association with rising levels of imperialism.

---

[3]Whether the Japanese replicated the same process undertaken by these Western nations is an open question. The Japanese accomplished a largely top-down transformation rather than a result driven by a restive middle class. This approach resulted in retaining some aspects of feudal institutions within the newly created structure. Of course it is unwise to lump all the Western powers together as well. Certainly the paths taken by latecomers such as Germany or Russia differed from the routes characterizing the US, Britain or France. A classic work examining the issue of a top-down approach to revolutions (reforms) is Skocpol (1979).

China, of course, provided Japan with all it needed to know about the dangers of becoming ensnared by European imperialism. Given this standpoint, demands by Western powers for special commercial privileges simply represented the thin edge of the wedge for reducing the Japanese to a repugnant colonial, or semi-colonial, status. The forced opening of Japan had meant a series of what the Japanese regarded as unequal treaties. The Meiji government consequently focused on becoming strong enough to be able to revise these agreements that had been foisted upon this powerless nation. If the Japanese could succeed, they would have sidestepped the trap that had befallen so many of their other Asian neighbors. Avoiding outright colonization was of course imperative. But Japan also wanted to escape the common fate of domination as exemplified by Thailand (then Siam) and Indonesia. However, as a "latecomer" to the integrated world system, the Japanese, pursuing a path of practicality, had little choice but to acknowledge their country's inferiority, materially if not culturally, to the West in terms of wealth and power. Yet, Japan not only wished to elude Europe's domination but hoped to emulate their dominant position in Asia. This notable "love–hate relationship with the West" came from an ambiguity intrinsic to the process of "catching up" (Dower, 1993, p. 315). Different groups of passionate Meiji-era intellectuals reflected this basic ambiguity by proposing two basically different paths for Japan in world affairs.

One group of these Japanese intellectuals was taken by the idea of "civilization and enlightenment." They believed passionately that Japan needed to emulate the superior ways of Western culture. For instance, Yukichi Fukuzawa[4] (1835–1901), who was not only an influential intellectual but a noted educator, argued for "Datsua ron" (a theory of separation from Asia):

> Adoption of western civilization is an essential tool to secure independence, therefore, Japan should leave Asia and emulate Western

[4] Born as a *samurai* of low rank, he devoted his life to teaching, writing, and translating while also finding time to establish Keio University. His aim was not only to bring to his people the benefit of foreign books, but to open the "closed" country and bring it entirely into the light of western civilization.

civilization in order to enrich and strengthen its country. In our relations with China and Korea, we should not feel obliged to make special allowances for these countries just because they happen to be our neighbours, but deal with them just the way westerners deal with them. Bad company ruins good morals. I refuse to keep company with bad acquaintances in East Asia (Fukuzawa, 1926 [translated by Hatakeyama]).[5]

In his discussions, Fukazawa avoided issues dealing with power politics and statecraft. Fukazawa's interest was confined to the advancement of civilization. But that did not prevent the paradigm he presented from being useful to Japanese leaders during the Meiji period. He provided a possible method for ordering resource priorities. Doing so created an allocation approach that might, if properly adapted, facilitate Japan's modernization process. However, in terms of concrete objectives, the government instead opted to pursue a more realistic or practical path, which emphasized military power as the key to achieving regional success and respect. In this widely shared view, expanding national power by creating a strong military force remained the most effective way to achieve Japan's fundamental goals.

A series of tests served to prove Japan's military strength and the efficacy of force over diplomacy. Japan first demonstrated its growing offensive capabilities in its clashes with China (Sato, 1977, p. 23).[6] Korea, the Ryukyus and Formosa defined a few of the most salient points of conflict characterizing the tense relations between the two countries. Korea in particular became a distinct flashpoint, with mutual antagonism inevitably leading to a declaration of war between Japan and China. Japan intended to use this contest to gain full recognition from the existing world powers. At this time, Japan thought it had now earned the right to be party to any agreement made between the "civilized" nations. The Japanese had fought hard to be acknowledged as an equal rather than being destined forever to toil in a subordinate position relative to these other major players. Achieving an overwhelming victory over the Chinese Qing dynasty in 1895 provided

---

[5] To get a fuller sense of Fukuzawa, see Keio (1960, p. 240).
[6] This article is one of many in a three-volume work edited by Scalapino (1977). It is also quite useful for the numerous archival documents it contains.

Japan with a foundation, from which it thought an accelerated burst of Japanese empire-building in Asia could proceed.[7] At the same time, Japan's iconic victory also set the rather repugnant course of future Sino–Japanese relationship. Japan's previous attitude of respect and even deference, soon turned to contempt for the defeated giant (Ikei, 1991, p. 77). This ingrained posture would continue to color relations between the two countries for more than half a century. However, despite this initial success, Japan soon learned that Europe was determined to be dismissive of any Japanese pretensions. Japan had failed to approach, let alone gain, the respect to which it aspired.

European attitudes became explicit a mere six days after the signing of the Sino–Japanese peace treaty. Japan submitted to heavy pressure exerted by Russia, Germany and France and reluctantly agreed to return Liaotung.[8] This European intervention humiliated the Japanese by highlighting the dismissive way in which these powers continued to treat them. Unfortunately, Japan was not in a position to ignore or refuse to follow "advice" issued by these Western powers. The hard learned lesson that Japan drew from this unhappy experience was a decided need to further strengthen its military standing. This quest first took the form of a 1902 alliance with Britain. The alignment, directed primarily against Russia, was hailed by the Japanese as the first solid proof that they were now worthy to sit at the same table with the acknowledged major nations.[9] At least as important was the recognition by Britain of Japan's interests in the Korean peninsula and that these interests encompassed political, commercial and industrial spheres. By doing so, Britain implicitly signaled its acceptance of Japan's subsequent expansion into Korea.

Japan was emboldened by these achievements to clash with Russia. The Russo–Japanese War of 1904–1905 was more than just another defeat for the hapless Russians. The victory over a European power

---

[7] Japan grabbed Taiwan and Liaotung as part of its reward for prevailing in the Sino–Japanese War (1895).

[8] Japan resented having to surrender Liaotung, which it viewed as its rightful desserts for defeating the Chinese.

[9] The treaty provided that each signatory would remain neutral if the other became involved in a Far Eastern war, while acting together if either were attacked by two or more other powers.

by a non-European state was not only a first in modern times, but symbolized Japan's ascendance as a rising imperialist power.[10] Japan then finalized this initial stage of its mainland adventures by forcibly annexing Korea in 1911. Other avenues of advancement serendipitously opened up soon after. With the European powers and eventually the US enmeshed in trench warfare, World War I provided a particularly fortuitous opportunity for Japan to extend its power on mainland China. Posing as a Western ally, Japan was able to take over the rights that had been ceded to Imperial Germany in Shantung. By this stage, Japan had covered a remarkable distance since the early days of the Meiji Restoration. The Japanese were now full-fledged players in the tough game of imperial politics.

However, trying to compete as equals in a Western devised game was bound to yield blows to Japan's self-esteem. Objectively, Japan was climbing up the rankings of powerful nations. Victory in the Russo–Japanese War had lifted Japan to number eight. The subsequent German defeat in World War I had moved Japan, by default, up to the fifth spot. With the war at an end, Japan assumed it now would be respected for its military might, if not for its contributions to winning the largely European conflict. As one of the victorious allied nations, Japan felt that it had earned a seat at the Versailles Peace Conference in 1919. Reality and racism soon corrected this illusion. Japan's proposal to include a principle of racial equality in the Covenant of the League of Nations was met with dismissive opposition. The collected British dominions, but in particular the Australian contingent led by its combative Prime Minister, Billy Hughes, adamantly rejected any such clause.[11] The Australians regarded the Japanese proposal as a virtual attack on its "white Australia" policy, refusing any possible compromise

---

[10]As a result, Japan

- gained Russian recognition of its freedom of action in Korea,
- took over the Russian lease of Liaotung plus part of the associated railway,
- secured the southern half of Sakhalin.

[11]The Australians harped on the sheer numbers of casualties they had sustained over the long years of war and demanded recognition of their sacrifice in terms of blocking the Japanese. Japan lacked any real champion willing to take up their cause.

or alternative (Kajima, 1976, p. 9). This episode only fed into Japanese perceptions of an intractable racism that aimed to keep Asians isolated and an ingrained discrimination against which there was no appeal. A repugnant and prevailing sense of white supremacy allied to unyielding domination left Japan extremely sensitive to any perceived slight or unequal treatment (Dower, 1993, p. 258).[12]

Japanese feelings were further aggravated just three years after the Versailles Treaty. The Washington Naval Treaty of 1922 provided additional fuel for their bruised egos and consuming rage at the deliberate unequal treatment they were asked to endure. The agreement prescribed that the American, British and Japanese Navies would remain in the ratio of 5:5:3. The ostensible objective behind such an agreement was to forestall the sort of arms race that had helped to precipitate World War I. The Japanese, however, perceived this arrangement as an attempt to lock in their inferior position relative to the prevailing powers. The idea that military restraint was to be largely borne by them, only served to fuel Japan's festering sense of unfairness and implicit racism. This Western attitude of contempt would later rationalize Japan's self-serving justification for its coercive expansionism. Seizing the moral high ground, the Japanese would claim, rather self-righteously, that they were liberating the East, not only from the arrogant domination of the Western colonial powers, but from the heavy hand of their contemptuous racism.

These actions by the Western powers neatly fed into rising domestic resentment, which was effectively exploited by self-interested parties, specifically factions within the Japanese military. They were able to generally convince the public that Japan was in an inherently disadvantageous and desperate position relative to its Western oppressors. This widely felt animosity was then increasingly inflamed by

---

[12] For the role of racism, see Dower (1986, p. 8):

> In the United States and Britain, the Japanese were more hated than the Germans before as well as after Pearl Harbor. On this, there was no dispute among contemporary observers. They were perceived as a race apart, even a species apart — and an overpoweringly monolithic one at that. There was no Japanese counterpart to the "good German" in the popular consciousness of the Western Allies.

Japan's seemingly precarious position relative to secure access to natural resources. These basic commodities were of course essential to feed the sort of military machine that the Japanese high command insisted was a prerequisite for gaining the sort of dominant role that Japan deserved and the respect it had been denied. But Japan's attempt to finance a build-up on such an extensive scale had been thwarted, up to now, due to a basic lack of industrial competitiveness (Kosaka, 1977, pp. 212–214). This disadvantageous position was clearly reflected by a series of negative trade balances that Japan had been forced to bear since the start of the immediate post-war period (1919). The economic strain due to large budget allotments for military materials was undisputed (Kosaka, 1977, pp. 212–214; Ikei, 1991, p. 147).[13] This unwanted consequence of Japan's intensive modernization process had saddled the Japanese with budgetary problems for decades. A balance of payments problem had appeared during Japan's initial stages of industrialization, and thereafter its "strong army" focus caused the deficits to become chronic. This created a sort of chicken-and-egg dilemma in which the military insisted that only expanded power would procure the resources it needed. The resulting deficits were used as proof that even more such expenditures were urgently required.

If peaceful trade could not produce an unencumbered source of raw materials, Japan felt justified in exploring alternative routes to the same objective. In 1932, seeking to secure needed raw materials, the Kwantung Army, based in the Japanese concessions within Manchuria, created the puppet state of Manchukuo. (This dependency would become the site of an experimental, planned economy, and the opportunity for some serious self-enrichment by those attached to the Kwantung Army.) In response to Japan's seizures, the League of Nations united to condemn what was described as a blatant piece of expansionism.[14] Although the condemnation lacked any teeth at this early stage, the Japanese used the incident as an excuse for withdrawing from the

---

[13]During 1917–1921, Japan's military expenditure accounted for 43.54 percent of its total budget.
[14]Regarding the Manchurian incident, see Nihon Kokusai Seiji Gakkai (1987).

League the following year. They would no longer have to rationalize their inevitable rejection of that body's edict, but could now explicitly cast themselves off from any binding ties to such international organizations. As a result, Japan's isolation could only deepen. This Manchurian incident, driven by the unilateral and arbitrary decisions of the Kwantung Army, showed that the government lacked either the means or the will to reign in the army. Nor could any government hope to court public opinion by such targeted opposition. The Japanese people looked toward the military to reclaim Japan's lost honor through some daring and successful series of exploits.

This atmosphere filled with unrest, assassinations and widespread uncertainty proved a fertile breeding ground that helped create such hostile actions as the 1937 Marco Polo incident. However, this particular event, whether deliberately engineered or not, did lead directly to the desired war with China. Disappointing Japanese expectations, the war with China failed to enrich Japan but rather dragged on interminably, offering no quick conclusion to an increasingly costly conflict. The military at that point decided that the war could only be brought to a successful conclusion by having completely at its disposal the region's entire resources. This basic need to feed the growing Japanese war machine could only create fateful repercussions for Japan's relations with other nations. Fortunately for the Japanese, the European powers at this time were too preoccupied with the rise of Hitler and their experiment at appeasement in Munich. America was, for the most part, still stubbornly gazing inward and refusing to be drawn into distant conflicts.

For these reasons, as well as others, the major powers turned a temporary blind eye to Japan's exploits and failed to take any early concrete steps. Expansion of the sort undertaken by Japan on the Chinese mainland was not foreign to the widespread imperialism characterizing the Western powers. However, the rise of a competing Asian power eventually did create widespread apprehension. The long festering antagonism between the US and Japan quickly came to the fore with clear-cut American hostility to Japan's actions and policies in China. Embargoes of key raw materials, and other forms of economic pressure, culminated in a 1939 refusal by the US to renew its commercial treaty with Japan.

This led to the widely held Japanese opinion that the Americans were deliberately attempting to strangle them into submission.

But the confusion created by the European war in 1941 presented an increasingly aggressive Japan with the opportunity to drive southward to expand their sphere of influence. (Plans for a northern campaign had been effectively thwarted by the Soviets.) The aim was to break out of the continuing stalemate in China while simultaneously securing a reliable source of raw materials. To do so, the Japanese intended to first sweep through French Indochina and then into the Dutch East Indies. Upon occupying the former in September 1940, the Japanese became part of the Axis Powers by signing a Tripartite Pact with Germany and Italy. (This was clearly an alliance of convenience given Hitler's inherent racism, which extended to a sharp contempt for the Japanese and other Asians.)

The US retaliated by imposing a scrap metal embargo, as well as one on steel-making materials. The American move put a serious crimp into Japan's plans to stockpile strategic materials even before the subsequent total ban on oil supplies. By July 1941, the US had hardened its position. Not only did the Americans freeze Japanese assets and halt oil shipments, but they peremptorily demanded a total and immediate withdrawal of all Japanese military forces from China and French Indochina.[15] Both sides did attempt to negotiate their differences, but it is arguable whether either one was particularly serious or willing to compromise. Talks stalled as Japan insisted that it would withdraw from French Indochina only if the US agreed to lift the embargo. China was another story entirely, with the Japanese refusing categorically to withdraw unconditionally. Instead, the Japanese chose the military route of seizing whatever resources they deemed necessary.

Japan's military government almost compulsively rationalized Japan's territorial grab in Northeast and Southeast Asia. There was a perceived need to dress up a basic thirst for empire and the associated security of an assured flow of basic commodities. The Japanese cultivated a distinct ideological position based on the exaltation of the Asian race (though with a distinct Nipponese slant). The intention was

---

[15] Japan was dependent on the US for 80 percent of its total oil imports.

to insure domestic and regional support by providing a feasible rationale for their actions, one which would place the Japanese in the best light possible. They held out the promise of establishing a new world order in East Asia. This Japanese-inspired regional structure would break from the unjust Western-imposed framework that had exploited the East in the past. More formally, in 1938, the Japanese proclaimed the beginning of an "East Asian New Order" that would lift the fortunes of the entire region under a benevolent order imposed by Japan. Within this newly designed Commonwealth, Japan would form the hub uniting the now diverse nations of Asia.

This new order would stress the importance of Pan Asian unity in the formation of the region's economics and politics. A united China, Manchukuo and Japan would represent the necessary initial concrete steps that would inevitably lead to a higher objective. Once completed, a properly reconstituted Northeast Asia would spread prosperity throughout the region. This rationale for Japanese aggression quickly expanded to require the cooperation, or submission, of Southeast Asia as well in the even more grandly conceived "Greater East Asia Co-Prosperity Sphere." Within this vaunted landscape, Japan self-consciously took its place as the rightful liberator of Asia. Under the inspired Japanese leadership, other Asian countries would be enabled to throw off the bonds of Western colonialism. Japan, by destroying these despised Western bonds would act as an elder brother to the weaker, less self-sufficient Asian nations. The Japanese promised that they would erect a viable framework that would be constructed upon those unique Asian values that they shared with the rest of the region. Once successful, both Northeast and Southeast Asia in the following post-war period would share in the benefits accruing to this new Asian order. As was its due, Japan would assume the central position within its own creation.

Skillfully packaged and appealing to deeply felt Asian grievances, this Japanese vision did gain a number of initial followers in Malaya, Burma, the Philippines and Indonesia. The Burmese and Filipinos, under the firm hand and steady guidance of the all-powerful Japanese Army, even went so far as to declare their independence by 1943. Not surprisingly, Japan's utopian-like rhetoric failed to match the reality of its expansionist drive. Though professing to be battling on behalf of the downtrodden people of East Asia, the Japanese notably failed to garner the support of the Chinese or any other Southeast Asian country. Instead, the reaction to Japanese occupation was varying degrees of anti-Japanese resistance, often corresponding to the harshness with which the locals were treated. These movements seemed to gain ground over time in the areas occupied by the Japanese armed forces. Though hardly welcoming Western domination, many Asian nations found it difficult to exchange one form of exploitation for the version offered by the victorious Japanese.

In many ways, China became the crucible in which these opposing ideologies were tested. Neither the Kuomintang nor the Communist party showed the slightest interest in Japan's ideological manifesto, although not displaying any eagerness to embrace the West. Pragmatically, they aligned themselves with either the US or the Soviet Union in order to dispose of the hated Japanese. This antagonism between the two nationalities extended beyond limited geographical boundaries. In Malaya, it was the Chinese population that formed the main source of resistance. In general, the Chinese refused to swallow Japanese dreams, especially when faced with the harsh reality of their implementation. The leader of the Kuomintang forces, Chiang Kai-shek, repeatedly scoffed at this Japanese notion of a future "Greater East Asia Co-Prosperity." They promised a peaceful entity that would extend over the width and breadth of the region. To him, as to others, this example of Japanese propaganda was full of naked hypocrisy (Irie, 1991, pp. 26–27).[16] In fact, Japan's treatment of the resident Chinese in these fully "liberated" areas, as well as in the other conquered Asian countries, only served to confirm the worse of these suspicions.

Naturally, unconditional surrender by the Japanese ended these dreams of a New Asia engineered and dominated by the Japanese. Yet, Japan's record of conquest was not without its consequences. The colonial order that had defined Southeast Asia vanished, as did the centralized imperial order that had prevailed in China. Inadvertently, Japan

---

[16]For Chiang Kai-shek's speech in regard to Japan's "East Asian New Order," see Yoshibumi Wakamiya (1995, pp. 83–85).

did create a new regional order by utterly destroying the basis of the old one.

After the war, a Japan, flattened by defeat, nonetheless discovered that it did not have to entirely surrender its dreams of leadership and pre-eminence. Under the newly evolving post-war regional order, Japan could still maneuver to gain some elements of leadership, at least given time and the sufficient will and skill to persevere. This coveted position would be won this time, not by brute domination, but by employing a more subtle, consensual approach. Force and the overt flexing of military might would prove to be denied to the Japanese in the aftermath of a disastrous war. New tools focusing on diplomatic finesse and positive inducements might, however, accomplish the same objectives where more forceful and overt strategies failed in the years preceding Japan's overwhelming defeat.

2.3 Japan Attempts to Position Itself Strategically: Finessing US Cold War Diplomacy

An unforeseen twist of fate changed the direction of Japan's post-war future. The Cold War altered US priorities from remaking and re-educating Japan to the more compelling need to create a reliable Asian surrogate to help withstand communist aggression. Defeat in World War II led to a largely American occupation that would continue until 1952. Japan then would endure an extended tutelage under the watchful eye of its American conquerors. The occupation forces were led by the often overweening General Douglas MacArthur, acting as the Supreme Commander of the Allied Powers (SCAP). MacArthur, who would reign in Japan like some sort of latter-day emperor, came to have a profound effect on Japan's post-war development.

The occupation itself can best be divided into two distinct periods. The early days were more idealistic, with New Dealers from the Roosevelt administration dominating strategic thinking. The Americans were intent on disarming Japan and ensuring that they would never pose a future threat to the Pacific region. The major objective was to forestall what many saw as an inherent tendency toward militarism and empire building. This conception rejected fostering a strong Japanese economy, which would only be the basis for renewing Japan's old aggressive dreams. For these reasons, no economic aid would be forthcoming, nor would there be any future regional integration. From this standpoint, the Japanese must by necessity be humbled by the occupation forces, with living standards forced to match those of the surrounding countries (Borden, 1984, pp. 62–67).

Months after surrender, in December 1945, America's first mission investigating the current state and future course of Japan was headed by its newly appointed ambassador, Edwin Pauley. The conclusion drawn by the mission urged that Japan be kept weak through a series of reparation payments that forcibly would relocate Japan's remaining industrial facilities to other countries. An impoverished Japan would inevitably lack the means of mounting any future attempts to dominate the region.

As it turned out, Japan soon found itself being marched toward a completely different destination. The Americans quickly came to the realization that "containing communism" was not coincident with weakening Japan. Guided by this new inspiration, the attempt instead to produce an economically strong Japan would deliver a vital opportunity to stabilize the region and further facilitate resistance to the communist menace. The Cold War turned out to be a fortuitous break for Japan, at least when viewed from a certain vantage point.

The world was clearly veering away from its wartime realities. The Truman Doctrine (1947), along with the Marshall Plan to revitalize Europe, were both meant to hold the Soviets in check. By 1947, few doubted that the Cold War had come to dominate all other diplomatic efforts. In this framework, Soviet communism was monolithic. Each and every conflict had, by definition, a single cause. This would remain an unassailable Cold War verity, whatever the underlying reality of a specific problem might be. Though the problems in Asia would seem closely linked to the difficulties attendant on decolonization, the Americans preferred to operate on a more simplistic scenario.

By 1945, anti-colonial, independent governments had sprouted in Indonesia and Vietnam, the consequence, in part, of Japan's wartime activities. These consequences did not only alarm their former European colonial masters but the Americans as well. Vietnam became an instant trouble spot as the Vietnamese leader, Ho Chi Minh, was

labeled a communist and thus dangerous to the regional status quo.
The former colonial powers were able to play upon these American fears
to try to reinstate their previous positions. They argued that only the
former arrangements would allow these European countries to shore
up Asia against an encroaching Soviet Union. Examples abounded
throughout the region. Korea, for instance, was the site of a classic Cold War face-off with the American-backed regime in the South
confronting their Soviet counterparts in the North. Similar flare-ups
occurred in other former, and reclaimed, possessions. In 1948, the
Malayan Communist Party battled the British colonial administration
for control of the country. But most importantly, psychologically as
well as strategically, American-supported Generalissimo Chiang Kai-
shek seemed incapable of holding off the resurgent communists under
the guidance of Mao Tse Tung.

Circumstances thus had fortuitously changed Japan's status from
that of a despised, defeated enemy into a budding, Western-style
democracy that would act as a designated bulwark in turning back the
spread of Asian communism. A transformed US policy now seemed
inevitable. Regimes in China, Korea and Vietnam were all teetering
on the brink. These geopolitical shocks, quite expectedly, caused the
reshaping of American strategy to move ahead rapidly. A radically different environment meant that the negative after effects of the Pacific
War would largely vanish as Japan made its first tentative steps back into
the realm of international politics.

Looking back at the start of those long years of occupation, rehabilitation was never the central concern of this period, at least not the type
that would yield equal status to a hard-fought and now defeated foe.[17]
Initially, the Americans were more focused on eradicating the political
and economic structure that they believed had pushed the Japanese into
a suicidal war. Japan needed to be shoved firmly back into the periphery and maintained there. American policy makers could not imagine
that the Japanese had anything positive to contribute to forwarding

---

[17] This was proposed by George F. Kennan, Chairman of the State Department's Policy Planning
Council. The core of Kennan's Soviet containment vision in the late 1940s was the rehabilitation
of Germany and Japan as centers of regional power.

US interests. Instead, democratizing the country by making it over in the image of America would supposedly tame the aggressive tendencies that had characterized the Japanese since the Meiji restoration.

The US also had to take into consideration the sensitivities of their European allies. These countries often felt quite differently when it came to framing a future for Germany and Japan (Schaller, 1985, p. 88). But, as previously pointed out, circumstances and unforeseen events soon made the exigencies of the Cold War the top agenda item rather than any redressing of old wrongs by former enemies. By the time (February, 1948) that Percy H. Johnston headed up the third investigative mission into the future of Japan, the punitive focus on reparations had been discarded in favor of reconstructing the Japanese economy. In a parody of past Japanese aspirations, after adroitly reversing course, the US now thought in terms of "strong economy, strong ally." With Japan's economy left devastated by the war effort and ally bombing, "an end to reparation payments" became of prime importance. Marking the turnaround in 1948, the National Security Council (NSC 13/2) not only stopped that lethal financial drain of imposed repayments, but also insisted on making "economic rehabilitation" a priority. Clearly, accomplishing this daunting objective, reviving the devastated Japanese economy, could not be achieved quickly. Therefore, the report also insisted on a "postponement of an early peace treaty" implying extended years of occupation (US Department of State, 1974, pp. 858–862).

During this time, when America was reconsidering its best path forward, William Draper, Assistant Secretary of War, was in charge of both German and Japanese Occupation policy. He insisted on the need for a dramatic "shift in emphasis" from reform to recovery policies. If not adopted, Draper warned that the Japanese trade imbalance would continue to create a dangerous "dollar gap." This looming crisis needed to be addressed by completely revamping the Japanese economy. To do so would require an initial coordinated aid scheme, swiftly followed by the economic integration of Japan within a regional framework that could best be provided by Southeast Asia (Borden, 1984, pp. 77–81). To carry out these goals, the US imposed a set of nine stabilization principles that would kill off the crippling inflation, boost investment, and lay the grounds for economic growth. Carried out in early 1949, this program became known as the "Dodge Line," after the US banker brought in to implement this rather draconian initiative.[18] The ultimate aim was to create a strong and viable economy by transforming Japan into a "low-cost, high-volume industrial exporter linked to its Asian neighbours" (Schaller, 1985, pp. 145–146).[19] The overwhelming reason for these shifts in American occupation policy no doubt lay with a series of conflagrations, first in China, but followed soon after by Vietnam and Korea.

In October 1949, the Chinese communists achieved victory over their Kuomintang foes and almost immediately concluded a Sino–Soviet Treaty of Friendship and Alliance. Ho Chi Minh's communist-led government in Vietnam received support in the form of diplomatic recognition from other communist states. Finally, the outbreak of the Korean War in June 1950 unexpectedly made Asia, not Europe, the center of Cold War confrontations. With the US, backed by a UN resolution, plunging into war in the Korean Peninsula, a new round of balancing and counterbalancing began in Northeast Asia.[20] Emboldened by their early success in pushing back the North Korean forces, troops under the command of Douglas MacArthur moved relentlessly toward the Chinese border. The predictable response saw "volunteers"

---

[18] The program was more emblematic of the virtues of a small-town American banker than containing any reflection of the Keynesian revolution that was then sweeping the economics profession. The aim was to curb the excesses of domestic consumption and its inflationary companion and promote instead exports, which could rebalance Japan's trade accounts. These ideas, as well as that of a balanced budget, would continue to haunt Japan's economic planning up until the 1970s.

In December 1948, Washington announced nine principles of economic stabilization that were to be imposed on Japan, and then two months later dispatched to Tokyo a highly publicized mission aimed at putting the country back on its feet as a viable market economy. The mission was headed by a dictatorial "economic czar," Joseph Dodge, whose conservative "Dodge Line" was vigorously imposed until the outbreak of the Korean War. Under Dodge's stern supervision, the nine principles quickly became know as the "Nine Commandments;" and in this near-theological atmosphere, the redoubtable Detroit banker essentially joined Douglas MacArthur as another supreme being in occupied Japan (Dower, 1999, p. 540).

[19] Dodge also believed Japan would serve as a "key border area in the world-wide clash between communism and democracy" (Schaller, 1985, pp. 145–146).

[20] Having walked out on the Security Council, the Soviet Union found itself unable to veto the resolution. For that reason, the Western forces in Korea were nominally under UN command.

from the relabeled People's Republic of China (PRC) pour over the Korean border (November 1950), driving Western forces back toward Seoul. Some form of confrontation between the US and China became unavoidable. The stalemated Korean War featured few clear successes, but it did end up promoting the expansion of American military forces in the East, as called for in a National Security Council document (NSC-68) at that time.[21] These measures paralleled the build-up of NATO forces in Europe.[22] Responding to these current threats, American strategy now regarded Japan no longer with contempt, but rather as a key Asian surrogate in the ongoing battle developing between the communist and the Western blocs. With the Cold War outbreak, geographical destiny inevitably changed Japan's value to the US. As pointed out, old considerations were jettisoned for a diplomatic program of rehabilitation. Japan would emerge from this process with the past cosmetically erased and the future shaped by its role as a stalwart US ally.

Other considerations also played a part in creating such a decisive shift in US policy. Economic imperatives worked as an effective accelerant in overturning previously expected outcomes (Kolko and Gabriel, 1972, pp. 300–328, 510–533).[23] An extended American occupation of Japan undoubtedly would be costly. Even as early as 1947, Washington planners had not been reluctant to point out this obvious fact. Maintaining the decrepit state of the Japanese economy with continued assistance could only prove to be an expensive necessity over the coming years. Japan's extreme weakness at this time becomes depressingly obvious by examining just a few comparative statistics. For instance, by the end of 1947, Japan's industrial production was still only 45 percent

---

[21] Traditionally, the end of each American conflict had seen a drastic demobilization of its armed forces.

[22] NSC-68 called for a major expansion of America's armed forces, adding military instruments to the political and economic means of containment. This approach would significantly alter the form and content of US foreign policy and would eventually lead to direct American military involvement in conflicts such as those in Korea and Vietnam.

[23] As presented, the argument largely dismisses the effects that events taking place in China and Russia had on the reappraisal of occupation policy, which commenced in Washington (1947). Instead, according to this analysis, America's considerations in Japan were first and foremost economic.

of its 1930–1934 average. The status of trade was even more forlorn with exports accounting for only 19 percent of those pre-war levels, while imports managed a 39 percent level (Kolko and Gabriel, 1972, p. 518).

Without the ability to produce valued exports, Japan automatically lacked the wherewithal to import key resources. Under these conditions, Japan's trade deficits became chronic. From September 1945 to 1948 the deficits amounted to $978.1 million. Providing a minimum counterbalance to save Japan from complete collapse, US assistance during the same period totaled $1.0583 billion. Japan's devastated economy was just eking by, barely sustained by this lump of continuing US aid (Shiraishi, 1990, pp. 6–7). In the estimation of the National Security Council, Japan's inability to develop a self-sufficient economy was simply the crux of the problem. The US contribution was temporarily staving off economic collapse, but only at the cost of making Japan a permanent American dependency. The size of such assistance was simply too large. Instead of boosting economic rehabilitation, US largesse was becoming an unintentional impediment (Kolko and Gabriel, 1972, p. 522).

Ironically, Japan's saving grace turned out to be the outbreak of the Korean War (Kolko and Gabriel, 1972, p. 528). War had destroyed its economy and would now be instrumental in saving it. However, Japan, once again, plunged into recession after the momentary reprieve provided by the Korean War disappeared. The US, looking to end its occupation, formulated and decisively accelerated its policy shift. To these American policy makers, a rapid economic recovery now became equivalent to combating communism. An economically vibrant Japan would henceforth become one of the keystones of US Cold War strategy.

As mentioned, the economic strategy plotted out for Japan by US officials called for growing trade ties with the rest of Asia. However, the Chinese market had vanished with the fall of Chiang Kai-shek's forces, as had Japan's former colonial markets of Korea and Formosa. Japan seemed incapable of achieving a semblance of balanced trade, let alone using trade to spur its economic growth. Interests within Japan itself pushed for freer trade with communist China as a means of transcending its unyielding trade constraints (US Department of State, 1985, pp. 1413–1415). From a US standpoint, such trade was simply non-negotiable. With the Americans unequivocally shutting the door to mainland China, Japan's trade policy was made unarguably more difficult. In fact, faced with implacable US pressure, the Japanese government saw no other recourse than to conclude a peace treaty with the Kuomintang government in Taipei.[24] Of course, doing so made any sort of straightforward trade relations with either communist China or the Soviet Union much more difficult.[25] These externally imposed barriers ran counter to the more pragmatic thinking espoused by a number of Japanese officials, including Prime Minister Yoshida. To them it appeared obvious that trade with China could help offset post-war losses of import and export markets. In fact, entry into foreign markets was proving difficult for the Japanese in light of their failure to be admitted to the General Agreement of Trade and Tariffs (GATT) that largely defined post-war trade. Moreover, Japan faced intractable problems now that the economic boost deriving from US procurements inevitably vanished once the Korean armistice was in place.

Not surprisingly, the US was not eager to see a future marked by expanding trade between Japan and communist China. One of the last things that the US administration was anxious to facilitate in any way was a Japan increasingly dependent on China either as an export market or as a source of raw materials. Handing the Chinese a bargaining chip of that size would eventually undermine US strategic and political objectives.[26] Once the Americans had decided to pursue the creation of a revitalized Japan, the obvious trade connections to push were renewed partnerships, not with Northeast Asia, but with Southeast Asia, perhaps even stretching as far away as Australia.

---

[24]The US interpreted Finance Minister Ikeda's message to mean that the Japanese government wanted "the best they can get under the circumstances and as quickly as possible," whether or not China and the Soviet Union participated. See US Department of State (1976, pp. 1194–1198). Also see *Gaiko Kiroku*. Ministry of Foreign Affairs, B'-0010 0566.
[25]Before World War II, about 18 percent of Japanese exports went to the Chinese mainland (including Manchuria) and about 25 percent of its imports came from there.
[26]Yoshida explained Japan's position in a letter to John Foster Dulles:

The Sino–Soviet treaty of Friendship Alliance and Mutual Assistance concluded in Moscow in 1950 is virtually a military alliance aimed against Japan. In fact, there are many reasons

The rationale behind such a strategy was relatively straightforward. As a newly democratic ally of the US, Japan's contribution to the Cold War effort could only be economic in shape. This objective implied sustained growth spurred by a serious boost in productivity. Assured overseas markets may have been necessary for this strategy to succeed, but not those that were tinged red by communism. As an alternative, the US emphasized focusing southward toward South and Southeast Asia. These countries were certainly capable of supplying the necessary food and raw materials that Japan required to assist its economic reha-bilitation (US Department of State, 1985, pp. 1413–1415). The result-ing increase in productivity from this advantageous trade would make Japan increasingly competitive with other industrialized countries. The Japanese would then find markets for their manufactured goods. Such a move would effectively pre-empt the China option. Otherwise, the US foresaw that Japan, increasingly entangled in Chinese trade, would drift almost imperceptibly toward the Communist bloc (US Depart-ment of State, 1985, p. 414). Vice President Nixon, representing the voice of US policy, publicly explained the underlying rationale for this American strategy in December 1953.

> If Indochina falls, Thailand is put in an almost impossible position, the same is true of Malaya with its rubber and tin, the same is true of Indonesia, if this whole part of Southeast Asia goes under communist domination or communist influence, Japan, who trades and must trade with this area in order to exist, must inevitably be oriented towards the Communist regime (Kolko, 1971, p. 5).

Nixon's statement can be viewed as a sort of trial balloon that later allowed President Dwight D. Eisenhower to follow up, in April 1954, by making the "falling dominos" analogy official (Kissinger, 1994, pp. 623–624). Asia became characterized as an essential battle zone because of its natural resources and the fear that an overly

---

to believe that the communist regime in China is backing the Japan Communist Party in seeking violently to overthrow the constitutional system and the present government of Japan. In view of these considerations, I can assure you that the Japanese government has no intention to conclude a bilateral treaty with the communist regime of China (*Gaiko Kiroku*, B'-0009, 1069).

For Japan's relationship with China, see Soeya (1995, pp. 64–67).

trade-dependent Japan would be forced to turn in the Chinese direction to survive economically (Gravel, 1971, p. 597).[27] The context of these warnings came while the old European colonial empires were crumbling in Asia. The French were decisively defeated at Dien Bien Phu in Vietnam, which left no effective barriers standing to stem the inexorable communist advancement, or at least, this was the view firmly held by the Americans. Walling off this encroachment with a series of alliances (such as the American-led formation of the South East Asian Treaty Organization (SEATO)) seemed to promise a viable strategic response to contain communism. Southeast Asia would become the bedrock supporting America's Asian policy. Building upon this base, Japan could evolve into a dependable ally by redirecting its economic focus in a more southerly direction. Bowing to US pressure would still present Japan with a receptive market and a source of abundant resources. In this way, the Japanese could still prosper while staying well within the limitations set by Cold War constraints. Temptation would then be intentionally removed from Japan's policy planners. No need for them to play the China card when US-nurtured allies would prove to be even more amenable to Japan's economic needs.

To further its Cold War objectives, the US deliberately constructed a convenient framework within which Japan could fulfill a prescribed role in an increasingly complex struggle. An economically strong and growing Japan would be firmly in the Western Camp and offer a key staging post for the US military forces. Unintentionally, post-war communist success translated into an American strategy that was intent on securing an increasingly productive and growing Japanese economy. Thus it was hardly accidental that Japan chose to cultivate links with Southeast Asian countries rather than with the Chinese communists. China was at odds with the US and it was American strategy that was developing Japan's future diplomatic path. Japan obediently took the required, if tentative, steps in this direction by first initiating reparations to these

---

[27] It should be noted that ultimately Japan did not pursue a stereotypical program of what would later be labeled as export-led growth. In contrast to other Asian countries that followed, Japanese growth, until the first oil shock in 1973, was balanced between the need to rebuild its domestic market and the inter-related export trade.

favored Southeast Asian countries as well as promoting anti-communist ideology by becoming a member of the Colombo Plan in 1954.[28]

2.4 No More Warrior Nation: Understanding Anti-Militarist Constraints

We have seen how Japan's economic rehabilitation under strict American guidance was transformed from barely appearing on the US policy radar to moving to the center of those concerns. In pursuing these ends, US interests were not particularly driven by any overt concern with Japanese well being, but rather came to the fore as an offshoot of the evolving international situation. Japan, due to its US-devised constitution, was effectively sealed off from playing any direct military role in the ongoing Cold War struggle. But being geographically positioned in the forefront of potential Asian confrontations, an economically strong Japan became essential to US interests. This was a path both the Japanese and the American officials could view with equanimity. By appearing to be mutually beneficial to both sides, this strategic policy easily attracted influential supporters. The objectives of the US have been sufficiently discussed. But this tentative arrangement also worked well for the Japanese, not just in forwarding their long-term objectives, but in also playing adroitly to domestic public opinion. In the aftermath of an overwhelming defeat, the Japanese people were now overwhelmingly anti-militarist and unlikely to accept any role that was even faintly redolent of Japan's military past. Moreover, the US desire for economic expansion raised the prospect that the lives of the average citizen might be noticeably improved. Hopes for political stability, therefore, became increasingly dependent on the expectations of rising family incomes.

---

[28] The plan was essentially composed of a loose framework of countries in the Asia-Pacific region which aimed to promote the economic and social development of its members. By stressing foreign aid and technical assistance, the program fitted in well with Japan's broad diplomatic strategy. In particular, the emphasis was on human resource development through scholarship and other training programs. The initiative was launched at a Commonwealth Conference in 1950 in what was then Colombo, Ceylon, which subsequently gave its name to the policy.

On the Japanese side, the key individual shepherding this vision of a mutually advantageous US–Japan alliance was Shigeru Yoshida, prime minister between 1946 and 1947, and then again between 1948 and 1954.[29] The traditional Yoshida line dominated Japanese thinking during the post-war period. He stressed a Japan that was fully aligned with the US and a foreign policy that was largely economically determined. Following Yoshida's vision, a Japan nesting comfortably under the umbrella of US military power would only need light armaments at best. Anything more would court the danger of undermining Japan's own objectives. Fortunately, Japan could pursue this line without difficulty. If pressed, Japanese politicians could honestly claim that despite their wishes they were simply constrained from pursuing more offensive rearmament by Article 9 of the 1947 SCAP drafted and imposed constitution. The exact wording of what remained a controversial peace formulation is as follows:

> Aspiring sincerely to an international peace based on justice and order, the Japanese people forever renounce war as a sovereign right of the nation and the threat or use of force as means of settling international disputes. In order to accomplish the aim of the preceding paragraph, land, sea and air forces, as well as other war potential, will never be maintained. The right of belligerency of the state will not be recognized.[30]

Article 9 conveniently allowed Japan an escape hatch, keeping it from being fatally drawn into what would become an almost obsessive US Cold War strategy of containing communism on mainland Asia. The constitutional prohibition then provided an immediate tactical advantage as it managed to reassure a war-weary Japanese public while saving

---

[29]Yoshida was adopted by a rich trader and became a diplomat soon after the Russo–Japanese war, that is to say, he had been a diplomat before and during the Pacific War (Yoshida, 1957).

[30]Hitoshi Ashida, then Chairman of the Lower House Subcommittee established to review the draft constitution, inserted the phrase "in order to accomplish the aim of the preceding paragraph" at the beginning of the second paragraph to make it clearly possible that armaments for self-defense could still be permitted. For a more detailed discussion see Jitsuo Tsuchiyama (2000, p. 138). Ashida's amendment opened the way for the creation of the Self-Defense Forces in 1951. However, whether Ashida himself seriously intended, by the amendment, to make room for the future formation of the SDF is unclear (Saigunbi no ito uageaezu, *Asahi Shimbun*, September 30, 1995). As Dower points out, however, the actual motivation behind and reason for this particular amendment is ambiguous at best.

Japan from the worse excesses of America's anti-communist crusade. However, it also meant that Japan was highly constrained should it wish to develop a more assertive or even independent approach to regional security matters.

But with the Cold War growing and being relentlessly pursued by all parties concerned, the likelihood of maintaining the status quo characterizing the immediate occupation years grew ever smaller. Despite having largely written and imposed the singular peace imperative (Article 9), the US quickly revised its position as circumstances changed. With the Cold War suggesting the need for a more aggressive stance, the US now demanded that the Japanese jettison their newly acquired pacifism and rearm. The Americans pushed hard for this objective. First, MacArthur in imperial mode, only a month after the outbreak of the Korean War (July 1950) created by means of a *de facto* order, a newly constituted National Police Reserve of 75,000 men.

Then, in January 1951, with American forces rapidly retreating in Korea, US Secretary of State, John Foster Dulles, urgently pressed Japan to rearm. He considered that Japan was now one of the relatively few democratic countries, and thus automatically responsible for actively containing communist totalitarianism. Prime Minister Yoshida, however, was fully aware of the potential folly of pushing ahead with rearmament. Forestalling the Americans, Yoshida skillfully argued that the strongly pacifist Japanese public would recoil at any attempt to reinstitute a formal military structure. Moreover, with a weak and barely recovering economy, rearmament would entail levels of expenditure that would basically impoverish the Japanese. Yoshida concluded that combined with Japan's new found repugnance to anything military,

---

Ashida himself later claimed that it had been his purpose from the outset to open the door to future armament for self-defense through this change. This never emerged in the Diet discussions, however; and the secret records of Ashida's subcommittee, which remained classified for many decades, reveal that neither he nor his fellow committee members ever explicitly discussed their revision in terms of allowing "self-defense," nor was there any evidence of an implicit understanding that this is what was being done (Dower, 1999, p. 396).

For Yoshida's position on Article 9, see Dower (1979, pp. 378–383).

acquiescing to American demands would only generate the sort of domestic unrest that the communists could exploit.

A sudden reversal of policy then would not work in a country where the psychological scars of such a recent defeat are still largely unhealed (Yoshida, 1983, pp. 160–161). If communism was to be contained or even pushed back, first consideration should be given instead to Japan's devastated economy. Yoshida insisted that US aims could then best be served if Japan, for the time being, continued to pursue a narrowly defined national purpose (the promotion of economic recovery, not military build-up). This could work if the US was willing to guarantee Japan's security needs and leave the Japanese to tend to their domestic economy. Somewhat more formally, Yoshida set out this explicit position in a 1949 Diet address.

> It is my belief that the very absence of armaments is a guarantee of the security and happiness of our people, and will gain for us the confidence of the world, and will enable us as a peaceful nation to take pride before the world in our national politics (Pyle, 1996, p. 23).

Yoshida though was not categorical about the issue. He understood the need to rearm in terms of internal and external security (Yoshida, 1983, p. 168). To facilitate matters, while hewing to his public pronouncement, he opted for a more backroom route to insure an initial move to rearmament. Contrary to his explicit statements, he sought to secretly appease Dulles by setting in motion a limited level of rearmament. Security forces of 50,000 men were established. With peace treaty negotiation underway, and an implacable desire to witness the swift end to such a prolonged occupation, Yoshida hoped that this gesture would be sufficient to accelerate the signing of an acceptable agreement (Tanaka, 1997, pp. 61–64).

Yoshida generally dug in his heels despite the best attempts by the US to shape Japanese policy. He realized that the military route was hardly the best way to regain the prestige and respect that Japan had thrown away in the war. In this view, economic, rather than military, strength was both more achievable and more effective.

But the Yoshida administration was sufficiently wise to know that Japan could not foreswear security concerns even if the Japanese chose not to provide for these objectives themselves. Instead, Japan would have to depend on an alliance with the US in terms of a mutual security treaty that would treat the Japanese as equal partners while providing the country with crucial external protection. Fortunately, Japan did have a bargaining chip to play in the treaty negotiations that commenced in January 1951. The Korean War was raging, the Cold War was settling into a long haul stalemate, and the US needed strategic military bases. This meant that the US wanted to maintain forces on Japanese soil following the official end of the occupation. Both parties were well aware of America's newly developed strategic interests in Japan (US Department of State, 1976, p. 1264). As an enticement to encourage an early end to this post-war aftermath, Yoshida offered to host American bases in Okinawa, using UN Charter Article 51 as camouflage for this implicit trade-off. With its security assured, Japan could then concentrate on engineering an all-out economic recovery.

> The American occupiers had anyway pushed Japan in a conservative direction as early as 1948, when the risk of communist revolution in Japan and China — to say nothing of the Soviet threat — had come to be seen as a greater peril than militarism. The Korean War reinforced these priorities, while adding an economic dimension: the United States needed Japan's economy to be humming again to help the war effort (*Economist*, July 19, 2009, p. 28).

The bargaining did result in an American guarantee in terms of a US–Japan Security Treaty. Unfortunately, the reality of the treaty was a serious disappointment. Contrary to Japan's wishes and expectations, the terms did not leave the two countries on anything like an equal footing. Although the agreement allowed US military forces to be based in Japan, there was no reciprocal obligation for them to defend the Japanese. Moreover, the treaty provided US forces with the repugnant right to suppress domestic disturbances in Japan, an option normally deemed to be unacceptable in an independent state. In reaction to the unequal status that was the fundamental basis of the treaty, Foreign Minister Aoi Shigemitsu visited US Secretary of State, John Foster Dulles, in 1955. The purpose behind the visit was to gain a revision which would commit the US to defending Japan. Dulles refused straight out. In his opinion, Japan, given its constitutional restrictions, would be incapable of returning the obligation by defending such American territories as Guam in the Western Pacific. This dismissive US approach only emphasized the unequal nature of the relationship. Viewed as American contempt, this attitude left a residue of bruised feelings among Japanese politicians.

The end of the occupation in no way marked a cessation of pressure by the US to remilitarize (US Department of State, 1985, pp. 1450–1451). Though Yoshida had made a significant concession by establishing the first security forces, more was expected. What the US considered a reasonable military presence diverged widely from Japan's idea on the subject. The Japanese public was in no mood to accept the need for rearmament. Ever the clever politician, Yoshida was naturally cautious about boosting his embryo forces any further. With Japan desperately needing public stability, deliberately treading on public sensitivities was no way to ensure it. He made this point sufficiently clear to the then Ambassador Murphy.

> Time is necessary to adjust public opinion. As a result of the war, great prejudices exist especially on the part of the Japanese women against the military National Police Reserve and it has suffered because of these prejudices and that is why it is necessary that the new national safety force appear to the public in a favourable light (US Department of State, 1985, p. 1354).

Economically, it might have been barely feasible for the Japanese in the 1950s to have focused more of their attention on insuring national security by increasing their military expenditure. They had managed the equivalent during the Meiji era, even though they had been noticeably less wealthy then (Irie, 1991, p. 92).[31] But this time, concentrating almost exclusively on economic growth seemed the better option. Pursuing this strategy, the Japanese government did make concerted attempts to countermand US pressure during this decade. These were, however, only partially successful. Japan yielded to the extent of creating a Self-Defense Forces (SDF) in 1954. Fortunately, with the Korean War concluded, US demands became more attuned to Japan's current realities. The Americans shifted from expecting a military build-up to a more general level of satisfaction with an economically strong Japan. They in part conceded that recovery and growth would be the way in which Japan could play an indirect, but more effective, role in securing

---

[31] Per-capita GDP in 1900 was estimated at approximately \$8. In contrast, per-capita GDP in 1955 was \$200.

US Cold War strategy. As pointed out previously, a scenario that would leave the Japanese wealthier was bound to generate more popular acceptance than a return to anything resembling, however faintly, wartime militarism.

In fact, Japanese politicians were relatively powerless to do much except acquiesce to this diplomatic alternative. Pacifism and simultaneous anti-Americanism was widespread, held not only by the general public, but by a sizeable number of the political class. The absolute intransigence on this point became a worry not only to the US, as might be expected, but to the majority of the Japanese government as well. This irreconcilable contradiction between the Japan which was regarded by the Americans as a firm ally and the Japan which refused to contribute militarily to its own national security necessarily sowed the seeds of future conflicts. These underlying frictions burst into flame during the attempt to renew the US–Japan Security Treaty. Not only was any type of military role automatically rejected by the Japanese public, but as events proved, domestic feelings could make even a simple renegotiation of such agreements a matter for concern.

During these controversial treaty negotiations, Nobusuke Kishi served as prime minister (1957–1960). A bureaucrat who had made a name for himself as economic czar of the puppet Manchukuo administration, he later was able to enter the Tojo War Cabinet.[32] Ever the unscrupulous deal maker, he successfully resurrected his political career after his release, along with 18 other suspected war criminals, on December 24, 1948. As prime minister, he attempted to finesse widespread anti-Americanism and generally negative reaction to the US–Japan alliance by trying to engineer a renewal of the Security Treaty on more equal terms. In his metaphorical gun sights were the two greatest sticking points between the two countries. Kishi focused on getting a commitment from America to defend Japan against aggression and deleting the clause allowing US forces to suppress Japanese domestic disorder. Kishi though faced an uphill battle as Japanese politics turned

---

[32] He was born to one of the notable "power elite" families. For generations they had grown wealthy as highly successful operators of a number of sake breweries. Subsequently he was jailed, but not convicted, as a Class A war criminal. Part of the charges stemmed from accusations that he had been responsible for thousands of Chinese serving as forced laborers.

confrontational. Left-wing parties, especially the Japan Socialist Party (JSP) and of course the Japanese Communist Party (JCP), unconditionally opposed any form of treaty renewal. They had both unreservedly opposed the original agreement as unconstitutional. Moreover, the recently formed SDF was placed in the same unenviable category.

By October 1956, popular unrest focused on the loathed American bases. A large-scale demonstration mobilized the Japanese public to protest the planned extension of an airfield near the village of Sunakawa. At risk was the loss of agricultural land, seen as a sacrifice made to satisfy the continuing demands of the US (Beasley, 1990, p. 237). The prevailing ugly mood mounted with the 1957 Girard case. An army specialist, W.S. Girard, shot an unarmed Japanese woman who was approaching him. (Sadly, all she desired were some empty brass cartridge cases.) As viewed by the Japanese public, incidents such as these only served to inflame the already rising anti-American sentiment. The US took this widespread unrest quite seriously. President Eisenhower went so far as to request that the National Security Council compile a special study weighing the possibility of developing bases in Australia and New Zealand as a viable alternative to remaining in volatile Japan (Eisenhower, 1965, p. 141). Such a persistent and disruptive campaign made a continued military agreement between the two countries increasingly difficult. The Japanese public had become convinced that the security treaty represented the thin edge of an American wedge. In their view, acceptance meant that step by step, pliant Japanese politicians would allow the country to become forcibly remilitarized at the behest of the US.

The left-wing parties launched a campaign to completely abandon the security treaty in any form. Though the movement to end the treaty may have been spearheaded by political opposition, support was dispersed widely throughout the Japanese public. University students, in particular, became vocal opponents of these treaty negotiations. Ignoring the potential for unrest, the House of Representatives adopted the renegotiated treaty in May 1960. As anticipated, passage was met with violence and recurrent demonstrations, not only outside the Diet building, but throughout Japan as well. In June 1960, 5.8 million people gathered at a mass demonstration reflecting their unyielding opposition to the renewed alliance. Fearing to be the proverbial kerosene sprayed on a blazing fire, President Eisenhower cancelled a state visit deliberately timed to honor the ratification of the controversial treaty.[33] Ignoring the widespread unrest, Kishi was willing to sacrifice his own term as prime minister as the price required to push the treaty through the Japanese Diet.

For these reasons, the signed treaty did not enlarge Japan's defense forces or allow the country to play a greatly enlarged role in security matters. Domestic sensitivities, and Asian suspicions of Japan's motives, still greatly constrained the ambit of Japan's diplomacy. Using military means was clearly not a viable option, at least not in the foreseeable future. The only practical alternative remaining was an adroit use of economic initiatives, especially if Japan was ever to regain the trust of other Asian countries and exercise even an implicit degree of leadership. In this way, 1960 represented a reconfirmation, once and for all, of Japan's post-war direction. By that time, the last great protests by radical labor unionists had been crushed by the government, which had also weathered the unrest over the US alliance. The Japanese government had had to jettison a prime minister to appease the public, but Japan was now free to follow an economic route to regional influence. This was perhaps symbolized when Hayato Ikeda, Kishi's successor, inaugurated his much publicized "income doubling" program. The public, with the success of this plan, would peacefully pursue wealth instead of manufacturing unrest. Sanctioned by the Americans, Japan would generate the means to embark on a form of economic diplomacy. Strategically applied wealth would become the major method for carving out a distinctive Japanese role in Asia.

2.5 The Phoenix Economy: Pursuing Influence Through Other Means

Although Shigeru Yoshida became Japan's iconic statesman of the immediate post-war period, he had been a noted diplomat in the years

---

[33]This incident was used, however, as a device to persuade Americans, who were not supportive of the American Mutual Security Program, what they were up against in containing communism. See Eisenhower (1965, p. 563).

leading up to the conflict. During those years, his manifest goal, shared widely in ruling circles, was to establish Japanese hegemony in Asia. However, he diverged from the prevailing majority by wanting to achieve that shared objective by cooperating with, instead of opposing, Britain and the US. The inevitable and disastrous war only succeeded in confirming his goals and objectives. After the war, he pursued his long-held vision by seeking to nurture co-existence and co-prosperity with the rest of Asia. By establishing such a realm, Japan would be instrumental in stabilizing the region. The Japanese would consequently draw their power, at least in part, by acting as a sanctioned ally of the Western democracies (Dower, 1979). Post-war realities caused Yoshida to exchange the iron fist for the more acceptable velvet glove. His new stance emphasized cooperation, foreswearing any actions that could be classified as a form of regional domination. Yoshida's outlines of a new diplomatic direction would come to shape Japan's relations with the rest of Asia. Reflecting in 1957 on his time as prime minister, Yoshida wrote:

> The principle of Japan's diplomacy is and will be maintenance of good relationships with the US. Given its domestic politics, economy, industry and structure of society, Japan is similar to western countries, rather to Asian countries. Nevertheless, it is quite natural to think that Japan can understand Asia better than western countries since Japan belongs to Asia geographically (Yoshida, 1995, pp. 112–113 [translated by Hatakeyama]).

As Yoshida points out, Japan during this period faced a rather complex balancing challenge. The Japanese had to position themselves as though they were some sort of Western country, while at the same time effectively carving out a leadership role within Asia. Economic wealth was meant to be the basis for squaring the circle of this complexity. The necessity of pursuing two seemingly conflicting aims presented a distinctly ineradicable problem in those early post-war years, since its economy was basically floundering. Playing the *de facto* leader was an old Japanese dream, but it was not a proper fantasy for a country in straitened circumstance. Before any serious diplomatic forays could be made, Japan's fundamental economic failings needed to be addressed.

The US fully comprehended the Japanese dilemma. To assist in the American Cold War effort, Japan's economy needed to be placed on a sound footing. The obvious implication, as previously pointed out, was to foster a US policy which would relentlessly pursue a Japanese economic recovery.[34] An essential first step in this process was to accelerate the drawn out negotiations that were characterizing the attempts to conclude a final peace treaty. Moreover, the terms of such an agreement needed to be lenient so that no stumbling blocks would be placed on this potential Japanese road to recovery.

With measured diplomacy seemingly ineffective in achieving this result, circumstances arose that helped break through the impasse where more careful deliberation had failed. As noted, the perceived need for American bases created a powerful incentive for concluding a treaty. Moreover, the Korean War created a boost in demand for wartime necessities. By creating this sort of indirect boom, American purchasing power succeeded in bailing out a number of floundering Japanese firms and thus rescuing the Japanese economy, at least temporarily. The Americans found the end result of this fortuitous circumstance understandably agreeable. The resurrection of the Japanese economy meant a stabilized Asian ally, in other words, a country saved from the potential scourge of communism (US Department of State, 1985, p. 1413).

At the same time, Japan fully realized the seriousness of its economic situation and the dire need for reconstruction. Such concerns are clearly reflected in a 1946 Foreign Ministry's report, "Problems in the Reconstruction of Japan's Economy." This attempt to specify Japan's precarious economic state marks something of an official beginning of Japan's post-war recovery, at least if one assumes that recognition of the problem is the necessary first step toward solving it. The working assumption of the document insisted that due to Japan's grievous lack of natural resources, only recreating Japan as a major trading nation would make economic growth viable (Sudo, 1992, p. 36). Under these broad guidelines, Japan would still dominate Asia, but subtly as a peaceful trading partner. These efforts bore fruit in 1955 when Japan was admitted to the world's trading club (the General Agreement on Trade and Tariffs)

---

[34]The US implemented aid programs, such as the Government and Relief in Occupied Areas (GARIOA) and the Economic Recovery for Occupied Areas (EROA), after the immediate post-war period.

at the behest of American prerogatives (Akaneya, 1992). This US strategy was partially motivated by the American attempt to provide Japan with a viable alternative to the prohibited Chinese market. With economic rehabilitation becoming a reality and with acceptance by the world's clubs and institutions, Japan could now think more concretely about its role within Asia.

Japan was finally in a position to accept the Yoshida approach as providing a viable framework for post-war Japanese diplomacy. The core of Japan's initiative would consist of economic development as the basis for all regional relationships. As might be expected, the peace treaty that did eventuate was largely orchestrated by US Cold War needs. This meant that no such treaty was simultaneously concluded with such communist nations as China and the Soviet Union. For somewhat different reasons, South Korea, Japan's former colony, also declined to come to a formal peace arrangement. Though the success of Japan's dash for growth hung in the balance for a number of years, by 1954 a lasting economic recovery seemed Japan's most likely prospect. Only by establishing a solid economic base could a developing Japan hope to implement something resembling a unique Japanese form of diplomacy. As Japan's economy succeeded, so did Japanese diplomacy expand to fill up the Asian stage.

The economy then would come to dominate Japanese political and diplomatic discourse through the 1950s and 1960s. Key speeches would be defined by the use of economic terminologies like "production," "industries," and "exports," rather than the intricacies of international entanglements and political balances (Tanaka, 1994, pp. 5–12). As previously indicated, becoming a major trading nation did not mean cultivating the obvious Chinese market. The Americans, for instance, would be far from pleased to see the thrust of their Cold War strategy contravened. Nor were the Chinese themselves, staunchly communist and still smarting from Japanese occupation, overly eager to re-establish relations with their former oppressors. Moreover, the possibility that Japan would even consider such an option was formally constrained by the US-inspired Coordinating Committee (CoCoM) established in 1949. This unyielding restriction was further buttressed by the establishment of a China Committee (CHINCOM) in August

1952. Perhaps the conclusive step came with the signing of the San Francisco peace treaty in that same year. With the Taipei regime as one of the signers, Japan was now essentially shut out from either recognizing or trading with the mainland government.[35] With few other viable options left, and at the not-so-subtle behest of the Americans, Japan during these early years grew increasingly attentive to the opportunities presented by Southeast Asia.[36] With no other avenue available to pursue its newly designed diplomatic strategy, this region became the staging platform for future attempts at moving inexorably to center stage in Asia. The almost impossible challenge, however, was to foster such an objective despite possessing seriously limited economic means.[37]

Japan at this time made no secret of these twin and interrelated goals. The Japanese intended to pursue economic prosperity for its own sake as well as to create the means of gaining Asian influence. This particular diplomatic strategy was clearly expressed in the inaugural 1957 volume of an annual foreign ministry's series entitled *Waga Gaiko no kinkyo*. The volume highlighted the significance of Japan's return to the international community, as reflected by its newly won UN membership. The document went on to imply that Japan was linking its economic cooperation to its political aspirations in order to create a place for itself in Asia.

> … the Asian countries have reciprocal economic relationships with Japan. Few days have passed since most of the Asian countries became independent. They

---

[35] US Cold War strategy made normalizing relations between China and Japan a ticklish proposition. Both the Chinese President, Chou En Lai, and the Japanese State Minister, Tatsunosuke Takasaki, privately expressed their strong wish to regularize diplomatic relations at an April 1955 meeting. Japan was forced to maintain a disjuncture between its public stance and its more pragmatic actions. In line with its standard Cold War posture, Japan maintained a public stance which disapproved of communist China. However, exhibiting a less publicized practically, Japan under Hatoyama and then subsequently under Prime Minister Tanzan Ishibashi (1956–1957) maintained economic relations and private contacts with China.

[36] China accounted for 17 percent of Japan's total exports and 12 percent of its imports during 1934–1936. Korea accounted for 17 percent of its exports and 14 percent of imports during the same period. See Shiraishi (2000a, pp. 12–13).

[37] The challenge of creating a vibrant two-way trade with Southeast Asia differed radically with the circumstances attending Japan's pre-war trade with China and Korea. As colonial master and occupier, terms of trade were largely dictated and contracts mandatory. Encouraging voluntary trade would entail ensuring that such trade was clearly mutually beneficial.

therefore have not yet launched their economic plans despite having abundant raw materials. Given a lack of plans, there was room for Japan, which possess advanced technology and industry, to help promote their economic development. ... Given that Japan's growth cannot be achieved without Asia's peace and prosperity, economic cooperation towards Asia is an essential tool in our economic diplomacy (Ministry of Foreign Affairs, 1957, p. 9 [translated by Hatakeyama]).

Japan as the leading engine driving Asian economic prosperity by facilitating increased integration was essentially a recapitulation of Japan's traditional vision, adjusted for current circumstances. Linking Asia with its own economic strategy had motivated Japan to drive both south and north to secure raw materials in both the pre-war and Pacific war periods. Pursuing the same goals through non-military means was a tactical, rather than a deeply strategic change. In the reality of the post-war environment, there were simply more effective ways to pursue these central goals than by applying military force.

Unexpectedly, but quite fortuitously, the adroit use of war reparations proved to be a convenient tool for initiating this form of diplomacy. As Japan's master statesman Yoshida clearly stated, reparations were not meant only to compensate countries, but also to promote shared prosperity between Japan and the rest of developing Asia (1983, pp. 162–163). By employing reparations in the appropriate manner, Japan could begin to establish a workable link between Asian economic security and its own. Economic ties could validate Japan's regional aspirations, in contrast to military occupation, which essentially had failed.[38] The US, quite naturally, also wanted to see Japan well integrated with the rest of Southeast Asia and promoting a regime of mutual growth. For these reasons, the Americans readily supported

---

[38]In 1954, the Japanese government concluded its first post-war reparation convention. Japan offered Burma some $200 million in goods and services over a 10-year period. Soon after, in 1956, the Philippines agreed to a total of $800 million with $550 million in the form of goods and services over 20 years and in the rest in private loans. In 1958, agreement was reached with Indonesia. Japan granted $400 million in loans plus the cancellation of Indonesia's $170 million debt. Japan also offered an additional $223 million in reparations. In 1959, Japan agreed to provide services and products worth $30 million to South Vietnam along with a $7.5 million loan. In 1965, South Korea accepted a $300 million grant on top of a $200 million loan. The package also included some $300 million in economic cooperation from the private sector. Japan provided quasi-reparations to eight other countries including Laos, Cambodia, Thailand, Malaysia, Singapore, and Micronesia.

the inclusion of a lenient reparations clause in their negotiated peace treaty. In 1951, John Foster Dulles underscored this objective.

> If these war-devastated countries sent to Japan the raw materials which many of them have in abundance, then Japan could process them for the creditor countries and by these services, freely given, provide appreciable reparations (US Department of State, 1951, p. 457).

Because of Japan's critical shortage of American dollars, the reparation clause delineated Japanese obligations strictly in terms of services. Any other method would only further aggravate Japan's dangerously low dollar reserves (Ministry of Foreign Affairs, 1958, p. 29). Running parallel to any moral obligations, which might be tied to such reparation payments, was the specific aim of increasing the prosperity of all of the recipients. In a sense, America's Cold War strategy was two pronged. The more obvious thrust was the selective use of military force and military aid to blunt communist expansion. But the gentler side recognized that a country characterized by rising incomes was less likely to find the allures of communist ideas attractive. For Japan, the economic openings to Asian nations also provided the recovering country some initial room in which to nourish its political aspirations, as well as boost its economic needs. Thus early on in the post-war period, Japan was developing a diplomatic approach that could further its own regional objectives within the constraints created by that period's Cold War obsessions.

As hoped, reparations contributed greatly to the rehabilitation of the war-damaged Japanese economy. By stimulating Southeast Asian countries, these payments provided new outlets for Japan's developing heavy industry. In line with American expectations, developing these Asian markets offset the loss of Japan's more traditional export destinations, namely mainland China and Korea. They further cushioned Japan's economy from the precipitous drop in US procurements following the Korean armistice.

Though government reparations proved to be the vanguard of economic flows within the region, the private sector was also strongly encouraged to supplement these efforts by seeking closer economic links with Southeast Asia. During these crucial decades, which saw Japan create a new economy on the ruins of its old one, this sort of private–public partnership became characteristic of Japan's initiatives at home and abroad (Shiraishi, 1997, p. 179).[39] The reparations paved the way for new trade relations that could be gradually developed by private industry and financial institutions (often cooperating with government agencies). This breakthrough meant not only new export markets, but sources of secure raw materials leading to growing regional interdependence (Mendle, 1995, p. 98). For more than 20 years (ending with the Philippines in July 1976) reparations to East Asian countries would continue to act as a flagship displaying Japan's intention to promote greater economic cooperation overseas (Fukushima, 2000, p. 155).

Reparations were in effect a trial run for Japan's later intensive foreign aid program, achieving many equivalent results and furthering the same political objectives. The parallel can be demonstrated in the case of Laos and Cambodia. Both voluntarily renounced any claims to reparations. Instead, they implicitly accepted direct assistance in lieu of foresworn reparations (Ministry of Foreign Affairs, 1957, pp. 16–17).[40] Both programs, of course, ran parallel to Japan's Official Development Assistance (ODA). This form of foreign aid grew steadily and eventually completely replaced the wartime-induced repayments.

The full blossoming of its aid program as a lever of political influence would need to wait until Japan became a full member of the club of Western democracies. This milestone occurred in 1964 when Japan earned admittance to the Organization of Economic Cooperation and Development (OECD). However, the relatively late date of that particular event does not imply that using foreign aid strategically was held in abeyance until it could be employed decisively. Small steps had been assayed in the years preceding this occasion. As early as 1954, Japan had taken its first official tentative steps down this road by becoming a donor in the technical cooperation program of the Colombo Plan for Southeast Asia. Quite naturally, the Japanese were still too poor to contribute

---

[39] These collusive public–private relations are noticeable in the multinational arrangements encompassing LDP politicians, leading Japanese business figures, and influential Southeast Asian politicians and their business cronies. The North Sumatra Oil Development Cooperation Company, established in 1960 with Overseas Economic Cooperation Fund's (OECF's) loans, was one of the examples of this type of arrangement.

[40] As noted above, the government referred to these as quasi-reparations.

anything but in-kind service to international aid programs. In fact, during the critical conception of this economically driven diplomatic approach, the Japanese were still the recipient of World Bank funds (from 1953 through to the mid-1960s) that were deemed necessary to keep their economy afloat (Ministry of Foreign Affairs, 1985, p. 109).

This did not prevent "economic cooperation" from becoming the watchword of successive governments. The essential importance of this idea was continually confirmed by frequent appearances in those weighty tomes symbolizing Japan's Foreign Ministry, namely the yearly *Diplomatic Bluebooks*. Locked into an assigned role during the obsession-ridden Cold War period, Japan was effectively blocked from cooperating with any other part of Asia than the American designated Southeast.[41] Only in this direction were the rigid constraints attached to its US alliance loosened to a degree that allowed for Japanese initiatives.

Unfortunately, foreign assistance as a potent means of political leverage did not initially translate into any significant level of application. Japan still lacked both the economic and diplomatic capabilities to employ such a strategy successfully. To compensate, Japan would somehow have to finesse these deficiencies in embarking on a major aid program, one which might begin to regain Japan's status within the region. To succeed, Japan would need to convince the US to fund its Japanese-inspired "Asian Marshall Plan" under the guise of boosting Asia economic development (Shimizu, 2001, pp. 93–95, 100). Yoshida efficiently encapsulated this proposed policy whereby the US would essentially underwrite Japan's program for Asian development. "Japan's future role would be to promote and contribute to the development of Asian countries by linking Japan's technology to American funds" (Yoshida, 1995, pp. 112–113). (Necessarily left unsaid was the edge such policy would deliver to the Japanese.)

This Japanese-devised approach gained a degree of credibility since it cleverly accorded with clear US Cold War objectives. The Japanese could work within US-imposed constraints by giving the Americans

---

[41] South Korea, of course, was tied firmly to the US and its Cold War policies. However, wartime, and even colonial, grievances had not been resolved during these early years, making any serious level of co-operation infeasible.

what they wanted, while simultaneously furthering Japanese aims. As pointed out, increased economic development was viewed as an effective antidote to communism. Meanwhile, Japan would grow richer by riding this wave of American greenbacks (Tamaki, 1995, p. 238). If done cleverly, the Japanese could use the pretext of anti-communism to cultivate its own regional influence through a program of cooperative assistance. Although the Americans failed to buy this particular formulation, Japan would return with a similar approach in subsequent years.

Further steps toward diplomatic rehabilitation saw Japan become the 80th member of the UN in 1956. (Achieving this breakthrough required negating a potential Soviet veto by first establishing official diplomatic relations.) The UN became another arena in which Japan could strive for increased recognition and greater influence. During Prime Minister Kishi's administration, UN membership presented the possibility of a new avenue that might be useful, but only if it could deliver the political and economic rehabilitation of Japan that Kishi desired (Kitaoka, 2001, p. 58). Kishi, leading the recently amalgamated Liberal Democratic Party (LDP), developed a multifaceted policy for working within US imposed constraints. Part of the foundation of this approach lay in an unquestioned alliance with the US and support for its policies (Kitaoka, 2001, p. 167). Within these boundaries, however, Kishi still promoted an Asian-centered diplomacy. Though confined by US leadership, he continued to insist that Japan could act effectively as an Asian spokesman promoting Asian concerns (Shiraishi, 2000b, p. 58).[42]

Clearly Prime Minister Kishi had not departed sharply from the Kishi who had made his mark in Manchukuo and subsequently the Tojo cabinet; same dreams, different methods. He continued to press his idea of Japan's Asian role in subsequent meetings with Eisenhower. Unremarkably, his vision placed Japan at the very apex of Asian activity. In Kishi's judgment, a leadership role for Japan would bring the added advantage of moving toward a more equal relationship with the US. In more concrete terms, Kishi believed in buying off any

---

[42] Shiraishi (2000b) presents an interesting viewpoint on the purpose behind Kishi's position.

residual Asian fear or distrust with a sufficient package of development money. A Kishi-proposed "Asian Development Fund," would
construct a virtual Sino-proof barrier by surrounding China with a
wall of unyielding prosperity. Achieving this Cold War dream would
take only the adroit mixture of American capital, Japanese goods and
skills, and of course Southeast Asian labor and essential raw materials
(Shimizu, 2001, p. 195). In effect, Japan would resurrect the East Asian
Co-Prosperity Sphere, only this time the Americans would underwrite
this Japanese endeavor instead of trying to destroy it.

The US failed to be quite as ingenuous as Kishi wished. Japan's
effectiveness was severely limited by US power. The proposed initiative
gained support neither from the Americans nor other Asian "beneficiaries." The US declined to share its unquestioned power with some
yet-to-be-determined multilateral organization. It preferred to control
its own funds and choose its own projects. Other Asian countries continued to suspect Japanese motives. Japan, however, seemed unfazed
by what was at best a tepid reaction to its initiative. Undaunted, the
Japanese then proposed that Washington support a multilateral committee in Tokyo "to consider projects in South East Asia for which
Japan would provide 'know how' and materials and the US would
provide finance" (Rix, 1989–1990, pp. 466–467; Shimizu, 2001,
pp. 194–198). Japan's enthusiasm to move forward with this proposal
was balked by failing to arouse a shred of US interest. The Americans saw little advantage of funding a Japanese-centered organization,
which would then support Asian economic development. Surely it was
in principle wiser that American funding for such a project should go
through a US-formed and carefully controlled institution.

Forced to resign, Hayato Ikeda (1960–1964) succeeded the
now unpopular Kishi. Ikeda had started his career as a Ministry
of Finance bureaucrat.[43] His policies tended to be shaped by this
background. Ikeda, a post-war Japanese conservative technocrat,
opted to forego diplomatic forays in order to focus on and promote domestic economic growth. In fact, following the turmoil

---

[43] Similar to, but not quite like Kishi, Ikeda was born to a family engaged in the brewing of sake,
but not a particularly rich or influential one.

ending Kishi's administration, Japan required a powerful vision of middle-class wealth and tranquility to calm the broad majority of the population. Ikeda introduced an "income doubling plan," a deliberate effort to raise living standards and improve social infrastructure. The actual results surpassed even these ambitious objectives. However, to accomplish this proposed growth, the government not only promoted exports and severely restricted imports, but also restrained most forms of investment abroad. Additional controls clamped down heavily on foreign direct investment. Japan's economy took off. Even during the boom years that most of the world enjoyed during the 1960s, Japan's average growth rate of 10.9 percent was remarkable. As an offshoot of this "miracle" growth, Japan was now able to initiate an extensive aid program. As always, Ikeda's focus remained steadfastly domestic. Assistance, when given, should primarily benefit and spur Japan's own economic growth. However, he did show a definite interest in East Asian development assistance. Ikeda's initial steps in this direction would create a pattern further developed by future prime ministers.[44] His policy was of course based on the economic realities then facing Japan. Providing assistance to developing countries made perfect sense, since Japan at that time depended on those countries for 45 percent of its total trade (Ministry of Foreign Affairs, 1961, p. 15).

The pursuit of US dollars to finance Japanese initiatives gradually fell into disuse as Japan succeeded economically in its own right. Negotiations between the US and Japan now focused on the use of Japanese foreign assistance to promote Asian development (Watanabe, 1992, p. 116). To facilitate this shift in responsibility, the US sponsored Japan's inclusion, as a founding member, in the Development Assistance Committee (DAC).[45] The Americans meant this as a not-so-subtle encouragement for Japan to seriously increase

---

[44] Ikeda's position on foreign assistance is indicated in a joint statement made by Japanese Prime Minister Ikeda and US President Kennedy (1961).

[45] In the march of acronyms beloved by bureaucrats, the DAC was an offshoot of the OECD. The anomaly in this situation consisted of Japan being boosted to become a founding member of the DAC, although not yet included in the OECD.

its level of Asian aid. Japan willingly acquiesced. Any other response might have hindered the timing of its inclusion into the OECD. This organization was just the sort of exclusive club Japan yearned to join, in part as a type of "coming of age" recognition (Fukushima, 2000, p. 156). But even these coveted memberships were insufficient. To gain the level of respect driving the Japanese meant establishing the basis for more independent diplomatic initiatives. The Ministry of Foreign Affairs, looking to the future, established an economic cooperation department in 1959. Even at this early stage, when funding was still a major sticking point, government officials perceived a distinct need to simplify, as well as to unify, all the bureaucratic machinery necessary for running a successful aid program. The Japanese clearly intended to make prior preparations for conducting what they envisioned as a diplomatic strategy based on foreign assistance.

Soon after the successful Tokyo Olympics (1964), Foreign Minister Shiina could mark something of a culmination of Japan's economic struggles in a statement to the 49th National Diet (1965). "Japan has finally realized its desire, which is the major pillar of Japan's economic diplomacy in the post-war era, to obtain a position as a developed country internationally through the realization of the status of IMF Article 8 and affiliation in OECD."[46] At least from a Japanese viewpoint, Japan's international status was rising coincident with its economic wealth. This trend would be further accelerated by the US-triggered Vietnam War. While World War II might have smashed Japan's hopes, post-war conflicts would prove to be advantageous for rebuilding Japan. The Korean War helped pull the Japanese economy back from the brink of disaster. The Vietnam War would provide the Japanese with new diplomatic as well as economic opportunities. Newly created wealth would encourage Japan to trace out a relatively more independent path on the world stage, though one still highly constrained by American objectives. What remains clear is that Japan now seemed committed to shaping foreign aid into its chief diplomatic tool.

---

[46] For those interested in ascertaining Japan's foreign policy at this juncture, the complete speech by Shiina can be found at http://www.ioc.u-tokyo/~worldjpn/.

2.6   Conclusion: Prospering Within the Realm of Peaceful Diplomacy

Given the harsh international circumstances during the pre-war period, Japan concluded that explicit expansionism, resting on military strength, provided the best way to gain respect and join the ranks of Western imperial powers. As a slight of hand, the Japanese attempted to camouflage their own ambitions under the banner of anti-colonialism. After the realities of defeat in the Pacific War made such a path infeasible, Japan pragmatically accepted American tutelage and rapidly transformed itself into, at least the semblance of, a democratic country.[47] Defeat meant that the Japanese would be forced to face once again in a parallel fashion the challenges that arose at the start of the Meiji restoration. This time, the reconstruction blueprint was largely created and imposed by the victorious Americans.[48] The striking difference with the pre-war period was the substitution of economic for military power when dealing with the larger international community. Even without constitutional limitations, opting for a military approach was clearly unrealistic. These nominal constraints remained non-binding.

In post-war Japan, a war-tired population had turned its back on military solutions. Any potential slippage away from this entrenched pacifist posture would quickly initiate a consequential response. Moreover, a flattened economy made such spending an extravagant folly. Domestic political stability demanded growing wealth for the general population rather than more sacrifices in pursuit of military glory. Added to this inherent domestic resistance, international sensibilities, and in particular the still raw memories of neighboring countries, made the resurrection of a military state a non-starter. Even the semblance of such an initiative would be seen as proof of Japan's unquenchable ambitions.

---

[47]Whether a democratic country simply means one in which people have the right to vote for a representative government is an unsettled question. Certainly, Japan's government was as responsive to its voters as that of many other indisputably democratic countries. It would however be unreasonable to expect Japan to turn out to be a carbon copy of the US simply because its government was formed during the American occupation. As mentioned, other imperatives quickly came to dominate US policy, leaving the promotion of Japanese democracy a distant second.

[48]How much was actually imposed remains debatable. It can be argued that the Japanese were more skilled at adopting the institutional forms that the Americans imposed, while adroitly adapting (or subverting) the intentions driving the reforms to serve their own purposes.

No other viable option then remained but a concerted concentration on economic growth. Fortunately for the Japanese, this economic strategy was in perfect accord with broader US Cold War policy in the immediate post-war period. To American strategists, an economically strong Japan would act as a key bulwark against spreading Asian communism.

Though constrained to accept this path by the prevailing economic environment, such an acceptance did not represent a renunciation of past Japanese ambitions. Though foreswearing force, the reformed Japanese would come to see economic might as an alternative path to an old objective. Wealth would enable them to ease their way back into the Asian community. Reparations made to Southeast Asian nations would mark an initial step in Japan's political aspirations to move to the center of Asian policy making, though, at this early stage of the post-war period, Japan was still insufficiently wealthy to take anything except the smallest of steps. But while lacking military strength, or even its potential, an economy that was displaying rapid and unstoppable growth appeared to be moving Japan, at least tentatively, in the right direction.

References

Akaneya T. (1992) *Nihon no Gatt Kanyu Mondai*. University of Tokyo Press, Tokyo.

Beasley WG. (1963) *The Modern History of Japan*. Weidenfeld and Nicolson, London.

Beasley WG. (1990) *The Rise of Modern Japan*. 1st ed. Weidenfeld and Nicolson, London.

Borden WS. (1984) *The Pacific Alliance: United States Foreign Economic Policy and Japanese Trade Recovery, 1947–1955*. The University of Wisconsin Press, Wisconsin.

Dower JW. (1979) *Empire and Aftermath*. Council on East Asian Studies, Harvard University, Cambridge.

Dower JW. (1986) *War without Mercy: Race and Power in the Pacific War*. Pantheon, New York.

Dower JW. (1993) *Japan in War and Peace*. The New Press, New York.

Dower JW. (1999) *Embracing Defeat*. W.W. Norton & Company, New York.

Economist (2009) Banyan: End of the line for the LDP, *The Economist*, July 19, p. 28.

Eisenhower DD. (1965) *Waging Peace*. Doubleday and Company, New York.

Feis H. (1950) *The Road to Pearl Harbour: the Coming of the War Between the United States and Japan*. Princeton University Press, Princeton.

Fukushima A. (2000) ODA as a Japanese Foreign Policy Tool. In: Inoguchi, Takashi, Purnendra J (eds.), *Japanese Foreign Policy Today*, pp. 152–176. Palgrave, New York.

Gravel M. ed. (1971) *The Pentagon Papers: The Defense Department History of United States Decisionmaking on Vietnam*, Vol. I. Beacon Press, Boston.

Hatano S. (1996) *Taiheiyo Senso to Ajia Giako*. University of Tokyo Press, Tokyo.

Ikei S. (1991) *Nihon Gaikoshi Gaisetsu*. Keio Tsushin, Tokyo.

Irie A. (1981) *Power and Culture*. Harvard University Press, Cambridge.

Irie A. (1987) *The Origins of the Second World War*. Longman, New York.

Irie A. (1991) *Shin Nihon no Gaikou*. Chuo Kosho, Tokyo.

Kajima M. (1976) *The Diplomacy of Japan 1984–1922*, Vol. I. Kajima Institute of International Peace, Tokyo.

Keo Gijuku ed. (1960) *Fukuzawa Yukichi Zenshu*, No. 10. Iwanami Shoten, Tokyo.

Kissinger H. (1994) *Diplomacy*. Simon and Schuster, New York.

Kitaoka S. (2001) Kishi Nobusuke-Yashinto Zasetsu. In: Watanabe A (ed.), *Sengo Nihon no Saisho Tachi*, pp. 143–174. Chuo Koron, Tokyo.

Kolko G. (1971) The American goals in Vietnam. In: Chompsky N and Zinn H (eds.), *The Pentagon Papers: Critical Essays*, Vol. 5, pp. 1–15. Beacon Press, Boston.

Kolko J, Gabriel (1972) *The Limits of Power: The World and the United States Foreign Policy 1945–1954*. Harper and Row, New York.

Kosaka M. (1977) International economic policy. In: Scalapino RA (ed.), *The Foreign Policy of Modern Japan*, pp. 207–226. University of California Press, Los Angeles.

Mendle W. (1995) *Japan's Asia Policy: Regional Security and Global Interests*. Routledge, London, New York.

Ministry of Foreign Affairs (1957) *Waga gaiko no kinkyo*, No. 1. Okurasho Insatsukyoku, Tokyo.

Ministry of Foreign Affairs (1958) *Waga gaiko no kinkyo*, No. 2. Okurasho Insatsukyoku, Tokyo.

Ministry of Foreign Affairs (1961) *Waga gaiko no kinkyo*. Okurasho Insatsukyoku, Tokyo.

Ministry of Foreign Affairs (1965) *Nihon Gaiko Nenpyo Narabini Shuyou Bunsho*. Hara Shobo, Tokyo.

Ministry of Foreign Affairs (1985) *Diplomatic Bluebook 1985 edition*. Okurasho Insatsukyoku, Tokyo.

Nihon Kokusai Seiji Gakkai ed. (1987) *Taiheiyo Senso Eno Michi*, Vol. 2. Asahi Shimbun, Tokyo.

Pyle KB. (1996) *The Japanese Question: Power and Purpose in a New Era*. AEI press, Washington, DC.

Rix A. (1989–1990) Japan's foreign aid policy: A capacity for leadership. *Pacific Affairs* 26(4), 461–475.

Sato S. (1977) The foundations of modern Japanese foreign policy. In: Scalapino, RS (ed.), *The Foreign Policy of Modern Japan*, pp. 367–390. University of California Press, Los Angeles.

Scalapino RS, ed. (1977) *The Foreign Policy of Modern Japan*. University of California Press, Los Angeles.

Schaller M. (1985) *The American Occupation of Japan*. Oxford University Press, New York.

Skocpol T. (1979) *States and Social Revolutions: A Comparative Analysis of France, Russia, and China*. Cambridge University Press, New York.

Shimizu S. (2001) *Creating People of Plenty*. The Kent State University Press, Kent, Ohio, London.

Shiraishi M. (1990) *Japanese Relations with Vietnam: 1951–1987*. Southeast Asia Program, New York.

Shiraishi T. (1997) Japan and Southeast Asia. In: Katzenstein PJ, Shiraishi T (eds.), *Network Power*, pp. 169–194. Cornell University Press, Ithaca and London.

Shiraishi T. (2000a) Asia's regional order: A two-century perspective. *Japan Echo* 27(3), http://www.japanecho.co/jp/docs/html/270304.html, accessed in April 2002.

Shiraishi T. (2000b) Nihon no Tonan Ajia Seikaku no Saikentou. *Kokusai Mondai*. March, 53–64.

Soeya Y. (1995) *Nihon Gaiko to Chugoku*. Keio Tsushin, Tokyo.

Sudo S. (1992) *The Fukuda Doctrine and ASEAN*. Institute of Southeast Asian Studies, Singapore.

Tamaki K. (1995) Nihon to ASEAN No Partnership. In: Okabe T (ed.), *Asia Seiji No Mirai to Nihon*. Keiso Shobo, Tokyo.

Tanaka A. (1994). Rhetorics[sic] and Limitations of Japan's New Internationalism. *Japanese Studies Bulletin*, 14(1), 5–12.

Tanaka A. (1997) *Anzenhosho: Sengo 50 Nen no Mosaku*. Yomiuri Shimbunsha, Tokyo.

Tsuchiyama J. (2000) Ironies in Japanese defense and disarmament policy. In: Inoguchi T, Purnendra J (eds.), *Japanese Foreign Policy Today*, pp. 131–151. Palgrave, New York.

US Department of State (1951) *Department of State, Bulletin*, 17 September. Government Printing Office, Washington, DC.

US Department of State (1952–1954) Foriegn Relations of the United States, 1952–1954 China and Japan volume XIV, part 2, Government Printing Office, Washington, DC, pp. 1063–1822.

US Department of State (1974) *Foreign Relations of the United States 1948*, Vol. VI. Government Printing Office, Washington.

US Department of State (1976) *Foreign Relations of the US, 1950, VI: East Asia and the Pacific*. Government Printing Office, Washington, DC.

US Department of State (1985) *Foreign Relations of the United States–Japan, 1952–54*. Vol. XIV. Government Printing Office, Washington, DC.

Wakamiya Y. (1995) *The Post War Conservative View of Asia*. LTCB International Library Foundation, Tokyo.

Watanabe A. (1992) Ajia Tai heiyo no Kokumilcankei to Nihon. Tokyo University press, Tokyo.

Yoshida S. (1957) *Kaiso Junen*, Vols. 1–4. Shinhosha, Tokyo.

Yoshida S. (1983) *Kaiso Junen*, Vol. 3. Shirakawa Shoin, Tokyo.

Yoshida S. (1995) Nihon Gaiko no Ayndekita Michi. In: Senngo Nihongaikouron Shu, Kitaoka S (ed.), pp. 99–114. Chuo koron, Tokyo.

Chapter 3

A Junior Partner: Japanese Entanglements with the United States and Asia 1965–1980

3.1 Life as a Second-String Player: Japan Searches for a Viable Diplomatic Role

In the early post-war period, the need to resuscitate a nearly non-functional economy dominated any other objective including any desire to exert decisive diplomatic influence. Necessity limited Japan to a near obsession with economic consequences. However, once the "miracle economy" was reliably ticking over in the mid-1960s, Japan started to regroup and regear its policy initiatives. The result was a more activist diplomatic stance tilted toward the regional, if not global, stage. The Japanese slowly expanded not only their economic forays abroad, but their political reach as well. Not surprisingly, these tentative measures were able to operate only within the overarching framework of the ever-present Cold War "containment" policies devised by the US. Still, as the regional strategic situation changed over the decades, Japan's growing economic power would eventually enable it to play a larger role, not only as a junior partner of the US, but as the wielder of an increasing degree of political leverage in its own right.

This chapter examines the ways in which Japan's attempts to recapture a regional leadership role were thwarted, as well as the manner in which the Japanese attempted to overcome these imposed barriers. The intent of the following analysis is to pinpoint the objectives

Japan struggled to accomplish as it attempted to redefine and extend its post-war diplomatic role. Our contention is that Japan consistently sustained and even reinvigorated its long-held dreams of gaining regional influence. To do so, the Japanese shrewdly employed their growing economic leverage to effective advantage, despite the still circumscribed nature of their post-war power.

3.2 Japan Tries to Make Its Mark: Operating Under US-Imposed Constraints

During the period under consideration, the US dominated its anti-communist allies in the Asia-Pacific region (Japan, South Korea, Taiwan, the Philippines, Australia, and New Zealand). Countries structured their security policies to accord with US military needs. The bilateral defense treaties struck in this era largely reflected these very American imperatives.[1] A lack of alternatives left the compliant allies with little scope for engineering any potentially independent foreign policy or entertaining divergent defense initiatives. This concession to American security concerns made it possible and even permissible for Japan to conduct only a rather one-dimensionally biased foreign policy, essentially circumscribed within the boundaries of "economic diplomacy." Even inside these rather limited boundaries, the US still expected the Japanese to operate in a derivative and highly partisan fashion. However, the advent of the Vietnam War changed the cosiness of the existing status quo. In fact, the war triggered an effort by the Americans to drag Japan into assuming a more activist pose, although one largely designed to continue fostering US objectives.

In many ways, the long-running Vietnam conflict replicated the basic structural constraints that defined these two key actors during the earlier Korean War. But with Japan now representing an even more essenialally, its realized role in the Cold War geography of the mid-1960s increased. Japan at this time was endowed with more in

---

[1] In Bruce Cummings' opinion, these countries became semi-sovereign states and "hermit kingdoms" (1997, p. 154).

the way of political weight, given the context of America's prevailing Asian strategy. In exchange for this more consultative role, the US felt justified in expecting Japan to acquiesce to what it viewed as more than a slight modification in the existing relationship. Japan would shoulder additional responsibility for sustaining regional security, but this would take the form of increasing its financial share of the burden. This newly imposed challenge potentially set Japan directly on the path of becoming a dominant player in Asia, though one clearly limited by the acknowledged and essentially undisputed dominance of American leadership.[2] At the same time, the extent to which Japan could accomplish any such US-sanctioned goal still depended largely on those political, constitutional, regional and military constraints that were a distinct legacy of World War II. For instance, as part of its Asian-Pacific strategy, the US persuaded South Korea, the Philippines, Australia, New Zealand and Thailand to provide at least a token contingent of military forces to support the war effort in Vietnam. (Concerned over the likely communist Chinese reaction, Taiwan limited its contribution to the field of covert operations.) The aim was an attempt to manufacture a seeming endorsement of US policies throughout the region, if not within the world. However, widespread public resistance in Japan and predictable Asian suspicion of their motivations precluded any direct military role for the Japanese. Unfortunately, this did not excuse Japan, when viewed with American eyes, from making at least some form of minimum contribution to the war effort.

Nearly 30 other American allies and friendly nations unwilling to become militarily involved in Vietnam were still pushed, somewhat heavy-handedly, to provide non-military aid of varying degrees. Meanwhile, the rising cost of the war, in human as well as economic terms, meant that the US was struggling as much to maintain domestic support as it was in attempting to steady international opinion. This peculiar confluence of impediments led a distracted US to turn a regrettably blind eye to the unique historical factors shaping Japan's defense

---

[2]A clear first sign of a policy modification came in 1963. At that time, Senator Frank Church spoke against continuing economic and military aid to Japan because it had become economically independent (Momoi, 1977, p. 353).

policy. Actually sending troops to Vietnam, of course, was unthinkable. But more importantly, a strong pacifist sentiment in Japan undercut potential support of any kind for America's ambiguous war in Vietnam. Despite recognizing these unresolved difficulties, facing its own pressing demands translated into increasing US pressure for a newly wealthy Japan to assume a more significant role in financing the anti-communist struggle in Asia.[3]

This was the dilemma faced by Prime Minister Eisaku Sato, whose long rule from 1964 to 1972 succeeded that of Ikeda. From a political family, Sato was a brother of the former Prime Minister Kishi. Like most of Japan's population, he personally opposed the Vietnam War.[4] Yet, he firmly believed that the US–Japan Security Treaty had a key role to play in sustaining Japan's own national interests. The type of neutrality, fiercely advocated by the opposition Japanese Socialist Party and supported by a substantial portion of the population was, in his eyes, no more than a foolish illusion (Sato, 1966). Given his characteristic pragmatism, Sato felt obligated to respond positively to these unambiguous US overtures. To demonstrate Japan's willingness to partner with the US in Asia, he acted as a sort of unofficial ambassador by visiting an array of neighboring countries, even including the Democratic Republic of Vietnam (North Vietnam), prior to a crucial November 1967 meeting with US President Lyndon Johnson.

Not surprisingly, Sato had an ulterior motive that to a substantial degree guided his decision to provide support for US efforts in Vietnam. In exchange for dutifully following the path laid out by the US, Sato hoped to gain the much desired return of Okinawa. Pulling this off would rank as a major political, as well as diplomatic, coup. Similarly, he signaled his willingness to have Japan shoulder a greater role in providing for Japan's self-defense in order to achieve this same specific objective. His 1967 Diet speech reflected these overriding strategic considerations. Because Lyndon Johnson faced increasing financial constraints domestically, as well as decreasing popular support in pursuing his Vietnam policy, Sato felt that he could gather sufficient

---

[3] At the time, William P. Bundy was Assistant Secretary for Far Eastern Affairs (Bundy, 1965).
[4] For further analysis, see Tanaka (1997) and also Eto (1987).

bargaining chips to ensure that Okinawa would once again be part of Japan.[5]

We can conclude that the Okinawa issue, combined with the continuing Japanese dependence on American military might, sufficiently explains Sato's officially sanctioned, though far from enthusiastic, support of the Vietnam War. Yet this policy was not without some obvious costs. America's intervention created sharp anti-US sentiment in Japan, as it did in many other countries including those of America's erstwhile allies. Parties on the left of Japan's political spectrum, including those closely allied to the trade union movement, led demonstrations that further exacerbated domestic opinion. Dissatisfaction became widespread with some 75 percent of the public opposing the war in Vietnam (Shiraishi, 1990, pp. 33–37). To most Japanese, the conflict had little to do with communist aggression. American pig headedness had trapped the US into making a foolishly dogmatic intervention into what was essentially a civil war (Department of State — United States, 1965). This antipathy to US policies was further aggravated at this time by a surge of Japanese nationalism focused on Okinawan restoration. Such aroused opposition led the US to reconsider the wisdom of maintaining its post war occupation for any extended length of time.[6] Equally, the Japanese government would have been foolish to entirely ignore the rising anti-American feelings that had taken hold of the public and the not unrelated nationalist sentiments, with Okinawa forming one of the focal points. Encouraged, if not forced, by these realities, the Japanese government seized on these trends to press harder for the island's return. The Japanese tried to impress the US with the very serious nature of their concerns.

The Tet Offensive in February 1968 managed to shake the faith of the Western World (and Japan) in the strength and reliability of US leadership. The continued Vietnamese stalemate presented a conflict that the US had proven incapable of controlling. With increasingly bitter domestic opposition demanding the withdrawal of US troops, America

---

[5] Officially, such an agreement can be found in the 1969 Nixon–Sato Joint Statement.
[6] Kosaka argued that the issue of Okinawa had an enormous impact on public opinion and affected future relationship between Japan and the US. See Kosaka (1998, p. 546).

became hard pressed to maintain its commitments. The result of these rising pressures was reflected in the Nixon Doctrine of 1969. Under the guiding hand of this policy, America would stage a phased retreat from Vietnam and shift the responsibility for containing communism to its Asian allies. Countries such as Japan recognized this policy as a clear indication of America's intention to disengage from the region. The consequences of this dramatic shift was clearly driven home when Nixon specifically emphasized that "the United States would not undertake the kind of policy that would make countries in Asia so dependent upon us that we are dragged into conflicts such as the one we have in Vietnam" (Nixon, 1971–1975, pp. 548–549). When this newly developed, non-interventionist stance was combined with Japan's continued concerns over Okinawa, the role of the Japanese in providing for the collective security of Asia was ripe for renegotiation.

Despite comprehending the direction that the US was choosing to take, the Japanese government still felt incapable of shouldering the implicit security burden, given the dominance of pacifist feeling that still defined public opinion. Politically, such a policy shift was simply not practical. However, Japan still felt the need to appease US expectations (or at least give the appearance of doing so) to some degree. The Japanese government proceeded to make a series of announcements in the late 1960s indicating its intention to strengthen self-defense measures. The same set of politicians then made such policy initiatives somewhat more publicly palatable by painting them in terms of developing an independent approach to security matters. They claimed that Japan would now be able to take a more active role in insuring regional peace and security.[7] Sato also took the opportunity of advancing his own agenda by assuring President Richard Nixon (November 1969) that the restoration of Okinawan would have no noticeable effect on America's ability to continue using its existing military bases on the island. Such

---

[7] At a meeting between Foreign Minister Miki and Secretary of State Rusk, Miki emphasized that its defense strength depended upon Japan's own voluntary decision to support the peace and stability of Asian countries, not the degree of pressure the US exerted on Japan to share more of the burden (*Gaiko Kiroku*, 01–531, October 6, 1968).

reassurance was vital, since Okinawa had played a key strategic role in America's Asian initiatives, especially during the Vietnam War.

Sato continued balancing the perceived need to strengthen Japan's American ties against the political necessity of soothing public opinion. The Sato–Nixon Joint Communiqué of 1969 tested his ability to calm any lingering apprehensions generated by the strong commitments seemingly implied by the statement. "The security of the Republic of Korea is essential to Japan's own security and the maintenance of peace and security in the Taiwan area is also a most important factor for the security of Japan" (Sato and Nixon, 1969; Sato, 1969a; Kono, 1991, p. 215). The communiqué in fact represented the first official pronouncement explicating the proposed nature of Japan's Asian security stance. However, the statement, rather than sketching out the future direction of Japan's policy initiatives, was no more than a bald attempt to win the return of Okinawa. The Japanese hoped that by mouthing the words the US wanted to hear, their goal could be achieved. While appearing steadfast in terms of promises, Japan's pledges lacked any concrete measures or obligations. Though the intention was only tactical, the public unfolding of this apparent commitment had to be minimized in order to avoid ruffling domestic opinion over a perennially sensitive issue. This was especially apropos since controversy was already slated to arise over the extension of the US–Japan Security Treaty (Momoi, 1977, p. 355). As drafted, the treaty came up for automatic renewal every 10 years.[8] In turn, American intentions in returning Okinawa would not be just a simple reaction to Japan's calculated efforts and attempted manipulations. The US had broader strategic concerns to implement, which made a potential return of the disputed island diplomatically convenient.[9]

---

[8] The uproar created at the last renewal under the Kishi administration is detailed in Chapter 2 of this volume.

[9] Ultimately, the Americans (or at least Richard M. Nixon) would think that the Japanese had not provided fair value for the return of Okinawa. Even a master of realpolitik, like Nixon, would become so angry at the way in which Eisaku Sato had dealt with trade issues, the problem of China, and other matters that he would simply boycott the ceremony celebrating the reuniting of Okinawa with the Japanese mainland.

By the late 1960s, the US was initiating an exit strategy from Vietnam. The war had proven fruitless and an unwonted drain on the economy. The US believed that Japan could facilitate its intended disengagement from Asia by assuming a greater role in security matters, even if such cooperation did not extend to the military realm. Okinawa was a small price to pay for such a desirable outcome.[10] To expedite this result, Nixon unreservedly demanded that Japan develop a "significant military capacity." By doing so, Japan would be more capable of assuming greater responsibility in the region. Sato assured the US that Japan had every intention of carefully examining its self-defense stance following the restoration of Okinawa. But it was clear, even at this stage, that Japan was reluctant to extend its role beyond a limited form of self-defense. Sato flatly refused to bow completely to US pressure.[11] To the Japanese, restoration would bring a more active role in terms of security responsibilities, but nothing further. Japan was willing and even keen to contribute toward regional stability, but only in the limited form of economic aid.[12]

The Japanese though did recognize a particularly fortuitous opportunity to shape American pressure so that it could prove conducive to taking concrete steps toward retrieving lost regional influence. However, the Japanese government preferred to do its string pulling in the background, trying in this way to avoid a politically serious backlash from prevailing public opinion. The government decided to defuse any potentially lethal fallout by equating security concerns with regional economic assistance. This approach allowed Sato to maintain his tightwire act. The Japanese could assuage US demands by directing more aid money to strategically chosen Asian countries. At the same time, such targeted economic support could potentially boost Japan's regional profile, thus serving its own wish to expand its role while appearing to be simultaneously boosting US Cold War aims.

---

[10] At that time, Nixon was under pressure from the textile industry which demanded protection from cheap Japanese imports. It would be a mistake then not to factor in the settlement of the textile issue when considering the nature of the agreement.

[11] At a meeting between Sato and Nixon (November 1969), Nixon urged Japan to assume greater responsibility, saying "it is not a demand but a statement of fact" (*Gaiko Kiroku*, 01-527-2.).

[12] For additional verification see *Gaiko Kiroku*, 01-527-2.

As we have seen, the shift in US policy toward a more disengaged stance with Asia was to some extent a reflection of the desire to withdraw from the Vietnamese conflict. The ramifications of such a shift affected not only Japan, but China as well. A rapprochement between the US and China was a natural development of America's wish to shift away from Asia. Change started with a series of dramatic developments including the validation of travel to China by American citizens and liberalizing policies regarding Chinese goods purchased by US travelers (Department of State — United States, 1969). The US government then normalized relations with China. This surprising about-face came to be known as the "Nixon Shock" of 1971 for obvious reasons.[13] The dramatic extent of this shift could be feasibly accomplished within the US political arena only by a figure such as Richard Nixon, who carried as part of his accumulated baggage impeccable anti-communist credentials.

However, US regional disengagement was met with a strong dollop of Chinese suspicion. Despite Japan's observed reluctance to develop a military capability extending beyond self-defense preparedness, China still feared that Japan might substitute its own military ambitions for those which the US claimed to be foregoing. In this nightmare scenario, Japanese troops would simply replace American soldiers in South Korea and Taiwan.[14] Chinese Prime Minister Chou En Lai went so far as to seek assurance from Assistant to the President for National Security Affairs, Henry Kissinger.[15] China was worried that Japan's growing economic might could possibly spill over to a concerted military expansion, only loosely masquerading under the banner of strengthening its self-defense stance.[16] The US, though encouraging Japan to take a more active role in security matters, was also wary of an independent, militarized Japan venturing beyond its own self-prescribed defense limitations. The US left no doubt that it considered its bedrock alliance

---

[13]This came on top of Nixon's suspending the redemption of dollars for gold, the erection of trade barriers to imported Japanese textiles and also the soybean embargo.
[14]This derives from the tapes made of the meeting between Kissinger and Chou En Lai (Nixon, 1971, pp. 32–33).
[15]*Ibid.*, pp. 10–11.
[16]*Ibid.*, pp. 19–20.

with Japan to be imposing a clear "restraint on the Japanese," especially on their ability to act independently.[17] This position was emphatically reiterated by Nixon in a February 1972 meeting with Chou En Lai. According to the US president, American leadership, as embodied in its security treaty with Japan, could "restrain Japan from following a course which the Prime Minister correctly pointed out could happen, of economic expansion being followed by military expansion."[18] Both China and the US tacitly shared suspicions that a military buildup could certainly follow from Japan's growing economic strength. However, opposed to these uncomfortable scenarios was the reality of Japan's political situation. The Japanese themselves were markedly unwilling to extend their military readiness beyond the comforts of their own unilaterally imposed self-defense prohibitions. Given the existing domestic distaste for overseas adventures and the lingering regional suspicions of Japanese motives, any path constructed upon diplomatic practicality favored emphasizing Japan's economic, rather than its military, capabilities.

Unfortunately for Japan, both the US and China preferred to accept a more standard view confirmed by traditional wisdom. Achieving economic growth inevitably led to the pursuit of military power. This assumption in fact proved to be mistaken. Quite contrary to these conventional concerns, the Japanese themselves were extremely reluctant to expand their militarily beyond the realm of self-defense. From the Japanese perspective, fashioning their country into an economic power, while eschewing military might, could effectively quell regional apprehension. Conveniently, such a strategy could also stave off the worst effects of an overwhelming domestic backlash, which would ensue by deliberately arousing latent anti-militarism.

Normalized relations between the US and China in 1971 was quickly followed in 1972 by the first Strategic Arms Limitation Treaty (SALT I) between the US and the Soviet Union, leading to a policy of détente between these post-war foes. Together, these two milestones represented a perceived thawing of Cold War tensions. Under

---

[17] *Ibid.*, p. 24).
[18] *Ibid.*, p. 19.

such favorable circumstances, American military presence along with much of its influence visibly declined, as troops withdrew from the region. This was noticeably the case in Vietnam after 1973. American military presence shrank (776,000 troops in 1969 to 176,000 in 1973) and US influence quickly dissipated. But the Vietnamese pullout did not encompass the magnitude of this policy shift. With another 62,000 troops departing Japan, South Korea and the Philippines, a major disengagement was clearly under way.[19] Added to this by 1974 was a cessation of free military assistance to Taiwan, as well as still more troop withdrawals, this time from Taiwan and Thailand. The regional vacuum created, especially on the Korean Peninsula, worried both the Japanese and the South Korean governments. The seriousness of the situation caused an unlikely cooperative effort to be staged by the Japanese and South Koreans (Cha, 1999, pp. 141–168). They joined hands to lobby the US, hoping to alter the shape of the planned disengagement. Responding, President Gerald Ford tried to assuage allied fears by reaffirming US intentions to maintain its presence in Korea (Watanabe, 2000, pp. 297–300). Unfortunately, the subsequent decision by the Carter administration to backtrack somewhat from the Ford era commitments further roiled relations with Japan and South Korea.

The pledge by President Carter to withdraw US military forces from their Korean bases reinforced Japan's perception that America was irresistibly drifting toward a policy of non-intervention following the 1975 fall of Saigon. Carter was making a deliberate effort to construct a foreign policy that placed greater reliance on economic issues and human rights. In other words, this strategic shift rejected the more traditional policy of "power politics," that depended essentially upon coercive force. Partisan mobilization against the communist menace appeared to be increasingly peripheral to America's vital security interests, given the growing interdependence of the world's economy. Buoyed by South Korea's increasing wealth and the easing

---

[19] For this and related matters, see *Gaiko Kiroku* 01-956-1, June 16, 1973, Appendix.

of international tensions, Carter felt encouraged to proceed with his idiosyncratic policy agenda.[20]

Yet, Japan did not entirely welcome this development, as it ran at cross purposes to some basic Japanese objectives. Though Japan desired to structure a more independent and influential regional profile, this could only be accomplished under the American security umbrella. Prime Minister Takeo Fukuda reminded US Vice President Walter Mondale that the safety of the Korean Peninsula, as well as Taiwan, still remained of prime importance to Japan. Given the potential consequences, the US (in Fukuda's opinion) needed to reconsider its strategy of withdrawal without delay (Watanabe, 2000, pp. 302–303).

Countering this position, the US instead made its expectations clear. Japan was obligated, as a dependent ally, to play a key role in facilitating this planned American disengagement, even if it was politic to stop short of making a formal commitment to do so. Although the Japanese retained an abiding interest in the "security of the Korean Peninsula," and had even made this point abidingly clear at a 1969 meeting with Nixon, they were reluctant to become directly involved in such touchy security issues. Given ever-present regional suspicions, namely the apprehension created by any possible remilitarization of Japan, and the embedded anti-militarist stance characterizing Japanese public opinion at this time, the government distinctly preferred to cling to a more familiar role. As always, it chose to remain the ever-quiet bystander when dealing with security concerns.

In any case, in terms of direct military participation, Japan's hands were firmly tied. The Japanese opted instead to demonstrate their required loyalty by increasing financial support for those US forces stationed in Japan. Showing a degree of sensitivity to Japanese concerns, the US provided a degree of reassurance by reaffirming its intention to retain a balanced and flexible military presence in the Western Pacific. This stance certainly extended to the Korean Peninsula, which was a key element in ensuring stability in the region as well as maintaining

---

[20]For greater detail of the US withdrawal from the Korean Peninsula during the Carter Administration, see Murata (1998, pp. 161–180).

its commitment to defend South Korea.[21] Despite these significant gestures, the shrinking US presence in Asia was an overwhelming reality. Reduced American foreign aid clearly signaled an ebbing of US influence. In this one respect, Japan was ready and more than willing to substitute its own style of aid, acquiescing in this idiosyncratic fashion to US pressure. Ironically, this particular aspect of American pressure was ideally suited to Japan's new activist policy and its objectives. Bowing to US demands, at least in this guise, conveniently allowed the Japanese to pursue its "alternative approach" to gaining regional influence.

However, disengagement did not translate into an end to America's partisanship approach within the region. Adopting this new diplomatic twist inevitably (and almost by definition) required communist China to be transmuted into a sympathetic friend and a bulwark against a hostile Soviet Union. As a result, the US pressed Japan to conclude a peace treaty with the Chinese. This maneuver aroused the Soviet Union, which now viewed Japan as a potential threat (Iokibe, 1995, p. 351). Due to an anti-hegemony clause in the signed treaty with China, Japan was effectively blocked from engaging in similarly productive bridge-building with the Soviet Union. Exacerbating these increasingly precarious diplomatic relations was the Soviets' 1979 intrusion into Afghanistan. This not only triggered a distinct heightening of the previously quiescent Cold War, but in doing so strictly limited any potential Japanese success in influencing regional developments. However, if attention is kept focused solely on the region's smaller powers, the possibility for Japanese success within this much more limited sphere could not be entirely ruled out. Still, the renewal of the Cold War temporarily blocked Japan's longer-term objective of creating a more independent, regional policy. We now turn to the way in which the Japanese attempted to implement their new strategic pose by employing both diplomatic skills and economic means.

---

[21] Carter reaffirmed US security commitments within the region in a March 1977 Joint Communiqué with Japan. For the complete text, access http://www.ioc.u-tokyo.ac.jp/~worldjpn/documents/texts/JPUS; or see "The Joint Statement at the US-South Korea 11th security meeting, July 1978," *Waga Gaiko no kinkyo No. 23*, 1979, pp. 433–435.

3.3 Japan Tries the Diplomatic Route: Practising the Art of Persuasion

Following the occupation period, Japan's Asia policy from 1952 onward ran in tandem with America's Cold War diplomacy. In a sense, Japan relinquished its option for any strictly independent action by signing the US–Japan Security Treaty. At that time, Japan was grappling with a devastated economy and something of a political power vacuum. Faced with regional apprehension and animosity, hewing to a path undeniably laid out by US policy seemed to be the wisest choice. In fact, ever since 1952, US influence has dominated, to a lesser or greater extent, Japan's Asia policy. It is then foolhardy to attempt to comprehend the contours created by Japan's post-war endeavors without realizing the enforced effectiveness that the constraints created by the US had on Japanese action.

As the Cold War intensified in Asia, so did US pressure to toe the prescribed policy line. This partisan demand for alignment left only a very limited scope for independent action and almost none in regards to the communist states in Asia. Despite these rather rigid constraints, Japan during these early years did not remain an entirely subservient entity. Though always consistent in action with US leadership, Japan seized whatever opportunities arose for greater independence and more daring aspirations within the ostensible solidarity expressed and demanded by the US–Japan Security Treaty. Prime Minister Sato reflected this precarious balancing act, seeming to accept whatever Asian policy the US suggested (or dictated), while still emphasizing the need for Japan to be more active in pursuing peace and stability throughout the region. This more subtle approach contrasted with his predecessors who had focused exclusively on economic relations. Sato preferred when possible to wiggle his way out of the all encompassing American strait jacket. As he succinctly explained:

> Japan, as one of the few countries in Asia enjoying political stability and possessing a highly industrialized economy, considers herself to be in a unique position to offer as much of a contribution as possible within her own capacity towards the achievement of stability and prosperity in Asia ... Japan is also fully aware that for the ultimate

purpose of contributing to the promotion of peace in Asia she must promote her own friendly relations with other Asian countries … (Sato, 1967).

In 1965, Sato concluded that a propitious start in this direction could be attempted by sending a special envoy, Masajiro Kawashima, to the Afro-Asian conference in Jakarta. Appropriately, part of his mission included mediating the conflict between Indonesia and Malaysia ("Fumidashita Ajia Gaiko," *Asahi Shimbun*, April 20, 1965). Yet, despite its professed objective, Japan stood out in a crowd characterized by an almost automatic adherence to the abstract concepts of anti-colonialism, anti-imperialism and nationalism. Other participants stigmatized the Japanese for being firmly aligned with the despised Western camp when evaluating geo-political considerations. Kawashima could only sit in silence listening to the flow of inflammatory oratory. At least though, by attempting to mediate the Indonesia–Malaysia dispute, Japan could still demonstrate a beneficent willingness to play a more active and productive role within the region. Kawashima continued to act as a catalyst, trying to ameliorate ruptured relations, like the one that had grown between Jakarta and Beijing. Despite a 10-year break, he still hoped to bring these two nations closer together (*Asahi Shimbun*, April 20, 1965).

The continuing Cold War confrontations of the 1960s encouraged the Japanese to focus more on improving relations, even if only unofficially, with China. The potential economic and state security advantages drove Japan to explore these opportunities despite the very nature of these uncharted waters. On the surface, Japan's diplomatic stance was careful not to stray an iota from the path pursued by the US. However, the Japanese were convinced that a policy based on cultivated hostility toward the Chinese people was probably unwise, especially in the long run. Adopting this viewpoint meant that there would be no sustainable peace in Asia as long as the perennial "Chinese" problem remained unresolved (Sato, 1967, pp. 692–693; Department of State, 1965, p. 775). The US appeared to be surprisingly sensitive to these Japanese concerns. In response, the Americans attempted to downplay the seriousness of these divergent paths by insisting that this particular issue was the "only major matter on which US–Japanese views differ significantly."[22] However, at a more fundamental level, Japan's desire to blaze an independent diplomatic path in cultivating China did not fail to rankle the Americans, who continued to pursue their own restrictive agenda. The US viewed Japan as naively underestimating the regional threat posed by this classic sleeping giant.[23]

Japan, however, remained desperately unenthusiastic about mechanically hewing to the dictates of US Cold War strategy. Instead, the Japanese were determined to balance its obligations to support American policy against the advantages of building and maintaining good relations with its Asian neighbors, including the communist ones. Prime Minister Sato, for instance, when meeting with President Nixon, stressed the mutual advantages that would accrue should Japan success- fully establish itself as a bridge between democratic and communist Asia. The direction of this proposed role can be distinguished when catego- rizing Japan's Vietnam strategy. As a matter of course, Japan supported South Vietnam in its role as America's most loyal Asian ally. Still, Japan saw the necessity of promoting North Vietnam's welfare and encour- aging it to co-exist with other entities in the region. Instability could not only threaten regional prosperity, but have a distinct impact on the Japanese economy.[24] Pursuing this goal of peace and growth, Japan continued post-war trading relations with North Vietnam, even though the actual level of trade remained negligible. Japan, when convenient, could overlook any lack of formal diplomatic relations and even to a certain extent ignore a given level of outright hostility. Instead, Japan skillfully employed separate tracks in pursuing economic and political aims. For example, Japan tried to construct a niche role for itself by mak- ing unofficial contracts with North Vietnam in Paris during 1971 and by sending to Hanoi the first director of the Foreign Ministry's newly established Southeast Asia Division (Inada, 1993, p. 113). The extent

---

[22]For further insights refer to "Future of Japan," Department of State Paper, June 26, 1964, National Security Files, Lyndon B. Johnson Papers, Lyndon B. Johnson Library. This relevant work is cited in Hosoya (1999, p. 605).

[23]*Ibid.*, pp. 775–776).

[24]This is discussed in *Gaiko Kiroku*, 01-681-1, 1970.

of this bridging function was of course highly limited by the operative international environment. However, greater opportunities did open up as Sino–American relations changed dramatically.

With *rapprochement* between the US and China starting in 1971, the balance of power in Asia was relentlessly transformed. Having achieved the unanticipated objective of establishing diplomatic relations with the US, a newly energized China next explored the possibility of creating similar links with Japan.[25] Seizing on the "Nixon shock" as a rare opportunity, Sato's successor, Kakuei Tanaka weighed up China's new attitudes as offering a potential strategic opening. He traveled to China in September 1972, meaning to nail down official diplomatic relations between the two Asian powers. This initial success marked the first step toward a better and more workable relationship with the Chinese. With the traditional Cold War barrier removed by America's own hands, the Japanese now felt free to more openly pursue and even realize its long-held objectives.[26]

With Sino–American relations warming, Japan could initiate an increasingly autonomous Asian policy without offending the ideological strictures formerly dictated by US-inspired Cold War blinders. Ignoring differences in social, political, or economic systems, Japan pursued its diplomatic advantage by improving relationships with all neighboring countries. Such tactics, if managed properly, might provide the Japanese with the ability to act more flexibly while still pursuing national objectives (Ministry of Foreign Affairs, 1971, p. 104). In effect, Japan would no longer be strictly identified with the US, but would edge more toward the middle ground between East and West. That at least was the hope. Foreign Minister Ohira clearly indicated

---

[25] In September 1972, Chou En Lai handed a normalization proposal to Takeiri of the Clean Government Party (now merged into the New Komeito Party), and this became known as the "Takeiri memo."

[26] There were three important steps in the normalization process. First, the Prime Minister went further than Nixon by stating that Japan would recognize Beijing as the sole legal government of China, thereby abandoning official ties with Taiwan. This acceptance included an acknowledgement that Japan fully understood and respected China's insistence that Taiwan remained an inalienable part of its territory. Second, both countries willingly pledged not to make any attempt to establish hegemony within the region. They pledged to oppose such efforts when mounted by other countries. Third, China renounced its demand for war reparations from Japan.

that this was Japan's intention in 1972 while attending the Seventh Southeast Asia Development Ministerial Conference. He emphasized Japan's newly explicit desire to ignore differences in political systems when providing international aid.[27]

For this reason, Japan intended to use the American withdrawal from Vietnam to do more than simply substitute for the US as some sort of surrogate power. Instead, by becoming an acknowledged mediator between contending powers, Japan saw its regional influence as growing in a satisfactory manner. As the international environment shifted more dramatically and the US ingloriously fled from Vietnam, Japan skillfully responded by accelerating its strategic makeover. In concrete terms, this implied greater dialogue with previously ostracized nations such as the Soviet Union, communist China, North Vietnam and North Korea.[28] In line with this transformation came a rising sense of identity and nationalism. The return of Okinawa came to be seen as the historic fruit gained by taking a much more active role on the world's stage. Such an unambiguous success was something of a defining moment in Japan's post-war attempt to construct a more independent and precisely structured political role within regional diplomacy (Sato, 1969b, p. 374). Part of Japan's need to transform its previous stance was a compelling recognition that it could no longer shirk the burden of actively contributing to regional stability (Sato, 1969b, p. 374). The restoration of Okinawa provided Japan with a sense that it was now competent to exercise a large degree of political freedom. Events such as these served to restore Japan's fragile confidence.

Japan's tactical departure from past policy came to define the 1970s. As a symbol of this attempt at broad-based renovation, in 1973, 17 years after former Prime Minister Hatoyama had made a similar journey, the then Prime Minister, Kakuei Tanaka, made his own Moscow. The ostensible object of his pilgrimage was to conclude a lasting peace with the Soviets, which had remained in abeyance since World War II. However,

---

[27] Further insight can be gained at *Gaiko Seisho*, 1972, pp. 461–465.

[28] Ministry of Foreign Affairs (1973, p. 14). Japan had anticipated being part of the Paris Peace Conference. Japan based these hopes on its willingness to help reconstruct Vietnam in whatever way proved feasible. Despite its optimism, Japan was not one of the 15 nations invited to the Conference.

it was not in fact particularly fatal when this attempt floundered. Tanaka instead was willing to settle for a joint communiqué touching on the Northern Islands, the status of which had long remained unresolved.[29] The inherent symbolism of narrowing the unbridgeable gulf that had existed between the two countries more than outweighed any more concrete results. Expanding this diplomatic offensive, the Japanese next recognized North Vietnam in September 1973 with an embassy opening soon after in the capital of Hanoi. Building on these actions, Foreign Minister Miyazawa took this opportunity to emphasize (1973) Japan's policy objective, namely improving regional relations. In practise, this would involve increasing Japan's explicit dealings with all Asian countries rather than excluding those of a communist stripe. This outreach program might even extend to the outright pariahs. The Japanese assumed that taking a more independent approach, concentrating critically on mutual cooperation, would almost inevitably promote regional peace and stability.[30] Such a policy appeared feasible, now that the heavy hand of US policy had been relaxed at least momentarily.

However, intentions alone proved insufficient. Actual relations between Japan and the relevant communist regimes seemed destined to remain fractious. Instead, searching for what might prove to be a viable alternative, Japan came to regard the Association of Southeast Asian Nations (ASEAN) as the most reasonable regional option. ASEAN had been gaining in stature and influence since its formation in 1967. The Ministries of Foreign Affairs and that of International Track and Industry (MOFA and MITI) harbored some initial suspicions about the wisdom of edging closer to ASEAN. They saw the potential for conflicts of interest dominating any such relationship. These fears seemed validated by Malaysia's proposal to establish a Zone of Peace, Freedom and Neutrality (ZOPFAN). This proposal appeared to be potentially at odds with the type of US-designed security policy to which Japan

---

[29] The Soviet Union's consistent stance had been that the territorial issue was settled already. The new Joint Statement made clear that territorial issues did exist between the two countries. This meeting then can be regarded as having opened the possibility for a settlement of the Northern Territorial issue.

[30] Foreign Minister Miyazawa's speech of July 1975 can be found in *Waga gaiko no kinkyo* 1976, 41–45 accessed at http://www.iocu-tokyo.ac.jp/~worldjpn. See also Ministry of Foreign Affairs (1977, p. 27).

had faithfully adhered (Hook *et al.*, 2002, p. 186). To these MOFA-tinged concerns was added those of MITI, which viewed the ASEAN alliance as the nucleus of an exclusive economic confederation. These fears proved to be largely groundless. ASEAN in the late 1960s and early 1970s managed to contribute directly to stabilizing the previously unsettled relations between Indonesia, Malaysia, and Singapore. Even more so, ASEAN also acted as an effective mediator between member countries at the bilateral level (Jeshurun, 1993, p. 84). Recognizing ASEAN's future importance, Prime Minister Tanaka refocused diplomatic attention in that direction, following the rapid normalization of relations with China.

However, the newly transformed political environment was not the sole incentive generating Japan's diplomatic shifts. Japan's economic growth translated into a greater flow of funds that allowed for additional economic cooperation. Japan could use its new-found wealth to assist targeted developing countries. Unfortunately, the benign aspect of this economically buoyant Japan was undervalued. Instead, Japan, the new powerhouse, tended to arouse regional suspicions. To some neighboring countries, Japanese assistance amounted to nothing more than regional aggrandizement, masquerading behind a more innocent label. This potential conflict flared up in 1971 as ASEAN claimed that Japan's synthetic rubber industry was gutting the traditional sector that continued to be a pivotal export for some of the ASEAN countries. To pacify these qualms, the Japanese established an ASEAN–Japan synthetic rubber forum to adjudicate any such disputes. Japan attempted to demonstrate its good faith by curtailing its own production and providing technical assistance to affected countries. Through such conflicts, Japan came to appreciate the sensitivity of most of the Asian countries to what they viewed as Japanese expansion. These fears were in no way limited to expressly military matters. Given the redefinition of Japanese growth into worrisome regional dominance, Japan necessarily modified its Asian policy. ASEAN was elevated to the role of equal partner, rather than relegated to simply following Japan's clear but unwelcome lead (Yamakage, 1991, p. 158).

These diplomatic initiatives then formed the background to Tanaka's visit to Southeast Asia some 6 years after Sato's tour. This excursion became the occasion for Tanaka to enunciate and clarify the emerging shape of Japan's Asian policy. In particular, he defined five key principles that would characterize Japan's diplomatic efforts in Southeast Asia:

- The promotion of good relations with the Southeast Asian states,
- A respect for their independence,
- The promotion of mutual understanding between states,
- A dependable Japanese contribution to the future economic development of these states;
- A continuing promotion of respect for voluntary regional cooperation among them (Ministry of Foreign Affairs, 1973, p. 25).

However, despite the best of intentions, the populations of these countries greeted Tanaka with sharply divisive protests. Such episodes as the rubber conflict had served only to enflame regional suspicions of Japanese economic expansion. This underlying lack of trust among Japan's neighbors would continue to limit the potential for Japan to take dramatic and independent initiatives within the region. Instead of promoting Japanese objectives, these tactics set off almost immediate anti-Japanese feelings, which flared uncontrollably in these ASEAN countries. The local populace classified an active, expanding Japan as no more than a later day version of the unlamented "Greater East Asia Co-Prosperity Sphere" which had formed one of the key rationales for Japanese domination during the Pacific War. This perception was hardly helped by the behavior of some Japanese business transplants and those individuals closely associated with such firms. These transplants seemed to display a short-run mentality that focused on narrowly defined objectives. Their limited aims provided little, if any, perceived benefits to the host country (Kosaka, 1999, pp. 213–227; Ministry of Foreign Affairs, 1973, p. 25). Public protests to Tanaka's visit in Thailand and Indonesia reflected this antipathy to a dramatically increased Japanese presence. Such raised voices generally succeeded in drowning out Tanaka's message of goodwill.

These foreign reactions, of course, also reflected more domestically rooted problems in each specific country. However, Tokyo still felt compelled to conduct a thorough review of its Asia policy.

The goal was to shift the emphasis away from a purely private sector focus. Japan sought to discover a strategy which would allow for continuing economic expansion without simultaneously triggering virulent anti-Japanese sentiment. The subsequent Fukuda (1976–1978) administration would successfully transform such objectives into concrete diplomatic behavior.

Politics in Japan has been to a significant degree largely a family business (and remains so today (2009) with the current Prime Minister (Aso) and Opposition Leader (Hatoyama) closely conforming to this specification). Fukuda, a former Ministry of Finance bureaucrat, was no exception to this rule. His experience and background helped him recognize quite clearly that any such sustained foreign revulsion against the Japanese could only be overcome by adopting a distinctly different approach to diplomatic relations. He summed up the core of the problem facing Japan in an August 1977 speech:

> Diplomacy towards Southeast Asia until now was contact through money and goods. It was not contact based on the policy of good friends acting for mutual benefit. Even when viewed from our country there was an impression of economic aggression and arrogant manners. It was a situation which was symbolized by the expression 'economic animal' (*Mainichi Shimbun*, August 5, 1977, cited in Sudo, 1992, p. 158).

The Japan–ASEAN Forum inaugurated in March 1977 reflected Fukuda's new emphasis on promoting greater "dialogue" between Japan and the ASEAN member nations. The forum itself would evolve into a conduit allowing ASEAN countries to lobby for more Japanese assistance and economic cooperation during widespread economic downturns (Yamakage, 1991, p. 178). The Japanese government supplemented these initiatives by attempting to improve relations on a leader-to-leader basis. Stronger ASEAN links were cultivated through a series of invitations. President Marcos of the Philippines arrived with Prime Minister Lee of Singapore twice, once in April and then in May. Both the Thai and Malaysian Prime Ministers were able to visit in September of that same year (Ministry of foreign Affairs, 1977, p. 33). By August 1977, a tentative fit was growing between ASEAN expectations of greater economic assistance and Japan's perceived need to structure a new regional policy. This led to a series of top-level meetings that year with the ASEAN heads of government. This new-found level of activity grew out of broader Japanese objectives.

At the end of a fevered six-country tour throughout the ASEAN nations, Fukuda appeared ready to enunciate a striking doctrine built upon three main commitments:

> First, Japan is committed to peace and rejects the role of a military power. Second, Japan will do its best to consolidate the relationship of mutual confidence and trust based on "heart-to heart" understanding with the nations of Southeast Asia. Third, Japan will cooperate positively with ASEAN while aiming at fostering a relationship based on mutual understanding with the countries of Indochina and will thus contribute to the building of peace and prosperity throughout Southeast Asia (Ministry of Foreign Affairs, 1977, p. 30).

Contrasting sharply with the controversial Tanaka visit of 1974, Fukuda found himself well received. By this time, the ASEAN nations actually welcomed a decided Japanese regional engagement. Two factors, one political, and the other economic, provided this noticeable change of heart. Politically, Vietnam's emergence as a socialist military power within the region threatened to destabilize the existing status quo of security arrangements (Shiraishi, 1990, p. 73). ASEAN governments at least, though not perhaps their populace, now expected Japan to contribute economically, if not militarily or politically, to stymie Vietnam's possible ambitions. This re-evaluation of Japan fortuitously coincided with its emerging diplomatic approach of "bridging" potential conflicts between the regional powers and helping to resolve any sensitive issues. With the still recent *rapprochement* between the US and China creating an encouraging environment and the Vietnam War now a fading memory, the easing of international confrontations allowed room for a more activist diplomatic policy to be pursued by the Japanese.

Regional economic development can be viewed as gaining increased importance during this period. Japan's economic policy, if properly executed, could therefore smooth the way for the rest of Japan's diplomatic initiatives during this era. Expectations of material assistance proved the driving force behind Fukuda's warm welcome in Thailand and Indonesia ("Gaishi kangei no kankyo zukuri," *Asahi Shimbun*, August 16, 1977). Asian countries looked to Japan's economic dominance as an

effective bulwark supporting their own specific nation-building agendas. This eagerness to tap proffered Japanese economic cooperation
generated numerous press releases and joint communiqués during
the Fukuda period, with only a fraction of this output eventually
meaningful.

This overall eagerness may not have reflected the sentiments of the
respective populations in these countries, but such potential discord
did not discourage most ASEAN governments from pursuing Japanese
largesse during the economic slump of the mid-1970s.[31] Renewed
Japanese investment could act as the very elixir needed to revive flag-
ging economies.[32] The 1973 oil shock had led to a sharp curtailment of
Japanese foreign direct investment. By 1976, Japan's Indonesian investment had fallen to one-fourth its previous level. During 1975–1977,
investment flows into Thailand had practically disappeared.[33] Singapore's Prime Minister, Lee, at this time managed to concisely express
ASEAN's hope for a life line. In his statement Lee "...urged Japan
to express a firm commitment to ASEAN by extending more aid and
particularly to help their proposed industrial projects" (cited in Sudo,
1992, p. 104).

Although rejected by Fukuda, Lee's suggested structure for a pref-
erential tariff arrangement perfectly illustrated ASEAN's attempt to
turn Japan into a dependable economic engine capable of pulling the
regional train of nations out of its unwanted slump.[34] This choice
was accentuated by a distinct lack of viable alternatives. Thus, the
desire for increased Japanese investment dramatically changed regional
attitudes.[35] Certainly an America determined to disengage would not
possibly wish to play such a burdensome role. Japan provided the
only valid substitute actually interested in nourishing their economic
ambitions.

---

[31] See the various joint communiqués and press releases disseminated by the Japanese government
and the governments of a variety of other Asian countries. For example, The 1974 Joint Press
Release of Japan and Malaysia can be accessed at http://www.ioc.u-tokyo.worldjpn~/.

[32] For example, see *Waga gaiko no kinkyo 1978*, 377–379, found at http://www.iocu-
tokyo.ac.jp/~worldjpn.

[33] *Ibid.*

[34] More information is available at *Gaiko Kiroku*, 01-946-2.

[35] For example, see *Waga gaiko no kinkyo 197*, 377–379.

Clearly, ASEAN hopes were limited to economic, rather than anything resembling military assistance from Japan. The Fukuda doctrine distinctly ruled out any intervention of this type. But the Japanese still thought that attaining the trust of these countries would allow Japan to use its economic might to fashion a greater political role within the region. The Fukuda doctrine again marked a real departure for Japan's diplomatic ambitions. The key was Japan's willingness to adopt a negotiating position of equality when dealing with its regional neighbors. To achieve its aims, Japan deliberately eschewed anything that could be dismissed as a self-serving hierarchical view of Asian relations. Japan shied away from assuming a dominant position that could be perceived as justification for demanding some sort of leadership role.

Fukuda's approach did not only encapsulate Japan's regional aspirations, or even simply represent an initiative that coincided with ASEAN's economic goals and objectives. Providentially, it was a strategy that proved capable of aligning itself with current US interests in the region as well. After withdrawing from Vietnam, America's military presence also declined regionally. However, Southeast Asia did not lose its importance as a major component of US security strategy.[36] An unstable Southeast Asia could threaten the security of Japan and South Korea. Both countries represented key US allies. American disengagement strategy could only work if countries like Japan and South Korea proved willing to pick up a good deal of the remaining burden.[37] This American strategy extended to the various ASEAN countries as well.[38] They too had their prescribed roles to play if the US scheme was to be made practical.

Under this view, more regional cohesion and economic development might end up stabilizing the region and keeping it secure despite US disengagement. Given the thrust of American thinking, the Fukuda doctrine, which encouraged such results, was capable of gaining support from US policy makers as well as the group of ASEAN countries

---

[36] Those interested can analyse the speech by Vice President Mondale in Hawaii (May 10, 1978) (*Waga gaiko no kinkyo No. 23*, 1979, p. 417).

[37] *Ibid.*

[38] This can be found in the 1977 US-Japan Joint Communiqué. This Joint Communiqué can be found at http://www.ioc.u-tokyo.ac.jp/~worldjpn/documents/texts/JPUS.

that benefited more directly and unequivocally. For once, independent Japanese objectives and US goals sufficiently coincided. Tokyo wished to play a more influential regional role by increasing economic aid. Financial underwriting of this category would in turn provide general support for ASEAN and, by doing so, help safeguard the region against communist encroachment. This approach would of course perfectly supplement US commitments within the region.[39] In essence, the removal of the heavily binding American constraint, which had reduced Japan to a very auxiliary role, created much more scope for Japan to pursue its traditional objectives.

Unfortunately, even with increased room to maneuver, ideological divisions within the region meant that actually gaining a position of influence posed some increasingly difficult problems. Vietnam, for instance, proved less than completely predictable. According to Japanese expectations, Vietnam should have carved out a policy characterized by "independent diplomacy," locating itself at some distance away from the extremes of the polar powers, the US and the Soviet Union. If the Vietnamese had been sufficiently tractable to follow this Japanese-inspired script, Vietnam would have become a prime target for Japan's proposed bridging attempts to bring the East and the West closer together.

Japan's objective, however, was more ambitious than a simple attempt to close the diplomatic distance separating Japan from Vietnam. The Japanese also wanted to bridge the much wider gap still existing between the US and Vietnam. Doing so would have transformed the Japanese into one of the most influential playmakers of the world. It was quite predictable then that on September 1978, Japan would urge the Americans to normalize relations with the Vietnamese, hoping that accomplishing this practical goal would encourage greater regional stability, as well as reflecting well on the Japanese themselves (Sudo, 1992, p. 200). The Soviet Union, quite naturally, was ready to counter such obvious diplomatic maneuvering. Responding to the new (and too cordial) understanding among the US, China, and Japan, the

---

[39]Those who are interested in this wordy communication can examine the "Speech by Vice President Mondale in Hawaii, 10 May 1978," *Waga gaiko no kinkyo No. 23*, 1979, p. 417.

Soviets made every effort to lure the Vietnamese firmly into their orbit. Japan's mediation efforts then proved to be largely ineffective, with the Soviet Union successfully engineering a peace treaty with Vietnam by November 1978. This posed a serious setback to Japan's clever diplomatic ploy. Little leverage could be captured now by serving as a midwife capable of improving US–Vietnam relations. Nor did the already unsettled regional situation improve with the 1979 Vietnamese invasion of Cambodia.

Similar difficulties confronted Japan in its attempts to edge ASEAN countries closer to Vietnam as well. Thus, the potentially fruitful opportunity to mediate between opposing forces proved largely illusory. The apparent room in which the Fukuda doctrine could prove to be effective was largely history in less than two years. Still, Japan did not entirely lose its sense of proportion by going so far as to support China when it invaded Vietnam. The Japanese proved resistant even to Chinese Vice-Premier Teng Hsiao-Ping's most persuasive arguments. However, Japan did fully align itself with the US, China, and the ASEAN countries in opposing Vietnam, now closely aligned with the Soviet Union. Given the geo-political climate, opportunities to carve out a too distinctively independent posture proved evanescent. Once again, the international environment had frustrated Japanese ambitions. Pivotal roles that effectively would promote Japan's desire to gain regional recognition and influence seemed depressingly elusive. However, despite these disappointing setbacks, the Fukuda Doctrine did represent a useful experiment that encouraged Japan to play a more active role on the international stage. More practically, it encouraged Japan to pursue a closer, and potentially more productive, relation with the various ASEAN nations.

3.4 Japan Follows an Economic Path: Financing Regional Influence

As previously discussed, the Vietnam War represented a rather dramatic turning point for Japan. Because the war completely upset the prevailing status quo, the American world view was forced to make some significant adjustments. The US began to consider and include Japan as a fundamental building block in containing the communist threat. This new-found consideration included an unquestioned expectation of Japanese support for the war. In line with this current US strategic thinking, Japan, as a result, had to step up economic aid to neighboring Asian countries. Fortunately, this policy not only served US Cold War strategy, but also fell in line with Japan's emerging efforts to play a greater role in regional determinations. Initially, Japan focused most of its diplomatic efforts on backing America's containment policy in Asia, with the sole exception being its clear push to restore Okinawa to Japanese rule. Japan's primary target still centered on stemming the Cold War communist threat rather than any more independent and distinctly Japanese objective. Though Japanese diplomacy would continue to be heavily constrained by US imperatives, the Vietnam War forced the US to let Japan off its very short leash. In a sense, more activities, such as financial aid, were delegated to Japan, given the growing US reluctance to remain overly committed in Asia.

This new role as America's junior partner started innocently enough, as a growing Japanese economy brought with it greater expectations and responsibilities. The US visualized a more developed Japan as playing an active role in providing the financial underpinnings of American-structured diplomatic efforts. The January 1965 joint statement by Sato and Johnson confirmed the shape of future directions. There would be more economic cooperation and consultation between the two allies over Asian-specific issues. In those early days of developing a new policy landscape, such statements were largely created to reflect US necessities rather than essential Japanese objectives. Still, Sato saw clear advantages to expanding Japan's role in development and technical assistance, even if forced to be conducted under the guise of toeing the US line. This initially nebulous role became increasingly specific as Japan enlisted in the American scheme for Southeast Asian development. Johnson's April 1965 Johns Hopkins speech on the eve of the Vietnam War made this policy's direction manifestly clear.

America's rising demands on Japan paralleled Japan's own rising economic strength. Augmented by the deepening US involvement in the Vietnam quagmire, America almost automatically translated Japan's role as a trusted ally into implying an obligation to bear more of the burden in advancing Western interests in Asia. (Notice the clear identification between Japanese and Western interests by the Americans.) Faced with such overarching demands, Sato tried to finesse a difficult position by establishing a beachhead at the Asian Development Bank (ADB). Japan initiated this policy departure by making a contribution of $200 million to the Bank, while at the same time providing direct aid to South Vietnam.[40] Under increased US pressure, Sato then upped Japan's ADB support to $300 million, still some $200 million less than what the US had requested.[41] Johnson, however, also demanded additional Japanese aid to Indonesia, where Suharto was struggling to solidify his new regime. Such timely assistance might also enable Indonesia to send a desired number of troops to South Vietnam.[42]

The denouement of this new style of diplomacy was marked by increased Japanese assistance from 1967 onwards in the form of direct loans.[43] Economic relief also took the form of playing a leading role in the Inter-Governmental Group in Indonesia. Japan in fact ended up hosting a meeting of Indonesia's creditors and subsequently matching the US by financing one-third of that aid request.[44] More broadly, the US now expected Japan to share responsibility for future Asian development, since growing economies were thought to be largely immune from any communist infection. In effect, this meant following the lead or "general path" laid down by the US. In American eyes, this was an attempt to reprise the "Marshall Plan," with the US and Japan closely cooperating to achieve a common objective.[45] Employing the pretext of aid, Japan ended up shouldering some of the burden of the Vietnam War. However, the very indirect manner of its contribution meant that any potential domestic controversy was effectively forestalled.

---

[40] Further discussion can be found at *Gaiko Kiroku*, 01-534-2, November 1967.

[41] *Ibid.*

[42] Japan started to provide aid to Indonesia in 1966. *Ibid.*

[43] For more details explore the following: *Gaiko Kiroku* 01-534-2, November 1967; *Gaiko Kiroku*, 01-678-2; 01-684-1, 1964; 01-534-2, 1967; *Gaiko Kiroku* 01-534-2, November 1967; *Gaiko Kiroku*, 01-678-2; 01-684-1, 1964; 01-534-2, 1967.

[44] For Japan's ODA to Indonesia, see Kingston (1993).

[45] This is based on what occurred at a meeting between Foreign Minister Miki and Secretary of State Rusk (October 6, 1968) (*Gaiko Kiroku*, 01-531).

US pressure for Japan to measure up as a worthy ally meant that as American intervention in Vietnam grew after 1965, so did the flow of Japanese yen. Japan's Official Development Assistance (ODA) had commenced quite modestly in 1954. By 1964, aid had reached $116 million. Financial flows thereafter started to jump by leaps and starts. The total read $245 million in 1965, $283 million in 1966, and finally $384 million by 1967 (Development Assistance Committee, 1969, p. 298). Japan's financial underwriting had more than tripled in just three years. Though this level was far lower than the US outlay, it was still 2.5 times that of another close American ally, Australia (Development Assistance Committee, 1969, p. 298).[46] Of course, the Australians contributed boots on the ground in Vietnam, something that the Japanese were fortuitously prevented from doing.

But it is misleading to attribute the veritable gush of ODA solely to US demands and insistence. It is true that the Japanese had to operate within strict, US-designed limits, but Japan was more than a ventriloquist's dummy in setting the parameters of its diplomatic policy. By 1964, Japan was the only developed (or near developed) country in Asia. With this greatly relished status came the requisite obligations tied to its full membership in the OECD, its full role in the Development Assistance Committee, as well as being bound by "Article 8"[47] status as a member of the IMF and "Article 11" status as part of GATT.[48]

---

[46]Total American foreign aid in 1967 amounted to $3,559 million.

[47]Japan at the time had an obsession with its balance of payments that went back to the Meiji period. Though occasionally justified in the past, balance of payment problems had become an all-purpose excuse to restrict imports. Accepting "Article 8 status" by joining the IMF removed this excuse from Japan's policymaker's bag of tricks.

The key issue regarding Article 8 status at the IMF was whether balance of payment problems could be used as a reason for temporarily restricting imports beyond previously existing import levels — a proviso that applied to developing countries. Thus, in accepting Article 8, Japan agreed not to use balance of payments to justify import protection. In 1964, the balance of payment issue was much more critical for Japan than that of liberalizing cross border capital flows, which only gained importance in the 1970s and 1980s (Schaede, 2000, p. 94n).

[48]In return for being recognized as a grown-up, Japan gave its acceptance to being forcefully weaned from some standard protectionist barriers.

Prime Minister Sato at that time emphatically recognized these obligations. He saw sharing the burden of development assistance as being congruent with broader Japanese objectives.[49] Japan could use such an opening to make economic forays into the heart of Asia (Langdon, 1973, p. 189). Prime focus would be on Southeast Asia, where Japan could further its own ends while staying adeptly within US guidelines. In essence, Japan would conduct a virtually "autonomous policy" based on its newly found economic strength.[50] This eagerness to expand its influence via economic assistance was clearly signaled by the enthusiasm with which Japan embraced Johnson's 1965 "Asian Marshall Plan."[51] In reality, the policy was more of a public relations exercise to soften criticism of America's Vietnam adventure. Nonetheless, Sato seized the opportunity provided by Ambassador Reischauer's request that Japan become an active participant in this proposed assistance strategy. Given his own ambitions to expand Japan's Asian presence, Sato suggested that the US proposal for a $10-million-a-year package was woefully inadequate. In his estimation, at least $20 million per year would be needed to provide the minimum required ante ("Seifu ga Kento wo Kaishi," *Asahi Shimbun*, April 14, 1965).

Japan showed itself willing to surpass America's Asian aid budget if it meant greater recognition for the Japanese within the targeted Asian region. Remember that in the 1960s, Japan was much smaller economically than the US, and was just emerging as an industrial power. This made Sato's initiative all the more daring. Even at this early stage, Sato could envision an advantageous "division of roles" that would

---

At the 1959 IMF general meeting and the 1959 GATT conference, Japan was sternly criticized for its heavy import controls and received substantial pressure to change to an "Article 8" status in the IMF (which, among others, required liberalizing cross-border capital flows) and an "Article 11" status in GATT (which prohibited levying heavy tariffs (Schaede, 2000, pp. 94–95).

[49] A speech by Sato given to the 51st National Diet in January 1966; also see another speech by Sato given to the 58th session of the National Diet in January 1968. http://www.ioc.u-tokyo.ac.jp/~worldjpn, accessed in March 2002.

[50] By 1967, Japan's economy (ranked by GDP) had become the world's third largest after the US and West Germany (excluding the uncertain accounts of the communist countries).

[51] It clearly stated that economic cooperation was important as a means of political leverage. See *Waga gaiko no kinkyo*, No. 12, 1968, p. 315.

serve Japanese interests in the future. If the Japanese proved willing to underwrite the cost, then the US should reliably bear the burden of enforcing Asian security. Sato forcefully made exactly this case in 1969:

> The US has played a vital role and taken a great responsibility not only for the maintenance of the peace and stability in the world but also for the security of Asia. Therefore, I think Japan should play a role in the field of economics, including technical cooperation, to contribute to the economic development of Asian countries.... there has emerged an awareness among the Japanese that we should contribute to the world in any way possible.[52]

Based on its newly discovered economic strength, Japan now felt capable of gradually revealing its core objectives in a series of initiatives. The concrete manifestation of this policy shift came not only in the form of more Japanese aid, but in the very scope of its foreign forays and Japan's increased contributions to an array of multilateral funds. This policy result can be evaluated as the culmination of a series of diplomatic efforts beginning in the 1960s and coinciding with Japan's final escape from the worse of its dire post-war economic situation. Even as early as the mid-1960s, Japan displayed definite leanings toward the erection of more multilateral frameworks, albeit clearly bounded by the strictures of US-determined Cold War policies. Unfortunately, with the exception of the Asian Development Bank (ADB), all these often Japanese-instigated proposals were ultimately aborted. Still, even the failures demonstrated a distinctly Japanese preoccupation with Asia-Pacific regionalism.[53] Yet, despite a lack of early success, the future foundations for Asian development initiatives were taking root, along with the potential for subsequent direct Japanese involvement. Regional frameworks would spring up by 1966, just as the Vietnam War was also being geared up to a more intense level of conflict.

As pointed out, the one clear success from this period was the establishment of the ADB. Japan would prove capable of using this institution as an appropriate vehicle for pursuing its legitimate interests.

---

[52]This can be found in a speech given by Sato to the National Press Club (November 1969) (*Waga gaiko no kinkyo*, No. 14, 1970, p. 374).
[53]See Diet speech by Foreign Minister Aichi at the 63rd session of the National Diet, February 1970. Likewise, examine the speech by Sato at the 63rd session of the National Diet, February 1970, http://www.iocu-tokyo.ac.jp/~worldjpn, accessed in July 2002.

As early as 1962, some Japanese officials sought US support for such a regional facility. This move anticipated the subsequent decision by the UN Economic Commission for Asia and the Far East (ECAFE) to explore this possibility (Yasutomo, 1983, pp. 28–40, 69). When plans came to fruition, the Japanese government became deeply involved in establishing the bank. Japan harbored quite natural hopes of becoming a central player in this new financial institution, which would help promote its broader diplomatic agenda. At the same time, Japan specifically acknowledged that the bank was meant to support America's Cold War vision circa 1966. The implementation of this regional organization in fact saw both the US and Japan contribute 20 percent of its start-up capital. The very size of Japan's share displayed the depth of importance with which Japan was willing to invest this particular scheme. At the time, the US economy was some 7.8 times that of Japan.[54] But the Japanese hoped that the new bank could play a transformative role in Asia. Japan had grown weary of playing the very junior partner to America's behemoth. The size of Japan's financial contribution clearly signaled its sharp desire to use the bank for its own substantive initiatives.

As a key first step, Japan campaigned vigorously to establish the bank's headquarters in Tokyo. To the Japanese, this small measure of international respect seemed clearly deserved, given its sizeable contribution toward the bank's start-up capital. As the Japanese would continually discover in the following decades, they nurtured an unfortunate tendency to completely underestimate the predictable apprehension than any sign of naked Japanese ambition would evoke in neighboring countries. In fact, Japan's post-war diplomatic policy can only be fully comprehended by understanding the extent to which this potential regional reaction continued to positively constrain Japan's limited options. In all probability, the majority of Asians at this time were still painfully sensitive to the political symbolism of choosing Tokyo to be the bank's central location. They "were not ready to acquiesce in Japan's self-appointed Asian leadership role" (Yasutomo, 1983, pp. 67–82).

---

[54] Japan's willingness to encourage and support such Asian initiatives was repeatedly stated in the *Diplomatic Bluebook* and policy speeches of then foreign minister (*Waga gaiko no kinkyo*, No. 13, 1969).

Japan was perhaps alone in being shocked when Manila was selected instead. But Japan's ambitions were not entirely thwarted. It did manage to secure some strategic positions in the bank, such as the Presidency and the Director of Administration. In fact, it may be possible to judge the success of this particular policy move by the high percentage of Japanese representatives in managerial positions. This outcome was unprecedented, given the then current employment of Japanese in other international organizations. The advantages gained from securing a strategic beachhead in the Asian Development Bank worked in two ways. Japan could use the bank to shape regional economic matters. The Japanese would also be able to direct the bank's procurement requirements toward Japanese firms. During the initial decade of its existence (1967–1976), Japan actually captured some 41.67 percent of all such contracts, though during its second decade (1977–1986) this amount would dip to 23.65 percent as other Asian firms began to match efficiency levels and as other Asian countries were able to exert more political clout (Wan, 1995–1996).[55]

Japan, as mentioned, did not limit itself to utilizing the Asian Development Bank solely to forward its own narrow economic objectives. To begin with, Japan hosted its first international meeting in 1966, the Ministerial Conference for the Economic Development of Southeast Asia (MCEDSEA). Baldly stated, this was yet another attempt, like the Asia Pacific Council (ASPAC) by the US to sell its increasingly criticized Asian policy. This particular proposal took the form of financing poor Asian nations, but deliberately made the purely political point of excluding North Vietnam. Japan, however, could see how even a highly politicized promotion like the MCEDSEA might be utilized to launch particularly advantageous Japanese programs under the rubric of economic cooperation.[56] Officially, Japan stated its willingness to provide assistance, but did so always with a weather eye out to calculate exactly how such aid would translate into a measure of Japanese influence.

---

[55] Calculated from the figures in *Waga gaiko no kinkyo*, No. 13, 1969, Appendix 2. Of course, the total number of contracts also would have grown during this period.

[56] For example, Foreign Minister Shiiha's speech given at the 49th special session of the National Diet on July 30, 1965, makes this clear (*Waga gaiko no kinkyo*, No. 10, 1966, Appendix 7).

Japan's growing economic strength became a tool with which to leverage and even dominate other member nations. Japanese intentions were clarified by Foreign Minister Aichi at the 1968 third conference of the MCEDSEA. As Japan's economy grew, so would its economic assistance, with the bulk of it going to Asia.[57] The conference served as a platform by which the Japanese could direct growing amounts of aid to Southeast Asia. (The conference itself would cease to exist with the subsequent terminal postponement of the 1975 meeting.) Such structures would eventually outlive their usefulness with America's exit from Vietnam (Yamakage, 1991a, p. 14).[58] However, as pointed out, the US decision on troop withdrawals ultimately led to a policy of extended Asian disengagement. Such a move quite naturally weakened the US-inspired "containment" architecture within Asia. This structure had been the mechanism within which American-dominated allies, like Japan, had successfully navigated. This startling new reality caused by the emerging US vacuum called for a general reassessment of their diplomatic efforts by the Japanese.

The Japanese, in the past, had proven to be quite selective when choosing subsequent regional organizations. As previously explained, Japan wanted to advance its diplomatic objective using the guise of economic cooperation. It was though thoroughly reluctant to become enmeshed in anything redolent of security issues or having the potential for military confrontations, even when somewhat sanitized by operating under a multilateral framework. This reluctance, if not downright trepidation, was ably encapsulated by Japan's hesitation to participate in the South Korean-inspired, and implicitly anti-communist-defined, Asia Pacific Council (ASPAC). Japan eventually did decide to participate, but only under certain conditions. The Japanese joined only when they gained the appropriate reassurance that ASPAC's remit did not extend beyond issues of regional cooperation. Membership was only acceptable if the organization explicitly foreswore all involvement

---

[57] Foreign Minister Aichi's speech to the fourth conference of the MCEDSEA can be explored for additional insights (*Waga gaiko no kinkyo*, No. 13, 1969, Part III, p. 22).

[58] See Foreign Minister Aichi's speech to the fourth conference of the MCEDSEA which emphasizes this point (*Ibid.*, pp. 20–22).

with either security or ideological matters.[59] The 1973 *rapprochement* between China and the US rendered treaty organizations of this type essentially obsolete.

By this time, Japan was straining at the boundaries mandated by the US-inspired diplomatic framework. Japan's growing economy loosened the traditional dependency that had up to now defined Japanese diplomacy. Nixon's willingness to engineer the demise of the Bretton Woods system by allowing the dollar to float characterized a distinct break with past policies. This dramatic decision, scuttling the post-war, financial architecture, meant the end of the favorable fixed exchange rate ($1 = 360 yen) that had assisted Japan's post-war miracle growth by spurring exports. The new exchange rate would more closely reflect Japan's changed status as a major Asian economic power.[60] Economic strength undermined the standard rationale Japan had adopted as a developing nation to defend its protectionist policies. Up until the late 1960s, the Japanese government had actively discouraged direct foreign investment into Japan to provide Japanese firms with space to grow. Japanese overseas investment was strictly limited as well, to protect scarce foreign currency reserves. Such investment was for the most part limited to promoting Japanese exports and securing natural resources (Pempel, 1993, pp. 110–111).

This approach conflicted with the policies adopted by other Western industrialized countries. After finally achieving implicit recognition of its economic status by becoming one of the select OECD countries, Japan was expected, given its new status, to open its markets to a much greater extent and to liberalize the restrictions attached to capital inflows and investment.[61] Taking a first step in 1967, Japan announced its intention of opening up its borders to more foreign direct investment (Hirono, 2001, pp. 10–12). This action preceded, and to some extent anticipated, a 1968 UN Conference on Trade and Development

---

[59]There was of course no reason not to believe this (*Waga gaiko no kinkyo*, No. 10, 1966, p. 15).
[60]Speech by Sato regarding the appreciation of yen, December 1971. http://www.ioc. u-tokyo.ac.jp/~worldjpn, accessed in July 2002. As a result of Nixon's new economic policy, the yen appreciated from ¥360 to ¥306.
[61]Further information is available at *Waga gakiko no kinkyo*, No. 11, 1967, pp. 179–180.

that decreed a new generalized system of trade preferences. But with 1970 drawing near, Japan focused on expanding regional investment and trade, reacting to both domestic and international pressure. Japan soon became the major trading partner of other Asian nations. By 1970, Japan controlled 25.5 percent of Malaysia's total trade, 39.9 percent of Indonesia's, while at the same time dominating trade with Thailand (33 percent) and the Philippines (34.6 percent) as well (Sudo, 1992, p. 102). The floating dollar and corresponding appreciating yen encouraged Japan to increase its economic commitment within its immediate neighborhood. During the 1968–1973 period, direct investment by Japan surged throughout Asia. Such increased expenditure was easily supported by the booming Japanese economy. In contrast, the US economic presence shrank as America decided against staying the course and prolonging the war in Vietnam.

All of these changes coincided with a power struggle that periodically arose between the American Presidency and the US Congress. Reacting to the disastrous Vietnam War, American attention quite obviously had become more inwardly directed. The imperial presidency characteristic of the Vietnam War era was now hauled in. The 1973 Foreign Assistance Act linking both security and economic assistance to human rights proved to be a watershed legislative act. Cuts to aid packages became a routine event with military assistance to Thailand, Indonesia, and the Philippines all reduced.[62] In a parallel measure, Congress terminated the Military Assistance Advisory Groups, clearly indicating a phased disengagement away from Asian security concerns. The US Congressional prohibition, making assistance dependent on human rights, was consistent with one traditional strand of US foreign policy. But in this case, in a rather retributive mood, the restrictions were also intended to deny any future aid to North Vietnam (Yasutomo, 1983, p. 90). These congressional efforts sought to deliberately tie the hands of American policy in Asia. Whatever their proposed objective, they definitely did limit the degree of US responsiveness to a number of ASEAN economic initiatives. We can then be hardly surprised that

---

[62] For example, US aid towards IGGI (Indonesia) declined from $268 million in 1972 to $150 million in 1973 and then to $61 million in 1975 (*Kokusaikyoryoku suishin kyokai*, 1977, p. 294).

following the fall of Saigon, the percentage that aid (including military and economic) to Asia comprised out of the total US assistance package plummeted from 67 percent in 1973 to 34 percent in 1975 and then to a mere 14 percent in 1976 (Kusano, 1991, p. 298). The sort of power vacuum arising from a directly diminishing US presence provided corresponding scope for a newly confident Japan to flex its economic muscle.

As mentioned, a declining US presence in Southeast Asia provided Japan with the opportunity to substitute its own interest, symbolically as well as concretely, instead of simply following standard American prescriptions. As a result, Japan's regional aid surpassed that of the US by 1975. There was no better indication that America's vanishing influence and interests were being supplanted by Japan's growing economic power than this shift in foreign assistance. Japan, in this instance, revealed its determination to gain regional influence by establishing a solid foothold upon which to build its new policy. Essentially, a significant relaxation in the perennial post-war ideological confrontation that had closely characterized the 1970s managed to clearly reveal Japan's underlying policy ambitions. Simply put, in that early post-war period, Japan's ambitions were almost fatally limited by the prevailing international climate combined with its fundamental economic weakness. Diplomatic focus, at that time, seemed defined solely by Japan's economic agenda. However now, the Japanese were more than willing to provide not only the required backup to sustain US strategy, but also to actively push for initiatives that would expand the operative range of its own interests. Changing international circumstances had provided Japan with the chance of more closely matching tactical aims to political ambitions. Japan planned to use an expanded aid program, not only as a replacement for the one abandoned by the US, but also as a means to develop its own version of an activist Asian policy.

To support its revised strategy, at the 1975 Economic Summit in Rambouillet, Japan continued to display its willingness to accept a growing degree of international responsibility. This new Japanese pose was widely recognized and often appreciated by the conference's participants. Japan further advanced its status by completing war reparations to all impacted countries, finalized by a last payment to the Philippines.

Japan's slate, financially if not morally, could now be regarded as completely clean. Using this moment to symbolize a new beginning, Japan's preferred vehicle for implementing its evolving policy was an expanded and increased Official Development Assistance (ODA) initiative that accurately reflected Japan's newly discovered confidence. This pose, which entailed a significantly larger regional role for the Japanese, was encapsulated in a March 1977 Joint Communiqué with the US. According to the stated terms, "Japan would contribute further to stability and development in the Asia-Pacific region in various fields including economic development."[63]

The precise nature of this new style of diplomatic approach had its unveiling at the 1977 Conference on International Economic Cooperation. Japan emphasized to the assembled delegates that it intended to double ODA disbursements every five years. This was a strategy the US could willingly embrace.[64] Boding well for the success of such an initiative, Japan at this time was buoyed by an environment of general acceptance. The 1978 Bonn Summit provided an occasion for Prime Minister Fukuda to promise that the first doubling of aid would take no more than three years instead of the previously proposed five. To achieve these ambitious objectives, net ODA soared by 134 percent, increasing from $1126 million in 1974 to $2637 million in 1979 (OECD, 1980, p. 179). Such a drastic enlargement of what had been a rather modest aid program was driven by two objectives.

The first purpose of the dramatic increase in aid was a compelling desire to alleviate the chronic criticism from a combined chorus of overseas countries. Japan faced almost automatic censure for pursuing a strategy characterized as one which allowed the Japanese to enjoy the fruits of rapid economic growth while effectively dodging any security responsibilities. Japan could do so by being conveniently situated under a US-provided security umbrella. This perceived lack of responsibility extended to trade policy where, once again, the Japanese were thought

---

[63]The 1977 Joint Communiqué between the US President and the Japanese Prime Minister can be found in Database of the World and Japan, which can be accessed at http://www.ioc.u-tokyo.ac.jp/~worldjpn/documnets/texts/JPUS/19770322.D1E.htm.
[64]This is taken from a speech given by Secretary of State Cyrus Vance (June 1976). It can be found at http://www.ioc.u-tokyo.ac.jp/~worldjpn/index.html.

to be avoiding their free trade obligations implicitly required by the GATT system. The Japanese hoped that a generous ODA policy would provide the means by which they could distract international attention away from a sizable and growing trade surplus. This surplus had started to accumulate sometime in the late 1970s. By the 1980s, it would be reaching historic and threatening proportions, particularly in the eyes of the US.

The second purpose was to expand its influence in the region through the provision of foreign assistance. An overriding desire to dominate, one way or the other, had always defined Japan's diplomatic policy. Overseas aid to Southeast Asia (via its ODA program) merely provided a convenient vehicle to carry out this characteristic objective. Moreover, Japan now possessed the added confidence, previously absent, that flowed from its newly generated economic strength. With this type of potential leverage, Japan was emboldened to pursue a more activist form of diplomacy within the region. As mentioned, the changing economic environment presented a favorable, though not perfect, opportunity with some of Japan's traditionally binding constraints now loosened, if not entirely vanished.

During the depths of the Cold War, for instance, ideology clearly ruled. The Ministry of Foreign Affairs at that time would have quietly supported US policy under most any conceivable circumstances. Japanese ministers would never have had the temerity required to propose, for example, an Indochina Recovery Fund (for regional reconstruction) as part of the primary agenda of the Asian Development Bank.[65] In the 1970s, however, at least some of its former hesitancy started to dissipate. Once the US had disengaged from Vietnam, Japan boldly recognized North Vietnam in 1973, setting the stage for an initial 1975 aid package to the newly reconstituted Socialist Republic of Vietnam to assist in its post-war reconstruction.[66] Such assistance

---

[65] Japan had always realized that it was essential to take into consideration American wishes and objectives before initiating any diplomatic endeavor. For example, Japan realized the need to handle both the US and South Vietnam delicately prior to extending aid towards North Vietnam (*Gaiko Kiroku*, 01-681-1, 1970).

[66] Aid to Mongolia in March 1973 was the first bilateral aid to a socialist state. See Inada (1991, p. 296).

signaled a concerted attempt by Japan to engender the necessary level of trust that might enable it to successfully mediate between the West and communist counties like Vietnam.[67] The underlying hope was that financial support could be the tool that would help to create a more independent Vietnam, rather than one strongly under the sway of either China or the Soviet Union. Japan would then be able to make use of such vital economic ties with a quickly recovering Vietnam when bargaining with the US, China, and the USSR. Unfortunately, the Japanese seemed to be deliberately deluding themselves into believing that Vietnam was not yet irretrievably under the influence of either China or the Soviet Union.[68]

This forlorn hope spurred the Japanese into providing some 8.5 billion yen in 1975 to the Vietnamese plus an additional 3.5 billion yen to construct a cement plant. Japan refused to relinquish its brave hopes even though Vietnam had been participating in the Council for Mutual Economic Assistance (COMECON), the communist answer to the European Common Market. The Japanese still persisted in making every effort to maintain an open channel with Vietnam by lubricating relations with a continuing flood of cash. The Japanese underpinned its assistance strategy by pledging a 4 billion yen grant in 1978 as well as an additional 10 billion yen in credit loans.[69]

At the same time, in July 1978, Japan attempted the seemingly impossible task of encouraging the US to also extend economic assistance to its former enemy, all done with the ostensible aim of stabilizing the region. Key to this diplomatic approach was the overriding objective of ensuring an independent Vietnam. Realistically, Japan had little hope of influencing Vietnam's direction solely by employing a series of economic carrots. Despite regional realities, Japan clung to the hope of somehow drawing the Vietnamese more in the direction of the prevailing Western Bloc, despite Vietnam having concluded a decisive peace treaty with the Soviet Union. Japan seemed to doggedly

---

[67] Japan had long hoped to play a leading political role in settling the issue. For example, see *Waga gaiko no kinkyo*, No. 13, 1969, pp. 107–108. This includes Aichi's speech in 1968.

[68] Japan's policy towards the DRV, March 1976 (*Gaiko Kiroku*, 01-944-02).

[69] In return, Hanoi agreed to repay over a period of 26 years the debt which had been incurred by the Saigon Government.

pursue its ultimate aims even against insurmountable regional realities. Foreign Minister Sunao Sonoda made such delusions amply clear when speaking to his Vietnamese counterpart in December of 1978, "Japan can provide an appropriate amount of economic aid if Vietnam contributes to the peace and stability of Southeast Asia, but if not, it will be necessary to restrict Japan's cooperation" (Sudo, 1992, p. 201; Inada, 1993, p. 131).

However, Japan persevered in continuing to wish that its economic leverage was in fact sufficiently effective, despite all evidence to the contrary. This irreconcilable hope extended to adopting a non-confrontational stance in regard to Vietnam. At the July 1979 ASEAN Ministerial Conference in Bali, Japan essentially was ready to ignore Vietnam's recent Cambodian incursion in order to maintain the groundless and rather vague hope that Vietnam might yet respond to the power of its economic blandishments. Despite these undeniable desires, there were still clear limits to what even Japan could attempt to deny. The Cold War was still quite alive at this time, as was Japan's active alignment with the US. Keeping its new friend China sweet also placed a serious limit on Japan's scope for independent action. In fact, the Cold War took a decided turn for the worse with the Soviet Union's December 1979 invasion of Afghanistan. To say the least, this made further attempts to continue wooing the Vietnamese, now a close Soviet client state, more than a trifle difficult.

Lacking any previous success from its assiduous efforts at persuasion, Japan was forced to officially freeze aid to Vietnam following the Soviets' invasion. In the case of the Cambodian incursion, Japan managed to equivocate and avoid labeling that incursion as something more akin to a human rights violation. In that way, Japan successfully avoided adding its voice to the combined chorus of the US and China that was determined to seize this fortuitous opportunity to condemn Vietnam. However, the opprobrium heaped on the Vietnamese had more to do with its position as a Soviet ally, than with any serious concern for Cambodia or for the plight of its people. Unfortunately, the Afghanistan situation went beyond the limits of Japan's diplomatic abilities to spin bleak realities. So, though Japan clearly yearned to use its economic capabilities to create a more independent diplomatic stance, Cold War imperatives rendered Japan's concerted efforts less than successful, as once again pragmatic necessities blocked more optimistic objectives.

3.5 Conclusion: Looking Toward a More Independent Japan

During the 1960s and the 1970s, US interests had determinedly pushed Japan into assuming a more active diplomatic role, though one clearly defined by its status as no more than America's junior partner. Quite practically, Japan's position in Asia was inevitably redefined by the Vietnam War and the subsequent US reaction to its aftermath, namely a policy of regional disengagement. These events made it increasingly attractive for Japan to assume an all-encompassing economic role that could help to implement and supplement US Cold War strategy.

Fortunately, the US was pushing Japan in exactly the direction that Japan had long yearned to traverse. Taking advantage of the given situation, Japan succeeded in expanding its scope of action within the region. A dramatic increase of its Official Development Assistance in the 1960s and 1970s illustrated Japan's willingness to play a larger role by using its growing economic wealth as a convenient lever. With the announcement of the Fukuda Doctrine in 1977, Japan clearly manifested its long-held aspiration to play a more political role in Asia by establishing a potentially productive partnership with ASEAN. With the disappearance of key external constraints, although only for a relatively brief period of time, Japan sensed a real shift in the international environment. This change presented Japan with the potential of performing a more vital regional role, given its developing economic muscle. Unfortunately, Japan's new assertiveness faced a serious challenge when the Cold War revived in the 1980s.

References

Bundy W. (1965) Speech. *Department of State Bulletin*. November 15, 771–776.
Cha VD. (1999) *Alignment Despite Antagonism*. Stanford University Press, Stanford.

Cummings B. (1997) Japan and Northeast Asia. In: Katzenstein PJ, Shiraishi T (eds.), *Network Power: Japan and Asia*, pp. 136–168. Cornell University Press, Ithaca and London.

Department of State — United States (1965) *U.S. Department of State Bulletin*, November 15, 779–780.

Department of State — United States (1969) *U.S. Department of State Bulletin*, September 1, 180.

Development Assistance Committee (1969) *1969 Review: Development Assistance*. OECD, Paris.

Eto S. (1987) *Sato Eisaku*. Jiji Tsushinsha, Tokyo.

Hirono R. (2001) Changing Japanese Development Cooperation Policy toward ASEAN in the post-war period. In *ASEAN no Taigai Kankei ni Okeru ODA no Igi (Significance of Official development assistance in the external relationships of ASEAN)*: Hirano R. (ed.), Nihon Kokusai Mondai Kenkyusha, Tokyo.

Hook GD, Gibson J, Hughes CW, Dobson H. (2002) *Japan's International Relations: Politics, Economics and Security*. Routledge, London.

Hosoya C. (1999) *Nichibei Kankei Shiryoshu 1945–1997*. University of Tokyo Press, Tokyo.

Inada J. (1991) Hatten Tojoukoku to Nihon. In: Watanabe A (ed.), *Sengo Nihon no Taigai Seisaku*, pp. 285–314. Yuhikaku, Tokyo.

Inada J. (1993) Stick of carrot?: Japanese aid policy and Vietnam. In: Koppel BM, Orr RM (eds), *Japan's Foreign Aid: Power and Policy in a New Era*, pp. 111–134. Westview Press, Boulder, Colorado.

Iokibe M. (1995) Fukuda Takeo. In: Watanabe A (ed.), *Sengo Nihon no Saisho Tachi*, pp. 311–354. Chuo Koko, Tokyo.

Jeshurun, C. (1993) ASEAN as a source of security in the Asia-Pacific region. In: Millar TB, Walter J (eds.), *Asia-Pacific Security after the Cold War*, pp. 81–100. Allen & Unwin, Sydney.

Kingston J. (1993) Bolstering the New Order: Japan's ODA relationship with Indonesia. In: Koppel BM, Orr RM Jr. (eds.), *Japan's Foreign Aid: Power and Policy in a New Era*, pp. 41–62. Westview Press, Boulder, Colorado.

Kokusai Kyoryoku Suishin Kyokai (1977) *Kaihatsutojokoku no Infrastructure Seibi ni Taisuru Enjo Taikei Chosa*. Ministry of Foreign Affairs, Tokyo.

Kono Y. (1991) Sengo No Owari. In: Watanabe A (ed.), *Sengo Nihon No Taigai Seisaku*. Yuhi kaku, Tokyo.

Kosaka M. (1998) *Kosaka Masataka Chosaku Shu No. 1*. Toshi Shuppan, Tokyo.

Kosaka M. (1999) *Kosaka Masataka Chosaku Shu No. 2*, pp. 213–227. Toshi shuppan, Tokyo.

Kusano A. (1991) Kokusai Keizaito Nihon. In: Watanabe, A (ed.), *Sengo Nihon no Taigai Seisaku*. Yuhikaku, Tokyo.

Lagdon FC. (1973) *Japan's Foreign Policy*. University of British Colombia Press, Vancouver.

Ministry of Foreign Affairs (1971) *Diplomatic Bluebook for 1971*. Okurasho Insatsukyoku, Tokyo.

Ministry of Foreign Affairs (1973) *Diplomatic Bluebook for 1973*. Okurasho Insatsukyoku, Tokyo.

Ministry of Foreign Affairs (1977) *Diplomatic Bluebook for 1977.* Okurasho Insatsukyoku, Tokyo.

Momoi M. (1977) Basic trends in Japanese Security policies. In: Scalapino RA (ed.), *The Foreign Policy of Modern Japan*, pp. 341–364. University of California Press, London.

Murata K. (1998) *Daitoryo no Zasetsu.* Yuikaku, Tokyo.

Nixon RM. (1971–1975) *Public papers of the Presidents of the United States, Richard Nixon : containing the public messages, speeches, and statements of the President, 1969 to August 9, 1974.* U.S. Government Printing Office, Washington, D.C.

Nixon RM. (1971) "Memorandum of conversation between Chou En Lai and Kissinger," October 22. *Nixon Presidential Materials Project*, NSC Files, box 1034, pololl-HAK China trip; transcript of meetings. http://www.gwu.edu/~nsarchiv/nsa/publications/DOC_readers/kissinger/.

Organization for Economic Cooperation and Development. (1980) *Development Assistance 1979.* OECD, Paris.

Pempel TJ. (1993) The thrust for economic success — from exporter to investor: Japanese foreign economic policy. In: Curtis G (ed.) *Japan's Foreign Policy: After the Cold War, Coping with Change*, pp. 105–136. M.E Sharpe, Armonk, New York.

Sato E. (1966) Prime Minister Sato's speech in the 51st session of the National Diet. *Waga gaiko no kinkyo No. 10*, Appendix, 5.

Sato E. (1967) Japan's role in Asia. *Contemporary Japan*, 4 (May), 693–696.

Sato E. (1969a) Sato's speech at National Press Club in November 21, 1969. http://www.ioc.u-tokyo.ac.jp/~worldjpn/documents/texts/docs/1969, accessed in June 2002.

Sato E. (1969b) Sato's speech at National Press Club in November 21, 1969, *Waga gakiko no kinkyo No. 14.*

Sato E, Nixon RM. (1969) Joint statement of Japanese Prime Minister Sato and US President Nixon, *Ministry of Foreign Affairs.* http://www.ioc.u-tokyo.ac.jp/~worldjpn/documents/texts/docs/19691121.DIE.html, accessed in June 2002.

Schaede U. (2000) *Cooperative Capitalism: Self Regulation, Trade Associations, and the Anti-Monopoly Law in Japan.* Oxford University Press, Oxford.

Shiraishi, M. (1990) *Japanese Relations with Vietnam: 1951–1987.* Southeast Asia Program, New York.

Sudo S. (1992) *The Fukuda Doctrine and ASEAN.* Institute of Southeast Asian Studies, Singapore.

Tanaka A. (1997) *Anzenhosho: Sengo 50 Nen no Mosaku.* Yomiuri Shimbun Sha, Tokyo.

Wan M. (1995–1996) Japan and the Asian Development bank. *Pacific Affairs*, 68(4), 509–528.

Watanabe A. (2000) *Taikoku Nihon no Yuragi.* Chuo Koron Shinsha, Tokyo.

Yamakage S. (1991a) Asia Taiheiyo to Nihon. In: Watanabe A (ed.), *Sengo Nihon no Taigai Seisaku*, pp. 135–161. Yuhikaku, Tokyo.

Yamakage S. (1991b) *ASEAN: From Symbol to System.* University of Tokyo Press, Tokyo.

Yasutomo DT. (1983) *Japan and the Asian Development Bank.* Praeger, New York.

Chapter 4

Rising Power: Japan Attempts
to Recapture Its Traditional Role
in the 1980s

4.1 Seizing Opportunities: Japan Flexes
Its Economic Muscles

The 1970s witnessed tentative measures by Japan to carve out a more independent, as well as increasingly influential regional role in Asia. Growing economic wealth during this period became the means of achieving this consistent goal. In initiating this shift in approach, the Japanese made no serious attempt to break away from their tradition of US diplomatic tutelage. By necessity, such departures had to still operate within the well-defined scope of America's broader strategic objectives. Nonetheless, the changing international environment created new opportunities for a wealthy and newly confident Japan.

The 1980s saw the US pull in its horns in Asia, not only militarily, but economically as well. By attempting to disengage regionally, the US created something of a security policy vacuum which could be filled, but only to a limited degree, by America's acknowledged junior partner, Japan. The impact of these strategic decisions allowed the Japanese to use this regionally created opportunity to counter-balance the distinct drop in applied American economic assistance. By dramatically increasing its selective use of targeted financial grants, Japan hoped to redefine its regional presence and increase its diplomatic leverage. Directed assistance became a selective tool insuring regional security.

The efficacy of this strategy was then directly augmented by inducing leading Japanese corporations to extend their overseas reach. Greater economic integration played out on an ever-expanding canvas could, with an appropriately timed boost of luck, raise Japan's diplomatic visibility by creating a greater regional role for itself.

Japan hoped to construct an essential platform that would succeed in launching its leadership ambitions. This specific form of internationalization held the potential to deliver a number of welcomed benefits. By expanding overseas, Japan could gain access to badly needed, low-cost labor, as well as opening up new markets overseas. Not only would such a strategy further strengthen the Japanese domestic economy, but by doing so buoy their regional ambitions. Growing wealth would quickly equate to a growing confidence within the country and a noticeable willingness by the government to take a more aggressive role, even if often constrained to do so in a distinctly indirect manner.

This growing self-assurance, built on a foundation of economic success proved timely, given the trend of US policy during this period. It was in the 1980s that the need for Japan to take a more assertive stance could be so easily justified by a perception that the Japanese were compelled to do more to ensure their own comprehensive security. Concurrent with these demands and feeding into such concerns, the Government came to believe during this same period that internationalization was the key to the country's continued economic growth. For the first time in the post-war period, Japan seemingly had managed to align all the necessary policy elements to achieve its newly enunciated objectives. These now explicit goals reflected Japan's long-held drive (or near obsession) to regain a measure of regional influence despite internal and external constraints that seemed to be working intractably against such an achievement.

The difference in the 1980s is that mounting wealth provided Japan with a new face with which to meet its increasingly complex regional challenges. Japan would be encouraged, perhaps to an unreasonable degree, by reaching a seemingly irresistible level of economic might. However, the ability to deploy this unquestioned strength would remain hobbled by its intractable constitutional limits on employing military force. In this chapter, we trace out this distinctly Japanese drive to attain influence and increase regional leadership. This allows us to evaluate Japan's limited success in constructing new strategies to overcome old constraints.

4.2 No Shrinking Violet: Japan Deals with Its Security Issues

4.2.1 *Dealing with Defense*

While growing *détente* and rapprochement characterized the 1970s, a more turbulent history marked the early years of the new decade. By the end of the previous decade (1979), fundamentalist Islamic revolutionaries had toppled the long reigning, and heavily US-supported, Shah of Iran. In the post-revolutionary aftermath, youthful Islamic Guards invaded the American Embassy, seizing US hostages. To further bedevil the Carter administration, the very same year saw the USSR on the offensive. The Soviets sent 80,000 troops into Afghanistan to buttress a faltering allied regime. The troops were soon beset by fundamentalist *mujahedeen* insurgents backed increasingly by the Americans and aided by the Pakistani intelligence service.[1]

Hoping to force a Soviet withdrawal, an increasingly desperate Carter administration suspended grain sales to the USSR, withdrew from the unratified SALT II agreement, boosted defense spending and even boycotted the 1980 Summer Olympics, held that year in Moscow. *Détente* was now an abandoned relic of a failed US strategy. The election of Ronald Reagan as US president only accelerated a policy shift emphasizing an assertive containment of the Soviet military machine. The first term of the Reagan administration was characterized by a further and even more rapid expansion of the military budget. The winds of the Cold War once again chilled political debate, as the Reaganites pushed for a "new revitalization of the US" and proclaimed that they were building a "strong America."

---

[1] The link between the *mujahedeen* and the Pakistani intelligence services would have rather dire consequences during the following decades.

Like most viral changes, the tension initiated in a few specific flash-points spread to the Asia-Pacific region. In 1978, confident of Soviet backing, the Vietnamese flooded into Cambodia focused on replacing the ruthless Khmer Rouge regime. As a result, the pro-Chinese government fled back into the jungle leaving the country to be ruled by Hanoi friendly faces. The resulting tension, as Chinese leaders faced potentially hostile forces on two fronts, pushed the Chinese into the arms of a willing US. As a concrete signal to a newly belligerent Soviet Union, China reversed course by endorsing the US–Japan mutual security treaty. Even an alliance with the detested Japanese now seemed feasible, as China sought a ring of alliances to protect itself against hostile Soviets and their equally militarized allies.[2] As tensions grew, a border war between China and Vietnam erupted for some 17 days in February 1979. The alleged border incursions by the Vietnamese enabled Chinese leader Deng Xiaoping to justify his harsh reaction. As the 1970s ended, the region had clearly become less secure. The increasing closeness among the Soviet Union, Vietnam, and Cambodia had tipped China into retaliating in the guise of a land invasion against the neighboring Vietnamese. Given this hostile preamble, it was hardly surprising that the 1980s opened with a Vietnamese incursion into Thailand. Clearly the region was growing less stable with the future increasingly uncertain.

With Cold War animosity rising in Asia as well, the new Reagan Administration swiftly reversed the partial troop withdrawal from South Korea previously promoted during the Carter era. Circumstances now forced Washington to turn increasingly to Japan for assistance in shoring up its regional position. Economics lay at the heart of this shift in tactics and focus. The stagflation of the 1970s, fuelled by the dual oil shocks of that decade, created slowing economic growth, inflationary fears, and calls for greater economic protection. As US exports faltered, and with its unquestioned dominance no longer a certainty, America's growing trade deficit during this decade seemed to symbolize the almost inevitable economic replacement of the US by the Japanese.

---

[2] Japan refused to support China's policy towards Vietnam and the Soviet Union (*Gaiko Kiroku*, 01-959, February 13, 1979).

By 1980, Japan's economy had come to represent 10 percent of the world's GDP. For the Americans, it was the symbolism as well as the reality of its ever-expanding trade imbalance that seemed to rankle more than anything else. An out-of-control deficit ballooned with an almost planned ease, growing from $10.1 billion in 1978 to $13.58 billion by 1981. Domestic public opinion turned harshly anti-Japanese once the trade issue was swiftly equated to the ensuing loss of well-paid, blue-collar jobs. In Washington, at the height of the political frenzy ignited by what are usually rather mundane issues, Japanese consumer goods were smashed on the steps of the Capitol Building in a somewhat mindless protest. Faced with the practical certainty of punitive tariffs, Japan sought to forestall the inevitable by accepting a system of supposedly voluntary restraints on exported cars. More than any other single good contributing to the trade deficit, cars had become the visible trigger point separating the two countries.[3]

Recognizing Japan's growing economic strength, Washington sought to turn a potential liability into a source of advantage by shifting some of the traditional regional burden for insuring security onto Japanese shoulders (Kusano, 1991, p. 270). This new US approach did not stem simply from Japan's growing ability to pay, but more broadly from a significant realignment of America's strategic focus. Given limited resources, strengthening of America's Middle Eastern position implied a balanced redeployment away from Asia. The US came to view the Japanese as a convenient means for plugging an inconvenient gap created by this policy shift. A corresponding expansion in Japan's defense budget seemed a logical necessity, given the Japanese-perceived obligation for maintaining a measure of the peace and stability in their own neighboring region.[4]

In the face of US disengagement, Japan had little choice but to shoulder some of the security burden, if only indirectly, in order to supplement the diminishing reach of the US. With the 1980s characterized by rising clashes and an unstable regional and international

---

[3] Automobiles accounted for 32 percent of Japan's exports to the US in 1980.
[4] For example, see the Statement made by Secretary of Defense, Harold Brown on January 13, 1980 ("Nihon ni Boueihi Yosei e," *Asashi Shimbun*, January 14, 1980).

environment, a reform of its diplomatic posture seemed inevitable. The Soviet build-up in the Far East and the concomitant Cold War tensions also encouraged Japan to focus more intently on defending its national security. The 1980 *Diplomatic Bluebook* explicitly signaled this shift. Japan had started to regard itself as a major industrialized country with a growing responsibility for ensuring regional security.

> In order to effectively restrain Soviet actions, which have the danger of disturbing world peace and stability, the advanced democracies must fully cooperate with each other for the appropriate policy response (Ministry of Foreign Affairs, 1980, p. 26).

Engendering this new awareness of its changed role in the 1980s, Prime Minister Masayoshi Ohira (1978–1980) in December 1980, not only established the Comprehensive National Security Ministerial Council, but included it within the operating sphere of the Cabinet. Although still narrowly limited by Japan's post-war pacifism, the Council's writ extended to examining "alternative approaches" and weighing a number of options to Japan's traditional position within the regional security framework. The Japanese government had explicitly acknowledged the urgent need to formulate a concept of "comprehensive security." This recognition marked a watershed in Japanese policy. Japan's revamped strategy now sought:

> ...to secure Japan's national survival and protect its social order from various kinds of external threats which will or may have serious effects on the foundation of the nation's existence, by preventing such threats from arising, or by properly coping with them, through a combination of diplomacy, national defence, economic and other policy measures. In other words, the most important thing for our comprehensive national security policy is to always keep our external environment as peaceful and stable as possible, thereby preventing crises from arising (Ministry of Foreign Affairs, 1980, p. 30).

The committee's report emphasized the changing international situation which was no longer simply defined through the lens of overwhelming US economic and military power. Its analysis delineated the way in which the disappearing "*Pax Americana*," due to the ebbing of US power, had been counterbalanced by Japan's growing economic strength and the new role that attached to this rise (Tanaka, 1997, p. 278). International relations could no longer remain as a diplomatic after thought or something that could be taken for granted. Japan was now the equivalent to any other major Western democracy. With this achievement came responsibilities for assisting in the formation, application, and financing of security initiatives. However, as can be expected, the report did draw the line when it came to seriously exploring military options. Any such discussion at this time would have been clearly premature. Despite this self-imposed restriction on the strategic use of military power, Prime Minister Ohira made it abundantly clear that Japan fully intended to explore feasible alternatives which would serve to boost Japan's security profile.

> Japanese security will be concretely realized, but not by military power alone but through the linked support of economic power, information, political power and diplomacy, it will not do if one link in the chain is too strong or too weak. My meaning is that they should be well-balanced (Yasutomo, 1986, p. 25).

Ohira's stance became something of a blueprint for successive prime ministers who proceeded to adopt selected elements of this broadly formulated "comprehensive security" concept. Over the years, this approach has managed to become entrenched as an implicit cornerstone of foreign policy, although one that has not always been explicitly emphasized. Recognizing the need for a "comprehensive security" approach and adopting it as an underlying diplomatic policy represented a significant step for a Japan that was now acknowledged as a rising power. For the first time, the Japanese clarified their intention of taking full responsibility for their own security. This step automatically implied a limited involvement in global issues, including formulating initiatives to ensure regional stability. By filling these obligations, Japan hoped to develop a position of leadership and a solid international standing.

As could be expected, the direction indicated by the report met largely with unequivocal US acceptance. However, while America welcomed a more active Japanese stance, a security policy limited only to economic aspects was not deemed to be sufficient. The US expected Japan to extend its reach into more explicitly military venues. The Japanese were envisaged as playing something that resembled a facilitating role in the ongoing transition of American policy. The US seemed to have little choice but to restructure its strategic initiatives in light of a newly recognized set of limitations. Economically, the defining dominance of the US was no longer left unquestioned. This eroding power was almost symbolically represented by a trade deficit that seemed to grow in an almost unstoppable manner. America's military posture was now anything but self-sustaining. To nourish the requisite posture of possessing overwhelming power now implied significant and targeted support from its traditional allies. This necessity only became more intensified as the Soviet military build-up continued, partially symbolized by its accompanying military incursion into Afghanistan.

Japan faced an international situation that had become more unstable and fragile as the US seemed to founder upon a series of economic shoals. As pointed out, with the focus of US policy increasingly shifting to the Middle East, Asia was in danger of becoming something of a strategic afterthought. This refocusing created the risk of an emerging vacuum defining regional Asian policy, with America being largely preoccupied with other concerns. An American transformation of this magnitude and the accompanying ebbing of confidence were largely consequent on the withdrawal of US armed forces from Vietnam. Given these reduced circumstances, American policy eschewed the folly of continuing to believe that the US was capable of doing everything. Rather, given the reality of these new set of circumstances, America deemed it to be entirely reasonable for Japan to step up to the plate and bear its rightful share of mounting security burdens. Such a move by the Japanese, if correctly targeted, could serve to assist the continuing feasibility of the US global position. The most obvious and concrete manifestation of this shifting Japanese stance that characterized the 1980s was reflected in the growing defense budget. During the decade, expenditure jumped by 73.3 percent.[5] For obvious reasons, given its many years of explicit and near total dependency, the starting point for Japan's concerted attempt to gain international recognition and achieve greater self-respect began with the attempt to enhance its standing vis-à-vis the US.

---

[5] Figures are taken from *Japan's ODA 1990*, p. 13.

Essentially, the Americans hoped to see a Japanese defense budget capable of supporting a full-fledged effort to contain Soviet communism. An expansion of this type would allow the US to shift its forces and more of its attention to the Indian Ocean and the Middle East. Success would require an improved alignment of troop allocations that was more consistent with the evolving US global strategy (Sado, 2003, pp. 328–338). Specifically, Japan would take up some of the slack by ensuring the safety of sea lanes for up to 1,000 miles in either direction of its home ports. At a May 1981 joint summit meeting with the US, Prime Minister Zenko Suzuki (1980–1982) demonstrated, at least partially, a new-found Japanese willingness to embrace its very recently conceived doctrine of "comprehensive security."

Suzuki signaled a growing Japanese ability to recognize that the time had come to take greater responsibility for bearing a reliable share of the burden of international security by pursuing a more active defense posture. The Japanese had in fact unambiguously recognized the changing global environment. Their acceptance of a new Japanese role was clearly indicated by Prime Minister Suzuki after this critical 1981 summit meeting. In issuing the summit's Japan–US Joint Communiqué, Suzuki, for the first time in the post-war era, described the long-standing Japan–US relationship as an "alliance." By examining this terminological shift we can conceptually visualize Japan's acceptance of, and implicit demand for, an increasingly equal, rather than dependent, relationship with the implacable American leviathan. Suzuki further clarified Japan's intentions by spelling out the extent of Japan's defensive objectives. "Japan will seek to make even greater efforts toward improving its defense capabilities in Japanese territories and in its surrounding sea and air space, and towards further alleviating the financial burden of US forces in Japan" (Suzuki, 1981). As could be expected, Suzuki's declaration was met with unquestioned acceptance by Japan's US counterparts. The promised alleviation of a substantial share of the ongoing financial burden was especially welcome to American ears (Sado, 2003, pp. 328–338).

Unfortunately, Suzuki had become careless by making a unilateral commitment that was essentially impossible to achieve. A Japanese military role extending outside its clearly defined domestic reach (a promised 1,000 miles) seemed neither constitutionally nor politically realizable. Once surrounded by the realities of Japan's political environment, Suzuki was quick to retreat from and adamantly deny any intention to create a direct military role for Japan. Such an obligation would not be a corollary of the proposed burden-sharing arrangement. To escape these politically treacherous waters into which he had precipitously cast himself, Suzuki attempted to dodge responsibility by predictably pointing his finger elsewhere. He vehemently castigated the Ministry of Foreign Affairs for being willing to specify an enlarged role for Japan's defense establishment.

Though Suzuki now found it expedient to display a decidedly reserved attitude toward any expansion of Japanese military activity, MOFA and the Defense Agency took a more independent stance that betrayed a near eagerness to support a more active military policy (Sado, 2003, pp. 328–350). The ensuing arguments and divisive views within the government on this matter indicated that a ruling consensus seemed only to have conceded a growing need to shoulder more of Japan's international responsibilities. In contrast, some individual ministries and politicians had realized the necessity of exploring alternative means to accomplish such a goal. They were ahead of their time. More generally, most politicians and bureaucrats were still unwilling to embrace an expanded security role.

As Suzuki was forced to admit, the raw gap in perception between what an enlarged security role meant to the US, as compared with what Japan was willing or capable of doing, proved to be too large to overcome.[6] As is so often the case, Suzuki's careless statement inevitably provoked domestic controversy. Once again, the public proved to be more sensitive to Japan's potential activism in security affairs than either their elected politicians or their policy-making bureaucrats. Even using the term "alliance" generated an almost allergic public reaction. However, opinion polls did demonstrate that these objectives were not entirely devoid of popular support. In fact, there had been a growing acceptance of this new policy approach. The proportion of Japanese in

---

[6]This rationale is clearly set out in *Gaiko Kiroku*, Brief on Hawai meeting, June 23, 1981, 2009-00292.

favor of increased defense spending rose from 12 percent in 1974 to 19 percent in 1978 and then to 20.1 percent by 1981 (Japan Defense Agency, 2000). Certainly, public opinion was continuing to change. However, despite all the profound shifts that had occurred, Japan was starting from an extremely low level of support for such initiatives. When examining this period, it would therefore be misleading to exaggerate the actual support that such changes reflected. As these figures testify, an overwhelming majority of the public unarguably supported only peaceful diplomacy, especially the kind that successfully avoided any regrettable entanglements in security matters.

Such equivocation was unlikely to please the US. As could be anticipated, the Americans at subsequent meetings met Japanese hesitancy with even more urgent insistence. They unequivocally argued that only by taking up a more direct military role could Japan effectively contribute to the necessary containment of Soviet aggression. Unsatisfied with Japan's perceived inconsistency, the US persisted in demanding that Japan take a more direct military role if they were to usefully contribute to thwarting the ever-increasing threat posed by the Soviet Union. The Americans attributed only the basest of objectives to the latest Soviet obsession in building up its military strength and increasing its global presence. Specifically, the Americans feared that the Soviet Union intended to expand its influence and presence in Southwest Asia. The American strategy for containing this aggressive Soviet policy depended, in part, on the willingness of its professed allies to follow its lead.[7]

As part of the tactical consequences of its policy position, the US felt obliged to repeatedly pressure the Japanese government into increasing its defense budget and expanding its military role. The US concluded that given the ever-present Soviet threat, Japan should not shy away from counterbalancing the USSR by defending some 1,000 miles of sea lanes (Sado, 2003, pp. 328–350). However, Suzuki's implied promises and some of his more assertive statements turned out to be more of a mirage than emblematic of any pragmatic reality. Without a

---

[7] The response to the Soviet threat is taken up in *Gaiko Kiroku*, A report on 13th SSC meeting, June 23, 1981, 2009-00292, p. 4.

public consensus, or even one within his own government, an expanded Japanese military role turned out to be a complete non-starter. Even increases in the defense budget under Suzuki turned out to be limited to approximately 7 percent. Though Japan's government might be fully aware of the necessity to back a diplomatic policy characterized by "comprehensive security," the political wherewithal, or perhaps political nerve, needed to extend this approach to encompass a more direct military role simply did not exist.

However, with the advent of a new prime minister (Yasuhiro Nakasone, 1982–1987) the status quo that had dominated Japanese diplomacy no longer reliably determined policy decisions. Nakasone had distinct ideas of Japan's proper place in the global security framework. In his view, only by increasing the role played by Japan in securing US objectives could Nakasone hope to elevate Japan's position vis-à-vis the sceptical Americans. Fortunately, the new Nakasone and Reagan administrations largely saw eye to eye on key diplomatic issues. Four summit meetings between Nakasone and Reagan (January 1985 to April 1986) highlighted the developing close relationship between the two leaders and demonstrated Japan's focus on strengthening its relationship with the US. Nakasone's diplomatic stance became characterized by essentially a 'realist' view of the world. If at all achievable, "world peace was to be preserved by obtaining a workable balance of power" (Ministry of Foreign Affairs, 1985a, pp. 8–9). Translated, this meant that the Japanese government now tied the preservation of its own peace and security to its ability to ensure continued success in cultivating the smooth and effective operation of the US–Japan security treaty. It goes without saying that all of these strategic steps were inevitably constrained by well defined constitutional boundaries (Ministry of Foreign Affairs, 1985a, pp. 8–9).

Nakasone was keenly aware of the prevailing international environment in which Japan by necessity had to navigate, as well as the overly ambitious American expectations that at time required subtle forestalling. While signaling Japan's willingness to share some of the security burdens falling by default on the US, Nakasone was sufficiently circumspect to insist that any Japanese contribution be limited exclusively to a defensive posture exclusively. However, his desire to advance Japan's security profile, while toeing the line on constitutional limitations, often resulted in transgressing the requisite balance between those two conflicting objectives. Remarks committing Japan to act as something like an "unsinkable aircraft carrier" that would assist the US to thwart any proposed aggression by the Soviet Backfire Bombers was bound to create public controversy. Again, this was simply a case of Nakasone overstepping the bounds in which Japan was forced to operate. His desire to impress his American allies and to expand Japan's security reach was a not unexpected reflection of his drive to increase Japan's regional visibility. More concretely, he was able to signal Japan's new international stance and defensive strength by disclosing secret information intercepted by the Japanese Self-Defense Forces. Through this dramatic disclosure, the rest of the world gained unassailable insights into the Soviet's involvement in shooting down a Korean Air Liner in 1983. Defense Agency operatives had strongly resisted any release of this information, claiming that revealing Japan's success in intercepting messages in this way would undercut its ability to successfully make such vital diversions in the future. However in this case, Nakasone pressed forward with a more opportunistic strategy, focusing almost exclusively on the public relations value that such a feat might contribute to enhancing Japan's international standing and garnering additional respect (Nakasone, 1996, p. 461).

Nakasone expanded Suzuki's more modest initiatives by continuing to strengthen the US–Japan alliance and bulking up the defense budget. In 1985, the Nakasone administration took a significant step in carrying out these objectives by approving the Mid-Term Defense Program. The US strongly supported this less tentative strategy, which to American eyes demonstrated the extent to which Japan could move aggressively to shore up its defense responsibilities while still operating within its constitutional constraints. Even though Japan's military build-up necessarily occurred within the self-imposed limits of self-defense, such a transformed Japanese policy would still enable the US to contain the threat now posed by the Soviet Union much more effectively.

Continuing with this approach, Nakasone in 1987, managed to remove the long-standing 1 percent of GDP cap on defense spending. This ceiling had proved to be a cornerstone of Japanese defense policy since being instituted by the Miki administration in 1976 under the National Defense Program Outline. Observers could easily understand this to be a subtle blow to the entrenched public policy of state pacifism since up to this time, the imposed spending limitation had been a clear signal of Japanese more reticent intentions. These major changes were meant as a mere down payment in achieving Nakasone's more ambitious objectives. Seeking to further strengthen military coopera-tion within the alliance framework, Nakasone partially lifted the pre-viously imposed export ban on defense-related technology. Applied to the US, this represented a major acquiescence to US demands that had been previously rejected by the Suzuki administration. At the World Economic Summit (1983), Nakasone was far from shy in his staunch and explicit support of the US security policies that were articulated at that Williamsburg meeting. He made it sufficiently clear that Japan's objectives would extend to creating an expanded role in maintaining regional, if not international, security.

Nakasone, however, was not satisfied with simply inaugurating an expanded security role. This expansion was merely a prelude to achiev-ing the far more serious aim of assuming the role and responsibilities of a major power. By championing an aggressive form of "international-ization," Nakasone hoped to provide Japan with at least the appearance of being an influential country. This semblance of influence was viewed as a gateway to becoming an acknowledged regional leader.[8]

> Japan would no longer be a follower nation; Japan would be pre-pared for global leadership by being remade into an international state; a new liberal nationalism would be based on the concept of the country's national interests beyond traditional nationalism and would assume an active role in global affairs (Pyle, 1996, p. 89).

Nakasone attempted to finesse Japan's military limits by making demonstrable contributions to the international community. With a measure of good fortune, a successful portrayal of its newly conceived

---

[8] Nakasone was the first Prime Minister who openly advocated "internationalism." However, the idea of internationalism had existed, at least at governmental levels, before he espoused it. The *Diplomatic Bluebook* of 1980 underlined a need to gain public support for Japan's foreign policy and to deepen the public's understanding of international affairs. It also insisted that the issue of Japanese responsibilities and its role in the world should be publicly debated and its role in the world be publicly debated.

role would noticeably increase Japan's level of influence. By making significant and continued contributions to peace and stability in the world, Japan would transform itself into an "international state" capable of "walking proudly" among other developed countries.[9] Symbolically, Nakasone established this position at the Williamsburg Summit. He successfully positioned himself next to Ronald Reagan in the official group photo of the event. Nakasone later claimed that "if I had not stood next to Reagan in a central position, I would have lost face in the eyes of the Japanese people, as this would not have properly reflected Japan's international position as an economic power" (Kusano, 2001, p. 434).

Nakasone limited his grand security strategy, for the most part, to repairing and improving Japan's relationship with the US. His goal was to have the Americans come to regard the Japanese as an equal partner in containing the Soviet threat. Nakasone was cautious in the way he supplemented US Cold War strategy since he was obligated to stay within the somewhat arbitrary bounds of self-defense. The basis then for Japan's transformed security posture was confined to demonstrating its unshakable commitment to being a completely trustworthy US ally and aspiring to an equal relationship within this touchstone alliance.

4.2.2 'Comprehensive Security' Comes into Its Own

Japan's Asia-Pacific diplomacy in the 1980s continued to be characterized by its economic focus. Given Japan's operational restrictions, regional initiatives, almost by definition, tended to rely heavily on economic cooperation. Buying one's way to respectability hardly represented an entirely novel approach, but the way in which Japan employed its growing economic power did denote something of a notable change as the 1980s unfolded. The core of Japan's policy departure was

---

[9] See the 1983 *Diplomatic Bluebook*. Despite its desire to become an "international state," to foreign eyes Japan seemed to have been pursuing only its own economic interests without linking its economic strength to diplomatic goals. Extending exchanges in various fields between Japan and other countries often produced only increased international frictions. Given these circumstances, it is not surprising to find growing support for a theory that posited Japan's "exceptionalism." Proponents of "exceptionalism" attempted to explain the rapid success of the Japanese and their unorthodox behavior in terms of its unique social, economic, and other institutions and practices. These were broadly lumped together under an all-weather cultural umbrella.

aptly encapsulated by Japan's new-found insistence on promoting its doctrine of "comprehensive security." This approach signaled Japan's intention to employ any feasible means to protect its security and external environment. Until this decade, economic assistance had for the most part been employed as a tool for furthering Japanese growth and economic influence. Wealth under the "comprehensive security" doctrine now became a means of ensuring security objectives as well. In lieu of deployable military power, foreign aid became the leading edge advancing Japan's perceived security requirements.

As is often the case with diplomatic departures, though "comprehensive security" might well represent a remarkable redirection of Japan's strategic policy, the concept itself was hardly original. Prime Minster Yoshida expressed a somewhat similar view some 30 years before without actually embodying it in any defined policy statement. His firm belief was that diplomacy and other alternative creative methods could ensure national security more effectively than military power (Maeda and Iijima, 2003, p. 17). Unfortunately, Yoshida never clearly enunciated any details that could define those alternative means. Nor is it even certain that he was capable at that time of listing them. It took the Ohira administration, and decades of evolving initiatives, to take up a rather vague policy formulation and transform it into a fully articulated and concrete doctrine.

For the first time in the post-war period, the Japanese government was able to elaborate on its perceived need to examine and formulate the future of Japan's national security. Out of this implicit introspection came a new willingness to commit to a set of protective security measures. Given its constitutional limitations, these measures by necessity differed from the more traditional steps taken by other countries. Faced with inherent anti-militarist norms commonly accepted by the public and the inherent reluctance of many Japanese officials to challenge these guiding assumptions, the new doctrine of "comprehensive security" perfectly suited the prevailing conditions by placing Japan firmly on a road leading away from pacifism, without explicitly making such issues the center of open debate.

Unfortunately, the road ahead, even when paved over by Nakasone's skillful tactics, was not without its bumps and potholes. The key issue constraining any attempt to formulate a Japanese security policy lay in the binding nature of its constitutional constraint. As a result, any diplomatic efforts focused on national security, or in playing a part in international settlements, had to be finessed using alternative means. In terms of policy objectives during that decade, security aims were achievable only by using "all measures possible to pursue." Japan was fortunate in having at its command growing economic power and the diplomatic possibilities arising from that. By necessity, this strength would have to provide the basis for self-protection. However, ambition ran beyond self-preservation. The Japanese wanted to use that newly developed capacity to go beyond narrowly based calculation and provide positive assistance to their regional neighbors as well. Japan had once again discovered a new-found determination to assume a leading role in security matters. In previous decades, the Japanese had bided peacefully, seemingly content to ignore such dormant imperatives. The only real difference now was that the Japanese, with their growing wealth, had the means to achieve influence and leadership through non-military means. For decades, possibilities had been narrowly limited. Wealth would provide the ammunition to open up a new array of alternatives. The 1981 *Diplomatic Bluebook* makes this sufficiently clear.

> That Japan should have a common basic perception and strategy with the advanced democracies, including the US, does not necessarily mean that this country's specific policies should be the same as those of other countries...The role of Japan, which has its Peace Constitution, is greatly limited in the military field, and it is natural that its role should be focused on the political and economic fields (Ministry of Foreign Affairs, 1981, p. 26).

In Japan's case, diplomacy was assisted by generous foreign aid, which was why the economic base became particularly crucial to the success of this alternative strategy. Employing assistance tactically was in fact the concrete realization of the rather ambiguous "comprehensive security" doctrine. Lacking the constitutional ability to send in troops, cash could play the role of Japan's proxy soldiers when sent to a "country in a bordering conflict." (This terminology actually referred to a country which bordered another country currently in turmoil.) To qualify, a potential country at risk would need independent certification by the Japanese government that the assistance proffered was "important for the maintenance of world peace and stability." The explicit financial link was aid targeted to economic development, which would help to stabilize the political state of the recipient, and by doing so improve security within the given region. Official Development Assistance (ODA) became the price the Japanese were willing to pay to ensure international security. Thereafter, the cost–benefit analysis performed by the Ministry of International Trade and Industry (MITI) would necessarily employ a security dimension when evaluating any given aid package.

As we have seen, weighing decision on the scales of "comprehensive security" meant that the ministry came to equate economic cooperation and industrial R&D expenditure as inextricably linked with military spending (Arase, 1995, p. 225). Specifically, government officials saw aid as an extension of such spending. With military expenditure limited and military action strictly confined, foreign aid could operate as an effective substitute in lieu of an expanded defense capability (Arase, 1995, p. 225). Twisting the traditional budget argument of "guns or butter" inside out, under Japan's new diplomatic stance, butter essentially became the equivalent of guns. Japan would use its financial weight aggressively to boost its international profile and to become a vital player within the field of international security without firing a shot or making an angry gesture.

Clearly, a new diplomatic initiative of this sort based on such a radical rationale must have significant implications for both partners of the US–Japan alliance. The concept of "comprehensive security" provided Japanese policy with a useful edge of flexibility. The doctrine allowed Japan to take a rather broad approach when tackling overly convoluted security matters. Hamstrung militarily, Japan thought that it had found an effective way around this institutional limitation, one which would allow the Japanese to assume, at least indirectly, a respectable measure of responsibility for regional stability. The Americans would get the support they had insistently requested by having Japan supplement traditional US military might with some serious flexing of the country's newly found economic muscle. With Japan making a credible commitment in terms of financial underwriting, the US felt more capable of continuing its steady Asian disengagement without upsetting regional peace and stability. At this time, the US was willing to accept Japan's economic contribution in recognition of its inability to pay in more militarized coin (*Yomiuri Shimbum*, January 27, 1987).[10]

Of course, without brisk and dependable economic growth, the newly structured framework would inevitably collapse. But at that time, with Japan appearing to have found the key to economic success, the policy seemed to be a perfectly workable solution to the problem that Japan's particular post-war situation presented. Up until the 1980s, Japan appeared to have deliberately evaded any real responsibility for maintaining peace and stability within the East Asian region. This reticent stance was deemed to be particularly inappropriate, at least from an American standpoint, as Japan's trade surplus with the US expanded almost effortlessly. Populist opinion, expressed quite vehemently at the time, caricatured a Japan that was triumphing largely at the expense of the US. From this perspective, Americans saw themselves as subsidizing Japan's trade surpluses against their will by paying for Japan's defensive safety with their hard-earned tax dollars.

With trade imbalances in 1985 appearing to threaten its economic viability, the US by employing the equivalent of a force majeure, attempted to rebalance trade patterns. The tool of choice would prove to be the manipulation of foreign exchange rates. Success proved to be limited and the unperceived consequences far more destructive than could have been imagined.[11] The growth of the US trade deficit may have been somewhat hampered by such measures, but failed to reverse itself in any significant sense of the term. Even after the 1985 Plaza Accord (see below for details), the trade deficit still stood at $14 billion

---

[10] *Yomiuri Shimbun* (January 27, 1987) conducted an extensive interview with Kissinger. He stressed that Japan had an obligation to contribute to peace and stability in Asia through aid, rather than by increasing its defense budget.

[11] It can be argued the Japanese reaction to the Plaza Accord essentially initiated the "bubble economy" that defined the last half of the decade. Ultimately, the aftermath of this period of asset inflation would undermine the subsequent growth path of the Japanese economy. Other analysts would stress unresolved structural problems. The bursting of the bubble under this scenario merely acted as a catalyst in bringing these inherent stress lines out in the open.

in 1986. US frustration at the failure of the agreement to make any serious inroads into the existing situation, despite a serious appreciation of the Japanese yen, goaded the US into escalating its demands. Americans were becoming increasingly uneasy at the contrast of a Japan that was constantly pictured as a rising economic power compared to a US that was in obvious decline. To help salvage a worrying tense confrontation between the erstwhile allies, Japan committed itself to a foreign aid program which would alleviate some of America's financial burden within Asia. Thus the boost in overseas assistance was not only an attempt by Japan to seize a measure of leadership given the vacuum created by the US policy of disengagement. The expanded initiative was also an attempt to placate the growing wrath of the US at slipping into an economically inferior role.[12] Rectifying this situation, or at least maintaining the semblance of doing so, required a partial underwriting by the Japanese of some of the financial maintenance attached to continued foreign aid within the region. This was deemed by both sides to be Japan's essential contribution to the alliance's security strategy, accurately reflecting its economic strength.

US disengagement from the region can be measured unequivocally by the dramatic decrease of aid to the region (see Fig. 4.1). Following its Vietnam retreat, in 1976 US aid to Asia still accounted for some

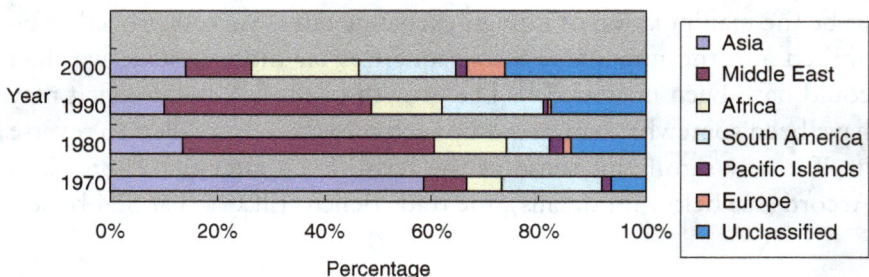

Source: ODA Hakusho, 2002, p. 579.

Fig. 4.1   US aid by region.

---

[12]The voluntary export restrictions on the Japanese car industry were also of the same vintage and motivated by much the same reasons. Popular opinion in the US saw Japanese success as being gained through deceit and unfair tactics.

31.2 percent of all assistance provided by the Development Assistance Committee (DAC) countries to the region. Yet this percentage continued in its downward spiral. By 1986, it had dropped to 26.4 percent. This decline was reflected across the individual countries as well. In 1970, at the height of the Vietnamese conflict, 63 percent of US aid went to Asia, mainly to India and South Vietnam. After the war, the slice heading to the East almost halved, falling to 33 percent in 1985. East Asian assistance was no more than 7.6 percent (Ministry of Foreign Affairs, 1985b, p. 9). By 1986, US regional aid of just $192 million trailed not only Japan's total of $1.35 billion, but also Germany's contribution of $324 million (Ministry of Foreign Affairs, 1987, p. 11). By this time, America's focus and wallet was directed increasingly towards the Middle East. Both Israel and Egypt became major recipient countries, with 40.36 percent of the US total aid being disbursed just between those two countries (Ministry of Foreign Affairs, 1987, pp. 86–87).

However, even in the midst of this paced American withdrawal, Japan's diplomats still were forced to operate within the larger bounds of US policy. A "country in a bordering conflict" would receive Japanese aid, but the recipient would be largely determined by American interests rather than solely those of Japan. Thus, key American allies like Pakistan and Turkey would become new recipients of Japanese assistance, even though the countries had previously had only tenuous connections with the Japanese.[13] Labeling countries like the Philippines, South Korea, and Thailand as strategically important also qualified this trio for dramatically larger aid packages. The Japanese, of course, were loathe to admit to any such strategic bias. They quite naturally insisted that all such decisions were entirely independent and based solely on a country's strategic value. Despite such protestations, Japanese decisions reflected its need to signal Japan's worthiness to serve as America's moneyed partner. This arrangement was made somewhat explicit

---

[13] Japan's aid to Turkey demonstrated a willingness to contribute more broadly to global security. With Turkey's external debt problem reaching serious proportions, the turbulence in Iran led to fears of increased Soviet influence in the region. In response to American and European requests, Japan responded by pledging $100 million in bilateral aid to Turkey.

in 1985. Following a US–Japan consultation on aid, America made its objectives clear by strongly encouraging the Japanese to target aid to "countries strategically important" (Armacost, 1996, p. 149). While inevitably having its decisions constrained by US priorities, the government still seized whatever opportunities arose under this limited scenario to expand its reach in security matters. The Japanese successfully employed the cover of "comprehensive security" to move their own agenda forward.

4.2.2.1 *Applying the doctrine: The Case of South Korea and the Philippines*

Japan's strategic aid to the Philippines and South Korea illustrated Japan's attempt to expand its role within the security field. Justifying such targeted assistance required a rather creative employment of the "comprehensive security" doctrine. The actual reasoning was much more pragmatic. Both countries were important US allies in Asia, each one harboring vital military bases. By supporting these allies, Japan was essentially furthering US policy in the Far East. In addition, at least South Korea and to a lesser extent the Philippines were geographically linked to Japan's extended security. Fortunately, under the all-purpose rationale of "comprehensive security" any and all such contingencies were covered quite adroitly. As a result, Japan's aid to these countries jumped in the 1980s. Assistance of this character obviously represented a departure from past patterns of behavior. Japan could no longer be convicted of simply pursuing its narrow economic interests by dramatically increasing aid to these two countries.

Seriously Seoul

During the post-war period, South Korea, Japan's former colony, had been the second major recipient of aid from the time of the first Japanese quasi-reparation. However, in August 1981, a sluggish economy persuaded South Korea to request a substantial loan of some $6 billion to finance a new 5-year development plan. According to Korean reasoning, such a request could be justified based on military and security grounds. Since its defense efforts had benefited Japanese national security, Japan should in turn feel obliged to extend economic assistance to South Korea. In other words, the Japanese should prove willing to reduce some of that country's financial burden in return for services rendered. South Korea's attempt to squeeze such a significant loan from Japanese coffers was partly a response to the May 1981 Regan–Suzuki Joint Communiqué. The presented position provided a sufficient rationale for almost any South Korean request.

> To promote the maintenance of peace on the Korean peninsula is important for peace and security in East Asia, including Japan... The President and the Prime Minister place a high value on the respective role each country is playing... (Ministry of Foreign Affairs, 1982, p. 426).[14]

The communiqué illustrated a developing strategy that was quickly becoming the keystone of the US–Japan relationship. The incipient stages of the policy can be traced back to the Vietnam War. Following a rough division of labor, the US claimed complete responsibility for any required military response. This left Japan to substantially underwrite the financial requirements attached to any such initiative. In June 1981, the US further delineated the specifics of such a partnership. While attending the Security Sub-Committee meeting in Hawaii, US representatives laid out Japan's responsibilities for South Korean economic development. The package, supported by the US, required not only simple economic assistance to the South Korean government but also additional logistical support for the US troops stationed there.[15]

With unwavering US support for such an approach, and with clear advantages accruing from the proposed program, the South Korean government added its insistence that the Japanese were under an indisputable obligation to follow the path drawn by American priorities.[16] To drive home this point, South Korea's Prime Minister felt free to criticize Japan for capping its military spending below 1 percent of GDP.

---

[14] Prime Minister Suzuki again admitted that South Korea's defense efforts contributed to Japan's security. See the Speech by Suzuki in September 1981 at the Shimoda conference.

[15] The details are reported in *Gaiko Kiroku*, June 23, 1981, 2009-00292, p. 8.

[16] In an interview, one South Korean foreign official disclosed that the US government asked the Korean government, before the Reagan–Suzuki meeting, if the Korean government wanted the US to direct Japan's economic assistance to South Korea (Kim, 1993, p. 225).

The implication could be easily drawn, namely that like the Americans, South Korea considered Japan to be intentionally shirking its responsibility to its closest allies. The South Koreans found it comparatively easy to point out Japan's very limited sacrifice in face of the Koreans' willingness to spend approximately 6 percent of their GDP on military preparedness (*The New York Times*, January 14, 1981). On its part, the Japanese government was not so willing to accept this brand of rationalization since it neatly implied an obligation for Japan to subsidize such South Korean spending via its program of overseas aid.

Though much more in the limelight in the 1980s, Japan's foreign assistance program had a long history behind it before becoming an essential tool of foreign policy. The new aid strategy, however, added precise aims, objectives, and a philosophical motivation that had either been missing or not clearly articulated up to this time. Structuring aid packages to boost domestic economic growth was as far as Japanese intentions extended, or at least nothing more subtle than this obvious goal had ever been explicitly spelled out (Rix, 1980).[17]

In contrast, by the beginning of the 1980s, the Ministry of Foreign Affairs' new aid philosophy (1980) had sufficiently formulated at least a rough set of criteria for future loans. This conceptualization built on a 1978 resolution previously adopted by the Foreign Affairs Committee of the Japanese House of Representatives. These instrumental steps were counterbalanced by a more precautionary measure (March, 1981) obliging anti-corruption strictures to be put in place prior to any such assistance. The thrust of this legislation was to introduce a greater degree of accountability to such rapidly expanding assistance in order to avoid any conflicts, whether constitutional or otherwise. In this particular case, recipient countries were deterred from using such aid to directly advance its military objectives, or what is worse, to employ it as a means of underwriting a military build-up (Yasutomo, 1986, p. 64).[18]

---

[17] See Rix (1980) for more details.

[18] The earlier resolution was passed by the 84th House of Representatives Foreign Affairs Committee on April 1978. This effort was followed by the March 1981 resolution, which constrained the government to refrain from providing aid either for military purposes or to parties engaged in conflicts.

These limitations created something of a roadblock for the ambitious South Koreans. Their demand for a 14-fold aid increase was unfortunately linked to the reciprocal role Korea was to play as Japan's military surrogates. The South Koreans expected to receive financial grants, although ultimately they proved willing to accept them concealed as development payments. The actual purpose, understood by both sides, was a simple return for providing a portion of Japanese national security. Unfortunately, the South Koreans at times seemed almost deliberately oblivious of the fact that the Japanese were constrained from providing either aid or loans if they were destined for military purposes. Moreover, strategic necessity, in terms of overall US policy objectives, meant that this surge of purported development aid would still need to be provided, despite the fact that by 1983, South Korea's GDP had already surpassed the per-capita income cut-off level of $1,635 per year. The South Koreans by this time had topped the $2,000 mark.

All interested parties to this arrangement could easily recognize that there was no economic urgency behind South Korean demands for assistance. Obviously, a number of other countries were truly in dire straits and could have made greater use of Japanese aid, if the actual objective had been measured strictly in terms of economic development. However, despite this clear lack of any perceived need or urgency, the Japanese government agreed to provide up to $4 billion in aid. Japan's ODA program had become a mere conduit for channeling money to the South Korean defense budget. The subversion of Japan's foreign aid program appeared to vex none of the interested parties. This is underlined by the fact that as part of the final agreement, both sides managed to save face by having the South Korean government drop its explicitly military rationale for such assistance.[19]

Japan essentially chose to ignore implicitly prohibitions against using aid dollars for military purposes. Once again, the flexibility of its "comprehensive security" doctrine provided a rationale for doing what the government deemed necessary. Loosely speaking, "comprehensive security" had come to mean "whatever it takes." The

---

[19] See the 1983 Joint Communiqué between Japan and Korea. *Gaiko Seisho*, 1982, pp. 454–456.

Japanese government found that it could effectively respond to US pressures cloaked in the camouflage of this useful cover. Such an all-purpose doctrine presented wide-ranging options to meet American demands, while at least technically remaining within the bounds set by its constitution and other legislative restraints. As noted, this approach did not represent the first best strategy in terms of US requirements. From an American viewpoint, increased military spending by the Japanese, along with a corresponding military build-up, remained the most efficient way of countering Soviet military growth in the Far East. By substituting Japanese troops, the US could continue to forestall any Asian threat, while allowing a number of its own forces to be shifted more easily to the Middle East. This bit of geography became the growing focus of US strategic initiatives in the 1980s.[20]

American expectations were bound to be disappointed, given such unrealistic hopes. Prescribed limitations on defense spending, combined with a prohibition on military initiatives abroad, inherently thwarted these grand objectives. Forced to locate an alternative, the US turned to South Korean troops financed out of Japanese pockets ("US pressing Tokyo to buttress forces", *The New York Times*, January 14, 1981). South Korea wasted no time in seizing the opportunity created by the prevailing American–Japanese dynamics and by doing so, successfully grabbed a considerable share of Japan's available foreign assistance. Given an acknowledged inability to commit troops, Japan chose the alternative route of providing funds to signal its commitment to regional stability. With a large contingent of US troops stationed in South Korea, Japanese foreign aid was clearly intended to "demonstrate to America, Japan's efforts to promote stability in Northeast Asia" through economic means ("Negotiations on Japanese aid to Seoul near impasse", *The New York Times*, April 19, 1982). As with many interactions between the two alliance members during this period, the choice of providing such assistance to South Korea was hardly voluntary. Japan, in fact, perceived that it had few options, given the constraints imposed by its American alliance. Lacking any viable alternative, the Japanese could only meet their obligations by employing economic means rather

---

[20] For US policy towards the Middle East, see the Carter Doctrine, January 1980.

than providing direct military support. Fortunately, Japan seemed capable of finding ways to transform such necessities into opportunities by invoking the conveniently formulated doctrine of "comprehensive security."

Mainly Manila

Parallel strategic positioning provides a useful rationale for understanding Japan's unanticipated generosity to the Philippines in the 1980s. Dominated by key American military bases, the Philippines had long played a vital role in US Cold War strategy. Japan, by a flexible employment of its "comprehensive security" doctrine, was persistently carving out an increasingly visible profile within the Asian security apparatus. As pointed out, the Japanese were able, and seemingly willing, to provide financial support in lieu of the troops they were incapable of offering. US pressures, plus Japanese ambitions, aligned themselves dramatically in the case of the Philippines after 1986. America had, for decades, backed the corrupt Marcos regime in exchange for a dependable measure of loyalty and commitment. The unanticipated overthrow of their compliant ally left the US with a potentially vulnerable point in their web of strategic alliances. Aid to the new democratic government, under President Corazon Aquino, now became a matter of some urgency.

In response to, or parallel with, this rising level of US anxiety, Japan rapidly expanded its aid program to the Philippines by some 60 percent. Not only was this a dramatic increase, but Japan soon overtook the US as the largest donor to the new, struggling Aquino government. In response to a bloated foreign debt level of $28 billion, a legacy of the former and quite reckless Marcos government, the US in April 1987 formulated a joint economic aid plan, which would help float the current regime through the financial turmoil it was forced to face. As expected, the official justification for this US-initiated stabilization drive was the need to support an infant democracy. Without acknowledging any ulterior motives, the Americans simply claimed that doing so would provide encouragement to other such countries throughout the world. Moreover, they insisted that without support for this democratic experiment in the Philippines, the obvious vulnerability of the

Aquino government could only fuel and encourage the long-running communist insurgency in the south of that country.

However, the underlying reality that characterized such a significant increase in foreign aid was clearly an attempt to once again buy the loyalty of the Filipino government. These hearts and minds were deemed crucial if the continuing leases of US bases on the Islands were to be made secure. These leases were in fact at the crux of the problem, given their 1991 expiration date.[21] Consulting its immediate strategic requirements, the US considered the option of departing the Philippines to be clearly unacceptable. Working in tandem with the Americans, the Japanese government responded to this developing problem by attempting to play a major role in this critical situation. It called and hosted a Tokyo donors meeting in July 1989. Japan was also loathe to see the US military pushed out of the Philippines. In Japan's view, these troops and bases were essential in ensuring regional peace and security. Therefore, placating Filipino demands, at least to a limited extent, was deemed to be in Japan's self-interest.

In this specific case, prevailing motivations are not particularly difficult to fathom. For clearly strategic reasons, the Japanese took an initial step in their quest to re-establish the Philippines as a dependable ally. They sought to do so by unequivocally supporting the US-initiated mini Marshall-type Plan for the Philippines. This allied effort became known as the Multilateral Aid Initiative. Japan pledged a startling $10 billion to underwrite this endeavor compared to the mere $1 billion offered by the US. This proposed aid package would hike Japan's contribution to the Philippines by an additional $4 billion over its previous level. As suggested previously, the Japanese were becoming skilled at using the idea of "comprehensive security" to explain and justify almost any diplomatic initiative.

By the late 1980s, the Japanese were clearly scavenging for any way to signal its continuing status as a reliable ally. Bankrolling US objectives seemed a clear way to placate the Americans and shift attention away from any potentially disagreeable conflict between the two. In line with this strategy, in 1987, Nakasone succeeded in removing the

---

[21] Further verification is available at *Gaiko Kiroku*, 01-956-7, April 18, 1988.

1 percent ceiling on military spending. Clearly, the ceiling had been largely symbolic. As it turned out, abolishing this supposedly binding restraint failed to induce any further flood of military spending. Making matters worse in terms of its alliance partner, Japan's commitment to regional security became suspect with the revelation that Toshiba Machine Company had violated the strictures laid down by the Multinational Coordinating Committee for Multilateral Export Controls.[22] Although this was clearly a private action, rather than a government-instigated policy application, the Japanese as a whole could not avoid being dismissed as once again being driven by narrowly defined, economic interests.

The proposed Multilateral Aid Initiative provided an attractive opportunity for the Japanese. They could placate their US allies by signaling their reliability while also increasing Japan's profile in the Philippines' economy and those security-related aspects. Moreover, by portraying its aid as simply a means to support a struggling democracy, Japan could neatly escape any potential domestic backlash. As with much of its developing diplomacy in this era, Japan managed to appear to be quietly serving US objectives while subtly maneuvering to further its own agenda. Accumulated wealth would increasingly enable the Japanese to pursue such objectives while remaining within the limits set by a demanding US government and a reactive public at home.

4.2.2.2   *The imprimatur of "comprehensive security"*

Japan had discovered a method for forging a seemingly viable defense partnership with the US. Using its newly discovered doctrine of "comprehensive security" Japan found it feasible to extend its reach through the strategic use of foreign aid. As pointed out, flexible definitions allowed assistance to flow to "countries in bordering conflict" such as Thailand and South Korea. Extending this initiative to the Philippines then proved simple to accomplish. A clear division of labor between the two allies in tackling security matters appeared to be gaining traction,

---

[22]The Toshiba Machine Company had supplied eight computer-guided propeller milling machines to the Soviet Union between 1982 and 1984. The technology greatly improved the ability of Soviet submarines to evade detection, creating an increased security risk for the US.

buoyed by Japan's growing wealth. A Japanese diplomat stationed in Manila during this period was able to confirm the advantage of separating out these two functions. "We can play a major role in enhancing economic stability and progress in the Philippines — the US can concentrate on building its (Manila's) defense capability against the (communist) insurgency" (*Financial Review*, January 18, 1989). The ever-flexible doctrine of "comprehensive security" rationalized this strategy, which, given Japan's domestic constraints, perfectly suited Japan's reality.

With its economic strength and the one-size-fits-all approach inherent in the idea of "comprehensive security," Japan was able to contribute, although indirectly only, to the stability of the region. To do so required operating as the close ally of the US. Though far from dominant, the role Japan played cannot be dismissed as trivial. Successive governments continued to assume that they had found a way to make a substantial and recognized contribution. More to the point, fashioning this distinctive approach seemed to prove a successful substitute for Japan's inability to provide military support. Japan had discovered a ploy that could circumvent an intractable weakness pervading the heart of the alliance. The trajectory of such a policy would potentially help ensure international stability by combining Japanese wealth with American might. Such stability would not only bolster Japan's ever-growing prosperity, but it would increase, over time, Japan's regional influence, even if Japan could only wield such leadership as the approved junior partner of the US.

Despite Japanese expectations, other countries viewed these financial contributions with somewhat different eyes. Though welcoming the increased flow of funds, they tended to dismiss the validity that such contributions had in supplying desperately needed stability. Even more unsettling, the domestic base of such an approach was far from assured. Given the sectionalism and conflicting interests that often characterized government bureaucracies, MOFA could not counterbalance bureaucratic opposition by appealing to any domestic constituency. These vaunted programs of "strategic aid" often lacked any broad support (Yasutomo, 1986, pp. 67–70). A potential ally such as MITI was more apt to be focused on the strictly economic aspects of any such initiative. Diplomatic and policy implications were likely to be dismissed as irrelevant by key MITI officials. According to the insular view adopted at this time, "Political considerations are the Foreign Ministry's responsibility" (Yasutomo, 1986, p. 68). Strategic aid then never proved to be quite the weapon envisioned by the Foreign Ministry. Without the ability to garner unquestioned support by an array of policy makers, the political influence of this strategy remained doubtful. Rather than establishing a clear-cut diplomatic direction, the aid lever could prove to lack any resilience under more difficult circumstances.

4.3 Japan's Economic Diplomacy: Deploying Internationalism for Strategic Gain

The Ministry of Foreign Affairs may have had difficulty in transferring Japan's economic strength into diplomatic leverage even with the convenient camouflage provided by its ingenious doctrine of "comprehensive security." In retrospect, Japan's success during the 1980s in portraying itself as a useful and competently successful ally to the more skeptical Americans remains in question. However, Japan's impressive approach to achieving economic growth was a formulation eagerly emulated throughout the region. Japan had managed to position itself as the lead goose in its "flying geese" development analogy.

In response to such overwhelming success, Singapore launched a "learn from Japan" program in 1978. The aim was to encourage its citizens to emulate the Japanese by working hard to build their own economy. Even more remarkable was Malaysia's Prime Minister Mahathir's "Look East Policy" — a plan to boost economic development by following in the footsteps of Japan and South Korea. The Asian reach of Japan's success extended to a growing number of people who thought that learning Japanese might prove to be a useful or strategic tool. In the Asia-Pacific region alone these numbers almost doubled, growing from 484,000 in 1984 to 890,000 in 1990. North Americans and Europeans, however, unlike their Asian counterparts, seemed much less infected by all things Japanese. Language students remained almost the same, growing only from 55,000 in 1984 to 62,000 in 1990 (Ministry of Foreign Affairs, 1986, p. 110).[23] With an economy enhancing the Japanese regional presence, the Ministry of International Trade and Industry sought to turn this growing recognition into explicit advantages that could be efficiently exploited by individual Japanese firms. The ultimate goal was an economically integrated region, but one that was clearly under the direct influence of the Japanese.

Meanwhile, Prime Minister Nakasone sought to seize a public relations advantage by staunchly advocating increased "internationalization." For the bureaucrats of MITI, such "internationalization" pragmatically translated into the employment of Japan's growing funds to further the country's economic advantage. Given these pursuits, the Asia-Pacific region became its natural operating theatre in implementing these plans. This change of vision lifted foreign assistance to another level of importance. In previous decades, Japan had been content simply to employ regional aid to promote its own economic recovery and to establish good regional relationships. (Of course such relationships also advanced the Japanese revival.)

During the 1980s, other aims and policy aspects were now able to rise to a more prominent position. As previously noted, Japan used the leverage provided by financial aid to carve out something of a regional security role for itself. A convenient doctrine ambiguously defined as pursuing "comprehensive security" provided an all-purpose tool with which to pursue more ambitious diplomatic objectives. Whether explicitly intended or not, foreign aid by furthering economic integration and contributing to the much vaunted "internationalization" of Japan's economy, also successfully promoted and disseminated Japan's development model to its Asian neighbors. Aid then was no longer simply a device to further Japanese growth. Promoting dynamic Asian economies would do that, but it would also extend and deepen Japanese influence (Lincoln, 1993, p. 190). This approach meshed with MITI's broader objectives during this period. In its view, further integration and "internationalization" of Japan's economy would create and

---

[23] Japan had promoted cultural exchange by teaching Japanese language in the region since the mid-1960s. For further information see *Waga gaiko no kinkyo*, 1968, p. 415 and *Gaiko Seisho*, 1993, p. 285.

cement interdependent regional relationships. As pointed out previously, this represented Japan's classic "flying geese pattern" of regional economic development. (Needless to say, there could be only one candidate for "lead goose" in the MITI scenario.) As this framework inevitably developed, other Asian states would predictably follow quite dutifully behind Japan, confirming its natural leadership role (Pempel, 1997, p. 52).[24] The certainty harbored by Japanese bureaucrats that the country's growth was unstoppable, as was its ever-increasing wealth, encouraged MITI to single-mindedly pursue this somewhat grandiose goal during this period.

Quite predictably, Japan's rising economic power was met increasingly with suspicion and fear. Criticism grew of Japan's trade policy as its surplus expanded to what Japan's counterparts viewed to be unacceptable levels. Trade frictions were growing particularly intense with the US. During the 1980s, America found itself in the unenviable position of operating under historically high twin deficits encompassing both its current account and federal budget. Given the problems envisaged by these looming deficits, the very size of Japan's growing trade surplus with the US could only result in ever more acrimonious trade frictions. The US faced the unwelcome prospect of becoming economically dominated by the Japanese, at least if rising trade deficits were any indication.

Without any noticeable market corrections, the increasing severity of the situation encouraged an American move to rebalance the existing financial environment by better correlating it to US objectives. Given the treacherous trade imbalances, the immediate focus of any such initiative naturally fell to exchange rate adjustments. With trade continuing to be one-sided, the almost automatic reaction was to blame out of line terms of trade (reflected by the exchange rate) for the apparent market maladjustments. The argument, in essence, pinpointed the dramatically undervalued Japanese yen as failing to reflect the existing

---

[24]The "flying geese model" was initially advanced by Japanese professor Kaname Akamatsu in the 1930s. Subsequently, the model gained wider currency during the 1970s in the writings of Kiyoshi Kojima. In his formulation, Kojima referred to this model in the context of a catching-up product cycle.

economic reality. Instead, the managed currency provided Japan with an unfair edge. In essence, the badly undervalued Japanese yen should reflect the existing economic reality rather than providing Japan with an unequitable trade advantage.

The G5 countries (the US, Japan, France, the UK, and Western Germany) hoped that they had managed to achieve a successful solution by agreeing to the terms of the 1985 Plaza Accord. The reconfiguration of exchange rates would, in terms of the prevailing beliefs held by the participants, succeed in lessening the out-of-control trade balances. The reality proved otherwise. Undeterred by policy recipes such as the 1985 Plaza Accord, the US trade deficit still amounted to $144.3 billion a year later. In particular, Japan's trade surplus with the US, the focus of the Accord, managed to reach $54.4 billion in 1986. Weighing in at more than a third of the total deficit, the Plaza agreement had, in fact, accomplished little to abate the acrimony between the two countries.[25] Not only did the Plaza Accord fail to achieve the desired outcomes that had driven the meetings, but also, ironically, served mainly to increase Japan's economic influence.

The continuing realities of international trade left the Japanese with few options. Clearly they had to find a way to recycle these rising trade surpluses in such a way as to deflect growing US animosity. Part of their response consisted of an unprecedented expansion in foreign assistance during the 1980s. Japan tackled the foreign aid issue rather systematically by setting out a series of targets. The First Medium Target formulated in 1977, preceded, as one might guess, Japan's Second Medium Target. But facing pressures to expand the reach and scope of its program, Japan resorted to contriving another and much enhanced objective. The Third Medium Target originally aimed at doubling the 1985 level by the year 1992. The end date was then shortened to 1990 to allow for a quicker disbursement of available funds. On a dollar basis,

---

[25] During the time when trade frictions were rising, Wolferen (1986/87) published an article entitled "The Japan problem." According to the author, Japan was perceived as a "threat" by America. As he pointed out, "Japan bashing" a term gaining common parlance in the debate raging over trade, was a word concisely illustrating the problematic relationship between the US and Japan at the time.

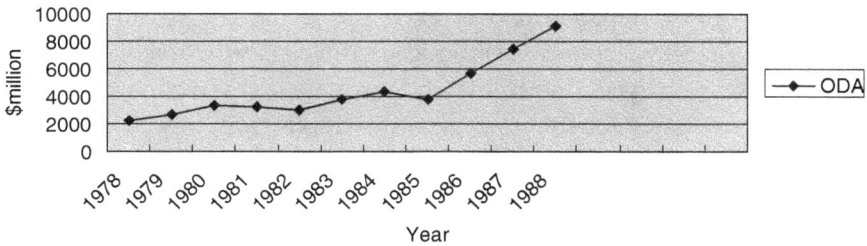

Source: Ministry of Foreign Affairs, 1989a, p. 87.

Fig. 4.2   Japan's ODA (net disbursement basis).

in the space of just 10 years (ending in 1988), foreign aid increased by 4.12 times (see Fig. 4.2) (Ministry of Foreign Affairs, 1989a, p. 87). Compared to a total of $105 million provided in 1960, aid increased in 1986 by a factor of 50 times ($5.634 million). Even when adjusted for inflation, the increase in Japan's ODA over that extended period was impressive, if not outright overwhelming.

The growth rate of its foreign aid was twice that of any other Development Assistance Committee member. In comparison, total government budgets increased 41.9 percent between 1981 and 1990 with spending on education and science practically stagnating at 7.8 percent, and social security expenditure crawling upward by only 31.4 percent. Meanwhile, during the same period, foreign aid enjoyed a remarkable 106.2 percent increase. Not coincidentally, the nearest rival in increased spending was defense, which showed a boost of 73.3 percent (Ministry of Foreign Affairs, 1990, p. 13). Such figures would at least indicate the emerging centrality of security and regional leadership during that decade.

As expected, Japan's drastic increase in aid was mirrored by its regional recipients. ASEAN countries in particular; Thailand, the Philippines, Indonesia, Malaysia, Burma, and Singapore became major beneficiaries with Japan solidly in place as each country's largest donor. In 1987, Japan's assistance accounted for 63.1 percent of the total aid received by Indonesia, 78.5 percent by Malaysia, 53.7 percent by the Philippines, 69.4 percent by Thailand, 50.6 percent by Singapore, and 88.6 percent by Brunei. Overall, from 1982 onwards, China became Japan's largest recipient country (Ministry of Foreign Affairs, 1989b,

p. 12). By 1991, Japan had overtaken the US as the world's largest donor. Regionally, Japan's economic might clearly had replaced that of the US. Japan was determinately constructing a noticeably more independent stance for themselves by developing a comprehensive aid policy based on an ever-expanding fountain of economic wealth.

The amount of ODA, consisting of aid and other official flows of capital, exceeded all expectations. Foreign assistance packages totaled more than $20 billion of completely untied official and private funds, all directed to developing countries. Smoothed by government aid programs, sizeable inflows of Japanese private capital followed into the region. The combination generated increased regional economic expansion and more interdependence.[26] A steadily appreciating yen only accelerated this movement.

The strength of the yen helped to increase Japan's foreign direct investment. For Japanese corporations, the misfortune of a significantly stronger yen encouraged increased off-shoring to maintain a continued level of international competitiveness. During this period, as its domestic economy boomed, Japanese investment in the Asian region grew to outstrip that of the US.[27] Domestically, the Japanese economy not only faced an appreciating yen, but a growing scarcity of blue-collar workers. The resulting increase in wages also encouraged traditional Japanese manufacturers to seek cheaper wages throughout Asia. Much of the lower value added end of production began to shift to other Asian destinations. This trend, however, was not simply a reaction to a changed economic environment, but rather one encouraged by MITI. The ministry had been hoping to rationalize production through a regional division of labor by confining the high value added end to the domestic market. Such a policy, if completed successfully, would deliver rising incomes to Japanese voters while maintaining Japan's competitive edge in manufacturing.

---

[26] See Orr (1990) for more details. He emphasizes the significant influence that MITI had over aid policy. These bureaucrats continued to regard aid as only an offshoot of export policy.
[27] These countries accounted for 8.3 percent of the world's exports in 1988. This level represented a 6.4 percent increase when compared to the 1965 level.

The manufacturing strategy, at least, triumphed as trade imbalances with the US continued to dominate media outlets. But this chronic problem was by no means confined to increasingly irritable Americans. Asian countries were also running trade deficits with Japan. Generally, they managed to ameliorate the worse effects by maintaining concurrent trade surpluses with the US, a safety valve, by definition denied to the Americans (Hatch and Yamamura, 1996, p. 175). Thailand, for instance, served largely as an export platform for Japan's corporate affiliates. Most of the goods manufactured there were sent abroad rather than remaining in the domestic market. (Only a relatively small amount went to Japan itself, as firms were wary of threatening domestic jobs.) Despite a growing trade deficit with Japan, Thailand showed increased surpluses with the rest of the world, especially the US (Fallows, 1994, p. 268). Regional countries, including Japan, depended heavily on those American markets. In stark contrast, Japan's growing dominance did not translate into greater regional imports for Japan's domestic market. To the rest of the world, Japanese trade policy seemed badly skewed, even within its own region.

MITI was aware of the need to absorb more exports from ASEAN countries (Ministry of International Trade and Industry, 1988). An increased flow would appease those Asian countries frustrated by their trade deficits with Japan. With a view to reducing its persistent surpluses, MITI encouraged Japanese firms to move overseas and establish off-shore branches. In this way, Japan would increase its regional imports, since such subsidiaries would produce low value added components, which subsequently could be imported back to Japan. As previously noted, MITI viewed this particular category of Japanese investment in ASEAN countries as encouraging a greater regional division of labor. ASEAN countries would produce low-cost components, enabling Japan to absorb more exports and establish itself as the dominant regional economy.[28] MITI aimed to promote the ongoing restructure of Japan's economy by encouraging Japanese companies to move offshore (Ministry of International Trade and Industry, 1987). This

---

[28] A broad outline of this policy appears in Prime Minister Takeshita's speech at the National Press Club in Washington, January 14, 1988, *Gaiko Seisho No. 32*, 1988, pp. 343–344.

was what MITI meant when it called for the greater "international-ization" of the Japanese economy. An emergence of a "Japanese pro-duction alliance" in the region, one that was dominated by Japan, was not only the result of Japanese firms pursuing competitiveness, but also the result of the Japanese government pursuing a specific foreign eco-nomic policy. The surge in Japan's FDI did successfully create a division of labor, first producing a number of regional "sub-contractors" and then a growing intra-industry trade. As a consequence, Japan's trade with Asia doubled in the 1980s.

To further pursue its stated internalization objectives, MITI sup-ported a number of policy initiatives to promote regional economic integration. Japan's ever-growing capital underpinned these steps. To examine just one concrete measure, in January 1987, MITI introduced the 1987 New Asian Industries Development Plan. The underlying aim motivating its enactment was to recycle Japan's over-abundant surpluses by encouraging the dispersion of private and official cap-ital throughout the region (Arase, 1988, p. 29; Rix, 1993, p. 29). The plan intended to provide the funds needed to develop economic infrastructure in the recipient countries. Investment of this sort was a means of facilitating further private investment. As a supplement to this primary purpose, it also encouraged joint industrial projects between Japan and recipient countries. MITI's aim was to accelerate grow-ing interdependence between Japan and these same countries, while ensuring that Japan would continue to be at the center of these lucra-tive economic relationships. Though not explicitly mentioned, MITI bureaucrats assumed that the transfer of Japanese technology and of its business model (characterized by the close relationships between gov-ernment and business) would also result in the transfer of Japan's devel-opment model. MITI hoped that by putting this development plan in place it would strengthen "control over an emerging Asian regional economy" and increase the "integration of the Asian economies under Japanese leadership" (Katzenstein and Rouse, 1993, p. 230; Hatch and Yamamura, 1996, p. 139). This hope was not realized. To suc-ceed, Japanese policies needed to minimize bureaucratic infighting and elicit a semblance of consensus support. In this specific case, MITI, whether intentionally or not, had been acting at cross purposes to its counterparts at MOFA. As a result, lacking any involvement or support from the Ministry of Foreign Affairs, which had been trying to sanitize assistance of all previous commercial aspects, the initiative quietly faded away (Rix, 1993).

Undaunted by this remarkable lack of success, the same year saw yet another government attempt to further its policies. The third ASEAN summit in Manila (December 1987) was an epoch-making event in Japan–Southeast Asian relations. Japan stood out as the only non-ASEAN country attending, but its presence reflected an ulterior motive. A highpoint of the summit turned out to be the formation of a Japan–ASEAN Development Fund. The Japanese provided more than $2 billion in hopes that the Fund would serve as an effective financial recycling program. By ploughing back Japan's accumulated private and official funds, the Development Fund hoped to facilitate a major leap forward in the economic development of ASEAN private sectors. Some successful transition was clearly necessary. With a few exceptions, industries in these ASEAN countries were neither internationally competitive nor particularly efficient. Those behind the fund were also quite aware that due to the inefficiency of these governments and the crucial lack of workable management systems, a large proportion of the Japanese aid had not been utilized properly. Waste attached to these foreign grants needed to be removed (Byrnes, 1987).

With a view to promoting private sector development in the region, the purpose of the fund was to specifically encourage Japanese investment into ASEAN countries. The most direct way of doing so was by reducing the risk to Japanese firms attached to these projects. ASEAN countries would be able to jump-start their growth, if assisted by these Japan–ASEAN joint ventures. Ostensibly, the rationale behind the fund's creation was simply an attempt to facilitate economic development. But without needing to dig too deeply, other, more essential motivations can be found. It seems likely that the Japanese government aimed to create asymmetrically dependent relationships between Japan and ASEAN countries by making these economies tightly linked to the fate of these proliferating Japanese subsidiaries. Under such a scenario, Japan's version of economic integration or interdependence apparently would reduce to no more than private sector activity, motivated purely by the self-interested pursuit of competitiveness and profits. But this type of exegesis would be a bit too simplistic. More accurately, the underlying strategy encompassed more than just the advancement of private capital. That it would be the result of governmental initiatives is essential in understanding the broader connotations underlying this effort.[29] The Japanese government attempted to use the strength of its private sector in positioning itself to reach a more dominant role within the region. Foreign Minister Abe's statement at the ASEAN Enlarged Foreign Ministers' Conference clearly demonstrates the great emphasis placed on continued collaboration between the government and the private sector. His speech emphatically indicated that more was at stake than simply narrow economic considerations.[30]

Despite the boldness of this approach, actually accomplishing such broader and challenging objectives proved to be vulnerable to unforeseen circumstances. As the unfortunate CoCoM violation by the Toshiba Machine Company indicated, private companies were not always perfectly aligned with governmental goals. However, in the 1980s, for the most part, government interests and those of the private sector roughly converged in their Asian operations. Investment and establishment of off-shore companies brought clear benefits to the private sector throughout the region, which previously had suffered from the appreciated yen. The government officially facilitated this capital dispersion through policy initiatives. Following this blueprint, private sector expansion would smooth the way for further regional integration, with Japan naturally leading the way forward. The transfer of technology and investment by the private sector, which was greatly encouraged by the government, further enhanced Japan's image by creating employment opportunities in the host countries. Investment also served to rectify the niggling current account imbalances between Japan and these selected countries (Ministry of Foreign

---

[29] This increase in Japanese off-shore companies was welcomed by Foreign Minister Abe. To savor the subtleties of his encouragement, readers are refereed to the 1986 speech by Foreign Minister Abe to the ASEAN Enlarged Foreign Ministers' Conference found at http://www.ioc.u-tokyo/~worldjpn/.

[30] For a nuanced understanding of Abe's 1986 speech at the ASEAN Enlarged Foreign Ministers' Conference, interested readers are directed to http://www.ioc.u-tokyo/~worldjpn/.

Affairs, 1986, pp. 22–25). A clear convergence of interests had facil-itated this bureaucratically sanctioned internationalization of Japan's economy.

At this stage, many Japanese ministries were confident that through aid and a variety of other economic activities they finally had moved to a position in which to exercise greater influence over other Asian countries. As Cold War tensions eased, the Japanese government, encouraged by the initial results, became even more assertive. It believed that by effectively employing its economic strength it could target and increase Japan's political clout. This assumption, unfortu-nately, proved to be valid for only a very brief period. The forthcoming Gulf War, together with the inevitable collapse of the bubble econ-omy, would soon expose the limits of an economic-contribution-only approach. These more complex diplomatic efforts will form the subject of the remaining chapters.

4.4   Conclusion: Japan Transforms Its Diplomatic Policy

Although it was not widely perceived at the time, the 1980s did repre-sent a major step forward for Japan's diplomatic policy. It was during this period that the Japanese quietly assumed a larger, more substantial role within the prevailing architecture of regional security. Encouraged by the upheavals and uncertain strategic environment during this time, the Japanese government methodically modified its approach to secu-rity matters. A doctrine of "comprehensive security" became the touch-stone for this new way of thinking and dealing with issues which had to some extent been avoided until this critical period. Constitutional and domestic constraints quite naturally limited the reach of this rather daring (at least in Japanese terms) diplomatic initiative. However, the underlying intention was quite clear. Japan should use whatever means feasible, especially those heavily dependent on economic options, to ensure its future security and to forge a new, more aggressive regional leadership role.

Out of this need to signal a changed position came an increased defense posture which aimed, implicitly, at supplementing the US Cold

War strategy. One of the implications of this more sharply defined objective was a greater flow of aid funding. The target recipients were largely defined by America's broader diplomatic aims. Unsurprisingly, the bulk of the funds found their way to America's strategic Asian allies.

Despite, or perhaps even because of, the nature of its policy initiatives, Japan, at this time, was often dismissed as a purely one-dimensional country, obsessed with its growing economic power. But this chapter has demonstrated that Japanese concerns transcended the purely economic. Although crucially limited by its post-war pacifist tradition and legal restrictions, Japan made persistent efforts to broaden its security presence beyond simple economic issues. The fact that such efforts were either not widely perceived or dismissed as ineffectual does not change the distinct objectives that the Japanese persistently pursued.

Economically, however, no question existed regarding Japan's success. By the 1980s it had become the very center of Asian economic activity. This development ensued as a result of Japan's continuing path and style of development. As the Japanese grew richer, the corporate sector accomplished a successful regional division of labor by locating a growing number of foreign subsidies throughout Asia. This expansion continued to create tensions, grounded on the historical fears of Japanese ambitions. Such fears were only amplified by the basic asymmetrical relationships between these relatively low value added countries and the increasingly wealthy Japanese.

But as Japan's corporate sector grew, so did the economic dependency of those Asian countries receiving Japanese foreign investment. Unhappily for Japan's diplomatic efforts, such economic leadership did not always translate into political influence. However, the multiplying Japanese subsidies, as well as the example Japan provided for an alternative Asian development path, imbued Japan with a certain degree of unstated (or even acknowledged) influence. Unfortunately at this stage, the government was still slow in promoting the Japanese model of development, at least when compared to the potent marketing power of the US. This reticence, or lack of confidence, undercut some of the potential influence such growing economic dominance could provide. While Japan pushed ahead in achieving its economic aims, its achievements at the diplomatic or political level were still only modest.

References

Arase D. (1988) *Japanese Objectives in Pacific Economic Cooperation*. East West Center Resource Systems Institute, Honolulu.

Arase D. (1995). *Buying Power: The Political Economy of Japan's Foreign Aid*. Lynne Rienner, Boubler.

Armacost M. (1996) *Friends or Rivals?* Columbia University Press, New York.

Byrnes M. (1987) Big Boy Japan brings $US2 billion to play in Australia's economic backyard. *Australian Financial Review*, 18 December.

Fallows J. (1994) *Looking at the Sun*. Pantheon Books, New York.

Hatch W, Yamamura K. (1996) *Asia in Japan's Embrace: Building a Regional Production Alliance*. Cambridge University Press, Cambridge.

Japan Defense Agency. (2000). http://www.jda/go.jp/j/library/yoron/2000/a0302/htm, accessed in December 2002.

Katzenstein PJ, Rouse M. (1993) Japan as a regional power in Asia. In: Frankel JA, Kahler M (eds.), *Regionalism and Rivalry*, pp. 217–244. The University of Chicago Press, Chicago, London.

Kim H. (1993) Japanese ODA policy to the Republic of Korea. In: Koppel BM Jr, Orr RM (eds.), *Japan's Foreign Aid*, pp. 203–229. Westview Press, Boulder.

Kusano A. (1991) Kokusai Seijikeizaito Nihon In *Sengo Nihon no Saisho Tachi*: Watanabe A (ed.), pp. 405–448. Yuikaku, Tokyo.

Lincoln EJ. (1993) *Japan's New Global Role*. Brookings Institution, Washington, DC.

Maeda T, Iijima S. (2003) In: Maeda T, Iijima S (eds.), *Kokkai Shingikara Boueiron wo Yomitoku*. Sanseido, Tokyo.

Ministry of Foreign Affairs. (1980) Okurasho Insatsukyoku, Tokyo.

Ministry of Foreign Affairs. (1982) *Gaiko Seisho 1982*. Okurasho Insatsukyoku, Tokyo.

Ministry of Foreign Affairs. (1985a) *Diplomatic Bluebook 1985*. Okurasho Insatsukyoku, Tokyo.

Ministry of Foreign Affairs. (1985b) *Wagakuni no Seifu Kaihatsu Enjo*. Okurasho Insatsukyoku, Tokyo.

Ministry of Foreign Affairs. (1986) *Diplomatic Bluebook 1986 edition*. Okurasho Insatsukyoku, Tokyo.

Ministry of Foreign Affairs. (1987) *Wagakuni no Seifu Kaihats Enjo*. Okurasho Insatsukyoku, Tokyo.

Ministry of Foreign Affairs. (1990) *Japan's ODA 1990*. Okurasho Insatsukyoku, Tokyo.

Ministry of Foreign Affairs. (1989a) *Diplomatic Bluebook 1989*. Okurasho Insatsukyoku, Tokyo.

Ministry of Foreign Affairs. (1989b) *Japan's ODA 1989*. Okurasho Insatsukyoku, Tokyo.

Ministry of Foreign Affairs. (2003) ODA Hakusho 2002, Kokuritsu Insatsukyoku, Tokyo.

Ministry of International Trade and Industry. (1987) *White Paper*, http://www.meti.go.jp/hakusho/index.html, accessed in April 2005.

Ministry of International Trade and Industry. (1988) *Tsusho Hakusho*, http://www.meti.go.jp/hakusho/index.html, accessed in April 2005.

Nakasone Y. (1996) *Tenchi Yujo*. Bungeishunju, Tokyo.

Orr RM, Jr. (1990) *The Emergence of Japan's Foreign Aid Power*. Columbia University Press, New York.

Pempel TJ. (1997) Transpacific Torii. In: Katzenstein P, Shiraishi T (eds.), *Network Power: Japan and Asia*, pp. 47–82. Cornell University Press, Ithaca.

Pyle KB. (1996) *The Japanese question: Power and Purpose in a New Era*. The AEI Press, Washington.

Rix A. (1993) Managing Japan's Aid: ASEAN. In: Koppel BM, Orr RM (eds.), pp. 19–40. Westview Press, Boulder.

Rix A. (1980) *Japan's Economic Aid*. St. Martin's Press, New York.

Sado A. (2003) *Sengo Nihon no Boei to Seiji*. Yoshikawakobunkan, Tokyo.

Suziki Z. (1981) *Joint Communiqué Following Discussions with Prime Minister Zenko Suzuki of Japan*. May 8, http://www.reagan.utexas.edu/archives/speeches/1981/50881b.htm, August 21, 2009.

Tanaka A. (1997) Anzenhosho: Sengo 50 Nen no Mosaku. Yomiuri Shinbunsha, Tokyo.

Wolferen K. (1986/87) The Japan problem. *Foreign Affairs* Winter, 288–303.

Yasutomo DT. (1986) *The Manner of Aid Giving, Lexington*. DC Heath and Company, Washington, DC.

PART II

The 1990s — Case Studies in Diplomacy

> This question the Dodo could not answer without a great deal of thought, and it sat for a long time with one finger pressed upon its forehead (the position you usually see Shakespeare in the pictures of him), while the rest waited in silence. At last the Dodo said, '*Everybody* has won, and all must have prizes' (Lewis Carroll, *Alice's Adventures in Wonderland*).

The core of our argument lies in whether we can discover a consistent and unifying objective in the various examples of practical Japanese diplomacy. What follows is a series of case studies which, despite their disparities, effectively exemplify what we identify as a very persistent Japanese imperative. The implied need for Japan to exert power and influence in the East Asian region is the best way to understand this series of seemingly isolated instances of applied foreign policy. It has been the circumstances rather than the underlying goals that have superficially differentiated these cases. Our analysis demonstrates that Japan has not been a special case or dogged by incoherent policy approaches. Although not always successful or effective, Japan's policy objectives have remained remarkably consistent.

Chapter 5

Becoming a Full-Fledged Power in the 1990s: The Purpose Behind Peacekeeping Operations

5.1 Putting a Toe into the Ocean: Cambodia as a Test Case

In the post-war period, Japan depended entirely on the US to maintain an acceptable level of national security. During those decades, the Japanese had enjoyed peace and stability free from the burden of constructing its own security system or engaging in a military build-up of any significance. Focused on rebuilding a shattered nation, Japanese political leaders accepted the limitations that both the international and domestic environments imposed, and opted to rely on the US to provide the requisite comfort yielded by a reliable national defense. If such an alternative had been feasible from a practical standpoint, rearmament still would have presented insurmountable difficulties in those early post-war years. Even ignoring economic landmines standing in the way, there were other barriers with which to contend in the prevailing Cold War structure. The fears of Japanese remilitarization still harbored by neighboring countries and an embedded general repugnance among the Japanese public concerning any military adventure dominated the post-war era. When taken together, these factors made a possible re-emergence as a military power a rather whimsical alternative. Besides the explicit limits mandated by Article 9 of the constitution, cultural norms deeply rooted in the post-war era limited the possibility of any Japanese military expansion. However, as the century's last decade began, Japan finally signaled that its long-held attitude toward all things military were headed in a new direction.

As previously mentioned, Cambodia in the post-Pol Pot era presented an unresolved challenge for those willing to grapple with all the inherent difficulties. Hoping to influence future eventualities in Cambodia, Japan aggressively pursued both diplomatic and economic opportunities, as they arose, to remain at the forefront of this particular issue. But despite its concerted efforts, Japan was unfortunately unsuccessful in the early stages of these initiatives. By the 1990s, however, new tactics and a transformed environment gradually enabled Japan to achieve its goals.

This chapter analyses the reasons behind Japan's Cambodian involvement. Rather than an isolated departure, this initiative was a coherent piece of a consistent, but often only implicitly expressed, objective driving the Japanese foreign policy. Japan nurtured a desire to gain influence by becoming a de facto leader in the Asia-Pacific region. This was the unvarnished reason for pushing through the legislation that authorized the heretofore neglected Self Defense Forces (SDF) to participate for the first time in actual peacekeeping operations. Therefore, this explicit policy change represented more than just a response to allied pressure or a fulfillment of Japan's international responsibilities in a new post-Cold War climate. Without adopting a broader perspective, the reasons for Japan's turning away from its post-war anti-militarist stance, and an almost stubborn degree of persistent pacifism, would remain as mysterious as they were unanticipated at the time. The goal then is to dig beneath readily available, but superficial, explanations in order to unearth the specific environmental changes that induced Japan to play a more active and independent diplomatic role.

5.2 Advancing New Tactics: Diplomatic Efforts in Cambodia

Cambodia, with a small population of about 11 million and few natural resources or business opportunities, has never provided sufficient scope for Japan to pursue its more narrow economic interests. However, since the promulgation of the Fukuda Doctrine, Japan had been eager to play a major political role in Indochina. As we have seen, the Ministry of Foreign Affairs (MOFA) on several occasions did attempt some rather tentative initiatives, even though forced to act only within the scope defined by its narrowly circumscribed boundaries. However, given the conflicts of interest characterizing the major powers at that time, nothing of importance flowed from these limited efforts Japan mounted in the 1970s and 1980s. The perennial clash among China, the US and the Soviet Union seemed insurmountable, leaving Japan with little room to operate in a world composed of fixed powers and entrenched opposition (Ministry of Foreign Affairs, 1988, p. 42). The collapse of this existing status quo spurred the Japanese into finally risking some new and more explicit diplomatic initiatives.

With a gradual easing of the previous major power conflicts in Indochina (see Chapter 4), the Ministry of Foreign Affairs accelerated its mediation attempts under the all-purpose banner of bringing peace and stability to Cambodia. Despite Japan's newly found enthusiasm for uncharted waters, the US was less than happy with these freshly baked initiatives. To make matters worse from the American standpoint, these diplomatic departures tended to be taken independently. In the case of Cambodia, Japan clearly was willing to exceed the collective intentions of the Permanent Security Council members. In January 1990, aware of these growing tensions, the Ministry of Foreign Affairs accordingly dispatched Masaharu Kono, the Director of the Southeast Asian Division, to try and allay US fears. Japan, as ever, was most reluctant to pursue its settlement proposals for Cambodia without at least tacit American approval. For this reason, the Japanese sought American agreement prior to Kono's proposed, but unofficial, Cambodian visit.[1] Unfortunately, the US fiercely opposed not only Japan's plan but even the proposed visits by Japanese officials. Instead, the Americans firmly requested Japan to be careful not to impede those initiatives already commenced by the Permanent Security Council members (Ogura, 1999, p. 135). Only after Japan reluctantly

---

[1] For a discussion of Japan's initiatives in Cambodia, see Kono (1999).

conceded a willingness to bear the financial burden attached to the desperately needed Cambodian reconstruction, did the US provide grudging approval for Kono's Cambodian visit (Ogura, 1999, p. 135). Note that at this stage, the US still envisaged Japan as limited to a defined economic role rather than engaged in any serious diplomatic efforts. Japan was to remain the check writer, not the policy creator. Despite these US-imposed blinders, Kono's visit did manage to bring about a change in Japan's Cambodian posture.

Kono's report, written soon after his visit to Cambodia, instigated a policy shift, which up to then had often seemed in virtual lockstep with that of the US. The Tokyo Conference in June 1990 signaled a discernable departure from America's Asian policy. Although the US hardly welcomed MOFA's diplomatic efforts, the Japanese refused to back down. Based on its strong connections with key players of each one of the major Cambodian factions (Sihanouk, Ranariddh, and Hun Sen), Japan began to call in some favors.[2]

Japanese officials believed that an agreement between two of the key players (Sihanouk and Hun Sen), rather than all four recognized parties engaged in the current conflict, would prove sufficient to move the country toward a lasting settlement.[3] Japan collaborated with Thai Prime Minister Chatichai Choonhavan in staging a June 1990 meeting in Tokyo. Although Khmer Rouge spokesperson Khieu Samphan boycotted this meeting, the achieved outcome was the formation of a Supreme National Council (SNC) represented by a tripartite coalition of the multilettered opposition parties [Front Uni National Pour Un Cambodge Independent, Neutre Pacific et Cooperative

---

[2] Sihanouk was known to be pro-Japanese. He visited Japan some seven times before he reascended the throne in 1993, illustrating this very close connection. Furthermore, Prince Ranariddh visited Japan 7 times, with Hun Sen visiting 12 times prior to 2001. Hun Sen had ties to many Japanese politicians and governmental officials. Prior to official recognition for his regime, Hun Sen visited Japan under the Japanese name "Ichiro Yamauchi" in 1991 to receive medical treatment. These connections proved advantageous for MOFA when arranging subsequent negotiations.

[3] Hun Sen, the ruling Cambodian leader, had come to power with the Vietnamese invasion of Cambodia. Prince Sihanouk had ruled Cambodia as its constitutional monarch for many years from independence in 1953 until 1970. He had managed to maintain his country's neutrality even in the face of the Vietnamese conflict. The Lon Nol government, acting under the guidance of the US, forced Sihanouk to abdicate in 1970.

(FUNCINPEC), Khmer People's National Liberation Front (KPNLF), and Khmer Rouge (PDK)] and the ruling Phnom Penh government. Vice Foreign Minister Kuriayama described Japan's diplomatic efforts that precipitated the meeting as being *"taikoku zura shinai naikoku gaiko,"* namely major power diplomacy that is not strong-armed. For the first time in post-war history, Japan was able to bring about a concrete result by performing the essential role of mediator.

As the next step, in February 1991, Japan proposed a disarmament agreement that would verify the successive stages of the military cease-fire and the general disarmament. This arrangement would establish the UN Transitional Authority in Cambodia (UNTAC) to oversee this initial peacemaking process. Not unexpectedly, the US State Department was far from supportive of Japan's initiatives. Nonetheless, the Japanese government managed to successfully gain support from key Cambodian participants. At the second session of the Paris Conference in October 1991, all the relevant parties accepted the brokered Paris Peace Accord. The treaty created a UN force, the UN Transitional Authority in Cambodia (UNTAC), that would establish and supervise an immediate ceasefire. Despite its vigorous diplomatic efforts, the Japanese government predictably ran up against the limitations of its own power. In reaction to Japan's previous initiatives, the Permanent Members of the UN Security Council demanded that the Japanese be excluded from the Thailand meeting of the Supreme National Council (SNC) held in December 1991 (Ogura, 1999, p. 142). Yukio Imagawa, Japanese representative to the SNC, fiercely protested this unwarranted maneuver. After some significant delay, permission was subsequently granted. As this incident indicated, despite its economic strength, Japan still had not yet positioned itself to play a major diplomatic role. The traditional international power structure, despite Japan's economic wealth and power, had failed to recognize Japan's bid to be acknowledged as a major player.

Limits to Japan's actions extended beyond the realm of political or even diplomatic tactics. Japan's scant post-war policy record conveyed a persistent shallowness underlying its actions. For instance, its non-participation in any peacekeeping opeartions signaled a seeming disregard of its international humanitarian obligations. This marked reluctance had been met with a wall of studied disinterest during the Cold War when loyalty transcended all other relevant foreign policy characteristics. However, once the ideological confrontations between the two Cold War superpowers had vanished, a plethora of civil disputes erupted to fill this newly created vacuum. The largely unanticipated reaction to the post-Cold War climate meant the increased deployment of UN peacekeepers. Between 1948 and 2004, the UN and other international alliances had conducted some 56 peacekeeping operations of varying success throughout the world. However, 43 of these missions had occurred between the short span bookended by the years 1988 and 2004 (Ministry of Foreign Affairs, 2004, p. 3).

These figures demonstrate a sudden and partially unexpected increase in peacekeeping demands during the post-Cold War period. Consequently, participation in these operations under UN auspices came to provide an increasingly valuable political currency in the continuing competition for international influence. At least momentarily, such missions seemed to underlie any successful resolution of international or civil conflicts in this new world order. The increasing political weight attached to peacekeeping operations transformed a previously seldom used option into a diplomatic device that now resembled something of an international "norm." In this new era, a global consensus now insisted that all states, whether weak or strong, rich or poor, be obliged to respond to conflicts by making some sort of a humanitarian contribution according to their capacity (Dobson, 2003, pp. 26–48). Belatedly, even Japan realized the necessity for getting behind this now fashionable strategy.

As is its wont in such matters, Japan's progress toward participating in selected peacekeeping operations was extremely slow and painstaking. Foreign Minister Taro Nakayama, aware of the need to finally make some contribution that could be categorized as humanitarian assistance, demonstrated a distinct willingness to provide not only financial but humanitarian assistance as well once Cambodia achieved a sustainable level of peace and stability (Nakayama, 1990). However, both the government and the public had hoped to remain aloof from the actual grittiness associated with international military matters. Instead of direct involvement, a widespread domestic consensus still believed Japan could adequately fulfill its international obligations by contributing economic assistance alone. Such largesse had long been seen as providing adequately for regional security, even though only in an indirect fashion. In the prevailing Japanese mindset, a sufficient donation of economic assistance at this level obviated the need for any further contributions. As a result, the Japanese persistently failed to consider peacekeeping participation as being particularly urgent. But it was not merely a case of Japan proving typically obtuse. Other countries equaled the Japanese in their lack of any enthusiasm for having Japan extend its diplomatic efforts beyond this self-imposed economic focus. Taken in tandem, these distinctive domestic and international attitudes limited Japan from doing much more than simply signaling its willingness to think about extending the scope of its obligations (*Gaiko Kiroku*, 01-906-7, March 1990). The prevailing reality at this time imbued any quasi-military involvement, even if masquerading as a humanitarian commitment, with the dangerous potential for generating a backlash against Japan.

The US fully understood these constraints that narrowly defined Japan's actions. As a result, instead of requesting direct participation, America insisted that the Japanese act as underwriters by financing at least part of the burden that any proposed UN peacekeeping operation might produce in Cambodia. The US had increasingly characterized the Japanese as deliberately dragging their feet in this regard. For example, by the early 1990s, the pro-rated US financial contribution to the UN peacekeeping budget had reached 30.4 percent. In contrast, Japan supported a mere 12.45 percent of that total budget. This imbalance stirred the US Congress into insisting that the Japanese bear a noticeably greater proportion of any future cost of these operations, starting with those proposed for Cambodia (*Gaiko Kiroku*, 01-910-8, March 1992). The American ability to continue to finance such missions had been heavily restrained by an increasingly recalcitrant Congress. In contrast, Japan's growing economy, rather than the sluggish one then burdening the US, better equipped the Japanese with an ability to float these high-cost operations. Given the prevailing financial realities, both countries conceded that Japan should from then on assume the leading role in reconstructing Cambodia (*Gaiko Kiroku*, 01-910-8,

March 1992). In June 1992, Japan took its first step along this path by providing a sizable contribution to UNTAC. This amount was largely viewed as a significant down payment that might insure regional peace and stability since cash is seldom turned away. These initial measures quite naturally won the approval of all the countries directly participating in the peace process (*Gaiko Kiroku*, 01-910-24, July 1992). Despite this encouragement, the Japanese government came to realize that economic assistance would not suffice if its underlying objective was to garner significant influence within the existing regional environment.

One way to extend beyond the purely financial was to make a contribution to the proposed peacekeeping mission in Cambodia. Soon after his appointment as UNTAC head, Yasushi Akashi advised the Japanese government that sending Japanese police officers would be one way for Japan to measure up to international expectations (Dobson, 2003, p. 111). Failure to participate in UNTAC would unduly limit any opportunity Japan had to play a leading role in Cambodia. Any refusal to embrace this risk would once again reduce Japan to nothing more than a tired cliché, a country more willing to shell out cash than to take on the necessary but dangerous task of peacekeeping. Without providing this specific type of humanitarian assistance, Japan would continue to stand on the sidelines, demeaning itself in the eyes of Cambodia and other affected countries. All its substantial economic and diplomatic contributions would largely go for naught, discounted by the wider world.

Aware of these dangers, the Miyazawa coalition government, succeeding the fallen administration of Prime Minister Kaifu in November 1991, felt duty bound to expedite an International Peace and Cooperation Law (hereafter the peacekeeping bill). This piece of legislation would free Japan from its self-imposed constraints by allowing the SDF to fully participate in the proposed Cambodian mission. The bill represented a coherent part of the new government's broader policy goals. Miyazawa had set out to increase Japan's international political stature from the moment he took office. By being part of a future Cambodian peacekeeping mission, Japan could finally signal its willingness to sweat blood and tears in its quest to bring peace and stability to the region.

For Miyazawa, the post-Cold War era presented a set of opportunities that could provide "the start of a time of building a new order for global peace." This implied that Japan was determined "not only to be active on the economic front but also to broaden the opportunities for political dialogue and to play a vigorous political role" (Miyazawa, 1992, p. 334). By making a concrete contribution to regional security, Japan would be able to increase its presence as a full-fledged power. As part of this strategy, Miyazawa also intended for Japan to take its place as a permanent member of the Security Council sometime in the future. The perceived importance of this long-term diplomatic initiative meant that the peacekeeping legislation was expeditiously pushed through the Diet. Accomplishing such broad targeted objectives required a solid legal framework that would legitimize full-blown peacekeeping operations. The proposed bill intended to provide the necessary groundwork for the sort of fresh strategic thinking which could successfully shape future Japanese diplomacy.

For these reasons, Miyazawa's perceptions that Japan needed to participate in the Cambodian mission managed to put some steel in his backbone (Iokibe, 2001). Specifically, in the immediate future it meant pushing ahead with the scheduled peacekeeping operations under the auspices of the UN. In terms of Japanese sensitivities, such a carefully orchestrated first step would fit in perfectly with the prevailing environment at that time. This approach might quell domestic unease, while reassuring all countries still apprehensive about a potential remilitarization. Fortunately for Miyazawa, the current government coalition was willing to accept an enlarged role in security matters if it could be effectively camouflaged as a humanitarian contribution. Subsequently, Miyazawa's unwavering support for this second effort to pass peacekeeping legislation provided the required lubrication needed to achieve ultimate success (Iokibe, 2001).

The challenge facing Miyazawa then was not so much to convince his own LDP members but to gain the support from his other partners, Komeito, as well as the allied Democratic Socialist Party. To achieve such a significant policy departure, compromise became essential if he was to bring seemingly irreconcilable standpoints together. Therefore, the legislation made a clear distinction between peacekeeping and peace enforcing, with the later effort strictly prohibited. A cautious approach of this type would avoid violating a constitution that does allow scope for international cooperation to preserve peace. However, this leeway would be permitted only if the following "five principles" were maintained:

1. an agreement on a cease-fire in place,
2. the consent of all parties involved in the conflict to the deployment of a peacekeeping force, and to Japan's participation,
3. the impartiality of such a peacekeeping force,
4. a means of withdrawal in case of a suspension of the above three agreements,
5. the minimum use of weaponry, with employment restricted to those protecting the lives of personnel (Ministry of Foreign Affairs, 1992).

These "five principles" considerably narrowed Japan's scope for military action. The constitution essentially limits the SDF from employing force in more traditional ways. On the other hand, these imposed limitations did make it easier for Japan to explore a significant policy departure by ameliorating some pointed public concerns. Despite these positives, opposition parties, such as the Japan Socialist Party and the Japanese Communist Party, fiercely opposed the bill. Their actions intentionally delayed passage through the Diet. Ignoring this intractable opposition, the government still managed to force the legislation through with the help of its coalition partners.

In June 1992, following the passage of the peacekeeping bill, Japan, for the first time since World War II, sent troops overseas. Only three months elapsed between legislative approval and departure of the troops. The close timing indicates that the Japanese constructed the peacekeeping bill with a view to expediting the movement of SDF personnel to Cambodia. The legislative initiative represented a dramatic policy change, but at the same time, this new course only reflected aspirations long nurtured by the Japanese to step out of the diplomatic shadows and instead gain explicit recognition as a full-fledged power. The Cambodian mission provided an initial step toward a policy transformation that would turn long-held desires into concrete reality. Specifically, Japan would fulfill its perceived responsibility as a major power by demonstrating its willingness and ability to engage in humanitarian activity, using UNTAC as a representative test case. Operating under UN auspices would also salve not only domestic sensibilities but any regional anxiety over possible Japanese remilitarization. This policy departure could potentially enhance Japan's international reputation while at the same time strengthening its influence in Cambodia. However, given the strictures mandated by the constitution, tasks allocated to the SDF were limited to such lower-risk activities as election monitoring, road building, transport improvements, and the provision of medical assistance. Despite the inevitably circumscribed scope of its actions, Japan's contribution to this particular peacekeeping mission marked a historic and critical first step.

In addition to these new tactics, the Japanese government continued to employ more traditional means as well. The 1992 Tokyo Ministerial Conference on the Rehabilitation and Reconstruction of Cambodia [later reformulated in September 1993 as the International Committee on the Reconstruction of Cambodia (ICORC)] followed by the 1995 Ministerial Meeting of the Forum for Comprehensive Development of Indochina (also held in Tokyo) together formulated the required level of effective economic aid. By coupling its traditional leading role in coordinating continued financial assistance with its newly established humanitarian efforts, Japan could take pride in a policy approach that had finally come of age.[4]

As noted in previous chapters, starting with the Meiji restoration, Japan had aspired not only to avoid foreign domination but to be recognized as a major power in its own right. By 1990, despite the restrictions imposed by its "Five Principles," Japan had succeeded in becoming a full-fledged economic power with hopes of expanding beyond its currently limited sphere. Clearly, these peacekeeping operations were not capable of directly improving Japan's material well-being. The limited trade and investment opportunities that Cambodia provided indicated the absence of any compelling economic advantage driving this policy departure.

---

[4]The Japanese government expressed its intention to resume aid to Cambodia in January 1994.

An examination of the relevant investment figures following the resolution of destabilizing political conflicts in Cambodia makes this essentially unarguable. Starting in August 1994, new legislation allowed foreign direct investment (FDI) into Cambodia. Between 1994 and 1998, Malaysia became Cambodia's largest investor, accounting for 45.4 percent of the total approved by the government. The US was second with 9.7 percent (Ebashi and Onozawa, 2000, p. 279). Meanwhile, between 1997 and 2001, Japanese firms committed only a total of $3 million in actual investments. This compares with the $129 million made by the US or the $145 million by Malaysian firms during this same period. Even the Chinese contributed more ($20 million) to the sum of foreign investment flowing into Cambodia (International Monetary Fund, 2004). The more cautious Japanese lagged far behind. In fact, Japan clung to a low-key, risk-averse approach when deciding whether to commit to joint ventures. As of 2002, the Japanese backed only one project involving routine wood processing, despite a total of 10 joint ventures agreed to by the Cambodian government (Ebashi and Onozawa, 2000). Likewise, in terms of trade, Japan remained a minor player. The Japanese represented a mere 7.5 percent of total Cambodian imports, only the fifth largest total in 1997 (Ebashi and Onozawa, 2000, p. 277). Even in 1998, after the settlement of a second Cambodian political upheaval, exports to and imports from Cambodia were valued at only 5.8 billion yen and 2.1 billion yen, respectively. In contrast, similar trade with Vietnam were worth 173.8 billion yen and 228.9 billion yen, respectively, as of 1998 (Japan Customs, 2004). This absence of any credible economic inducements reflects a lack of critical financial reasons for Japan adopting an active Cambodian policy. Instead, the engagement indicated that long-term goals were focused on gaining regional influence rather than chasing after some narrowly defined economic opportunity.

Predictably, Japan's participation in the Cambodian operation did serve to enhance its presence and influence as a mature power. Hun Sen's unequivocal support of Japan's subsequent bid for a UN Security Council seat indicated Japan's continuing influence in that country, well after all troops had departed (Kawamura, 2000). MOFA claimed that Japanese activism in Cambodia led to increased respect on the international front. Asian countries increasingly expected Japan to assume the lead in any cooperative regional framework (Takahashi, 2001). Motivations that had been quietly concealed beneath a broad pacifist political culture were now emerging. After decades of effective cloaking, the intrinsic aspirations underlying Japan's diplomatic efforts seem to have achieved an initial fruition.

5.3 Prometheus Bound: Overcoming Intrinsic Limitations to Japanese Action

Using peacekeeping operations as a start, Japan in the early 1990s began fashioning a new framework for its military strategy. Such tactics would have been a clear non-starter during the Cold War period. Anti-military sentiment was simply running too high among the Japanese public at that time. The peacekeeping bill, timed to expedite the dispatch of troops to Cambodia, represented the second attempt to achieve this particular goal. The first attempt was obviously thwarted. Among other factors, this previous effort had been unable or unwilling to overcome the public's ingrained pacifism. However, despite this previous setback and Japan's post-war history of anti-militarism, the Miyazawa government refused to be effectively discouraged from making another attempt to push through similar legislation. We now turn to an analysis of the environmental factors that had changed sufficiently to encourage the then ruling coalition to risk its political capital by going against what appeared to be an embedded and even intractable post-war tradition of eschewing military involvement. To understand why this moment seemed to offer previously unavailable possibilities, we need to first trace out the development and the basis for the norms that shaped foreign policy.

5.3.1 *Embedded Pacifist Norms and Cold War Contributions*

Since World War II, when then Prime Minister Shigeru Yoshida first set the direction of an economy-first policy, Japan had pursued its own prosperity under the umbrella of the US–Japan Security Treaty. During the Cold War, any open discussion of security issues was strictly taboo. Despite these apparent prohibitions, successive Japanese governments did not have the luxury of carelessly free-riding off the alliance or of remaining vaguely uninterested. Though never explicitly formulated, beneath this surface indifference there lurked a deep-rooted desire to become more directly involved in its own security concerns. Japan had forfeited this alternative by being on the losing end of World War II. Given the subsequent constitutional prohibitions on the use of force, participation in peacekeeping operations that remained under the watchful eyes of the United Nations seemed the best and perhaps only option open to a deliberately circumscribed Japan. Moreover, peacekeeping was distinctly compatible with supporting a tried and tested position that emphasized a UN first policy. While devoting all its resources and attention to achieving an economic recovery during the early post-war period, quiet debates over dispatching the SDF for peacekeeping operations continued, at least at a discrete, bureaucratic level.

In 1954, the year in which the SDF was organized, the plenary session of the House of Councillors adopted a Resolution not to send Japanese forces abroad. Therefore, when in 1958, UN Secretary General Dag Hammarskjöld asked Japan to dispatch 10 officers to serve as military observers in Lebanon, the government refused on the grounds that restrictions placed on the SDF explicitly ruled out participating in anything resembling that role. However, at least constitutionally, Japan could participate legitimately in peacekeeping activity, as long as it was endorsed by the UN. The decision not to be part of these missions was strictly political in nature. The 1961 statement by the head of the National Legislation Bureau sufficiently clarified Japan's intentions on this point. Specifically, participating in a peacekeeping operation endorsed by the UN was in no way a violation of the constitution. However, the government was willing neither to participate in such operations nor revise the basic law under which the Self-Defense Forces operated (Tanaka, 1997, pp. 213–214). In effect, there was ample room for Japan to participate in a variety of UN peacekeeping initiatives once it chose to revise the existing operational structures imposed upon the SDF. But doing so would require something resembling a domestic consensus. Creating anything like a widespread agreement on Japan's security policy in those early post-war years appeared to be virtually impossible. Moreover, during that period, no urgent need or desire to initiate such a drastic change existed. Two insurmountable obstacles made even serious public discussion a forlorn hope.

Absolutely no middle ground seemingly existed between the perennially ruling party, the Liberal Democrats (LDP) and its traditional opponent, the Japanese Socialist Party (JSP), which remained the largest left-wing party for decades. Ever since the agreement on a US–Japanese security treaty, the JSP had adamantly refused to support either the treaty or the legitimacy of the SDF. This remained an article of faith for the JSP until 1994. The inauguration of a coalition government headed by Tomiichi Murayama saw the JSP, after so many years spent in the political wilderness, become part of a ruling coalition. Prior to this turn of events, even the legitimacy of the SDF had been an irreconcilable and highly divisive issue. A political culture of anti-militarism had created a policy-making pattern that effectively forestalled any defense initiatives (Berger, 1998). Political constraints proved highly effective at subordinating military issues to the dictates of economic policy (Berger, 1998, pp. 194–195). Explicit Cold War restrictions were not the only reason why security debates were so limited. At least equally important was public sentiment that had yet to warm toward either the military or to expanded operations by the SDF (Katzenstein, 1996, p. 22).

Perhaps the most compelling reason why Yoshida refused to meet the US demand for rearmament was not so much the economic burden attached to such a policy. Yoshida was always intently alert to the robust anti-militarism that continued to define public sentiment for decades. For instance, the so-called Mitsuya Kenkyu incident in 1965 revealed the peculiar Japanese sensitivity to even what would otherwise be dismissed as no more than a standard analysis of relevant security matters. The resulting uproar concerned a simulation study of war in the Korean Peninsula and a related examination of possible emergency laws by a few Defense Agency officials. The over-reaction when these efforts became public knowledge reflected fears that such a seemingly innocuous study might in fact be the first step on the road to remilitarization. This scandal temporarily froze the possibility of military cooperation with the

US and forestalled any substantial debate over national security (Smith, 1999, pp. 77–79). However, once the fury had had sufficient time to subside and was largely forgotten, the Fukuda administration demonstrated no qualms in secretly resuming a quite similar study in 1977. Encouraged, the Director General of the Defense Agency did attempt to draft a bill to allow for contingency planning. However, due to the predictably pacifist political culture then prevailing, the proposed legislation never made it out of the study and consideration stage (Watanabe, 2003). From the government's point of view, as long as the scope of any issue could be limited to questions of self-defense (setting guidelines on US military cooperation in case of an attack on Japan), no serious danger of touching off political controversy existed.[5] Yet, preparing for contingencies that went beyond a narrowly limited definition of self-defense had never been openly debated. Militant pacifism had made the issue highly sensitive and virtually taboo. This automatic reaction extended to government officials as well and created ideological confrontations both within and between political parties. Despite sporadic attempts to quietly examine the underlying issues, succeeding governments produced nothing concrete. Instead, governments easily opted to employ Japan's growing economic strength to meet national security requirements. The introduction of a burden-sharing arrangement underwriting US bases in Japan precisely reflected this approach. However, even though overtly constrained in this manner, the Ministry of Foreign Affairs still felt the necessity of quietly exploring a possible dispatch of troops as an enhancement of its international standing and influence.

Japan took its seat as a non-permanent member of the UN Security Council in 1965 for the first time. At least within government ranks, this event served to rekindle the debate over peacekeeping participation (Tanaka, 1997). At this time, MOFA clearly pointed out that Article 9 of the constitution did not prohibit either the dispatch or the participation of the SDF in a peacekeeping operation as long as it was endorsed and controlled by the UN. However, before such provisional

---

[5]For example, see the Guidelines for Japan–US Defense Cooperation as published in 1978.

expeditions could proceed, it was exigent for the sitting government to either enact special legislation or to revise the existing SDF law (*Gaiko Kiroku*, 01-899-21, October 11, 1965). The Ministry though wanted to go even further in introducing changes. In its judgment, dispatching troops was also constitutional as long as the requisite mission did not include any use of force (*Gaiko Kiroku*, 01-899-19, October 11, 1965). MOFA pointed out that prohibitions on the use of the SDF contradicted one of the three principles of Japanese diplomacy, namely its UN-centered approach. It quietly criticized the government for not fulfilling these Japanese obligations (*Gaiko Kiroku*, 01-899-4, January 1996). In the Ministry's view, the country required a UN peacekeeping operation bill. Only in this way could Japan hope to be seen as a major Asian country able to wield influence within the Security Council, whether or not it actually held a permanent seat (*Gaiko Kiroku*, 01-899-4, January 1966). Yet, there was no perceived urgency at this time to push forward a change in the existing law or even to review it. Japanese participation in peacekeeping operations remained unresolved due to the prevailing political sensitivity of these issues, which effectively acted to constrain government policy. Instead, from the time of Prime Minister's Ikeda's "income doubling plan" in the 1960s, economic growth had become Japan's dominant political objective. In contrast, defense policy remained controversial. Even the legitimacy of the SDF was wrapped in ambiguity due to the JSP-enshrined policy of questioning the constitutionality of these troops. Given the prevailing domestic situation, provoking a national debate would have been politically foolhardy. In these post-war decades, pacifist political culture and public anti-militarist sentiment brooked no alternative approach.

With a military approach effectively blocked, the Japanese government chose to help finance UN peacekeeping operations starting in the 1970s. The importance of these missions during that decade lacked any distinct parallel with the urgency of later events. However, even at that time, the Japanese government sensed the increasing importance that peacekeeping efforts would play in the international arena. The government soon realized that future commitments would require Japan to eventually make a more active contribution. Though administrations came and went, this considered judgment never noticeably changed. Peacekeeping operations, even to the extent of dispatching troops overseas, were not deemed unconstitutional as long as the SDF was not involved in anything resembling military activities (*Gaiko Kiroku*, 01-914-2, November 30, 1982). Participating in peacekeeping initiatives therefore, became a permanent item on government agendas, though necessarily recognized only implicitly.

With Japan again a member of the UN Security Council in 1982, Foreign Minister Yoshio Sakurauchi supported the dispatch of troops for non-military activities such as monitoring.[6] He went further that same year by citing a clear need to revise the relevant law in a way that would allow the SDF to participate in international monitoring.[7] Given the potential for domestic backlash and unwanted political turmoil, the incentive for the Japanese government to modify this law remained minimal. Afraid of stirring up domestic conflicts, Prime Minister Zenko Suzuki (1980–1982) flatly refused to even consider revising the SDF legislation during his term of office.[8] As we have seen, Suzuki did demonstrate a certain willingness to play at least a limited military role in bearing Japan's responsibilities to provide a degree of regional security. However, when donning its official Japanese face, the Suzuki government chose to outline a program limited to the economic aspects of this issue. To his domestic audience he insisted that this more restricted approach could assist sufficiently in maintaining regional peace and stability. Officially, the Japanese continued to strike a balance between their avowed State pacifism and bearing more responsibility for regional security. By strictly limiting its initiatives to making specific financial contributions, Japan hoped to finesse this dilemma.

Unfortunately, by the late 1980s, these practised evasions became more questionable. Peacekeeping operations had become an increasingly prominent tool in settling international disputes. The Japanese government had become aware that by themselves, economic

---

[6]Statement made by Foreign Minister Sakurauchi at the 96th National Diet, January 25, 1982.
[7]Statement made by Foreign Minister Sakurauchi at the House of Councillors budgetary committee on June 30, 1982, reported in *Gaiko Kiroku*, 01-914-2, November 30, 1982.
[8]Statement made by Prime Minister Suzuki at the House of Councillors on July 1, 1982, reported in *Gaiko Kiroku*, 01-914-2, November 30, 1982.

contributions would no longer suffice as a workable strategy if its aim was to gain any significant influence within the international arena. Faced with this reality, the Takeshita administration (1987–1989) responded by developing its "International Cooperation Initiative" in 1988. The policy championed three distinct pillars:

1. cooperating to insure peace,
2. enhancing ODA, and
3. promoting international cultural exchange.

For the first time, Japan officially accepted its responsibility to underwrite global peace and stability. The Takeshita government went so far as to bring participation in Peacekeeping operations within the realm of political possibility. Takeshita considered such participation as potentially enhancing its power regionally if not internationally (*Gaiko Kiroku*, 01-911-1, April 28, 1989). However, at this stage, such a policy break still existed only as a bureaucratic potential. Japan had not yet formed a national consensus embracing the country's appropriate security role. In practical terms, the government was still quite unwilling to take anything resembling decisive action. Instead, as a tacit preliminary step, the government quietly examined the way in which other countries managed and ran their peacekeeping systems (*Gaiko Kiroku*, 01-906-18, February 27, 1990). Despite launching a study group, the move toward what eventually would be packaged as making "a humanitarian contribution" to peace and stability failed to gain any real traction. The government, let alone the public, still considered economic contributions as more than sufficient to fulfill any international responsibility that Japan might have. Extending this obligation to humanitarian efforts or even military ones seemed unnecessary (Hatakeyama, interview with an anonymous official in Ministry of Foreign Affairs, April 2004). The public, in fact, thought that Japan should limit itself to providing assistance which would promote economic development.[9] Moreover, resorting to peacekeeping missions had only begun to gain a respectable degree of international credibility. No substantial pressure,

---

[9] 50.4 percent of the Japanese opted for playing a role in providing economic assistance (*Yoron Chosa Nenkan*, 1989, p. 116).

domestic or otherwise, existed to shift Japanese policy into supporting a more active role. However, as a gesture of a good will, the Japanese did end up dispatching one token individual although not SDF affiliated, to the UN Good Offices Mission in Afghanistan/Pakistan. Dispatching yet another solitary person to the UN Iran–Iraqi Military Observation Group in 1988 followed next. After these very modest initial forays, Japan next sent a total of 27 personnel to the UN Transition Assistance Group (Namibia) in 1989. But Japan was still not ready to deploy SDF troops for overseas peace keeping. Such a clear rerouting of policy would require a dramatic change in the domestic constraints inhibiting any further action.

5.3.2 *Paper Tigers: The Gulf War Fractures the Japanese Consensus*

The 1990s opened with a dramatic and largely unanticipated change, namely the end of the Cold War. The 1991 START treaty (the first treaty to cut strategic nuclear weapons) coincided with a reduction in Soviet forces that eased East–West tensions. This reduction in what had been an all-encompassing superpower conflict potentially opened up some space for Japan to maneuver within the newly emerging international order. Japan expected that it could now play a more positive international role, one that might be more commensurate with its growing economic power (now accounting for 14 percent of the world gross domestic product). For Prime Minister Toshiki Kaifu, this decade seemed to present a perfect opportunity for Japan to play a decisive role, even one that helped contour the shape of the future international environment. Backed by its seemingly impregnable economic strength, Japan was now able to play a significant role in establishing a more stable and economically interdependent world. The thrust of this idea is encapsulated by a 1989 *Diplomatic Bluebook* pronouncement. This explicit reference clearly conveys an attempt to establish Japan's responsibility as, and right to be, a major power. "We can no longer accept the international climate as an external given. Japan is an important determinant influencing international developments" (Ministry of Foreign Affairs, 1989, p. 13).

Reinforcing this approach, in 1990, Kaifu specifically emphasized the importance of having Japan take part in building an international order that would prove congenial to an environment that was full of hope. He expressed his willingness to embark upon the pursuit of "a foreign policy of aspirations."[10] The government was also aware that with the end of the Cold War, peacekeeping operations were evolving into the moral equivalent of making a serious contribution in terms of humanitarian assistance. Full-fledged participation in these missions would certify Japan as a member in good standing of the international community. Peacekeeping provided Japan with a low-risk option to enhance its reputation. The government establishment generally comprehended the requirements needed to achieve these higher goals. However, these people also understood that bringing such aspirations down to a more applicable level remained fraught with difficulties.

The Gulf War of 1990–1991 shocked the nation by revealing to the Japanese their chronic inability to respond quickly to pressing issues. As a result, the Japanese ambition of building a new international order lay in tatters.[11] Not only did the war expose Japan's failure to handle strategic issues, but also posed a challenge to its policy of quiet diplomacy and economic sweeteners that had largely composed Japan's approach to international relations. First, the Gulf Crisis demonstrated that Japan could no longer depend on its rationale of "one-country pacifism" as a means of avoiding military controversies. This turn of events forced the Japanese to re-examine the way in which they related to the rest of the world (Ito, 1991, p. 281). Second, the war raised constitutional issues, presented alternative approaches to US–Japan relations and perhaps most importantly questioned the exact status of the SDF. The

---

[10]Policy speech by Prime Minister Kaifu at the 118th Session of the National Diet on March 1990. According to Kaifu, the international order Japan should pursue consisted of:

- ensuring peace and security,
- respecting freedom and democracy,
- guaranteeing world prosperity through open-market economies,
- preserving an environment in which all people can lead rewarding lives, and
- creating stable international relations founded upon dialogue and cooperation.

For further details see Ministry of Foreign Affairs (1990, pp. 276–277).

[11]For factors shaping Japan's response to the Gulf Crisis, see Inoguch (1993, pp. 98–114) as well as Okamoto (2001).

Gulf War, for the first time in Japan's post-war era, created a serious challenge to its comfortable, economic-centric approach. This series of doubts and questions over Japan's diplomatic practises gave birth to future national debates over security issues.

The war generated a wide-ranging domestic debate focusing on how Japan might extend its international contribution to peace and stability in a manner that transcended the merely economic.[12] Realizing that the time had come for its traditional financial contributions to be supplemented by those of a more humanitarian description, the Kaifu government submitted a bill proposing limited cooperation with UN peacemaking efforts during the Gulf Crisis. Unsurprisingly, these policy shifts coincided with increased US pressure as well. SDF support troops could at least indirectly contribute to ongoing military actions undertaken by the multinational forces committed to the conflict.

However, the MOFA-inspired bill was not sufficiently vented within key bureaucracies and political groupings prior to submission. Any semblance of consensus soon broke down. Appearing before the Diet, Kaifu had assured members that SDF troops would not be stationed in harm's way, despite having had the Ministry of Foreign Affairs already contradict the prime minister by conceding this unfortunate possibility. In the ensuing tussle, Kaifu himself lacked the staying power required to garner the necessary approval for his measure. Nor did the rest of the LDP demonstrate any backbone in this matter. But the wobbly support provided by the government merely reflected the public mood at that time and thus the political reality. According to opinion polls conducted by *Asahi Shimbun* in 1990, 78 percent of those polled opposed any overseas dispatch of the SDF in general, with 58 percent opposing the specific bill and only 30 percent supporting sending troops under

---

[12] Newspapers (Mainichi, Yomiuri, Asahi, and Sankei) referred to the term "international contribution" 48 times but did not refer to "international contribution and the SDF" even once between August 1, 1989, and July 30, 1990. In contrast, they referred to "international contribution" 1393 times with "international contribution and the SDF" 789 times after the Gulf War from August 1, 1990, to July 30, 1991. This clearly demonstrates a change in what the media thought would be acceptable to the Japanese public and also what that public would consider to be of interest. Additional information can be found at: https://gateway.nifty.com/service/g-way/mmdb/aps/RXCN/main.jsp?ssid=20070528171417193acropolis02.

any circumstances ("Jieitai Haken 78% ga Hantai", *Asahi Shimbun*, November 6, 1990). In part, the attempt to push through legislation lacked any prior serious discussion that could have provided an invaluable groundwork in forming a consensus behind the bill.

As a result, any serious consideration of making this type of humanitarian contribution remained an option devoid of any credibility. The Gulf War reconfirmed strong public opposition to seeing Japanese troops abroad, even if they were serving in an UN-endorsed peace-keeping mission. But this sentiment was not restricted to the general Japanese public. Politicians and bureaucrats alike resisted any change, especially of such a dramatic nature. As pointed out, with the JSP vehemently opposed to such LDP-inspired policies, it was quite natural that the bill would soon be dropped. The more left-wing opposition maintained that both the SDF and the US–Japan Security Treaty were simply unconstitutional. Consequently, this meant that the LDP Strategy of cloaking the SDF under the guise of a humanitarian gesture did not go far in placating the JSP. For these socialists, a humanitarian contribution by the SDF remained a contradiction in terms and was definitely not acceptable. In contrast, the LDP relentlessly interpreted Article 9 of the Constitution, which renounces belligerency and forbids the possession of military forces, as not limiting the right of self-defense. Under this analysis, the SDF was unquestionably constitutional. However, both parties ultimately appeared reluctant to enter into or to participate in a national debate that might challenge their entrenched positions. Even 45 years after World War II, sensitivities over military matters were acute. Reinforcing these difficulties were the still unresolved legal issues as to whether the SDF itself or sending troops overseas might be legitimate.

Bereft of either the strong leadership which could pull an issue forward or the type of government consensus that could push steadily from behind, the bill authorizing a troop dispatch lay abandoned even before legislative deliberations had been fully completed. A similar attempt to use SDF forces to transport refugees was likewise dropped. However, this episode did provide an opportunity, at least, to make a stab at initiating a proper debate over the constitutionality of dispatching the SDF abroad to settle armed conflicts.

5.4 Letting Loose: Factors Creating a New Path for the Japanese

Precipitated by the Gulf War, the resulting crisis provided a much needed opportunity for both the public and the government to reconsider their stands on security matters. Despite an absence of any immediate change, a fertile seed was planted. Certainly, no immediate change could be noted. However, the harshness of international criticism subsequent to the Gulf War did have an enormous impact on Japan's wider perceptions, especially that of the government. Even though the Japanese had ultimately contributed $13 billion to help finance the war effort, Japan's erstwhile allies scorned Japan as once again providing support that was judged to be "too little, too late." However, it was the gratuitous snub administered by the Kuwaitis that registered most sharply with the Japanese government. The *New York Times* advertisement, meant to acknowledge Kuwait's appreciation and debt to the allied effort, deliberately contained no mention of Japan, nor did it deign to note its overwhelming financial support that had floated the allied effort. This flood of criticism (both explicit and implicit) caught the government unawares. As a result, the heretofore sacrosanct limitations on troop deployment appeared vulnerable.

These prohibitions had reached a stage where they might be challenged. A newly emerging political consensus was for the first time open to the argument that Japan's humanitarian contributions should not continue to be restricted to economic assistance. The Japanese had to at least consider supplementing its more traditional efforts with a willingness to deploy the SDF in peacekeeping missions and exercises (Ministry of Foreign Affairs, 1991, p. 23). Even more to the point, the very size of the financial largesse extorted from the Japanese by the multinational alliance changed the shape of the ensuing debate. The Japanese found it distasteful to finance such a large proportion of a military expedition without being permitted to influence or shape its subsequent deployment or the goals it hoped to achieve. A growing consensus within the country concluded that any future demands to share financial burdens should be shouldered only if it coincided with Japan's ability to exercise an independent and separate identity for its foreign policy (Ministry of Foreign Affairs, 1991, p. 24).

Soon after the conclusion of the war, a new strategy emerged that supported dispatching Marine Self Defense minesweepers to the Gulf region as part of a humanitarian mission. Initially Kaifu was again reluctant to act, but this time the proposal garnered both public and business support. This new-found domestic approval encouraged the government to send six mine sweepers to remove any devices still lurking in the open sea off Kuwait. The government promoted this initiative as a breakthrough in devising new and successful ways to play a significant international role without contravening Japan's peace constitution. This policy departure met with clear foreign approval, thus pushing forward Japan's changing perceptions about its role in the currently evolving international environment.

A public opinion survey at this time reflected the changing domestic perception following an extensive series of open debates and the successful operation of the mine sweepers. The overwhelming majority had been sceptical of any direct Japanese involvement in security affairs, especially those conducted by the SDF. The preferred option had remained the long-standing strategy of never venturing beyond economic assistance (Katzenstein and Okawara, 1993, p. 101). However, the end of the Cold War and the ensuing Gulf War gradually shifted public debate. The focus now centered on the exact nature of Japan's legitimate contributions to peace and stability rather than rehashing previously controversial issues such as those surrounding SDF legitimacy. This was a remarkable turnaround. As late as the 1980s, a clear majority still favored a strict policy limiting all initiatives to economic cooperation. After the Gulf War, however, poll results from October 1992 indicated that 68.7 percent of the Japanese people now thought that Japan's responsibility as a member of the UN extended to the "area of peace and stability of the world." Only 39.7 percent now limited Japanese actions to "economic assistance to developing countries" (*Yoron Chosa Nenkan*, 1993, p. 102). However by the 1990s, the actual dispatch of troops overseas was still a divisive issue. In 1985, a poll indicated that a clear majority of 63.6 percent opposed sending the SDF, with only 23.9 percent in support (*Yoron Chosa Nenkan*, 1985, p. 530).

But by 1993, those against were down to 47.3 percent, with 43 percent now being in favor (*Yoron Chosa Nenkan*, 1993, p. 418). These later figures still demonstrate that the public remained more receptive to limiting deployment to humanitarian missions alone. Public support had clearly moved away from restricting contributions to financial assistance. Such an approach had of course defined Japanese policy for some four decades. It was this change in public opinion that essentially enabled the government to explore new policy approaches.

Not coincidentally, Yoichiro Funabashi, an influential journalist, provided a new policy formulation at just this moment. He advocated a Japan that would become a global civilian power by shaping international outcomes through non-military means. This approach would include foreign aid, humanitarian relief, and peacekeeping operations.[13] Similarly, a leading LDP politician at that time, Ichiro Ozawa, promoted a vision of a Japan transforming itself into a "normal country." This formulation shared many of the same core ideas as that presented by Funabashi.[14] For him, becoming a "normal country" meant contributing militarily, when necessary, to sustain peace and stability in the world. In other words, Japan should strive to emerge as a fully fledged international power. Although these two proposals had somewhat different approaches, they did share a common view. Japan needed to make an international contribution that extended beyond the purely economic. In the future, Japan should not be satisfied with playing the role of a passive bystander, contributing large amounts of money without receiving anything tangible in return. By this time, the emergence of newly developed ideas had conclusively rejected the ideology behind more traditional policy approaches. This changed domestic situation worked to facilitate long-held LDP ambitions. Based on this perceived sea change, these politicians could now gain newly discovered support and cooperation from both the Komeito and the Democratic Socialist Parties in pushing through the peacekeeping legislation. (Although, as might be expected, the LDP had to make some key concessions before achieving this desired consensus.)

---

[13]This view was advocated by Japanese journalist Funabashi. See Funabashi (1991/92).
[14]Ozawa emphasized the need to debate security matters openly and to set clear rules on the use of Japan's military power. For Ozawa's insights, see Ozawa (1993, pp. 102–179, 1995).

In addition to the fortuitous change in public opinion, Prime Minister Miyazawa, unlike his predecessor Kaifu, was intent on repairing Japan's international reputation. He viewed Japan's one-country pacifism and yen diplomacy during the Gulf War as responsible for precipitating Japan's currently degraded posture.[15] Miyazawa calculated that Japan could only consolidate its power and revive its reputation by making a decisive gesture. Participation in the Cambodian peacekeeping operation seemed to provide a perfect opportunity to signal a major policy departure. In Miyazawa's estimation, giving the SDF a wider international scope represented a key first step in restoring Japan's reputation (Mikuriya and Watanabe, 1997, p. 89). His determination to push Japan down this path was clearly illustrated when a Japanese UN volunteer, Atsuhiko Nakata, and a Japanese civilian police officer, Haruyuki Takata, were killed in 1993. Although it was true that the public had gradually changed its evaluation of humanitarian assistance, the Japanese were still largely unprepared when it came to accepting such deadly risks. Only 8.8 percent of the population showed support for Japanese missions involving a real level of danger (*Yoron Chosa Nenkan*, 1992, p. 116). Despite a clear and increasing public unease with the decision to continue Japan's role in Cambodia, Miyazawa stood firm and refused to withdraw. He was afraid that a withdrawal now might fatally damage Japan's reputation and largely nullify all the good that Japan's efforts had so far accomplished.[16]

Public opinion then, while often divided on details, had started to swing sufficiently to allow for a transition to a historic policy departure. But besides this quantifiable shift, another essential change that created the possibility for this new direction was an absence of the destructive, but highly predictably "turf battles" that characterized the Japanese bureaucracy and often fragmented policy formation. Former Finance Minister Hashimoto had attributed Japan's slow and inconsistent response to the financial demands of the Gulf War to the

---

[15] Japan's vigorous diplomatic efforts invited international criticism. These critics viewed Japan as hastily attempting to enhance its political standing to compensate for its diplomatic failure during the Gulf War. For further analysis, see Hirata (2001, p. 109).

[16] Miyazawa remained confident that he would able to sway the public if only this one time. However, he was less sure that he would be able to repeat the performance. For details, see Iokibe (2001).

bureaucratic immobility caused by "turf consciousness" (Iokibe, 2002). This hesitant style of policy making had been largely responsible for generating harsh and unwanted international criticism. It was then natural for Hashimoto to suggest that the Cabinet Office take the lead in drafting the proposed legislation rather than acquiescing to MOFA's customary guidance. Employing standard practise, a bill encapsulating clear international implications would ordinarily rely heavily on MOFA's drafting skills. Alternatively, dispatching SDF troops was a matter falling within the jurisdiction of the Defense Agency. Considering the decidedly mixed nature of the legislation and the aggressive battles to maintain turf boundaries, in the ordinary conduct of business, reaching a consensus would remain outside the realm of possibility without efficient strong arming by a supremely confident Cabinet Office. The government overcame this potential fragmentation, which had constrained Japan's effective policy formation, by giving decisive authority and legitimacy to the Cabinet Office (Shinoda, 2006, p. 72). By granting such power, the government managed to break the log jam that had doomed previous policy initiatives.

With fragmentation ceasing to be a stumbling block, the government was free to exploit the perceived change in public sentiment. Adopting some variety of legislation permitting peacekeeping operations would no longer reliably attract the same degree of political risk. For this reason, despite the expected fierce opposition from the JSP, the government proved willing to force the bill through. This new approach was meant to forestall any future international criticism of the type painfully garnered during the Gulf War. The proposed bill would enable Japan to perform as a major power, not only economically, but in the military sphere as well.

The JSP, which had remained a strong advocate of a "pacifist Japan," had suffered electoral losses subsequent to the adoption of the peacekeeping legislation. These losses underpinned two changed circumstances. One entailed the recognition that the JSP was perhaps irretrievably losing its influence. The second indicated that the Japanese public had largely shed its apprehension of an expanded role for the military, provided it was restricted to humanitarian missions. The government took advantage of this historic shift in public opinion to embark on some essential steps that might make Japan's long-term aspiration of employing its potential power a reality. It was able to use the idea of fulfilling humanitarian obligations as its rationale. The Gulf War changed both public and political perceptions. The government opportunistically seized this opening to elevate Japan's standing and influence.

Triggered by the Gulf War, the Japanese government accomplished an impressive strategic shift. Japan's ability to do so reflected a transformation in both public and government perception. It was not simply a response to foreign pressure nor did it represent a real change in Japanese objectives. The shift in fact would greatly help Japan achieve its long-term goals by upgrading its status from a partially fledged power centering only on economic matters to one willing to bear its full responsibilities.[17] Japan had discovered an alternative approach that would allow for future international contributions without depending purely on its economic might.

5.5 Japanese are not Economic Animals: Lessons Learned

Unarguably, Japan had concentrated on economic matters throughout the post-war period. However, it is too simplistic to conclude that Japan's objective was strictly limited to increasing its economic muscle. While by necessity directing resources to economic growth, Japan had never given up searching for a chance to play a significant political-military role, albeit as a responsible member of the international community. Under its long-term pacifist culture, however, this desire to perform as a full-fledged power had not been translated into concrete policy. Domestic obstacles were overwhelming. Without a legitimate reason to involve itself in security matters, the Japanese government had either kept its distance, or engaged indirectly by utilizing economic leverage. Constrained by domestic factors, no alternative avenues existed during the Cold War period.

---

[17] Japan's contribution to peacekeeping operations, starting with Cambodia in 1992, was followed by missions in Mozambique, Rwanda, El Salvador, and the Golan Heights.

However, when a departure became possible, Japan was willing to abandon its traditional approach of economic assistance and quiet diplomacy. In its place, Japan adopted a new strategy to achieve its goal, namely, justifying the deployment of troops to achieve commendable humanitarian goals. Cambodia, where successive Japanese governments had hoped to play a political role, provided an opportunity to make a remarkable policy shift. Changed perceptions by the Japanese created the possibility for a new strategic direction. This chapter has demonstrated that the Gulf War cut through limitations implicitly imposed by public opinion and perception. Once this obstacle was effectively removed, the LDP-dominated government of the day could adopt a set of congruent tactics to move closer to its goals.

That Japanese sensitivity to military matters would continue to circumscribe the extent and nature of overseas operations cannot be denied. However, international humanitarian assistance within a UN framework tempered any possible public hypersensitivity provoked by military issues. Consequently, by participating in a peacekeeping mission in Cambodia, Japan managed to move one step closer to achieving its desire for international leadership and influence. An opening had been created by determined policy makers, which in the future could allow the SDF to play a larger political/military role.

References

Berger TU. (1998) *Cultures of Anti-Militarism: National Security in Germany and Japan.* Johns Hopkins University Press, London, Baltimore.

Dobson H. (2003) *Japan and United Nations Peacekeeping.* Routledge Curson, London.

Ebashi M, Onozawa J. (2000) *Asia Keizai Handbook 2001.* Zennichi houki, Tokyo.

Funabashi Y. (1991/92) Japan and the New World Order. *Foreign Affairs*, 70(5), 58–74.

Hirata K. (2001) Reaction and action: Analyzing Japan's relations with the Socialist Republic of Vietnam. In: Maswood SY (ed.), *Regionalism and Japan: The Bases of Trust and Leadership*, pp. 90–117. Routledge, New York.

Inoguch T. (1993) *Japan's Foreign Policy in an Era of Global Change.* Pinter Publishers Ltd, London.

International Monetary Fund. (2004) Direction of trade statistics. *IMF Statistics.* http://www.imfstatistics.org/dot/, May 2004.

Iokibe M. (2001) Nihon Gaiko interview series (1) Miyazawa Kiichi. *Kokusai Mondai*, November, 56–79.

Iokibe M. (2002) Interview series 3, Hashimoto Ryutaro, Kokusai Mondai. 504(March), pp. 62–79.

Ito K. (1991) The Japanese state of mind: Deliberations on the Gulf crisis. *Journal of Japanese Studies*, 17(2), 275–290.

Japan Customs. (2004) Trade statistics. *Japan Customs Statistics*, http://www.customs.go.jp/toukei/srch/, accessed in May 2004.

Katzenstein PJ. (1996) *Cultural Norms and National Security: Police and Military in Post-War Japan*. Cornell University Press, Ithaca and London.

Katzenstein PJ, Okawara N. (1993) Japan's national security: structures, norms and policies. *International Security*, 17(4), 58–74.

Kawamura Y. [MOFA press secretary] (2000) Visit to Southeast Asia by Prime Minister Keizo Obuchi and details of his meeting with Prime Minister Hun Sen of the Kingdom of Cambodia. Press Conference by the Press Secretary, 12 January 2000. http://www.mofa.go.jp/announce/press/2000/1/112.html#2, accessed July 2003.

Kono M. (1999) *Wahei Kosaku: Tai Kanbojia Gaiko no Shogen*. Iwanami Shoten, Tokyo.

Ministry of Foreign Affairs. (2004) Kokuren Heiwa Iji Katsudo kanren shiryo. Unpublished Paper 3.

Ministry of Foreign Affairs. (1992) *Diplomatic Bluebook 1992*. Okurasho Insatsukyoku, Tokyo.

Ministry of Foreign Affairs. (1991) *Diplomatic Bluebook 1991*. Okurasho Insatsukyoku, Tokyo.

Ministry of Foreign Affairs. (1990) *Diplomatic Bluebook 1990*. Okurasho Insatsukyoku, Tokyo.

Ministry of Foreign Affairs. (1989) *Diplomatic Bluebook 1989*. Okurasho Insatsukyoku, Tokyo.

Ministry of Foreign Affairs. (1988) *Diplomatic Bluebook 1988*. Okurasho Insatsukyoku, Tokyo.

Mikuriya T, Watanabe A. (1997) *Shusho Kantei no Ketsudan: Naikaku Kanbo Fukuchokan Ishihara Nobuo no 2600 Nichi*. Chuo Korn, Tokyo.

Miyazawa K. (1992) Policy speech by Prime Minister Kiichi Miyazawa to the 122nd Session of the National Diet on 8 November 1991. *Diplomatic Bluebook 1992*.

Nakayama T. (1990) Foreign Minister Nakayama's foreign policy speech to the 118th session of the National Diet. *Diplomatic Bluebook*. March.

Ogura S. (1999) Kenshou: Kanbojia Wahei to Nihon Gaiko. *Sekai*. November, 129–148.

Okamoto Y. (2001) Mata Onaji Koto ni Naranaika. *Gaiko Forum*, 158(September), 12–20.

Ozawa I. (1995) Futsu no Kuni ni Nare. In *Sengo Nihon Gaikou Ronshu*: Kitaoka S (ed.), pp. 461–482. Chuo koron, Tokyo.

Ozawa I. (1993) *Nihon Kaizou Keikakku*. Kodansha, Tokyo.

Shinoda T. (2006) Reisengo no Nihon Gaiko: Anzenhosho Seisaku no Kokusai Seiji Katei, Mineruba Shobo, Tokyo.

Smith SA. (1999) The evolution of military cooperation in the US–Japan alliance. In: Green MJ, Cronin PM (eds.), *The US–Japan Alliance: Past, Present, and Future*, pp. 69–93. Council on Foreign Relations Press, New York.

Takahashi T. (2001) Hatten to Hanei no 10 Nen no Jitsugen ni Mukete. *Gaiko Forum*, 159(October), 86–91.

Tanaka A. (1997) *Anzenhosho: Sengo 50 Nen no Mosaku*. Yomiuri shimbun sha, Tokyo.

Watanabe A. (2003) Has Japan crossed the Rubicon? *Japan Review of International Affairs*, 17(1), 238–254.

Chapter 6

More Peacekeeping Operations:
The Case of East Timor

6.1 East Timor: Opportunity or Pitfall

We have previously examined the way in which the shock of the Gulf War forced both the Japanese government and the public to re-evaluate their standard assumptions about security issues. With public opinion concerning military matters evolving, the usual no-go zone created by embedded post-war pacifism was gradually vanishing. Without these traditional roadblocks created by hitherto predictable popular reaction, the Japanese government was now able to think "the unthinkable" in terms of discussing and even initiating new approaches to security matters. For decades, overseas policy had been defined by the limits that using economic assistance as its major diplomatic tool created. As we have seen, Japan was encouraged by perceived changes in public sentiment to push forward with an uncharacteristic peacekeeping operation in Cambodia, albeit strictly under the auspices of the UN. This new look to foreign policy promised an approach that would make a more direct and explicit contribution, whatever the issue might be. Japan hoped this policy departure would effectively boost its international standing from the depths achieved during the Gulf War, and do so without stirring the predictable regional fears about emerging Japanese ambitions. However, the preferred multilateral approach was engineered not only to avoid regional complications, but to placate previously hypersensitive domestic opinion. In the past, any indication, or even mention, that Japan intended to dispatch Self-Defense Forces (SDF) overseas would have caused an immediate and politically uncontrollable backlash.

With a successful operation in Cambodia behind it, East Timor presented a perfect opportunity for Japan to continue and extend its reach. The Japanese could use the occasion to provide an unmistakable signal of their intention to play a leading role in securing regional stability. According to the Minister of the Defense Agency at that time, Hajime Nakatani, Japan intended to give clear priority status to peacekeeping operations within the region (*Asahi Shimbun*, August 22, 2002). This seemed the most direct way to achieve Japan's regional objectives. However, quite at odds with such a precisely specified claim, in practice Japan remained at best diffident to the deteriorating local situation in East Timor. Japan's government seemed incapable of seeing in this situation a clear opportunity to pursue a more active and aggressive regional policy. This was possibly justifiable when initial peacekeeping efforts were limited to an Australian-led multinational force. But Japan still dragged its feet when a UN-sanctioned operation replaced that of the Australians. Only with time, and with what might be perceived as an unfortunate reluctance, did Japan finally dispatch a contingent of SDF troops to assist in the reconstruction of East Timor.

In this chapter we examine Japan's apparently inconsistent approach in East Timor, namely the desire to expand its regional profile overlaid by an older, lingering hesitancy not to get involved. These contradictory motives generate two distinct and pertinent questions.

1. Before 2002, why was Japan determined to avoid dispatching even civilian officers to this particular UN peacekeeping operation? As a natural follow-up to its Cambodian contribution, joining the East Timor effort would have reinforced Japan's avowed intent to make more than just a financial contribution toward securing regional peace and stability. Maintaining this consistent strategy was clearly Japan's most effective route to achieving its desired level of influence. Is such a contradictory behavior explicable?

Actions so seemingly at odds with intentions can often become more comprehensible once a believable set of strong, mitigating factors can be identified as operative during the period in question. Without discovering such a rationale, Japan's foreign policy could only be described as erratic. Such a categorization would deprive Japanese diplomacy of the underlying consistency which forms the core assumption at the heart of our analysis.

2. Equally mystifying are Japan's initiatives after 2002. A complete turnaround saw Japan refigure its diplomatic position by dispatching a record number of peacekeeping troops. What, in fact, motivated such a dramatic change of heart? In other words, the following pages delve deeply into the factors that first impeded Japan's underlying drive for regional recognition and influence. The same controlling factors then seemingly vanished just as suddenly as they appeared. To resolve these paradoxical events, we will demonstrate that East Timor does not represent a diplomatic aberration for Japan, but is rather consistent with both the tone and objectives defined by Japanese foreign policy.

6.2 Conflict in East Timor: From Peripheral to Central Concern

Over the decades, East Timor had remained in the very periphery of Japan's diplomatic concerns. In stark contrast, Indonesia had always featured as a key player in America's Cold War strategy. This position meant that Japan had long extended economic assistance to support Indonesia's development in accord with its own interests and that of its American ally. Given this context, Japan was left largely unmoved by Indonesia's unilateral annexation of this former Portuguese colony in 1976. The pretext of communist containment was a sufficient justification to lull any Japanese suspicions, as well as that of other regional players like Australia or the US. Indonesia had counted on meeting the minimum requirements necessary to retain support by providing a rationale which was convenient for the Japanese, among others, to believe. In contrast to such expediency, the UN never recognized the legitimacy of this act of Indonesian aggrandizement. But at the time, the US had more pressing concerns than evaluating elements of justice or fairness in this act of aggression.

Despite a broader Asian disengagement following the Vietnam War, the US was still focused on communist containment. Consistent with this strategy, America had no intention of ruffling a key ally, namely the Suharto regime in Indonesia. This strong vested interest made it all too easy to acquiesce in the brutal takeover of what was regarded as a rather insignificant bit of geography. As has almost always been the case, ASEAN countries were loathe to chastise one of their own. Bowing to this dominant reality, Japan followed suit in ignoring the status of East Timor. However, even such tacit regional agreement failed to settle the matter. After the annexation, confrontations continued between pro-independence and pro-integration groups in East Timor. Despite the relative legitimacy of the opposing sides, Japan continued to take a strictly pragmatic line. As an ASEAN leader, Indonesia would quite naturally exert some measurable influence on Japan's foreign policy. Japan was thus complicit, along with the other Western collaborators, in propping up a questionable East Timor policy. However, despite the widespread show of support, the status quo was eventually upset. After years of being on an international slow boil, by the 1990s, East Timor began to gain increasing attention.

The situation in East Timor started to deteriorate rapidly by 1999, with Indonesia no longer capable of keeping the local strife contained. Confrontations between pro-independence and pro-integration groups grew on an almost weekly basis. However, hope did momentarily blossom. A tenable settlement between the Indonesian-backed militia and the East Timor independence movement seemed possible with the fall of Suharto and the installation of the Bacharuddin Jusuf Habibie government. Habibie took a new approach to East Timor, agreeing that a direct referendum would be staged in August 1999. One result of this policy shift was the creation of a United Nations Mission in East Timor (UNAMET) in June of that same year. Falling prey to the bureaucratic measures beloved by UN administrators, that organization by October 1999 had been reborn as the UN Transitional Administration in East Timor (UNTAET). This UN-led mission seemed to present a golden opportunity for the Japanese government that was purportedly intent on flexing its diplomatic muscles. It had done so previously by taking a series of tentative steps in Cambodia. Instead, the Japanese government deliberately chose to maintain a consistently low profile.[1] Rather than supporting such measures, Japan opted to signal its displeasure with this multilateral style of intervention by contributing few personnel to UNAMET. Even once the United Nations had Indonesia's backing, the Japanese still persisted in limiting their contribution to a token gesture of dispatching only three officials (including civilian police) by July 1999 (*Asahi Shimbun*, July 8, 1999). Contrasting sharply with its Cambodian experience where 75 civilian officers made up the Japanese contingent, only three among the 280 officers in UNAMET contingent hailed from Japan. This seemed a curious pose to strike, given Japan's long-held wish to function as a major regional power.

The September 1999 referendum led to a landslide victory (78.5 percent) by pro-independence groups. The Indonesian government in turn, announced its intention to honor and accept the result. Unfortunately, this acceptance did not end the matter. Instead, the East Timor situation deteriorated rapidly. Pro-integration militia, allegedly backed by the Indonesian military, staged a fierce resistance. These militiamen murdered East Timorese while many others were displaced in the ensuing conflict. Renegade forces even went so far as to attack the personnel serving with international organizations. This outbreak caused the Indonesian government to dispatch a military force to East Timor, ostensibly to restore order. As a first step, Indonesia declared martial law on September 7, 1999. Such measures did nothing to actively resolve the building crisis. Even worse, these events caused mounting suspicion to be focused upon the Indonesian military, who were thought to be backing and in fact manipulating the pro-integration militia.

Faced with these atrocities, independence leader, Jose Ramos-Horta, strongly reminded the West of its humanitarian obligation to intervene (*Washington Post*, September 9, 1999). This call was heightened by the atrocities committed by the pro-integration militia

---

[1] Prime Minister Hashimoto did not see Ramos Horta, a leader of the East Timorese independence movement, when he visited Japan in 1997. However, Foreign Minister Koumura met a pro-independence leader, Xanana Gusumao, who was under house arrest in Jakarta, after the establishment of UNAMET.

and broadcast throughout the international community. As a result, rising worldwide pressure insisted that the Indonesian government take matters in hand and restore stability and order to this troubled island. Undergoing a serious change in policy, Australia responded to the deteriorating situation by suggesting a more direct form of intervention. Priding themselves on being the self-appointed sheriffs of the region, the Australians rapidly dispatched troops to enforce peace in East Timor. However, the US was not yet quite so keen to see peacekeeping forces unleashed without the explicit consent of their staunch regional ally, Indonesia. Given its broader strategic interests, the US viewed such aggressive measures as imposing an unwanted risk on its potentially fragile relationship with an Indonesia still in transition from the Suharto military government (Hadar, 1999). Japan following suit also looked for an explicit American go ahead before committing itself to any such mission.[2]

However, by September 10, the Clinton administration decided that given the way the East Timor situation was evolving, it was now unambiguously expedient to change previous US policy. The Americans proceeded to switch positions by threatening to re-evaluate future aid unless the Indonesian government agreed to accept peacekeeping troops (Harder, 1999). Fortunately, the concerned powers, including Indonesia, managed to reach an international consensus on intervention during the September 9–10 APEC meeting in Auckland (Gorjao, 2002). Facing increasing international pressure, the Japanese government began trimming its diplomatic sails so as to align its policy with the emerging regional consensus. Though unwilling to apply direct pressure, the Japanese did attempt to persuade the Indonesian government that it would be wise to agree to an Australian-led multinational force. In fact, on September 11, the very day after the US policy shift, Japanese Foreign Minister Koumura met with Dr Ir Ginandjar Kartasasmita, Coordinating Minister for Economy, Finance, and Industry, to persuade Indonesia to accept such a multinational force. The Indonesian government agreed on that same day and informed Japan of its intention, before Indonesia officially announced its acceptance

---

[2] MOFA, Press Conference by the Press Secretary, September 17, 1999. The full transcript can be found at http://www.mofa.go.jp/announce/press/1999/9/917.html#5.

(*Asahi Shimbun*, September 24, 1999). Indonesia's agreement finally opened the way for the implementation of UN Security Council Resolution 1264, which endorsed the dispatch of a multinational force to East Timor.

At this time, there was no question of Japan participating as part of the proposed expedition. Japan technically could not do so (Komura, 1999). Even if the force had been officially under the UN command, Japan would have found it legally impossible to release the required troops. At this relevant moment, a certain portion of the law legitimizing peacekeeping operations was in a virtual legal "freeze." To "defreeze," the law required another piece of enabling legislation. Facing unsympathetic reaction to what appeared to be no more than a technical excuse, the Japanese government faced the contradictory and irreconcilable expectations held by the United Nations, Indonesia, and many of the other involved countries. Japan had created something of a self-inflicted diplomatic wound by previously choosing to portray itself as a regional power. However, staking out this policy position implied that the Japanese now had to be prepared to accept the burdens and even disagreeable responsibilities that came with assuming such a role. Given its professed commitment, Japan could no longer afford to cling to its convenient post-war position of the non-involved bystander. From a practical point of view, these raised expectations meant that the Japanese government needed to demonstrate its position as a regional player both domestically and internationally and to do so as soon as possible (*Gaiko Kiroku*, 2004-469, September 19, 1999). Instead, to avoid confrontations, the Japanese tried to stave off potential criticism by resorting to a number of ad hoc measures. In November 1999, the Japanese government dispatched an SDF unit to help transport aid resources to those East Timorese displaced in West Timor. In this instance, Japan was responding to a direct request by the UN High Commissioner for Refugees.

Seeking to provide yet another alternative, Japan fell back on its tried and true method of easing a troubling dilemma by making a financial contribution. In December 1999, the Japanese government held the first Donors' Meeting for East Timor. Japan immediately set the standard by pledging the largest aid package, consisting of approximately $100 million for reconstruction and development assistance and $30 million for humanitarian relief. The package also provided $2 million to the multinational peacekeeping force. Responding to an Australian demand, it gave another $100 million to underwrite those Asian countries directly participating in the multinational force (*Asahi Shimbun*, September 16, 2002). (Indonesia had made it abundantly clear that they wished for more ASEAN participation in the multinational force to counterbalance the Australian contingent.) The Indonesians welcomed the Japanese contribution, which by keeping Australia's growing political influence in check, helped to alleviate their fears. But the Australians had actually requested the support in the first place. They welcomed Japan's financial contribution, since it tempered Indonesia's anti-Australian sentiment by offsetting their own forces with more acceptable soldiers from the ASEAN countries (*Asahi Shimbun*, September 16, 2002). Since money is seldom turned away, all the relevant countries agreed in welcoming Japan's economic contribution. Still, Japan shied away from taking the final step and committing troops to enforce and maintain the peace. The ruling SDF law effectively blocked this possibility. Fortunately for the Japanese, the East Timorese situation subsequently improved, providing Japan more numerous and less controversial opportunities for involvement.

Soon after the deployment of the Australian-led multinational forces, the situation on the ground took a turn for the better. This change allowed UN-sanctioned peacekeepers to replace the more controversial multinational force as of February 2000. By this means, such a substitution, at least technically, provided the Japanese with the opportunity to participate in a peacekeeping operation under the aegis of UNTAET. Participation of this variety would not require any new enabling legislation (Ministry of Foreign Affairs, 2002). However, the security situation unpredictably shifted in the opposite direction. Renegade militia staged a series of armed attacks aimed at the UN troops and those East Timorese people residing along the border and in refugee camps located within West Timor. This change of events overrode the technical feasibility of any proposed troop contribution. Responding to the new developments, the Japanese government remained reluctant to move forward on the peacekeeping issue. Instead, Japan sought a rationale for avoiding such an urgent problem. Japan explained its inaction by discovering reasons to question the validity of the cease-fire agreement between the two warring parties. Uppermost in Japan's thinking was the memory of casualties sustained in Cambodia. Japan would now do its best not to test its resolve in that way again.

For a country with professed regional power aspirations, Japan, during this initial period, had opted for a curiously minimalist approach. Though officially restricted in its use of SDF troops, Japan deliberately chose to send only a few civilian officers. Even after it became technically possible, Japan carefully avoided participation in any of the UN-sponsored peacekeeping operations. The Japanese claimed that the fragile situation in East Timor meant that the circumstance did not sufficiently comply with its five principles of commitment (agreement on a ceasefire; consent of all parties in the conflict to the deployment of the peacekeeping forces, etc.). However, the Japanese, when faced with a somewhat changed environment would later find that it could quite easily switch to a more active role. When convenient, its position as a regional bystander could be abjured.

In fact, by February 2002, the Japanese government had altered its position by belatedly dispatching a SDF Engineering Unit to participate in East Timorese reconstruction. The troop's purpose was to support logistic operations as well as assisting in road and bridge repair. By this time, with many troops on the ground and NGOs operating freely, there was really no pressing need for any SDF soldiers of this type to augment the existing ground forces. Fortunately for the Japanese, an expedient face-saving opportunity arose. The withdrawal of Pakistani forces created something of a vacuum that the Japanese could then conveniently fill. In April of that year, Japan replaced the departing Pakistanis in East Timor by taking on the previously described tasks including repairing bridges and roads (Japan Defense Agency, 2002). By international standards, this belated contribution to peacekeeping operations was still relatively small. Of the 85 nations with representatives in the UN force, Japan ranked only as high as 17th in the number of participating troops.

However, for Japan, East Timor represented another watershed. The actual number of SDF personnel represented its largest peacekeeping contribution yet (Ministry of Foreign Affairs, 2003).

Japan hoped that the size of its contingent would cause the lateness of the contribution to be largely overlooked. Though tardy, the Japanese wanted to believe that the very enthusiasm with which they finally shouldered their obligation would erase any lingering impression that Japan was willing to remain coolly indifferent to deteriorating and life-threatening situations, like the one that had unfolded in East Timor. As is often the case, the dispatch of the SDF was expeditiously followed by a public relations visit from Prime Minister Koizumi. This appearance was clearly a media event aimed at boosting Japan's international profile as well as securing domestic support within Japan. Subsequently, Koizumi was also at hand in April 2002 to celebrate East Timorese independence. The official ceremony served to highlight Japan's positive involvement in East Timor's reconstruction through the exemplary work performed by the SDF.

As it had done in other situations during the post-war period, once again, Japan showed a certain naivety in its diplomatic expectations. The Japanese government had anticipated that its efforts in East Timor would pay-off in terms of tangible influence. Japan's policies had, after all, been tailored specifically in order to portray Japan as a fully fledged power. Unfortunately, in the case of East Timor, such recognition and influence was not to be. Japan's belated participation and partisanship could not entirely negate its previous indifference and lack of commitment. At the independence ceremony, the name of Masatake Sugiura, Vice-Foreign Minister, far from being honored, was excluded from the official list of appreciation as part of a deliberate snub (*Asahi Shimbun*, May 21, 2002).[3] At this early stage, it seemed that the immediate pay-off from Japan's participation in this particular peacekeeping operation was neither impressive nor productive.

6.3 Deviant Behavior: Japan's Stubborn Reluctance to Join the Party

The mystery then is why Japan seemed to deliberately eschew the opportunity provided during the initial stages of the East Timor crisis.

---

[3] A MOFA official explained that Sugiura was neither Prime Minister nor Foreign Minister.

Clearly, Japan could have dispatched the SDF as a component of UNTAET or compromised by sending a reasonable number of civilian operatives to either UNAMET or UNTAET. As a relatively conservative measure, such personnel movements would have openly signaled Japan's readiness and dedication to playing an expanded role in insuring regional peace and stability. Since its Cambodian experience, Japan had shown itself willing by sending off troops to five different peacekeeping operations. However, none of these efforts were located within a relevant neighboring nation. If carried out, peacekeeping in East Timor would represent only Japan's second regional effort. Instead, Japan turned down the opportunity provided by the East Timor crisis. Perceiving it to be the only wise alternative course of action, Japan cautiously dispatched only three civilian officers to either UNAMET or UNTAET during the first, and most vital, stage of the crisis. The Japanese stuck with their decision, seeming to ignore the fact that this initial period was when the situation on the ground provided the greatest potential for harvesting gains. Given the chance to demonstrate its willingness to contribute to regional stability, Japan was not to be moved.

It could be argued in Japan's defense (as previously noted) that the Japanese were technically restricted from allowing SDF troops to be part of a multinational force. It is possible to counter that such obstacles had been seemingly overcome in the past (and would be in the future) under different circumstances, when the required will to do so was present. Moreover, this rationale fails to explain Japan's continued reluctance even after February 2000 when UN peacekeepers had replaced the multinational force. Given the key changed circumstances (operating under the arc of a UN-sanctioned intervention), participation under the newly organized UNTAET should have posed no problems (Ministry of Foreign Affairs, 2002). It was an almost heaven-sent opportunity for Japan to pose as a leader by demonstrating its readiness to contribute to a workable regional architecture that assured stability. Yet, given this tempting situation, the Japanese government initially chose not to participate. Instead, it seemed to almost relish dodging its expected role by hiding behind a rather rigid interpretation of the peacekeeping operations law. Almost two years would go by before the Japanese government was willing to send the SDF to East Timor as part of a peacekeeping initiative. Is it possible then to explain satisfactorily what would otherwise appear to be a glaring inconsistency in Japan's diplomatic practises?

6.3.1 *Holding Off: The Story behind Japan's Initial Non-participation Decision*

Without question, East Timor had played at best a marginal role in Japan's Asia policy. East Timor was the focus of no economic, political, or discernible strategic interest within Japan's diplomatic reach. In contrast, Indonesia had long been central to a variety of Japanese concerns. As has been previously emphasized, the thrust of the Fukuda Doctrine, and the objectives driving that administration, positioned ASEAN as one of the pillars of diplomatic policy. Indonesia, which viewed itself as a self-anointed leader of ASEAN, would almost automatically then become of central concern to the Japanese. Of course, minimizing the importance that a country rich in oil and natural gas would hold for a resource-hungry nation like Japan would be unwise. Japan's almost desperate efforts to assure guaranteed sources of energy supply had led to initiatives like North Sumatra Oil in the 1960s and the Asahan Project a decade later.[4] With Indonesia long established as a key supplier of vital resources, assuming a critical or otherwise controversial stance to Indonesian policies became unlikely.

---

[4] North Sumatra Oil involved a joint project with the national oil company of Indonesia, Permina (now Pertamina) and the North Sumatra Oil Development Corporation (Japan) to explore for oil in North Sumatra. This was less important than what became known as the "Asahan formula." For Japan, this marked a new approach to foreign aid (mentioned in Chapter 4). The Japanese government would not only assist the host country for the proposed project (Indonesia) but simultaneously assist Japanese corporations to develop the project. This would be the model for foreign assistance adopted in many subsequent initiatives. For the Asahan Project, three agencies [Overseas Economic Cooperation Fund (OECF), Japan International Cooperation Agency (JICA), and the Ex-Im Bank of Japan] provided funding.

> The Asahan project involved the construction of *a large dam, a hydroelectric power station* on the Asahan River and *an aluminium refinery* that would use the power generated and related infrastructural facilities in Sumatra, Indonesia. The idea was first brought by the Indonesian government to the attention of Sumitomo Chemical, which organized a feasibility study team in August 1970 — in collaboration with two other Japanese smelters,

With the economic importance of Indonesia being basically unchallengeable, the Japanese were more likely to placate rather than confront. To add to its importance, between 1990 and 2002, the Indonesians managed to establish themselves as one of Japan's top six sources for imported goods (Japan External Trade Organization, 2005). Moreover, Japan's dependency on Indonesian natural resources grew to reach a level of $12.6 billion by 1999. In contrast, Japanese exports, limited to mainly machinery, registered only some $1.9 billion in the same year. Cementing that vital flow of imports made Indonesia automatically one of Japan's largest aid recipients. When the East Timor crisis gained prominence, nothing much had occurred to change this situation. The Japanese assistance program to Indonesia started in 1966. By 1999, a package worth some $1.6 billion made the country one of the biggest recipients of Japanese aid, in fact trailing only behind China. The breadth of Japan's development investments in Indonesia amounted to 1,361 projects and 1631.8 billion yen, all established between the years of 1989 and 2002.[5] Such figures did fall short of the 4,141 projects and 2105.8 billion yen sunk into China, but emphatically exceeded the 885 projects and 1008.5 billion yen poured into the Philippines. Indonesia, geographically, also occupied a central position within Japan's maritime transport system.

Therefore, both the Japanese government and the Japanese business community had ample reasons for currying Indonesia's favor. Bucharuddin Jusuf Habibie more than adequately summed up the essence of the two countries' close relationship and virtual interdependence by stating, "Japan is not our friend but our family" (*Asahi Shimbun*, September 24, 1999). Given these vital, yet potentially fragile ties, Japan had every reason not to roil the waters by taking on board the highly charged issue of East Timorese independence. To deliberately undermine the years invested in establishing a good relationship with

---

Nippon Light Metal and Showa Denko. Soon afterwards, the group was expanded to include Mitsubishi Chemical Industries and Mitsui Aluminum, thus becoming a collaborative venture among Japan's top industrial group (Ozawa, 2008, p. 16).

[5]Calculated from Ministry of Finance Statistics. The statistics are available at http://www.mof.go.jp/fdi/sankou01.xls, accessed in April 2005.

Indonesia would have seemed to be the height of insanity. Japan had every reason, both economic and strategic, for toeing a perhaps overly cautious line when it came to Indonesian concerns.

Even before East Timor became something of an international cause celebre in the late 1990s, the incident that became known as the Santa Cruz massacre sadly had failed to register with the Japanese public. At this earlier stage, the underlying constraints on Japan's behavior were holding quite effectively. The incident in question was an attempt to brutally suppress pro-independence demonstrations in 1991, leading to a few hundred deaths in East Timor. The massacre attracted international attention. The US responded by demanding the dispatch of a UN investigation team. Taking a clearly contrasting position, the Japanese government clung desperately to the sidelines by simply abstaining when the motion reached a vote in 1993 (*Asahi Shimbun,* July 8, 1999). The Japanese government obviously hoped that the appearance of assuming a hands-off policy would be sufficient to placate the Indonesian government. The potential for grabbing a leadership role in East Timor's affairs simply failed to measure up against the assured comfort of fostering an increasingly valuable relationship with Indonesia.

This episode established a distinct pattern which made it almost natural for Japan to shy away from any apparently volatile situation. The Japanese preferred to cling to what they perceived as the low-risk option in any crisis. Quite naturally then, even when faced with a rapidly deteriorating situation in East Timor, the Japanese government still staunchly supported the Indonesians. The government was quite reluctant to exert any controversial influence, even though by this time, the international community was pressuring the Indonesian government to accept a multinational force. The presence of a mounting international consensus, not any exigent humanitarian considerations, ultimately moved Japan to "advise" Indonesia on this issue in September 1999. In other words, fear of becoming internationally isolated forced the Japanese government to suggest to the Indonesians that the time had come to rectify the situation. Japan claimed to be providing this advice as a "friend" (Numata, 1999). This nuanced shift should not be taken as evidence that Japan's policy had become more sympathetic to an independent East Timor. Each Japanese step signaled what might, with only a touch of exaggeration, be characterized as policy making under extreme duress. Japan's continuing partisanship attached to this issue displayed where its true sympathies lay.

Back on the ground, the East Timorese situation had failed to stabilize even with direct Indonesian intervention. The Report of the High Commissioner for Human Rights stated that on September 23–24, 1999, Indonesian military personnel acquiesced as local militia continued a campaign of violence. The militia was now armed with automatic weapons and hand grenades, although they had depended on homemade guns prior to the vote (United Nations Commission on Human Rights, 1999). However, along with Indonesia, China, Cuba, India, the Philippines, Russia, and Sudan, the Japanese government voted against establishing a committee to investigate killings and disturbances in East Timor (United Nations Commission on Human Rights, 1999). Japan justified its vote on the grounds that the Indonesian government already had announced its own investigation into abuses allegedly attributed to Indonesian-backed militias (Hatakeyama, interview with an anonymous MOFA official, April 2004). Father Bello of East Timor, a Nobel laureate, harshly criticized Japan's partisan and self-interested stance in continuing to support the Indonesian government (*Asahi Shimbun*, October 9, 1999).

Japan, however, maintained a strikingly consistent, though highly biased, position relative to this issue. Its strong ties to Indonesia meant that Japan, whenever possible, would oppose investigative committees, be reluctant to send civilian officers to UNAMET or participate in any UN peacekeeping operations. Akira Takahashi, from the Japanese International Cooperation Agency (JICA), had been appointed Deputy Representative of the reconstruction division of UNTAET. The government insisted that he should be obliged to consult closely with the Indonesian government, rather than with leaders of East Timor's independence movement (*Gaiko Kiroku*, 2004-467, p. 17). Self-defined Japanese interests in Indonesia effectively constrained Japan from taking the sort of leadership role that it would have otherwise adopted. Instead, Japanese diplomats seemed intent on stalling any proposal that might embarass their Indonesian friends. Under these circumstances, the Japanese considered the potential benefits of being in the East Timor vanguard, not worth the perceived risks.

Moreover, it was not just Japan's Indonesian policy that restricted its willingness to participate in peacekeeping operations. Domestic reaction, once again, acted to limit the Japanese government politically. East Timor did not register strongly with the Japanese public. The East Timorese issue remained muddled for most voters or simply ignored. Without sufficient public sympathy, the Japanese government remained reluctant to seize such a high-risk option. In contrast, when Iraq invaded Kuwait, this was deemed indisputably intolerable, even by the usually disinterested Japanese citizens. The prevailing perception was that Iraq had clearly violated international law. Faced with such open aggression, the Japanese public was able to grasp that unilateral invasions of this type could not be tolerated. As we have seen, the issue at that time was not whether to respond, but the nature of the response. The invasion created a debate, centered on the means by which the Japanese might contribute to endangered stability and the legitimacy of such means, not whether involvement was justified. Such a discussion inevitably focused on the employment of the SDF. As a result, Japan was able to adopt a peacekeeping operations law which legitimized future participation in UN-sanctioned forces (Hatakeyama, interview with an anonymous MOFA official, April 2004). East Timor, unfortunately, was not characteristically a simple picture of good versus evil, at least not in the eyes of the Japanese public. This lack of sympathy became one of the reasons that East Timor had trouble gaining traction in Japan, while the Kuwait invasion, at the time of the Gulf War, did.

The underlying questions of self-determination and independence did not greatly grab the attention of the Japanese public or any of the more important media outlets. A distinct lack of domestic concern assisted the government in remaining stubbornly uncommitted. In the midst of a battle for the LDP's presidency in September 1999, Prime Minister Obuchi saw no potential payoff in taking a proactive and sympathetic stand (Green, 2001, p. 187). The replacement of the multinational force by UN-sanctioned peacekeepers in 2000 did nothing to alter the prevailing politics of the situation. As a result, no pressing need for Japanese intervention appeared on the horizon. The government could only perceive the security risk associated with any hasty dispatch of SDF troops. As for any sufficiently large benefits flowing from a decision of this type, there appeared to be none worthy of consideration.

In addition, the Japanese were naturally reluctant to contribute even civilian officers while the situation in East Timor was still dangerous and unsettled. The police themselves, because of their previous two losses in Cambodia, balked at dispatching any additional officers as part of the peacekeeping operation (Ministry of Foreign Affairs, 2002). The Japanese, when it suited them, could always invoke the "five principles" test which employed ambiguous standards depending on flexible and difficult-to-verify interpretations. These convenient principles provided suitable camouflage to suit any Japanese purpose. As a result, the replacement of the multinational force with UN-approved troops changed little, if anything. Much more important in determining its decision, the government, especially that part represented by the Police and the Defense Agency, was not eager to participate unless the safety of Japanese personnel could be assured (Hatakeyama, interview with Kenji Isezaki, June 2009).

In this particular case, it would be misleading to try to dismiss Japanese diffidence as yet another typical instance of the country's long embedded anti-militarist sentiment. By the late 1990s, an automatic and undiscerning pacifist reaction had been declining, notably among the general public. There were a number of definable reasons why such a hypersensitive response could no longer be taken for granted. The left-wing Japanese Socialist Party (JSP) had rather carelessly frittered away its perceived integrity and corresponding influence in 1994 by joining an overly pragmatic coalition government (including the LDP) with the Socialist leader, Tomiichi Murayama as Prime Minister. The JSP appeared to the public eye, willing to compromise their professed principles, so desperate were they to wield power. This tactical move by the Socialists was particularly significant since they had established a long post-war record of attempting to contain a more active Japanese role in security issues. Their principled opposition ostensibly was based on an uncompromising insistence that both the SDF and the Japan–US security treaty were unconstitutional. Despite this long-term stance, the party proved remarkably willing to abandon these long-standing principles when it came down to expediency, namely seizing the opportunity to form a coalition government.

The successful operations in Cambodia helped make the public aware of the fact that the Self-Defense Forces were capable of contributing to regional peace and stability. Furthermore, such actions had the potential to enhance Japan's status as a responsible international citizen. This positive note was combined with a dose of real concern engendered by the North Korean missile launch in 1993. Publicly, a clearly perceived threat of this nature elevated the importance of the US alliance in protecting Japanese national sovereignty. According to opinion polls at that time, 77.9 percent of the Japanese felt that they needed the SDF, while 62 percent of the Japanese were supportive of the US–Japan alliance (*Yoron Chosa Nenkan*, 1994, p. 519; *Yoron Chosa Nenkan*, 1995, p. 498). The JSP recognized that the public was turning away from traditional pacifist leanings and instead providing growing support for the SDF. Even more important was a widespread realization of how dependent Japan was on US military power. By opting expeditiously to embrace a new-found level of pragmatism, the JSP discovered that it was incapable of continuing to hew to its long-held pacifist principles. This abandonment was the price the party was willing to pay in order to lead an incoming coalition government.

In this way, the formation of the Murayama government marked a real transition away from the public's reliably anti-military sentiments, and thus the disappearance of this binding constraint on Japanese diplomatic policies. Ironically, though not unexpectedly, this ideological abandonment delivered a body blow to the future hopes of the JSP. In fact, a dramatic loss in the 1996 election of the House of Representatives opened the way for a LDP revival, as they once again seized the reins of government. A later attempt to unite the much battered party and generate greater appeal by repacking themselves as the Social Democratic Party proved fruitless. Given the changing times and their almost casual disposal of a principal that had defined the party in the eyes of the voters, the role of the JSP could only rapidly decline in the years to come.

More, though, was occurring on the political scene than just a general consensus on the SDF and the US alliance. A realignment within the LDP resulted in a new culture that proved to be more receptive to Japan playing a larger role in security matters. The LDP shake-up led to establishment of new parties such as *Shinshinto* (New Frontier Party) in December 1994 and the later formation of both the *Jiyuto* (Liberal Party) and the *Minshuto* (Democratic Party of Japan) in 1998.[6] All these parties adopted a position basically favoring increased international involvement, even if it included deploying the SDF. There were, of course, slight dissimilarities between the parties. However, after first reaching a fundamental consensus in 1994, Japan's political establishment, from that time onward, managed to accommodate two, or even three, major parties all committed to the US alliance and to supporting a larger role for the SDF (Hughes, 1999, pp. 16–17). This new domestic environment, encouraged by the increasingly unstable and uncertain regional situation created by the second North Korean missile launch, encouraged an expanding role for the Japanese military, though always within the framework created by the US alliance.[7] Japan's military position still remained defensive in nature, but now had acquired a more active edge to its delegated role.

Both the Gulf War and the seemingly unresolvable North Korean crisis served as shocks to Japan's usual complacency. Rising uncertainty could only encourage a greater fixation on security matters. Taking the opportunity created by an unstable and worrisome environment, the Defense Agency successfully cultivated an increased influence in matters concerning policy formation. Starting with peacekeeping operations in Cambodia, the Defense Agency's influence started to grow incrementally. Quite expectedly, so did that of the SDF. Military assistance during the Hanshin earthquake and the subsequent terrorist attack by the Aum Shinrikyo Cult in 1995 generated a more positive impression

---

[6]These parties finally united as *Minshuto* (Democratic Party) in September 2003.

[7]For example, see both the 1996 redefinition of the security treaty with the US and the 1997 New Guidelines.

among the Japanese. Public sentiment was now capable of viewing the SDF as a potential contributor to world peace and stability. Widespread indicators pointed to anti-SDF sentiment declining at a slow but steady rate.

Given a population more amenable to the Japanese military and with a Japanese government now intent on strengthening cooperation and increasing dialog on security matters with the US, the Defense Agency found it quite feasible to seize a more central role in determining security policy coordination. Uncertain regional security architecture also played a contributing role in this instance (Funabashi, 1997, pp. 112–116). In short, part of the new political landscape of the 1990s was characterized by the legitimatization of the SDF and its overlord, the Defense Agency. A new and more tempered sensitivity had evolved when dealing with issues concerning national security. However, as the East Timor dilemma amply points out, the Japanese were still quite hesitant to embrace what they viewed as unwarranted risks. Achieving peace and stability in a remote country such as East Timor did not really register as a compelling matter. The resistance of the Police Force and the reluctance of the government showed that Japan would exert extreme caution in the face of potential casualties. Perceived risk remained a key mitigating factor that clearly outweighed what could only be defined as a rather small Japanese stake in that emerging nation.

Nor did Japan receive any essential encouragement toward making such a risky commitment. Despite the announcement that a new Clinton doctrine now prevailed, in the case of East Timor, the US displayed no great eagerness to become involved in that country's shifting sands. Conveniently, America was willing to overlook the precepts of a policy that openly declared that both the US and "the international community have an obligation to violate the principle of state sovereignty to protect the rights of a persecuted minority" (Hardar, 1999, p. 1). Though this provided the rationale for widespread US intervention, such action was hardly automatic at a more pragmatic level. In practise, the Americans proved to be far more selective. In East Timor, at least at the early stages of the conflict, maintaining good relations with Indonesia clearly outweighed any humanitarian considerations. The US did later find it expedient to change its position and apply pressure on the Indonesian government to accept a multinational force. However, this initial US reluctance to confront Indonesia and the low level of public awareness in Japan kept East Timor a low-priority item on its diplomatic agenda and enabled the Japanese to remain quiet.

In addition, Japan was less than eager to evoke the perennial fear of revived Japanese militarism among other Asian countries, unless it seemed possible to construct a compelling rationale which justified deploying the SDF. Appearing to be overly hasty in joining UN peacekeeping operations could only fan the flames of regional apprehension or at least provide an excuse for the sort of populist rhetoric that Asian politicians could indulge in at Japan's expense. Opinion surveys conducted in Indonesia, Malaysia, the Philippines, Singapore, and Thailand in 1983, 1987, 1992, and 1997 displayed their continuing ambiguous feelings toward a larger security role for Japan. Responding to a question focused on Japanese military security, more than 20 percent of the people polled in these countries (excepting Thailand) retained the perception that Japan's overwhelming military power ensured its national security. Surprisingly, even in 1997 more than 30 percent still assumed that Japan was capable of becoming a military threat. However, despite these residual fears, the majority in these countries now expected Japan to play a leading role in economic development rather than in maintaining regional peace and stability (Ministry of Foreign Affairs, 1998).

Clearly, there were strong and even overwhelming factors which discouraged Japan's participation in peacekeeping operations. These effective constraints created an unpropitious environment for any attempt by Japan to assist in restoring order to East Timor. However, despite these binding factors effectively limiting Japanese actions, Japan's position somehow managed to undergo a striking transformation in the later stages of the East Timor crisis. This change of heart led to a comparatively rapid deployment of troops. It is however essential to point out that despite the dramatic policy shift, the lengthy delay before Japan made a commitment reduces the troop gesture to no more than a symbol. The actual causes behind this seemingly dramatic diplomatic shift, form the next part of our story.

6.3.2   *Better Late than Never: Explaining Japan's Enthusiastic Second Stage Involvement*

As we have seen, in the initial stage Japan was intent on maintaining a low profile and therefore remained reluctant to confront the Indonesian government. Even after the situation in East Timor improved in 2000, symbolized by the substitution of UN-sanctioned troops, the Japanese government still delayed in dispatching the SDF. But in 2002, Japan underwent a sudden and seemingly unexplained change of heart by willingly sending troops to East Timor. Officially, the decision arose out of the newly stabilized situation in that country. The Japanese government insisted that only at this point were all "five principles" sufficiently met. In this version of reality, only this restriction and this restriction alone had kept the SDF safely at home. Yet, more believably, there were other, quite compelling, reasons that actually induced the government to modify its stance from one of avoidance and seeming indifference to one that emphasized responsibility and regional leadership. By examining the precise timing of this key decision, we can locate the probable motivations underlying this apparent change in direction by the Japanese government.

To begin with, the international confirmation of East Timor's independence removed an overwhelming stumbling block. As mentioned, Japan had been sensitive to Indonesian interests, assuming a studiously neutral position as long as possible. While the fate of East Timor's independence remained in balance, maintaining good relationships with Indonesia dominated any other political or strategic consideration. However, the emerging international consensus managed to change the prevailing picture. Widespread recognition of the need for East Timorese independence mitigated the necessity of deferring completely to Indonesia's interest. Japan now faced a broader set of viable diplomatic options.

A MOFA official clearly admitted that one reason for Japan's enthusiastic second stage engagement lay in the growing international agreement over East Timor's independence (Hatakeyama, interview with an anonymous MOFA official, April 2004). At this stage, Japan began to see an opportunity to create another reliable regional sympathizer.

Therefore, only after independence came firmly into sight did Japan dispatch its forces for reconstruction work. As always, Japanese diplomacy worked from what it perceived to be the low-risk option. The timing of the troop deployment, just three months before East Timor's independence, serves to confirm this supposition. Though late coming to the party, Japan viewed it unwise to swim against such a widespread agreement on the East Timor situation. Perhaps in the long run, Japan's enthusiastic (and transparently opportunistic) involvement in East Timor's nation building might come to outweigh its initial stubborn reluctance. Sadly for larger Japanese ambitions, only under this not entirely credible scenario will Japan's slow dispatch of troops serve retrospectively to elevate Japan's international position and create a new Japanese sympathizer.

In addition, as has been the repeated case when assessing Japanese diplomatic policy, natural resources cast a deciding vote in this case. An independent East Timor became a country endowed with potentially valuable resources. Engaging in East Timorese nation building could then be considered as a sensible method for obtaining access to valuable commodities in the future. Prior to Japan's troop deployment, East Timor's instability and unpredictability had hampered planned investment by the American energy corporation Phillips Petroleum. As a practical response, Phillips suspended the Bayu Undan oil project off East Timor's coast (*World Market Research Centre Daily Analysis*, March 15, 2002). However, by December 2001, Phillips and East Timor successfully agreed to a workable tax and fiscal regime. Once such an arrangement was in place, Japanese firms felt encouraged to open their own negotiations and frame their own agreements (in conjunction with Phillips) (*World Market Research Centre Daily Analysis*, March 15, 2002).

In March 2002, just a month after the arrival of SDF troops, a new gas supply contract for some 3 million tonnes per year was signed by Phillips in partnership with two Japanese energy companies (Tokyo Electric Power and Tokyo Gas).[8] Importing liquefied natural

---

[8] In addition to the two companies, INPEX Corporation has held 10.53% of the right in the Bayu Undan project.

gas (LNG) from the Bayu Undan field off East Timor's coast started in January 2006. Further supply is slated to continue through 2023. Three million tonnes per year may not appear to be particularly significant on its own merits. Viewed in isolation, the signed agreement was unlikely to directly affect decisions made by the Japanese government. However, when compared to Japan's total import of some 58 million tonnes of LNG in 2004 (Japan Bank for International Cooperation, 2006), the Bayu Undan deal no longer appears entirely trivial, but rather rates as a biggish type of project (Hatakeyama, interview with managers of the Tokyo Gas Co. Ltd., April 2009). Placing the deal in a broader context, Japan has long seen itself as burdened by a habitual lack of natural resources. It has also, for some time, had on its agenda a perceived desire to reduce its reliance on oil imports from the war-torn Middle East. Considering these deeply entrenched policy positions, simply dismissing the possibility that a deal securing LNG might carry little or no political weight would probably be mistaken. By this time, China also had emerged as a resource-importing competitor. The Chinese had noticeably signed new contracts for liquefied natural gas with both Australia and Indonesia, from which Japan also imported LNG. These competitive considerations undoubtedly made a deal with East Timor seem even more exigent and encouraged the Japanese government to reconsider its relationship. However, the connection between the two events is hardly air tight. Being able to discern an implicit consideration or advantage of this particular type does not necessarily create a direct link tying the decision to dispatch troops to the subsequent LNG agreement.

As mentioned, Japan's shift should also partially be viewed as a response to increasing international expectations. The end of the Cold War, instead of ushering in widespread peace and stability, brought with it an increasing number of conflicts. As a result, the political leverage attached to peacekeeping operations grew. Acknowledging this new reality, the UN's "Brahimi" Report, issued in August 2000, recommended strengthening support for peacekeeping by augmenting the authority of the UN Department of Peacekeeping Operations. With the security threat posed by North Korea growing increasingly urgent, Japan became ever more receptive to assuming a larger military role, though one positioned within the framework provided by its US alliance. Hitherto, Japan had flexibly employed a stated rigid adherence to its "five principles" to limit (if rather conveniently) its peacekeeping contributions.

Following this assessment, in October of the same year, the "Armitage" Report (informally named after Vice Secretary of State Richard Armitage) demanded that Japan, as a prominent member of the international community, fully participate in peacekeeping operations in order to share more of America's global burden (Institute for National Strategic Studies, 2000). Further, at a June 2001 meeting between US representatives and the Secretaries of the ruling parties (the LDP, the New Conservative Party, and the New Komeito Party), Armitage demanded that Japan revise its peacekeeping operations law. Under the current restrictions, Japanese forces were prohibited from deploying weapons, which obviously limited peacekeeping possibilities. Consequently, Japan could only participate if other countries agreed to protect SDF personnel (*Asahi Shimbun*, June 2, 2001).

Again, in September 2001, just before the 9/11 Al-Qaeda attacks, US Secretary of State Colin Powell strongly suggested that Japan play a larger role in the maintenance of regional stability and security by fully participating in strategic peacekeeping missions (*Asahi Shimbun*, September 10, 2001). US policy obviously had shifted from assigning Japan a purely supportive economic role to a more comprehensive one, including engaging directly in military operations. The UN apparently concurred with this position. This demand for a changed Japanese stance arose despite Japan's continuing role as a major underwriter of UN peacekeeping deployments (second only to the US). As pointed out previously, Japan had managed to avoid playing a more direct role by falling back on explicit constitutional restrictions prohibiting any use of weaponry. But now a purely financial contribution was deemed to be an insufficient substitute for concrete military action. The UN expected Japan to begin playing a more practical role through active participation (*Asahi Shimbun*, November 9, 2001).

In line with these demands, the Bush Administration's crusading call for a "war on terrorism" inevitably had a distinct impact on Japan's East Timor policy. Japan's active support of the US, in the aftermath of the attacks, would almost inevitably lead to a dramatic change in its previous stance. While unanticipated by Japanese decision makers, this event proved more influential than any other in shaping Japan's revised diplomacy. The 9/11 attacks dramatically changed the international, as well as domestic, situation. One of the ripple effects was an evolving need to signal Japanese solidarity with its American ally. Participating in the East Timor peacekeeping operation presented a handy opportunity to better realign Japan's policy more closely with that of the US.

The likelihood of such strategic policy shifts was boosted when Junichiro Koizumi, an unequivocal nationalist, took power in April 2001. With Koizumi at the helm, Japan's focus on security matters gained momentum. Early in his tenure, Koizumi flagged his intention of revising the constitution. His vision was one in which Japan played a much more active role in ensuring international peace and stability. Koizumi also believed that the "SDF is substantially Japan's military" and "the day should come when the SDF is recognized as the military under a revised constitution" (Green, 2003). This unequivocal stand broke a long-running "taboo" in Japanese society and consequently elevated the status of the SDF. A studied ambiguity when discussing military matters no longer seemed a political necessity. Though Koizumi's political support within the LDP was weak, his fresh approach to politics, especially his use of the media (an acknowledged master of the sound bite), caused initial public approval to reach an almost stratospheric 90 percent at its peak. This extreme popularity helped to entrench Koizumi's leadership position within the LDP. With such solid public support he could more easily set aside opposition from within his party and instead pursue his own agenda.

Structural reforms, exemplified by a 1999 Cabinet law, also augmented the Prime Minister's ability to exercise greater leadership in policy matters (Hughes, 2004, p. 63). With more room to maneuver, Koizumi was able to staunchly support the US-led war against terrorism. Justification for his controversial decision relied on two basic rationalizations. He first employed the image of the North Korean bogeyman by pointing out that a dependent Japan more than ever required US assistance to contain the security threat posed by that inscrutable regime. Koizumi also stressed that the US under these strained circumstances expected Japan to act forthrightly as a major power. By this the Americans specifically meant using military means to contribute to international security. Koizumi forcefully reiterated these two rationales when pushing through special legislation, which enabled the SDF to cooperate with US-led forces in Iraq and Afghanistan.

Complementing Koizumi's strong leadership at this time, the afore-mentioned rough consensus among the prevailing political parties served to facilitate his bold steps. No real organized opposition among the major factions now existed. Disagreements tended to be minor on this specific issue. The *Shinshinto* (New Frontier Party) formed in 1994 by Ichiro Ozawa and members from other small parties regrouped into either *Jiyuto* (the Liberal Party) or *Minshuto* (Democratic Party of Japan) by 1998. Unlike the traditional stand espoused by the left-wing and rapidly vanishing JSP, these parties were supportive of a larger international role for Japan. They did not shy away from extending this involvement to include some degree of military effort as well. However, this superficial consensus did not mean in any sense that a hasty expansion of Japan's military role could be quickly anticipated. An almost seismic shift of this sort would require lengthy debate and take a corresponding measure of time.

Fortunately for Koizumi's diplomatic agenda, the two main opposition parties and the LDP shared similar policy positions on this issue. While the Democratic Party of Japan and the Liberal Party might not embrace an unconditional change, all three parties, including the LDP, agreed in principle that Japan's military should undertake a wider range of tasks abroad. A new generation of policy makers, uninhibited by the shared histories of their predecessors were more likely, in varying degrees, to support the proposed reform. This consensual backing provided real momentum for a change (Hughes, 2004, p. 53). Moreover, the still bitter memory of their traumatic failure to handle the Gulf Crisis with any degree of adeptness encouraged government officials subsequently to take more assertive and more rapid action (Ina, 2002, pp. 178–179). Special legislation, adopted immediately after the 9/11 attacks, converted this desire into reality. From this time forward, Japan would significantly increase its military cooperation with the US, though perhaps not always at the pace envisioned by the Americans.

This policy shift, fuelled by the "war on terrorism," would consequently inform the entirety of Japanese diplomacy.

It would, however, be careless to conclude that linking its expanded pursuit of an international role with its position as a key US ally permanently resolved the ongoing military controversy. This supposition remained far from the actual case. Japan's peacekeeping operations were still heavily constrained by the rigidity of existing laws. To overcome this obstacle, Koizumi pushed to amend the basic peacekeeping law in December 2001. The aim behind his move was to provide the SDF with greater leeway by at least partially lifting the existing restrictions (Hatakeyama, interview with an anonymous MOFA official, April 2004). Despite such future hopes, the actual revision of December 2001 did not manage to eliminate the intentionally rigid "five principles." As previously demonstrated, these principles had effectively limited Japan's military participation and activities in the past. However, the legislation did enable the SDF to conduct previously prohibited actions such as monitoring disarmament, stationing and patrolling in buffer zones, and collecting and disposing of abandoned weapons. Previously, SDF troops had been allowed to use weapons only in self-defense or to protect other Japanese personnel. The revision permitted SDF troops to protect the life or person of anyone who was with them and had come under their *de facto* "control." Partially lifting some of the more stringent restrictions certainly broadened SDF's activities while peacekeeping and made the laws more applicable.

In evaluating such changes, it might be natural to assume that the revised law was driven by a need to dispatch troops to East Timor given the prevailing international climate. However, the timing of the two events remains essentially coincidental (Hatakeyama, interview with an anonymous MOFA official, April 2004). By the time of the revision, the East Timorese situation already had improved significantly due to a successful mop-up operation of the remaining militia by October 2000. Dispatching forces under those conditions no longer required the existing law to be amended. Moreover, the activities proposed for SDF personnel in East Timor remained firmly within the range of the former legislation. Since operations performed by these soldiers would be essentially limited to repairing roads and bridges, an urgent need to revise the existing law did not directly influence the government's decision to send troops to East Timor.

Instead, the timing of the amendment demonstrates that the actual troop deployment represented an attempt to balance Japan's increasing military role in the "war on terrorism" with its relatively more minor role in localized peacekeeping operations. The government felt that it should show a willingness to contribute to international peace and stability by participating in such interventions. Amending the peace-keeping operations law was meant to transmit this specific signal. The revision aimed to achieve a balance by enlarging Japan's security role through bilateral cooperation with the US, while at the same time making a broader international contribution as a "good citizen." Otherwise, without the buffering provided by more humanitarian actions, Japan's unquestioning support of US military actions, even when cloaked by the "war on terrorism" banner, might have been interpreted as an unwelcome return to militarism. Stable public support of the Koizumi administration, fluctuating between 70 and 80 percent, facilitated the government's revision of the law and neutralized any widely organized pacifist reaction (*Yoron Chosa Nenkan*, 1996–2002).

Given these considerations, sending troops to East Timor can best be placed within a policy framework that required careful, balanced diplomacy. Clearly Japan's late move to release troops did not reflect any pressing security considerations. After the mop-up operations of October 2000, the UN was able to gradually reduce and withdraw its forces (Hatakeyama, interview with Kenji Isezaki, June 2009). However, Japan could not remain uncommitted after it had broadened the scope of its peacekeeping activities by loosening some restrictions. This degree of selectivity would have called into question Japan's motivations. It had long faced accusations of too forcefully pursuing its own narrow self-interest while uncritically accepting US leadership. To demonstrate Japan's willingness to take a decidedly wider role in international as well as regional security matters, the Japanese perceived the need to balance their overt efforts to fight terrorism with less controversial peacekeeping efforts to sustain East Timorese stability.

Thus, the dispatch of the SDF was not precipitated by the achievement of a more conducive ground situation towards the end of 2000, but rather due to the aftermath of the 9/11 attack. The arrival of the troops was essentially a public relations exercise aimed at creating a beneficent image, one that would effectively circumvent potential domestic and international criticism over Japan's newly enlarged security role. As expected, the achievements by the SDF in East Timor generated popular domestic reactions, facilitating those more contentious governmental decisions which subsequently enlarged Japan's security role. Such publicity helped to dispel potentially undesirable reactions to more controversial efforts, such as Koizumi's later decision to dispatch troops to Iraq.

In retrospect, the dramatic turnaround in Japan's policy reflected the almost simultaneous disappearance of some major behavioral constraints. East Timor's independence meant that Japan could actively pursue peacekeeping operations without offending Indonesian sensitivities. Added to this fortuitous turn of events, international expectations grew, requiring greater Japanese activity in maintaining security. Eager to demonstrate Japan's active support for the US-led "war on terrorism," Prime Minister Koizumi pushed through special legislation which consequently freed the Japanese to pursue a larger, more independent regional role as a counter-balance to its increased prominence as a US ally. Quite conveniently, by the time SDF troops did arrive in East Timor, the situation had significantly stabilized. This agreeably limited any potential risk to personnel, effectively muting any military domestic outcry. Lastly, even after taking potential domestic reaction into consideration, successfully engaging in East Timorese nation building opened up future possibilities for the government to broaden its security role. The pay-off was clearly demonstrated by Japan's later engagement in Afghanistan and Iraq. Without a preliminary paving of the way, such a road could not have been so easily taken.

6.4 Conclusion: Lessons from East Timor

Participating in peacekeeping operations in East Timor seemed to be a chance for Japan to demonstrate its willingness to contribute to regional peace and stability and to display some concrete signs of leadership. However, an array of factors narrowed Japan's diplomatic options, constraining its behavior until order was restored in East Timor. At a later stage, the Koizumi government completed a policy turnaround by dispatching troops to East Timor. This deployment seemed to lack any compelling rationale at the time since the critical moment for peacekeeping had passed. Instead, East Timor was now in desperate need of nation-building assistance. But regard for the East Timorese played little role in this aspect of Japanese diplomacy. The peacekeeping operation can be more accurately seen as something of a Trojan horse that paved the way for an enlarged Japanese role within a regional security framework. Essentially, when a number of constraints that had inhibited Japan's drive to become a regional power disappeared, the Japanese dropped any compunction in dispatching troops. Thus Japan's apparent reluctance, at least initially, to pursue its broader agenda in East Timor is anything but a mystery. Rather, its diplomatic shift reflects a perfectly explicable realignment with more overarching Japanese objectives, once its actions were no longer effectively constrained.

References

Funabashi Y. (1997) *Doumei Hyoryu*. Iwanami, Tokyo.

Gorjao P. (2002) Japan's foreign policy and East Timor, 1975–2002. *Asian Survey*, 42(5), 754–771.

Green MJ. (2001) *Japan's Reluctant Realism*. Palgrave, New York.

Green S. (2003) Japan ready to strike first if threatened. *Sydney Morning Herald* May 22.

Hadar LT. (1999) East Timor and the 'slippery slope' problem. *Foreign Policy Briefing* (*Cato Institute*), 55(December 20), 1–12.

Hughes CW. (1999) *Japan's Economic Power and Security*. Routledge, London and New York.

Hughes CW. (2004) *Japan's Re-Emergence as a 'Normal' Military Power, Adelphi Paper 368-9*. Oxford University Press, Oxford.

Ina H. (2002) Document-9.11 no Shougeki. In: '*Atarashii Senso*' *Jidaino Anzenhosho*: Tanaka A. (ed.), pp. 171–206. Toshi Shuppan, Tokyo.

Institute for National Strategic Studies. (2000) The United States and Japan: Advancing towards a mature partnership. *INSS Special Report*. October 11, pp. 1–8, National Defense University Press, Washington.

Japan Bank for International Cooperation. (2006) Energy security for Japan: Support for stable supplies of energy from strategic regions. *JBIC Today*. November, http://www.jbic.go.jp/en/report/jbic-today/2006/11/index.html, accessed in April 2007.

Japan Defense Agency. (2002) Report of international troop deployment. http://jda-clearing.jda.go.jp/hakusho_data/2002/honmon/frame/at1404020200.htm, accessed in July 2004.

Japan External Trade Organization. (2005) Japan's outward and inward foreign direct investment — by country and regions (historical data — inward). *Japanese Trade and Investment Statistics*. http://www.jetro.go.jp/en/reports/statistics/, accessed in 2005.

Komura M. (1999) Statement by Foreign Minister Komura. MOFA Press Conference, September 17, http://www.mofa.go.jp/announce/press/917.html#5, accessed in December 2003.

Ministry of Foreign Affairs. (2003) Extension of the term of the dispatch of the Self-Defense Force engineer group and other personnel to the United Nations Mission of Support in East Timor (UNMISET). *MOFA Announcement*. June 20, p. 1, http://www.mofa.go.jp/announce/announce/2003/6/0620.html, accessed in November 2003.

Ministry of Foreign Affairs. (2002) Report of the Advisory Group on International Cooperation for Peace. *Japan Development Policy Update*. December 18, pp. 1–8, http://www.kantei.go.jp/foreign/policy/2002/1218houkoku_s_e.pdf, accessed in May 2004.

Ministry of Foreign Affairs. (1998) *ASEAN Shokoku ni Okeru Tainichi Yoron Chosa*. Daijin Kanbo Kaigai Kohoka, Tokyo.

Numata S. (1999) Press Conference by the Press Secretary/section II: Overview of the current situation facing East Timor. *Ministry of Foreign Affairs*. September 17, http://www.mofa.go.jp/announce/press/1999/9/917.html, accessed in April 2004.

Ozawa T. (2008) History repeats itself: Evolutionary structural change and TNC's involvement in infrastructure overseas, flying-geese style. *Working Paper Series — Center on Japanese Economy and Business*, 261 (March), pp. 1–40. Columbia Business School, New York.

United Nations Commission on Human Rights. (1999) Report of the Commission on Human Rights on its Fourth Special Session. *Commission on Human Rights* (Geneva). September 23–24, http://www.unhchr.ch/Huridocda/Huridoca.nsf/(Symbol)/E.CN.4.1999.167.Add.1,E.1999.23.Add.1.En?Opendocument, accessed in July 2004.

Chapter 7

Hampered Diplomacy: Japanese Overtures to North Korea

7.1 Introduction: Mission Impossible

In the post-war period, Japan had failed to normalize diplomatic relations with just two countries, North Korea and Russia. However, small volumes of trade had allowed Japan to maintain, at least marginally, unofficial relations with North Korea. During the decades of continuing confrontation between the two Cold War superpowers, there was neither room nor any pressing need for Japan to regularize relations with North Korea. But this particular status quo failed to survive.

The end of the Cold War created a significant change in the international balance of power. As the old ideological confrontation disappeared, East and West Germany united. Eastern European countries largely opened themselves up to democracy and transformed into semblances of liberal market economies. Finally, the Soviet Union itself collapsed into a jigsaw of component pieces. Nevertheless, the authoritarian regime in North Korea seemed to remain unfazed as its nominal allies and ideological stable-mates fell to the wayside. The Korean Peninsula still featured what was now a unique standoff. North Korea, however, did not completely escape the ramifications of the demise of the Cold War. The North Koreans had maintained close political and economic relationships with the Soviet Union. Its collapse pushed

252 Snow on the Pine

them into a difficult position, leaving the country as something of a diplomatic orphan. But unlike the other former socialist states, North Korea's authoritarian leadership, and its propensity for brinkmanship, transformed the events that had normalized relations elsewhere into an emerging crisis that demanded immediate redress.

Japan, unfortunately, did not seem to be entirely up to the challenge. Domestic public opinion, particularly an embedded anti-militarist culture, combined with an enduring status quo that was characteristic of the post-war Japanese party political structure, had heavily constrained successive governments. Whenever possible, their embedded political instincts warned them away from tackling complex security matters. This seduced many analysts and observers into reducing Japanese goals to the mundane and the minimal. These observers largely dismissed Japan as being merely concerned with pursuing its own narrow economic advantage whenever possible. However, Japan's response to the perceived North Korean security threat clearly demonstrated that this supposition is simply at odds with the available evidence. If Japan's ultimate goals were simply organized around economic issues, Japan, under this analysis, would have remained cautiously silent when threatened by North Korea. Under this scenario, Japan would have been wiser to defer to the US for a solution. Instead, the Japanese government took a bold and independent step to insure its own national security. In this particular instance, trusting solely to US initiatives would have appeared to be far too passive and ineffective. To meet its objectives satisfactorily, Japan felt compelled to put forward its immediate security concerns in a more unrestrained manner. Such bold action might bring with it multiple dividends. Diplomatic forays aimed at insuring peace and stability, not only could have the potential to contribute to Japan's own immediate security, but also would boost its leverage and prestige as a regional leader.

This chapter examines whether Japan responded to the imminent threat posed by North Korea in a manner consistent with its long held goal of regional leadership. Doing so will require an analysis of Koizumi's historic visit to North Korea in 2002. An assortment of factors led to this groundbreaking visit, which, if successful, might have contributed to ensuring Japanese national security. Moreover, the visit could have boosted Japan's international reputation by demonstrating an ability to act independently and responsibly when dealing with security matters. Unfortunately, the Japanese government felt constrained to alter its behavior midway through the process. Despite a central focus on protecting its national security, the Japanese government felt obligated to deal simultaneously with more peripheral concerns. In particular, the politically sensitive issue of abduction eventually overwhelmed all other considerations. Japan's deviation from its more overarching objectives clearly limited Japan's options. Why did the Japanese government become obsessed by the kidnapping question? Behind such a shift in focus was a specific factor, namely, domestic public opinion. Japanese politicians lacked the deftness required to pursue these dual and somewhat conflicting goals. Coupled with subtle and not so subtle American pressure to ameliorate and more closely align Japan's rising conflicts with broader US strategies, these factors transformed themselves into insurmountable obstacles undermining Japan's grand strategy, namely bringing peace and stability to the region. However, it is important to keep in mind that Japan did in fact initiate its Korean diplomacy in the hope of increasing its regional influence, while simultaneously insuring its own national security. This chapter then explains Japan's quiet pursuit of its diplomatic goals and the subsequent failure to achieve them.

7.2 Diverging Streams: Japan Re-Examines US Intentions

Even after the end of the Cold War, North Korea remained no more than a remote country for the Japanese — psychologically, diplomatically, and economically. A contingent among Japanese leftists, such as those associated with the Japanese Socialist Party and the Japanese Communist Party, had at times even held positive views of this mystery enshrouded country. Although North Korea previously had demonstrated certain "terrorist" behavioral aspects (the 1983 Rangoon bombing and the blowing-up of a Korean airline in 1987), until the 1980s, most Japanese did not consider North Korea to be either a major or an imminent threat. During the Cold War, it was the Soviet Union that was perceived as indisputably representing Japan's major challenge. Only North Korea's nuclear development program and the subsequent launch of two missiles in the early 1990s eventually tripped Japanese alarm bells and converted a relatively obscure and somewhat forgotten country into a major security threat. This sudden break from the past spurred a decisive rethinking and reappraisal of the situation. Japan distinctly realized that its post-war strategy of total dependence on the US translated into a corresponding absence of any separate and employable framework insuring Japanese security.

With the collapse of the Soviet Union (1991), North Korea could no longer count on a dependable and subsidized flow of oil. Supplies dropped dramatically. Subsequent floods further devastated its stagnant economy. In contrast, economically as well as ideologically, South Korea's successful liberal reforms seemed to brand that country as an economic powerhouse and a clear winner. This left North Korea's debilitated and steadily shrinking economy definitely languishing in the loser's circle (Johnson, 1995, p. 71). Pressed by its precarious existence and lacking any other strategic hand to play, North Korea deliberately provoked the international community by utilizing its nuclear hole-card. Undoubtedly, North Korea had signed the Nuclear Non-Proliferation Treaty (NPT) back in 1985. But now, as revelations of a secret nuclear construction program encompassing a large-scale reactor and reprocessing facility leaked out, the North Koreans renounced (March 1993) the same treaty and rejected its corresponding obligations.

The North Korean government saw provocation and brinkmanship as the only effective option which could possibly strengthen its bargaining position. Firing a No-dong One missile toward Japan (May 1993) might succeed in coercing US recognition of the regime. By attracting international assistance and potentially destabilizing the region, the North Koreans hoped that the US would attempt to neutralize the situation with a liberal dollop of economic assistance. The missile succeeded in rattling the Japanese who had not seriously considered its neighbors could pose anything resembling a pre-eminent security threat. Quite unexpectedly, this newly dangerous opponent had demonstrated the unfortunate ability and even proclivity for producing missiles and possibly nuclear weapons that were capable of reaching Japan. For the first time, the Japanese government regarded North Korea as posing an imminent threat to its security. Such visible danger required a definitive Japanese strategy for responding to this potential crisis on the Korean peninsula (Hughes, 1999). Unfortunately, at that very moment when decisiveness was most needed, the bedrock US–Japan alliance seemed to provide an undesirable degree of uncertainty. Quite naturally, with the end of the prolonged Cold War, some of the pact's standard initiatives had become outmoded. Moreover, the immediacy caused by a commonly perceived threat had faded with the disappearance of Soviet communism. Bonds once unassailable had loosened. Japan appeared to be stuck in a "drifting alliance" with the US just at a time when America's military presence was declining due to a strategy of regional disengagement. In this environment, Japan's considered response to the security threat posed by North Korea increased in urgency and significance (Hughes, 1996). One Ministry of Foreign Affairs (MOFA) official even questioned the US willingness to provide an effective shield if ever a serious disturbance on the Korean Peninsula was to eventuate (Tananka, 1994). Fortunately, while Japan dithered, concerted US efforts defused the unanticipated crisis. North Korea agreed to postpone its withdrawal from the NPT.

Unfortunately, North Korea soon unsettled this precarious status quo by impeding the scheduled inspections of the International Atomic Energy Association (IAEA) and by removing spent nuclear fuel rods. Due to these provocations, tensions along the Peninsula greatly escalated. During negotiations with former US President Jimmy Carter (June 1994), North Korea did show a willingness to freeze its nuclear development, but only in return for two specific concessions. The first required the resumption of high-level talks aimed at future diplomatic recognition. Looking to secure its future energy needs, the second encompassed financial support to develop North Korea's light-water nuclear reactors. Although Carter declined to meet Kim Il Sung's demand for financial assistance, he did mention a willingness to influence Japan into underwriting these controversial reactors. Carter later would demand that Japan share this burden after completing his negotiations in North Korea. Secretary of State Warren Christopher likewise insisted that Foreign Minister Yohei Kono provide economic cooperation (Miyashita, 2003, pp. 149–155).

Under the terms of the above-mentioned "agreed framework" between the two countries, North Korea promised to freeze three graphite-moderated reactors and remain in the NPT and the IAEA. In return, the US would coordinate international financial support for the provision of two light-water reactors and offer heavy oil until the Korean reactors could produce sufficient levels of energy. The US also undertook not to use nuclear weapons on the Korean Peninsula. In May 1995, the agreement established the Korean Peninsula Energy Development Organization (KEDO) with the proposed aim of providing the North Koreans with their much desired reactors. Deterring North Korea from developing a nuclear weapons program remained the key objective behind this multilateral framework. Japan, as a US ally, was incorporated within this treaty mechanism. By impeding North Korea from achieving a nuclear capability, this approach attempted to protect not only regional but also Japanese security.

As Carter promised, the US subsequently demanded that Japan financially contribute to KEDO. At this stage, the Japanese government resisted providing any support unless North Korea was willing in turn to release information on its reactors and nuclear development (Miyashita, 2003, p. 153). The stark lack of sufficient measures to ensure the North's compliance caused Japan to be suspicious of the future effectiveness of KEDO. In particular, Ministry of Foreign Affairs (MOFA) officials were skeptical that such promised financial support could prevent North Korea from developing a nuclear program (Miyashita, 2003, p. 166). Equally important, these financial obligations to KEDO would make it difficult for the Japanese government to employ economic assistance as a "carrot" in the parallel bilateral level negotiations that were then under way.

Japan had proved willing to experiment with a variety of bilateral tactics, employing an array of official and unofficial channels to normalize relations with North Korea. From the mid-1990s, the Japanese government had turned rice assistance into an implicit carrot by employing the services of the Red Cross Society. Japan deliberately intended this aid to be a direct response to North Korea's delayed admission in June 1994 that severe flooding the previous summer had generated a serious food shortage. The Japanese government, perhaps naively, expected such assistance to soften North Korea's attitudes and foster a better environment for normalization talks (Kono, 1995). Soon after, Japan's embassy in Beijing contacted North Korea in an attempt to sound out North Korea's willingness to engage in such talks (Lee and Moon, 2002, p. 100). To smooth the way, Japan provided not only rice assistance but also contributed an additional $500,000 to support the United Nations Development and Health Assistance (UNDHA) efforts in repairing North Korea's flood damage. Given these ongoing bilateral efforts, successfully establishing KEDO might have ultimately undermined Japan's diplomatic strategy. Although KEDO was a framework that purportedly aimed to assure Japan's security, the Japanese government was reluctant to provide support. Japan instead expressed its deep reservations regarding the basic safety surrounding the development of North Korean nuclear energy (Interview with Makoto Iokibe, *Asahi Shimbun*, July 3, 2003). This roundabout rejection of the proposed framework indicated that US and Japanese interests were working less than perfectly in tandem.

Japan was not the only country involved that doubted the efficacy of the "agreed framework." As might be expected, some hawkish US officials denounced the proposed framework as nothing better than a vile appeasement strategy. They claimed the agreement lacked any effective guarantees and that it would affect both the US–South Korea and the US–Japan bilateral alliances (Hughes, 1999, p. 106). South Korea was far from pleased that the US-negotiated agreement had failed to include any serious discussions with its own government. In Geneva, the then President Kim denounced the agreement, claiming that "any compromise [at this point] with North Korea will only help prolong its survival" (Oberdorfer, 2001, p. 354).

However, the Japanese could not continue to maintain their negative stance toward KEDO. Already, South Korea had changed its previously dissident attitude and displayed a new-found willingness to share the financial burden of the proposed reactor. Coupled with continuing US pressure on Japan to underwrite a proportion of the required cost, South Korea's newly cooperative attitude made it difficult for Japan to sustain its clearly negative approach. In addition, an assortment of major powers confirmed their support for KEDO at the Halifax G-7 Summit in June 1994. They had previously delineated their position by claiming that "the support of the international community can be made *inter alia* through participation in the KEDO" (Ministry of Foreign Affairs, 1996). In August of the same year, confirmation of support from 32 countries, including the US, the Republic of Korea, and the European Union, during the First General Conference of KEDO made it even more difficult for Japan to keep resisting.

Also, it would be unwise to overlook the prolonged trade conflict between the US and Japan, which at this time had soured relationships between the two. The trade deficit had reached $60 billion by 1994. The US responded by pressing the Japanese to open their domestic markets. The Americans in fact wanted the Japanese to agree to a set of aggressive numerical targets for US exports to Japan. Of course, when the full extent of Japan's floundering economy became apparent, those pressures quickly eased. However, for the time being, the confrontational economic relationship between the two contributed to making the financial issue of burden sharing contentious. As a US official speaking in October 1994 claimed, "I think there is a sense that we can use the trade surplus to win some Japanese help on other issues these days. We might as well get some indirect benefits from the deficit" (quoted in Miyashita, 2003, p. 157). This tough US attitude over trade issues made the Japanese side increasingly uneasy when gauging the depth of the existing security commitment. Given a growing sense of unquiet and anxiety about the enduring stability of the traditional US–Japan security pact, the Japanese could see no other viable option than yielding, once again, to US wishes. Just before the framework's formal agreement went through in October 1995, the Japanese government reconsidered and announced its grudging intention to provide financially support. Japan could not afford to weaken the keystone of its post-war security any further.

However, US expectations of Japan's share of this burden continued to escalate. In February 1996, Walter Mondale, the US ambassador to Japan, demanded that Japan also help underwrite the cost of heavy oil, which the US had pledged previously (Miyashita, 2003, p. 160).

Already harboring suspicions about KEDO's potential effectiveness, Japan was unwilling to step up its level of assistance. Unfortunately, the Japanese situation did not easily enable Japan to pursue an independent path. China's military exercises off the coast of Taiwan, first in July 1995 and then again in March 1996, meant that deliberately driving a wedge in its relationship with the US was far too risky an option.[1] Furthermore, by April 1996, South Korea feared that normalized relations between Japan and North Korea might cement the peninsula's existing division. As an alternative, South Korea proposed Four-Party Talks among China, North Korea, the US and South Korea. Its deliberate exclusion from these Four-Party talks caused the Japanese government to fear that it would be excluded from these crucial negotiations and be left without any way in which to redress its own security concerns (Green, 2001, p. 123; Fouse, 2004, p. 6). At this moment, the Japanese could hear the train pulling out of the station fully aware that they had yet to purchase a ticket.

Therefore, despite its substantial suspicions about KEDO's efficacy, Japan felt obliged to add its financial support. At the time, KEDO was the only available framework that would allow Japan to express its specific views and national interests. Meanwhile, negotiators had assumed that North Korea's staggering economy posed a serious threat to the continuing viability of its ruling regime. Providing an assured energy supply in the near future through KEDO was intended to stabilize the potentially unsettled peninsula. This presumed leverage over the North Korean regime would ostensibly restore calm to the region.[2]

However, a North Korean missile launch in 1998 revealed the essential ineffectiveness of KEDO. North Korea grew frustrated by construction delays of the promised light-water reactor and by the non-appearance of the heavy oil supply. In a 1998 statement, the North vigorously condemned the US and insisted that it live up to all its

---

[1] China conducted a series of major military exercises as a means of signaling its determination not to concede Taiwan's independence.

[2] Hughes examines whether economic power can be used to serve security ends (see Hughes, 1999).

obligations.[3] North Korea explicitly threatened the US by mentioning
its unambiguous willingness to press forward with its nuclear program
(Sakai, 2001, p. 68). To signal this discontent, North Korea again fired
a long-range missile toward Japan on August 31, 1998. The missile
flew over the island nation and landed harmlessly offshore in the Pacific
Ocean. These incidents served to convince Japan that as a deterrent,
KEDO was no more than an empty gesture. Even worse, Japan was
forced to weigh the extent of its own quite natural anger against what
appeared to be a US policy of appeasement. The gulf between American
and Japanese perceptions of the crisis was visibly growing.

An incensed Japanese government soon announced that it would
suspend all of its financial commitments. Japan followed up this action
by announcing that it would not join any forthcoming normalization
talks. For the time being at least Japan would suspend all food aid and
other assistance. Concurrently, the Japanese attempted to enlist international backing for their chosen position. The Japanese government
began its campaign by vociferously protesting to the UN. To create a
more broad-based appeal the Japanese characterized North Korea as
not just a relatively narrow threat to its own security concerns. According to Japanese analysis, this rogue nation was also undermining the
peace and stability of Northeast Asia by developing weapons of mass
destruction and possibly supplying them to other outlaw countries and
terrorist organizations.[4] Yet to Japan's obvious disappointment, the
UN refused to follow the lead that Japan had clearly indicated. Instead,
the UN officials issued a rather bland statement placing all responsibility and blame on the North Koreans. This lacked the weight of a
full-fledged Security Council resolution or an unambiguous statement
by the Secretary-General. Trying yet another alternative, at the Japan–
US Summit meeting (September 22, 1998), the Japanese succeeded
in getting both countries to agree that they would strongly pressure

---

[3]This is from a statement by the North Korean government requesting the US to carry out
the "agreed framework," May 1, 1998, http://www.ioc.u-tokyo.ac.jp/~worldjpn/documents/
texts/JPKR/19980501, accessed in December 2003.
[4]For example, see "Announcement by the Chief Cabinet Secretary on Japan's immediate
response to North Korea's missile launch," http://www.mofa.go.jp/announce/announce/
1998/8/831.html, accessed in July 2004.

North Korea not to launch, develop or export missiles (Ministry of Foreign Affairs, 1999, p. 15). In addition, Japan proposed that the trilateral consultations among Japan, the US and South Korea, ongoing since January 1996, should continue at the highest possible level. Japan's pointed demands resulted in a September 24, 1998 meeting held at the Foreign Ministerial level. On October 2, the Japanese co-sponsored, along with the US and six other countries, a resolution proposed by the International Civil Aviation Organization. The aim was to categorize North Korea's missile launch as an act that clearly jeopardized the safety of international civil aviation. On October 9, Japan continued its single-minded campaign by appealing to the Missile Technology Control Regime and obtaining a Chairman's statement placing all blame on the North Koreans. Japan had deliberately painted a portrait of North Korea as an imminent security threat, in order to shore up support from the international community. Yet, Japan's efforts still stopped short of successfully orchestrating an essentially effective campaign.

By demanding that North Korea fulfill its obligations as stipulated in the 1994 agreement, the US at least appeared to be responding to these critical Japanese concerns. However, in Japan's view, the US still proved to be far too flexible in its actual negotiations. Disregarding Japan's anxiety and the anger caused by North Korea's two provocative missile launches, the US agreed to accelerate the light-water reactor schedule under the terms laid down by KEDO. In return, by attending a September 5 meeting, North Korea demonstrated a basic willingness to undertake further discussions focused on the critical missile controversy (Green, 2001, p. 125). To emphasize the US position, KEDO's executive director, Desaix Anderson, went so far as to actually warn Japanese Vice-Foreign Minister Keizo Takemi that "if KEDO were to be destroyed, Japan would face the danger of both nuclear and missile developments" (quoted in Miyashita, 2003, p. 162).

Japan had not anticipated such a response. At the September 20, 1998, two-plus-two meeting, the US again pressured Japan to sign an agreement assuring financial aid for KEDO (Sakai, 2001, p. 69). Quite reasonably, the missile incidents had far less impact on the US than they did on Japan. The US was much more focused on preserving the wobbling non-proliferation treaty than with any perceived threats to Japanese security.

Recognizing its own limitations, the Japanese government eventually confirmed its intention to continue providing financial assistance to KEDO.[5] With that key commitment now in place, Japan, the US and South Korea announced their intention of maintaining the KEDO framework.[6] In less than a month, Japan found itself explicitly retreating from its determined pledge of suspending financial assistance despite receiving no equivalent concession in return. Foreign Minister Komura implicitly admitted defeat by saying on September 29, "The United States, South Korea and the international community do not want Japan to continue to do this any longer" (cited in Sakai, 2001, p. 69). In effect, US pressure had forced the Japanese to change its course despite Japan's broader strategic concerns. Japan had been obliged to concede on this difficult issue because of the increasingly divergent interests emerging between Japan and the US. American objectives once again succeeded in overriding Japanese long-term aims.

This outcome signified more than just a passing difference between the two erstwhile allies. The Japanese reacted accordingly. Soon after a scheduled trilateral meeting, Republic of Korean President Kim Dae-Jung visited Japan on October 8, 1998. Japan used this opportunity to shore up South Korea's cooperation by lobbying for its own position on the missile crisis. Japan did succeed, but only up to a point. The Japan–Republic of Korea Joint Declaration included shared concerns and expressed regrets regarding the missile launch and the security threat posed by North Korea (Ministry of Foreign Affairs, 1998). However, in return, the Japanese government had a price to pay. Japan had to renew its faith in and support of KEDO as the "most realistic and effective mechanisms for preventing North Korea from advancing its nuclear program" (cited in Sakai, 2001, p. 69). Eventually, the Japanese government substantially lifted all the measures it had taken

---

[5]This can be found in a joint statement by Japan, South Korea, and the US, September 24, 1998,   http://www.ioc.u-tokyo.ac.jp/~worldjpn/documents/texts/JPKR/19980924.D1J. html, accessed in July 2004.

[6]This intention is made clear in a joint press release by Japan, the US and South Korea, September 24, 1998, *Gaiko Seisho 1999*, 372, 373.

against KEDO and resumed financial cooperation on October 21. The Japanese diplomatic retreat was now complete, coming less than two months after North Korea's provocative missile launch. The Japanese weakly attempted to rationalize this policy turnabout by declaring that they refused to provide the Koreans with any excuse to resume nuclear weapons development (Ministry of Foreign Affairs, 1999, p. 15).

The second missile launch had highlighted a clear divergence between the US and Japanese interests. The Americans were focusing on containing the proliferation of nuclear weapons. Inevitably, to do so, the US would tenaciously provide continued life support to the KEDO framework. Secretary of State Warren Christopher clearly indicated that America considered stopping the proliferation of nuclear weapons to be its greatest concern. He stated:

> Our goal in crafting the framework was thus. Three-fold: to stop the North's existing nuclear program; to devise a larger strategy that would address the threat posed by North's missile program and conventional build-up; and to reduce tensions in the region by bringing North Korea out of its international isolation into the broader community of nations (cited in Hughes, 1999, p. 104).

The Japanese government did share the same ultimate goals as the US. However, without sufficient guarantees it was less than enthusiastic about providing sizeable and continuing financial support to KEDO. Japan doubted that KEDO would prove itself to be a framework that was particularly conducive to all of Japan's interests. Moreover, KEDO too starkly reflected the emerging conflicts of interest between Japan and the US. This ineffective level of deterrence convinced the Japanese government that it needed to somehow map out a more independent path without at the same time provoking or alienating the Americans.

The second missile launch was not the sole occasion that high-lighted potential rifts between the two allies. The entire US approach to North Korea exposed some fundamental strategic differences that had been adopted by the two countries. The Berlin Agreement between the US and North Korea in September 1999 did not suspend short- and mid-range missiles such as the No-dong, but dealt instead with more immediate American concerns such as missile export to Middle Eastern countries and the development of long-range missiles (Fouse, 2004,

p. 8). These bans were certainly a positive move, but this agreement also manifested the very different priorities held by the two countries. The Berlin Agreement, which for the most part ignored Japan's interests, created an amorphous fear among the Japanese. This uncertainty once again raised the critical question of US reliability. The Japanese government was forced to consider whether its security concerns could be fully met by the Americans or whether such security required some degree of unilateral action (Fouse, 2004, p. 8).

The Japanese government also found itself largely left out of the subsequent multilateral diplomacy. The US had agreed that South Korea would take a leading role on all peninsular issues. In April 1996, South Korea's President Kim Yong Sam and US President Clinton proposed Four-Party Peace Treaty Talks among North Korea, the US, South Korea, and China. Though North Korea's missile launch directly threatened its security, Japan remained an uninvited guest despite the high stakes involved. Still another unacknowledged complication ignored by the Four-Party negotiators was the continued allegations that North Korea had engineered the kidnapping of 11 Japanese nationals. But, except for KEDO, Japan was shut out of any of the key discussion groups. Exclusion from the Four-Party Talks quite naturally fed ever-present Japanese fears that its own security concerns would be left behind and largely forgotten (Green, 2001, p. 123; Fouse, 2004, p. 6). South Korean President Kim was distinctly hostile to Japan's attempts to employ the Japanese Red Cross as an alternative and independent channel of contact to the North Koreans. In January 1997, Kim made his displeasure explicit by pointing out that Tokyo's normalization talks would only complicate future Four-Party negotiations. Without a satisfactory framework that might advance its national interests or create a more beneficial environment, Tokyo's sense of isolation noticeably increased. Although the Four-Party Talks had lasted for two years and six meetings, these negotiations had made little, if any, progress. North Korea, for instance, persistently demanded the withdrawal of US forces from the peninsula. However, the Four-Party Talks did encourage the Japanese government to create a new participatory framework that was capable of pushing forward a more Japanese centered agenda.

In September 1998, Prime Minister Keizo Obuchi proposed enlarging the previous Four-Party Talks by adding Russia and Japan.[7] Foreign Minister Yohei Kono reiterated this idea in August 2000 while visiting China. Given the conflicting interests of the concerned countries, Japan was sufficiently realistic to view its own proposal as no more than a distant prospect (*Gaiko Kiroku*, 01-1279, August 31, 2000). Yet, South Korean President Kim Dae-Jung also proposed creating a framework of six-nation talks that would involve Japan and Russia and act as an improved version of the Four-Party Talks. Both proposals failed to engage either Chinese or American support at this stage of the negotiations (Kim, 2004).

As we have seen in the former chapters, Japan inevitably responded, however tentatively, to American winks, nods and shoves. By employing its economic muscle, Japan managed to share responsibility for regional stability, but only on US terms. As it had done in the past, the Americans had again strategically employed Japan's economic strength to achieve their own goals. KEDO, a multilateral framework of crisis avoidance, set up by US initiatives was an idiosyncratic burden sharing mechanism. Under US pressure, Japan reluctantly contributed a substantial amount of resources, thus buying its way into the negotiation process. Given its own lack of political/military power, the Japanese had no choice but to view KEDO as the only practical alternative that could defuse a particularly urgent security threat. However, the conflicting priorities of the two allies convinced the Japanese that it was unwise to entirely depend on the US to remove the threat posed by North Korean missiles. The Japanese government, if only belatedly, resolved to supplement US strategy with its own independent initiatives.

7.3 Koizumi's Pilgrimage: Shaking Off Conservative Constraints

As previously pointed out, since the end of the Cold War, the Japanese government had seen the wisdom of narrowly maintaining channels

---

[7] The idea was also supported by South Korea (see Aggarwal and Koo, 2006).

that could assist in normalizing relations with North Korea. Japan had made continuous efforts in this direction chiefly by exploiting unofficial visits by politicians and back channel links such as the Japanese Red Cross Society (Hatakeyama, interview with MOFA officials, April 2004). Shin Kanemaru's visit to North Korea in 1991 was one such attempt. However, many, if not most of these unofficial initiatives launched by politicians were made more in the hope of boosting their domestic profile than of achieving a positive outcome.[8] Similarly, since 1995, Japan had provided rice assistance via the Red Cross in an unsuccessful bid to soften North Korea's attitudes. Unfortunately, these Red Cross contacts failed to make any explicit impression. Instead, as demonstrated by North Korea's missile launch, signs of improvement proved scarce on the ground. Given this impasse, Japan had no other viable option than to seize upon a significantly changed international environment and take a bold and independent step.

The new Bush administration, in January 2001, signaled a drastic transformation in US–North Korean relations. Soon after his inauguration, US President George Bush ordered a review of US–North Korean policy.[9] Under the Clinton administration, the relationship had improved to a noticeable degree largely due to the softer approach taken by the Americans.[10] As a result, in October 2000, North Korea confirmed that it had suspended missile launches as part of a US–DPRK Joint Communiqué. This declaration was followed by Secretary of State Madeleine Albright's visit to North Korea in the same month. The Bush administration, however, maneuvered North Korea into a much more difficult position. Aware of toughening US attitudes, North Korea embarked on a series of vigorous diplomatic efforts to improve its international standing. They sought to establish diplomatic relations with other countries. The Koreans pledged their willingness to freeze missile launches until 2003 in the aftermath of an EU mission in May 2001.

---

[8] Michio Watanabe, a member of the LDP also visited North Korea in 1995. Former Prime Minister Murayama visited North Korea in 1998.

[9] For example, see Bush's statement on June 6, 2001, http://www.us.info.state.gov.

[10] William Perry supported the soft approach while serving in the Clinton administration (see Murata, 2002).

North Korea then followed up by announcing its intention to improve relations with major powers, including the US and Japan. In August 2001, Kim Jong Il visited Russia. He then met with China's Prime Minister Jiang Zemin in September. North Korea subsequently engaged in European diplomacy by establishing relations with Holland, Belgium, Spain, Germany, Luxembourg, Greece, and the EU.

This attempt to balance the major contending powers yielded mostly frustration for the North Koreans. The September 11, 2001, terrorist attacks on the US not only resonated in the Middle East but also rebounded on to the Korean peninsula. Soon after the attacks, the US declared its critical engagement in mounting a "war on terrorism." This declaration justified the subsequent US counter-attacks against terrorists in Afghanistan. Led by US President Bush, the "war on terrorism" relentlessly transformed major power relationships. After September 11, not only Japan, but also Russia moved quickly to support the US campaign. As a result, the US and Russia drew closer. China also lent its support to this American led "war on terrorism," resulting in improved relationships between the two countries. The international community clearly strengthened existing ties in reaction to the attacks.

North Korea now felt increasingly isolated. The regime feared for its survival more than ever before. Having clearly felt the imminent need to strongly differentiate itself from Iraq, North Korea vainly tried to clarify its determination to join the holy crusade against terrorism in the days immediately following the terrorist attack. Despite its best efforts, Bush proceeded to brand North Korea as part of an international "axis of evil" that also included Iran and Iraq. Despite this repudiation, North Korea continued to hint at its readiness to engage the US in dialog. In April 2002, the Koreans tried to improve their relationship with the Americans, but all such offers were summarily rejected. Sensing no other viable option available, North Korea once again opted to escalate its customary tactics of brinkmanship.

Bush's tough attitude combined with an adverse international situation compelled North Korea to modify its strategy in order to survive. North Korea's new found willingness to enter into direct talks with Japan came as something of a by-product of the unfavorable circumstances swirling around North Korea.[11] Pressed by hostile international circumstances, North Korea could only hope that Japan would function as an effective mediator between itself and the US. The Koreans also assumed that the Japanese might be willing to provide economic assistance in exchange for normalizing their relations. Anticipating some such assistance for their devastated economy, in July 2002, after a review of its price and distribution system, North Korea initiated a series of economic reforms. It created a "special administrative region" in the north-eastern region along the China–North Korea border, hoping to encourage business activity. North Korea's economic initiatives implicitly assumed that Japanese assistance would be forthcoming following bilateral negotiations.[12]

During this key period, Japan was itself dissatisfied with the existing situation. In addition to KEDO's limitations, Japan had failed to capture either American or international support to any desired extent. The Japanese government had dutifully protested North Korea's 1998 missile launch to the UN without obtaining a decisive condemnation of North Korea's actions. Trilateral coordination among the US, South Korea, and Japan had been the main pillar of Japan's North Korea policy. But nothing of use had come from this alliance. Rather, it only served to constrain Japan's actions further. Moreover, KEDO as a framework failed to deal with Japan's specific security concerns. The UN offered no effective alternative assistance. Japan could turn to no other multilateral frameworks to advance its agenda. The Japanese were quite conscious of the overarching reality they faced, namely that although they might share similar long-run goals or ultimate objectives with the US and Korea, these countries still could harbor distinct and perhaps conflicting concerns. The US was clearly fixated on the non-proliferation of nuclear weapons. In contrast, for the most part South

---

[11] In his article, C.S. Eliot Kang argues that North Korea was willing to trade its missile capabilities for economic development, therefore, its behavior can be explained by mercantilist realism (see Kang, 2002).

[12] In September 2002, North Korea changed Sinuijum into a special economic area which would tolerate private property rights, entry by foreigners without a visa and investment by foreign companies. The North Koreans granted these exceptions in the hope that they would be able to boost the lagging North Korean economy.

Korea was worried about the security threat posed by North Korea. But an expressed desire for future unification inevitably constrained the South's behavior. Meanwhile, Japan faced a distinctly domestic crisis as public outrage over the abduction issue threatened to boil over. Popular opinion, inflamed by media reports, demanded government action to resolve the outrage caused by these alleged kidnappings. An abiding concern over the potential security threat, aligned with pressure to expedite this increasingly emotional issue, combined to produce Japan's independent initiative.

Both North Korea and Japan shared some quite compelling reasons to proceed down this particular path. For North Korea, accelerated Japanese contacts, either at the official or unofficial level, created an opportunity to transform what was clearly a difficult situation. For Japan, North Korea's willingness to negotiate appeared to provide a chance to achieve a desirable breakthrough in the stalemated status quo. Consequently, the North Korean Labour Party suggested a summit meeting with Japan in January 2001 and demonstrated a seeming readiness to settle the "missing persons" issue (*Asahi Shimbun*, September 12, 2002). Up till then, Japan and North Korea had held meetings through their Red Cross Societies, but both were aware that these limited talks were unlikely to lead to any serious results. In comparison, an official meeting seemed to provide distinct possibilities. Responding to the offer, high-ranking officials of both governments secretly made contact in Singapore. Such attempts to build mutual confidence gained momentum in the Fall of 2001 when Hitoshi Tanaka, (Director-General of the Asian and Oceanian Affairs Bureau of MOFA) entered into additional high-level negotiations (Hatakeyama, interview with MOFA officials, April 2004).[13]

Promptly noticing a change in North Korean attitudes, Tanaka secretly approached Pyongyang.[14] He requested the release of a *Nihon Kezai Shimbun* journalist, who had been detained by the North

---

[13] Hitoshi Tanaka was appointed director around this time.

[14] Only two people in MOFA and two people in the Cabinet office including Koizumi were informed of these unfolding events. They were Tanaka and Kenji Hiramatsu of MOFA and Furukawa from the Cabinet.

Korean government for almost two years (Tanaka, 2005). In response, the journalist was released in February 2002. By March 2002, as a direct reaction to Japan's official announcement blaming North Korea for conducting abductions, the North Korean Red Cross Society announced that it would immediately resume investigations into the fate of those "missing persons." Through a variety of channels, North Korea indicated a clear willingness to talk. In April 2002, North Korean General Secretary Kim signaled that he would address the abduction issue in the near future. These softer attitudes clearly encouraged the Japanese government. However, whether Japan would be able to extract concessions through the judicious use of diplomacy and its economic inducements remained open to debate. Despite this essential ambiguity, Japan still felt capable of convincing North Korea that it faced a number of viable alternatives. The aim underpinning this strategy was to persuade the North Koreans that they need not repeatedly play their nuclear card.

In July 2002, the Japan–North Korea Foreign Minster's meeting was held to coincide with of the 9th ASEAN Regional Forum (ARF) Ministerial Meeting in Brunei. In August, further Japan–North Korea consultations at the Director-General level were held. Such meetings served as a convenient stepping stone to the ensuing historic visit by Prime Minister Koizumi. During the course of these talks, Tanaka of the Ministry of Foreign Affairs sensed that the North Koreans were willing to seriously negotiate normalization at an arranged summit meeting (Tanaka, 2005). He then managed to convince the US to accept such negotiations (or at least not interfere), although the Americans steadfastly and predicably had remained particularly unhappy with Japan's initiative. However, the US was well aware of the domestic volatility created by the abduction fracas. The Americans feared that these domestic considerations would lead Japan either to walk away from what they considered to be current and compelling security issues or even grant quite lenient terms when responding to Korea's nuclear development program. The US was particularly concerned that Japanese domestic opinion might be capable of derailing any serious attempt to come to grips with more pressing security concerns. To temper such dangerous largesse, the US repeatedly informed the Japanese government of the extent of North Korea's program for developing nuclear weapons prior to Koizumi's visit. American diplomats continued to express their deep concerns over the proposed meeting. They feared that Japan would be unable to properly handle vital security issues at the slated summit with North Korea.[15] Ultimately, the US, despite its qualms, did reluctantly agree to Koizumi's visit, but only on the condition that Japan would not fail to directly address the relevant security issues, as well as more specifically Japanese concerns (Yakushiji, 2003, p. 72).

On September 17, 2002, Koizumi traveled to North Korea carrying with him hopes that significant progress could be achieved. He planned to urge North Korea to "act responsibly as a member of the international community to wipe out the international community's concerns" over security issues including both nuclear and missile issues (Ministry of Foreign Affairs, 2002). As one of the key players, Tanaka left no doubt that the most important goal sought was enhancing peace and stability within the Korean Peninsula by normalizing relations. Japanese policymakers deeply involved in setting up this historic visit shared the belief that a normalization policy would contribute not only to Japan's security but also to that of the region.[16] Koizumi's statement after the summit meeting further confirmed this goal. He stated:

> An improvement in relations between Japan and North Korea does not just benefit those two countries. It will also affect peace and security in the Korean Peninsula and all of Northeast Asia. Moreover, it is linked to peace and stability for South Korea, the US, Russia, China, other neighbors and international society as a whole (*The Wall Street Journal*, September 18, 2002).

Needless to say, achieving such a result was never going to be an easy task. Despite harboring his own hopes, Tanaka himself did not realistically expect the visit to persuade North Korea to immediately abandon its nuclear ambitions. He cherished no illusions about North Korean strategy. Survival of the ruling regime depended on improving relations

---

[15] To arouse Japan's attention, the US informed Foreign Minister Yoriko Kawaguchi of North Korea's development program for nuclear weapons at the time of the ARF meeting in Brunei (July 2002) (see Yakushiji, 2003, pp. 3–6).
[16] He was one of the key persons involved in the decision-making process (see Furukawa, 2005, pp. 222–223).

with the US (Hatakeyama, interview with Tanaka, May 2006). Economic assistance from Japan was only of secondary importance. For
that reason, North Korea had failed to actively pursue normalization
with Japan until the international situation became unduly hostile. In
fact, North Korea's desire to strengthen an alliance with the US was the
primary driver which elevated Japan's bargaining position (Tanaka and
Tawara, 2005). Lacking nuclear weapons of its own, the Japanese were
in no position to extract concessions from an aggressive North Korea
(Hatakeyama, interview with Tanaka, May 2006). Nevertheless, Japan
realized that it lacked the luxury of remaining safely on the sidelines
while the US pursued its own solution.

Fully understanding that the only card it could play was an economic one, the Japanese government did not expect to achieve their
ultimate goal of curtailing North Korea's nuclear program. Instead, it
aimed, as a realistic alternative, to create a more inclusive framework.
This newly devised structure would ensure Japan's involvement in security talks and reflect Japanese interests. Setting such realistic targets did
seem feasible. Japan was, after all, a founding member of KEDO, which
dealt with such security issues. As we have seen however, this arrangement had failed to prevent North Korea from threatening regional
peace and stability. As far as Japan was concerned, KEDO was a distinct
disappointment. The diverging interests of Japan and the US had translated into certain failure for Japanese objectives. The Four-Party Talks
among the US, South Korea, China, and North Korea had served as a
framework meant to address peninsular problems. But it had the undesirable characteristic of excluding Japan. This situation had occurred
despite the large stakes that Japan had invested in the outcome. The
only tenuous recourse left to Japan was a combination of close consultations with the US along with a reliance on international institutions such as the UN. Achieving any of its aims now meant utilizing
more indirect routes. Without an existing framework that would allow
Japan to explore possible solutions, or express specific opinions to break
though what had become oppressive restrictions, the Japanese government turned to bilateral channels.

Fortunately, this historic meeting did result in achieving two important objectives. The Japan–Democratic People's Republic of Korea

Pyongyang Declaration provided a basis for settling security concerns by stating that North Korea "would further maintain the moratorium on missile launching in and after 2003 and comply with all international agreements related to the nuclear issue on the Korean peninsula" (Ministry of Foreign Affairs, 2003). The countries also agreed to settle historical issues. In return, North Korea would receive welcomed "economic cooperation" from Japan, while explicitly forgoing anything that might be labeled as "reparations." Total aid would add up to $10 billion. As a negotiating body, the summit meeting provided a potential opening for subsequent Six-Party Talks. Japan was finally able to structure a framework which would reflect its own views and resolve issues in a manner beneficial to Japan's national interests. Even though the framework would not yield instant results, it was far better than being virtually locked out of the process. By creating such a negotiating environment, Japan would establish a firmer basis for its national security concerns while contributing to regional peace and stability. The Tokyo–Pyongyang declaration provided the Japanese, even in the absence of military power, with a chance to take more responsibility for maintaining regional security (Hiramatsu, 2002). The declaration charted a specific course forward. In addition, the agreement did break the existing impasse over the abduction issue. North Korea finally admitted to the abduction of Japanese nationals in the past. Furthermore, the Koreans revealed that 8 out of 13 Japanese abductees were already dead.

Unfortunately, Japan's diplomatic glory soon faded. Two insurmountable hurdles surfaced, one domestically and the other internationally. These were, quite paradoxically, North Korea's acknowledgment of its history of abduction combined with its continued program of uranium enrichment. The two together effectively managed to frustrate Japan's grand strategy of settling its own concerns in such a way that the result would contribute to regional peace and stability.

7.4 Japan Trips over Its Own Feet: Backtracking on the Declaration

The Japanese government took advantage of public pressure to carry out its grand strategy. The historic meeting was supposed to achieve dramatic results. Even if not instantly, it was meant to secure Japan's national security in a way that would also contribute to regional security. Consequently, a successful visit would have elevated Japan's standing while demonstrating its readiness to perform as a leading regional power. Even without the benefit of military backing, Japan still would have helped to establish regional stability through clever diplomacy allied with its economic muscle. Other Asian countries could only welcome this new model of Japanese activism. Cambodian Foreign Minister Hor Nam Hong stated that it was a "very important step to guarantee security not only on the Korean Peninsula but also in the Asia-Pacific region and the whole world" (*BBC Morning Asia Pacific*, September 3, 2002).

Japan's decision to break through the existing diplomatic stalemate was entirely explicable based on the analysis previously presented in this volume. Moreover, the Japanese government was undeniably under public pressure to deal directly with a serious neighborhood problem. As we have seen, this considerable pressure was not the sole reason that encouraged the government to take such a historic step. Growing fears for Japan's national as well as regional security conspired with the more domestic abduction issue to drive government policy. These worries pushed the Japanese into taking a more independent path despite US preferences. Although Japan's bold step did not bring any immediate results, it did give birth to the subsequent Six-Party Talks that included Japan and provided a direct conduit for Japanese concerns. Momentarily, it did seem that Japan could be capable of taking a leading position in creating regional security.

Subsequently, Japanese behavior, both at and after the historic summit meeting, deviated from any more pragmatic expectations. The abduction issue soon achieved parity, if not priority with ostensibly more vital security matters. These emerging pressures became even more explicit after the summit meeting. Government resources and attention flowed instead to the abduction issue, largely ignoring any resolution of the more critical security issues. Priorities radically shifted from security to abduction concerns. This shift morbidly entangled these two different issues and, as a result, greatly limited Japan's options. In short, Japan's fixation on the abduction issue after the summit meeting undercut Japan's ability to chart a feasible course in pursuit of a bigger, and more long-term, picture. The Tokyo–Pyongyang declaration ceased to convey anything but the flimsiest of nominal values.

Rather than providing reinforcement, the summit meeting paradoxically nullified Japan's grand strategy. The actual outcome failed to protect Japan's national security by contributing to regional peace and stability. Instead, the Japanese government was forced to alter its planned course. Understanding the reasons for this non-productive shift requires an examination of those specific factors that ultimately shaped Japan's policy initiative.

7.5 Abducting Japanese Policy: Factors Altering Japanese Behavior

To emphasize the point once again, Japan's primary objective was to enhance its own security by contributing to regional stability. In addition, it wished to concurrently resolve the abduction issue. However, following the summit meeting, Japan's strategy to simultaneously resolve these two distinct issues failed abysmally. The change in priorities toward the more emotional issue made any success highly unlikely. The overwhelming factor shifting Japan's stance lay in the prevailing politics of the domestic situation. Public overreaction to the abduction situation swamped Japan's security concerns, thus forcing the government to alter its course.

North Korea's nuclear capability, including ballistic missiles able to reach Japan, had created negative, verging on hostile, reactions among the Japanese public. Growing anger generated by the increasingly publicized abduction cases served to effectively enflame public (and governmental) fears. Sections of the media acting in concert with opportunistic politicians ensured that public fear and anger were transformed into mounting and urgent domestic pressure to resolve this issue. The government was left with no other feasible option than to assume an extremely unyielding and truculent stand.[17]

---

[17] See Izumi (2000). In his opinion the abduction issues were relatively minor issues that the government could have easily contained.

The first explicit revelation that Japanese nationals had been abducted came in 1991. Kim Hyon Hui, a North Korean spy who conducted the 1987 bombing of a Korean Airlines jet, revealed that she was taught Japanese by a "Lee Un-Hae." The confession brought the issue to the fore. Suspicions arose that "Lee Un-Hae" might be a Japanese woman who had disappeared many years in the past. With the Kim Hyon Hui incident as a catalyst, growing numbers of Japanese came to believe that North Korea had abducted up to 11 Japanese. Adding to this conviction, North Korea's categorical denial of the "Lee Un-Hae" claim only served to heighten anti-North Korean sentiment. Public anti-North Korean feeling spilled over and spoiled unofficial normalization talks conducted by MOFA, which were then quietly under way.[18]

Fortunately, at this stage the alleged suspicions, although growing, had not been transformed into hardened conviction. Anti-North Korean opinion failed to gain a sufficient wave of momentum capable of preventing or even influencing the government's decision to financially underwrite KEDO. Public pressure was still far weaker than the strength it would eventually achieve at the time of Koizumi's fateful visit to North Korea in 2002. One MOFA official admitted that had there then been public pressure on the government to resolve the abduction issue, it would not have been able to financially support KEDO (Hatakeyama, interview with MOFA director, April 2004). The absence of any sizeable public pressure enabled the government to support and provide a substantial level of funding.

Prior to Koizumi's summit in 2002, the second wave of rising distrust had come in 1997. In February that year, the Japanese government officially admitted that nine Japanese nationals had been kidnapped by North Korea. In May of the same year, the government confirmed the possibility that a girl from Niigata prefecture was kidnapped as well. The official recognition by the government rekindled public resentment against North Korea's inhumane crime. Public anger then focused on the government's inability to protect the lives of Japanese nationals. The growing attitude among the general public

---

[18]For example, MOFA began to provide rice assistance through the Japanese Red Cross Society in the mid-1990s.

toward North Korea was already seriously negative due to the 1993 missile launch and its alleged nuclear development programs. The abduction cases tipped whatever balance remained. North Korea's defiant attitude of totally denying all allegations further fueled the public's adverse impression. The Association of the Facilities of Victims Kidnapped by North Korea (established in 1997) was a clear indication that public concern and apprehension increasingly revolved around this one issue. The organization also heralded the potential for using the abductees' plight as a vehicle for political gains. Only a shameless willingness to champion this emotional concern proved necessary. In short, the abduction issue was now impossible to ignore.

Despite growing public anger leading to widespread anti-North Korean sentiment, the Japanese government had no other option than to rely on the KEDO structure and/or the US to arbitrate this highly charged political problem. However, the capabilities defined by KEDO did not include dealing with specifically Japanese concerns such as the abduction issue. The Japanese government started to sense the emerging divergence of US and Japanese interests. A natural suspicion arose that any US–North Korean settlement might simply ignore the problem raised by the alleged abductions. A senior Japanese official pointed out that if the US negotiated while ignoring this issue, there would be a strong backlash from the Japanese public (*Nikkei English News*, March 11, 1997). A characteristic reaction of this type would place a serious strain on their long standing alliance with the US. Meanwhile, public resentment against North Korea increasingly edged on to the government's political radar. North Korean chronic misconduct further fanned public anger to the extent that the government dared not overlook the issue.

North Korea had initially attempted to soft pedal this increasingly emotional controversy by announcing its intention to investigate these "missing persons." However, a series of border violations by North Korean ships once again fueled Japanese resentment. In 1999, a naval clash between the two Koreas resulted in the loss of one North Korean warship and the deaths of approximately 30 sailors. In the same year, North Korean ships intruded into Japan's territorial waters. North Korea was perversely succeeding in strengthening its image as a renegade terrorist state. On top of this criminal type of behavior, North Korea continued to alienate public opinion with its provocative attitude. Public reaction had hardened, demanding that the Japanese government adopt a tougher line. Given a rising public chorus augmented, if not deliberately fueled, by some key LDP politicians, the matter of the abductees was bound to intrude into any bilateral negotiations. Without hope for a reasonable resolution, maintaining bilateral channels by providing rice assistance seemed increasingly difficult to sustain (*Gaiko Kiroku*, 01-541-2, May 2000). North Korea hardly helped itself by suddenly terminating the previously announced investigation into "missing persons" in December 2001 before it managed to produce any credible results. The Office of the United Nations High Commissioner for Human Rights also terminated its investigation on the alleged abduction issue in January 2002. Running counter to these moves, in March of the same year, the Japanese government again acknowledged that a Japanese woman was possibly kidnapped by North Korea. The total number of abductees was judged to be 11. Inflamed public opinion did not allow continued government inaction to be a feasible alternative.

North Korea's misconduct, the alleged abduction issue, missile launches, and suspected nuclear development program, all embellished country's very worst aspects. However, it was the abduction allegations that created an almost intractable diplomatic impasse for the Japanese. Even though they shared a number of ultimate objectives with other concerned nations, the Japanese government needed to ameliorate public opinion by giving first priority to settling the abduction issue. This one outstanding problem gained such political weight that it came to dominate the political landscape. A concerted Japanese chorus, led by the families of the abductees, created overwhelming public pressure. Japan's panoply of North Korea's intransigence seemed at times reduced to this one narrow issue: Japan's politicians saw no other option available than to deal with it urgently and independently. Public opinion compelled the government to attempt to balance both the abduction and security issues simultaneously. The 2002 *Diplomatic Bluebook* confirms this. Japan's purpose at the summit meeting was to "secure its utmost national interest, in other words, the safety and prosperity of Japan and its people" by making a "breakthrough toward the resolution of various issues such as the abduction issue" (Ministry of Foreign Affairs, 2002, Chapter 1).

Contrary to Japanese expectations, North Korea's acknowledgment and ensuing revelation of the appalling fates of the abductees resulted in an insurmountable public backlash. Faced with these sordid facts, the media ceaselessly reported the families' grief. Public resentment grew accordingly as this one story continued to dominate each day's top news. To make matters worse, MOFA's previous concealment of the dates when each of these eight abductees died, followed by the subsequent release of these dates, served to infuriate the Japanese public even further. The public now imagined MOFA as obsessed with normalizing relations with North Korea at the expense of these pitiful victims. This newly intractable public stance determined the course of subsequent negotiations.

In addition, the lack of consensus within the government itself hindered any effective response to the problem. An absence of coherence became obvious when the five abductees were allowed to return to Japan for a short time following the summit meeting. Deputy Cabinet Secretary Shinzo Abe was a leading figure championing the urgent concerns of the abductees. He appealed for public support, while extending his own governmental influence by striking a tough stance against the North Koreans. Abe opposed any normalization of relations without a prior resolution of the abduction issue. Backed by unyielding public opinion, he brazenly demanded that the five abductees remain in Japan despite previous arrangements between the two countries (*Nikkei*, December 24, 2002). In contrast, Tanaka kept his sights on the big picture. Since he was much more concerned with establishing North Korean ties, he insisted that the five abductees be returned. He was reluctant to jeopardize future relations with North Korea over what could be accurately described as a highly emotional dispute (*Nikkei*, December 24, 2002). Tanaka worried that any decision to keep the abductees at home might spoil all the efforts made so far to secure Japan's national security and to contribute to regional peace. Other politicians such as Chief Cabinet Secretary Yasuo Fukuda and Katsuya

Suzuki, a chief diplomat to KEDO, shared Tanaka's view. They joined in demanding that the government stick to the original terms of the declaration (*Nikkei*, December 24, 2002). Preserving a channel with North Korea for further talks seemed to be extremely vital, since it could provide Japan with a certain amount of future leverage (Soeya, 2003).

However, Koizumi, sensing the political winds, sided decisively with Abe. The most immediately advantageous stance in this controversy became increasingly obvious. Deciding to return the abductees would be a serious, if not fatal blow to his administration. Unlike his predecessors, Koizumi's political base tended to eschew the more traditional group of vested interests. His support did not rest on a coalition of LDP functionaries. Instead, he directly targeted public opinion by utilizing strategic sound bites to rally those disaffected by politics as usual. He frequently employed a catchy "one-phrase" (or sound bite) to attract and directly appeal to his core supporters. Almost perfectly understanding the role played by the media in influencing election strategy, he repeatedly appeared on TV, unlike the run of the mill traditional Japanese leaders (Nonaka, 2008, p. 64). As a result, Koizumi could ignore emotional public outcries only at his own peril given that it was still only his second year in power. In this particular calculus, losing public support would be equivalent to being forced to step down. With an opportunistic eye out for his political life, Koizumi insisted on a radical shift in priorities that would see his career remain afloat.

Countervailing factors that could have offset public opinion were largely nonexistent. While ambitious politicians, including Koizumi, sought short-term gains, an international deadlock over the Korean crisis left the Japanese government with little, if any, wiggle room. Added to the Koizumi administration's almost morbid sensitivity to public opinion, North Korea's acknowledgment of its nuclear development program ruled out any possibility of continuing scheduled security talks. Meanwhile, for the US, the first (and perhaps only) priority was to block North Korea from developing nuclear weapons. This concern only intensified as events unfolded. When meeting with Koizumi prior to the Japan–North Korea Summit (September 2002), Bush did not refer to the abduction issue even once. Instead, he chose to concentrate exclusively on the North Korean's development of nuclear weapons

(*Agence France-Presse*, September 15, 2002). Deepening this rift, in October 2002, US Assistant Secretary of State, James Kelly, produced startling evidence of North Korea's uranium-enrichment program. The US then demanded that its allies fall behind its strategy of applying pressure so that the Koreans would dismantle the program (*Agence France-Presse*, October 24, 2002). Given this approach, the MOFA's Senior Vice-Minister had to clarify Japan's position not to "proceed without progress in the security talks" with North Korea (*Agence France-Presse*, October 24, 2002). Coincidentally, this decision was made public on the same day as Koizumi decided that the five abductees would remain in Japan.

Faced with this bit of intransigence, North Korea again employed its development program as the key lever driving its characteristic strategy of brinkmanship. The Koreans unsealed nuclear facilities and expelled IAEA inspectors. In response, KEDO decided to suspend the entire supply of heavy fuel oil to North Korea from December 2002 onward. The situation grew worse with North Korea declaring its intention of withdrawing from the Nuclear Non-Proliferation Treaty as of January 2003. By taking such uncompromising positions, North Korea spoiled any potential agreement between Japan and North Korea. The result completely nullified previous Japanese efforts to bring North Korea back within the international community by providing reasonable alternative options. Japan's grand strategy of playing a leading role in establishing regional peace and security entirely vanished due to an unanticipated alignment of specific factors, namely, domestic pressure augmented by conflicting American interests.

7.6 Conclusion: The Limits to an Independent Foreign Policy

The missile launch and subsequent North Korean development of its nuclear capability challenged Japan's ability to establish its own security framework. However, subsequent revelations concerning the abduction issue added to an intractable and complex problem. Growing public pressure demanded that the Japanese government take decisive and concrete steps to resolve these issues. Aroused public opinion combined

with Japan's disappointment over KEDO and the difficulty of orchestrating divergent international interests pushed the Japanese into taking
a bold policy step.

This initiative was propelled by one clear objective. Japan's goal
was to protect its national security by contributing to regional peace
and stability. Diplomatic success would not only have strengthened its
security but also boosted Japan's regional reputation. Understanding
the intractable hurdles placed in front of any bilateral negotiations, the
government attempted to create a new framework to circumscribe any
difficulties that might arise. It hoped to devise a workable mechanism
which would reflect Japanese national interests and provide Japan with
a leading role in creating a new security order. In the absence of an
independent position which established room for Japan's objectives,
pursuing a national security agenda or building a role as a regional
leader would have proved futile.

Japan, trapped in this unavoidable crisis, clearly continued to pursue regional leadership during these initial stages of the Korean debacle.
However, irresistible domestic pressure, combined with an ultra sensitive Koizumi administration, derailed Japan's diplomatic direction.
Giving into public pressure, the government decided to deal primarily
with the abduction issue, much to the detriment of the security problem. North Korean acknowledgments during the summit served only to
inflame growing and highly emotional public resentment. From then
on, Japan's options were highly limited. Too much emphasis on the
abduction issue eventually blurred an initially clear determination to
foster peace and stability, not only to enhance its own security but
that of the region as well. Undermining this diplomatic direction, the
abduction issue ceased to be a subsidiary claim and came to dominate all
subsequent discussion. Nurtured and fostered by ambitious politicians,
the abductees created a nearly inflexible policy constraint.

A bit of unfortunate timing then saw a parallel, and equally unwelcome, additional development in this ongoing crisis. North Korea's
admission of a nuclear development program hardened an already
tough US policy position. Consequently, North Korea then had to
withstand even more pressure to dismantle its nuclear policy. This event
left Japan with little room to maneuver between these two committed

adversaries. For a crucial period, these two specific factors (domestic opinion and US pressure) were aligned, forcing the Japanese government to alter its short-term direction.

During this period, Japan had initiated a serious and independent effort to pursue its grand strategy of establishing the Japanese as a legitimate regional leader. However, the North Koreans proved too intransigent and Japan insufficiently determined. Though Japanese policy on the Korean peninsula was indicative of more fundamental diplomatic objectives, the specific initiative failed to achieve any lasting success.

References

Aggarwal VK, Koo MG. (2006) Shifting ground: Is it finally time? *Global Asia*, 1(1), 29–41.

Fouse D. (2004) Japan's post-Cold War North Korea policy. *Asia-Pacific Centre for Security Studies.* February, 1–14.

Furukawa T. (2005) *Kazumigaseki Hanseiki.* Saga Shimbumsha, Saga.

Green MJ. (2001) *Japan's Reluctant Realism.* Palgrave, New York.

Hiramatsu K. (2002) Leadup to the signing of the Japan–DPRK Pyongyang Declaration. *Gaiko Forum (English Edition)*, 2(4), 18–25.

Hughes CW. (1996) The North Korean nuclear crisis and Japanese security. *Survival*, 38(2), 79–103.

Hughes CW. (1999) *Japan's Economic Power and Security.* Routledge, London and New York.

Izumi H. (2000). Pyongyang grasps new realities. *Japan Quarterly* April–June: 11–16.

Johnson C. (1995) Korea and our Asia policy. *National Interest*, 41(Fall), 66–77.

Kang CSE. (2002) North Korea's security policy. In: Kim SS, Lee TH (eds.), *North Korea and Northeast Asia*, pp. 195–209. Rowman and Littlefield Publishers, Maryland.

Kim SS. (2004) Northeast Asia in the local global regional nexus: Multiple challenges and contending explanations. In: Kim SS (ed.), *The International Relations of Northeast Asia*, pp. 3–60. Rowman & Littlefield Publishers, New York.

Kono Y. (1995) Statement by Foreign Minister Yohei Kono on Japan's rice assistance to North Korea. *Ministry of Foreign Affairs*, 30 June, http://www.mofa.go.jp/announce/announce/archive_2/rice.html, accessed in June 2005.

Lee J-H, Moon C-I. (2002) The Korean Calculus. In: Inoguchi T (ed.), *Japan's Asia Policy: Revival and Response*, pp. 100–166. Palgrave, New York.

Ministry of Foreign Affairs. (2003) The Pyongyang declaration. *Ministry of Foreign Affairs.* http://www.mofa.go.jp/region/asia-paci/n_korea/pmv0209/pyongyang.html, accessed in September 2004.

Ministry of Foreign Affairs. (2002) *Diplomatic Bluebook 2002.* http://www.mofa.go.jp/policy/other/bluebook/2002/index.html, accessed in September 2004.

Ministry of Foreign Affairs. (1999) *Diplomatic Bluebook 1999.* http://www.mofa.go.jp/policy/other/bluebook/1999/index.html, accessed in July 2004.

Ministry of Foreign Affairs. (1998) Japan–Republic of Korea joint declaration, 8 October 1998. Ministry of Foreign Affairs. http://www.moga.go.jp/region/asia-apci/korea/joint9810htm, accessed in December 2003.

Ministry of Foreign Affairs. (1996) *Diplomatic Bluebook 1996.* http://www.mofa.go.jp/policy/other/bluebook/1996/index.html, accessed in July 2004.

Miyashita A. (2003) *Limits to Power.* Lexington Books, Lanham.

Murata K. (2002) America no Kitachosen Seisaku to Perry Hokoku. *International Affairs.* No. 479.

Nonaka N. (2008) *Jiminto Seiji no Owari.* Chikuma Shobo, Tokyo.

Oberdorfer D. (2001) *The Two Koreas: A Contemporary History.* Basic Books, New York.

Sakai H. (2001) Continuity and discontinuity. In: Akitoshi M, Sato Y (eds.), *Japanese Foreign Policy in Asia and the Pacific,* pp. 59–73. Palgrave, New York.

Soeya Y. (2003) Japan's diplomacy and the North Korean problem. *Japan Review of International Affairs,* 17(1), 55.

Tanaka H. (2005) Watashigamita Koizumi Gaiko 4 Nenkan no Shinjitsu. *Gekkan Gendai,* 11, 38–47.

Tanaka H. (1994). Kita Chosen Kaku Giwaku Mondai O Kensho Suru. *Gaiko Forum,* July.

Tanaka H, Tawara S. (2005) *Kokka to Gaiko.* Kodansha, Tokyo.

Yakushiji K. (2003) *Gaimusho.* Iwanami Shinsho, Tokyo.

Chapter 8

Using Economic Diplomacy: Japan and the Asian Meltdown

8.1 Introduction: Japan's Ache for Recognition

From the re-establishment of good relations with Asian countries after the Pacific War, up through the increasing economic penetration of the 1980s, economic considerations have been the hallmark of Japan's Asian strategy. By the 1980s, Japan's business sector had started to invest heavily overseas by establishing off-shore factories. This initiative significantly changed the nature of the economic relationship between Japan and other Asian countries. Mutual interdependence now defined this fundamental arrangement. In other words, through a "three-in-one approach," namely, a combination of aid, trade, and foreign direct investment (FDI), most Asian countries were incorporated into Japan's "production alliance" (Hatch and Yamamura, 1996, p. 175).

Given this environment, the breakout of the East Asian crisis in 1997 seemed to provide something of a litmus test for Japan's continued position as the dominant economic power in Asia. Japan had been actively attempting to spread its influence by forging a leadership role for itself. Although the crisis seemed to present Japan with a golden opportunity, its actions and policies instead received widespread criticism.[1] Japan was perceived as bowing to US pressure during the

---

[1] For example, see Lincoln (1998) and Drysdale (2002).

285

crisis, rather than assuming a leadership role in stabilizing the regional economy. However, when viewed through the prism of its long-run objective (Japan's pursuit of regional influence), the reality was in fact much more complex. Japan clearly attempted to initiate bold policy proposals while working within the bounds of a multilateral context. Unfortunately (or sometimes quite to the contrary) what a country aims to accomplish is not always what it achieves. Japan seriously tried to create a new economic order, but failed to realize this objective. Japan's behavior was constrained (as has often been the case) by running at cross purposes to US objectives. A post-war truism would reliably predict that whenever Japan develops a foreign policy strategy, whatever subsequent objectives it aims to achieve will inevitably be circumscribed by intractable US policy goals and decisions. As the East Asian Crisis progressed, Japan realized that it could only hope to perform an effective role by changing its tactics from a broad-based approach to a more bilateral one. By trying to fly beneath the US radar, Japan might be able to support narrowly specific initiatives without attracting undue opposition. To succeed to even a limited degree, Japan realized that it must choose a pragmatic, second best option in the hope that by stabilizing rising regional turbulence, this alternative strategy would also assist its own ailing economy. The subsequent transferal of substantial financial assistance to targeted East Asian countries manifested Japan's determination to enlarge the scope of its economic diplomacy.

The question remains whether the East Asian crisis displays a distinct Japanese failure to pursue its over-arching objective. Did Japan abdicate its preferred leadership role or was it simply thwarted by time-specific factors?[2] Two actions by the Japanese government will be examined: one is Japan's proposal to create an Asian Monetary Fund (AMF); another is the Miyazawa Initiative. These two attempts raise an array of issues. Traditionally, Japan had been reluctant to set up any type of regional mechanism that would not include the US. Given its previous reluctance to embrace any proposed regionalism that excluded the US, why did Japan at this time think that it could successfully ignore its

---

[2] Hughes (2000) also argues that Japan has been exercising "covert economic and political leadership."

dominant post-war ally? Why did it change its course by giving up its ambitious plan for an AMF? Subsequent to Japan's AMF failure, what factors enabled the Japanese, by employing the Miyazawa Initiative, to fund bilateral assistance after not succeeding with their multilateral strategy? In these instances, Japan can best be understood as having engaged in some required regearing of its economic diplomacy without changing its overall objectives. This is far from obvious since it was done, necessarily, very quietly. It is almost as though Japan aspired to increase its political influence by stealth, using more subtle tactics to achieve its goals while minimizing potential conflict.

8.2 Japan's First Attempt: The Multilateral Approach

8.2.1 *East Collides with West: Japan's Rising Ambitions*

During the post-war period, a combination of Japanese investment, trade, and overseas assistance contributed significantly to economic development throughout Asia. In addition to simple capital inflows, a relocation of Japanese manufacturing companies to these countries resulted in a new division of labor. Japan took its place, if not explicitly, as an innovative leader of new products and new technologies. As of 1993, technology transfers accounted for 47 percent of Japan's total exports within the region, illustrating the significance that such transfers play in facilitating development (Japan Science and Technology Agency, 1993, p. 348). Along with a quite tangible flow of capital, Japanese subcontractors also brought to these Asian countries a Japanese model of economic development. This approach is characterized by a close coordination between government and the business sector, with governmental interventions serving to protect targeted infant industries.[3] Successful duplication of Japan's developmental history

---

[3]There naturally has been criticism of Japan's "flying geese development model." Critics are willing to accept that technology transfer might occur due to an outflow of FDI and that these transfers could lead to regional economic development. However, they argue that the cost of start-ups and mastering this new technology would be prohibitive. Therefore, countries which follow the Japanese model cannot escape from a dependent status. They will inevitably end up as subcontractors of "Japan Inc."

to other Asian countries would nurture, perhaps only in a somewhat subtle degree, Japan's aspirations for regional recognition. Hoping to clone this model, the Ministry of International Trade and Industry (MITI) prodded the Thai government in the early 1980s to imitate Japan by creating parallel public institutions, such as a Thai Export–Import Bank, which would promote growth within the local business sector (Hatch and Yamamura, 1996, p. 142). Malaysia's "Look-East Policy"[4] also illustrated Japan's increasing influence as a role model. Given Japan's remarkable inability to articulate its policy, the extent to which Japan aimed to export its developmental model and the degree to which it expected Asian countries precisely to follow this distinctively Japanese path remains arguable. However, the undoubted combination of FDI, aid, and trade, strongly pushed by MITI, did serve as a backdoor for transferring its developmental model overseas. Given the rapid economic growth that distinguished this era, Asian countries did follow, perhaps not entirely intentionally, Japan's successful path in a requisite "flying geese" manner. In essence, Japan managed to achieve its desired goal of performing the role of the leading goose.

While Japan propagated its developmental philosophy with some success through its own economic activities, a new approach, immersed in the blessings provided by strong American support, gained increasing influence within the international financial arena. This became known as the "Washington Consensus," an apt shorthand for the dominant Western approach to developmental problems. With debt problems plaguing many poor and developing countries in the 1980s, the World Bank introduced a new approach based on a broadly supported model of Structural Adjustment Lending. Loans would become contingent on whether or not a recipient country was able to transform its economy to one which was more market based. Achieving this status required a concerted adjustment to both the country's economic and political structures. Building upon this idea, by 1986, the IMF had developed a fully operative Structural Adjustment Facility to help propagate this solution. The explicit intention in establishing such a framework was a

---

[4] See Chapter 4 this volume.

complementary attempt to push a recipient country toward adopting a more market-oriented economy. The unitary focus of the IMF was now centered on facilitating market-based initiatives. To accomplish this ordained end, the fund proved quite willing to impose harsh conditionality on its loan agreements. A distinct difference then emerged between the Japanese approach and that of the World Bank or the IMF.

As Japan's economic influence in the region expanded, the World Bank viewed Japan's development model, which countered the Fund's widely held mainstream values, as a challenge to the Western-based approach that it espoused. In September 1989, responding to this perceived threat, a Senior Vice President of the World Bank addressed a letter to the Overseas Economic Cooperation Fund (OECF), a Japanese financial institution that granted yen-denominated loans. The letter warned Japan that it needed to reconsider making subsidized, policy-directed loans to developing countries. Both the World Bank and the IMF regarded this type of loan as having a potentially negative impact on the development of the local financial sector. Such loans would only end up stalling necessary financial reforms. Without such an overhaul, ailing financial markets would never support a viable, growing economy. In contrast to this definitive view, during its catch-up period the Japanese government deliberately subsidized policy-directed loans. To the Japanese, these bureaucratically managed loans played a critical economic role, one that enabled its key infant industries to take off smoothly and expeditiously. As could be expected, this pre-emptive demand by these international organizations found scant acceptance with the Japanese (Shiratori, 1998, p. 77). Japan retained a firm and pragmatic belief, backed by its own successful track record, that its approach to economic development was quite effective. The Japanese also believed that this didactic approach was socially and economically ill suited to the realities of East Asian developing countries. They attributed the uncongenial nature of these ideas to Asia's intrinsic cultural differences from the West. This reasoning made little, if any, headway with these international organizations.

Although these very Japanese views remained low key during the Cold War period, Japan's self-confidence gained momentum as the

Cold War ended. It seemed to Japan that the end of the Cold War provided more room for it to take a commanding position, given its newly recognized economic power. The Ministry of Finance committee on Asia Pacific Economic Research declared: "It is necessary that what Japan used to do should be done by the Asian NIEs [newly industrialized economies]. What the Asian NIEs used to do, should be done by ASEAN countries" (cited in Pempel, 1997, p. 53). As might be anticipated, Prime Minister Kaifu's 1991 remarks while visiting Singapore clearly demonstrated the Japanese determination to establish its rightful position as an economic leader. "Japan will continue seeking to expand imports from the countries of the region and promote investment and further technology transfers to these countries" (Ministry of Foreign Affairs, 1991, pp. 426–427).

As Japan's confidence increased, its officials gained the courage to question the appropriateness of following Western recommendations. As pointed out, they doubted whether a Western approach, which urged the recipient countries to change the structure of their economies, suited Asian countries with different cultural backgrounds. Japan's Ministry of Finance (MOF), in order to support its preferred economic model, stepped up its continuing criticism of the laissez-faire strategies pursued by the World Bank and the IMF. Inevitably, such sharply pointed comments set the stage for an ideological confrontation. Beginning in October 1991, the OECF presented a paper which questioned the approach pursued by the World Bank.[5] In the same month, the then President of the Bank of Japan, Yasushi Mieno, speaking on behalf of the MOF, stressed the importance of the "Asian experience," which he claimed determined the role of the government sector. He emphasized the need "for a government to complement the market mechanism and create the kind of environment in which free markets can function effectively" (Shiratori, 1998, p. 77). Emboldened, a 1992 OECF report explicitly expressed its doubt of blindly adopting market mechanisms. It clearly emphasized the need to complement markets with an effective program of governmental intervention (Nishigaki and Shimomura, 1999). In sync with such efforts, the MOF released

---

[5] Masaki Shiratori was a key person in the drafting of this paper.

(1991) a critical report that demonstrated support for this approach, *Issues Related to the World Bank's Approach to a Structural Adjustment: Proposals from a Major Partner*. This analysis insisted that the World Bank needed to pay more attention to the role that government intervention could play, including government-led investment, subsidized interest rates, and the protection of infant industries (Hook *et al.*, 2001, p. 340). The MOF labeled the World Bank approach as being sadly one dimensional and out of date.

To emphasize the seriousness with which it defended its position, the MOF pressured the World Bank to consider alternative strategies. The Ministry firmly believed that any findings would inevitably validate the Japanese position. Under Japan's prodding and as a gesture of appeasement, the World Bank in 1992 embarked on a study of "Asian economic miracles" supported by a generous $1 million grant from Japan's Policy and Human Resource Development Fund (Yasutomo, 1995, pp. 64–81). This posed a serious challenge to the World Bank's mainstream approach. Consequently, the World Bank's 1993 report, *The East Asian Miracle: Economic Growth and Public Policy*, responded diplomatically by acknowledging the East Asian strategy of economic development, which differed from the Western approach based on more standard, if not textbook, economic thinking.[6] Japan through its persistence had managed finally to gain some international recognition for its own "development model." However, this acknowledgement did not lead to any realization of Japan's actual desire. Recognition did not inevitably translate into this model's increased presence within these quite powerful international financial institutions. The Washington consensus still prevailed. Alternative approaches failed to attract any serious consideration.

While Japanese influence continued to grow within the regional East Asian economies, its ability to shape the views of international financial institutions was still highly limited. It was true that Japan had played a leading role in establishing the Asian Development Bank (ADB). Moreover, reflecting this role, Japan held equal voting shares with the US in running this institution. However, despite Japan's larger presence in the

---

[6]For a critical analysis of the report, see Ono (1996, pp. 173–200).

administrative staff and its quite sizeable voting share, Japan's objectives persistently failed to be reflected in ADB policy. Opposing voices supporting the western approach to free market and trade successfully stymied any serious consideration of Japan's development model (Yasutomo, 1995, p. 91).

This clear lack of influence was even more pronounced when policy initiatives involved the IMF and the World Bank. Japan held proportionate voting shares in neither of these institutions. (Proportionate here signifies being geared to the country's economic size.) Within the IMF, while the US commanded 17.14 percent of the votes, Japan had to be satisfied with only 6.15 percent (IMF, 2005b). Japan held the second largest voting share after the US, but its still relatively small bloc failed to provide the leverage required to implement its views on actual policies. Due to Japan's strong lobbying, the disproportionate difference narrowed slightly in the 1980s. However, considering the relative size of the US and Japanese economies, the shares still remained significantly disproportionate. In this case, voting shares reflected the contributions made by these two countries to the IMF budget. Japan accounted for not quite one-third of the US levy. This is surprisingly small considering that in the case of the UN, Japan contributed 19.5 percent, which was nearly as large as the 22 percent provided by the US. However, Japan's basic dissatisfaction with the IMF was at least somewhat alleviated due to a significant new development.

The IMF awarded Japan, more specifically Tokyo, the Asian Pacific (OAP) regional office in 1997. However, though not an entirely negligible achievement, this bit of recognition represented at most only very limited progress. Japan first bid for a Tokyo branch office at the end of the 1980s coincident with its increased capital contribution. As Japan's economic strength grew, the Ministry of Finance became interested in gaining an increased share of financial influence, as measured on a more global scale. As part of this drive, the Japanese government continued to apply pressure to gain a regional office for Tokyo (Hatakeyama, interview with the former Secretary of the OAP, April 2005). It also requested the IMF to increase the number of Japanese staff until the level became commensurate with Japan's financial contribution. However, even these modest gains took several years to accomplish. It was not until the end of 1996 that the IMF finally decided to open an Asian regional office. At the beginning, most observers assumed that Hong Kong would be the designated city. By doing so, the IMF and its Western backers would hope to limit China's influence after Hong Kong returned to China in 1997. However, blessed by large financial contributions to the IMF and its tandem lobbying efforts, the Japanese managed to scoop the Chinese. As previously mentioned, the IMF designated Tokyo to be the new regional office in March 1997 (Hatakeyama, interview with the former Secretary of the OAP, April 2005).

The IMF established the OAP to keep itself informed of regional perspectives on various key issues. Japan's push in pursuit of proportionate influence and presence was partly realized, although the objectives of Japan and the IMF clearly differed in pushing for a regional office. On the Japanese side, as usual, the MOF ultimately wished to gain influence that was comparable to its financial contribution. Establishment of the regional office in Tokyo would provide a good channel to disseminate its views to the IMF. It would also convey, if only implicitly, the desired legitimization of its approach to economic development. On the IMF side, an Asian outpost seemed to be a good platform not only to track developments in the Japanese economy through contacts with political leaders, government officials, and major figures in the private business sector. Such an office also might achieve a "greater dissemination of IMF perspectives on the Japanese economy" (IMF, 2005a). In this instance, both sides had different dreams ending in the same result.

As a self-appointed economic leader of the region, winning the Asian office for Tokyo saved face for the Japanese. The Asia-Pacific Office also managed to serve as a channel between the opposing views of the IMF and Japan. However, contrary to the MOF's expectations, establishing such a channel did not lead to any noticeable increase in either Japan's influence or the wholesale dissemination of its views within the IMF. Given this deep-bred dissatisfaction among MOF officials, the Asian Economic Crisis presented them with a rare opportunity to create a new regional economic order. The 1997 crisis provided a chance for Japan to revive its economic diplomacy by employing a different set of tactics from those used in the 1980s.

8.2.2 *Responding to a Crisis: The Asian Monetary Fund*

The Thai baht had been pegged to the US dollar. Its dramatic collapse heralded the start of the Asian Economic Crisis in July 1997.[7] The crisis in Thailand was not entirely unexpected. The country's finances already had displayed persistent signs of deterioration.[8] The rapidly depreciating Thai baht enlarged not only its trade deficit, but also generated a large outflow of short-term capital, making a bad situation much worse. Investors became fearful that Thailand would be unable to sustain its growing current account deficit. With investors harboring such unresolved fears, a withdrawal of portfolio investment from Thailand was an expected and quite natural consequence. These withdrawals led, in turn, to further and more sizeable capital outflows. In a domino-like effect, fear became contagious. Foreign investors began to view other Asian countries, such as Indonesia and South Korea, with the same shade of pessimism. As a result, the crisis proved to be contagious.

With more Asian countries being sucked into this economic whirlpool, the crisis presented two fundamental questions for the Japanese government to tackle. One was whether the regional economies should undergo drastic structural changes under an IMF mandate. The Japanese also wondered what implications this widespread collapse would have for the spread of its developmental model, which had always stressed close relationships between the government and the private sector. This approach was the very opposite of the program being imposed by IMF officials.

Thailand was a veritable test case for the Japanese in terms of the crisis. Japan had been Thailand's largest aid donor, accounting for 82.7 percent of the total amount (Ministry of Foreign Affairs, 1996).

---

[7]Articles and books on the economic crisis are too numerous to list. However, those requiring useful background information might start with Pempel (1999). For some of the attendant controversy and criticism surrounding the IMF approach, informative articles are available by Radelet and Sachs (1997) and Feldstein (1998).

[8]Chalmers Johnson (1998) provides three possible and inter-related causes of the crisis:

1. China's growing competitiveness and Japan's depreciating yen,
2. over-borrowing from foreign lenders,
3. the US could no longer afford to maintain the economies of satellite states such as South Korea, Japan, Thailand, and Taiwan.

Japan also had been Thailand's largest creditor country, responsible, on average, for more than 50 percent of its debt. On July 18, 1997, immediately after the crisis began, the Thai government quite naturally requested assistance from the Japanese government in order to avoid a further deterioration of its economic circumstances. On July 28, Japan, contrary to Thailand's expectations, declined to provide such assistance. At this early stage of the crisis, the Japanese government preferred to operate within the prescribed IMF framework rather than hewing to the principles underlying their preferred development model. Being unsure of whether the Thai government possessed the potential wherewithal to repay any new loans, Japan opted for this more cautious stance. It firmly avoided offering any direct assistance. The Japanese based their gloomy estimation on a negative report provided by a government-directed mission, which doubted the genuine prospect for a rapid and sustained economic recovery in Thailand. Given these beliefs, Japan thought the less risky option was to restrict financial assistance to the more narrow channels defined by IMF structured loans (Sakakibara, 2000, p. 177).[9]

Unable to obtain Japan's financial support, Thailand, left without any better options, sought financial assistance from the IMF. On August 5, 1977, these two parties reached agreement on the conditions required for financial assistance. On August 12, hoping to coordinate international financial cooperation, the Asia-Pacific Regional Office of the IMF (OAP), invited 10 countries (the "Friends of Thailand") to a Tokyo meeting of financial ministers. The OAP excluded the US from that invitation list, as the US refused to provide any financial assistance whatsoever. After the 1994 Mexican bailout, the US Congress had put in place severe restrictions on any emergency funding to the IMF's

---

[9]The Thai economy had begun to crumble seriously already, attacked by speculative financial dealers even before the crisis. Both the IMF and the Japanese government shared the same view, namely that Thailand might fall into a serious economic crisis in the near future and, in that case, Thailand would need economic assistance. In response to these fears, the Japanese government dispatched a mission to Thailand before the crisis to investigate any problems or pitfalls the Thai economy might contain. The mission's negative report on the prospects of the Thai economy consequently affected future decisions made by the Japanese government. Therefore, when Thailand later asked for financial assistance at the early stages of its crisis, the Japanese government felt entitled to refuse the Thai request.

Exchange Stability Fund. These restrictions hamstrung the Clinton administration in persuading Congress to assist Thailand. Since the US did not seem to have a large stake in Thailand's recovery, such efforts proved to be essentially futile (Green, 2001, p. 245).

Yet, this did not signal a total US disengagement from the region. The US retained an effective means to implement its national interests. In the 1980s, in contrast to Japan's increasing economic power, the relative status of the US gradually declined due to its huge trade deficit. Unable to increase its aid because of a string of out-of-control budgets during this decade, the US became increasingly dependent on the IMF and the World Bank as surrogates willing to carry out US objectives. US dependency on these financial institutions became even more explicit after Congress restricted the direct provision of financial assistance to any country in the midst of an economic crisis (Altbach, 1997, p. 9). Therefore, the nature of the IMF gradually transformed, becoming akin to a false front that attempted to disguise the American national interests it so dutifully served (Johnson, 1998).

Seizing the initiative, the IMF in August 1997 responded to the developing crisis by holding a meeting in Tokyo. For the US-led IMF, the economic crisis in Thailand presented clear evidence invalidating the East Asian economic development model. This conclusion led the IMF to attempt a drastic restructuring of Thailand's economic relations. The well-established IMF strategy was to change as many of the existing Thai arrangements into those resembling more compatible with Western-type models. To accomplish this goal, the IMF felt confident in imposing harsh conditionality as a requirement for any loan granted, including liberalizing FDI, breaking up conglomerates, and dismantling close relationships between the Thai government and the private sector. All of these reforms aimed at encouraging competition that was fairer and much more open.

The Japanese government considered the IMF's requirements, which imposed substantial structural reforms, to be too harsh.[10] Prime Minister Hashimoto's statement (August 1997) reflected Japan's suspicion towards this "one-size-fits-all" IMF approach. "We have to ask

---

[10]For criticism of the IMF approach, see Radelet and Sachs (1997) and Feldstein (1998).

whether liberalism is necessarily superior to other sets of values and whether it is right to ask other nations to uniformly accept that."[11] Nevertheless, Japan was not yet ready to criticize the IMF approach or propose an alternative solution. Therefore, Japan, as a leading regional power, accepted the role of "lender of last resort" out of a perceived responsibility to stabilize the financial environment. Only by doing so, could Japan achieve some degree of financial security (Ministry of Finance, 1998a). Under the IMF-structured program, the Japanese government pledged to contribute $4 billion, the largest amount from any donor country. Japan was also influential in persuading other Asian countries to contribute financially as well. The total eventually amounted to $10.5 billion (Sakakibara, 2000). Although retaining its suspicions, the Japanese government ended up playing a leading role in this process by pledging a significant financial contribution. However, as anticipated by Japan, the stringent and drastic IMF approach did not ease Thailand's crisis. Rather, the prescribed cure seemed to exacerbate the situation. The economy deteriorated, with the Thai baht devaluing even further after the IMF announced bailout package.

The perceived failure of the IMF's approach presented the Ministry of Finance with a policy vacuum into which it was able to insert ideas that these bureaucrats had long harbored. Since 1996, MOF officials had proposed a deliberate strategy to strengthen and stabilize the regional monetary system. In tandem with this initiative, ASEAN countries had also formulated a strategy composed of similar monetary arrangements. However, this vague proposal, devoid of any Western support, soon faded away. An approach that lacked any substantial details would always face significant difficulties in gaining supporters. However, with a serious crisis clearly ripening the idea was once again proposed officially (September 18, 1997) by ASEAN countries at the Japan–ASEAN Financial Ministerial meeting held in Hong Kong. Following this event, on September 23, 1997, the Hashimoto administration, with ASEAN agreement, provided a concrete plan to establish an Asian Monetary Fund (AMF). The Japanese laid out their relatively

---

[11] For the original speech, see Ministry of Finance (1998a). For reports of the speech, see *The Australian*, August 19, 1997, 30–31.

radical departure from the prevailing wisdom at the annual World Bank–IMF meeting in Hong Kong. The initial fund backing this proposal would be $100 billion. Japan would contribute $50 billion and become the dominant share holder. The Asian Monetary Fund was nothing less than a regional monetary institution with Japan at its center. The leading role the US played in resolving the Mexican crisis (1994) provided Japanese officials with much of their inspiration (Ministry of Finance, 1998b). In a parallel fashion, Japan would assume the crucial, and possibly central, position in rescuing Asian countries. Just as the US dominated financial arrangements in Latin America, so too would Japan be the decisive player in East Asia. Japan would shoulder primary responsibility in this Asian crisis as the US did for Mexico (Ministry of Finance, 1998b). Japan's initiatives met with success at this OAP-instigated meeting in Tokyo. This small, but definite triumph at the early stage of the Thai crisis emboldened Japan to press on with its strategy.

Establishing and providing ample funding for the AMF should have (at least potentially) resulted in a dramatically different outcome, since the IMF's capacity to provide financial assistance to Asian countries was quite limited. In fact, just in the first six months of the crisis, the IMF's financial assistance to the devastated countries amounted to $35 billion, which was close to its available ceiling (Calder, 1998, p. 8). However, the Ministry of Finance was reluctant either to subscribe more to the IMF's fund or to cooperate financially in tandem with these sanctioned programs because it believed that the IMF's prescriptions were too economically destabilizing. The 1993 World Bank report and the establishment of the OAP had been merely small victories for Japan. Despite having better knowledge and understanding of Asian countries, its voice still had not been fully acknowledged in the world of Multinational Development Banks (the IMF, the World Bank, and the ADB). Consequently, the MOF was keen to establish a regional institution which would provide Japan with the chance to create a new Asian economic order, one that would have Japan at its center. Financial assistance, without stringent IMF-like conditionality, in Japan's view, could have ameliorated an otherwise harsh transition to the American advocated goal of ubiquitous market economies. Vice Finance Minister Eisuke Sakakibara, a key bureaucrat during this crucial period, seized the opportunity and attempted to convert Japan's economic power into a more legitimate and concrete form. Sakakibara viewed this proposed regional fund as a potential springboard that would allow Japan to exercise its new-found economic might in a mutually beneficial fashion.

To realize this plan, Sakakibara vigorously explored an array of diplomatic tactics to shore up support from key regional countries. US Treasury Secretary Robert Rubin could not fail to notice this Japanese attempt to establish itself as the leader of a new regional order. Preempting Japan's strategy, Rubin made America's opposition clear to Japanese Finance Minster Mitsuzuka, even before a specific proposal could be formulated at the World Bank–IMF annual meeting held that year (1998) in Hong Kong. Rubin explicitly rejected the plan by saying that it would undermine the effectiveness of the IMF, and in doing so cause irreparable difficulties in imposing requisite loan conditionalities. The result would be an inevitable and unwelcome increase in the risk of moral hazard.[12] Rubin's more honest concern was that the IMF, in which the US during the post-war period had played a dominant role, would lose its legitimacy and influence in the region. At the very least, its impact and importance would be eroded. The US and the American-dominated IMF were not alone in opposing this Japanese proposal. An odd alliance of these two plus China balked at accepting the plan. They argued that it was pointless to provide funds without first formulating a specific solution. Instead, they undoubtedly suspected that the hidden and only plausible purpose behind this Japanese ploy was to play the role of a Trojan horse acting to undermine the authority and effectiveness of the IMF. European countries at the G7 meeting in Hong Kong (September 20, 1998) followed suit by also expressing apprehension of this Japanese-inspired AMF proposal (Sakakibara, 2000, pp. 179, 188–189).

Faced with such unanticipated and concerted pressure, the Ministry soon gave up its initiative, deciding instead to support the IMF's programs. The rapid disappearance of the AMF as a viable alternative paralleled the demise of any serious Japanese financial leadership in the Asian region.

---

[12]For reports of this clash, see *Nihon Keizai Shimbun*, October 7, 1997.

8.2.3 *Thwarted Hopes: The Demise of the AMF*

Sakakibara had intended to establish the AMF as an IMF supplement in terms of financial resources, but one that remained essentially independent of the IMF in terms of conditionality. He shared, and helped to form, the general MOF belief that the IMF's approach (forcing recipient countries to privatize national companies within a condensed period of time) was too drastic. In his view, these recipes only caused the program to fail rather than achieving any positive objectives (Hatakeyama, interview with Eisuke Sakakibara, June 2005). In essence, the underlying nature of the "Washington consensus" was far too similar to that characterizing old style "colonialism" (Hatakeyama, interview with Eisuke Sakakibara, June 2005). Sakakibara concluded that the hidden policy objective carefully nurtured by the IMF was a transformation of the recipient economy into a market-based one which would be more conducive to US interests. In his view the aim, as usual, reduced to making the world safe for American domination. Assistance inevitably came with strings attached. The recipient country would be forced to trade away ownership of its policy-making process due to unrelenting pressure coming from the US-led IMF and its sister organization, the World Bank (Hatakeyama, interview with Eisuke Sakakibara, June 2005). He thought, therefore, that the creation of an institution out of the reach of Western control would be able to provide recipient countries more freedom to devise their own solutions. Japan also would be able to advance its economic development model by providing support for the recipient countries via this fund. The AMF could act as a platform, by means of which Japan would exercise its influence in a way that paralleled US capabilities.

Not surprisingly, US opposition caused the Japanese government to blink. Seeking to appease the US, the Ministry of Finance modified its stance. In its new version, the same IMF conditionality would serve as a necessary requirement for any country to receive assistance from the newly proposed AMF (*Gaiko Kiroku*, 2004–473). Despite this concession, the Ministry not only failed to win US approval, but it could not even manage to mitigate the US-conjured opposition. The plan had to be abandoned. The much-hoped-for proposal would have provided

Japan with the desperately desired legitimization needed to success-fully champion its developmental model. Despite the MOF's originally optimistic analysis, the AMF never saw the light of day.

After all of Japan's maneuvers and wrangling, the MOF ended up accepting what became known as the Manila framework. This arrange-ment served purely as a face-saving exercise for the MOF at both the APEC Economic Leaders' Meeting and its Ministerial Meeting (November 1997). The framework acted to provide a highly limited, but seeming acceptance of the AMF objectives. An institution of this type was given leave to act, but only according to parameters defined by two specific constraints. First, it could initiate cooperative financ-ing arrangements, as long as they would supplement IMF resources. Second, it was only permissible to undertake measures which would strengthen the IMF's capacity to respond to financial crises (Ministry of Finance, 1998c). Essentially, Japan needed to agree that the Manila framework would serve as a sort of dogsbody to the IMF. The accep-tance of IMF conditionality remained the crucial difference between the Japanese proposed AMF and the Manila framework. In addition, the Manila framework lacked a functioning structure and any associ-ated legitimacy. Its challenge would be to operate despite lacking any effective mechanism which could force financial cooperation within the region (Ministry of Finance, 1998a). Japan's intended strategy of gain-ing a leadership role within a multilateral context had failed miserably.

Recognizing its total inability to establish its desired regional institu-tion, the MOF instead adopted a very low key approach when Indone-sia fell into economic crisis (October 1997). Indonesia sought the IMF's help but again, the IMF-imposed conditionality was severe. As expected, the IMF sought to transform the Indonesian economy into one patterned after the American market model. The mandated program also had an associated political agenda as it attempted to break apart the close relationships that had grown up between gov-ernment and business. The IMF's price for financial assistance included non-discriminatory financial liberalization, a reduction of government expenditure, and the elimination of food subsidies.

Japan essentially had surrendered the chance to play any effective financial role during the Asian Crisis. Despite being unable to influence

IMF programs and disagreeing with their basic premise, Japan still ended up supporting its bailout packages. The Japanese pledged $5 billion in financial assistance to Indonesia. Likewise, it contributed $10 billion to South Korea under another IMF program. Thus, Japan decisively changed its behavior in a manner that ran contrary to its desire to influence key regional outcomes. Unable to gain a decisive position, the Japanese government instead adopted a more passive and supportive role by accepting IMF policies.

8.2.4 *Japan Agonistes: Constraints Limiting Japanese Initiatives*

As pointed out, Japan's move to establish a multilateral institution goes back to the 1960s. Successive Japanese governments made several attempts to establish regional institutions, both political and economic, during the early post-war period. It embarked on these initiatives despite lacking both economic and political strength during those early years. The almost automatic suspicions and apprehension aroused by Japan in other Asian countries limited Japanese alternatives. For post-war Japan, intent on launching initiatives through which it might restore Japanese influence, establishing regional institutions seemed to present a particularly effective framework. However, all these attempts needed to be made on the premise of US participation. Formulating plans that excluded the US from these regional alignments only served to create unrealistic scenarios within which Japan would be doomed to fail.

Open regionalism had long been an important pillar of Japan's foreign policy. The evolution of this position is clearly illustrated in the Foreign Ministry's yearly *Diplomatic Bluebooks*. Within those documents, examples that emphasize this idea are easy enough to find. Prime Minister Ohira openly advocated regional economic cooperation for the first time in 1980. However, Ohira generally limited such cooperation exclusively to the field of trade. His philosophy of regional cooperation reduced to "openness," which was consistent with a multilateral free trade system. Given Japan's strong inclination for open regionalism, it was natural that the Japanese government would be reluctant to support a 1991 Malaysian proposal to create an East Asian Economic Group. Japan's policy clearly opposed such examples of building closed regional alliances, especially ones aimed at excluding the US.

However, as we have seen, growing confidence as an economic leader, and a clash of opposing economic models between East and West, encouraged the Ministry of Finance to be bolder. Japan attempted to create a new economic order with itself at the center. In other words, the proposed creation of the AMF represented a challenge to the current economic order which centered on the IMF and the World Bank. In addition, it was an ideological challenge to US economic values, which the Americans liked to present as universal. The proposal implied a clash of economic norms between the Japanese government, which lobbied for a development model based on its own experience, and the IMF, which pursued an American style market model by imposing strict conditionality on its loans. Inevitably, strong US opposition frustrated the attempts by the Ministry of Finance to create a new economic order where Japan would play a leading and widely recognized role.

As a global leader and only remaining "superpower," the US remained convinced that it had a duty and a right to engage in the region. President Clinton, for example, insisted that the US did "not intend to bear the cost of a military presence in Asia and the burdens of regional leadership only to be shut out of the benefits of growth that stability brings."[13] As a means of protecting its own interests, the US intended to prevent any attempt to exclude it from even potential regional groupings. This predictable US sensitivity to any form of exclusion remained unchanged throughout this period and extended into the future. For example, the attempt to initiate an East Asia Community without the US met with determined opposition from former US Deputy Secretary of State Richard Armitage (*Asahi Shimbun*, May 2, 2005). Without exception, the US would never acquiesce to a Japanese initiative that challenged an existing world order supporting its economic dominance. Despite such US attitudes, Sakakibara thought that in this instance, the opposition would be more muted. Therefore, while

---

[13] Bill Clinton's remarks in Seattle, November 19, 1993, text by US Information Agency.

the MOF made vigorous diplomatic efforts to obtain the understanding of, and support from, other Asian countries, it did not bother to do its diplomatic homework to achieve a parallel agreement with the US. Unfortunately, Sakakibara chose to hold this over optimistic, if not naïve, expectation of the American reaction to this plan. The US was clearly furious with Japan. It did not react well to what it perceived as an attempt to bypass American interests by establishing an alternative regional framework. By rationalizing its own self-interested opposition, the US was able to maintain its moral position. It staked out the high ground by claiming that the establishment of the AMF would cause moral hazard and confusion within financial markets.

In addition to these foreseeable US factors, the internal structure of the Japanese government was hardly monolithic, or even particularly unified. The desire to forge new roles and new responsibilities drove only a select few of the assembled bureaucracy. Even among officials in the Ministry of Finance, views concerning the structure of the AMF were divided. Debates raged within the Ministry concerning the impact that the proposed institution would have on Japan–US relations. The financial domination of the IMF and the World Bank seemed to leave Japan without any obvious alternative position to adopt. Moreover, in the case of the AMF, internal divisions delayed the Ministry in developing the proposal's specific characteristics. An early version had yet to resolve the essential question of whether the AMF would be independent of the IMF or endorse the same brand of conditionality (Inoguchi, 2002, p. 10). The Japanese government proved incapable of acting with any degree of unity. In addition to the lack of consensus within the MOF, the Ministry of Foreign Affairs took itself out of the picture altogether by remaining stubbornly uncommitted (Hatakeyma, interview with the Director of the Economic Bureau, MOFA, April 2004). The MOFA neither opposed nor supported the Asian Monetary Fund at a critical moment when lack of support became little different from opposition. In a positive sense then, there was no actively conducted "turf" battle or deliberate immobilization within either ministry resulting in institutional inertia. However, the fragmented power that each ministry wielded meant that the absence of undiluted support for the AMP would tend to undercut the Ministry of Finances proposal.

8.3 Japan's Second Attempt: Accepting a More Bilateral and Pragmatic Approach

8.3.1 *Deus Ex Machina: The Miyazawa Initiative Rears Its Bilateral Head*

The Ministry of Finance failed to create a strategic financial institution. But, abandoning its leadership in campaigning for a new regional monetary system did not mean that the Ministry had lost confidence in its economic development approach. Criticism of Japan's development model, and its perceived responsibility for triggering the crisis, failed to make the Japanese government flinch. Nor did Japan appear bothered by its perceived leadership failure within the region. After assuming a low profile by supporting the IMF packages, the Japanese government once again roused itself by announcing a grab bag of measures at the 1997 ASEAN+3 meetings to help these countries recover from the crisis. One of the programs in the package supported ASEAN's small- and mid-size industries. The ostensible aim was to promote an industrial capacity which could produce parts and components needed by Japanese factories in those countries. As a quiet "leading goose," Japan still held the firm belief that since the Asian economy's fundamentals were basically sound, there remained a continued potential for high growth.[14]

Despite possessing unshaken confidence in its own ideas, Japan's current economy did not provide a very compelling exemplar. It was clearly staggering. Dealing with domestic problems became a priority overwhelming all other considerations. In fact, 1997 was the beginning of two consecutive years of negative growth for the Japanese economy, the first time ever in the post-war era (Ministry of Foreign Affairs, 1999a). An ill-considered rise in the consumption tax from three to five percent and an abandonment of a temporary tax-cut sliced deeply into a Japanese economy that was only beginning to revive. On top of these policy blunders, the collapse of the Hokkaido Takushoku Bank,

---

[14] This view was repeatedly affirmed by the APEC Economic Leaders' Meeting and the Ministerial Meeting in November as well as at the Japan–ASEAN Summit in December 1997. See Ministry of Foreign Affairs (1998b).

combined with the demise of Yamaichi Securities in November 1997, seemed to symbolize Japan's waning economic power. The failure of these supposedly unsinkable big financial firms, both regarded as being under the MOF's protective "convoy system," shocked the Japanese. This tumble into bankruptcy reflected the very serious condition of its financial underpinnings. More concretely, the banking system was in disarray with "non-performing loans" (unofficially estimated to be as high as 100 trillion yen), stifling Japanese credit creation both domestically and internationally. This predicament constituted an effective body blow to Japan's pretentions to be a financial as well as dominant economic power.

Despite Japan's waning credibility as a self-appointed regional leader, the Ministry of Finance could not afford to overlook the harsh conditions with which the IMF had deliberately burdened its loans. The Ministry still quietly opposed the IMF's prescriptions for both Thailand and Indonesia, criticizing them as too disruptive and unnecessarily tough. This attitude presented a clear contrast with those of Europe or the US, both of which supported the IMF's position. Given the united front presented by other wealthy nations, the Ministry of Finance was unable to influence IMF policies. Japan instead found itself on the defensive. Western industrialized countries were now busily lecturing and pressuring Japan to resolve its own deteriorating domestic financial problems by radically restructuring its economy along Western lines. This advice paralleled the type of requirements that the IMF had placed so unequivocally on its loans, namely market liberalization. A concurrent series of American demands and criticisms clearly reflected Japan's weakening economic position *vis-à-vis* the US. After imposing harsh conditions on Asian countries in the hope of achieving significant changes in their economic structure, the US turned its gaze on Japan.

In November 1997, Secretary of State Madeleine Albright insisted that Japan expand its domestic demand and further deregulate its economy. From her vantage point, only by complying could Japan hope to assist in stimulating other Asian economies (Ministry of Foreign Affairs, 1997). For the US, the collapse of some large Japanese financial institutions and the apparent weakness of Japan's financial sector provided further confirmation that a more laissez-faire, market economy was intrinsically superior to a state-interventionist one. Japan's faltering economy and policy quagmire provided the US with a fortuitous opportunity to lobby Japan to change its "exceptional" operating system.[15]

Unfortunately, the IMF's imposed economic programs in Indonesia did not yield prosperity, but instead gradually exposed the limits of those policies. Coupled with Indonesian President Suharto's uncooperative attitudes, which aimed to secure his regime's vested interests, the harsh IMF measures resulted in a deteriorating economic situation and subsequent social instability. The economic turmoil fuelled riots demanding additional political democratization, which eventually forced Suharto from power in May 1998.

Following the Indonesian crisis, the IMF once again exposed not only its inability to handle an economic crisis, but also its double standards. The financial crisis that started in Russia (August 1998), despite the nominal IMF supervision of the country, substantiated a flaw in the one-dimensional Western approach. The IMF's failure to quickly handle Russia's meltdown inflicted critical damage on Western financial firms. Further, Brazil in turn tumbled into its own economic crisis in September 1998. The US-led IMF rescue implemented an economic package to save Brazil, but the package was extremely lenient, without imposing harsh conditionality. The Brazilian package manifested a perceived US double standard. The Americans adopted a more relaxed attitude in the case of Brazil, because it was reluctant to support a harsh bailout regime that would cause additional damage to fragile American financial firms. These corporate giants had already endured considerable losses during Russia's meltdown (Sakakibara, 2000, pp. 50–81). Policy failure, coupled with a clear lack of consistency, undermined IMF credibility and created an opportunity for the Japanese to substitute their own financial initiatives.

To the Japanese government, Russia's meltdown and the subsequent economic crisis in Brazil proved that the cause of the Asian

---

[15] In the late 1980s, critics considered Japan's insistence on being an "exceptional" country as no more than a cloak to cover its "neo-mercantilism" policy, a classic case of putting old wine in a new bottle.

economic crisis was not its economic development model. Sakakibara thought the crises of these two countries verified his belief that the determining factor was not the nature of the capitalism in place, but so-called "hot money" — short-term capital flows moving quickly across borders (Sakakibara, 2000, pp. 50–81). Lessons drawn from the deba-cles known as the Russian and Brazilian crises definitely helped Japan to regain confidence in its own approach.

The MOF, now convinced of the IMF's inability to stabilize finan-cial crises, reported (May 1998) that the harsh approach adopted in Indonesia only made a precarious situation even worse. The Min-istry believed that the structural adjustment the IMF had imposed on troubled Asian countries were not necessarily appropriate (Ministry of Finance, 1998b). It also emphasized the need to take into account the differences in background and culture between Asian and Western countries. This stance spread throughout the Japanese government. In Singapore (September 1998), the Ministry for International Trade and Industry (MITI) joined forces with its colleagues at the MOF. MITI Minister Yosano Kaoru quietly laid the blame for the severity of the Asian Crisis on the IMF's one-size-fits-all approach. He pointed out that the "IMF had played an important role in the currency crisis, but that its response had been one of trial and error and it needed to develop a more flexible policy towards the region" (cited in Hughes, 2000, p. 243). Japan had become assertive once more.

Having failed to set up a regional institution at an earlier stage of the crisis, the MOF had learned that any attempt to create a broad frame-work in which the Japanese could exert significant influence would not be acceptable to the US. Therefore, it shifted its strategy from a multi-lateral to a bilateral approach, which might more easily escape foreign opposition. To the Japanese government, a bilateral approach seemed to be a good way to meet two seemingly incompatible demands — maintaining influence through the preservation and propagation of its economic norms while sustaining a good relationship with the US.

Learning from the clearly unsuccessful AMF initiative, the MOF suggested an alternative strategy which would allow Japan's proposed financial fund to bail out unsteady economies within the region. Thus, Japan's second attempt to exert financial influence was made in a more bilateral context. The Miyazawa Initiative, announced by the then

Finance Minister on October 1998, confirmed Japan's re-emergence as a country wishing to exert strategic economic influence. Miyazawa offered a bilateral financial scheme which deliberately would pose no threat to the current US-dominated international financial architecture. The widely anticipated initiative aimed to provide $30 billion. The fund was composed of $15 billion for medium- and long-term loans through the Ex-Im Bank and the Overseas Economic Cooperation Fund (OECF) (both were later reorganized into the Japan Bank for International Cooperation (JBIC)). Another $15 billion would be made available for short-term relief during periods of economic reform. These loans would go to those countries already suffering from the aftermath of an economic crisis. This sum supplemented the $44 billion pledged through the IMF, an amount aimed implicitly at appeasing the US. Using these far more subtle tactics, the Ministry of Finance shifted its strategy from a multilateral to a bilateral solution in order to avoid US opposition. Instead of working through a regional financial institution, Japan would try to achieve the same results on a case-by-case basis.

As expected, this strategy did not draw direct US fire because of its bilateral nature. The US did want Japan's financial assistance to stabilize the affected Asian economies. But the US did not want its financial leadership challenged by having its proxy institution, the IMF, facing any serious competition. The Miyazawa Initiative clearly accomplished the first while avoiding the inevitable conflict implicit in the second. As we have seen, given its continuing domestic difficulties, Japan was not in a comfortable position to provide sizeable amounts of assistance in addition to that already expended under the IMF programs. Yet, as a self-appointed regional leader, Japan was not happy to see those countries, where it had long supported economic development through foreign aid, fall completely under the influence of the US and the IMF's drastic economic packages. Japan considered these to be particularly disagreeable since they aimed at transforming regional Asian economies into something that resembled a pale imitation of the American model.[16] Japanese policy makers did not totally disagree with

---

[16] Japan had an undoubted economic interest in an Asian recovery. This extended to its financial and export sectors most directly.

the IMF's measures, but believed that some of their demands, which extended to overall structural reform, were not necessarily helpful. The conditions that the IMF placed on these recipient countries to open their financial markets to foreigners and to restructure their systems by removing governmental interference were contrary to Japan's own experience and to its ingrained beliefs. These strictures also ignored the pragmatic economic development of Asian countries, which the Japanese had long supported by means of its sizeable aid program. In their opinion, further liberalization of financial markets would chiefly benefit foreign investors, most of whom were Americans, by enabling them to buy local banks at cut-rate prices. In fact, the array of conditions placed on Asian countries usually included requests that the US had long demanded but which previously had been refused (Gilpin, 2000, p. 157). According to this view, acceding to these demands would assist Wall Street's profitability by creating a world of free capital mobility, which remained the motivating impetus behind these requirements (Bhagwati, 1998). Using this analysis, the American definition of structural improvement, via the IMF, was overly opportunistic and self-serving. It actually meant enhancing American economic interests, rather than those of the recipient countries (Bhagwati, 1998).

The Miyazawa Initiative provided a clear contrast to US strategies in the region. The Japanese intended to reinvigorate its political influence by reviving the local economies. They intended to provide financial funds and consultations without setting strict prior conditions. The Japanese expressed little interest in restructuring other Asian economies. Japan's priorities at this time are best illustrated by the imprecise conditions attached to these targeted loans.

The initiative was only a sketchy idea when first announced by the Japanese government. Although prepared to provide up to $30 billion in total, which was unquestionably substantial, the amount of assistance depended on the needs of each recipient country. The Japanese government declined to clarify what funds each country would receive. Officials explained that "in light of the urgent, specific, and clear needs of prospective recipient countries, the amount of money needed for such-and-such a country would be decided after examining closely the real needs of the respective recipient countries" (Ministry of Foreign

Affairs, 1998c). In other words, provision of the fund would depend on perceived needs, which had to meet the "criteria of the Miyazawa Initiatives" (Ministry of Foreign Affairs, 1998c). Yet, while the Japanese government emphasized the need to meet the "criteria," what these "criteria" might be was never sufficiently clarified. The announced, but rather ill-defined, objectives were to:

- support the restructuring of private companies' debt and stabilize the financial system,
- strengthen the social safety net for disadvantaged people,
- stimulate the economy to create more jobs,
- deal with any credit crunch or credit contraction (Ministry of Finance, 1998d).

In order to receive aid through the Miyazawa Initiative, a prospective recipient country had only to enter into discussions with the Japanese government in order to decide details and flesh out appropriate measures. When coupled with these essentially nebulous criteria, this approach provided Japan with an opportunity to exercise influence over recipient countries.

Japan's primary intention (preserve its influence and promote its economic model within the region) is also indicated by the deliberate exclusion of Russia from the initial recipient list. The Japanese anointed five countries (Thailand, Malaysia, Indonesia, South Korea, and the Philippines) as being within the eligible group. After substantial discussions, Thailand received $1.9 billion, Malaysia $2.2 billion, Indonesia $2.4 billion, the Philippines $1.6 billion, and South Korea $6 billion. Later, financial assistance through the Miyazawa Initiative was extended to Vietnam. Japan aided Vietnam's "pragmatic" development rather than insisting on the type of conditionality required by the IMF and World Bank. The grant made in 1999 was intended to support Vietnam's "pragmatic" economic strategy, especially in the agricultural area. This assistance ignored negotiations concerning conditionality among the IMF, the World Bank, and the Vietnamese government then under way. Ostensibly, the actions pursued by the Ministry of Finance did not explicitly intend to nullify or even hinder the ongoing negotiations among the three (Inada, 2001).

After its initial rollout, Japan continued to finance the Miyazawa Initiative. In December 1998, the then Prime Minister Keizo Obuchi promised that a $3 billion Asian Development Bank credit account would back bonds issued by Asian governments. An additional $5 billion loan facility was to be doled out over a 3-year period for infrastructure projects. With an interest rate of only 1 percent and a 40-year repayment period, this facility was available only to Asian members of the ADB. To support these programs, Japan established a $3 billion Asia Currency Crisis Support Facility in March 1999. MITI obliged by announcing its own plans to provide loans valued at 600 billion yen. At the APEC Financial ministerial meeting (May 1999), Miyazawa announced a further provision of funds totaling 2 billion yen as part of a second Miyazawa Initiative. The aim was to support a regional bond market by recycling Japanese private resources. This would reduce the region's dependency on outside capital and help to boost a stagnant Japanese loan market.

By shifting its strategy from a multilateral to a bilateral emphasis, the Ministry of Finance successfully implemented the Miyazawa Initiative. The objectives of both Japan's failed multilateral and more successful bilateral proposals were quite similar. They both aimed to protect and preserve the integrity of the Japanese economic model while gaining regional influence. To accomplish these goals, Japan was willing to provide significant sums of money as well as supply economic advice via continuing consultations. Poll results conducted by the Japanese government measured the success of this alternative strategy. When evaluating Japan's contribution at the time of the economic crisis, almost 90 percent of Thai officials appreciated the Miyazawa Initiative and attributed Thailand's recovery to it (Ministry of Foreign Affairs, 1999b). An official of the Thai government expressed satisfaction with Japan's economic assistance and praised its flexible approach. Polls of the Indonesian and the Philippine officials showed similar results as well. The then Thai Minister of Foreign Affairs, Pitsuwan Surin, gratefully admitted that without Japan's support, the Asian countries could not have overcome their economic crises (Surin, 2005). Thus, it is undeniable that the Miyazawa Initiative won a considerable degree of gratitude from an array of Asian countries. They viewed the policy as having provided the needed engine which propelled their economic recovery.

With the Miyazawa Initiative generating increased regional regard, Japanese influence correspondingly grew. The Asian countries' reciprocal support for Japan's controversial Early Voluntary Sectoral Liberalization (EVSL) package demonstrates this. Japan had been fighting a rearguard battle against Western governments that were intent on forcing open Japanese forestry and fisheries. Strong vested interests, with close ties to a select group of politicians and bureaucrats, have long distinguished these industries. At the Asia-Pacific Economic Cooperation (APEC) meeting in Kuala Lumpur (November 1998), Japan had refused to liberalize its trade in these areas. Instead, Japan successfully brought the EVSL package to the World Trade Organization for judgment. Strategically, this maneuver delayed any necessity to seek a compromise. The East Asian states, now under an obligation stemming from the Miyazawa Initiative, displayed a sympathetic understanding of Japan's response to the EVSL negotiations at the APEC summit (Hughes, 2000, p. 246). No indisputable evidence exists that demonstrates how the Miyazawa Initiative influenced the attitudes held by Asian countries on this issue. For instance, many of these countries might have regarded such intervention as a bad precedent for their own domestic economies. However, it is difficult to dismiss the distinct possibility that the Miyazawa Initiative, by creating an increased closeness between East Asian countries and Japan, tipped the balance in creating stronger support for Japanese positions.

Further ramifications of the Miyazawa Initiative also extended to Japanese relationships with South Korea. The South Koreans, initially quite sceptical of any effort originating from Japan, gradually changed their attitude after the Japanese extended loans to South Korea and turned one-third of its short-term loans (7.9 billion) into medium- or long-term ones. In October 1998, the Federation of Korean Industries endorsed the AMF and its associated Miyazawa Initiative by further agreeing to the internationalization of the Japanese yen (Lee and Moon, 2002, p. 157). South Korean Prime Minister Kim Dae Jung even called for a new AMF to resolve the crisis, emphasizing the importance of developing Asian solutions for Asian problems. South Korean public opinion was tilting toward the idea of an AMF, an institution that would not impose strict conditionality and that would offer low interest rates (about 6 percent, similar to those then operating in Japan) (Lee and Moon, 2002, p. 157). It was no mere coincidence that when President Kim visited Japan in December 1998 for a summit meeting, Kim accepted Obuchi's apology for past Japanese transgressions and emphasized his willingness to put the past aside and establish a friendly and constructive relationship. Under the Kim administration, this declaration led to increased cultural trade between the two nations. Japanese output, such as pop music and films, achieved wider distribution in South Korea, serving to promote a better understanding between the two countries.

Encouraged by this success, the Ministry of Finance again challenged the current international economic order, not by creating an alternative institution, but by articulating its views. Besides differences in economic norms and values, the MOF also viewed the crisis in purely economic terms. The Ministry believed that the international community should enhance its capacity to provide liquidity quickly whenever a financial crisis occurred (Miyazawa, 1998a). Creation of an adequately funded AMF could have achieved this aim. Even after failing to create such a financial institution, however, the MOF continued to insist on the need to change the current financial architecture.

Faced with the stark inappropriateness of the IMF approach in handling economic crises, the international community moved toward a new consensus. This new strategy shifted away from the previous one-size-fits-all thinking that had characterized IMF dealings. Instead, IMF policy in the future would be more responsive to ongoing economic changes by increasing its transparency and by adopting appropriate and specific reform programs (G7 Finance Ministers and Central Bank Governors, 1998a). At the meeting of G7 Finance Ministers and Central Bank Governors in October 1998, these usually conservative officials confirmed this new international consensus that emphasized IMF reform. Changes focused on IMF-lending policies, including the terms of the loans and the associated conditionalities (G7 Finance Ministers and Central Bank Governors, 1998b). Reform, however, did not imply precipitous change. It did not mean that, in the short run, Japan would achieve any real influence within the IMF. However, it did indicate that many other countries were changing their views and that the financial architecture of the global economy was gradually changing as well.

Sensing this new mood, the Japanese government increased its lobbying efforts aimed at reforming the existing international financial institutions. As noted, this policy had its beginnings with the announcement of the Miyazawa Initiative. Strategically, Japan had intended to use this proposal as a vehicle through which to exert influence. The goal was to affect financial decisions, especially those which had their greatest impact within the East Asian Region. In October 1998, soon after the announcement of the Miyazawa Initiative, the Japanese government openly had challenged an existing international economic order which was built around the IMF and the World Bank. It suggested a fundamental review of the IMF–World Bank-centered system so that these revitalized institutions would reflect the changing reality of the international financial system (Miyazawa, 1998b). Finance Minister Miyazawa bluntly stated at the 51st IMF provisional committee meeting that the IMF should modify its severe conditionality so that it would not trigger a further deterioration in economic and social stability (Miyazawa, 1998c). Stating Japan's official position, he urged the IMF to review its economic programs which essentially pursued structural adjustment while abstracting away from the particulars of a given situation, including the recipient country's background. Miyazawa concluded that the measures the IMF took were clearly neither appropriate nor necessary. He strongly suggested that the IMF review its economic adjustment programs, especially those that demanded severe conditionality. As Miyazawa pointed out, "fiscal balance improvements along with a tightening of monetary policy" could end up with more negatives than positives. Such an approach would only end up eroding vital economic confidence (Miyazawa, 1998c).[17]

In July 1999, Miyazawa once again openly questioned the IMF's approach and suggested a review of its economic programs. In a *Diplomatic Bluebook* of 1999, even MOFA bureaucrats were willing to openly state that it had become clear that "the current IMF

---

[17] Also see Miyazawa (1998b).

centered international financial system needs reform ... Japan is now addressing the urgent task of reforming the international financial system" (Ministry of Foreign Affairs, 1999c, p. 19). At the third meeting of the IMF committee in April 2001, Finance Minister Masajuro Shiokawa urged a re-examination and revision of the IMF's guidelines for conditionality, as well as a review of the allocation of quota shares, voting powers, and representation on the Executive Board. According to the Minister, the IMF should reflect more closely the existing international power balance in the economic arena (Shiokawa, 2001). Japan had persistently viewed an increased quota share as an essential step toward gaining more influence. The quota not only influenced voting share, but senior bureaucratic appointments as well. These are the very officials who carry out and interpret IMF policy. As mentioned before, during the 1990s, Japan's IMF quota improved compared to what it had been during the 1980s. However, it was still disproportionate, given the size of Japan's economy. Shiokawa's request reflected Japan's wish for due recognition by the international community. The Japanese wanted to exercise what they regarded as long delayed legitimate power in financial and economic matters.

8.3.2 *Modesty and Deference: The Keys to a Successful Initiative*

The AMF proposal failed due to strong US opposition. A characteristic reluctance by the Japanese government to confront its key ally only reinforced this outcome. Certainly, an inability by officials to coalesce behind the policy did not help, as even the MOF could not generate unified internal support for the Asian Monetary Fund. In contrast, the Miyazawa Initiative was successful by ensuring that regional countries facing economic turmoil received sizeable financial injections. The positive Asian response indicated the degree of its success. Encouraged by this achievement, Japan initiated subsequent attempts to influence the restructuring of the existing economic order. What factors enabled the Miyazawa Initiative to succeed?

The Miyazawa Initiative consisted of bilateral financial assistance which aided both Asian countries and the ailing Japanese economy.

Increased trade between this region and Japan yielded greater economic interdependence. Starting in the early 1990s, the Japanese economy had stumbled badly once its bubble economy had collapsed. Nevertheless, Japanese manufacturers continued to invest heavily in Asia as a way of offsetting the domestic downturn. Its direct investment within the Asian region (excluding China) continued to grow. Starting from a level of $5,865 million in 1991, FDI increased to $11,325 million by 1996. Asian regional FDI accounted for only 8.6 percent of Japan's total as of 1990, but 24 percent by 1996.[18] This deepening interdependence meant that initially the Japanese government would do whatever it could to avoid creating any negative impact on local Japanese subsidiaries. Subsequent policies would seek to buffer Asian-based Japanese companies against any regional economic turmoil (Ministry of Foreign Affairs, 1998d). Since Japanese banks had financed sizeable FDI projects in Asia, unsettled and even perilous economic conditions would create a serious blow for these institutions. They were already struggling, not entirely successfully, to survive in Japan's stagnating economy (Green, 2001, p. 255). Increased loans to Asia had been intended to offset a huge inventory of domestic non-performing loans. Given this burden, Japanese banks were simply incapable of writing off their Asian loans even though their US and European counterparts had already started to offset their delinquent regional loans (*Asian Wall Street Journal*, September 28, 1998, cited in Green, 2001). Japanese banks lacked the financial capacity to write off $114.7 billion worth of non-performing loans, amounting to more than 30 percent of their total loans to Asia. In contrast, non-performing loans comprised only 8 percent of all Asian debt held by US banks (*Asahi Shimbun*, March 19, 1998). Consequently, the Japanese business community expected their government to launch some initiative that would successfully assist economic recovery in Asia (Hatakeyama, interview with corporate representative in Asia; interview with Director

---

[18]This figure includes the ASEAN-10 countries, China, Hong Kong, Taiwan, and South Korea. For the source of this data, see http://www.jetro.go.jp/jpn/stats/fdi/data/jfdi1111_01.xls, accessed in January 2006.

of Kiedanren, April 2004).[19] The Miyazawa Initiative was a perfect plan to benefit both the crisis-racked Asian countries and the relevant at-risk Japanese business sectors (Katada, 2001).

It is undeniable that a strong revival of the Asian markets, which the Miyazawa Initiative sought to accomplish, would assist Japanese companies adrift in the prolonged economic recession. However, it does not mean that the government announced the Miyazawa Initiative as a direct response to pressure from the business sector. As previously pointed out, a long-standing and close relationship between the business sector and the government is a hallmark of Japan's economic policy. It was, after all, MITI that had encouraged business firms to go overseas by facilitating their entry through a "three in one approach" (trade, investment, and aid). JBIC stood ready to respond to business requests for overseas project facilitation. However, there has been little involvement by the business sector in direct policy making (Hatakeyama, interview with corporate representative, April 2004). The Miyazawa Initiative was responsive to business needs without being a simple reflection of direct lobbying. Rescuing faltering Asian economies would provide economic benefits for Japan as well. But the guiding principle behind the proposal was a determination to serve Japanese interests by creating the image of an effective economic leader, a Japan willing to contribute to regional well-being and continued stability.

To signal its role as a dominant economic power, the Japanese government felt obliged to assist Asian countries. Due to its own financial problems and the subsequent abortion of the AMF, Japan's status as an economic leader had eroded dangerously. As expected, at an ASEAN+3 meeting (December 1997), the Japanese government assumed a low profile by supporting the initial IMF packages. At that meeting, Prime Minister Hashimoto stated that financial assistance should be made under the IMF umbrella in order to induce a flow of capital from the US and Europe. Japan could not contribute to a worldwide depression by refusing to cooperate (*The Straits Times*, December 17, 1997). By taking this stance, Japan disappointed other

---

[19]The former represented one of Japan's biggest manufacturing companies. The Keidanren is the Japan Federation of Employers' Association.

Asian countries. They viewed the Japanese as once again acting more like an automatic teller machine than a country able to assume political and economic leadership.

In addition, Japan had been unable or unwilling to absorb a sufficient volume of exports from other Asian countries. Between 1995 and 1997, the yen depreciated 60 percent against the dollar and further depreciated to 147 yen in June 1998. This weak yen greatly helped the Japanese export industries suffering from the sustained recession, but was counter-productive for those Asian countries that expected Japan to absorb their imports. Even worse, low domestic demand meant that imports from other Asian countries actually decreased when compared to the previous year's (1996) total. Japanese policy makers denied that the depreciating yen was the result of any manipulation by the government and insisted that the government would not accept an undervalued yen (Miyazawa, 1998b). Whether this statement was true or not, the weak yen and the huge trade surplus of 1997 attracted criticism from other Asian countries. They saw this result as stemming from Japan's deliberate exchange rate manipulations which aimed to expand exports but limit imports from desperate Asian trading partners.

Criticism of Japan for not contributing enough to the economic stability of the region prevailed even among the European countries and the US, leading to severe criticism at subsequent G7 meetings. Japan did show a certain amount of enthusiasm for assisting devastated regional economies. This determination lay behind "Japan's Comprehensive Economic Measures" (April 1998) which set out a series of intended emergency actions and assistance measures to help resolve the increasingly worrisome Asian crisis. However, other countries deemed these efforts to be insufficient.[20] The international community did not hide its frustration with Japan. In January 1998, US. Treasury Secretary, Robert Rubin, demanded that Japan "deal with the issues in its financial system, to generate solid growth in domestic demand and open its markets." (Johnstone, 1999, p. 127) The "role of Japan in the Asian crisis" was much discussed at the London G7 meeting

---

[20]The package consisted of $120 billion in tax cuts and social infrastructure spending, including assistance worth $5.4 billion to the recipient Asian countries.

(February 1998). Members attending this meeting severely criticized Japan for not playing a role as an economic "stopper" (*Asahi Shimbun*, February 23, 1998). By March 1998, Asian countries had joined this growing chorus. At the ASEAN Financial Ministerial meeting (March 1998), the ASEAN countries demanded that Japan revive its economy by domestic demand-led growth and play a leading role in helping Asian countries pull out of their crisis (*Asahi Shimbun*, March 1, 1998). An opinion poll conducted in March 1998 among corporate owners and executives in 10 Asian countries found that 82 percent of those responding insisted that Japan's help was insufficient (*Asahi Shimbun*, March 19, 1998). The end result of Japan's worsening economic climate, and its related inability to assume anything like a leadership role, seemed to confirm the superiority of the US economic model. Further, in the Washington statement put out by the G7 countries in April of the same year, the importance of Japan's economic recovery was stated again as a matter of urgency. Meanwhile, President Bill Clinton, while visiting Hong Kong (July 1998), felt entitled to proclaim the undeniable triumph of US ideology. Somehow, those much touted "Asian values" had lost their validity, let alone their shine. Instead, critics insisted that Asia in the 21st century could only be built successfully on the shared values of freedom, democracy, and the market economy (*Yomiuri Shimbun*, July 5, 1998). Under these adverse circumstances, the Japanese government felt compelled to take measures which would revive its economic diplomacy. Asian countries and the US also awaited a more positive and effective Japanese role.

The US was furious when the Ministry of Finance responded by proposing the Asian Monetary Fund. In contrast to this furore, the US responded to Miyazawa's efforts with greater enthusiasm because of its non-threatening, bilateral nature. Rather, the Miyazawa Initiative, which provided large amounts of economic assistance to the region, was expedient since it removed any need for the US to contribute funds to float a broad-based, bail-out plan. Moreover, the recent financial crisis in Brazil had distracted American attention away from Asia. In return for acquiescing to lenient IMF programs for Brazil, the US, in turn, agreed not to oppose a leading Japanese role in Asia, as long as it remained within a bilateral context. Due to the mutually beneficial character of this arrangement, the US did not perceive the Miyazawa Initiative to be an explicit challenge.

Thus, the hopes of the Japanese business sector, the desire of the Japanese government to boost its influence, and finally US acceptance of a bilateral approach all came into alignment. Japanese underlying aims to boost its regional position were not thwarted by the needs of either domestic sectors or those of its chief ally. This enabled the government to confidently implement the Miyazawa Initiative. As a result, Japan was able to increase its regional influence.

8.4 Conclusion: Lessons Learned

The end of the Cold War appeared to provide Japan with greater opportunity to play a larger role within the realm of regional economies. However, Japan's increased confidence was not paralleled by any noticeable heightening of its influence relative to any of the international financial institutions. Conflicting views concerning economic development set the Japanese government and the IMF/World Bank at cross purposes. These conflicts remained submerged and did not surface openly, even during the Asian crisis. However, policy cross currents during this period did become more apparent.

With the economic crisis as a trigger, Japan boldly attempted to establish an Asian Monetary Fund that was Japanese focused and dominated. Besides featuring US exclusion, Japan's majority voting share in the fund would have enabled the Japanese to promote their views on economic development and influence actual policies. Using the proposed AMF as a first step, Japan could have continued by creating a new regional order, one that was based on its beliefs, especially those touching upon economic development. At the very least, the new institution would have served to promote and sustain this Japanese model of development and increase its effective influence. However the US had other ideas. The Americans clearly saw the AMF as a competitor to its own dominated institutions (the IMF and World Bank). Strong US opposition frustrated Japan's bold attempt to create a new economic order in the region and place itself in a central financial role. In addition, the lack of any coordinated agreement among the relevant ministries partly served to frustrate the Ministry of Finance's bold new initiative. An alternative route to an equivalent, if not quite as influential, result appeared possible.

Changing its tactics, the Ministry of Finance again attempted to exert its influence through the Miyazawa Initiative, despite Japan's precarious economic situation. The AMF proved to be a false start in Japan's crusade to construct a new economic order. In contrast, this alternative initiative managed to achieve a more modest degree of success because in this case, three crucial factors were aligned:

1. Japan's business interests,
2. US acceptance of the initiative due to its bilateral nature,
3. MOF's desire to enhance its own position by staking out a leadership role.

Clearly Japan's objectives did not change either before or after this episode. However, it did have to adjust its strategy when faced with key binding constraints.

References

Altbach E. (1997) JEI report. *JEI Report* 1. JEI, Tokyo.

Bhagwati J. (1998) The capital myth: The difference between trade in widgets and dollars. *Foreign Affairs*, 77(3), 7–13.

Calder KE. (1998) Japan's crucial role in Asia's financial crisis. *Japan Quarterly*, 45(2), 4–9.

Drysdale P. (2002) Beyond east Asia's economic crisis: Development paradise lost? In: Inoguchi T (ed.), *Japan's Asian Policy*, pp. 55–80. Palgrave Macmillan, New York.

Feldstein M. (1998) Refocusing the IMF. *Foreign Affairs*, 77(2), 20–33.

Gilpin R. (2000) *The Challenge of Global Capitalism: The World Economy in the 21st Century*. Princeton University Press, New Jersey.

G-7 Finance Ministers and Central Bank Governors. (1998a) Statement of the G-7 Finance Ministers and Central Bank Governors. *Ministry of Finance*. Washington, DC, October 3, http://www.mof.go.jp/english/if/e1e041.htm, accessed in April 2005.

G-7 Finance Ministers and Central Bank Governors. (1998b) Declaration of the G-7 Finance Ministers and Central Bank Governors. *Ministry of Finance*. Washington, DC, October 3, http://www.mof.go.jp/english/if/e1e049.htm, accessed in June 2005.

Green MJ. (2001) *Japan's Reluctant Realism*. Palgrave, New York.

Hatch W, Yamamura K. (1996) *Asia in Japan's Embrace: Building a Regional Production Alliance*. Cambridge University Press, Cambridge.

Hook GD, Gilson J, Hughes CW, Dobson H. (2001) *Japan's International Relations*. Routledge, London, New York.

Hughes CW. (2000) Japanese policy and the East Asia currency crisis: abject defeat or quite victory? *Review of International Political Economy*, 7(2), 219–253.

Inada J. (2001) Sekai Ginko, IMF no Kouzou Chousei Regime to Nihon no Seisaku. In: Inada J, Shimomura Y (eds.), *Ajia Kinyukiki no Seiji Keizaigaku*. Nihonkoku-saimondai kenkyujo, Tokyo.

Inoguchi, T. (2002) Japan goes regional. In: Inoguchi T (ed.), *Japan's Asia Policy: Revival and Response*, pp. 8–15. Palgrave, New York.

International Monetary Fund. (2005a) IMF regional office for Asia and the Pacific (OAP). *IMF*. http://www.imf.org/external/oap/about.htm, accessed in April 2005.

International Monetary Fund. (2005b) IMF Members' quotas and voting power, and IMF Board of Governors. IMF. http://www.imf.org/external/np/sec/memdir/members.htm#u, accessed in February 2005.

Japan Science and Technology Agency. (1993) Kagaku Gijutsu Hakusho. *White Paper* 348.

Johnson C. (1998) Economic crisis in East Asia: The clash of capitalism. *Cambridge Journal of Economics*, 22, 653–661.

Johnstone CB. (1999) Strained alliance: US–Japan diplomacy in the Asian financial crisis. *Survival*, 41(2), 121–138.

Katada, S. (2001) Determining factors in Japan's cooperation and non-cooperation with the US: The case of Asian financial crisis management 1997–1999. In: Miyashita A, Sato Y (eds.), *Japanese Foreign Policy in Asia and the Pacific*. Palgrave, New York.

Lee J-H, Moon C-I. (2002) The Korean calculus. In: Inoguchi T (ed.), *Japan's Asia Policy: Revival and Response*, pp. 137–166. Palgrave, New York.

Lincoln EJ. (1998) Japan's Financial Mess. *Foreign Affairs* 77(3), 57–66.

Ministry of Finance. (1998a) A report on Japan's contribution in the Asian crisis. *Ministry of Finance Reports*. http://www.mof.go.jp/jouhou/kyouka/14nendo/kekka/sougouhyoukasho/ajia.pdf, accessed in July 2005.

Ministry of Finance. (1998b) Gaikoku Kawase Shingikai, Ajia-Kinyu Shihonshijou Senmon Bukai Houkokusho. *Gekkan New Policy*, 19 May.

Ministry of Finance. (1998c) Meeting of Asian Finance and Central Bank Deputies. *Ministry of Finance Reports*. http://www.mof.go.jp/.english/if/if0001.htm, accessed in December 2006.

Ministry of Finance. (1998d) *Q & A about The New Initiative to Overcome the Asian Currency Crisis (New Miyazawa Initiative)*. http://www.mof.go.jp/english/qa/my001.htm, accessed in April 2005.

Ministry of Foreign Affairs. (1991) Policy speech by Prime Minister Toshiki Kaifu during his ASEAN visit. *Diplomatic Bluebook 1991*, pp. 426–427.

Ministry of Foreign Affairs. (1996) Taskforce on ODA. *MOF Report*. http://www.mofa.go.jp/mofaj/gaiko/oda/index/kunibetsu/taskforce.htm, accessed in April 2005.

Ministry of Foreign Affairs. (1997) Press conference by the Japanese delegation to the 1997 APEC meeting in Vancouver. *APEC meeting in Vancouver.* http://www.mofa.gp.jp/policy/economy/apec/1997/bilateral.html, accessed in December 2004.

Ministry of Foreign Affairs. (1998a) Speech by Prime Minister Hashimoto at Yomiuri kokusai keizaiai konwakai, 28 August 1997. *Gaiko Seisho 1998 [1998 Diplomatic Bluebook],* p. 226.

Ministry of Foreign Affairs. (1998b) *Gaiko Seisho 1998 [1998 Diplomatic Bluebook],* pp. 367–369.

Ministry of Foreign Affairs. (1998c) On-the-Record Briefing. *APEC meeting.* November 13, http://www.mofa.go.jp/policy/enonomy/apec/1998/brief13.html, accessed in April 2005.

Ministry of Foreign Affairs. (1998d) ODA and the Asian Currency and Financial Crisis. *Japan's ODA Annual Report (Summary) 1998.* http://www.mofa.go.jp/policy/oda/summary/1998/3.html, accessed in July 2005.

Ministry of Foreign Affairs. (1999a) Report of the Mission for revitalization of Asian economy: Living in harmony with Asia in the twenty-first century. *Mission for Revitalization of Asian Economy.* November, http://www.mofa.go.jp/policy/economy/asia/mission99/, accessed in July 2005.

Ministry of Foreign Affairs. (1999b) *Nihon no Shitenhoushin to Shien Jigyo.* http://www.mofa.go.jp/mofaj/gaiko/oda.shiryo.hyouka.kunibetsu/gai/asia_tuka/th, accessed in December 2005.

Ministry of Foreign Affairs. (1999c) *Gaiko Seisho 1998 [1998 Diplomatic Bluebook].*

Miyazawa K. (1998a) Towards a new international financial architecture. *Ministry of Finance.* Speech by Mr. Kiichi Miyazawa, the Minister of Finance, at the Foreign Correspondents Club of Japan, December 15, http://www.mof.go.jp/english/if/e1e057.htm, accessed in July 2005.

Miyazawa K. (1998b) Statement by the Hon. Kiichi Miyazawa at the Fifty-third Joint Annual Discussion. *Ministry of Finance.* October 6, http://www.mof.go.jp/enflish/if/e1e047hm, accessed in June 2005.

Miyazawa K. (1998c) Japan's Statement at the 51st IMF Provisional Committee. *Ministry of Finance.* http://www.mof.go.jp/daijin.1e039.htm, accessed in June 2005.

Nishigaki A, Shimomura Y. (1999) *The Economics of Development Assistance.* LTCB International Library Foundation, Tokyo.

Ohno K. (1996) *Shijou Ikou Senryaku.* Yuhikaku, Tokyo.

Pempel TJ. (1997) Transpacific Torii: Japan and the emerging Asian regionalism. In: Katzenstein P, Shiraishi T (eds.), *Network Power: Japan and Asia,* pp. 47–82. Cornell University Press, Ithaca.

Pempel TJ (ed.). (1999) *The Politics of the Asian Economic Crisis.* Cornell University Press, Ithaca.

Radelet S, Sachs J. (1997) Asia's reemergence. *Foreign Affairs,* 76(6), 44–59.

Sakakibara E. (2000) *Nihon to Sekaiga Furueta Hi: Cybernetic Shihonshugi no Seiritsu,* Chuo Koron, Tokyo.

Shiokawa M. (2001) Statement by H.E. Masajuro Shiokawa, Minister of Finance of Japan at the Third Meeting of the IMF Committee. *Ministry of Finance.* April 29, http://www.mof.go.jp/english/if/eko0732073.htm, accessed in July 2005.

Shiratori M. (1998) Afterword to the Japanese Translation of the World Bank Report 'The East Asian Miracle.' In: Ohno K, Ohno I (eds.), *Japanese Views on Economic Development*, pp. 77–83. Routledge, New York.

Surin P. (2005) Japan in the World, Japan in Asia. *Address by a former Minister of Foreign Affairs of Thailand, Pitsuwan Surin.* November 16, Tokyo Colloquium and Yomiuri International Economic Society Autumn Forum, Tokyo.

Yasutomo DT. (1995) *The New Multilateralism in Japan's Foreign Policy.* St. Martin's Press, New York.

Chapter 9

Intellectual Leadership: Japan's Relationship with Vietnam

9.1 Introduction: The ABCs of Aid

Lacking political and military power, Japan has often opted to employ foreign aid as a strategic tool for gaining increased influence. Starting initially in 1954 with its participation in the Colombo Plan for Southeast Asia (as well as paying concurrent war reparations), foreign aid gradually developed into a central pillar of Japan's diplomacy.[1] Assistance not only sweetened relationships with other Asian countries but also nurtured a favorable image that depicted Japan in the role of a selfless big brother supporting other developing countries. Although Japan's aid has been criticized as "faceless" and lacking distinct diplomatic aims, it is undeniable that Japan consistently and deliberately employed its Official Development Assistance (ODA) to elevate its international standing (Ministry of Foreign Affairs, 2003a).

However, a long-term refusal to articulate its aid policy or philosophy, despite years of financial commitment, attracted persistent international criticism. Opponents dismissed Japan's aid as no more than a simple excuse to further its own narrow commercial interests.[2]

---

[1] Japan's economic assistance to Laos and Cambodia, after both abandoned their claims for reparations, highlights the strong similarity between aid and reparations. See Chapter 1 for a more detailed explication.

[2] For example, see Arase (1995), Lincoln (1993) and Ensign (1992).

They claimed that although Japanese assistance emphasized large-scale infrastructure projects, the program lacked any underlying philosophic base. These critics used such observations to create a perception that the Japanese employed aid purely as an economic weapon, and not as a diplomatic one. Even after Japan introduced a peacekeeping operations law, allowing the Japanese to play a broader international role, its aid program still could not shake this rather dismissive characterization. Japan's low profile in the security field until the 1980s only confirmed this categorization. As a result, an analysis explaining not only Japan's aid policy, but also Japan's national objectives, in terms of economic interests prevailed. In this view, Japan "looked to development aid as an instrument to promote its own economic revival" (Guang, 1998, p. 17). Japan was also seen as lacking "political leadership or a national strategy, resulting in the expression of uncoordinated views by different ministries" (Takagi and Kawai, 2004, pp. 261–262). Given this approach, Japan was destined inevitably to "have a hard time assuming an international aid leadership role" in part because ministry rivalry inevitably fragmented Japan's aid policy (Hirata, 1998, p. 334). Japan's ill repute seemed to reduce any of Japan's diplomatic efforts to the level of simple "check-book diplomacy."[3]

In the late 1990s, however, Japan signaled a clear tactical change in its aid policy as well as in its approach to international affairs. Japan's low-key assistance program transformed itself into a high-profile one, which would more directly serve Japan's leadership aspirations and its perceived national interests. Concretely, Japan's strategy shifted, so that it tried to shape international aid initiatives by creating new structures and frameworks which would allow Japan to use assistance packages as a means of boosting its own influence.

This chapter examines whether, contrary to more traditionally held views, Japan's attempts to pursue intellectual leadership to a large extent reflects its desire to be a dominant regional power. Japan's strategy can be usefully illustrated by analyzing two specific instances. One is Japan's attempt to articulate precisely its approach to economic

---

[3] This criticism was common at the time of the Gulf War.

development and the role played by guided assistance. The other is Japan's actual and quite vigorous involvement in Vietnam's economic development program. The first section examines the background of this new approach. The second section looks at Japan's attempts to disseminate a new concept, namely its "Initiative for Development in East Asia" (IDEA). Though Japan's attempt to adopt a more aggressive posture quickly faded, the mere attempt indicates a deliberate policy to boost its presence as an intellectual leader. The third section evaluates Japan's involvement in Vietnam's economic development program. Both the Ministries of Finance and Foreign Affairs viewed Vietnam as a test case. These two ministries considered this initiative as a type of probe to determine whether Japan could develop a viable position as an intellectual and economic leader in either a bilateral or a multilateral context. Along with an examination of Japan's overarching objective, this chapter also examines the factors that enabled Japan to become more assertive and the extent to which economic considerations were interwoven in its pursuit of this goal.

9.2 Changes in International Aid Policy: The Japanese are Not Amused

In the late 1990s, the World Bank shifted its policy approach. Previously, it had focused on the various structural adjustments that supposedly would serve to assist economic development. Now it rediscovered poverty and saw development as a means to eradicate this widespread scourge. This shift culminated in the Comprehensive Development Framework (CDF) adopted at the Annual Meeting of the IMF and the World Bank in late 1997. The aim was to redirect attention to social aspects such as education, health, medical care, and welfare, all of which could directly reduce poverty.

The Poverty Reduction Strategy Papers adopted at the Annual General Meeting of the World Bank and the IMF in the following year greatly affected the international aid community and did not leave the Japanese unaffected. The aims depicted in these papers were: First, achieving tighter international coordination among aid donors and institutions. Second, convincing recipient countries to take ownership of a development program that mirrored the structure mandated in the Poverty Reduction Strategy Paper. From now on, any Heavily Indebted Poor Country and those countries targeted by the International Development Association (IDA) who wished to receive debt relief and the provision of IDA funds would need to produce a Poverty Reduction Strategy Paper as the first step in any assistance program. The paper was essentially a device enabling the World Bank and the IMF to influence the economic policies of developing countries. In this framework, international coordination would also indirectly influence the aid policies of donor countries as well. The Poverty Reduction Strategy Paper provided an overarching procedure that could be employed as a sort of roadmap to reduce global poverty.

In September 2000, the UN Millennium Development Goals endorsed the World Bank's new strategy. The emphasis was on developing the social sector as a means of reducing poverty. This new policy direction gained momentum with the September 11 attacks on the US in 2001. With failed states being defined as hotbeds of terrorist activity, developed countries re-examined aid programs and refocused them on alleviating poverty. By March 2002, even President George W. Bush at an Inter-American Development Bank Meeting dedicated his administration to poverty reduction in developing countries (Okuma, 2003, pp. 33–36). In September 2002, he again pledged to increase by 50 percent core development assistance through the New Millennium Challenge Account. By proposing an 18 percent increase in US contributions to the International Development Association (IDA) and the African Development Fund (see Fig. 9.1), the Bush administration reversed its previous downward trend. The EU followed suit. US and EU aid policies entered into a new phase. Opinion polls conducted in September 2002 indicated that some 91 percent of Europeans and 78 percent of Americans approved of fighting terrorism by expanding development aid (Okuma, 2003, pp. 33–36). Following the terrorist attack, poverty reduction became an overriding international consideration. Preventing the poor from supporting, or sympathizing with, terrorists gained increased urgency.[4]

---

[4]However, a counter-argument claims that economic conditions and education are largely unrelated to participation in terrorism. See Krueger and Maleckoba (2003) and Looney (2004).

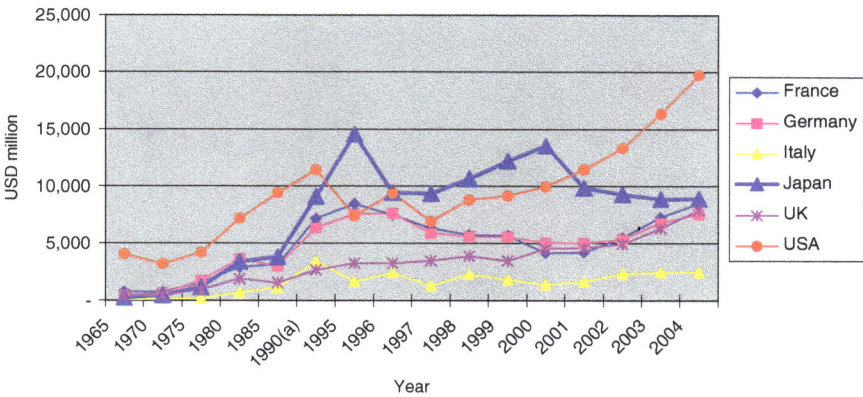

Source: OECD international development statistics online database.

Fig. 9.1   Net disbursement of ODA.

Japan was no exception. It had staunchly supported both the "war against terrorism" and poverty reduction. Prime Minister Koizumi's quick and controversial decision to send troops to Iraq left no doubt of Japan's position. Yet, its ailing economy and heavily constrained budget did not permit increasing Japanese aid in sync with other major donors. Moreover, a strategy emphasizing social development as the key to poverty eradication conflicted with the underlying rationale behind Japanese assistance.

During the earlier post-war decades, Japan to some degree had been influenced by economic considerations in providing foreign assistance. The Japanese regarded Southeast Asia as an important regional market and as a supplier of natural resources (Sudo, 2002, pp. 56–77). In fact, tied ODA during these early development stages meant that contracts for large-scale infrastructure projects would be awarded to Japanese firms. This mechanism undoubtedly contributed to the growth of Japan's economy. Unarguably, Japan's corresponding economic presence in turn increased its influence in the region, thus serving complementary objectives.

But concentrating on these purely economic considerations fails to tell the whole story. Based on its own experience (as well as what the Japanese believed to be a correct analysis of East Asian economic development), Japan had come to believe that large-scale infrastructure

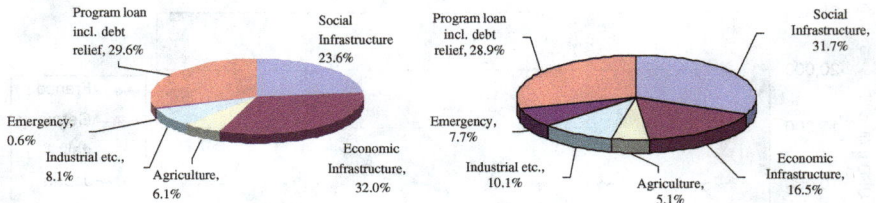

Source: ODA Hakusho, 2002, MOFA, p. 575, made by author.

Fig. 9.2   Japan's bilateral ODA (left) and DAC average (right) by sector, 2001.

projects were indispensable. This they believed to be the key to creating sustainable economic growth by encouraging the recipient countries' own self-help efforts. As Fig. 9.2 demonstrates, Japan showed a distinct bias for supporting the implementation of economic infrastructure. Japanese aid within this category is almost double the world average. Japan considered its particular emphasis to be a particularly effective form of poverty reduction since infrastructure projects, whose funds are provided mostly in the form of loans, would facilitate economic activity, leading to long-run economic growth and a subsequent increase in job opportunities. In more concrete terms, any assistance aimed at poverty reduction should not be narrowly limited to purely social-sector support, such as education, health, and medical care. Aid also needed to be extended to economic sectors including improving infrastructure. Such development could spur growth by expanding trade and investment, fostering the private sector, and promoting technology transfer. Growth promoted by these economic variables would eventually lead to reliable poverty reduction. Yet, the post-September 11 consensus took an almost diametrically opposite approach to aid strategy. The gap between Japan's view and that of the World Bank and the IMF grew ever more distinct.

Consequently, Japan found it increasingly difficult to support subsequent attempts seeking to create greater international coordination among donors. Unfortunately, the idea of donor coordination further transformed itself into a "common basket" objective, which would pool resources to achieve common goals. This multilateral approach would provide the Japanese government with even less opportunity to exert any type of meaningful influence on subsequent outcomes. Japan could either reluctantly accept this new aid agenda in order to avoid international isolation or risk taking independent action in the hope of influencing the global aid debate.

In addition, the Japanese government faced the domestic reality of an ever-tightening ODA budget. Rather than increasing aid, the growing budget deficit forced the government to make significant cutbacks. For the first time in the post-war era, the restrictive budget of 1998 decreased the aid budget by 10.4 percent compared with the previous year (Ministry of Foreign Affairs, 2005). Since 2001, this trend has become even more marked.[5] The domestic budgetary constraint forced the Japanese government to move counter to the direction adopted by the US and the EU, both of which dramatically increased aid after the September 11 terrorist attack. Japan's difficulties transformed it into one of the few countries which felt unable to pledge an increase in its own foreign assistance at the 2002 Monterrey Conference. Developed countries were expected to bolster their financial contributions to multilateral institutions, while also expanding bilateral aid. Japan's budgetary woes meant that it could do neither.

The Koizumi administration's focus on fiscal reform, intended to shore up a worsening budgetary situation, only created further complications. The Fiscal Investment and Loan Program (FILP) traditionally acted as something of a slush fund, enabling the Japanese government to easily access these interest-bearing amounts. However, in May 2000, with the intention of reforming the then existing system, the Japanese Diet passed a bill changing this status quo (Bill for the Amendment to the Trust Fund Bureau Fund Act and Others).[6] Once postal savings and pension reserves were no longer deposited automatically with the Trust Fund Bureau, the government found it difficult to dip into these fiscal pockets whenever augmenting ODA seemed strategically ripe.[7]

---

[5] In 2001, the total amount of US aid exceeded that of Japan's.

[6] It was slated to take effect on April 2001.

[7] ODA was funded from:

- the General account,
- the Fiscal Investment and Loan Programe, and
- interest payments and repayments from ODA loans previously provided.

The reform reduced resources available for ODA. The extent to which this specific reform impacted ODA spending requires further examination.

Table 9.1   Financial resources for ODA projects.

Year	2000	2001	2002	2003	2004
Fiscal loan and investment programs, etc. (billion yen)	677.8	635.6	574.1	552.8	526.0

Source: ODA White Paper, each year, made by author.

As a result, the government lost, to some degree, a flexible funding source for foreign assistance[8] (see Table 9.1).

In order to offset this array of difficulties and constraints, the Japanese government needed to influence subsequent international debate. It embarked on a new tactical approach which involved the widespread dissemination of its own distinct views on economic development. Japan needed to influence a previously one-dimensional discussion on aid by actively participating in and molding the international aid debate. Certainly, Japan also sought to reduce overseas poverty. Yet its methodology was clearly different. Japan's own successful experience in creating a successful program of post-war reconstruction provided the confidence the Japanese government required as it became increasingly assertive.

9.3 A New Concept: A Bold Initiative for East Asian Development

The Japanese government proceeded to reappraise its aid posture, responding both to shifts in the international community and to its increasing domestic budget limitations. To combat the pronounced changes in international aid policy, Japan articulated its own approach to economic development which it then disseminated, focusing especially within the Asian region. Japan operated under the firm belief that rapid economic growth throughout the rest of Asia would develop best under Japanese leadership. Starting in January 2002, a Proposal

---

[8] Abolition of the Trust Fund Bureau forced the Fiscal Investment and Loan Programme (FILP) agency to raise funds by issuing agency bonds and FILP bonds based on market-like principles.

for an Initiative for Development in East Asia (IDEA) represented a beginning attempt to realize this objective. However, the proposal at first failed to gain any significant traction, even within the Ministry of Foreign Affairs (Hatakeyama, telephone interview with MOFA official, Tokyo, February 2006).

Prime Minister Koizumi's Singapore visit in January 2002 led to the proposed IDEA. This newly developed concept, which encapsulated the Japanese experience, illustrated Japan's determination to influence international debate by attributing the success of East Asian economic development to Japan's massive foreign assistance, trade, and investment program. The new proposal was one of five objectives defined by Koizumi in his Singapore speech.[9] IDEA itself contained three goals:

> ... the first is to disseminate the development experiences and expertise of the region to the international community for the sake of other regions such as Africa, which has attracted international attention; the second is to shift the ongoing aid discussion and the third is to strengthen regional ties (Ministry of Foreign Affairs, 2002a).

This was an explicit attempt to influence the ongoing aid discussion by gaining Asian allies. Responding to Koizumi's call, the first IDEA Ministerial Meeting was held in August 2002 in Tokyo. China, South Korea, and the ASEAN countries participated. Japan's objective was to market the East Asian experience of economic development by emphasizing the necessity of its economic-oriented approach. Namely, Japan made an unequivocal claim that it had perfected the right formula to steer a country out of poverty. The Japanese government needed Asian support if it was to influence the new international debate. Given Japan's traditional lack of influence in both the international aid arena and

---

[9] The proposals are as follows:

- To promote education and human resource development.
- To designate 2003 as the Year of Japan–ASEAN Exchange, hoping to stimulate exchanges in all areas, including intellectual and cultural.
- To initiate Japan–ASEAN Comprehensive Economic Partnership.
- To initiate Development in the East Asia Meeting.
- To promote Japan and ASEAN security cooperation (Ministry of Foreign Affairs, 2002a).

multinational financial institutions, proceeding unilaterally would end up undercutting any chance Japan had of receiving a fair hearing.

At the first IDEA meeting, Asian ministers confirmed three points as prerequisites for sustainable economic growth:

1. building economic infrastructure,
2. sustaining human resource development,
3. enhancing institutional capacities in both the public and private sectors.

Building linkages between trade and investment would best support these requirements (Ministry of Foreign Affairs, 2002b). To the Japanese government, such steps represented the very pillars of economic development. Participants also reaffirmed the effectiveness of the East Asian strategy in reducing poverty. In this view, it was only by following such a specific prescription that East Asia had experienced remarkable economic growth in such a relatively short period. Other regions, such as Africa, could do so as well. Although Japan's contribution was not directly mentioned, its role in the successful East Asian experience was acknowledged by the other Asian countries.

To make this development concept more substantial, the ministers agreed to cooperate in three areas:

1. planning an IDEA project in line with the East Asian development model.
2. advancing analysis of the East Asian development experience in the intellectual community.
3. disseminating this experience to the international community and to international institutions such as the DAC (Ministry of Foreign Affairs 2002b).[10]

The purpose behind the agreement was obvious. The first point would prove the effectiveness of the model by constructing a concrete example. The second aimed at academically demonstrating this effectiveness, while the third aimed at facilitating and accelerating the dissemination

---

[10]The Development Assistance Committee (DAC, www.oecd.org/dac) is the principal body through which the OECD deals with issues related to cooperation with developing countries.

process. The Japanese government intended, quite explicitly, to persuade the international aid community that the East Asian economic development approach was effective. In fact, Japan created the IDEA as a vehicle to market its alternative views.

Japan intended this development initiative to be a mechanism for strengthening regional cooperation. These associated countries would share a common and systemic approach to economic development (Ministry of Foreign Affairs, 2002c). Joining with other ASEAN countries to develop such a unified approach would successfully increase regional solidarity. Japan, quite naturally, would assume a central position in packaging any development model focused on aid, trade, and investment.

In August 2003, the Japanese government was back heavily marketing the IDEA program at the Fukuoka Symposium. At this meeting, it again emphasized the Japanese style of economic development, which focused on the importance of private sector investment, a strong governmental role, intensive infrastructure, and human resource development. The Tokyo International Conference on African Development (TICAD III) in September 2003 provided another opportunity to present the IDEA concept. Japan's purpose here was to impress African countries with the effectiveness of these Japanese initiatives. Japan intended to use this approach to economic development to establish and extend its regional as well as international influence.

This new-found energy, edging almost on missionary zeal, contrasted with Japan's previous strategy. Heretofore, Japanese governments had not articulated an explicit philosophy of economic development. Its near invisibility did not change even when the idea of a "flying geese pattern" of regional economic development, with Japan as the leading goose, grabbed international attention in the 1980s. However, by this time, successive Japanese governments had covertly exported its "sunset industries" to other Asian countries (Korhonen, 1994, pp. 95–98). Tacit support for this approach can be found in a statement by the Japanese Ministry of Finance committee report on Asia Pacific Economic Research in 1990. "It is necessary that what Japan used to do should be done by the Asian NIEs, and what the Asian NIEs used to do should be done by ASEAN countries" (cited in Pempel, 1997, p. 53). Japan believed that this approach could contribute to the economic development. The model could succeed, not only in the specific case of Japan, but for other Asian countries as well. Economic development would then bring peace and prosperity to the region. In this view, Japan quite naturally reserved for itself the role of regional economic leader. Its firm grip on the dominant position in this scenario is underpinned by holding a clear lead in the possession and development of innovative technology.[11] Nonetheless, Japan had never formally articulated this belief into an officially sanctioned philosophy.

Japan's long-term recession after the collapse of its "bubble economy" would seem to have destroyed any credibility attached to its favored development model. But ironically this was exactly the moment when the Japanese government was practically forced to formalize a specific strategy that responded to its changing economic environment. By finally attempting to systematize a viable approach, Japan desired, once again, to project the image of a leader who illuminates, both intellectually and practically, the required path to economic development.

Exactly when the model was articulated is only of secondary importance. The IDEA concept did serve as a platform to market the Japanese vision of economic development. The proposal indicated Japan's willingness to counter what passed for new thinking in the realm of international aid. Japanese strategy provided a reasonable alternative that could be utilized to rally and consolidate the region in opposition to this new international consensus. By adopting Japan as their role model, Asian leaders would anoint the Japanese, at least implicitly, as controllers of the regional centre, intellectually as well as economically. The combination of aid, trade, investment, and an unshakable belief in this model, a sort of "four-in-one approach," emerged and became one of the most important tools of Japan's aid policy.

Lacking any urgent impetus, however, the IDEA bore no fruit. Never going beyond discussion and formalization, it generated no new projects. Additionally, it failed to directly influence aid discussions at the international level. Nevertheless, this very well orchestrated attempt

---

[11] However, the "flying geese pattern" is not a theory of domination. The dominating power of a leading goose will eventually loosen due to competition. See Korhonen (1994).

indicated a new Japanese desire to articulate its views explicitly. Though attempts to change minds were not successful internationally, Japan proved more adept at implementing its aid principles in the specific case of Vietnam.

9.4 Vietnamese Assistance: An Opportunity to Shine as Intellectual Leaders

9.4.1 *Determined Pursuit: Japan's Hunger for Influence*

As we have seen, the international consensus on aid contrasted sharply with Japan's position. This consensus became a type of pressure to be used against any potentially renegade donor government. The thrust of the program stressed aid allocation which would develop a recipient country's social sector in conjunction with a requirement that all donations go through multilateral institutions. Pooling meant that contributed resources could be used more effectively than by employing a myriad of individual and country-specific programs. This approach clearly was not conducive to Japan's aid policy. Its aid emphasized large-scale infrastructure projects. In addition, the orientation of Japanese programs was deliberately bilateral, serving as a tool to secure and improve relationships between the donor and the recipient countries. An overemphasis on social sector support would require a radical change in Japan's aid strategy. Moreover, pooling resources under the aegis of multilateral institutions was equivalent to renouncing aid as a means of influence.

Under these adverse circumstances, the selection in the late 1990s of Vietnam as a pilot country within the Comprehensive Development Framework program (under World Bank auspices) provided an opportunity for Japan to disseminate its own views. Since the end of the Cold War, Japan had played a committed and leading role in developing the Indochinese economy.[12] As always, the not-so-hidden agenda focused on the pursuit of regional stability and on a further deepening

---

[12]For instance, Japan had played a central role in the International Committee on the Reconstruction of Comboida (ICORC) and the Indochina Forum.

of economic integration. The absence of any significant US influence in Indochina provided Japan with an almost unique opportunity to play a substantial political role. More so than any other of the Indochinese countries, Vietnam has enjoyed a key position in Japan's foreign policy. As the Ministry of Finance had officially stated, Vietnam is and will continue to be an important country in terms of Japan's strategic positioning. Vietnam offers a potential future market, an energy supply base, as well as a manufacturing platform. Sharing a border with China also makes it strategically important (Ministry of Foreign Affairs, 2004a). In Vietnam, Japan had gained an initial foothold by being among the first to support Vietnam's Doi-Moi policy (economic liberalization combined with an open-door policy under its socialist regime). This position had been Japan's unvarying policy since resuming aid in November 1992. Despite persistent US opposition due to the unresolved MIAs controversy,[13] which continued to create strife between the US and Vietnam, Japan managed to successfully gain tacit US approval for aid resumption.[14] Since then, Japan, as Vietnam's top aid donor, had been quietly supporting its economic reform, not only through financial aid but also by extending "intellectual support."

The first such approach by the Japanese government was the "Ishikawa project" headed by Professor Shigeru Ishikawa. In response to Vietnamese requests in 1994, the Japanese government implemented a Comprehensive Policy Assistance Survey and collaborated in developing a legal system and formulating national economic plans.[15] Quite conveniently, when the World Bank nominated Vietnam as a pilot country, Japan already had a firmly established foothold through its previous policy of engagement. Taking advantage of this, the Japanese government launched a campaign, which it hoped would change the

---

[13]The bodies of a number of US soldiers who went missing in action during the Vietnam War have never been recovered. Rumors abounded that some of these men continued to be kept as prisoners of war in Vietnam.

[14]Vietnam established diplomatic relations with the US in August 1995.

[15]The Ishikawa project aimed at providing the Vietnamese government with policy recommendations and advice for its 5-year socio-economic development plan (1996–2000). The project covered a wide range of areas from macroeconomic to agricultural and rural development. For further discussion, see Ohno (2002).

direction of foreign aid. One objective was to achieve a more balanced discussion in the ongoing international debate, which had become fixated on developing a country's social aspects. To achieve this, Japan had to impress the rest of the international community with the significance and efficacy of the Asian way of economic development.[16] Starting with Vietnam as a pilot project, Japan hoped that it could establish viable new aid mechanisms, which could then be transferred successfully to other aid recipients.

Japanese involvement in formulating Vietnam's economic development program allowed Japan to push its own views at a more multilateral level, since the program required coordination by donors such as the various Multinational Development Banks. These included the World Bank, the Asian Development Bank, the French Development Agency, and the German KfW bank group. As a major donor, and one of the architects of the Vietnamese development plans, Japan expected that its views would be awarded their due weight in determining the appropriate program. Japan believed that its participation in policy formation would also create the opportunity to influence Vietnam's Poverty Reduction Strategy Papers so that they would reflect Japanese views, aims, and preferences. An official MOFA statement, at that time, reflected Japan's distinct intention of promoting a more assertive aid strategy. The hope was that effective assistance would enable Japan to "demonstrate intellectual leadership in global assistance trends and to convey Japan's concepts on development and assistance" (Ministry of Foreign Affairs, 2004a). The government clearly aimed at establishing Japan's approach as an internationally acknowledged and valid substitute for that of the World Bank. Japan aimed to use such success as a springboard that would increase its influence in international financial and political spheres.[17]

---

[16]For more on this, see Kitano (2003). He was Minister for Public Affairs while stationed in the Japanese Embassy in Vietnam.

[17]For a useful discussion, see Ishii (2003). She was Director of the Office of Development Finance, International Bureau of the Ministry of Finance. She admitted that there were some officials and politicians who put a priority on pursuing economic interests. She wondered whether such people were not interested in obtaining prestige and respect from countries.

Reflecting the existing consensus, however, Vietnam's Poverty Reduction Strategy Papers, structured as a guideline for Vietnam's economic development policy, initially focused only on providing social sector support that would directly reduce poverty. Japan consequently declined participating in an initial policy loan (the First Poverty Reduction Strategy Credit) implemented in June 2001. It had previously co-financed structural adjustment loans in conjunction with the World Bank. However, this time, Japanese officials showed little interest in helping to underwrite a policy loan under the aegis of the World Bank, which included a number of other donors.[18] As previously pointed out, the focus on developing only social sectors to achieve direct poverty reduction ran counter to Japan's stated beliefs (Kitano, Ishii and Karasawa, 2004, pp. 86–88). The 2001 paper, as formulated by Vietnam, lacked any reference to the importance of infrastructure in facilitating economic development. Japan's constrained budget categorically eliminated financial assistance for such unfavored and potentially ineffective projects. However, Japan's refusal to participate in the co-financing loan was not equivalent to the Japanese surrender of its own development approach. Rather, Japan counterattacked by marketing its strategy with renewed determination.

After first adopting the initial 2001 paper, the Vietnamese government changed its name from Poverty Reduction Strategy Paper to Comprehensive Poverty Reduction and Growth Strategy (CPRGS). The term "comprehensive" along with the insertion of the word "growth" was meant to underline the revised policy's economic development aspect. Despite changing its name, the CPRGS paper, presented at the informal Consultative Group meeting in May 2002, still did not sufficiently emphasize the importance of large-scale infrastructure development and the crucial role of economic growth (Ministry of Finance, 2004b). When adopting the CPRGS, the Vietnamese did not refer to the importance of economic infrastructure, but focused entirely on direct poverty reduction. In Japan's estimation, the end result would starve any aid budget of sufficient funds to implement

---

[18] See Kitano and Ishii (2003). Both of them played key roles dealing with this issue, one as an official of the Ministry of Foreign Affairs and the other as an official of the Ministry of Finance.

needed infrastructure (Kitano and Ishii, 2003). Without aid projects of this variety, Japanese officials believed that Vietnam's economic growth would never materialize. In reaction, Japan focused on persuading both Vietnam and the world of the wisdom of its approach.

The Ministry of Foreign Affairs, together with the Finance Ministry, launched a diplomatic offensive aimed at persuading the World Bank and Vietnam to shift their positions. Using her network of contacts, the then Director of the Ministry of Finance, Naoko Ishii, helped to convey Japan's distinct views on economic development (Hatakeyama, interview with JBIC official 2006).[19] Concurrently, the Japanese government established concrete evidence indicating that infrastructure development had had a significantly positive impact on economic development and growth. It ordered the National Graduate Institute for Policy Studies and the Japan Bank for International cooperation (JBIC) to conduct two studies quantifying the possible benefits that large-scale infrastructure projects might have on economic growth and poverty reduction. Both studies clearly demonstrated that developing large-scale infrastructure would lead to economic development. Rising employment would generate increased income levels, which would in turn reduce poverty (Ministry of Foreign Affairs, 2003b).[20] The fortuitous results of these studies effectively persuaded not only the Vietnamese authorities, but some influential donors as well (Ministry of Foreign Affairs, 2003c).

Japan's diplomatic campaign was not confined to Vietnam. Its broader efforts are reflected in an October 9, 2002 speech by Director General Furuta.[21] Providing the keynote address at an International Symposium held that year in Tokyo ("Towards Achieving Millennium Development Goals (MDGs): Focusing on Asia") Furuta emphasized Japan's approach to foreign assistance.

> The dramatic economic growth of six percent in the region during the past ten years and the decrease in the number of people earning less than one dollar

---

[19] Ishii had been seconded to the World Bank from 1997 to 2001.

[20] For more details about these findings, see Ministry of Foreign Affairs (2003b).

[21] Furuta was the Director General of the Economic Cooperation Bureau within the Ministry of Foreign Affairs.

a day (the line demarcating 'absolute poverty') to roughly half the number of ten years ago, both facts constitute objective proof that this approach to development has contributed in no small way to both economic growth in the region and progress in realizing the Millennium Development Goals (Ministry of Foreign Affairs, 2002d).

The Japanese government also extended its aid strategy to African countries. This region was rapidly gaining international attention as a prime target of the Millennium Development Goals. By dominating African aid discussions, Japan could position itself as an intellectual and economic role model. To market Japanese development leadership to the Third World, Japan's government held a side event during the World Summit on Sustainable Development (WSSD). The summit provided a perfect opportunity for Japan to seize intellectual leadership of the never-ending aid debate. Foreign Minister Kawaguchi stated that:

Japan would like to promote efforts for sharing global knowledge and for contributing to funding various approaches to the effective and feasible way of development in all regions around the world, including Africa (Ministry of Foreign Affairs, 2002e).

Japan's vigorous assault on the status quo represented by the international aid establishment, as well as in its more focused measures in Vietnam, did end up paying some dividends. To a degree, thinking on international aid began to shift. The first slight sign that this pronounced gap in approaches might be narrowing appeared at the annual meeting of the World Bank and the IMF held in September 2002. This occurred 3 months before the adoption of Vietnam's expanded CPRGS. At the meeting, the World Bank and the IMF admitted that imposing the standard formulation of a Poverty Reduction Strategy Paper on recipient countries was inappropriate. As a strategy to promote economic development it was ineffective. These institutions admitted that they had put too much emphasis on direct poverty reduction by focusing exclusively on higher welfare and education standards. The international aid community had clearly become more receptive to Japan's way of thinking.

In response, Vietnam and the World Bank agreed to consider an economic infrastructure development strategy. The agenda of the Consultative Group, scheduled for December 2002, reflected this change.

At that time, the group would discuss the appropriate ways in which the CPRGS could be improved. This willingness to reconsider, demonstrated that Japan's efforts had been partly rewarded. Japan was aware, however, that these future discussions amounted to nothing more than a diplomatic gesture and would not necessarily be reflected in actual policy decisions. It therefore did not participate in the Second Poverty Reduction Strategy Credit conducted in June 2003.

In the meantime, an emerging international trend receptive to Japan's approach continued to build. In April 2003, a DAC high-level meeting threw its support behind Japan's poverty reduction strategy. Attendees agreed that promoting trade and private investment while closely coordinating overseas development aid and business projects was the approach most likely to succeed (Ministry of Foreign Affairs, 2003d). Again in April 2003, the Development Committee of the World Bank confirmed that large-scale economic infrastructure was a key to successful development aid. At the next meeting in September 2003, the Infrastructure Action Plan acknowledged the importance of economic infrastructure in conjunction with social and economic service delivery in achieving the Millennium Development Goals as well as any sustainable development. Gradually, but definitely, Japan saw the gap between it and the international aid community begin to narrow.

The ultimate persuasiveness of Japanese views resulted in an additional chapter in the CPRGS devoted to the importance of promoting economic development through large-scale infrastructure. This addition, aligned with Japan's proposals, was finally completed in November 2003. The resulting revised CPRGS was partly due to a change in the international aid community, but it in turn served to generate yet a further change in the subsequent debate (Shimamura, 2005). Japan finally seemed successful in convincing the international aid community, as well as Vietnam, that economic infrastructure was a key to poverty reduction. Certainly in Vietnam itself, Japan's approach gained legitimacy.

The expansion of the CPRGS was not the only indicative sign that a shift in the debate was accelerating. Previously, the donors composing The Consultative Group Meetings for Vietnam had focused almost exclusively on developing welfare and education as the most effective, if not always the sole way to alleviate poverty. Although the ultimate goal remained poverty reduction, one additional topic discussed in the 2004 Consultative Meetings centered on the effectiveness that improving economic infrastructure might have on promoting economic growth (Hatakeyama, discussion with JICA officials, January 2006). This clearly indicated a distinct shift and potential reevaluation in the international aid consensus. Though hard to quantify, Japan did seem to gain success in influencing these aid discussions. The Japanese became a presence to be recognized in the donor community. One observer stated that other donor countries definitely came to respect Japan's views, thanks to its vigorous engagement in Vietnam's economic development program (Hatakeyama, interview with an anonymous academic, December 2005).[22] (Certainly Japan's willingness to withhold funds from programs running counter to its strategic beliefs must have had its impact as well.) Japan's development philosophy was able, at last, to gain acknowledgement at a multilateral level (Kitano and Ishii, 2003).

After having the validity of its economic development approach acknowledged, Japan's next challenge was to transform mere words into a workable, applied plan. Otherwise the expanded CPRGS would be in danger of degenerating into an empty rhetorical gesture. As mentioned, Japan did not support the First and the Second Poverty Reduction Credit Strategy. Japan remained at odds with the World Bank and the other donors due to its fundamentally different ideas. But Japan did take part in the policy formation process of the Third Poverty Reduction Strategy Credit (PRSC 3) once the desired substantive expansion of the CPRGS occurred. The policy now more closely reflected Japan's views. Remember, Japan consistently saw its guiding objective to be establishing itself as the economic and intellectual leader of Asia. A draft of the 2003 ODA Charter reflects this sense of Japan's mission. This draft, only the first since the previous 1992 Charter, underlined Japan's approach to economic development as providing the best role model that developing countries could possibly imitate.[23] However, a

---

[22] The anonymous academic had attended the Consultative Group meetings.
[23] For Japan's economic development model, see Kenichi Ohno (1996).

required level of diplomatic finesse caused Japan to drop this potentially provocative statement in the final version. Still, it does illustrate Japan's continuing fascination with being a self-appointed and widely recognized regional leader.

In the policy formation process of the Third Poverty Reduction Strategy Credit (PRSC 3), the Ministry of Foreign Affairs demanded that the Vietnamese government, prior to securing funds, strengthen its existing evaluation system of large-scale infrastructure projects. This necessitated the establishment of a set of effective mechanisms capable of coordinating government actions. Success would improve the resource allocation, continued operation, and effective maintenance of these projects (National Graduate Institute of Policy Studies, 2004). MOFA also insisted that the Vietnamese government necessarily should improve its aid management system. The reason was simple. Without improving Vietnam's management of its responsibilities, smooth implementation of large-scale projects would prove unviable. Economic development would fail to be achieved. Japan's aspirations to act as an intellectual leader would falter.

In concrete terms, the Ministry of Foreign Affairs concluded that Vietnam's lack of appropriate laws, as well as its poor management practices, posed definite obstacles for any development strategy. Particularly, Vietnam's Decree 17 resulted in slow, unclear, and complicated procedures, all of which created problems in implementing and maintaining ODA projects (Ohno and Niiya, 2004). Figures in Table 9.2

Table 9.2 Implementation Rate in Vietnam of the Past 5 Years.

Year	Percent
2001	9.8
2002	7.2
2003	11.5
2004	13.2
2005	12.4

Source: MOFA.
Implementation rate is the amount of disbursement in each year divided by the approved amount each year.

show that implementation of Japan's aid in Vietnam had been quite low, compared to the overall average yen loan rates. These only reached a level of 12.4 percent as of 2005. In contrast, Thailand managed to achieve a rate that was approximately 40 percent.[24] We cannot simply compare the implementation rates of Vietnam with those of other countries without taking into account the relative degree of development in place, the prevailing political system, and the period during which it was a recipient country. However, these figures do show that in the case of Vietnam, implementation of foreign aid did not proceed smoothly. From Japan's point of view, the reason for the low implementation lay in poor Vietnamese management (Ohno, 2004).

The Ministry of Foreign Affairs had been frustrated by the low level and slow rate of aid implementation in Vietnam and the subsequent shoddy maintenance of those projects in place. The Vietnamese were blamed for their poor management skills. A foreign assistance pledge bereft of effective implementation, no matter what its amount, inevitably would limit the success of Vietnam's economic development and thus undermine Japanese influence. Ambassador Hattori bluntly stated at the Consultative Group meeting in December 2003 that Japan was wasting its time and money. Despite a number of sizeable pledges, implementation had not gone smoothly. He urged the Vietnamese government to improve its management system (Mekong Watch, 2003). Pushed by the Japanese, the Vietnamese government reviewed Decree 17 hoping to achieve a smoother facilitation of aid funds. Following the review, Japan reminded Vietnam that pledges made by the Japanese government exceeded the total amount donated by the EU and the World Bank (Ministry of Foreign Affairs, 2004c).[25] As Vietnam's major donor, Japan seized on this advantage to gain influence over any subsequent economic policy and to expand its overall leverage.

Next, Japan proceeded to target the nature of Vietnam's business climate. MOFA concluded that Vietnam would fail to attract massive Foreign Direct Investment, even if aid did manage to improve

---

[24] This MOFA document was obtained privately by Kyoko Hatakeyama.

[25] Kyoko Hatakeyama obtained this document privately. Japan pledged $837 million for the Third Poverty Reduction Strategy Credit (PRSC 3) in 2004 with the EU pledging $625 million and the World Bank $750 million.

its infrastructure, without a substantial improvement in its business structure. Aiming at improving Vietnamese business practices, the Japanese government pushed Vietnam to accept "The Japan–Vietnam Joint Initiative" (discussed further below). This approach viewed increased competitiveness as the key to success. The Vietnamese government started off by resisting the "Joint Initiative" imperatives. Vietnam considered these demands as no less than an unacceptable form of Japanese intervention (Hatakeyama, interview with an unnamed academic, April 2005). After long negotiations, however, the Vietnamese government conceded by signing the agreement on December 2003. This capitulation left the Japanese government with a foothold from which to exert influence on Vietnam's economic policy.

It is tempting to start with the assumption that Japan's objective in implementing the Joint Initiative was only to increase the profits of Japanese firms. Vietnam's improved business environment would certainly facilitate the expansion of Japanese business. In fact, the practices prescribed by the "Joint Initiative" did improve Vietnam's business climate. Not surprisingly, Japan's Vietnamese investment surged, increasing from $300 million in 2003 to $810 million by 2005.[26] However, as might be expected, benefits flowing from this "Joint Initiative" were not confined to Japan alone. The Vietnamese government reported that the country attracted a total FDI of $5.9 billion in 2005. This represented a 30 percent increase over the previous year (Ministry of Foreign Affairs — Vietnam, 2005). A comparison shows, however, that Japan's investment in Vietnam was still relatively small. Figure 9.3 indicates that Vietnam had yet to occupy a significant economic position in terms of Japanese investment at this stage. While Japan certainly benefited from the "Joint Initiative," these gains were in line with those flowing to other countries as well.

9.4.2 *Mitigating Constraints: Defusing Bureaucratic Turf Wars*

The Japanese government successfully influenced the international aid debate and subsequently shaped Vietnamese behavior. It was a

---

[26]JBIC, Vietnam Economic News, this item was privately obtained by Kyoko Hatakeyama.

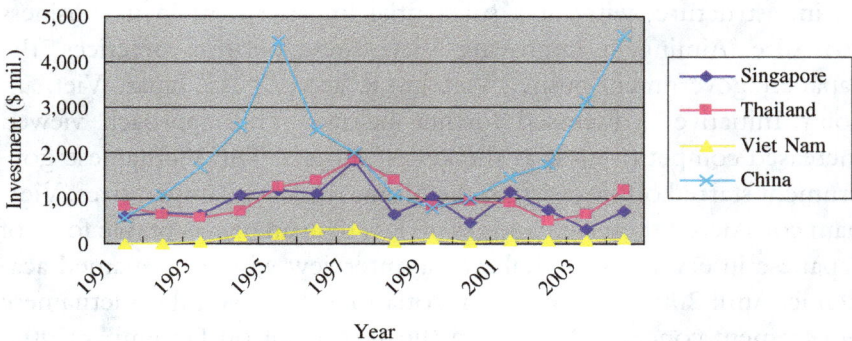

Source: JETRO, made by author.

Fig. 9.3   Japan's investment toward the region (1991–2004).

remarkable step for Japan, which had so far maintained a low profile in the aid debate, never venturing to articulate any specific views. What factors enabled Japan to succeed in gaining influence? A shift from the multipolarized decision-making system, which had characterized the government, to a more coordinated one contributed to edging the World Bank perspective closer to that of Japan. Finally, learning to speak with a unified voice inevitably provided Japan with more leverage in negotiations.

Japan's alleged "faceless" aid policy was, to some degree, attributable to the previous polarized structure of its decision making. Up until the 1980s, such Ministries as Foreign Affairs, Finance and International Trade harbored sharply divergent views on overseas assistance. MOFA had been particularly sensitive to foreign pressure since it defined its mission primarily as initiating diplomatic negotiations. From where it stood, bilateral aid was simply a vehicle to increase Japanese influence abroad. These ministers had lobbied for more focus on strategic interests and less fixation on trade and business. As shown previously in Chapter 4, the Ministry of Foreign Affairs had emphasized strategic aid that was in harmony with Japan's role as a junior partner of the US. Although decisions had to be necessarily consistent with those of the US, the ploy transformed foreign pressure into a fortuitous opportunity to enlarge the scope of the role played by Japan in the international arena (Hirata, 1998).

In contrast, MITI (later METI) obsessively aimed to facilitate business interests. MITI had strong and enduring connections with the Japanese private sector. These attachments translated into a focused drive to secure overseas business. To accomplish this objective, the Ministry ensured that aid was intentionally packaged to create increased trade and investment for corporate Japan. The government had prioritized a quick economic recovery followed by sustained growth in the early post-war period. During these years, MITI was able to exercise considerable influence over the direction of foreign aid by insisting that assistance be tied to the needs of Japanese manufacturers and suppliers. Later (at the end of the 1970s), the Foreign Ministry was able to use widening international criticism of these aid practises to overcome the powerful business lobby. Since then, about 90 percent of all yen loans have been untied.[27] Consequently, lacking any serious leverage, MITI began to lose influence. It could no longer pose as an effective champion of private business interests.

As might be expected, the Ministry of Finance's interests had been more budgetary in nature. Finance had been obligated to deal with yen loans and to contribute requisite funds to the various Multinational Development Banks. By making large contributions to key multilateral monetary institutions, the Ministry also aimed to gain increasing influence with the international financial system (Hirata, 1998). However, in contrast to Foreign Affairs, Finance had never demonstrated any substantial interest in increasing either Japan's political or even financial role in the international arena until the 1980s. The Ministry had quietly co-financed program loans in association with the World Bank and the IMF even though its ministers were not totally supportive of Structural Adjustment Lending Program Loans. (These loans were introduced by the World Bank and the IMF to pressure recipient countries into adopting more market-oriented macroeconomic policies. Accomplishing this depended on imposing harsh conditions as an associated cost attached

---

[27] The ratio of untied aid temporarily increased to 13.1 percent in 2000 due to the implementation of an outlay of special loans totalling 600 billion yen after the 1997 Asian economic crisis (1999–2001). The aim of these loans was to bail out the Asian economies as well as boost the staggering Japanese economy.

to any loan.)[28] Consequently, their disproportionate Ministerial influence resulted in Japan being criticized as a mere cash dispenser (Nakao, 2005). By the 1990s, however, the Ministry of Finance was pursuing a wider role that was more commensurate with the size of its financial contribution. MOF's attempt to establish the Asian Monetary Fund at the time of the Asian economic crisis exemplified how its objective had broadened.

Besides these conflicts of interests and divergent preferences, the simple lack of coordination between the ministries fragmented Japan's aid policies. Each ministry pursued its own particular interests and doggedly protected its specific and somewhat narrow "turf." Policies racked by conflict and lacking coordination proved unsurprisingly ineffective. For example, the slow Gulf War response, which created something of an international backlash, partly grew out of these "turf wars" created and fuelled by the contending ministries.[29]

Clearly, each of these Ministries, Finance, Foreign Affairs and International Trade and Industry, had diverse and even conflicting interests. As a result, implementation of aid was constrained by too many myopic objectives (Hirata, 1998). Moreover, the ability of the government to formulate a unitary aid policy by balancing diverse inputs was sometimes fatally impeded by an embedded absence of systematic coordination which could adjust these conflicting interests.

Hampered by this diversity of bureaucratic priorities which actively resisted amelioration, Japan was not able to articulate a succinct aid philosophy or detail its objectives until the adoption of an Official Development Assistance Charter (ODA Charter) in June 1992.[30] However,

---

[28] Juichi Inada (1993) argues that despite these differences, Japan consistently attempted to align itself with the World Bank and the IMF.

[29] Prime Minister Ryutaro Hashimoto criticised bureaucratic immobility caused by "turf consciousness." See (Makoto Iokibe, 2002).

[30] It stipulates:

- environmental conservation and development should be pursued in tandem,
- any use of ODA for military purposes or for aggravation of international conflicts should be avoided,
- full attention should be paid to trends in recipient countries' military expenditures, their development and production of weapons and missiles of mass destruction, and their export and import of arms so as to maintain and strengthen international peace and stability,

it is not an exaggeration to say that the Charter, which for the first time clarified political conditions by emphasizing a consideration for human rights, the environment, and increased democratization, was cynically announced for international consumption. The document reflected the prevailing international climate as well as Japan's consistent desire to achieve a more elevated position. It failed to articulate Japan's philosophy that the important role foreign assistance could play was to promote economic development by improving a recipient's business environment.[31] As a result, the Charter was not consistently applied to actual aid disbursement (Morrison, 2005). From Japan's point of view, foreign aid was not a tool through which to urge political change, but more a practical device with which to establish good relationships with other countries. By doing so, Japan hoped to gain the requisite level of influence which would create circumstances favoring its own national interest. Unfortunately, Japan often faced obstacles in articulating this distinctive view. Ironically, it was a long-term recession, weakening Japan's economic strength, that inadvertently triggered an opportunity.

The longer the Japanese economy was mired in recession, the louder public opposition to foreign assistance grew. Given the sluggish nature of its own economy, providing large donations to developing countries was domestically unpopular. Aid to China in particular lacked popular support. During this period, China had emerged as a potential economic superpower that threatened Japanese dominance. The lack of transparency clouding China's rapid increase in military expenditure also fuelled popular discontent. In the public mind at least, such Japanese aid became identified with subsidizing this worrying military build-up. These same critics extended their suspicions to encompass the

---

- developing countries should place appropriate priories on the allocation of their resources in order to support their own economic and social development,
- full attention should be paid to efforts for promoting democratization and introducing market-oriented economies,
- full attention should be paid regarding the securing of basic human rights and freedoms in the recipient country.

[31] Diplomat Kitano clearly stated the role of overseas assistance in his article. See Kitano and Yoshizawa (2003).

entire ODA program. Suspicions were further heightened by revelations concerning corruption among Foreign Affairs officials.[32] Regular accusations of misappropriation were increasingly bruited about. The only practical option open to the Japanese government was appeasing public opinion by improving the quality and effectiveness of aid. The need to counter both negative public perception and the international aid consensus pressured the government into producing clear and measurable results.

To accomplish this desired noticeable improvement, the government decided to centralize decision making. The Ministry of Foreign Affairs and the Japan International Cooperation Agency gained more authority. The Central Government Reform Law of June 1998 transformed the then "multi-polarized administrative system" characterizing Japanese ODA into a more centralized system with MOFA at its centre (Ministry of Foreign Affairs, 1998).[33] Building on this law, the Ministry of Foreign Affairs would be able to play a more pivotal role by providing loans and technical cooperation along with an essential policy-making and planning role. These initiatives would henceforth be "identified with Japan" (Ministry of Foreign Affairs, 1999).[34] Fractional budgetary components from related ministries and agencies for technical cooperation were also consolidated under JICA, which remained within MOFA's supervision. In April 1999, the Diet passed the Japan Bank of International Cooperation (JBIC) Law with a view to merging the Japan Export–Import Bank (JEXIM) and the Overview Economic Cooperation Fund (OECF) into the newly devised JBIC to create a more effective and better implemented aid.[35] In 2001, the Economic Planning Agency, the former supervisory agency of the OECF,

---

[32] A scandal surrounding Muneo Suzuki, former director general of the Hokkaido and Okinawa development agencies, was a serious blow for MOFA. He allegedly received bribes from 11 corporations that won ODA projects in Africa. See "Scandal Allegations dog Suzuki", *Daily Yomiuri*, February 24, 2002.

[33] It is notable that the government described its administrative system as being "multi-polarized."

[34] All of these structural changes were effectively in place by 2001.

[35] In February 2006, the government decided to abolish JBIC. As a result, the department previously in charge of ODA loans was merged into a new agency. This agency then supervised all ODA-related tasks. For additional information, see *Yomiuri Shimbum*, February 18, 2006.

as well as being an influential decision-maker was merged into the Cabinet Office. In addition, JICA, having played a supplemental role until then, found itself at the heart of implementing technical cooperation. In 2003, continued centralization of power made it more autonomous by changing its legal status. In October 2008, to facilitate this new strategy, government administrators transferred the department in charge of ODA loans, which previously operated within JBIC, to JICA. This left the newly reformulated JICA as sole supervisor of all ODA.

In combination with these organizational changes, the government initiated a new framework to enhance the effectiveness of its aid policy. In 2000, MOFA introduced a "country assistance program" whose objective was to charter a new aid direction for each recipient country. An evaluation of each assistance program would determine the future shape of its appropriate aid package.[36] The intention was to enlist and coordinate all the diverse views and interests among the concerned ministries. Three years later, MOFA also decided to set up an "ODA Task Force" for each recipient country. These task forces were meant to accelerate decision making when implementing ODA projects.[37] To smooth operations, the Task Force involved all the relevant agencies, including JICA, JBIC, and the Japan External Trade Organization (JETRO). In terms of administrative battle zones, JICA has had strong Foreign Affairs connections, while JBIC has been more under the influence of Finance. For obvious reasons JETRO, has been closely aligned with MITI. The Task Force provided a framework in which all concerned major ministries were automatically involved, if only indirectly, to coordinate the entire range of their various interests and views. It proudly purported to be an "all-Japan" framework. As desired, the introduction of the ODA Task Force system, which set-up a local office in each recipient country, succeeded in increasing the effectiveness of aid implementation. This approach has made

---

[36]Between 2000 and 2004, this involved the formulation of country assistance programs for 16 countries.
[37]The importance of timely decision making has been increasingly recognized internationally since the late 1990s. The World Bank sought to empower their local offices in recipient countries. Specifically, these local offices gained the authority to facilitate procedures and to increase the frequency of policy consultations with recipient countries.

a positive difference, increasing the potential for successful outcomes (Hatakeyama, interviews with JBIC and JICA officials, January 2006). The newly imposed system provided a framework that fostered cooperation beyond the limited "turfs" of the relevant actors. As a result, the sense of community within the decision-making process noticeably increased. Unity has in turn accelerated aid grants and strategic results.

JBIC and JICA officials attributed their Vietnam success to the concerted efforts by all those involved. This was only possible due to the introduction of the ODA Task Force. The officials claimed that "without the framework of the ODA task force, we would not have been able to coordinate our diverse views and interests and cooperate as an 'all-Japan' task force" (Hatakeyama, interviews with JBIC and JICA officials, January 2006). With each ministry and agency in Tokyo having diverse views and interests, it had been difficult to coordinate and adjust these differences when lacking a proper framework. However, working as a team in a local office created a tie among them and provided a cooperative atmosphere in which to accomplish goals prescribed by Japanese policy. This structure enabled them to leave aside their short-sighted interests (Hatakeyama, interviews with JBIC and JICA officials, January 2006). In particular, the concerted efforts by key figures like MOF's Ishii and MOFA's Kitano were successful in coordinating all concerned actors and, most importantly, persuading other aid donors to join these projects (Hatakeyama, interviews with JBIC and JICA officials, January 2006). Though not entirely, the strong traditional constraints created by "turf battles" gradually dissipated. Decision-making delays diminished and Japan's aid program in Vietnam became more consistent. To no small degree this resulted in Japan's increased influence in the aid community and its position as an intellectual leader in the case of Vietnam. A factor previously constraining Japan's ability to effectively implement its aid policy was mitigated. This allowed Japan to pursue its goal of obtaining regional influence.

9.4.3 *Deviant Behavior: Japan's Mixed Messages*

An easing of sectionalism and an improved coordination of Japanese efforts enabled resulted in the gap between Japan's view and that of the World Bank narrowing. Japan behaved in a manner consistent with its overarching goal of being recognized as an influential economic and intellectual leader within the region. However, the needs of the Japanese business community strongly influenced the "Joint Initiative." By doing so, the result deviated somewhat from Japan's ultimate aims of regional influence and intellectual leadership. The "Joint Initiative" delivered a mixed message to Vietnam, as well as to the rest of the world. To many interested observers, Japan once again was focused only in advancing its narrow economic interests. The impression conveyed was that Japan was using assistance, yet again, as a crude lever for expanding its business advantage. Why then the Japanese government push the Vietnamese government to conclude the "Joint Initiative"? Did this approach really represent business as usual for its aid program?

9.4.4 *The Reality Behind the Shadow Players: The End of Disunity?*

Japanese firms started entering the Vietnamese market when their government resumed aid in 1992. As a result, during 1992–1997, there was a rush of Japanese foreign direct investment (FDI) into Vietnam. However, in the absence of any notably improved commercial climate after the 1997 Asian economic crisis, not only Japan's but also the world's registered investment in Vietnam showed a downward trend (see Table 9.3). This slowdown contrasted sharply with the increasing flow of FDI into other ASEAN countries.

The reason for Vietnam's poor business climate lay in its economic policy. In particular, a noted lack of predictability had been the mainstay of an overall unsatisfactory environment. Vietnam accordingly paid the price of this government failure in terms of disappointing levels of economic development which consistently fell below its capabilities (Ohno and Niiya, 2005). The specific problems plaguing Vietnam were as follows:

- an inconsistent and insufficient legal system,
- an inconsistent interpretation of the law,
- an inappropriate empowerment of low level governmental officials resulting in a wide range of government corruption (Ohno, 2004).

Table 9.3   Amount of Registered and Implemented FDI Toward Vietnam between 1996 and 2001.

Year	Registered FDI (mil $)	Implemented FDI (mil $)
1996	9212	2371
1997	5548	2950
1998	4827	1900
1999	2156	2150
2000	2460	2150
2001	2384	2300

Source: Doanh LD. (2002) FDI in Vietnam: Results, Achievements, Challenges, and Prospects. Paper presented at the IMF conference on FDI, Ho Chi Minh City 2002. In: *Vietnam: Results, Achievements, Challenges, and Prospects.*

These obstacles remained the primary reasons that Vietnam had failed to attract large amounts of FDI from either Japan or other developed countries.

Vietnam's poor economic environment was characterized by a lack of appropriate laws, poor policy mechanisms, and inadequate structural systems. These not only nullified Vietnam's attractiveness as a destination for FDI, but also presented Japanese firms with insurmountable investment problems. Many Japanese firms, thinking of potentially expanding their Vietnamese business, repeatedly urged the Japanese embassy in Vietnam to exercise its undoubted influence on the Vietnamese to facilitate the entry process (Hatakeyama, interview with Director of JETRO, February 2006). Fully understanding the nature of Vietnam's poor business environment, Ambassador Norio Hattori tried to engineer an improvement by employing Japan's aid as a "carrot." Soon after the successful expansion of the CPRGS (including an economic infrastructure development strategy), he proposed a "Joint Initiative" at the Consultative Group meeting in December 2002. The intended aim was to persuade the Vietnamese government to improve its business environment so that it could attract more direct investment.

The "Joint Initiative" reflected at least to a considerable degree the interests of the Japanese business sector that was involved in negotiating the agreement. It encompassed a range of concerns and included

44 different action plans. Among these were:

- the development of economic infrastructure,
- tax incentives for FDI companies,
- a well-defined land law,
- a more efficient tax system,
- corruption eradication,
- an improvement of aid implementation judgments,
- a more fully developed legal system,
- public administration reform.[38]

Although some were specifically tailored to the requirements of Japanese business interests, most were universally desirable and would benefit all foreign companies, not only the Japanese. However, Vietnam proved reluctant to accept these proposals. The Ministry of Foreign Affairs responded by applying pressure on the Vietnamese government to agree. In a pointed message, The Ministry of Foreign Affairs indicated that the position adopted by the Vietnamese government would influence future flows of Japanese aid.[39] By utilizing these strong arm techniques, Japan persuaded Vietnam to conclude the "Joint Initiative." However, since this initiative clearly reflected the needs of Japanese business, the policy left an ineradicable impression that the proposal's intention was solely to advance Japanese economic interests.[40]

The Ministry of Finance worried about the possible damage to its reputation created by this "Joint Initiative." By attempting to seize a leadership role, the MOF was now determinately trying to expand its influence. This objective ran counter to a simple expansion of Japanese business interests. In addition to the "Joint Initiative," MOFA's more straightforward and simple strategy of independently supporting the 44 different action plans detailed in the initiative by pledging the "carrot"

---

[38]For details, see Ministry of Foreign Affairs (2003e).
[39]These views were garnered from interviews with JBIC and JICA officials in January 2006 as well as an interview with the Director-General of JETRO in March 2006. (He was a member of the Joint Committee of the Joint Initiative.) See also Kitano and Yoshizawa (2003).
[40]Consideration toward its future admission to the WTO provided a strong inducement for the Vietnamese government. See Kitano and Shimamura (2003) and Yoshizawa (2005).

of future Japanese funds, further worried the Ministry of Finance. From Finance's point of view, such a strategy was likely only to damage Japan's international image. The Japanese would seem once again to be self-absorbed by a concerted attempt to transform Vietnam's business environment into one that was favorable to Japanese investment requirements (Hatakeyama, interview with Naoko Ishii, May 2006).[41] In fact, the requirements posed by the agreements were universally beneficial. However, Japan's independent underwriting of the "Joint Initiative" would have nullified much of the efforts made by both Finance and the Foreign Affairs to create a credible position of influence within the international aid community. The Ministry of Finance insisted that the proposal lacked the support of PRSC3 as well as the World Bank and the IMF (Hatakeyama, interview with Naoko Ishii, May 2006). Finance unequivocally rejected the view that Japan's national interests should be defined solely in terms of a proposal's business potential (Hatakeyama, interview with Naoko Ishii, May 2006). However, the Foreign Affairs had a slightly different standpoint.

MOFA insisted that Japan's national interests could be defined quite broadly to include the permeation of Japanese business into the economies of recipient countries. As shown in Chapter 3, MITI strongly pushed for regional economic integration by encouraging Japanese firms to go overseas, especially in the 1980s. Concurrently, Foreign Affairs implemented a strategic aid policy that was meant to be consistent with the elastic terms of "comprehensive security." However, as MITI's influence declined, this corporate role had come increasingly under MOFA's wing. Since Japan's aid had been criticized as being "faceless," Foreign Affairs was keen to correct this image by employing Japan's business sector to help advance its aims. The direct participation of Japanese firms, in terms of engineers and managers working on projects sites, was meant to impress the locals with Japan's active involvement in development assistance. By these tactics, Japan's aid hoped to gain greater visibility. This strategy is what MOFA came to label as "aid with a face." To achieve this goal, the Ministry felt

---

[41] Naoko Ishii was at that time the Director of the Office of Development Finance International Bureau, Ministry of Finance.

obliged, quite independently, to support the action defined by the plans of the proposed "Joint Initiative". Aid programs would be accordingly designed to sustain these objectives. In contrast, co-financing alongside the World Bank and other donors would force the Japanese to share credit at these project sites (Hatakeyama, interview with Naoko Ishii, May 2006). Japanese contributions would become lost among a laundry list of multiple donors. MOFA assumed that acceding to this type of policy would once again reduce the Japanese to its familiar "faceless" status. Any chance to plant the national flag and claim full credit would vanish under these imposed adverse conditions (Hatakeyama, interview with Naoko Ishii, May 2006).

This variety of newly active involvement by the Foreign Ministry was emboldened by its approach to Vietnam. The Ministry also assisted Japanese firms to expand their business activities in other countries as well. This strategy became official in 2005 when MOFA launched a more widespread campaign to pursue this objective ("Kanmin de Nihon Urikomi," *Tokyo Shimbum*, March 6, 2008). For example, the Japanese embassy in Egypt financed and supported a party at the ambassador's official residence. The sole purpose of this gathering was to nurture a more favorable environment for Japanese firms. Ambassador to Egypt, Ishikawa, stated, "We have to sell Japan by means of an 'all-Japan'. This approach will eventually lead to increasing Japan's weight in Egypt" ("Kanmin de Nihon Urikomi," *Tokyo Shimbum*, March 6, 2008).

In a very narrow sense, the two ministries adopted a different approach due to different ideas on how employing aid could serve as an instrument to advance national interest. The Ministry of Foreign Affairs increasingly had become more concerned with purely economic interests. The Ministry of Finance, in contrast, has been more focused on expanding Japan's influence. Despite these minor differences, the two ministries continued to share a common desire to see Japan occupy a respectable position within the aid fraternity. Moreover, cooperative relationships nurtured by the ODA task force enabled them to compromise for the sake of achieving their ultimate goals. To accommodate these two different positions, the two ministries settled on supporting one-third of the requests proposed in the "Joint Initiative" by co-financing them with the World Bank, the IMF, and other

donors (Hatakeyama, interview with Naoko Ishii, May 2006). MOFA
independently supported the remainder (two-thirds). Undeniably, it
was always going to be difficult to entirely eliminate economic considerations when determining policy positions. Nevertheless, the distinctly changed perception that the first priority should always be one
consistent with Japan's national interests, rather than any more narrow
economic concerns, has worked effectively. The last few decades has
seen the growth of a Japanese presence compatible with the role of an
"intellectual leader."

9.5 Conclusion: The Secret of Japan's Success

Japan's newly created Initiative for Development in East Asia, combined with its enthusiastic involvement in Vietnam, clearly demonstrated its vigorous attempts to establish its influence bilaterally as well
as multilaterally. The criticism that Japan's aid was "faceless," limited
solely to narrow commercial aspects, was not only widely prevalent,
but a major contributor to Japan's poor image. On examination, this
criticism does not hold true today and was never entirely a complete or
accurate characterization. As stated, Japan has been attempting to take
a lead in the international aid debate by articulating its own views and
proposing new approaches. The Japanese have persistently attempted
to obtain international acknowledgment for its economic development
model. It took its marketing campaign one important step further, by
persuading the World Bank and other donors to support its position
concerning those aid policies which might best facilitate Vietnam's economic development. In short, Japan was successful in portraying itself
as an "intellectual leader" by utilizing a variety of channels.

This strategic shift was possible due to declining sectionalism among
Japan's ministerial actors. However, the implications of the "Joint Initiative" presented a slightly different image from that of "Japan as
an intellectual leader." MOFA's attempt to piggyback Japan's business interests created a mixed image. From the standpoint of Foreign
Affairs, the Japanese could strive to be "intellectual leader but they
could also pursue economic interests as well." The handling of this
landmark "Joint Initiative" not only demonstrated once again a series

of slight, but significant, differences in ministerial approaches, but also the difficulty governments have in completely separating entangled economic interests from diplomatic objectives. The desire to consolidate its regional leadership was, given a growing interdependence and the importance of those expanding regional economies, intricately linked with its need for economic security.

References

Arase D. (1995) *Buying Power: The Political Economy of Japan's Foreign Aid*. Lynne Rienner, Boulder.

Ensign MM. (1992) *Doing Good or Doing Well: Japan's Foreign Aid Program*. Columbia University Press, New York.

Guang Z. (1998) Japan's aid policy since the Cold War: Rhetoric and reality. *Asian Survey*, 38(11), 1051–1066.

Hirata K. (1998) New challenges in Japan's aid: An analysis of aid policy-making. *Pacific Affairs*, 71(3), 311–334.

Inada J. (1993) Stick or carrot? Japanese aid policy and Vietnam. In: Koppel BM, Orr Jr RM (eds.), *Japan's Foreign Aid: Power and Policy in a New Era*, pp. 111–134. Westview Press, Boulder.

Iokibe M. (2002) Interview series 3 — Hashimoto Ryutaro. *Kokusai Mondai*, 504(March), 62–79.

Ishii N. (2003) *Chouki Keizai Hatten no Jisshou Bunseki*, Nihon Keizai Shimbumsha, Tokyo.

Kitano M. (2003) Tai Viet Nam Keizai Kyoryoku no Shinjidai. *Kokusai Kaihatsu Journal*, June, 49–51.

Kitano M and Ishii N. (2003) Nihon no Koe wo PRSP e. *Kokusai Kaihatsu Journal*, March 37–39.

Kitano M, Ishii N, Karasawa M. (2004) Nihon no Koe wo PRSC e. *Kokusai Kaihatsu Journal*, August, 86–88.

Kitano M, Yoshizawa T. (2003) Viet Nam: Country Report No. 3 Toushi Kankyo Seibi e ODA wo Katsuyou: Nichietsu Kyodo Initiative. *Journal of International Development*, April: 42–44.

Korhonen P. (1994) The theory of the flying geese pattern of development and its interpretations. *Journal of Peace Research*, 31(1), 93–108.

Krueger AB, Maleckoba J. (2003) Education, poverty, political violence and terrorism: Is there a casual connection. *Journal of Economic Perspectives*, 17(4), 119–144.

Lincoln EJ. (1993). *Japan's New Global Role*. Brookings Institution, Washington, DC.

Looney R. (2004) Failed economic take-offs and terrorism in Pakistan: Conceptualizing a proper role for US assistance. *Asian Survey*, 44(6), 771–793.

Mekong W. (2003) Mekong River Development News, http://www.mekongwatch.org/resource/news/20031221_01.html, accessed in August 2005.

Ministry of Foreign Affairs. (2005) ODA Budget, http://www.mofa.go.jp/mofaj/gaiko/oda/kouhou/plaza/kp2005_2/chapter03.html, accessed in July 2005.

Ministry of Foreign Affairs. (1998) ODA: Its significance and recent trends. http://www.mofa.go.jp/policy/oda/summary/1998/1.html, accessed in July 2005.

Ministry of Foreign Affairs. (1999) Chapter 2. *Japan's ODA Annual report 1999.* http://www.mofa.go.jp.policy/oda/summary/1999/ov1_2.html, accessed in August 2005.

Ministry of Foreign Affairs. (2002a) Japan and ASEAN in East Asia — A sincere and open partnership. *Speech by Prime Minister of Japan, Junichiro Koizumi.* January 14, Singapore. http://www.mofa.go.jp/region/asia-paci/pmv0201/speech.html, accessed in March 2006.

Ministry of Foreign Affairs. (2002b) The joint ministerial statement of the initiative for development in East Asia. *Position Paper.* August 12, Tokyo, http://www.mofa.go.jp/region/asia-paci/idea0208-2.html, accessed in March 2006.

Ministry of Foreign Affairs. (2002c) Initiative for IDEA ministerial meeting. *Position Paper.* August 12, Tokyo, http://www.mofa.go.jp/region/asia-paci/idea0208-4.html, accessed in October 2005.

Ministry of Foreign Affairs. (2002d) The millennium development goals and issues in the international community. Keynote address (October) by Furuta, Director General of Economic Cooperation Bureau, MOFA, http://www.mofa.go.jp/policy/un/address/0210.html, accessed in October 2005.

Ministry of Foreign Affairs. (2002e) Opening remarks by Foreign Minister Yoriko Kawaguchi, Minister for Foreign Affairs of Japan. *The WSSD side event on the Initiative for Development in East Asia Ministerial Meeting,* September 1, http://www.mofa.go.jp/policy.environment/wssd/2002/event1_2.html, accessed in October 2005.

Ministry of Foreign Affairs. (2003a) Sekaino Ugoki, *Sakaino ugoki,* no. 666 (March).

Ministry of Foreign Affairs. (2003b) International assistance trends with respect to development issues. *ODA White Paper.* Part 2 (Chapter 2): Section 2. http://www.mofa.go.jp/policy/oda/white/2003/part2_2_2.html#Vietnam_rpsp, accessed in June 2005.

Ministry of Foreign Affairs. (2003c) International assistance trends with respect to development issues. *ODA White Paper.* Part 2 (Chapter 2): Section 2. http://www.mofa.go.jp/policy/oda/white/2003/part2_2_2.html#Vietnam_rpsp, accessed in December 2005.

Ministry of Foreign Affairs. (2003d) ODA White Paper. http://www.mofa.go.jp/policy/oda/white/2003, accessed in July 2005.

Ministry of Foreign Affairs. (2003e) Vietnam–Japan joint initiative to improve business environment with a view to strengthen Vietnam's competitiveness. *MOFA Report,* December 4, 1–118, http://www.mofa.go.jp/region/asia-paci/Vietnam/report0312.pdf, accessed in July 2005.

Ministry of Foreign Affairs. (2004a) Country assistance program for Vietnam. April, http://www.mofa.go.jp/policy/oda/region/e-asia/Vietnam.pdf, accessed in November 2005.

Ministry of Foreign Affairs. (2004b) Vietnam, http://www.mofa.go.jp/mofaj/gaiko/oda/shiryo/jisski/kuni/04_databook, accessed in October 2005.

Ministry of Foreign Affairs. (2004c) Vietnam: CG meeting pledge summary, Dec 1–2, obtained privately.

Ministry of Foreign Affairs — Vietnam. (2005) Investment Minister: Vietnam, a profitable investment destination. http://www.mofa.gov.vn/en/nr040807104143/nr040807105039/ns060103101714, accessed in July 2005.

Morrison K. (2005) The World Bank, Japan, and aid effectiveness. In: Arase D (ed.), *Japan's Foreign Aid: Old Continuities and New Directions*, pp. 23–40. Routledge, New York.

Nakao T. (2005) Wagakuni no ODA to Kokusaitekina Enjochoryu — Tokyni Kokusai Kinyu no Shiten kara. *Finance*, 472: 18–19.

National Graduate Institute of Policy Studies. (2004) Japan's new country assistance program for Vietnam finalized. *Japan News — Japanese Assistance to Vietnam*. Vol. III, June 14. http://www.grips.ac.jp/forum/pdf04/JapanNews3/JNIII.pdf, accessed in May 2005.

Ohno K. (1996) *Shijou Ikou Senryaku*, Chapter 7. Yuikaku, Tokyo.

Ohno I. (2002) *Diversifying PRSP — the Vietnamese Model for Growth Oriented Poverty Reduction*. August, http://www.grips.ac.jp/forum-e/pdf_e01/PN2.pdf#search='Diversifying PRSPtheVietnameseModelforGrowthORientedPovertyReduction', accessed in October 2005.

Ohno I. (2004) *Fostering True Ownership in Vietnam: From Donor Management to Policy Autonomy and Content*, GRIPS, November, 1–20. http://www.grips.ac.jp/forum-e/pdf_e01/VNownership.pdf, accessed in May 2006.

Ohno I, Niiya Y. (2004) *Vietnam Shuccho Hokoku*. Graduate Research Institute of Policy Studies, Tokyo.

Ohno I, Ohno K. (2005) Fostering true ownership in Vietnam: From donor management to policy autonomy and content. In: Ohno I (ed.), *True Ownership and Policy Autonomy: Managing Donors and Owning Policies*, GRIPS, Tokyo.

Okuma H. (2003) Kaihatsukara Heiwa He. *International Affairs*, 517, 21–39.

Pempel TJ. (1997) Transpacific Torii. In: Katzenstein P, Shiraishi T (eds.), *Network Power: Japan and Asia*, pp. 47–82. Cornell University Press, Ithaca.

Shimamura M. (2005) Betonamu ni Okeru Nihon no Seido, Seisaku Heno Noudoukanyo. *GRIPS Development Forum Discussion Paper*, No. 11 (April).

Sudo S. (2002) *The International Relations of Japan and Southeast Asia*, Routledge, London.

Takagi S, Kawai M. (2004) Japan's official development assistance: Recent issues and future directions. *Journal of International Development*, 16(2), 255–280.

Chapter 10

The Consequences of Japanese Diplomacy

10.1 The Mysterious East: Making Sense of Japan's Foreign Policy

The preceding chapters have examined Japan's approach to foreign policy during the post-war era. Our focus has been on the way in which Japan has applied its power resources to achieve designated results in the Asia-Pacific region. We have tried to employ the most salient available evidence in formulating a rationale behind a series of Japanese diplomatic initiatives. The only hypothesis that appears to provide a comprehensive and consistent explanation, of these often contradictory efforts, is that Japan has been doggedly pursuing a position as a regional power, namely that the Japanese have sought to influence the decisions and actions of their surrounding countries.

Allowing for differences in the nature of power between the pre-war and the post-war period, Japan's ambition to obtain political power, in a broader sense, has been continuously driving Japanese foreign policy, at least from behind the scenes, since the Meiji restoration of 1868. Bad choices characterized its attempt to gain hegemonic power through military means. The result was a devastating defeat in World War II. Obviously, the Japanese at this low point needed to reconsider, though not necessarily renounce, its deepest aspirations. With the end of the long American Occupation, Japan once again embarked on a transformed journey to capture quite a similar objective. This time, however, Japan would employ different means from those disastrous methods adopted in the pre-war period. No other realistic alternatives existed than to eschew military force as a means of advancing its goals. This unprecedented strategic approach in the post-war era attracted a considerable degree of scholarly attention. The growing conundrum faced by competing analysts was that Japan's diplomatic behavior seemed to be poorly explained by the prevailing theories of international relations.

Japan's behavior did appear to be exceptional. It was often dismissed as being a simple pursuit of economic interests. However, once we focus instead on the various constraints, including once-off affects, often operating behind the scenes of the decision-making process, Japan's behavior becomes much more comprehensible. As we have seen, due to mitigating international and domestic factors, the behavior of successive Japanese governments often has been bounded quite narrowly. The observed results of these conflicting forces usually have produced foreign policy that is so low profile as to appear invisible. This characterization seems directly at odds with the strong suggestion that Japan has been pursuing regional influence through power politics. But failure to achieve a set of given goals does not imply that Japan ever turned away from pursuing a dominant position in Asia. Both the overview and the detailed case studies from the 1990s demonstrate that, like other states, Japan has been seeking a leadership role, which would allow it to create a climate conducive to its economic and national security ambitions.

Thus, there is a surprising link with the Japan created by the Meiji restoration. During the pre-war period, Japan devoted all its resources and energy to joining the exclusive club composed of rich and powerful Western nations. The Japanese encapsulated their ambitions by proclaiming their intention to "enrich the nation, strengthen the military." Likewise, in the post-war period, Japan devoted all its efforts to recovering from the disaster that was World War II. Rehabilitating the economy was a necessary step in creating a future for Japan, but the key objective motivating subsequent Japanese foreign policy was the desire to regain the central position in Asia that it had so carelessly frittered away. As a consequence, Japan's aspirations were temporarily transformed into an economics-first policy. This represented a triumph of realism over more fanciful aspirations.

Economic difficulties clearly had to be resolved before Japan could think about pursuing political power. For this reason, Japan's early foreign policy seems largely determined by its need for economic growth. Pragmatically though, these ant-like endeavors had to precede any grander ambitions. By achieving a level of economic security in the 1960s and stabilizing a turbulent population, Japan could further its more political aspirations by making some tentative use of foreign aid during those early post-war years. Japan's political establishment could see no other viable option then to pursue leverage via economic muscle, given the prevailing international environment. Japan's growing economic power did allow the Japanese to move away from a purely subservient position by becoming America's acknowledged junior partner in the Far East. In a convenient division of labor, the US would continue to look after security matters while Japan would contribute economically by underwriting aid and assistance to US allies.

Japan also saw the creation of regional institutions as a parallel route to its desired objectives. This path, however, provided many more obstacles. Japan had to skate a badly defined boundary between directing the progress of its proposals and hiding its actual ambitions. In a region characterized by acute sensitivities and bruised egos, Japan had to tread carefully to avoid stirring up old fears and current apprehensions among its watchful neighbors. The 1977 Fukuda Doctrine marked the culmination of this first wave of attempts to pursue a regional political role. Unfortunately, many of these initiatives were effectively thwarted by the international environment prevailing at that time.

Bolstered by its growing economy, Japan in the 1980s extended the reach of its foreign assistance strategy. No longer would the main or sole thrust be limited to facilitating its own exports. This broader role covered a variety of purposes, including national defense and other security issues, though constrained by the boundaries set by US Cold War Policy. Enhancing economic resources was not in fact a simple objective but rather only a "means to ensure its security needs and to exercise its influence" during the Cold War period (Pyle, 2006, p. 17). In the meantime,

Japan was gaining some success in establishing its position as a regional economic leader by pursuing a strategy of providing widespread aid, trade, and investment.

In the 1990s, Japan incrementally expanded the scope of its action including some restricted use of its military resources. Though employment was limited to operating under either the UN aegis or the US alliance, the underlying purpose was still much the same. The deployment of its Self-Defense Forces (SDF) was intended to further Japan's leadership aspirations. At this stage, having largely overcome a deeply entrenched national pacifism, the Japanese public was now more willing to accept a new law redefining the role played by the SDF. Under these guidelines, the Self-Defense Forces could participate in peace-keeping operations as long as they remained under the auspices of the UN. As a result, Japan dispatched troops, first to Cambodia and then to East Timor. Digging beneath the public pronouncements, the Japanese hoped these efforts would succeed in increasing its regional prestige and position. To casual observers, these first military forays would appear to indicate a change in objectives, a clear break from previous policy goals. However, such apparent diplomatic transformations were more a reflection of the end of the Cold War than a rejection of the past. A dramatic environmental upheaval on this scale would almost automatically induce a noticeable shift in tactics as previous constraints were either loosened or simply vanished. Japan's expanded scope for military action in the 1990s thus runs counter to those models that reduce foreign policy concerns to a simple matter of economics. Only by combining evolving economic requirements with aspirations for influence and recognition can we arrive at a complete explanation.

These new tactics are visible in Japan's response to the North Korean threat. The Japanese were at pains to both secure their national security while enhancing their regional position. These dual demands created a tight-wire policy path that required exceptional balance. Had Japan not nurtured wider regional ambitions, achieving a successful outcome would not have presented so many daunting problems, nor would the actual approach taken by the Japanese appear to be so muddled. Japan did try to use economic incentives as a lever with which to manipulate the North Koreans. They hoped that the Kim regime could be bought

off on Japanese terms. Doing so would help to create a regional security framework more conducive to Japanese aspirations and gain Japan
some welcome recognition by producing an increased level of peace and
stability. The apparent failure of Japanese diplomacy in this case seems
to a casual observer to reflect a distinct and even inherent ineptness
on the part of the Japanese. However, a more informative approach
would need to examine the operative external and internal constraints
that Japan failed to negotiate successfully.

As noted, Japan played its traditional tool of promised assistance,
but the North Koreans found it either insufficient or unsatisfactory for
some other, unspecified reason. In fact, it appeared that they wanted
more than simple assistance, namely, they nursed demands that could
only be met by the US. Perhaps, more importantly for the Japanese
government, its broader goals became entirely sidetracked by domestic politics and pressure. The abduction issue, involving the deliberate
kidnappings of Japanese citizens, acted like a virtual tsunami sweeping all else before it. Whether the inroads Japan made during earlier
negotiations and the role it carved out for itself in dealing with North
Korea has any lasting significance is yet to be determined. Nevertheless,
we can note that economic measures were not always meant to simply
facilitate economic activity, but rather as a tool to advance diplomatic
goals. Failures are highlighted by the constraints in play rather than
any break in Japanese policy, or any ineptness specifically characterizing
Japanese negotiators.

Even policy initiatives with a seemingly straightforward economic
twist reveal greater levels of complexity when examined in terms of
fundamental Japanese ambitions. For instance, Japan's diplomacy at
the time of the 1997 Asian crisis was not simply intent on rescuing
its own floundering economy. Japan deliberately resisted the rather
draconian IMF's prescriptions aimed at transforming Asian economic
structures into American look-alikes. As a self-appointed Asian leader,
Japan provocatively challenged Western orthodoxy by proposing an
alternative Asian institution headed, of course, by the Japanese. These
ambitions, as could be anticipated, were thwarted by the fierce opposition of the US, quick to see the implications of such an initiative. Japanese objectives were not completely deterred, however. Still

intent on creating a key regional role for itself financially, Japan simply switched its tactics from a multilateral to a bilateral focus. Certainly, any regional economic stability would provide Japan's economy with a needed assist. But upon examination, it is clear that there was more at stake here than simply trade or investment issues.

This broader perspective rears its head once more in Japan's enthusiastic involvement in Vietnam's economic development program. Again, the stakes in terms of trade and investment were not overly large. Instead, Japan seemed to see Vietnam more as an opportunity to push itself forward as an active policy maker and leading intellectual light. The Japanese attempted to preempt US dominated institutions by pushing its own approach based on an alternative economic model of development. In essence, Japan was making a rather bold attempt to change what had been an international consensus on aid and its consequences. Certainly it would be foolish to divorce Japan's own business interests from such an initiative, but it is wiser also to see the broader picture of Japan's ambitions and aspirations within the region. Japan clearly wanted to lay siege to and conquer the intellectual high ground in this instance, to remake Asia, at least to some extent, in its own image. Given the changed circumstances at that time, Japan was actually able to make some discernable headway in overturning the prevailing Western consensus. Clearly, what all these case studies have demonstrated is that any analysis focused purely on economic objectives will be needlessly handicapping itself. Instead, each instance of diplomatic activity becomes more understandable if we accord the Japanese a credible, unchanging objective and then examine what relevant constraints were in play, ultimately limiting and shaping both policies and outcomes.

10.2 Constraints Versus Japan's Search for Political Power

In the past, analysts have found that Japanese foreign policy presents a rather difficult puzzle. One way to dismiss these complexities is too simply focus on the very visible economic aspect to Japan's post-war initiatives. As we have seen, such responses have been to varying degrees unsatisfactory. However, simply positing a consistent policy objective fails to explain why Japan seems incapable of transforming what has been described as its power assets into the political power that it supposedly seeks. Japan's diplomatic history seems more of a series of blunders than an attempt to achieve a definable goal. Fortunately, this initial confusion can be effectively cleared up if we put these policy efforts in their proper context. Post-war Japan has been very tightly constrained by both external and internal factors. If we then concentrate on these particular aspects and understand their role in shaping Japan's actions, this conundrum posed by its international relations begins to fade.

10.2.1 *Structural Constraints*

As pointed out throughout this volume, two superpowers shaped the Cold War environment. Other nations were forced to find their footing within this dominant architecture. A weak and flattened Japan could discern no wisdom in attempting to compete militarily or even carving out some low-level activity for itself. Instead, Japan settled comfortably under the nuclear umbrella provided by its former American occupiers. This essentially removed security considerations from Japan's diplomatic agenda. Japan retained a self-defense force while foreswearing the use of military intervention. This essentially sidetracked Japan from exerting any serious influence for a number of decades. Thus Japan's attempts to thrust itself into the limelight of recognition and influence as an independent mediator were bound to come up a cropper. Vietnam unremarkably rejected such Japanese offers in the late 1970s. Influence without military backup was not yet a viable alternative.

However, the 1990s represented a potential structural breakthrough with the Cold War finally coming to an end. The 1989 *Diplomatic Bluebook*, written at the peak of Japan's economic influence, looked forward to a more salubrious environment. "Now is the time for Japan to act in the international community in full awareness that we can no longer accept the international climate as an external given and that Japan is an important determinant influencing international developments" (Ministry of Foreign Affairs, 1989, p. 13). Japan anticipated, or at least hoped for, the emergence of a more peaceful world in which it could operate more independently or at least less constrained. To its great disappointment, Japan found that the demise of the Cold War had merely changed, rather than vanquished, its external constraints. Northeast Asia was still a sphere where military threats played a substantial, if not always dominant, role. Bereft of any offensive punch, Japan's attempts to create a new regional order were bound to be unsuccessful.

Moreover, while the US has furnished all of Japan's post-war defensive needs, this security blanket has come with an attached cost. The price has been the severe limitations America has sometimes placed on any individual Japanese action. For example, during the Asian economic crisis, the US successfully stymied Japanese efforts to establish a regional monetary institution. America considered this attempt at maverick diplomacy to clash with clearly defined US interests. Whether this Japanese-envisioned organization would have benefited regional economies and provided Japan with its desired recognition is naturally unknown. What is more significant is the way in which the US could, and did, close down this particular initiative. As long as the alliance between the countries remains badly asymmetrical, with America continuing to fill Japan's security needs, the US will remain a key consideration in any foreign policy calculation.

10.2.2 *Domestic Constraints*

As previously examined, pacifism has been a ruling characteristic of the domestic landscape throughout the decades following World War II. This aspect virtually ruled out any deployment or strategic use of Japan's military capacity. Any show of overt regional ambition would have precipitated sharp popular reaction. Thus, Japan's deliberate low-key profile diplomatically was largely imposed by domestic considerations, as well as the international structure previously discussed. It was not so much a lack of interest in grasping regional influence that determined Japan's stance, but the limitations within which it had to operate. With anti-militarism becoming less of a decisive factor following the first Gulf War, Japan's diplomacy and range became both broader and more active. For the first time, a role for the self-defense force abroad could be calmly and publicly evaluated. As well, some decline in regional apprehension (though not particularly noticeable in China or Korea) also allowed more scope for a military option. As one would expect, the simultaneous relaxing of these two previously binding constraints is reflected in the contour changes of Japan's foreign policy. The discussions and debates taking place in the run up to the August 30, 2009, election would be inconceivable some three decades ago.

Other attempts to project a more visible face in international relations have been hindered by the basic governmental structure underpinning the decision-making process. The dominant role played by the bureaucracy in initiating, executing, and operating policies enables key ministries to implicitly veto any proposal and certainly to undercut it. What has been denominated as bureaucratic sectionalism, or the basic incentive for administrative staff to protect their turf, makes it difficult to enact anything resembling a bold departure. In which case, the economy could flourish since ministerial incentives were basically aligned, while attempts to exercise even limited regional power could easily become derailed and lost as a victim of bureaucratic struggles. The difference in results is clear once the incentives motivating ministerial actions are in alignment. As previously pointed out, coordinated efforts between the Ministries of Foreign Affairs and Finance facilitated Japan's success in shaping Vietnam's development program. By being able to formulate a unified policy, Japan was able to establish its presence as an economic and intellectual leader.

10.2.3 *Casual Constraints*

While some binding constraints have had a constant presence in postwar Japan, others are more time and place specific. This simply reflects the way in which the relevant environment changes over time. Some factors transform at a glacial rate, while others resemble clashes of the tectonic plates of international relations, which both quickly explode and rapidly fade away. These converge to hinder or determine a given policy and seldom return as a consequential limitation. The previous discussion analyzing Japanese reluctance to contribute peacekeeping forces in East Timor demonstrates a combination of traditional limitations, such as the prevailing American posture, with more country-specific factors. In a parallel manner, Japan's North Korean venture came to grief due to domestic politics successfully stirring up public opinion. This episode demonstrated how momentary constraints, even those lacking any substantial long-run gravitas, can overwhelm all other considerations in diplomatic exchanges. Japan's path toward regional political power has been strewn with such stumbling blocks.

10.2.4 *Prospect of Future Constraints*

In the post-Cold War era, the emergence of "non-state actors" and new, largely unforeseen dangers such as terrorism, weapons proliferation, pirates, and climate change has caused a considerable redirection of focus toward containing these "new threats." In contrast to the fixed blocs that defined the Cold War period, these new international problems demand cooperation more than outright coercion to address such issues effectively. Military build-ups are still an essential feature of today's landscape, and the use of force has hardly been eschewed. But at least some of the basic threats confronting Japan do not require anything like overwhelming military power. To some degree, the Japanese approach has come into its own in the current global environment. Incremental steps and targeted contributions can yield positive results. Japan, for instance, is now able to employ its SDF and Maritime Coast Guard to protect ships, including foreign ones, against pirate depredation in the Aden Gulf. This is a small, but significant, intervention reflecting a broadening of its foreign operations and an increased ability to display leadership and international responsibility.

The increased independence of such actions is closely correlated with the easing of US dominance and the general failure of its attempts at unilateral measures. While still tethered to American policy, Japan has been more able to push its own agenda forward than ever before. Domestic pacifism, which had ruled out a number of military-tinged options for decades, seems to be gradually fading. With a general consensus among the major political parties, foreign policy is much less confrontational than in previous decades. This has added a level of increased flexibility to Japan's policy alternatives. However, new constraints have now come to the forefront, containing within them the ability to thwart Japanese ambitions in novel and untested areas. Domestically, the Japanese face weak political leadership and a less-than-robust economy. Internationally, future relations with China remain a question mark. Japan has become increasingly dependent on its economic relation with the Chinese. Yet, the Japanese often see themselves as simultaneous competitors. Japan then does not face an open road leading to the realization of its ambitions. There are new, yet equally serious limitations within which Japan is forced to now operate. Considering the enormous uncertainties shaping the future, the possibility that the Japanese will largely be blocked from realizing their continuing aspirations remains high.

10.3 Overcoming Confusion: Tentative Conclusions

- Japan appeared to change its fundamental objectives or direction in the 1990s. In fact, the Japanese only adjusted their tactics to the reality of their transformed environment.
- Japan's pursuit of power was sometimes interrupted by time- and place-specific factors. This need to bend to passing necessities often made Japanese policy appear to be indecisive and lacking any clearly defined goals.
- Since World War II, the US has been the dominant factor constraining Japanese foreign policy. For that reason, Japanese foreign policy was most effective when Japanese objectives aligned with those of the US. Alternatively, Japanese initiatives were badly thwarted when they ran counter to American intentions.
- The bureaucratic structure defining post-war Japan has often been divisive. These internal turf wars have undermined decisive policy initiatives, leaving the Japanese to appear bereft of anything other than narrowly defined economic interests.
- Japan has attempted quite actively to structure the economic architecture in which it must act, not only for purely economic gains, but extending to matters of security as well. These efforts have reflected a basic Japanese pursuit of regional influence and recognition.

10.4 Final Thoughts: The Meaning of Japanese Power

The diplomatic history of Japan's post-war years has been one defined by a pursuit of power. This objective has underlined Japanese policy since the time of the Meiji restoration. Of course, the cataclysm of World War II forced the Japanese to change their core strategy. However, the nature of the constraints they faced has forced the Japanese to employ different tactics to suit specific occasions. These necessities have often made Japan's diplomacy appear aimless, or motivated purely by its commercial interests. As a result, the Japanese, starting in the 1990s, seemed to have inexplicably switched to more heavily political, and from strictly economic, objectives. These preceding chapters have tried to indicate that Japan, in fact, has conducted a much more rational and consistent foreign policy than superficially would seem to be the case.

> So oft in theologic wars,
> The disputants, I ween,
> Rail on in utter ignorance
> Of what each other mean,
> *And prate about an Elephant*
> *Not one of them has seen!* (Saxe, 1973, p. 78)

References

Ministry of Foreign Affairs. (1989) *Diplomatic Bluebook 1989*. Okurasho Insatsukyoku, Tokyo.

Pyle KB. (2006) Abe Shinzo and Japan's change of course. *NBR Analysis*, 17.

Saxe JG. (1973) The Blind Men and the Elephant. In: *The Poems of John Godfrey Saxe, Complete edition*, pp. 77–78. James R. Osgood and Company, Boston.

PART III

The Economic and Political Context of Japanese Foreign Policy

"As to poetry, you know," said Humpty Dumpty, stretching out one of his great hands, "I can repeat poetry as well as other folk if it comes to that —"

"Oh, it needn't come to that!" Alice hastily said, hoping to keep him from beginning (Lewis Carroll, *Through The Looking Glass*).

The most staggering event in post-war Japan's history has been its economic revival. From a country unable to provide basic goods and services to its own population, some 40 years later, its unstoppable momentum seemed destined to take Japan to the very apex of economic power. No matter that Japan's rise to a lasting place in the sun proved to be no more than a day's outing to a *kaiyushiki* garden. To understand this period, including its diplomatic history, requires some understanding of the economic context that loomed particularly large no matter what aspect of events we care to analyze. What follows is an attempt to provide the reader with something resembling a political economy background to this period. Trying to reduce such a complex subject to a limited number of pages may seem closely akin to the *Monty Python* sketch where game show competitors vied to compress the entirety of Marcel Proust's *Remembrance of Things Past* into a 60-second summary. Our hope is that we have been a bit more successful than those trapped in that comedy sketch.

Chapter 11

Tatemae and *Honne*: Understanding the Post-War Japanese Economy

11.1 Introduction: The Japanese Enigma

> Those who flourish are destined to fall into decline (Former President and Founder of Honda Motor Corporation, Sochiro Honda, quoted in Sakiya, 1982, p. 130).

The transformation of the Japanese economy from "miracle" into "catatonic" produced an unnecessary bumper crop of works retrospectively pointing out Japan's errors, especially in respect to the conclusive demonstration of the long-run dominance of market competition.[1] Revisionism is no doubt entertaining. Moreover, many of these works did contain within themselves elements of truth and insight. What they lacked, however, was a coherent framework, or at least one that could be seen as being specific to Japan rather than characteristic of an abstract, general economy. Of course, if one is willing to dismiss history and other institutional constraints, this poses no problem whatsoever. But such an idealized approach fails to provide a compelling argument that can explain the remarkable post-war Japanese success, its subsequent failure or its more recent recovery.

---

[1]Such work can provide the opportunity, if not the excuse, of pushing ideologically inspired policy changes. Just as the decade of slow or no growth suggested that Japan needed a large dose of more competitive markets and less intervention, the current economic crisis (2008) is characterized by a rising call for the re-regulation of financial markets in an international context.

Equally unreliable are explanations and discussions that rely heavily on the uniqueness of Japan's culture. Culture is an explanation that simultaneously manages to explain far too little and far too much. Any observation that deviates from some prescribed norm can be reduced (and thus dismissed) to some intrinsic characteristic that describes the people and the institutions of a specific country.[2] It has for that reason found little favor with economists who prefer theories and concepts that lead to potentially measurable variables. However, even the most skeptical of economists would give credence to the idea that the same incentives will not have the same effect on all people. Unless we assume that preferences are globally identical, in which case only the relative constraints are significant, it makes little sense to dismiss out of hand the possibility of distinguishable national differences.[3] It might be wise to keep in mind that culture may imply no more than the simple idea that groups of people share similar backgrounds and relate to a commonly held set of experiences.

A useful understanding of post-war Japan begins with the acknowledgment that there is a Japanese tendency toward risk averseness.[4] Such a trait must be linked to the ways in which the prevailing group of corporate, political, and administrative leaders devised a set of incentives that were consistent with achieving a broad range of economic objectives. Post-war Japan did not take a path pre-determined by their culture

---

[2] Every one prefers to be unique. This is perhaps one reason for the popularity of *Nihonjiron* among the Japanese. It enables the Japanese to set themselves apart by explaining any observation by reaching into a customized cultural sack and pulling out some convenient aspect of Japanese history and customs. Befu (2001) forms a useful starting point for those wishing to understand this approach. In contrast, Western interpreters of the mysterious East prefer to rely on cultural explanations since it bars all but the cognizant from commenting on Japanese issues. Both of these approaches insist on the separateness of Japan and the importance of difference in understanding the country.

[3] Of course some economists take just that approach. See the classic paper by Stigler and Becker (1977).

[4] Every broad statement almost automatically provides distinct exceptions. What is commonly known as the Japanese "bubble" period, a reaction to the Plaza Accord of 1985 and ending as all bubbles must in the collapse of 1991, shows the Japanese as seemingly flinging caution to the wind. Under the spell that the price of assets (real estate, shares and others) could only rise, the Japanese acted like school girls released from their convent for the first time. Money was spent wildly on the seeming basis of buy high, sell low with the Japanese scooping up foreign assets only to dump them in the subsequent downturn.

but one deliberately synchronized with certain leading elements of that culture. Part of the success of the "miracle" economy depended upon this congruence between cultural beliefs and economic practice. More recent failures in part reflect a subsequent lack of synchronicity with beliefs lagging behind changing practises.

Given this somewhat more complex approach, the most plausible way to explain Japan's distinctive attitudes and concerns is to look back carefully on that economy's developmental history. Again, such an approach will not unearth a clearly deterministic growth path but instead explain the potential characteristics which could be channeled to achieve, under the appropriate circumstances, a specific set of objectives.

In analysing core constraints, Japan's economic development, like that of all countries, has been influenced heavily by demographic and geographic limitations. Though Japan has a total land area of 377,864 sq.km., only 13.6 percent is cultivated. Approximately 70 percent of the land is covered by largely uninhabited mountains, grasslands, forests, or waterways. Most of the population of 127,450,000 is huddled together on approximately 4 percent of the available land mass. Half of that population is centered around Tokyo, Osaka, and Nagoya, living in a low-rise sprawl consisting of single- or double-storey dwellings. Until quite recently, the history of Japan has always been a case of too many people living on too little land, or in purely economic terms, a country chronically rich in labor resources but traditionally capital poor. Without any substantial natural resources of note to fall back on, the Japanese have over the centuries come to see themselves as a country lacking the luxury of being able to afford mistakes.[5] Japan in fact does not differ greatly from a number of European countries in lacking a generous natural endowment. However, Japan has come to view itself as a unique case whether justified or not.

From this perception has flown a widely accepted, if not always carefully articulated belief, that unless the Japanese remained highly self-sufficient and inordinately careful, all would be lost. Namely, they

---

[5] This is diametrically opposed to the underlying optimism characterizing the United States where the idea of second chances and comebacks form the dominant mythology.

would cease to be an independent nation and become a vassal of a more powerful Asian neighbor or equally a colony of one of the Western empires.[6] The extended family or clan became a metaphor for Japanese society and the Japanese economy as well.[7] The clan looked after its own members and opposed any intrusion from outside. Change became a threat to contain, or at best a misfortune that needed careful management, rather than an opportunity opening up new possibilities. The later day reflection of this reactive response could be seen in the intrinsically conservative or highly risk-averse approach to economic and political decision making. Change has tended to come from outside shocks to the Japanese system rather than internal pressures.[8]

11.2 Political History

> Distrusting economic individualism ... their aim was to crystallize existing class relationships by submitting them to the pressure at once restrictive and protective, of a paternal government, vigilant to detect all movements which menaced the established order ... (Tawney, 1963, p. 166).

It can be persuasively argued that Japanese reluctance to take chances resulted in the transformation, but not rejection, of many aspects of the feudal system. Certainly from Toyotomi Hideyoshi's (1536–1598) misconceived adventure in Korea until Japan's even more foolhardy ambitions and over reach in World War II, the Japanese were

---

[6]It can be argued that during key periods, change was identified as equivalent to a threat. Certainly the closing off of Japan during the *bakufu* period was an attempt to regulate the rate of change. Western learning came through one official channel and could be employed judiciously by the ruling Tokugawa shogunate. The idea of outside threats formed the backbone of Japan's foreign policy with each aggressive action rationalized as a necessity.

[7]A reasonable working assumption would be that the Meiji restoration had less to do with anything resembling a revival and more to do with creating the concrete idea of Japan as a nation, especially one that was structurally suited to make rapid strides toward modernity.

[8]Here the reference is to the coming of the "Black Ships" under Commodore Perry which precipitated the crisis leading to the Meiji restoration and the aftermath to the Pacific War defeat and the long US occupation. In some sense the rapid change of these periods cloaked the incorporation of aspects of the existing order. In what was essentially a top down revolution, feudal characteristics of the shogunate continued far into the Meiji period. In the same way, what has become known as the 1940s system (see Noguchi, 1998) meant that the organizational structure of the post-war era leaned heavily on the building blocks of the wartime economy.

hesitant to pursue goals beyond their capacity.[9] A continuation and preservation of Japanese life against uncertain and outside elements of change remained the hallmark of political life. The use of the clan, or group, to provide stability did not die with the end of the great feudal lords (*daimyo*) and the loyalty of their trusted *samurai*. Echoes in more modern times still could be seen some 90 years later in the dedication of the post-war *salaryman* to his corporate overlord.[10]

11.2.1 *The closed country (Sakoku)*

The consolidation and unification of Japan under Tokugawa Ieyasu extended for the more than 200 years of the Tokugawa *Bakufu*.[11] Its hallmark was a deliberate strategy of isolation. The overriding policy objective was to slow down and control change in order to provide a stable platform for economic viability and to maintain continuing dynastic power. Once so warmly welcomed, trade, especially with Europeans, virtually ended.[12] The Tokugawa *Bakufu* granted the Dutch sole access at the island of Deshima (Dejima) off the port city of Nagasaki. This limited the damages which might flow from any and all outside shocks. Previous European missions (both religious and secular) had intrigued

---

[9]In the year building up to all out war in the Pacific, the Imperial Army had to essentially convince itself and the rest of the country that it had no other options. Under this analysis, aggressive action became transformed into a conservative form of self-defense.

[10]Thus the role of the *samurai* was democratized in the same sort of way that forming a national army of peasant recruits formed the basis of the new Japanese identity.

[11]Until the Meiji Restoration in 1868, Japanese Emperors ruled in name only while residing in the ancient capital of Kyoto. While everything was done in the name of the Emperor, including revolts against the existing power structure, the real power remained in the hands of a powerful clan headed by its leader (known in the West as the *shogun*). The Tokugawa *Bakufu*, for strategic reasons, established its working capital in Edo (later Tokyo) away from the ceremonial capital of the Emperor.

[12]Note is often also made of the banning of Christianity and the expulsion of Christian priests, mostly Franciscans from Spain. It is a misconception to assume that the objective in doing so stemmed from any sort of religious clash or was driven by intolerance. The Franciscans who had actively supported the opposing party battling the Tokugawa clan were seen as stalking horses for European powers and thus as a continuing threat to the existing regime. Moreover, the large number of converts, especially those centred around Nagasaki could easily be viewed as a fifth column poised to undermine the sway of the current rulers. Religious doctrine remained a curiosity rather than the basis for a successful crusade. The Japanese tended to absorb a number of irreconcilable religions without any seeming effort.

in the civil wars and politics of Japan. The highly regulated Dutch trade would provide a continuing window on the outside world. Knowledge would flow in, but unwanted interference or agents of change would be filtered out.[13]

11.2.2 *The Meiji restoration*

Outside shocks have long proven to be an effective impetus for major change in Japan. Change however, even that which on the surface creates dramatic transformations, has had a more enduring link to existing structures and hierarchies than is immediately apparent. Change has been perennially co-opted by elements of the old order and remained essentially conservative.

The forced opening of Japan is best symbolized by the entry of the "black ships" into Edo (Tokyo) Bay in 1853 and again in 1854. The US fleet under Commodore Matthew Perry left the Tokugawa Shogunate without a viable alternative. The inevitability of accepting this foreign ultimatum however, also revealed an underlying weakness in the existing status quo. Provincial clans from the Southwest of Japan, strongly supported by younger and opportunistic *samurai* retainers, seized upon the disruption created by foreign entry to overthrow Tokugawa rule in the name of the teenage Meiji emperor.[14] This same group of new leaders would form, from then on, the core of a ruling oligarchy for the next 50 years, providing Japan with remarkable and much needed political stability. In essence, they shared the same ultimate goals with the forces they defeated, namely expelling the barbarians. However they did not share the romantic reaction of some of the old guard. Pragmatically they were sufficiently realistic to accept the long-range nature of this goal. The shameful treaties (specifying foreign access and trade) dictated by the Western powers would be overturned, but only eventually. Japan would accomplish these goals by rapid modernization of its society and economy. Modernization would

---

[13]Channeling change by deliberately slowing down its effects is thus a very old Japanese strategy. Succeeding Japanese regimes of various guises would shy from any outright attempt to halt change but slowing down the pace was another thing.

[14]As noted already, the Tokugawa Shogunate also ruled in the name of the emperor.

bring the sort of military power ("strong army, strong country")[15] that the Japanese rulers saw as essential if China's creeping colonial fate was to be avoided. In the future, the Japanese would tend to view all treaties with the Western powers in a similar fashion, imposed by the West for the benefit of the West and demeaning to the honor and interests of Japan.[16]

But an economic transformation under these circumstances was not an internal class revolt against the existing power structure. The dominant cultural myths did not need to be displaced. Instead, under the guidance of a newly restored and powerful emperor, they could become the engine for rapid industrialization and capital accumulation. The peasantry was too dispersed and powerless to present a sustained challenge. Nor did the ruling caste have to contend with a burgeoning and somewhat independent commercial class. With the extended closure of foreign trade, merchants had become dependent on the government for the smooth functioning of internal commerce.[17] The marketplace, where price mechanisms usually reigned, was also subservient to government directives. The invisible hand would continue to defer to perceived national imperatives.

---

[15] The expression favored in Japan at this time was "*kyohei, fukoku*" or literally "strengthen the military, enrich the country."

[16] Some of this same attitude would continue to characterize Japan's foreign policy. To survive, there was no other option than to dominate Japan's geographical neighborhood. This common consensus was judged to be a defensive rather than an aggressive posture as noted previously. Whether this was to be obtained by military means or through economic might was more of a tactical question.

[17] Under the Tokugawa *Bakufu*, a policy of required attendance at the Edo court of all the ruling lords (in rotation) deliberately constrained their financial wherewithal to engineer a revolt against the centre. The unintended consequences were that such a policy spurred commerce as goods and services were required by such an extended trek to and from the capital. The merchant class in its role as an intermediary became if anything more beholden to Japan's rulers rather then becoming an independent source of influence.

> Key to the *bakufu*'s approach was the introduction of the *sankin kotai* system of alternative attendance whereby most *daimyo* were forced to come to Edo on a regular schedule, residing in the capital with their wives and children (who remained as prisoners in the capital when the *daimyo* returned to their domains) for a year at a time (Mosk, 2008, p. 56).

Japan rapidly adopted the leading systems of the industrialized nations and modernized itself over the next 50 years. The Japanese became a unified nation loyal to the emperor rather than to their clan. In effect, the Meiji Restoration created the concept or consciousness of Japan as a nation state. However, the old line samurai characteristics of loyalty, obedience, and self-sacrifice (the way of the warrior or *bushido*) remained dominant. To use a well-worn cliché, the over-riding motivating goal was a desire to achieve "a place in the sun" as a major military power. Economic modernization then was to a large degree only a means to that end.

The Meiji Government attempted to incorporate new industrial technology within the existing social structure by taking full advantage of long-standing hierarchical relations. This program gained currency under the slogan of combining Japanese spirit with Western ability (*wakon yosai*). Under State guidance, the unified people of Japan could be carefully shepherded and quite blatantly squeezed toward completion of this monumental task.

The first signs that these goals were within Japan's grasp came with a series of successful wars, first against China in 1895 and then against Russia in 1904–1905. While the first victory might have rudely surprised Western powers, the second came as an unwelcome shock to these same countries. By 1910, Japan's colonial domination extended over Taiwan and Korea. However, Japan's perceptions of unequal treatment by the West grew, at first cause by German, French, and Russian pressure to relinquish territory previously ceded by the Chinese government. Subsequently, the US-brokered treaty ending the Russo-Japanese War was again perceived by the Japanese as too favorable to the defeated Russians. This growing distrust of American motives was further aggravated in the post-World War I era by the Treaty of Versailles,[18] followed subsequently by US pressure on Britain to terminate its alliance with the Japanese and finally with the

---

[18]The Japanese entry into the war seemed motivated by the opportunity to snatch a number of German colonies while putting its own military at only a minimal degree of risk. During the negotiations at Versailles, Australia's Prime Minister, Billy Hughes, was adamant that Japan should not be treated as anything approaching an equal allied power.

Washington Naval Peace Conference.[19] In each case, the Japanese government, backed by popular sentiment, perceived American actions as deliberately depriving Japan of its just rewards while being laden with an almost reflex racism against the country.

The period following World War I encompassed a relatively brief, but significant deviation from more general patterns that seemingly dominated Japanese history. The Taisho era (1912–1926), displayed many less rigid, more open-minded characteristics. As opposed to the stereotype of a Japanese people heavily constrained by their group oriented culture, this period, boosted by an economically profitable World War I, moved the Japanese toward a more individualistic, market-oriented economy and society. These years were in one sense atypical. They did however display the possibility of a different type of Japanese society, perhaps one more in tune with Western values. Even at its height, this 1920s model never succeeded in dominating the whole of the country given its very short lifespan. The country was fiercely divided between rural conservative and the increasingly urban and liberal rest of the population (a 50–50 split by the 1920s). Perhaps with reliable economic growth, liberal parliamentary democracy might have survived. But slow growth marked the decade of the 1920s, slower than for any comparable span between 1880 and 1940. As in the Weimar republic, the Japanese people sought stability and an end to economic deprivation after a rather too tumultuous decade.[20] A financial crisis in 1927 and an unwise decision to return to the gold system (1930) sealed the fate of this era.[21]

Starting in the 1930s, economic and political freedom was simply the price paid for security. At the heart of this exchange lay a feudal mind set which substituted a clan-like governance system for one dominated by market relations. This system, which was only gradually imposed, borrowed elements already dominating the Japanese economy and the

---

[19] Japan saw the goal of these tactics as an attempt to maintain American dominance in the Pacific and to forestall Japan's own growing ambitions.

[20] The period was noted not only for its Westernized factories and culture but for political assassinations, the great Kanto earthquake, rice riots and an inability to curb growing military ambitions.

[21] See a parallel problem in inter-war England induced by Churchill's similar infatuation with the pre-war gold system.

Japanese character to redefine policy objectives. These elements were then cultivated while letting incipient moves toward more Western contractual relationships, and a reliance on parliamentary democracy, wither.

11.2.3 *Japan at war*

In a war-time economy, or one gearing-up for war, the major problem is trying to rapidly increase production. This is equivalent to producing to order (essentially defense-oriented goods) rather than producing for the market. The Japanese government needed to reconstruct its economy so that heavy industry could provide an expanded array of war materials. The government of the day eased a potentially binding capital constraint by shifting corporate finance from a system largely dependent on equity and retained earnings to one almost entirely based on bank finance. By doing so, the government could funnel investment directly to achieve specific ends. Banks became mere conduits for funds, while shareholders lost any real ability to hold corporate managers to account.[22]

Japan's Manchurian moves against China in 1931 initiated a war-time era that ceased only with Japan's unconditional surrender in 1945. The puppet state of Manchukuo (Manchuria) became Japan's operational base. However, US opposition continued to thwart Japan's dreams of Asian dominance. A US trade embargo, shutting off the flow of vital oil to Japan, brought past animosities to the surface. The military leadership, portraying Japan as having no other option, initiated war

---

[22] Mobilizing Japan's very limited resources for its dramatic war effort required removing as much risk and uncertainty as possible. A war economy meant that goods were produced on order as opposed to responding to market demand. Financing was assured so that the supply of war material always met requested demand.

> The decline of shareholders' power was accelerated by explicit government interventions, and, by the end of the war, managers were effectively free from monitoring. Financial institutions were turned into organizations which merely followed the government's leading orders. The evaluation and monitoring of borrowers, which is central to a healthy banking system, was no longer the banks' concern under the wartime economy (Hoshi, 1995, p. 307).

against the US with a surprise attack on the American fleet at Pearl Harbour (December 7, 1941). Japan's military took a calculated gamble that US and allied troops would not withstand an all-out attack and instead sue for peace, leaving Japan to control the East. Under the guise of liberating Asia from colonial rule (establishing the Co-Prosperity Sphere), Japan rapidly swept through Hong Kong, Malaya, Singapore, Java, the Indies, Burma, Indo-China, and most of the Pacific Islands. The brutality that defined military discipline in the Japanese army displayed itself in the treatment of enemy prisoners and the local Asian population. Despite early success, the tide of the war slowly turned. Given its limited resources, Japan's gamble was bound to fail over a longer time span. Badly underestimating the resolve of the Americans, British, and other allied troops,[23] Japan's refusal to surrender unconditionally led to the first atomic bomb falling on Hiroshima (August 6, 1945) followed by another on Nagasaki three days later.

11.2.4 *Post-war occupation*

Japan's refusal to surrender reflected a desire by Japan's rulers to preserve the existing militaristic order in Japan.[24] Ostensibly they failed miserably. An essentially American occupation (1945–1952) sought to install democratic institutions in place of the old order as a sort

---

[23] The Japanese high command essentially gambled that after a few quick defeats, the allies would sue for peace rather than persevere. Since this was the only strategy that carried with it any chance for success, the Japanese military largely convinced themselves of its likelihood thus nicely boxing themselves into a no-win war trajectory. Also playing a clear role was the basic contempt and outright racism each side held for each other. By reducing the relevant opponent to a caricature, any inherent threat could be casually dismissed. John Dower (1986) provides an intriguing look into the interplay between misrepresentation of one's enemy and the subsequent tactics and strategy adopted by both sides.

[24] Part of the difficulty lay with the Potsdam Declaration calling for Japan's unconditional surrender. This left ambiguous the future role for the Emperor in any post-surrender regime. Reasonably, Hirohito feared not only for his crown but for his life as well. This led not only to foot dragging on the part of the Japanese but also an official no surrender policy. In fact, the US occupation under the quasi-royal tutelage of General Douglas MacArthur made every effort to preserve the status of the Emperor. Advisors close to the General were quite convinced that a continuing constitutional role for Hirohito was essential to maintain post-war stability in Japan. Whether such an argument was in fact valid is still today highly debateable. Instead it can be properly claimed that both sides in post-war Japan shared parts of the same agenda. See Dower (1999) for a critical look at the US occupation of Japan.

of gift bestowed on the Japanese people much in the same way that GIs lavished chewing gum and nylons on their favorite *panpan* girls.[25] Beneath the perceived surface, one where change was the prescribed menu, the stated aims of democratization were subtly subverted. The former militaristic regime may have vanished with the allied victory, but many of the same institutions and even the same individuals associated with the war effort re-emerged, however superficially transformed.[26] The old guard eventually triumphed over attempted bottom up changes as well as the democratization by fiat practised by occupation forces.

There are perhaps two distinct stages during the occupation period, both of which were presided over, quite imperiously, by US General Douglas MacArthur. The initial stage bore the imprint of Roosevelt's New Dealers. Here the aims centered on insuring that Japanese militarism would not arise again and on democratizing Japanese institutions even to the point of ostensibly destroying existing one. The US-drafted Japanese constitution included an article (Article IX) limiting Japan to a strictly self-defense posture and seemingly eliminating the possibility of any future military adventures. In a parallel fashion, US occupation forces demanded land reform, released political prisoners (including communists), encouraged labor unions, provided women with voting rights, pushed for educational reforms, and broke up the large business trusts (*zaibatsu*).[27] This activist US stance was short lived with

---

[25] *Panpan* was the most popular euphemism for the Japanese prostitutes servicing the hordes of occupation soldiers.

> When prostitutes used the label themselves, it conveyed a similarly mixed impression — a sense of "desperation" and "misery," as popular accounts put it, couples with a proud defiance of conventional norms, a sensual *joie de vivre* (Dower, 1999, p. 132).

[26] Nobusuke Kishi indicted and jailed for war crimes until released with the onset of the Cold War would become Prime Minister in 1957 as later on would his younger brother Eisake Sato and his grandson Shinzo Abe. Post-war Japanese politics was, if anything, a family business.

[27] The breakup of the *zaibatsu* is an elegant example of the sort of shadow play that defined the stated reforms produced by the occupation authorities. As soon as those military bureaucrats departed in 1952, the *keiretsu* organizational structure showed a deep kinship to its earlier outlawed forerunner. No surprise that the biggest of these alliances bore the familiar names of

idealism being swiftly discarded as soon as political pragmatism reared its predictable head.

In the ongoing battle between those corporatist elements wanting to restore the previous status quo of power and those elements desiring either liberal reform, or the application of left leaning ideologies, 1945–1947 represented the high-water mark for the forces of change as well as general popular support. Shigeru Yoshida, the dominant conservative politician of this critical period 1946–1954, fought a successful rear guard battle against the New Deal reformers who initially surrounded MacArthur. His legacy was the Liberal Democratic Party[28] a political coalition which would form one of the bulwarks of the re-emerging "Iron Triangle." This subset of business, administrative, and political leaders would manage Japan successfully throughout the post-war period. Administrators, the Japanese bureaucracy, would play an essential coordinating role often pre-empting market processes in order to channel and retard any underlying forces of change.[29] This subset of business, administrative, and political leaders would manage Japan successfully throughout the post-war period. The key battles all involved transforming American reform initiatives into policies that achieved conservative business objectives. Japan would adopt the

---

Mitsubishi, Mitsui, and Sumitomo. As a Mr. Furuta of Sumitomo foreshadowed at the time of the official break-up:

> Now the *honsha* will disappear and the subsidiaries will be left on their own, but never forget that all the Sumitomo companies share the same history and roots and are brothers. Of course, we cannot offend the GHQ by holding meetings these days, but keep the spiritual ties, keep in touch with each other and co-ordinate your efforts to rebuild Japan (Tsuda, quoted in Hoshi, 1995, p. 314).

[28] Equally important and far more ruthless was Nobusuke Kishi. A wartime cabinet minister, jailed until 1948, he joined the then Democratic Party in 1952. In 1955, as head of the Democratic Party, he engineered the merger with Yoshida's Liberals ensuring conservative domination of Japanese politics. The party he bequeathed has often been lampooned as representing none of the ideas in its name and is in fact fairly devoid of any clear ideology. Its aim has been to maintain its power and barring one brief interlude in the early nineties has been surprisingly successful at doing so.

[29] Dower (1999) makes the reasonable point that the veneration of hierarchy and reliance on bureaucratic processes was not uniquely Japanese but rather heavily influenced by the stodgy administrative practises embedded during the US occupation period.

appearance (*tatemae* — outside face) of Western liberal democracy as a vehicle to promote a reality (*honne* — inside face) involving traditional feudal structures in which risk was minimized and collectivized. In exchange, conservative business leaders implicitly offered the vision of an all-inclusive middle-class society.[30] The defining issues of this transformational struggle would revolve around four inter-related aspects of the post-war economy:

- establishing a working agreement with labor,
- land redistribution,
- corporate business structure, and
- financial institutions.

The first, and most pitched, battle arose over labor. Without stability, conservatives and occupation forces saw no possibility for economic growth. Economic growth (the middle-class society) would placate the Japanese people and maintain conservative control. Together, stability and economic growth would insure that Japan would become a reliable surrogate and ally in strategic East Asia.

The turning point came on February 1, 1947 when MacArthur refused to allow a potentially crippling General Strike to go forward. This clearly marked a change in the US approach to the reconstruction of Japan. The Cold War was intensifying. Out went the New Dealers, in came the political and fiscal conservatives.[31] Then, following the fall of China to communist forces, Japanese unions in 1949 were purged of communist members. An estimated 10,000 workers lost their jobs, dissuading many times that number from aligning with them.

The Cold War marked a significant shift in labor relations away from Western-style confrontation, which had made the immediate post-war era in Japan one of rolling strikes and radical unions, to an era of consensus agreement in which enterprise unions accepted security (low risk) in

---

[30] Early work on the underlying promise of a middle class Japanese society is best typified by Murakami (1982).

[31] To be strictly accurate, the balance of power shifted to those taking a more conservative approach and one that was more aligned to US domestic and international concerns. MacArthur himself at this time was said to be harboring presidential aspirations.

return for delivering a dependable rising level of productivity (at least in a selective group of manufacturing industries).[32]

Two events at this time clearly marked the changeover in Japan's political and economic life. One was the arrival of Joseph Dodge in Japan on February 1, 1949. Dodge came with the expressed aim of reshaping the direction of the Japanese economy.[33] In a brief three-month tour of duty, Dodge laid a foundation that allowed traditional Japanese business interest to re-emerge. His insistence on conservative economic policies (balanced budgets, low inflation, and low exchange rate) would provide the opportunity to construct an economy that kept the appearance of an imposed Western-style system while undermining the reality through a program of clever risk sharing and ingenious income redistribution.

The Korean War[34] was the other great event of the time. Like some *deus ex machina* in a Greek tragedy, the sudden surge of war created demand rescued the Japanese economy. Firms, such as Nissan, would survive by producing parts and vehicles for the endlessly voracious US Army.

11.2.5 *The Post-War Japanese miracle*

The formation in 1955 of the Liberal Democratic Party sealed the shape of post-war Japan, with the Japan Federation of Economic Organizations (*Keidanren*) acting as a proud midwife. The LDP evolved into one of the most flexible of Japanese institutions. In fact it was hardly a unified party at all, existing more as a collection of party factions representing different special interests. Since the party firmly held no strongly grounded beliefs, it faced very small costs in changing direction whenever expedient. Over the years, the LDP has made few specific

---

[32] Sectors such as consumer electronics, cars and precision tools would eventually become major export industries.

[33] The Dodge program was essentially a scorched earth approach. By cutting off credit and squeezing employment, this approach provided Japanese industrialists with the opportunity to restructure the economy and shift bargaining power away from labor and labor unions.

[34] The Vietnam War would later be highly beneficial from an economic standpoint for Japan. US spending would accelerate Japan's catch-up policy of development in the 1960s.

ideological investments. Instead, the party's *raison d'etre* has been the distribution of spoils to its constituents.

In keeping with a pronounced penchant for political compromise, the Yoshida Doctrine came to define the foreign policy of post-war Japan. This approach substituted economic growth and eventual economic dominance for more overt military objectives. To accomplish this growth, Japan relied on the US to provide an essential security umbrella. With the coming of the Cold War, the US–Japan Mutual Security Treaty (1951) tied Japan firmly to the US. In return for the end of the prolonged occupation, the Japanese agreed to allow US military bases to remain on the mainland as well as in Okinawa (returned to Japan in May 1972). This approach fell foul of both right wing members of the LDP who wished Japan to rearm, as well as left wing parties that desired a total withdrawal of US troops. An attempt by Prime Minister Kishi to force through a revised treaty ended in his resignation in 1960 and a reversion to the Yoshida Doctrine. Notice that this approach in no way relinquished the dominant Japanese objective of regaining its status as the pre-eminent Asian power. Instead it turned away from the more explicit military option as being largely unworkable.

The decade of the 1960s focused obsessively on building an industrialized economy. Beginning with Prime Minister Hayato Ikeda's income doubling plan, this decade created the belief that the Japanese had built a miracle economy. Growth throughout this period expanded at a rate exceeding 10 percent per annum. By the start of the 1970s, the Japanese economy had become fully industrialized. Under Prime Minister Tanaka, a factional heavyweight who would continue to exert political power after his forced resignation, plans were laid for increased infrastructure projects and a widening of the social welfare net. Unfortunately, Japan was hit heavily by the first oil shock of 1973. As a reaction, Japan financed the increased cost of oil imports by an export led growth strategy.[35] Consumer electronic goods and cars made their

---

[35]While it is true that Japan served as a model for later industrializing countries in Asia, Japan's growth was quite balanced between the domestic and foreign markets. Japan's economy had basically caught up before an external shock in the 1970s tilted it toward export driven growth to maintain the basis of its economic success.

way in increasing numbers to US markets. This marks the start of an extended period of trade tensions that eventually would spill over into security matters facing the two erstwhile allies.

These problems were eased somewhat in the 1980s by the efforts of Japanese Prime Minister Yasuhiro Nakasone and US President Ronald Reagan. Nonetheless, the Japanese faced charges of unfair trade practices in both the US and Europe. The increasing direct foreign investment in the US by Japan caused tensions to continue to rise. The Plaza Accord between the G-7 large industrial countries in 1985 sought a resolution to these problems by drastically revaluating the Japanese yen. In reaction to the rising yen, an expansionary monetary policy in Japan laid the seeds for the Japanese bubble economy that characterized Japan until its collapse in 1992.

Unfortunately, political leadership at this time became bogged down in a share trading scandal centered on the Recruit Cosmos Company. This set up a period characterized by a lack of leadership, with a series of very short-term prime ministers, and a marked inability to deal with pressing economic issues. Even before the economic bubble burst, Japan's foreign policy had come under fire. The Gulf War (1991) clearly illustrated the constraints Article IX of the constitution could exert. Attempts by Prime Minister Kaifu to send 200 non-combatant personnel to the conflict met with defeat in the Diet. Instead, Kaifu offered $4 billion to defray the cost of the war, only to be met by American pressure for an even more substantial contribution. Japan would gain the unwanted laurels of being the king of cheque book diplomacy. Financial support would mount to an additional $9 billion, making Japan by far the largest financial contributor of the war. Such efforts met with neither appreciation nor gratitude from the Kuwaitis or their US allies. Instead, Japan was largely scorned and derided for attempting to buy itself out of its obligations with wads of cash. The US–Japan alliance was clearly beginning to show the strains of embracing conflicting objectives.[36]

---

[36]A decade later this would see the crumbling of the Yoshida Doctrine as calls for the repeal of Article IX became increasingly common amongst the more conservative and right wing elements of the political spectrum. The mysterious appeal of becoming a "normal country," though

In July of 1993, the LDP itself, racked with dissension and scandal, lost control of political power for the first time since its 1955 formation. A multi-party coalition, centered on two new political parties created by breakaway LDP members, formed government with Morihiro Hosokawa as Prime Minister. The coalition did manage a successful reform of the electoral system which helped break the stranglehold of rural constituencies (though a rural vote continued to be weighted more than that of an urban one). This move seemed to indicate that a major change in the very structure of the country was possible. Broad range reforms put forward by the Hosokawa coalition took clear aim at the Iron Triangle that had essentially run Japan since the war. The reforms made a particular target the bureaucratic control characterizing so much of the economy during the post-occupation period.

Such an unstable collation was clearly unsuited for an extended life in the tumultuous Japanese political environment. Forced to resign in April 1994, Hosokawa was succeeded by Tsutomu Hata who was gone almost as soon as he arrived. (A lack of leadership stability would characterize the country throughout the decade until the atypical interlude during the reign of Junichiro Koizumi.) By 1994, the LDP was once again in control, using the Japan's Socialist Party as a stalking horse for their return to power. Though Tomiichi Murayama would become the first socialist prime minister in 47 years, he would best be remembered for his failure to deal adequately with the January 1995 Kobe earthquake and the March 1995 sarin gas attack by the Aum Shinrikyo religious sect. The LDP was clearly back in charge by January 1995 with Ryutaro Hashimoto as prime minister. Initially, he pushed what for Japan was a bold reform package centered on a Japanese version of the "Big Bang." This essentially accelerated financial decontrol while reforming accounting practices and encouraging more transparency in corporate matters.

However, the overwhelming problem by 1996 was whether Japan's post-bubble economy would finally revive. Traditionally, Japanese

---

ill-defined, would see the Japanese send non-combatant troops to Iraq (2004–2005). These 1500 troops, protected first by Dutch and then Australian soldiers, were no more than symbolic. However it did represent a potentially major shift for Japanese international policy. Such debate intensified in the post-Koizumi era.

governments faced with economic downturns regarded them as short-term phenomena. Nothing drastic needed to be done.[37] Fiscal expansion would limit the duration and damage of any recession. Adjustment schemes would ensure that no particular sector or company suffered inordinately. Japan's post-bubble policy followed predictable steps. Expansion of fiscal policy did seem to mute the depth of the recession. However, money, as could be expected, was not well spent. Most expenditure went toward highway and similar projects which favored rural districts and the construction industry (a major LDP contributor as well as heavily indebted to the main banks). Despite the limited effectiveness of this approach and the efforts of the Ministry of Finance to cover up rather than resolve banking problems, the economy by 1996 seemed on its way back to sustainable growth.

The Hashimoto government then ran head on into a combination of bad policy moves, bad luck and increasing financial scandals. Urged on by the Ministry of Finance, the Hashimoto government sought fiscal rectitude by raising taxes, particularly the VAT. Unfortunately, the largely unforeseen Asian Crisis (1997) dealt a staggering blow to Japan's already troubled banking sector. Japanese banks had sought to earn their way out of a rising post-bubble bad debt problem through loans to fast-growing East Asian countries such as Thailand and Indonesia. A collapse in these economies saw Japanese banks pull in their loans and worsen the Asian Crisis. The collapse also uncovered the underlying fragility of the banking system and spotlighted all the ineffectual government attempts to disguise the problem.

In response to a faltering economy, the LDP performed poorly in May 1998 elections. Hashimoto was out, replaced by LDP stalwart Keizo Obuchi, a triumph of factional politics over any potential reform program. His death in April 2000 brought in a Prime Minister, Yoshiro Mori, possibly the very epitome of the party machine politician. With the economy floundering, Mori proved to be particularly

---

[37] In the current (2008) economic crisis, there is now a general consensus that the one lesson to learn from the Japanese experience is not to dither. It is far less risky to do too much rather than follow the Japanese example of doing too little in the rather Micawberish belief that the economy will largely right itself.

maladroit in his public dealings. His approval ratings bottomed at 10 percent. Fearing an overwhelming loss in the upcoming elections Mori bowed out. (He would however, in the abiding LDP tradition, remain a factional heavyweight and kingmaker.) In a surprising outcome, perennial leadership contender, Junichiro Koizumi managed to triumph over party stalwarts who backed ex-Prime Minister Ryutaro Hashinoto. Koizumi raised hopes for fundamental change by championing economic reform and a new way of conducting political business.

Koizumi took the LDP to an unexpected victory, although he did need support from both the New Komeito and Liberal Parties to gain a ruling majority. The reality of Koizumi's policy turned out to differ from the promise. Adept at forming media sound bites, Koizumi brought American-style pizzazz to the traditionally gray-on-gray style characteristic of Japanese politics. Unfortunately, Koizumi proved to have little abiding interest in economic reform or economics in general. He can best be seen as a political reformer determined to break the factional nature of LDP politics and the power of both the *zoku*[38] politicians representing vested interests and the bureaucrats of the powerful ministries. The more cynical might suspect that his real aim in all his reform policies was simply to consolidate the power of his own supporters by cutting off financial flows to opposing LDP factions.

Starting in 2003 and certainly by 2004, Japan had poked its way out of the worst of its economic misery and was at the start of its longest post-war expansionary period.[39] Little responsibility for Japan's very limited success could be laid at the door of Prime Minister Koizumi.[40]

---

[38] The Japanese are much more forthright about politics as a conduit for representing specific vested interests. The *zoku*, or tribes, are members of the Diet whose main (or seemingly only) purpose is to push for the interests of a narrow group of backers.

[39] While hardly a boom, the Japanese economy throughout this five year period (ending in 2008) would average a bit more than two percent growth per year. When placed in terms of per capita growth, Japan would compare favorably with the US over this relevant period.

[40] This is a controversial point. Some commentators are eager to award credit for rescuing the Japanese banking sector to Koizumi via his Economic Tsar, Heizo Takenake. However more attention should be shifted to the change in banking policy initiated by the Bank of Japan in 2002 and the fortuitous boost in exports largely due to the booming Chinese economy in 2003.

He seemed more interested in pushing forward a revived nationalistic foreign policy than in regenerating Japan's uncertain economy. The result of his new look diplomatic approach bore fruit in the steadily worsening relationships with both China and South Korea. Koizumi has gone on to become one of Japan's longest serving, though perhaps not necessarily the most successful, prime ministers. Though he was determined to transform the LDP, the political structure he attempted to form before stepping down in 2007 soon crumbled in the hands of his three far less skilful successors. Koizumi did seem able to transform the LDP to fit his predetermined objectives forming a stark contrast with what followed after his retirement. As his attempt to push through a postal reform bill demonstrated in August of 2005, he was willing to gamble on the collapse of his party rather than resort to the business as usual strategy of political compromise. The subsequent September 2005 election demonstrated the new found importance of spin in Japanese elections. By ignoring all other issues and simply asserting that his plan for postal reform was the equivalent of forging ahead with the pressing need for economic revitalization, Koizumi was able to achieve the LDP's biggest electoral victory since 1986.[41] Winning 296 of the Diet's 480 seats, the LDP in coalition with its New Komeito partner held a two-thirds majority. This would stymie attempts by the Upper House to veto any of his bills. What was merely a hypothetical situation would become reality when public opinion shifted firmly against his successors.

Koizumi was followed by the relatively youthful Shinzo Abe who seemed to ride in on Koizumi's popularity and set to work mending the damaged relationships with Japan's near neighbors, namely China and South Korea. Unfortunately Abe, even for an LDP politician, seemed blessed with a tin ear. The major concerns manifested by the electorate were economic in nature. Continuing economic growth devoid of real wage increases focused concerns on providing for old age, rising health

---

[41] There is a common belief that Koizumi did not bother to actually read the postal reform bill as formulated by the Ministry of Finance. As reported above, Koizumi demonstrated no real interest in economics. The bill had less to do with economic reform and more to do with breaking the cash nexus supporting opposition factions of the LDP.

costs, and concerns that educational quality was inexorably slipping away. These were all very practical concerns. Abe though focused on patriotism, security matters and building something he referred to as a beautiful country.[42] A pension scandal where the Japanese ever arrogant bureaucracy admitted to losing untold pension records was a fatal nail in Abe's hopes for a successful term as prime minister. Days after an APEC meeting held in Sydney in December of 2007, Abe found himself resigning for convenient reasons of health. With former foreign minister Aso primed to succeed, the LDP proved itself capable of surprise by giving the prize to Fukuda in a "back to the future" style strategy. After the difficult to anticipate Abe, Fukuda represented safe hands. The old guard of the LDP was back in the saddle and the undramatic and somewhat gray Fukuda seemingly proved a popular choice. But instead, Fukuda appeared ineffectual in dealing with a resurgent *Minshuto* (Democratic Party of Japan). Having changed the balance of power in the Upper House as a result of the elections, Japan faced the novel situation of the Diet being held by different political coalitions. With Fukuda's popularity steadily dropping, he also failed to survive the year as Taro Aso on his third attempt managed to win the now dubious prize. However, his timing was unfortunate to say the least. With economic recession hitting one country after the next, Japan, more than ever export dependent, also fell into recession. Despite rapidly sinking confidence in either the economic future or his leadership, Aso's major concern seemed to be to put off new elections as long as possible. Instead of providing a way forward, as 2009 began, Aso seemed more interested in lecturing the Japanese population on the need to work harder and sacrifice more. The Japanese people in turn responded by awarding the prime minister with an approval rating of 19 percent, a rate that in February 2009 plumbed single digits, figures unseen since the ill-fated Yoshiro Mori held office. With 2009 looking less than promising, whether the Japanese government ultimately remains headed by Aso, another LDP aspirant or even the leader of the Democratic Party seems largely immaterial.

---

[42] It was difficult not to wonder how many politicians ever explicitly promoted building an ugly country.

None of the current gaggle of aspiring politicians seems capable of avoiding what almost seems a characteristic tendency to dither, a code of conduct that largely had underwritten the still remembered lost decade.

11.3 A Look at the Japanese Economy

11.3.1 *Reforms and post-war trends*

The Japanese post-war miracle had two basic cornerstones. By implicitly promising the Japanese people a secure, low-risk economy where living standards would predictably rise, the allure of achieving a universally middle-class economy allowed the Iron Triangle (business, bureaucrats, and politicians) that essentially created war-time Japan to maintain its hold on the reins of power and insured the political stability needed for a vibrant economy. Socializing risk and redistributing income required economic growth of the steady and rather significantly large variety.

Three particular reforms defined the future path of post-war Japan. In each case, traditional and conservative Japanese interest subverted the intentions of the initial reformers that defined the immediate occupation objectives. While successful in driving economic growth during the catch-up stage of development, the structures growing out of and transforming these post-war reforms eventually became an impediment to growth as the Japanese economy grew ever larger and more successful.

The first of these reforms saw the enactment of a new set of labor laws. The occupation forces hoped to establish industrial labor unions similar to those operating in the US. Given the 55 percent unionization rate of the early, post-war work force, this Western adversarial approach to union organization initially led to industrial unrest, with the Japanese worker characterized as unreliable and confrontational. The fall of China in 1949 to communist forces, followed soon after by the Korean War changed the initial US predilection for keeping Japan economically weak and unthreatening. From this somewhat adversarial relationship, Japan rapidly graduated to a more privileged position as

America's main industrial client state in Asia. In return, Japan implicitly received approval to reassert something resembling the war-time status quo. Companies in the early 1950s embraced a union-busting strategy. More compliant, hierarchical structures conveniently became reframed as representing true, traditional Japanese order. Employers utilized and encouraged the strong type of group identification so common in Japanese society. They managed to redefine the relevant economic and social group in a way that supported and drove corporate growth. The company unions, which supplanted the industrial-based ones, resembled, not coincidentally, the *Sanyo Hokokukai* (in-house unions) characteristic of war-time Japan, where maximizing production was the guiding objective of union and corporation alike. However, the security promised in return for labor compliance and productivity would create an unending pressure for corporate growth and expansion.

The dissolution of the large financial conglomerates *zaibatsu*) was the second major reform. Vertical and horizontal groupings of firms (*keiretsu*), often around a main bank and a trading company, took on many of the properties of the war-time conglomerates. The ostensible break up simply acted as a means to redistribute wealth and remove any residual control from the old *zaibatsu* families. Effective control shifted to an entrenched, new management elite. US-style anti-trust legislation lacked enforcement, as both government officials and corporate management failed to accept the competitive rationales driving such laws.

The associated emphasis on bank financing had its origins in the 1930s when strict limitations on dividend policy made it difficult to raise funds on equity markets. While initially seen as a way in which management could focus on long-term investments, the subsequent loosening of links to main banks and the concomitant failure of these banks to perform their implicit monitoring requirements, ultimately led in the late 1980s and 1990s to poor investment choices. Structures which had assisted economic growth during the 1950s and 1960s began to create problems once Japan completed its catch-up phase.

Widespread land reform was the third influential change. Land reform would seem to be the most US-inspired and successful occupation achievement.[43] The enacted program seemed to adhere closely to its explicit objective. Its stated aim was to end the era of large absentee landlords, labeled as being the mainstay of Japanese militarism. In fact, the hoped for and underlying objective promoted by Japanese politicians and bureaucrats was to create a hard core of support for conservative parties (the forerunners of the LDP) via rising rates of subsidization. This insured that a sufficient core of voters would remain in these rural districts, but doomed Japanese agriculture to increasing inefficiency.

There is a clear lesson to be learned from the way in which the Japanese cleverly subverted the aims of the occupation's reforms. Japan faced the challenge of a devastated industrial structure not by transforming itself into the sort of liberal capitalist economy envisioned by its occupiers, but by using structural elements developed in the 1930s and 1940s to compete in the post-war era against Western industrialized societies. This effort was guided by sheer necessity, utilizing the co-operative, group mentality that often has characterized Japanese society.[44] Growing rigidities and other associated problems started to emerge in the 1970s, as Japanese economic structures drifted inexorably out of step with changing world markets, eventually leading to the stagnation of the 1990s and beyond.

Four distinct growth periods reflect both post-war Japan's internal institutional and structural development and also its reaction to external factors. The first period (the "miracle economy" of 1945–1973)

---

[43] The reality, as was frequently the case, differed noticeably. Influential bureaucrats had pushed for a similar program of land reform during the war years. What appeared to be a radically inspired American departure in fact met with little concerted Japanese opposition. The reform allowed the Japanese bureaucrats to accomplish their own objectives without having to take responsibility for such a change.

[44] Explaining this as a reflection of deep seated and unchangeable Japanese culture is fraught with difficulty. Certainly the structural incentives of Japanese society and its associated economy has often emphasized and rewarded such behavior. The long lasting feudal aftertaste that has defined Japan even after the Meiji Restoration maintained strong links to this tradition. Yet the *Taisho* era of the 1920s was a time when urban Japanese were keen to imitate western sophistication and western ways. The arts and literature of the time reflected that trend perhaps best summarized by the popular label, "modern boy, modern girl." Economic stress and political turmoil ushering in the *Showa* period of Emperor Hirohito brought an end to this incipient move toward stressing individualism.

recorded double-digit growth. These rates were markedly above those of Western industrial countries, which were, for the most part, also enjoying an unprecedented post-war boom. This initial growth period lasted until the first "oil shock" in 1973. Japan as a major petroleum importer,[45] was quick to register the effect on its economy, but unlike many Western industrial countries, the Japanese were able to rapidly adjust to these changed circumstances.

During the second period of economic growth, which lasted until 1992, although slower than the initial years of rapid expansion, Japan still outperformed most other economies by having higher growth, lower inflation, and lower unemployment. Per-capita growth declined from its previous unsustainable levels to only three-fifths of its former rate, with other comparable economies experiencing a similar or even more drastic decline. However, while Europe in particular would struggle with high unemployment levels in the 1970s and 1980s, the Japanese seemed immune to these difficulties as well as to the "stagflation" which became the defining characteristic of the US economy in the 1970s. Japan's reputation for resilience, was enhanced in the 1980s, by avoiding the fluctuations experienced by the economies of the US and the UK and definitely escaping the growing and ineradicably high levels of unemployment that plagued Western European economies. By the end of the 1980s, the myth of Japan's invincibility was taken seriously not only by outsiders but by the Japanese themselves.

The Japanese were increasingly accused of unfair trade practices by Western industrial nations that felt unable to compete with what by then had become known as Japan Inc. The height of confusion occurred when it was assumed that Japanese financial muscle would inevitably come to dominate all Western competitors. This forecast served only to demonstrate how little outsiders knew about Japanese banks and, as it transpired, how little Japanese banks knew about banking. During the late 1980s, instead of laying the foundation for the Japanese economy to become dominant, the financial sector created and fanned an asset inflation which led inevitably to the collapse of those unsustainable

---

[45] Japan imports just a bit under 100 percent of its petroleum needs.

price levels and to Japan's economic growth. The end of the "bubble economy" in 1991 marked the start of a reassessment of Japan's accomplishments.

In the decade following 1992, the third and most recent period completed, Japan can be characterized as having an almost narcoleptic economy. During those years, Japan averaged no more than one per-cent per annum growth of real GDP. This was amongs the lowest of any developed economy in the post-war era and came in the midst of a period of strong gains in much of the rest of the world.[46] From seem-ing unable to make one wrong move, the Japanese appeared incapable of taking any decisive step to initiate the required policy changes or recommended structural reforms.

An extended period of growth did begin in 2003 (technically the last quarter of 2002) and extended until 2008. Though not comparable to the booms of the earlier post-war years, it did manage to be the longest. Unfortunately it was characterized by being uncomfortably dependent on ever increasing exports which in turn triggered sizable business investment and profits. Domestic spending (nearly 60 percent of the Japanese economy) stayed flat as wages were held down to remain competitive in the global economy. When Western Economies faltered and reversed one after the other in 2008, Japan's narrowly focused export market collapsed as sales of cars and consumers electronics flat lined in these countries.[47] Whether Japanese officials would manage to be more aggressive in tackling its economic problems this time around is far from clear. However, what is certain is that Japan will need a higher rate of per-capita growth to handle the demographic changes

---

[46]The Asian crisis was a distinct setback for many of the newly industrialized economies of the region. But this only interrupted a strong period of growth for these countries and barring a few exceptions like Indonesia, the expansion continued after this very sharp but relatively short break.

[47]Before the worldwide recession in 2008, much speculation centred on the idea that the Asian economies were decoupling from those of the West, particularly the Chinese. With China acting as an Eastern locomotive, Asian economies would not be dramatically affected by what occurred in the West and particularly not by America. This proved illusionary when the US, home to the World's reserve army of consumers, collapsed. This sent ripples through Asian economies directly and also indirectly via China as its roaring economy slowed along with its import demand.

characterizing an ageing economy. A more detailed assessment of each one of these periods follows.

11.3.1.1   *1945–1973 — the "miracle economy"*

Japan's development has been characterized by a pattern that could be denominated as capitalism from above. Since the Meiji Restoration, this has meant a degree of indicative planning on the part of the government. During both the Meiji Restoration and the immediate post-war years, Japan focused on the development of human capital.[48] Given the scarcity of physical capital, this strategy was the only possible way to escape the limitations of an economy that would otherwise be characterized by cheap, labor-intensive goods. The ability of the Japanese to work co-operatively proved to be their greatest strength and source of flexibility.

Labor relations and corporate structure

Job security, promotion heavily based on seniority, and a high cost of job loss all promoted an exceptional degree of loyalty and trust between management and workers. An early retirement age mandated by large corporations (55 or 60) and an influx of workers from the primary sector made a seniority system feasible (or at least a seniority system modified by merit criteria). Reluctance to recruit established employees from other corporations limited the options available to a typical "*salaryman*" working his way up a corporate ladder. By leaving, a corporate employee would be forced to seek work among smaller firms, which offered significantly lower remuneration. The belief that corporate hierarchies would ensure individual well-being created a workforce more willing to adopt and adapt to new technology, without the fear that such acceptance would translate into fewer jobs.

In the immediate post-war years, the Japanese toured US factories looking for those most advanced industrial techniques and technologies that would lend themselves most easily to the Japanese workplace.

---

[48] Japan's growth was underwritten more by process than product innovation. In particular the Japanese peculiar talent lay in their ability to utilize inputs more efficiently, especially in regard to labor.

This allowed Japan to develop and emphasize such ideas as total quality production and the *kanban* system. Both reflected the shortage of physical capital in the 1940s and 1950s. Avoiding mistakes (instead of correcting them after the fact) saved on working capital and eventually provided Japanese output with a dependably high standard of quality. Given the shortcomings of the transport system and the need to minimize working capital requirements by reducing inventory, just-in-time production provided an obvious solution to this problem. Highly skilled workers, scientists, and engineers were available to abet the development of consumer manufacturing (cars and electronics), owing to the mandatory restrictions on the growth of the defense sector. Japanese firms soon became world leaders in a number of heavy industries and later in the field of consumer electronics. Although not in these years a noted innovator (developing countries steal, borrow, or license), Japan's strong commitment to research and development did lead to an improvement of existing industrial products.

The corporate sector remained dominated by firms established and certainly shaped by the war-time years. Toyota, Nissan, Toshiba and Hitachi were at best an evolutionary extension of those formative years, rather than an attempt to depart from a familiar mold. Firms formed loose associations (*keiretsu*), reflecting the structure of dominant war time conglomerates (*zaibatsu*). These associations reduced the risk otherwise inherent in competitive markets. Vertical *keiretsu* contributed needed flexibility and certainty to production. Commitment to a limited number of suppliers, providing that their quality and price met required standards, allowed greater sharing of knowledge and especially development of new products. The structure also allowed parent corporations more easily to shift the cost of economic adjustment on to these suppliers, providing them with a strong incentive to pursue continual and incremental improvements. Horizontal *keiretsu*, with their strategy of interlocking ownership, made hostile take-overs an improbable event, allowing corporate management largely to ignore shareholder objectives. Removing this particular constraint supposedly permitted long-term planning rather than the sort of unquestioning obedience to short-term indicators that would increasingly characterize their Western counterparts. In lieu of this familiar type of corporate accountability, main banks provided loans as well as a check on imprudent corporate decision making.[49]

The *keiretsu* approach was part of a widespread attempt to reduce overall market risk. This form of sporadic cross-subsidization allowed firms affected by temporary cash-flow problems to recover. Unfortunately, a cash-rich *keiretsu* might decide to subsidize an unprofitable operation to insure continued organizational expansion. This aspect of corporate welfare may be sustainable in a growing economy, but is increasingly difficult to maintain in any prolonged economic contraction.

Government policy

The role of government policy in initiating and sustaining Japan's era of high growth remains immersed in continuing and unresolvable controversy. Recent revisionist work indicates that industrial policy merely served to sustain non-competitive, declining sectors. Even if true, this contention overlooks the fact that government protection of low productivity sectors defused potentially dangerous social pressures. These instabilities were the unintended consequences of the dislocations caused by rapid economic growth. Low productivity sectors served to absorb otherwise excess workers.

In the first period of growth, a reserve of low-cost funds financed governmental infrastructure and export industries via the Fiscal Investment and Loan Program (the FILP). What was essentially a second government budget did not require Diet approval until 1972.[50] The source of these funds was the postal savings system, as well as additional funds

---

[49]Also crucial to this particular set-up was the trading company. It allowed Japanese firms, critically short of working capital during this period, to obtain needed credit by being allowed a grace period before paying for inputs and being able to sell off inventory instead of having to hold on to it pending a sale. Risk was adeptly shifted to these larger organizations which were more capable of bearing it. Trading companies also served during these early years as unofficial diplomats, carrying Japan's economic policy to overseas ports. See Sheard (1989) for a useful discussion on the risk shifting capabilities of the major trading companies.

[50]This represents yet another classic example of the need to look for the *honne* (inner face) and avoid simply accepting the *tatemae* (outer face) provided for public consumption. The Dodge line described previously made the idea of the balanced budget a long lasting occupation tenet of economic faith. The FILP allowed Japanese lawmakers to hew to the accepted gospel while gaining access to additional required funds.

arising from various nationally administered insurance and pension schemes. Postal savings were virtually tax free and attracted a considerable share (up to one-half) of all private bank deposits. Given the high personal saving rate during this period in Japan, infrastructure and other growth inducing projects could be funded while maintaining a balanced and relatively small governmental section.

From 1949 until 1971, the yen was pegged to the dollar at the fixed rate of 360 yen to the US dollar. This clearly became an artificially low rate (partially a reward for Japan's role as loyal ally) as the Japanese economy grew. Nonetheless, given Japan's initially small economy (GDP per capita was $1873 in 1950 compared to $11,017 in 1970), and the fact that until 1973 domestic and export growth was balanced, Japan's trade surplus remained relatively small. Owing to the pegged yen and capital controls, monetary policy remained almost entirely immune to changes in international capital markets. In other words, a generation of Japanese bankers felt no need to evaluate the underlying risk of their operations, protected as they were from outside shocks.

Government protection combined with cheap funds encouraged industrial development. By the end of the 1950s, only about 20 percent of Japan's imports were free of either bans or quotas. During the post-war occupation (1945–1952), US vehicles filled the Japanese market, owing to limited domestic production and the suspension of pre-war restrictions on imports. MITI (Ministry of International Trade and Industry) subsequently restricted foreign exchange allocations and imposed a value added tax of 40 percent on imported automobiles. As a result, domestic production blossomed. Between 1951 and 1961 the ratio of imported cars to domestic sales declined from 44.6 percent to 0.7 percent. Imports remained at this negligible level for the next 20 years. It is doubtful that an entirely indigenous Japanese car industry would have existed without direct post-war government protection designed to foster that sector. Government and industry enthusiastically embraced this policy since it maintained limited foreign reserves while providing a large outlet for a revived steel industry.[51]

---

[51] It is unlikely that the industry that did develop would have been as capable of taking advantage of the "oil shocks" of the 1970s in the absence of such assistance.

Household sector

Post-war Japan placed a distinctive emphasis on economic growth, focusing on the need to draw level with Western industrialized countries, much as it did during the Meiji restoration. Although living standards did rise rapidly during this period, Japan was a society with a distinct focus on production rather than consumption. Government welfare expenditures were initially very low given the limited economic capability that characterizes any developing country. Even by 1965, these outlays consisted of less than one percent of national income, leaving Japan at the very bottom of the spending tables formulated by the Organization for Economic Co-operation and Development (OECD). This was feasible due to several factors. In the 1950s, Japan was still a very young country with just five percent of the population over 65. The extended family, in particular the heavily burdened daughter-in-law, took care of the elderly. Even in the early 1990s, 60 percent of the elderly were still living with their son and daughter-in-law (compared with 20 percent in the US). Employers came to be major providers of social services. This included housing and recreational activities, as well as pensions and health care. The fact that such a large percentage of welfare services remained in the private sector would emphasize the need for a predictably growing economy. Private rather than public provision would increase the role played by job security and insure a relatively stable work force. Japanese employees would change jobs much less frequently than their counterparts.

Lacking publicly provided security, Japanese workers responded to demands for corporate loyalty. (The Japanese of this era took fewer than nine days leave per year.) The evolving hierarchical structure cultivated a perceived Japanese desire to belong, to be part of a group. Widespread consultations (*nemiwashi*) became the norm before decisions were taken. This allowed responsibility to be shared broadly as well as rewards. Rapid responses might be fraught with difficulty, but implementation was highly effective once a decision was taken.

From the Western viewpoint, the Japanese were still no more than "workaholics living in rabbit hutches." Population density ensured that housing remained small and expensive. The problem was exacerbated by legal restrictions and societal norms. Agricultural subsidies meant that land, even in urban regions, remained farm land rather than shifting into the ever growing housing sector. Land itself as an asset, was lightly taxed, with agricultural land taxed below residential or commercial use rates. The belief in an ever rising value of land-led owners to hold on to their property.

The Japanese however do share a desire to own their own homes, and considering housing costs, the percentage privately owned is quite high (approximately 60 percent). The enormous postal savings system helped to underwrite home ownership. Tax exempt postal savings could be lent at below market rates to the government Trust Fund Bureau which could turn around and lend at subsidized rates to the Housing Loan Corporation (HLC). In this way, the HLC became Japan's biggest housing loan originator.[52]

The social safety net showed signs of expansion with expenditure on health care growing rapidly, although from a very low base. The rate of physicians per 1000 inhabitants however still lagged behind Western standards, and the quality of care remained variable. Government protection of the pharmaceutical sector resulted in a non-competitive and non-innovative industry, riddled by scandals involving the dubious approval of dangerous drugs. The production psychology that dominated these early post-war years led the government to provide little protection for ordinary citizens against possible corporate misdeeds. Nor were funds expended on public and recreational facilities to any marked extent. In a work-saturated environment, the driving force was rebuilding Japan into a dominant economic power. The Japanese continued their drive for regional influence through other than military means. However, at this stage of its economic development, Japan remained a country clearly looking to its future.

11.3.1.2 *1973–1992 — A period of dominance*

Japan depends heavily on imports for its petroleum supply (by the 1990s, 99.7 percent of its requirements were imported, with

---

[52]The purpose of such housing loans was middle class welfare. The structure of loans eliminated their usefulness for low income families, while limitations on the size of qualified property meant that it held little appeal for wealthier members of society.

79.4 percent coming from the Middle East), prior to 1973, with petroleum prices remaining at low levels, Japan followed the West in fostering energy intensive industries. The sudden increase in petroleum prices, combined with the ending of the Vietnam War, was a severe setback for the Japanese economy. Industrial production declined by nine percent in 1974, profits disappeared, and some 11,000 firms shut down. How to pay for the dramatically increased outflows of capital without institutionalizing either inflation or a cyclically stagnating economy became the paramount problem. In resolving this major challenge, Japan would make a decided break with common Western practices. The "oil shock" turned into an opportunity rather than a catastrophe. By 1983, Japan would have withstood both the first and second (1978) oil shock to emerge as the world's second largest economy. Japan's success in resolving this unforeseen challenge would set in motion not only measures to maintain its current account position and to permit the economy to grow in an uninterrupted fashion but also would foster structural distortions. These eventually led to the "bubble economy" of the late 1980s and its subsequent collapse in the 1990s.

From the early 1970s, growth in aggregate demand began to fall short of growth in output, a pattern that has become increasingly pronounced since the late 1970s. From 1979, Japan's growth in domestic demand has, on average, lagged a full percentage point behind the pace of output growth. (Reflecting this gap, the current account surplus widened dramatically, growing to more than four percent of GDP in 1986.) Japanese administrators attempted to offset the additional expense of higher petroleum costs by increasing its exports. With productivity rising faster than wages, domestic demand therefore gave way in importance to rising exports.[53] Docile in-house unions co-operated in a cost sharing effort aimed at keeping

---

[53] The myth that equates the export driven growth of South Korea or more recently China to the development of the post war Japanese economy needs closer scrutiny. An examination of trends prior to the first oil shock indicates a balanced growth pattern with the domestic economy growing in stride with that of the export sector (based on contributions to GDP increases). It was the initial need to pay for suddenly more costly oil that led to a more deliberate export strategy. Once the catch up period was for all intents and purposes complete, with capacity constraints no longer an issue, the key macroeconomic problem shifted to one of deficient demand. The initial resolution, until the mid-eighties, was a strategy of ever increasing exports.

wages internationally competitive. Workers accepted a smaller share of productivity increases in return for secure jobs. This was crucial, as during this period Japanese productivity increases were clearly the highest among OECD countries. Consensus driven Japanese employees did not engage in inflationary wage demands. As a consequence, wage increases varied little among industrial sectors. The close collaboration that had developed between union leaders, employer associations, and government bureaucrats resulted in the unions agreeing to make the maximum possible concessions.

The government supported employment in structurally depressed heavy industries (such as steel and shipbuilding), while such value added industries as cars, consumer electronics, and machine tools gained an increasing percentage of exports, as well as absorbing a greater share of the work force.[54] By 1987, road vehicles accounted for 25 percent of total exports compared with 15 percent in 1975. The contribution of the iron and steel industry however, declined from 18 percent in 1975 to five percent in 1987. Japanese manufacturing breakthroughs delivered higher quality output at lower costs. This allowed Japan to maintain a substantial high value-added manufacturing sector in con-trast to other industrialized countries that were rapidly switching to more service dominated economies. In Japan, the number of employ-ees working in the primary sector decreased from 53.4 percent of the work force in 1947 down to 17.4 percent in 1970 and then only a mere 7.2 percent by 1990. However, the numbers employed in the secondary sector (manufacturing, mining, and construction) rose from 23.3 percent in 1947 to 35.2 percent in 1970 and only tailed off to 33.6 percent as late as 1990.

The success of the manufacturing sector, particularly in exporting to the US and Europe, enabled the Japanese not only to subsidize their agricultural markets by increasing amounts, but to continue to

---

[54]The potential weakness of this targeted export strategy became apparent more than twenty years later in 2008. Slumping markets in North America and Europe compounded by a slowing Chinese economy hit Japan particularly hard given that its engines of growth had become heavily dependent on just a handful of export sectors. Japanese export strategy was noticeable for a lack of intra-industry trade during this period. Manufactured goods formed a relatively negligible proportion of its imports. This stood in contrast to other developed countries where intra-industry trade was steadily gaining in importance.

protect jobs in unproductive service and financial sectors. Protection (and income redistribution) extended as well to declining industries such as textiles, steel, and shipbuilding.

When compared with the export performance of the US during this critical period, Japan began to be regarded in the 1980s as invincible. Appearances, at least superficially, conveyed the impression of an economy that had come out of nowhere to rapidly dominate international trade. Both the US and its European counterparts saw Japan's growing exports as a threat to their domestic manufacturing industries. The disappearance of US-manufactured television sets, for example, became for many US politicians a warning of the dire future in store for the entire domestic manufacturing industry.[55] Less competitive countries ascribed Japan's success to unfair practices such as "dumping" overseas while protecting domestic markets.[56] The Japanese responded by making straightforward efficiency claims. Accurate analysis was beside the point. Japan's reluctance to import inevitably increased trade tensions. Political solutions led to "voluntary" quota restrictions on Japanese exports such as steel, televisions, cars, and semiconductors.

Attempts to open up the Japanese market encountered little success during this period. Debate over whether or not non-tariff barriers were the root cause of the problem remained an unsolved issue. Both sides simply chose to interpret data to support their preconceived objectives. Whatever its true cause, the Japanese export success was even more remarkable given the steady strengthening of the yen once it was allowed to float from 1973. Starting in that year at 301.5 yen to the US dollar, by 1992 the yen's value against the dollar had then risen to 158.8.

Labor relations and corporate structure

The special characteristics of what might be termed the "Japanese System" became more pronounced during this period. Internally

---

[55] A popular opinion of the time equated a strong and sizeable manufacturing sector with a strong and vibrant economy. Doomsayers warned that the US could not expect to sustain an economy where everyone performed services for one another. An economy produced goods and the US was letting the manufacture of one good after another slip into the Japanese sphere.
[56] The assumption here was that the Japanese could only be succeeding by cheating in one way or another. See the parallels (Dower, 1986) with US sentiment toward Japan during World War II.

generated cash flow enabled many of the largest firms to become largely self-financing. The indirect system of financing through the main bank, and the associated restraints exerted by these generally more conservative organizations, weakened substantially. The need for the government to draw on national savings through bond issues in the years immediately following the first "oil shock" (expanding the social safety net for example) initiated a loosening of financial control, leading to the beginning of financial deregulation. This further shifted the balance between main banks and their borrowers as more funds began to be raised directly. Corporate investment, although not at the insupportable rates of the previous period, was still considerably higher in absolute terms than in corresponding industrialized countries. Critics contended that the essential lack of accountability to any stringent monitoring agent allowed Japanese managers to push for market expansion whatever its profitability. Even so, corporate investment could not sufficiently absorb the huge lump of national saving produced every year. Japan inexorably accumulated a current account surplus. It rose steadily from $4,700 million in 1981 to $87,000 million in 1986, before a strengthening yen reduced it to $35,000 million in 1990. However, this ineradicably persistent surplus reached $117,500 million just as the Japanese bubble burst in 1992. A result of this expanding surplus was a corresponding increase in direct foreign investment abroad. Although initially a way to overcome trade barriers or to secure essential raw materials, rising wages and a steadily appreciating yen began to make Japanese exporters less competitive, especially when faced with improving performances by foreign firms.

Moving production offshore, especially to East Asia, became one way of constraining cost. Starting from $227 million in 1966, investment reached a record $67,000 million in 1989 (17 percent of that year's world total). This was nearly equal to the US ($40,000 million) and the UK ($37,000 million) combined. Projecting continued expansion into the foreseeable future, Japanese firms increased their hiring, in effect attempting to hoard labor in anticipation of a future shortage. Job stability became even more entrenched, especially in large firms. Mid-career recruits became rarer, with most workers entering corporate life directly from school and seldom switching employment after the age of 30. Japanese workers came to expect secure employment and an absence of risk.

Government policy

The "oil shock" plus rising demand for social services caused the Japanese to deviate from the conservative budgeting approach laid down by their occupation mentor, Joseph Dodge. Japan was obliged to address the dual threats of stagnation and inflation, while learning to accept a floating exchange rate. Consumer prices increased 24.5 percent in the 12 months proceeding December 1974. For the first time, Japan recorded budget deficits, seeking to stimulate the economy while using constrictive monetary policy to restrain inflation.

An ensuing thrust into world capital markets led to a gradual deregulation of the financial system. In 1980, foreign exchange controls were abolished and large security companies were allowed to borrow in the call market. In the following year, city banks were permitted to buy in the *gensaki* (repo market). Having been given the okay to sell government bonds over the counter in the previous year, in 1984 a government bond futures market was established. By 1993, interest rates on time deposits had been completely liberalized and in 1994, interest rates on non-time deposits (including postal savings) were also liberalized. This signaled a breakdown of the traditional role of corporate lending as the almost exclusive focus of city banks (the main bank role). The search for alternative financial functions in part fueled the lethal bubble economy ending this period of growth.[57]

Household sector

While the US was agonizing over the problem of its growing underclass and Europe worried about increasing structural unemployment, the Japanese were busily maintaining their position as the archetypical middle-class country. Income distribution remained relatively equal

---

[57] Financial regulation has for a number of decades proven to precede an inevitable financial crisis. Banks when let free to compete inevitably seem incapable of meeting these new demands. Tending to underestimate risk, they overextend, placing themselves and the financial system in a perilous situation.

when compared with other industrialized countries. Despite the rapid expansion of the corporate sector, executive management staff did not achieve gains similar to those won by their US counterparts. While executive compensation in the US reached 30 times that of the wages earned on the factory floor, Japan's levels barely reached a multiple of 10. The Japanese idea of creating a low-risk society where no one was excluded seemed within reach.

However, despite, or perhaps more accurately, because of the rising sums being spent on government subsidized mortgages, the increase in house prices in the 1980s started to raise the cost of housing beyond the reach of younger people attempting to enter the market for the first time, thus denying to many the very symbol of middle-class life.[58] Houses were bought by an increasingly older demographic group. Children tended to remain with their parents longer, while trying to save for the necessary down payment required to secure their first home. Correspondingly, marriages were delayed and the birth rate edged steadily down. Given the increase of single children in these late marriages, this change tended to amplify the problem since traditionally the eldest son bore responsibility for the care of aged parents. With a greater percentage of eligible men being single children, women faced the prospect of becoming the primary carer for their in-laws and further delayed any marriage commitment.

Urban land prices increased fivefold between 1970 and 1991. In the six biggest cities (Tokyo, Yokohama, Osaka, Nagoya, Sapporo, and Kobe), these prices increased six-fold. The major cities continued to expand, creating ever lengthening commuter journeys to work. With husbands often at home only at weekends, the households increasingly became the sole domain of women. Education became the domain of "the education crazed mamas" left by their "*salarymen*" husbands to look after the household and raise the children. The path to a successful career increasingly lay in securing entry into a good university. Places were awarded according to examination results, which stressed prodigious memorization skills. Given the very limited places, competition

---

[58] As the housing bubble gained impetus, home ownership declined. In 1988, 62 percent of all households owned their own home, by 1993 only 60 percent.

for them steadily increased, and children spent more time studying. Not only did they attend their required classes, but spent additional hours at "cram" schools (*juku*). Ironically, once in university little in the way of serious education or training occurred. Corporations conducted their own extensive and specific on-the-job training, while universities served mainly to screen potential applicants.

The "bubble economy"

The Nikkei average index of stocks plunged from a record high of 38,915 in December 1989 to 14,309 in August 1992, a decline of 63.2 percent. This was an unprecedented drop by post-war standards, and made clear to even the most optimistic observer that Japan's "bubble economy" had definitely ended. While other countries successfully managed post-bubble recoveries, the Japanese economy displayed a surprising paralysis going from stagnation to fitful growth and then into recession.

Asset inflation implies an underlying miscalculation of risk. Credit expands rapidly, in part because borrowers undertake increasingly dubious projects and fanciful investments encouraged by low interest rates and easy lending regimes. Lenders underestimate the riskiness of providing credit by overvaluing the underlying asset purchase with the loan.[59] In Japan's case, an extended period of success led business leaders and bankers to confuse asset inflation with real economic growth. Since the start of the decade, the Bank of Japan had steadily decreased its discount rate (9 percent in 1980 to 2.5 percent by 1987). Even more importantly, to jump start domestic demand after the Plaza Accord strengthened the value of the yen, the Bank of Japan used its traditional tool of window guidance to foist large flows of cash into the hands of the banking establishment.[60] Given that the worst strategy a

---

[59] This phenomenon is hardly new, characterizing every financial bubble since at least the time of the tulip mania. Keynes (1964) describes the basis of asset inflation in his discussion of borrower's and lender's risk and the way uncertainty affects decision making. Such lessons have been routinely forgotten as was made evident in the sub-prime mortgage crises. Accumulated bad judgment came due in 2007 and subsequently extended further to affect the wider global financial system and world economy.

[60] See Wenner (2005) for evidence of this policy of force-feeding the Japanese banking system.

bank can adopt (other than losing funds) is simply to sit on cash, banks aggressively expanded their lending practises.

The historically low rates achieved in 1987 (2.5 percent) were sustained for another two years by a central bank determined to demonstrate that Japan was immune to the type of economic instability that plagued foreign countries. Easy credit, combined with rising confidence in the assured destiny of the Japanese economy, led to an unfortunate sense of overconfidence. Borrowers believed that their loans would inevitably be rescheduled. Owing to the widely held view that land prices were incapable of falling, banks did not take the trouble of evaluating the basic riskiness of the loans. Ignoring whether the proposed project was able to generate the required level of cash flow, lenders simply adhered to the widely held expectation that the value of any underlying collateral (often real estate) could only appreciate. Profits seemed assured to those bankers able to make the greatest quantity of loans no matter who the recipients might be.[61] Government bureaucrats emboldened by a successful resistance to the 1987 foreign stock exchange crashes, assumed that they could control and rectify any conceivable difficulty that might be encountered as opposed to their more fallible foreign counterparts. Memories of failure dimmed, remaining in the minds only of the pre-war elderly. Government expenditure and taxes were necessarily low, given the security provided by a reliably growing economy and a private sector that protected jobs. Japan while gaining a corresponding reputation for invincibility, failed to recognize the underlying problems that were emerging as a result of this period of prolonged asset inflation. The economy as a whole depended on a narrow group of manufacturing firms that in turn faced increased competition from revived US and European rivals, as well as new East Asian entrants.

Main banks became ever more aggressive lenders. This was a typically unforeseen effect of the initial stages of financial deregulation, coupled with the continued success of corporate Japan. Main banks were

---

[61]Widespread loans to criminal elements (*yakuza*) and associated front companies were estimated to comprise at least twenty percent of all loans made during this period. Often banks assured recipients of such loans that there was no downside risk attached.

forced to turn elsewhere for lending purposes given the ability of large corporations to tap credit markets directly (through commercial paper) or the attraction of selling shares in a rising market. As in the US or Australia, inexperienced lenders facing an increasingly competitive loan market gravitated toward making more questionable loans including murky deals in collaboration with organized crime (*yakuza*).[62] Corporations also realized that money could be made quickly and more easily through speculation (financial engineering or *zaitechi*) than by solid investment. Households contributed to this economic souf-flé by pouring in their own net financial assets (13,000 million yen) which also fueled the rapidly expanding bubble. The inevitable price collapse occurred as the Bank of Japan, finally taking action after a two-year delay, rapidly raised the discount rate from 2.5 percent in 1989 to 6.2 percent in mid-1990 and maintained that level for nearly a year.[63]

The underlying weakness in the banking sector would ultimately limit recovery and by 1997 push Japan into its worst post-war recession. Much of the difficulty in implementing any fundamental structural change lay in a refusal on the part of leading members of the "iron triangle" to accept the possibility that what had worked in the past would not continue to so in the future. Equally, if not more responsible, was a monetary policy that largely starved the Japanese economy of credit at crucial periods. The Bank of Japan seemed determined to push their agenda of structural reform without regard to the short-term economic fallout. Previous post-war success led the Japanese government and business leaders to feel no sense of urgency. Instead, Japanese bureaucrats followed the standard formula of protecting each particular sector of the economy from bearing too much of the pain of any economic downturn and of protecting their business clients such as those located in the financial sector. Because of this approach, the Japanese economy

---

[62] Peter Hill (2003) makes some interesting points pertaining to this matter.

[63] Despite the impression that many central bankers desire to convey, interest rate adjustment is rather a blunt tool with which to attempt to control a complex economy. The danger of maintaining an inappropriate interest rate for too sustained a period is obvious. Perceived inflation threats are thus remedied by flattening a given economy.

would miss out on the economic growth most other economies enjoyed in the 1990s.

11.3.1.3 *1992–2003 — The anorexic economy*

In 1996, compared with the previous year, real GDP growth of 3.9 percent was recorded. In 1997 however, GDP expanded by only 0.9 percent. By 1998, the rate of unemployment exceeded 4.0 percent of the labor force (compared with 2.2 percent in 1992). The second quarter of 1998 yielded an even bleaker result than anticipated. GDP contracted for the third consecutive quarter making this downturn the worst in Japan's post-war history. A decline of 0.8 percent (an annualized decrease of 3.3 percent) made it clear that Japan could be approaching a dangerous deflationary spiral. Growth essentially stopped between 1998 and 2002 with the economy growing only by a negligible annual rate of 0.2 percent per annum. Private corporate investment in the second quarter of 1998 had fallen by 5.5 percent. Between their peak in 1991 and sober reality of mid-1998, land prices for residential sites had decreased by nearly 50 percent while those for commercial property had declined by as much as 80 percent. Housing starts continued to fall, with housing investment in the second quarter of 1998 down by 1 percent. Reflecting stock market movements, the Nikkei average fell below 14,000 and started to approach historic lows (eventually dipping below 8,000). By mid-1998, the large amounts of funds being invested in 10-year government bonds had driven the yield down to a record low of 0.77 percent, the call rate being an insignificant 0.25 percent. Despite tax cuts and fiscal stimulus measures, worried citizens continued to place funds in postal-savings accounts. Consumers remained concerned about employment and their pensions, feeling betrayed by bureaucrats and business leaders whom they had implicitly trusted.

Consumers who had largely sustained the meagre growth of the early 1990s had simply stopped spending. They would not resume any significant spending thoughout this period with real wage growth virtually stuck at zero. To simply maintain their standard of living, Japanese households would start spending out of their savings. From a rate of 11 percent in the mid-1990s, household saving would drop steadily to

Percent Disposable Income

Patterns of Household Saving
2008 data includes recent quarter forecasts

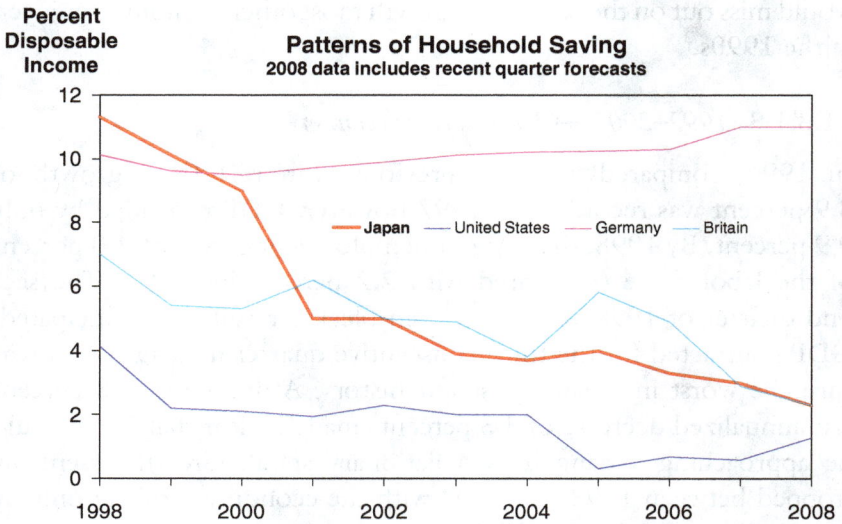

Japan — United States — Germany — Britain

1998   2000   2002   2004   2006   2008

Fig. 11.1

rates nearing 3 percent by the end of this slow growth period.[64] Japan would come closer to resembling the spendthrift Anglo-American model than those of continental Europe.

A zero-interest-rate policy failed to have any noticeable effect when combined with a too tight credit policy. Nor was fiscal policy able to boost aggregate demand. Government spending deficits were financed by bond issues largely taken up by the banking community.[65] Any potential expansionary tendency from deficit spending was largely nullified with funds being withdrawn almost simultaneously from the private sphere.

---

[64] A common assumption of many writers had been that Japanese households were culturally conditioned to save significant portions of their income. The historical record however shows that high rates of saving were deliberately induced in the war time economy and maintained in the post war period. In periods of rapid economic growth, household spending typically lags behind increasing income in developing countries. Household saving soars especially where social safety nets are weak or non-existent. In Japan, however, faced with stagnating real incomes, the Japanese reacted more like verifiers of Milton Friedman's permanent income hypothesis than culturally determined actors.

[65] Banks could borrow funds at zero percent from the Bank of Japan and gain risk-free income from purchased government bonds.

Given the bad loans Japanese banks labored under (at its height an estimated 100 trillion yen worth), the sort of lending and borrowing required for economic expansion simply did not occur. Businesses intent on cleaning up the excess debt on their balance sheets moved from a negative saving regime that characterized the "bubble" years to one that was strongly positive. Banks played accounting tricks, rolled over or forgave bad loans, but essentially tied up funds in failing businesses instead of extending new loans to expanding concerns. During this decade, Japanese financial markets operated in a strictly perverse manner. Funds flowed to the least instead of the most productive borrowers. Because of the quantity of dubious loans granted, banks could only stay afloat by extending lifelines to their most dubious customers. To recognize reality would have been to acknowledge their own insolvency.

Despite the apparent seriousness of the economic situation throughout this period, the urgency of the problem was reflected in the words of politicians and government officials rather than by their deeds. Slow growth was not immediately alarming, with the dire warnings focused on an imminent financial collapse failing to materialize. Gross national income by 2003 was $35,497.46 per person, still second highest amongst nations. Continuing trade surpluses created the world's largest foreign currency reserves. Unemployment would creep above five percent at its highest point, but any pain resulting from this persistent slow growth seemed widely diffused. Tokyo for instance continued to appear a vibrant, growing metropolis throughout all these economic woes.

Response to the end of the "bubble" economy

Superficially, the economic downturn that began in 1992 appeared to differ little from the distortions representative of any business cycle. An excessive build-up of investment stock would normally imply a decrease in investment (business fixed investment did decline over a three-year period), falling asset prices, and an eventual recovery resulting from the depreciation of existing business stock and a much lower level of asset prices. Unfortunately, underlying the expected weak level of investment was a more fundamental problem that curbed any potential recovery.

The banks and the financial system at large symbolized much of what was wrong with the Japanese economy, particularly its corporate governance and accompanying betrayal of trust. Scandals at the largest brokerage house, Nomura securities, and at one of the major banks at that time, Dai-ichi Kangyo, in late 1995 and early 1996 revealed that a basic "protection racket" was being utilized to transfer funds to *yakuza* (organized crime) in the form of loans never intended to be repaid and stock purchases with no downside risk (losses were made good by the brokers). Regulators, such as those at the Ministry of Finance, were clearly more concerned with the best interests of banking officials than with economic growth or welfare. (Bank examiners forewarned the relevant corporate officials of audits, allowing funds to be moved around in such a way as to disguise the weakness of a bank's capital base.) The Japanese bureaucrats, almost totally responsible for policy initiatives, maintained their status quo position in the expectation that asset prices had reached a record low and were about to recover.

The "convoy" mentality held firm as Ministry of Finance officials made only marginal attempts to prevent any abrupt or considerable disruptions to the financial system. This meant that stronger banks, for instance, would be expected to support their weaker counterparts, either via forced mergers or cash infusions. In turn, banks would bail out corporations by rolling over their loans at subsidized interest rates or by directing additional funds in their direction. In contrast with how efficient financial markets should work, this convoy system insured that resources flowed to the most inefficient sectors of the economy during a recession. This was an effective recipe for prolonging rather than minimizing the length of any downturn. However, this approach did reduce the burden borne by any one sector or firm. As noted before, such risks and costs were effectively socialized.

To boost the economy and restore confidence, policymakers fell back on traditional remedies. The export led growth of the 1970s became a paradigm of post-bubble strategy. (After a long delay, this approach did partially pull Japan out of the worse of its problems, thanks largely to an inexhaustible Chinese market.) Accordingly, current account surpluses rose steadily. However, during the 1990s, some strength of this strategy was undermined by rising yen values, especially against the dollar (reaching a high point of 80 yen to the dollar) and by the threat of US reprisals.[66] Japanese manufacturers responded to the strong yen and high wages by shifting more operations offshore, both to re-export back into Japan and to sell into booming East Asian markets (especially those of Indonesia and Thailand). As the East Asian boom gathered momentum in 1996, 44.1 percent of Japanese exports went to other Asian countries with 37.3 percent of imports being of Asian origin. Japanese banks shoveled funds into East Asia in the hope of recouping their domestic losses.

The other policy was one of fiscal stimulus. Budgets that had reverted to surpluses during the era of asset inflation quickly changed direction. As a percentage of GDP, the budget deficit increased from 3.0 percent in 1994, to 3.9 percent in 1995, and then 4.1 percent in 1996. Unfortunately, the primary driving force behind fiscal stimulus was repayment for political support of the LDP rather than an attempt to revive the economy. Much of the money was spent on dubious construction projects intended to reward key constituencies and more importantly, to float insolvent, but very large construction companies.[67]

Whatever the actual wisdom of the exact nature of the fiscal stimulus program, it did seem to yield results. The 3.9 percent increase in GDP recorded for 1996 easily surpassed the OECD average of 2.7 percent. Investment surged. What abruptly halted this incipient recovery was a concatenation of three basic events. The first involved the Ministry of Finance acting on dubious economic principles and backed by insufficient evidence. Assuming that the Japanese economy was solidly established on its course of long-term growth, the Hashimoto government dutifully pushed fiscal consolidation forward. Despite still fragile

---

[66]As the decade of the nineties wore on and Japan's economic problems became more apparent, trade issues with the US became less pressing. For instance, as a candidate, Bill Clinton ran on a "get tough" approach to trade conflicts with Japan. By his second administration, such problems no longer registered as part of his political agenda.

[67]By 1998 the total interest bearing liabilities owed by the 119 largest builders totaled 10,400,000 million yen. Indirectly, this financial support also maintained the viability of barely solvent banks as well. Japan, a country with slightly less than one-half of the population of the US and covering a considerably smaller geographic area, deployed more cement annually than did the entire US economy.

consumer spending, policymakers cut government expenditure while increasing consumption taxes. This had predictable results.

At the same time, from mid-1997, the Asian crisis, as it became known, led to the contraction of the regional export market while loans that were once regarded as a life saver thrown to the capital base of the Japanese banking system now threatened to turn into a depth charge undermining that base instead. Banks had outstanding East Asian loans totalling $265 billion. These largely unrepayable debts were mostly the responsibility of Indonesia, Thailand, and South Korea. The Asian crisis also temporarily removed an investment destination for opportunity starved Japanese corporations with domestic expansion limited. In 1998, the EPA (Economic Planning Agency) estimated that in total, the 4,500 major Japanese companies surveyed planned to reduce direct foreign investment by 57 percent. That would indicate a fall in such investment from 4.2 trillion yen in 1990 to 1.8 trillion yen in the space of eight years.[68]

The last and ultimately most negative factor, one exacerbated by the previous two, proved to be the emergence and realization of the extent of the bad loan problem, deliberately shrouded until 1997–1998 by the efforts of bureaucrats and bankers. Policy under succeeding LDP governments (Hashimoto, Obuchi, Moro, and Koizumi) underplayed the seriousness of the banking sector problem while providing some needed emergency funds to keep large banking concerns afloat. Large city banks did not actually go under. The very largest merged into four mega-banks (soon after three as the weakest, UFJ, merged successfully with the Bank of Tokyo-Mitsubishi in January 2006). This merger movement, encouraged by MOF bureaucrats, had more to do with creating banks too big to fail and in that way boosting customer confidence than with any conceivable economies of scale or scope.

Foreign direct investment into Japan grew significantly with Renault gaining control of a failing Nissan Motors and successfully turning it around. (Daimler had less joy with running Mitsubishi and has since relinquished interest in that concern.) Prime Minister Koizumi

---

[68] Total foreign direct investment outflows went from 20.5 percent of the world's total in 1990 to 2.6 percent in 1999.

appeared to actually court foreign investment.[69] Working counter to such encouragement, it has still proven difficult for even Japanese, let alone an overseas firm, to launch hostile takeovers against poorly performing corporations.

The period between 1998 and 2003 alternated between cautious optimism and black-hearted despair. In fact, Japan's failure to either recover some of its former glory or to sink into a total miasma of despair helped China to become the new economic epicenter in East Asia with Japan going off-radar to some extent. It should be noted that recovery seemed possible in 2000. Share values were rising smartly, growth picked up from its low or even negative base with price deflation easing. Unfortunately, superficial appearances were misleading. Share values largely reflected an influx of "stupid foreign funds" gulled by a false belief in a growing recovery. However, any stock rally was bound to falter since the desire by Japanese banks to unload their share holdings led ultimately to an implicit cap on prices. As it turned out, increased foreign holdings merely replaced bank (and other *keiretsu* type) shareholdings.

Also unchanged was consumer spending (composing approximately 55 percent of aggregate demand). Stagnant wages, a sustained drop in housing prices, and the need to support both ageing parents and stay at home children put strains on household budgets. Moreover, an on again, off again monetary policy that seemed to tighten credit at the first sign of any recovery doomed Japan's economic prospects.

11.3.1.4 *Future prospects — 2003 and onwards*

It must be said that despite government policies, including the supposed reform agenda put forth by Prime Minister Koizumi, the Japanese economy pulled out of recession in late 2002 and noticeable growth began during 2003. This latest cycle of economic growth would average 2.1 percent as measured from the trough of the recession (fourth quarter of 2001) to the peak of the expansion (first quarter

---

[69] Foreign direct investment into Japan was negligible before the turn of this century. In 1985 it amounted to 1.1 percent of total world inflows. By 1999 Japan's share was virtually unchanged at 1.3 percent of total world inflow.

2008). Two causes sustained this recovery. The remarkable growth of China boosted exports. Initially up to one half of the increased growth derived from this single source. Soon China (including Hong Kong) became Japan's largest single trading partner with trade amounting to 22 trillion yen or 20.1 percent of total trade in 2003. This compares with bilateral trade of 20.48 trillion yen with the US. Moreover, unlike Japan's trade with the US, that with China remained largely complementary. An ever rising trade surplus would provide approximately one-third of GDP growth over this five-year expansionary period.

Responding to this steady and seemingly endless increase of exports, business investment, including business inventories, also grew steadily with business profits booming. Like trade, business investment, looking toward an ever growing Chinese market, would also account for a third of the growth during Japan's recent expansion. In the post-bubble decade, business focus tended to be limited to reducing costs and paying down corporate debt loads. After a period of excess, Japanese executives were intent on restoring their balance sheets and ridding themselves of excess capacity and dubious assets. Net business saving turned resolutely positive, constraining any expansion of aggregate demand. Weak consumer demand belied the robustness of the recovery. Without the expansion carrying over into the domestic economy, apparent Japanese strength remained at the mercy of overseas economies. With Japanese corporations intent on remaining competitive and relying increasingly on part-time labor, real wages fell in every year during this period except in 2005. Only the willingness of Japanese households to reach into their savings maintained domestic spending. Even though total real compensation for workers 2007 rose only 2 percent above its 1997 level, spending increased by 12 percent.[70] So though unemployment in June 2005 dropped to 4.2 percent from its 2003 peak of 5.5 percent

---

[70]The fragility of domestic demand has been a persistent problem since the end of the bubble economy with real income largely stagnating. This problem has become distressingly clear during this financially inspired economic crisis. Japan's per capita gross domestic product, a measure of economic prosperity, had been third highest in 1991. In 2008, Japan achieved a rather dismal 18th place according to World Bank figures. Average household income peaked in 1994. The figure of 5.56 million yen ($58,000) in 2007 represents a 19-year low.

this did not translate into a substantial flow on effect from the booming trade sector to household budgets. Even the trade surplus itself remained particularly fragile with almost all of the growth limited to cars and IT equipment although these sectors account for only a fifth of all manufacturing activity.

Japanese economic health was therefore deceptive, especially if one focused on the honne rather than the tatemae of the prevailing situation. Any continued economic buoyancy had become overly reliant on overseas trade. Japanese manufacturers by 2008 depended on exports for 57 percent of their sales compared to only 35 percent 10 years ago. Although as the world economy and especially that of China boomed, theories promoting a decoupling of Asia from any serious dependency on North American or European well being also rose proportionately. With Japan gearing up for unlimited Chinese growth, the initial financial crisis developing in the US in 2007 seemed relatively trivial. Japanese banks had learned hard lessons from its post-bubble decade. Its three major banks had cleaned up bad assets and pursued a very low risk, conservative strategy.

Reality hit as a financial problem supposedly limited to the subprime mortgage market inevitably spread to major worldwide financial institutions. As the US and European countries fell into recession in 2008 (the US shrinking by more than 5 percent in the last quarter while Britain decreased by 6 percent), the fallacy behind a decoupled global economy became apparent. With Americans no longer acting as a reserve army of consumers, Japan was hit directly and indirectly. An ever strengthening yen against the US dollar (slipping below 90 yen to the dollar) combined with a weakening US economy hit exports directly. China also started to falter as its export-oriented economy found world markets no longer eager for its output. (Exports fell in dollar terms by 13 percent in the last quarter of 2008.) Growth by the end of 2008 (on a year to December basis) was down to 6.5 percent. Healthy compared to the rest of the world but not anything like the double digit results that preceded this outcome. (More importantly for those countries depending on the locomotive power of the Chinese economy, imports were down by 21 percent in the 12 months to December 2008.) With China being Japan's leading trading partner, such a drop in growth would inevitably lead to serious repercussions. In fact Japanese exports would drop 35 percent in December 2008 compared to the previous December. Far from being led by growing trade surpluses, Japan recorded two consecutive months of trade deficits (October–November), the first such occurrence since the oil shocks of 1980. Even worse news came in January 2009 with exports dropping by 46 percent compared to that month one year earlier.[71] Those sectors which had powered Japanese growth now led its collapse. November 2008 shipments of vehicles were down 31.9 percent while microchips and other electronic components fell 29 percent during the same month. The result was a 13-percent drop in manufacturing output for 2008. In response to these woeful results, forecasters at UBS, HBSC, and Morgan Stanley believe that a GDP decline of anywhere between 6 and 6.5 percent. In fact, for the four quarters ending March 2009, Japanese GDP fell by an unprecedented 8.4 percent.[72] This was a little more than double the average 4.5 percent drop in the European Union and almost three times the drop in the US of 3.6 percent.[73]

As a result, by November 2008, the jobless rate had pushed up from 3.7 to 3.9 percent and household spending dropped by 0.5 percent for the ninth monthly dip in a row. December 2008 proved even worse with production falling 9.6 percent and unemployment rising at its fastest pace in the post-war era. The rate approached a three-year high (at 4.1 percent) with further bad news expected in the coming months. There are fears that by the end of 2010, 1.5 million people will lose their jobs pushing the unemployment rate over 6 percent. These are levels

---

[71] The collapse of Japan's key export sector becomes even more apparent when comparing the six month results to the end of March 2009. Japanese exports plummeted some 37 percent which represented twice the drop of China and three time that of India's export driven economies.

[72] The nearest equivalent by another G7 country (Japan, Germany, Italy, France, Britain, the US and Canada) was −6.9 percent endured by Germany. Notice that both, before the financial clash, were both heavily exports dependent.

[73] What this meant when placed in context of Japan's recent economic history was even more alarming. Some 75 percent of the gain in GDP engineered during the years of post 2001 recovery was wiped out. Similarly a drop over those same four quarters of business investment by 22 percent meant that 92 percent of the growth over the past seven years had disappeared. In the same manner a plunge in exports of 37 percent translated into a loss of 80 percent of the recovery era gains. Clearly without the trade surplus powering business investment, the narrowly focused Japanese economy was unmistakably in trouble.

not seen since the immediate post-war period. Such worries became aggravated when in January 2009 new job offers fell by 18.4 percent when compared to the same month in the previous year. The ration of jobs to applicants in that month hit a five-year low with only two jobs for every three applicants.

Fears have been rising that production for the five months ending in February 2009 would see a fall of one-third. Such a drop would push output down to levels not seen since 1983. Aggregate levels were equally gloomy. With the last quarter for 2008 showing an economy contracting at an annualized rate of 12.7 percent, the worst since the 1974 oil crisis, the country was rapidly becoming the basket case of the G7 countries.[74] The immediate future appeared equally pessimistic. Japan was clearly facing its worse recession since the darkest days of the interwar period. The very keystones of the Japanese economy, Toyota, Nissan, and Sony planned to idle capacity and lay-off employees. Toyota on 22 December 2008, forecasting its first operating loss in seven decades, announced that it would fire some 3,000 temporary employees.[75] Certainly, Toyota faces its worse crisis since the 1950s with the size of the potential loss for 2008 estimated at around $5 billion. With its losses continuing to rise, numbers grew to 6,000 temporary employees in Japan alone. Meanwhile, Sony, facing a predicted operating loss of $2.6 billion, planned to chop 16,000 jobs worldwide while Nissan's job cuts were scheduled to equal 12,000 domestically. Some more dismal estimates expect up to 400,000 contract and temporary workers to be laid off between December 2008 and March 2009.

Clearly, as 2009 began, Japan faced economic difficulties certainly rivaling those of its post-bubble decade and perhaps problems essentially more serious. While during the previous period, parts of the

---

[74]This 3.3 percent drop in GDP for the fourth quarter compared badly with the 1.0 percent reduction in the US or the 1.5 decline in the Euro Zone. Japan's heavily focused export trade is largely dependent on cars, machinery and IT equipment, sectors that were particularly hard hit. Net exports accounted for 2.3 percentage points of the last quarter's (2008) contraction. The fragility of the previous economic expansion has now become obvious. By putting all its economic eggs in one basket, Japan has shown itself to be especially vulnerable to the collapse of overseas markets.

[75]Whether Toyota has gone seven decades without an operating loss is far from clear. If true it would make its bailout in the fifties a quite curious episode.

global economy remained strong, this crisis finds few safe havens from this downward spiral. This is particularly troublesome for an economy such as Japan that has too often depended on exporting its way out of economic difficulties. As was the case during the post-bubble period when a good deal of the problem centered on political dithering, the question again arises as to whether the current cast of political characters will be bold enough to prevent the worse of this developing recession.

So far there has been something unsettling familiar about the political response. While there would appear (*tatemae*) to be bold measures either already in place or urgently planned, the reality (*honne*) is quite different. The reality of fiscal policy after 1997 was that it was not at all expansionary. Yet an appearance of activity was provided through deceptive announcements and accounting maneuvers. (Programs previously announced were rolled into any new initiatives with headline figures badly inflated.) So far, since the crisis hit only two small stimulus packages actually have been passed. The Diet approved the second package on 13 January 2008 adding to the budget deficit by a figure equal to only 1 percent of GDP.[76] So far the proposed 2009 budget includes no new stimulus measures. Again the announced increase of spending of 6.5 percent is illusorily. When the original 2008 proposed budget is adjusted upwards for the supplementary budgets passed, any increase vanishes. The Bank of Japan is again acting hesitantly, playing symbolically with a near zero interest rate while still avoiding the sort of quantitative easing that helped pull the Japanese economy out of its previous difficulties. The more drastic measures mooted in other

---

[76]The problem also arises in the nature of the stimulus being pushed by Prime Minister Aso as well as its size. Altogether, the total package is priced at 75 trillion yen. (Though based on past experience, no one would be wise to take such figures at face value.) Quick handouts of cash, even when spent create a once off impulse that does little to create a sustained increase in aggregate demand. A centrepiece of the bill is a 2 trillion yen handout to the Japanese population with each individual receiving 12,000 yen while those 18 and younger or 65 and older would receive an additional 8,000 yen. Similar programs appeared during the post bubble period and had little effect in pulling the economy out of its chronic stagnation. The aim seems a clear political attempt to focus on the *tatemae* of action rather than the *honne* of effective policy. Such a decision comes at a time when Japan's public investment at 3.5 percent of GDP is lower than any other time in its post war history. With Japan near the bottom of OECD statistics in areas such as sewerage and water treatment, opportunities for productive investment are not lacking.

countries so far remains off the discussion table.[77] Rumors abound that if the LDP somehow succeed in pushing through their proposed budget, the current leadership will unveil another stimulus package, possibly as large as 30 trillion yen.[78]

As Japan moves toward a critical 30 August (2009) election, some hopeful signs of economic recovery have appeared though probably not enough of a boost to save the LDP. The recession had so far caused a loss of 8.8 percent of GDP with unemployment at a six-year high of 5.4 percent. Optimists can place their hopes on a 0.9 percent upward tick in GDP for the second quarter of 2009 (a healthy annualized rate of 3.7 percent growth). The worrying edge to the good news was the possible temporary nature of those factors driving the rebound. Once again, it was a recovery of critical export markets that boosted the economy. Exports grew by 6.3 percent from the previous quarter with imports falling by 5.1 percent. This was helped by a 1.2 percent increase in public spending offsetting the 1.3 percent drop in private sector demand. This still leave the Japanese economy extremely vulnerable to foreign demand especially when government stimulus packages start to dry up.

> Unless Japan can maintain robust growth into next year, the country will have suffered another "Lost Decade" of economic growth, after limping through

---

[77] The Minister for Financial, Economic and Budgetry Matters in the Prime Minister's Office, Kaoru Yosano, responded to charges of dithering by claiming that although the government has budgeted and is ready to spend some 12 trillion yen to stimulate the economy, that same government has not found a good way to spend it even after examining all possibilities. Given the state of some of the country's infrastructure and other services, such a statement would have to raise at least a few eyebrows.

[78] Faced by a collapse in business confidence as demonstrated by a historic low in the Tankan index, Prime Minister Aso moved boldly by proposing a Good Friday (April 10, 2009) supplementary budget calling for a record actual expenditure of 15.4 trillion yen or some three percent of the gross domestic product. Calculating the value of all the programs and government guarantees the budget on a project basis sums up to more than 56.8 trillion yen. Possibly grasping at straws, Aso goes into the election pledging to spend some 25 trillion yen which would include a cash handout and public spending programs including such thing as quake-proofing public schools. More extravagantly, the contending Democrats promise cash allowances to families with children, free tuition and lower gasoline taxes. This would represent a permanent boost in government spending rather than a once off stimulus. Neither party seems willing to explain how wages and the number of full-time jobs might be boosted. Weak domestic consumption seems destined to plague the Japanese economy. The problem is reflected by the share of GDP going to workers' salaries falling from a peak of 73 percent in 1999 to only 65 percent in 2007.

much of the 1990s with little growth, Yutaka Harada, chief economist at the Daiwa Institute of Research, wrote in a recent note. "Ten years after our Lost Decade, we're finding ourselves in the midst of a second Lost Decade," Mr. Harada said (Tabuchi, 2009, p. 2).

Desperate times call for desperate remedies. However, with Prime Minister Aso's reputation in shreds, given his approval rating registering at times in single digits, the chances of pushing such a bill through a divided Japanese Diet seem slim. Nor are there great hopes invested in alternative leadership. The opposition, given the chance to rule, fails to generate confidence as well.[79] A decisive moment may come in with the August 30, 2009 election. Hoping that time would lessen the dissatisfaction felt by Japanese voters with his leadership and his party, Prime Minister Aso persistently delayed setting a date for new elections. After five straight by-election defeats, even the ever optimistic Aso implicitly conceded that nothing was likely to turn up which would divert what seems to be an almost unstoppable momentum generated by the opposition. Whether this change of parties will represent a decisive political moment, remains to be seen. Not much more than four years previously, Koizumi's landslide victory seemed to mark an irreversible political revolution, only to quickly dissipate once the initiator had left the public stage.

Once again it appears the Japan's basic economic problems will be compounded by political inaction. As has been the case for a number of decades, the key to the country's economic problems seem mostly political at heart. This has effectively sidelined the plans of such LDP leaders as Abe or Aso to foster a more explicit and dominant role for Japan in world affairs. Instead, more pessimistic observers envision a country being forced to turn inwards as the country finds itself reprising some of the worst conditions characterizing Japan during the Great Depression. Though quite possibly an exaggeration, Japan's policymakers will

---

[79] In the run up to the August 2009 election, a public opinion survey released in the previous month by the government-financed Institute of Statistical Mathematics showed that 57 percent of 3,302 respondents said they expected their lives to get worse, with only 11 percent saying they would get better. This reflects almost the mirror opposite of replies to the same survey 30 years ago.

once again be reminded of the exigencies that domestic problems create for any grand overseas initiative.

11.4 Problems and Outlook

The OECD toward the beginning of the recent expansion estimated that annual GDP growth would average only 0.8 percent per annum. Forecasters for the Ministry of Health, Labor and Welfare competed to deliver an even gloomier outlook with a forecast of 0.7 percent until 2015. (Later consensus revisions put growth capacity at a more reasonable 1.5–2.0 percent.) Propelling this limited growth is a shrinking labor base that is still not being sufficiently counter-balanced by increased productivity. So far any significant up-tick in productivity has not been apparent with growth in this crucial measurement limited to 1.4 percent.

The decade of anorexic growth Japan had endured up to 2003 may have some decided effects on the chance for needed productivity growth to compensate for Japan's shrinking workforce. The younger generation of workers are receiving insufficient training. In the post-war era, most training has been of the on-the-job variety, encouraged by stable, long-term commitments between employer and employee. Amongs the current crop of young Japanese, NEETs (not in employment, education, or training) have at times accounted for as many as 850,000 people between 15 and 34. Freeters (young people working short-term, low-skill jobs) are estimated to compose up to 15 percent of those young workers. The latest (pre-recession) figures show that the number of irregular workers (temporary, contract, and part-time) measure 43 percent of the cohort between 20 and 24, and 28 percent of those from 25 to 29. The idea that the Japanese workforce can count on secure jobs (the key to the post-war low-risk, middle-class society) seems more a historical memory than a current reality with one-third of those employed working non-regular jobs. The trend shows no sign of abating with firms looking to temporary workers to keep down costs and provide a requisite measure of flexibility.

In effect the idea of creating a middle-class society is dying, if not already dead. In 1981, the Japanese Gini coefficient, measuring the equality of income distribution was 0.349 before government redistribution efforts and 0.314 after. By 1999, the relevant numbers were 0.472 and 0.381. While still a bit better than the US or the UK, Japan was now only the 15th most egalitarian country amongs the 20 OECD members. Accordingly, perceptions within Japan had changed greatly. In 1994, surveys found 90 percent of the population thinking of themselves as middle class. The post-war goal of creating a middle-class society had been seemingly achieved. However, in a similar survey conducted a decade later, 60 percent now saw themselves as below middle class. In 1995, 600,000 Japanese households needed welfare benefits to survive, with this number jumping to 1,000,000 by the end of the decade. The rising use of the terms *kachigumi* (winners) and *makegumi* (losers) to describe the divisions becoming clear in Japanese society, indicates that the dream of creating a low-risk, middle-class society had badly frayed if not disappeared. Also disappearing was the model of dutiful and studious children studying long hours. Discipline within classrooms were reported as deteriorating while long-term truancy increased by 80 percent in the past decade.

This has the potential to create future economic difficulties since a poorly educated or insufficiently trained workforce can hardly be expected to boost productivity growth from 1.4 percent to a more welcome rate of over 2.0 percent. Dithering Japanese politicians has as of yet done little to compensate for this trend. Job retraining is highly limited and the Japanese government spends a rather trivial amount (0.04 percent of GDP) on vocational training. Such a failure has the potential to transform a manageable demographic adjustment into a much more serious problem. Japan's population is rapidly ageing. Projections have the percentage of people over 65 rising from 17 percent in 2000 to 23 percent by 2015.[80] Further projections see this figure as peaking at 30 percent by 2025. This must inevitably put a serious strain on the public budget in terms of increased demand for health care.[81]

---

[80] The Japanese population over 65 had already reached 22.8 percent by 2009 and was now estimated to achieve 29.2 percent by 2020. Japan was the only G7 country to see a population decrease in 2008 (0.1 percent).

[81] Some of the problems caused by an ageing population may be exaggerated by not fully considering savings due to fewer babies and children in the population. Needed educational facilities and childcare services would naturally decrease.

Higher taxes are not necessarily a problem where income is also rising at a healthy rate. But there is no assurance that in those critical years of the next few decades per-capita GDP will grow sufficiently.

Part of the problem is that welfare costs are gradually being shifted back to the public sector and away from the corporate or family arenas. Once, the wife of the eldest son was expected to care for her in-laws. Japanese women are now less willing to live up to these expectations. The multi-generational household is also becoming less common as well. The role of women also has been changing in Japan, but like most such changes, it is proceeding quite slowly and from a clearly low base. In 1999, the difference between male and female median full-time earnings as a percentage of male median full-time earnings was 39 percent, the second largest disparity among developed economies. (Only the South Koreans were able to better that result.) Judged by an international gender empowerment index, Japan is at the very bottom of 17 industrialized countries.[82] Even today (2009), only 9 percent of administrators and managers in Japan are women.[83] It is hardly surprising that some of the brightest women (often with good language skills) are opting to work for foreign corporations where they see a chance for real advancement. Clearly, one way to overcome the potential workforce problem is to make better use of, by providing more opportunities for, women. The days when women were employed in make work, pre-marriage jobs as "office ladies" are no longer viable.

11.5 Conclusions: Is There Life After Miracles?

In the very short term, Japan faces yet another serious economic downturn with its last relatively lengthy expansion having done too little to resolve its underlying economic problems. In the longer run, it

---

[82] The index takes into account: Seats in parliament held by women (%); Female Administrators and managers (%); Female professional and technical workers (%); Women's GDP per capita.

[83] Not surprisingly, few women are noticeable in the political sphere at the federal level. As a percentage of women holding office at this national level, Japan in 2008 ranked 104th in the world.

needs to increase its growth capacity if it is to handle potential demo-graphic changes that will arrive during the next few decades. Increasing growth capacity requires more radical reforms, including the selling off of stagnating assets, even if the buyers are overseas corporations. The biggest challenge consists of the necessity to implement funda-mental changes to transform the economy from one focused on sim-ply reducing risk to one where risk-taking is appropriately rewarded. Although the dangers of getting fundamental incentives wrong and fundamentally underestimating inherent risk could be fatal, there is no going back to the days of the middle-class, low-risk society. In fact, the current reality has moved irretrievably away from that standard. The challenge however is to move to a viable alternative, one where the social safety net is no longer largely privatized.

Major Japanese corporations have been moving away from tradi-tional hierarchic structures featuring job security and seniority systems, but change has been limited. Neither the tax system, nor the financial and social environments that dominate corporations create sufficient incentives for Japanese managers to actively foster innovation. As long as they avoid bankruptcy, managers with poorly performing firms seem still to manage to hold on to their positions.

The past decade has demonstrated that neither politicians nor bureaucrats intend to take the lead in this regard. The momentum behind any such change must come from the increasing disillusion-ment of the Japanese people. In a sense, an implicit agreement has been broken. The Japanese had been assured by their business, politi-cal, and government leaders that, if they were loyal and worked hard, they would be provided for. The assurance vanished abruptly after a very few years of striking success in the 1980s. The Japanese now find that they were largely being taken advantage of, rather than taken care of.

Many Japanese politicians, whether in the long-ruling LDP or the opposition want to change the face of Japan's foreign policy. They want Japan to become a "normal" country. Whether or not this stated desire makes a good deal of sense, what we have shown is that this repre-sents no grand departure from Japan's post-war past. This proposal is simply another way in which Japan can carry out its long-standing program of dominating the East Asia region and influencing decisions made by those countries. To do so however, Japan must first get its economic house in order. Though Japanese policy has not been simply driven or determined by economic objectives, no diplomatic program can be successfully and continuously carried out without the strength of a vibrant economy. This was long recognized in Japan. The recent run of political leaders has at times seemed to lose sight of this underlying requirement. Some of them even appeared entirely uninterested in the Japanese economy. The current economic crisis has once again reminded the foreign policy establishments of its vital importance.

References

Befu H. (2001) *Hegemony of Homogeneity.* Trans-Pacific Press, Melbourne.

Dower J. (1986) *War without Mercy: Race & Power in the Pacific War.* Pantheon Books, New York.

Dower JW. (1999) *Embracing Defeat.* W.W. Norton, New York.

Hill P. (2003) Heisei Yakuza: Burst Bubble and *Botaiho. Social Science Japan Journal,* 6(1), 1–18.

Hoshi T. (1995) Evolution of the main bank system. In: Okabe M (ed.), *The Structure of the Japanese Economy,* pp. 287–323. Macmillan, London.

Keynes JM. (1964) *The General Theory of Money, Interest and Employment.* Macmillan, London.

Mosk C. (2008) *Japanese Economic Development.* Routledge, Abingdon.

Murakami Y. (1982) The age of new middle mass politics: The case of Japan. *Journal of Japanese Studies,* 8(1), 29–73.

Noguchi Y. (1998) The 1940 system: Japan under the wartime economy. *The American Economic Review: Papers and Proceedings,* 88(2), 404–407.

Sakya T. (1982) *Honda Motor: The Men, the Management, the Machines.* Kodansha International, Odaka.

Sheard P. (1989) The Japanese general trading company as an aspect of interfirm risk-sharing. *Journal of the Japanese and International Economies,* 3(3), 308–322.

Stigler GJ, Becker GS. (1977) De gustibus non est disputandum. *American Economic Review,* 67(1), 76–90.

Tabuchi H. (2009) Japan's economy shows signs of improvement. *New York Times.* August 17: 1–3. www.nytimes.com/2009/08/17/business/global/17econ. html?_r=1&ref=asia. Retrieved on August 18, 2009.

Tawney RH. (1963) *Religion and the Rise of Capitalism: A Historical Study.* P. Smith Gloucester, Mass.

Wenner RA. (2005) *A New Paradigm in Macroeconomics: Solving the Riddle of Japanese Macroeconomic Performance.* Palgrave, Macmillan, London.

Sources for Statistical Information

Bank of Japan website August 2008; *CIA World Factbook*, March 2008; International Standards Organization (ISO), The ISO Survey of ISO9000 and ISO14000 certificates; UNDP, *Human Development Report 1998* (Oxford University Press, Oxford 1998); *The Oriental Economist*; Development Assistance Committee, 2002, DAC Online Database, Paris; World Bank 2002, *World Development Indicators 2002*, CD-ROM, Washington, DC; *World Investment Report 2002*, Annex Table B.1, 303–306; *World Bank 2002 Correspondence on GDP Per Capita Annual Growth Rates*, March, Washington, DC; *Human Development Reports*, UN 2002; *World Bank Economic Outlook Databases*, calculated for the Human Development Report Office by the World Bank on the basis of data on the consumer price index from the World Bank (2002); *IMF World Economic Outlook Database*; Porter, Michael and Jeffrey Sachs (eds.), *The Global Competitiveness Report 2001–2002*, New York: Oxford University Press, 2001, p. 104; WIPO (World Intellectual Property Organization), 2001, *Intellectual Property Statistics*, Publication A, Geneva; *GECD Historical Statistics* (CD-ROM), OECD Development Assistance, p. 253; *UN Development Program Human Development Report 2001*, New York: Oxford University Press, 2001, Table A2.1.

Chapter 12

The Long Arm of the Japanese Economy: The Role of Foreign Direct Investment in Post-War Japan

> Harry had heard that the moon was different in Japan, the cherry trees were different, the seasons were different, the mountains were different, the rice was different. Add them all up and he supposed that reality itself was different (*Tokyo Station*, Martin Cruz Smith, 2005, p. 227).

A debate has lingered on for nearly a half century as to the exact nature of Japanese overseas investment. The question remains as to whether there is anything unique about the way in which the Japanese have strategically approached and even managed these decisions. However, much of the mystery dissipates if we only seek and identify the ruling imperatives that have defined such investment as Japan has progressed from a developing to a dominant economy.[1] What might seem odd at times about the Japanese approach can upon reflection be reduced to more ordinary dimensions if we succeed in identifying Japanese objectives and constraints within any given period. Once understood, Japan's off-shoring and other overseas ventures become as understandable as that of other industrial countries.

---

[1] Some of the confusion was undoubtedly created by much of the early literature on direct foreign investment which took as its model highly developed western economies like the US. In such modelling, earlier developmental stages were ignored as were earlier historical periods. The Japanese propensity to seek comfort in its own uniqueness also tended to mislead many researchers. A constant background hum proclaiming uniqueness is enough to bias anyone's judgment. This created a tendency to generalize into universals rather historically specific investment strategies.

In any investigation of this sort, what is perhaps crucial is trying to discern whether differences dominate similarities. A mistake in
either direction can prove analytically fatal. This becomes glaring in
the work of those theorists who start with *a priori* conceptions. Thus
the very success of post-war Japan created a cottage industry devoted
to explaining Japan as a special case. In the 1980s, bookshops pro-
liferated with works by Ronald Dore or Ezra Vogel explaining the
culturally determined uniqueness of the Japanese brand of managed
capitalism.[2] As with any strong thrust, a matching counter-thrust, con-
spicuous in the voluminous work of such stalwarts as Gary Saxonhouse
or J. Mark Ramseyer, insisted on placing standard market explanations
at centre stage. Often these authors resembled the fable of the blind
men confronted with an elephant. Each grabs a portion of the whole
and insists that his generalizations based on partial knowledge encompass the entirety. But this only muddles understanding and relegates
analysis to a contest between two contending camps. More prefer-
able would be an honest attempt to look at what facts there are as
well as any and all contending explanations. When we look at foreign
direct investment (FDI), certainly there should be some differences in
the way Japanese firms approached this issue in the post-war period
when compared to other corporate entities. Japanese firms faced constraints that were to some degree unique to their own domestic base.
But that does not preclude that these firms were motivated by similar incentives as their western counterparts. Again, the problem is
making sure we compare like with like instead of looking for similarities in firms facing quite different situations. There is also a danger of overlooking the obvious fact that patterns of foreign direct

---

[2]In the 1980s, there were related uniqueness arguments among Japanese opponents in the US
(the Japan bashers) as well as in Japan itself. The American contingent might have caricatured the
idea of unique practises as a polite subterfuge that cloaked what was in their view manipulative
cheating. That this new-found position enjoyed by Japanese firms could not be legitimate was
true by definition. The Japanese unaided by such wiles could in no sense out-compete Americans.
The mirror image of uniqueness in Japan (associated with *Nihonjinron* studies) saw this triumph
as demonstrating that the Japanese could do what others were incapable of achieving. Such a
stance has roots in the sort of universalized samurai ethic popularized in the 1930s and 1940s.
For a good introduction to *Nihonjinron*, see Befu (2001).

investment change over time as the incentives of the operative firms evolve, as do the key characteristics of each and every potential host country.[3]

What should be examined is the way Japanese foreign investment has changed in the post-war years and the underlying determinants of that change. Not surprisingly, these changes closely reflect the evolving Japanese domestic economy. In this, Japanese firms are little different than their Western counterparts. By taking such an approach we will be able to discern something of a trend that might give us an insight into the future direction of this investment.

12.1 The Story of Japanese Foreign Investment as an Odyssean Saga[4]

> Outward investment is a way of maximizing the rents on the accumulated knowledge and skill of a country's firms, or preserving them as long as possible when the country itself has lost its comparative advantage in their industries, and the industries, or parts of them must relocate (Blomström *et al.*, 2000, p. 2).

The great epic poem, *The Odyssey*, is divided into two parts indicated by Odysseus' own name. It can be translated as "hated by the Gods" or as "man of wrath." What this counterpoises is the dual nature of the hero as determined by his own abilities and the constraints he faces. Without sufficient knowledge and development, Odysseus is a plaything of the

---

[3] Notice the parallel problems in analyzing foreign policy. By comparing two dissimilar situations, Japan may appear to be an outlier when measured against western counterparts. Likewise changes over time may bury the underlying consistency of such a policy.

[4] In what follows there may be at times some difficulties with the FDI data presented. It is a truth universally acknowledged that different agencies use different measurements for what is ostensibly the same output. In Japan, the Ministry of Finance provides FDI data based on prior notifications by the relevant Japanese firms. There also exists another series based on balance of payments statistics. The latter has more appeal since it represents actual movements of capital overseas. However, the series published by the Ministry of Finance has the advantage of being disaggregated by country of destination and industrial sector. The two series track closely. Bayoumi and Lipworth (1997, p. 29) estimate that their contemporaneous correlation coefficient is 0.92. Which series is chosen for relative movements over time is not that significant. However, absolute numbers will vary noticeably. See the Appendix on Data provided by Bayoumi and Lipworth (1997, p. 29).

Gods who must simply respond to the forces and situations he faces. This could be construed as the passive, or reactive, stage of the poem. With greater self-knowledge and on the familiar ground of his home island, he becomes an active force to be reckoned with.

Consequently, for the first few post-war decades, Japanese firms also needed to learn and develop. The limited foreign investment under-taken was a direct extension of domestic imperatives and to some extent characterized by the type of administrative guidance provided by the Japanese bureaucracy. Only with the coming of age of the Japanese economy in the 1980s did Japanese firms begin to break free and invest independently and actively instead of simply as a response to an eco-nomic environment others created.

Although economists are wont to use short hand designations like "Japanese foreign direct investment," decisions to invest overseas must by definition be made by individual firms. This is reflected in most of the more recent economic research done in this area.

> The theoretical refinements have focused on the individual firm, studying its choices in response to its own characteristics, the nature of the industry in which it operates, and the opportunities afforded by foreign trade and investment (Helpman, 2006, p. 589).

These individual decisions are in turn constrained not only by a firm's own internal limitation (efficiency and size) but by obstacles placed by both home and foreign governments.[5] To then understand the changing nature of Japanese foreign direct investment we must analyze the changing objectives of these individual firms as well as the domestic market in which they operated. We would then expect that

---

[5] It is also incorrect to assume that firms within the same industry will make similar FDI decisions. Each firm represents a set of different capabilities, the result of unique histories, and is guided by distinct management teams. Therefore, each firm will see distinct opportunities in the same set of circumstances as well as separate ways of exploiting them. Of Japanese car makers, Honda was the first to move manufacturing operations to the US. Honda, being the newest of Japanese car firms, found opportunities within the domestic market to be limited. Given the 1970s, with the US market unexpectedly opening to smaller, fuel-efficient cars, Honda took the riskier path of US production instead of simply exporting as its competitors were satisfied to do until faced with government brokered restrictions. In contrast, Toyota took the least risk path, attempting a joint venture with General Motors in California (NUMMI) to gain first hand knowledge of the US market before committing to a more risk prone "go it alone" option.

the more Japanese firms reflected the same concerns as firms in other developed economies and were faced with many of the same binding constraints, the more Japanese FDI would be roughly similar to the FDI undertaken by western economies.[6] This is the direction in which the existing statistics, economic history, and current anecdotal evidence seem to point quite strongly. Trends are always difficult to clearly discern, however, in the case of FDI it seems far more useful to focus on common incentives motivating such decisions than to fix upon any unique characteristics which can be easily explained and which over time has played a reduced role in such decisions.

12.2 Post-War Japan: Establishing a Low-Risk, Middle-Class Society

> Many argue that the above features are reflections of the unique aspects of Japan's cultural and social norms whose origins can be traced back to the history of Japan. I will argue that these are not necessarily "intrinsic Japanese" and that most of them were introduced as the wartime system during the years around 1940, and hence can be called the "1940 system" (Noguchi, 1998, p. 404).

To understand the economic system in which Japanese firms made their initial post-war FDI decisions requires an understanding of the economic approach that system ostensibly replaced. As can be argued, the Japanese during the occupation period preferred the appearance of acquiescence rather than the reality.[7] Necessity and the objectives of the traditional ruling classes led them to opt for the simpler choice of adopting those institutions that had already served them sufficiently well. In essence, the post-war Japanese government substituted "strong

---

[6]Given that the bulk of economists tend to be US-centric in their research, US or Anglo-American companies are often implicitly assumed to be something of a benchmark. This can be deceptive given that Japanese firms and the Japanese economy tend to resemble more closely those of Continental Europe with the US standing as an outlier. Nonetheless, in the case of FDI, Japanese multinationals (firms that decide to invest overseas) will be seen as becoming less distinguishable from their US counterparts over time. We need to remember here that multinationals of all types and countries inevitably evolve by aligning with their environment.

[7]Those interested in this Japanese strategy of appearing to acquiesce would benefit by looking at Dower (1999).

economy" for "strong army" in the traditional recipe of building a strong country. The key to building that strong economy, however, was achieving a secure level of political stability. This accomplishment required an implicit working promise to build a middle-class, low-risk society; an inclusive economy where everyone who worked hard and obeyed the rules (both explicit and implicit) could be assured of a secure job and an ever-rising living standard.[8]

By the 1960s, this underlying objective became even more exigent in Prime Minister's Ikeda's income doubling promise (a response to the rising unrest at that time). To achieve this, post-war Japan borrowed heavily from the structures that had guided Japan through the war. While the war itself was certainly misguided, the system had performed remarkably well, mobilizing severely limited available resources. These military era strategies provided a familiar institutional framework for the millions of veterans returning from military service. More specifically, prior to actual hostilities, FDI had largely been focused on expediting exports and securing raw materials.[9] Japan's colonial empire imitated the western model in which colonial investment yielded key commodity imports. Moreover, economic growth depended in part on competitive exports. Such trade needed financing and distribution channels.

> Mitusi Bussan (in English, Mitsui Trading) had by 1876 established an overseas marketing organization for selling Japanese coal in China, Hong Kong, and Singapore. In time, this distribution network had grown and new products were included reflecting the expansion of the business activity. The distribution web extended to London, Paris, Bombay, Sydney, as well as New York and San Francisco ... Mitsui & Co. also served as a transmitter of American technology to Japan (Wilkens, 1982, pp. 506, 508).

It should come as no surprise that of the $41 million of Japanese direct investment in the US in 1937, 16.5 million reflected distributional needs with 21.8 million going toward financial services (Wilkens, 1982, p. 507).

---

[8] Early work on the underlying promise of a middle-class Japanese society is best typified by Murakami (1982).

[9] The US embargo of oil and iron ore was a key rationale for the Japanese attack on Pearl Harbor. American actions were portrayed as leaving the Japanese with no other option if they were to survive and not to capitulate to self-dealing US demands.

It might be argued somewhat convincingly that this type of simple vertical integration characterized such overseas investment both prior and subsequent to the war. In adopting this tack during the post-war recovery, Japanese firms reflected the reality of the constraints under which they operated.[10] Imposed constraints in the form of government directives limited the foreign exchange available for overseas adventures. The immediate challenge was to rebuild domestic capacity and create employment for returning war veterans. Japanese manufacturing firms at this stage lacked the efficiency required to compete overseas, making the question of direct investment a moot one.[11] It might be safe to say that in those early post-war years the restrictions imposed by government authorities were not particularly binding. Few firms were in any condition to attempt extensive overseas investment with most lacking the size or efficiency required.

> A small fraction of firms engage in FDI, and these firms are larger and more productive than exporting firms. A lot of within-industry heterogeneity exists, and the distribution of firms by size or productivity varies substantially across industries (Helpman, 2006, p. 590).

---

[10]James Fallows in what might be described as a classic period piece of Japan bashing, tried to depict the Japanese drive to secure basic commodities as unusual if not unique.

> Last year Japan agreed to reduce its barriers against beef imports, in stages over the next few years. One immediate effect was to increase the sales not of US beef in Japan but of US beef *ranches*. ... "The whole point in opening up the Japanese market was for American producers to be able to sell here," Bill Cody, of Oregon's Japan Representative Office, told Fred Hiatt, of *The Washington Post*. "So what is the mentality that refuses to buy our products? What is the necessity to come and buy our producers?" (Fallows, 1989, p. 8).

However, Western colonial empires were premised on this basis. One possible underlying reason for George Bush's 2003 Iraqi invasion is thought to have been the likelihood that the Saddam Hussein regime was about to strike oil development deals with French, Russian, and even Chinese multinationals instead of Anglo-American ones. Moreover, the rationale behind China's persistent support of such questionable regimes as those in the Sudan or Myanmar reflects an almost unquenchable desire to secure key resources.

[11]The now rightly admired Japanese car industry was in 1964 largely incapable of producing a car that would be competitive in the US market. It is sometimes claimed that Nissan marketed its first exports under the Datsun logo so as to not damage its brand name. These early cars proved incapable of the demands of freeway driving in California. As expected, FDI by the Japanese car industry at this time would have been minimal since relatively few units were even exported to the States.

Clearly imposed constraints did start to be felt starting with the 1960s and every following year until all such restrictions were removed by 1982.[12] In general, these changes reflected rising pressure exerted by those firms most limited by government impositions. At such moments, barriers interfered too crucially with the ability of these firms to exploit potential opportunities. What is noticeable is that although in popular myth Japan Inc. was characterized as a reflection of the power held by government bureaucrats, their role should be more accurately seen as that of adjudicators and coordinators that attempted to slow down and channel the standard adjustments made by competitive markets.[13] Such implicit administrative guidance through vehicles like

---

[12] Controls over foreign direct investment were implemented with the Foreign Exchange and Foreign Trade Management Law (promulgated December 1949) and the Investment Law (May 1950), allowing MITI to veto all FDI proposals, particularly in the case of outward flows to prevent "reverse exports" (Cowling and Tomlinson, 2001, p. 3). In June 1960, the Cabinet announced easing of regulations including "gradual easement" of capital account transactions, mindful of the possible negative effects on the domestic economy. Easement was further foreshadowed by Japan's move to IMF Article 8 status in April 1964.

Liberalization of outward FDI flows lagged easing of restrictions on inward flows, the latter being encouraged and the former discouraged especially in times of Balance of Payments constraints. The volatility of short-term capital flows, in particular, meant that partial liberalization was often followed by subsequent re-regulation, depending on the conflicting needs such as preventing a too rapid yen appreciation or controlling payments deficits.

The liberalization of outward FDI flows commenced in October 1969, with a series of five foreign capital liberalization packages. The last occurred in June 1972, with broad "in principle" (Aramaki, 2006, p. 188) liberalization of FDI, though subsequently there was a general reversal of policy back to facilitating inflows and restricting outflows, given the Balance of Payments problems surrounding the first Oil Shock.

The Foreign Exchange and Foreign Trade Management Law was revised, with promulgation in December 1979 and implementation in December 1980. Under these regulatory changes there was a shift to a general and permanent liberalization of the capital account. Remaining impediments included prior notification requirements for transactions such as external borrowing and portfolio securities investment flows, with ministry approval required for transactions likely to disturb financial markets or exchange rates (Aramaki, 2006, p. 189). Sources cite these regulatory changes of 1979–1980 as eliminating "most controls on outward FDI" (Bailey, 2003, p. 10).

[13] The idea that corporate leaders simply took their marching orders from MITI bureaucrats was no more than a gross exaggeration. In some industries, like steel, firms saw a certain mutual advantage to adopting a cooperative approach with government officials mediating conflicts and suggesting probable paths and strategies. But even in the steel industry, often seen as the prime example of this approach, disputes would rage among firms and with the relevant bureaucrats.

> The *Jishu Chosie* [self-regulation] system institutionalised MITI's earlier capacity co-ordination. With MITI's help, the leading steel company managers assumed the task of co-ordinating capacity increases to protect firms

indicative planning sought to stabilize markets and reduce a significant degree of their underlying variability. A lower-risk environment would after all encourage more investment. Greater investment in these early decades translated into greater growth and a quicker movement toward achieving the desired middle-class, low-risk society.

Given its status as a capacity-constrained, developing economy until sometime in the 1970s, FDI could be expected to play only a relatively small role in Japan's rapidly growing post-war period.

> The total book value of manufacturing investment abroad in 1972 was no more than $1.74 billion about 5 per cent of the comparable figure for the United States, but almost half the total investment has taken place during the most recent three years, and it is growing ... Almost one-half of the total investment is found in three industries — textiles, timber and pulp, and steel. Among firms surveyed, the foreign manufacturing operations, on the average accounted for only 1.3 per cent of the total output, 1.6 per cent of the total assets, and less than 5 per cent of the employees of the parent companies. The total sales of the manufacturing subsidiaries are only 6 per cent of the export sales of all the companies surveyed (Yoshino, 1974, pp. 357–358).[14]

A useful way to grasp the purpose and reactive nature of FDI during this period is to focus on the textile industry. Patterns would be formed here that would foreshadow future overseas investment strategies. As in many other developing countries, textiles established itself as a key domestic and export industry for the Japanese. Its labor-intensive quality created jobs, and the low-wage structure of the Japanese industry immediately following the war made this industry export competitive. Textiles also represented familiar corporate ground. This had been one of Japan's flagship export sectors prior to the war, with the Japanese

---

from overcapacity, low operating rates, and rising unit costs. ... Of course, while the firms agreed that a common solution was desirable, negotiating an agreement was far from orderly or harmonious. *Jishu Chosei* meetings were intensely heated, described by some participants as 'boxing matches' among the companies (O'Brien, 1992, pp. 146–147).

[14]To provide some perspective on the limited size of Japanese FDI in 1972, the accumulated stock of such investment was only 5 percent of the US total. However, the Japanese economy of that time was one-third the size of its American counterpart. Overseas investment was still only a minor economic appendage for the Japanese of that era.

acknowledged as a technological leader. Access to cheap cotton imports and a pool of low-wage labor made the Japanese a formidable competitor. However, the industry would have to react to two potentially damaging constraints. Exports could be shut out by developed countries trying to protect their own domestic industry or by other developing economies trying to build a strong market sector given the import substitution strategy popular in those years.

Then as the 1960s progressed, Japanese textile firms were forced to respond to rising wages as the supply of farm labor (especially of the female variety) started to dry up. With other employment opportunities arising, wage costs steadily increased, making output less competitive.

> Access to cheap and productive labor was increasingly difficult after 1960 as well. Many young women either continued their education or went into new and more attractive sectors. Higher wages and longer-term employment (longer than three years) had to be offered to attract enough staff. While textile wages in Japan increased much faster than elsewhere, the growth in labor productivity was comparable to that of other countries (Delanghe, 2005, p. 81).

The solution was twofold. Initially, investment in third-world markets was intended to overcome cases where Japanese exports faced limited, if any, entry. This would provide needed access not only to the domestic market, but also in many cases to raw cotton and low wages. Exemplifying a classic case of horizontal integration, little, if any, output was intended to be shipped back to Japan. Such goods would only spoil the domestic sector and disrupt the status quo of Japanese labor markets.

> Most of these manufacturing facilities were established to serve the foreign market. Approximately 75 per cent of the total output of the manufacturing affiliates surveyed is marketed locally; 20 per cent is exported to a third country, and only 5 per cent is shipped back to Japan (Yoshino, 1974, p. 359).

The focus of such investment changed in the late 1960s when Japanese textile industries ceased to be internationally competitive. FDI (especially in Brazil) allowed a paced withdrawal from this sector in terms of the domestic economy. Lower-valued production was shipped abroad while Japanese manufacturers of power looms (such as Toyoda) maintained the higher value added end of operations by exporting technologically advanced machinery to Brazilian mills. Thus, as efficiency in a sector slid, MITI would act as an industrial midwife, allowing domestic production to shrink without disrupting the Japanese economy or relevant labor markets. This is where producer cartels and administrative guidance came to the fore. In fact, it can be safely claimed that such strategies more closely characterized sunset rather than sunrise industries.[15]

The pattern set by the post-war textile industry foreshadowed future Japanese FDI both in its purpose and the category of investing firms. In this case, some of Japan's largest corporations were behind this move.

> Eight Japanese companies undertook cotton textile FDI in Brazil in the postwar period. Four companies entered in the first wave. These were Kanebo, Toyobo, Tsuzuki, and Unitika. ... Kanebo ranked 171st out of the 200 largest non-US companies in 1962, and Toyobo ranked 163rd. Both companies continued to move up the ranks of the largest non-US companies until 1973 (Delanghe, 2005, p. 87).

The Brazilian example also makes clear that Japanese firms, when choosing overseas ventures, preferred low-risk options. One of the attractions of the Brazilian market lay in the Japanese immigrants making their home there who were willing to raise and provide the raw cotton. The link was further secured by establishing and operating cotton gins in concert with the mills.

> The cleaning and classification problems that plagued the processing of Brazilian raw cotton were solved by firms that linked up with raw cotton producing Japanese immigrants and that integrated backward into cotton ginning. ... Operating one's own cotton gin had additional advantages. It provided information on the quality of the season's crop and, by cutting out intermediaries, further

---

[15]To a degree, this does contrast with the Anglo-American approach. (Note that there is no compelling reason to see the US as any sort of desired or even dominant standard. Continental European countries often deviate in their own various ways.) However, in the case of textiles, it is useful to remember that for many years the domestic US sector was heavily protected. There was also initially no need for investment overseas as the US South served the same purpose, providing lower-wage, non-union labor in contrast to the original New England home of textile mills. However, the key difference is that the US originally made little effort to alleviate the disruption caused by abandoned mills and lost jobs.

reduced the price of an already cheap raw material (Delanghe, 2005, pp. 88–89).

Vertical integration, or strong vertical relationships, traditionally reflects a need to reduce risk in uncertain markets by improving informational flows. In such markets, the reliability of suppliers, as well as the quality of their output, is often an unknown. It is then unsurprising that in later decades, Japanese suppliers often followed the lead of their key corporations in making parallel overseas investments. As Japanese car makers shifted production out of Japan, suppliers to these firms followed. Statistics showing the relatively low use made of local producers by Japanese firms reflect this ingrained risk avoidance based on a lack of information and experience in operating overseas. As expected, over time, use of such local suppliers became more common.

> The relative value of local materials and components in products assembled in Taiwan, for example, ranges from almost 100 per cent for standard lines of transistor radios, to 50 per cent for black-and-white television sets, to 15 per cent for color sets. The significant increase in local content is due largely to similar expansions abroad by specialized parts and components manufacturers. There are now half a dozen medium-size Japanese components manufacturers which produce as much as one-third of their total output overseas [as of 1973] (Yoshino, 1974, p. 359).

In these early days, foreign investment often depended on a collective effort involving trading companies, local firms, and financial institutions as well as a pivotal Japanese manufacturer. Given the capital constraints, lack of experience, and often dire lack of local information, it is unsurprising that a number of early examples of overseas investments reflect joint efforts, with government input constraining corporate decisions. This was not so much a typical example of culturally determined preference for a cooperative strategy but rather a reasonable economic response to restrictive necessity.

> 'Group' investment (i.e. where a number of Japanese firms, usually involving trading companies, participate in a given overseas venture as co-investors) is a popular form of overseas investment among Japanese firms. The Overseas Economic Co-operation Fund, a government agency, also participates, as a shareholder, directly in overseas ventures that have an overtone of economic assistance. ... Japanese firms are highly dependent on external

sources of funds to finance their direct foreign investments. As of the end of March 1975, for example, 34.2 per cent of their overseas investment capital came from government-affiliated financial institutions ... 32.8 per cent from private financial institutions (mostly city banks whose liquidity was, in turn, created by the Bank of Japan), and the remainder from the investing firms' own internal funds (Ozawa, 1979, p. 75).

In some cases, joint ventures with local firms reflected a binding constraint imposed by the host government. However, the role played by Japanese trading companies was especially significant during this period. These firms were unsurprisingly central in the first few decades of Japan's export drive when most products could be fairly described as unbranded commodities. (Not until the advent of such consumer electronics as transistor radios did Japanese firms start building brand name reputations abroad. This necessitated overseas investment in the form of marketing and specialized distribution centers.) Given their superior knowledge of foreign markets and larger capitalization, trading firms could sell a portfolio of Japanese goods, and reduce the risk of those Japanese producers wanting to sell abroad or even produce overseas.[16] In these early days, provided with sufficient assistance, even small companies were as likely to venture abroad as larger, more efficient ones. Twenty-five percent of parent companies were capitalized at less than ¥50 million ($167,000 in 1973) (Yoshino, 1974, p. 358).

> Trading companies, traditionally an essential element in the distribution of textile products, were also mobilized. They performed useful integrative functions linking the large fiber manufacturers with a myriad of downstream operators and distributors. A particular value of the trading companies was their financial strength and their close contact with many small enterprises (Yoshino, 1974, p. 363).

Clearly during this period, domestic imperatives largely dictated these foreign investment strategies. Higher value added production where Japan remained competitive, and this provided rising wages for Japanese workers, deliberately remained bound within the domestic

---

[16] Paul Sheard (1989) develops the numerous ways in which trading companies were able to shift risk away from manufacturers, thus allowing them to invest and expand more rapidly.

market. However, production with undesirable side effects, especially in a rapidly developing country with aspirations toward middle class comfort, was carefully shifted overseas.[17] This led to an intentional exit of the petro-chemical industry.[18] The 1970s saw an increasing concern with excess capacity coupled with a public unwillingness to tolerate further plant sites. As incomes rose domestically, so did demand for less pollution, specifically fewer "dirty" industries. Shifting out of these undesirable sectors became even more compelling than leaving behind such labor-intensive industries as textiles which dominated overseas investment in the 1960s (see Fig. 12.1).

> Meantime, finding plant sites has become increasingly difficult; virtually all attractive locations have been occupied and even more basic is a change in the social climate. Concern for environmental protection has heightened, and any efforts to expand existing capacity or to create a new complex would almost inevitably meet serious opposition from local citizens (Yoshino, 1974, p. 378).

---

[17] It is important to emphasize that shifts out of declining industries were not conducted precipitously. Off-shoring of production, which allowed foreign subsidiaries to send back components and other inputs to their home base, was clearly discouraged.

> Initially, the Ministry of International Trade and Industry discouraged such moves for fear of oppressing small-and-medium-size enterprises in Japan. In fact, the MITI had once insisted on a written pledge that none of the output from the overseas facilities would be shipped to Japan (Yoshino, 1974, p. 371).

[18] Again there is an active coordinating role played by Japanese bureaucrats. Thus not only are firms in this era reacting to the changing domestic environment but to the government's posture on the perceived environment as well. The result shifted the processing of raw materials toward sites where wages were more competitive and/or raw inputs more secure.

> In the face of the uncertain supplies of overseas resource, the irremovable scarcities of labour and industrial sites at home, and the ever-deteriorating environmental conditions, the Japanese government adopted an epoch-making policy to restructure Japan's industry, a proposal made by the Industrial Structure Council, a consultative organ for Japan's Ministry of International Trade and Industry. The policy emphasized a shift from 'pollution-prone' and 'resource-consuming' heavy and chemical industries towards 'clean' and 'knowledge-intensive' industries, and assigned overseas investment, a new role to serve as a catalyst to houseclean the economy (Ozawa, 1979, p. 88).

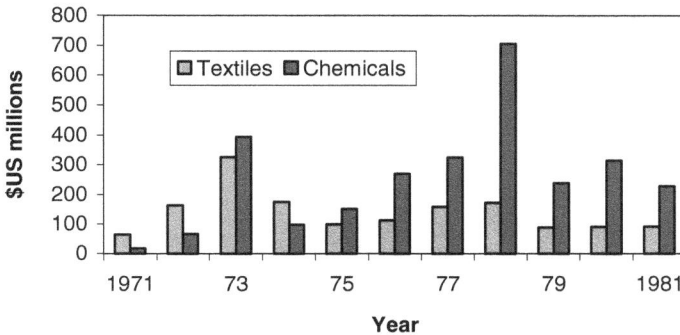

Source: JETRO

Fig. 12.1   FDI in the 1970s selected industries.

The defining characteristic toward the end of this reactive period became a rather distinct shift away from investment in developing countries (initially Latin America and then Asia) to more developed countries in North America or Europe.

> Most striking is that the relative importance of flows to North America (Canada and the US) has doubled since the mid 1970s, accounting for about $24 billion in 1988 (more than half of the total outflow). Similarly, the European share of FDI has risen from about 12 to 20 percent of the $47 billion outflow in 1988. These increases in the share of FDI to developed countries have come at the expense of developing-country shares (Froot, 1991, p. 8).

This unmistakeable change of course which refocused FDI toward developed economies can again be understood as largely reactive in nature (see Fig. 12.2). Its clear objectives were to ensure export markets and to overcome export restrictions. Notice once again the conservative, risk reduction aspect of this strategy. It is hardly a coincidence that this shift coincided with the distinct creation of international Japanese brand names which came of age in the 1970s. Such a changed focus complemented the continuing move into value-added areas, leaving more competitive markets, characterized by generic type products, behind. Continuing to produce consumer electronics that were simply rebranded by established US companies held too much risk and provided unattractively low margins. As Japanese wages rose, demand

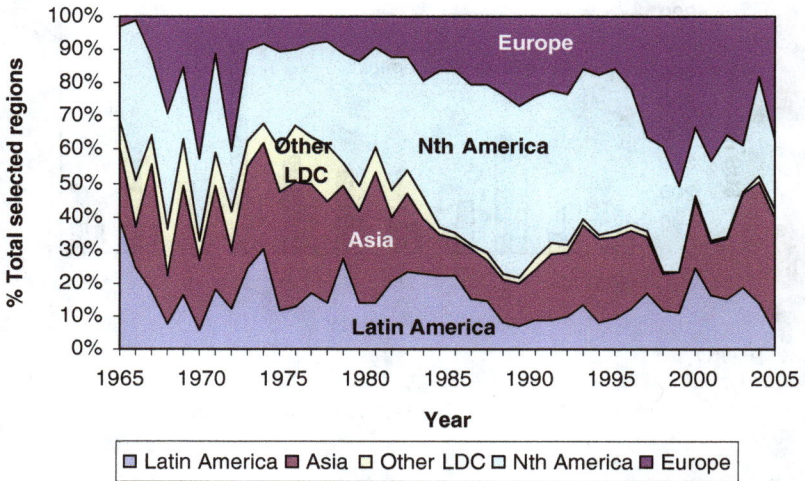

Source: JETRO (2005–2006 data on BoP net basis)

Fig. 12.2   Japanese FDI by region.

for such no-name products could shift easily to lower cost producers. An oligopolistic brand advantage would eliminate such dead-end options. This impetus, moving FDI away from its more traditional destinations, was augmented by two other unavoidable factors that gained prominence after 1972. First, Japanese firms feared the likelihood that rising concerns in countries like the US would soon see attempts to block the flood of Japanese imports. Second, the expanded opportunities created by the continued liberalization of constraints on foreign investment, driven by the Japanese bureaucracy's attempt to retard any further appreciation of the yen.

> The suddenly swollen coffers of international reserves and the steep appreciation of yen triggered by the successive devaluations of the dollar in the early 1970s compelled the Japanese government to go through three stages of the so-called 'yen defense programme' to reduce an embarrassingly large stock of reserves and to 'defend' the yen from further appreciation. ... Various measures were taken to encourage imports and capital outflows, each time more progressively than before, and to discourage exports and capital inflows on a temporary basis. All overseas investments were in principle completely liberalized in June 1972 (Ozawa, 1979, p. 87).

Efficient and innovative Japanese firms made the unsurprising choice to promote their brands abroad, first through distributional and marketing investment but next in the hope of eluding potential barriers to trade by producing locally. As previously pointed out, the textile industry provided something of a template for this strategy. Sony was a clear pioneer in this movement which would build and peak in the late 1980s and early 1990s. Again, this reactive strategy provided a relatively low-risk alternative considering the rapidly changing economic circumstances.

> In the late 1960s, the company became increasingly concerned with its ability to continue serving the American market from Japan in the face of mounting pressures for import restrictions. Having established a strong market position, and given the overriding importance of the US market to the company (roughly a third of its total sales), Sony began to contemplate the establishment of a plant in the United States. Because it was a rapidly growing company, Sony was faced with the need to expand its capacity at regular intervals; it made good sense to build an incremental capacity in the United States. No doubt, some production costs would be higher in the U.S., but the wage gap between the two countries was narrowing, and there would be some savings in tariffs and transportation costs. Most importantly, Sony had the distinct oligopolistic advantage of a well-accepted brand, which made it easier to pass any increased costs on to consumers (Yoshino, 1979, p. 375).

This set the pace for an onslaught of manufacturing investment which would be the hallmark of the 1980s.

> Significant investment in manufacturing sectors of the industrial countries, especially the United States, began only in the 1970s, as two necessary conditions came to be satisfied. One was the considerable successes scored by many Japanese industries during the 1960s in exporting sophisticated goods that won substantial goodwill in the US market. The second was changes in conditions that began to make the United States an attractive base for Japanese firms to supply the US market — depreciation of the dollar following the collapse of the Bretton Woods system and the rise of pressure to protect US industries against Japanese exports (Drake and Caves, 1992, pp. 230–231).

With Honda making the initial move in 1982, other Japanese car makers followed suit. Capacity expansion meant shifting plants to the US.[19] The Japanese manufacturers had responded rapidly to an opportunity provided by an unanticipated shift in demand. The first oil shock in 1973 created a new opportunity for small car sales in the US. Japan, given the nature of their domestic market, had managed to produce quality small cars efficiently. The "Big Three" US manufacturers, eschewing low-profit margins provided by small car sales, largely chose to ignore this sector, believing demand for larger-sized vehicles would rebound. They were correct initially, but the industry was soon overwhelmed by a second oil crisis later in the same decade. Rapidly falling sales led to intense pressure by domestic car makers on the US government to provide them with what they claimed was a much needed period to recover.

Breathing space came mostly from government-to-government negotiations. In 1980, the Big Three car manufacturers had lost a total of $4 billion. Domestic sales dropped 1.5 million and factories were running at only 60 percent capacity. Faced with the possible collapse of two major car companies (Ford and Chrysler), the US government successfully pressured the Japanese into limiting their annual exports to 1.68 million cars compared with the 1980 sales level of 1.9 million cars. Rapid recovery of the US industry would see import restraints raised to 1.85 million.[20]

Japanese car makers in the early 1980s were stuck in the small economy end of the market where margins were thin and competition, if only among themselves, was fierce. To gain any lasting success, that is, to hold on to and increase their current customer base, the Japanese would need to expand their model line. Translated, this meant more expensive cars loaded with more options in order to widen profit margins. Further, if they were to become immune to political pressures and foreign exchange fluctuations (achieve a lower risk profile), production would need to be shifted to the US. Sticking mainly to the lower end of the market would make such a transition more perilous.

---

[19] Not surprisingly, these were "greenfield" investments, since the opportunity to buy out an existing manufacturer was not a feasible possibility. As noted, the one exception was the intial joint venture between Toyota and General Motors, but this reflected basically the cautious nature of Toyota's decision-making process. Subsequent investments were all "greenfield" in nature.
[20] See *Automotive News* — Annual Report 1987 for details.

The quotas allowed Japan to limit its imports, to more profitable models and to charge prices some 15–25 percent higher than otherwise by artificially limiting supply. This brought Japanese car makers an additional $3.25–$5 billion in 1985 alone.[21] In a sense, these import restrictions financed the Japanese invasion into domestic production and their move into the more upscale market. Without such an assist, these companies would have had to borrow heavily, taking on additional commitments and additional risk. These imposed constraints allowed the Japanese to raise prices by only 25 percent despite the yen's doubling in appreciation between 1985 and 1988.

Notice that the Japanese car makers were largely reactive in this situation. To prosper they had no other viable option. But such an opportunity had scarcely been foreseen. This was a case of essentially horizontal integration driven by the host country's imposed limitations. Given export constraints, Japanese car makers could only continue to exploit the existing opportunity and build their sales base by shifting part of the production process overseas. A similar strategy operated in Europe with a number of Japanese firms choosing to expand into the UK to avoid similar restrictions.[22]

Not only did Japanese FDI grow rapidly[23] as firms expanded horizontally to overcome imposed restrictions and maintain viable export markets, but the nature of this overseas investment was also evolving as well. Ozawa (1979), focusing on the developmental stage of Japan's post-war economy, could easily contrast the sharp differences with the US during this same period.

> Other than her commerce-oriented investments, Japan's overseas investments are aimed mostly at exploiting natural resources in

---

[21] See *Economist*, February 6, 1988, p. 69 for additional details.

[22] Nissan came to Northeast England as a result of a deal between the British Government and Nissan Motors in 1984. Seeking to alleviate unemployment and economic downturn in the region, the land was provided at subsidized rates. Production began in 1986. Between 1999 and 2004, Nissan Motor Manufacturing UK became the largest British car exporter with one in five exported cars in 2004 having Nissan as its origin. For a quick sketch of Nissan Motor Manufacturing UK, see the Wikipedia entry, which can be easily checked against other sites for reliability and accuracy.

[23] The rapid rise of Japanese FDI reflects the way in which the "miracle economy" of the 1960s was changing the Japanese domestic economy. Buoyant growth led to an increased ability and a corresponding utility of investing overseas.

resource-rich countries or manufacturing labor-intensive products
in labor-abundant developing countries ... Most outputs from the
first type of investment are shipped back to Japan, while the man-
ufactures from the second type are increasingly exported back to
Japan or to third-country markets. In contrast, American overseas manufacturing investments are designed mostly to produce
highly sophisticated, technology-based products for local markets,
as envisaged in the oligopoly theory of direct investment. Kojima[24]
characterized the Japanese type as 'trade oriented,' the American
type as 'anti-trade oriented' (Ozawa, 1979, p. 79).

Ozawa was contrasting this approach with the then prevailing theory emphasizing the monopolistic nature of international investment.
What is important here is that as he was writing these conclusions, the
very nature of Japan's investment was changing to reflect its evolving
domestic economy. By the late 1970s, the prominent features characterizing FDI were no longer those of the 1960s. And indeed, even
American strategies so concisely characterized by Ozawa would also
shift away from any simple manifestation of horizontal integration.

Thus, the profile of Japanese manufacturing investments five years
from now is likely to be quite different from the present picture. The
motives of investment have become more diverse; the commitments
will become larger. Not only is a pull generated by Japanese industrialists' desire to defend export markets, but internal forces are

---

The growth of Japan's direct foreign investment has become significantly
large ever since the mid 1960s, particularly since 1968. (The value of overseas investments approved by the government in fiscal 1968 was $557 mil-
lion, which added as much as 38.4 per cent to the previous level of outstanding investment, $1,451 million, made during the 17-year period of
1951–67. Then, from 1968 up to the end of fiscal 1975, overseas investment
increased at the average annual rate of 35.4 per cent, reaching a cumulative
value of $15, 943 million as of 31 March 1976, the end of Japan's fiscal
year.) The outward expansion of Japanese industry is, therefore, a sudden
and relatively recent phenomenon — instead of an evolutionary one like
that of its US counterpart — and engulfs practically all industrial sectors,
including the iron and steel industry in which Western multinationals rarely
make overseas investments (Ozawa, 1979, pp. 73–74).

...the Japanese presence in world outflows has indisputably risen, growing from 6 percent in the 1970s to 15 percent in the 1980s and to about
30 percent in 1988 ... (Froot, 1991, p. 6).

[24]The reference here is to work done by Kojima in 1973.

now pushing a number of them abroad. The character of the invest-ment has shifted from small, labor-intensive, fragmented operations to more capital-intensive and technologically oriented ones. The behavior of large, oligopolistic Japanese firms has begun to man-ifest characteristics commonly associated with their US counter-parts, but the Japanese enterprises are forging distinctive patterns of cooperation which may have important ramifications for the future (Yoshino, 1974, p. 381).

This new wave, peaking in the early to mid-1980s featured what would become a roster of dominant Japanese multinational firms. Along with these manufacturers came associated suppliers and firms that largely existed to service such corporations. These included finan-cial firms, realtors, and others who initially came to facilitate the needs of this growing contingent of Japanese firms (see Fig. 12.3). Characteris-tically, and as expected by theory, firms that dominated this activity were large and apparently efficient. With the players in place and the nature of overseas investment evolving noticeably from the earlier developmen-tal stage, the transition toward a more individualistic and independent FDI profile was in the making.

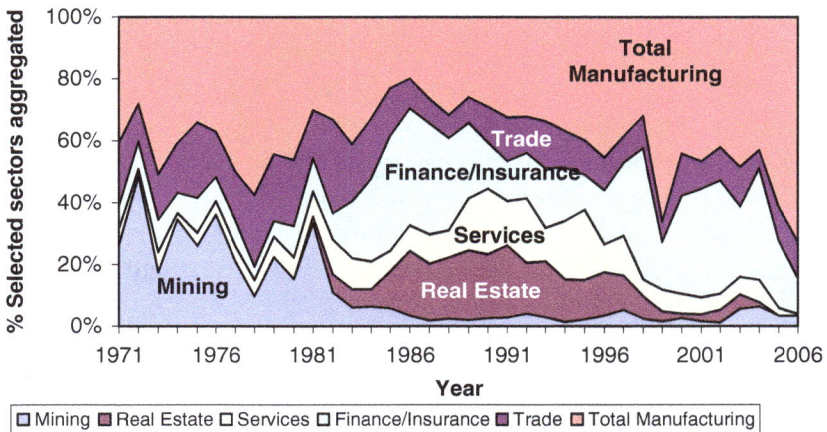

Source: JETRO (data post-2004 is on BoP net basis)

Fig. 12.3   Japanese FDI by selected sectors.

12.2.1 *The Bubble Transition: A Drunken Sailor Paradigm of Overseas Investment*

> Ishizaki, ever the fixer, would arrange the art deals with the help of a female French friend who was a retired prostitute. "She had grown too old to be a hooker," Ishizaki said, "she had a few too many wrinkles, so she decided to become a freelance art dealer." Though she had switched careers, the Frenchwoman had not lost her accommodating ways. 'I'd ask her to draw up a valuation certificate for, say, ten million dollars," Ishizaki later explained, "and then the bankers would come and look at this painting. The bankers didn't know a Cezanne from a Monet, but they'd nod and say, 'Yes, this is worth ten million, so we'll lend you eight million against it.' Then my French friend would sell us the painting, probably under a different name, and take a commission on the deal" (Tett, 2003, p. 55).

Back in 1988, there was a widespread joke in Australia which played on a ubiquitous ad for Queensland tourism. The original had as its hard-to-forget tagline "Beautiful one day, perfect the next." The joke quickly transformed into "Beautiful one day, Japanese the next" which perfectly summed up the anxiety, xenophobia, and downright paranoia surrounding Japanese overseas investment of the time. The Japanese were seemingly buying up any asset they could get their hands on with swaths of real estate falling into their clutches. There was talk of Japanese retirement villages and a Japanese Multi Function Polis to be located somewhere north of Adelaide in South Australia.[25] The reality was that in the late 1980s, Japanese FDI seemingly exploded, peaking at nearly 20 percent of total world FDI for 1988 (see Fig. 12.4). To outside eyes, Japanese firms were acting like convent-educated young ladies left unchaperoned in the big city for the first time. In contrast to the previous conservative, risk-averse nature of its FDI ventures, this new era seemingly disregarded the issue of risk altogether. This "bubble period" provided a necessary shock that would largely change the

---

[25]This rather bizarre episode evolved from a plan cooked up by Japanese Trade Minister Hajima Tamura and Australian Industry Minister John Button. The vision was of a "greenfield" development incorporating future-oriented high technology and leisure activities. Controversial at the time, the project stirred up visions of a successful Japanese invasion and takeover. With Australian Federal funding withdrawn in 1996, and the Japanese for a number of years more occupied with other urgent matters, the ill-fated project was allowed to die a natural death in 1998. See Australian newspapers of the late 1980s and early 1990s for the popular reaction to this plan.

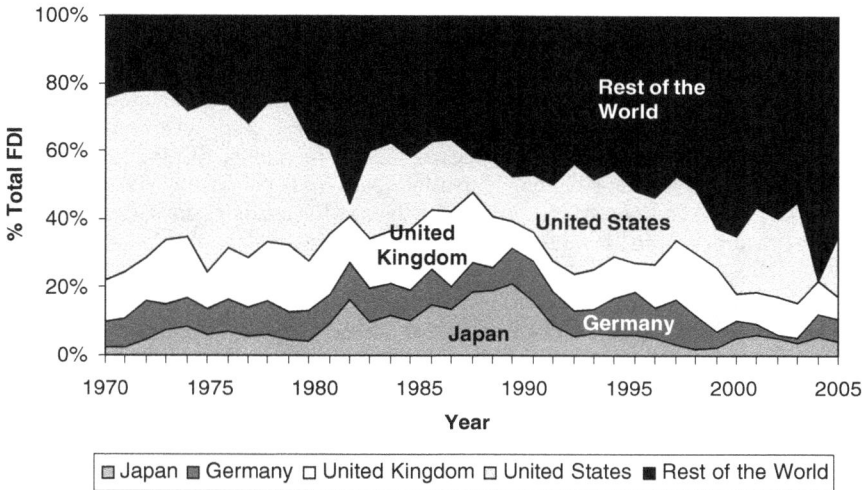

Fig. 12.4 Japan FDI as proportion of world FDI.

Source: UNCTAD

nature of Japanese overseas investment. But it would be a transition that would come at an enormous cost and which would provide lessons that have only started to be fully absorbed in the last few years (2007–2008).

Flooded with cash, Japanese firms moved away from boring investments in manufacturing to the more enticing option of speculative assets. The Japanese bought other firms, real estate, and just about any asset that an abundance of funds could purchase. The rule of thumb seemed to be to buy anything as long as it was selling for top dollar. In some distorted way, Japanese ventures overseas during this period seemed to operate on the basis of a "buy high, sell low" tradition.[26]

> Meanwhile, outside Japan, some American brokers estimated that Japanese companies had acquired about two-thirds of the value

---

[26] Foreign firms would continue to buy US assets long after the boom-crazed Japanese had folded up their tents. More recently, there has not been quite the public uproar over these purchases as there was some 20 years ago. Although in the post-Olympic period, China can be seen to occupy a similar position that Japan did 20 years earlier. According to a July 2008 CNN poll, 70 percent of Americans fear China's economic might. (China's rise however includes a military aspect that Japan's lacked.)

of real estate in Manhattan. Mitsui Real Estate had spent $610 million to buy the Exxon building in New York, even though the building was initially valued at just $375 million. Mitsubishi Real Estate bought Rockefeller Center in New York for $850 million, at its time a record deal in New York. Japanese companies were also spending lavishly on other trophies: Sony acquired Columbia Pictures for $3.4 billion. Matsushita paid $6.6 billion for MCA. Yasuda Fire and Marine paid $39 million for a single Van Gogh painting (Tett, 2003, pp. 49–50).

This extended buying spree simply imaged the parallel domestic economic changes at that time in the same way as Japanese FDI had during previous periods. The difference was that firms were now awash in cash and free from all constraints. They could pursue their objectives and search for easy profits unimpeded by Japanese or even foreign host governments.

The domestic economy was at this time encapsulated in the self-delusion of a "bubble economy" whose hallmark was, of course, extreme asset inflation. In reaction to the Plaza Accord which led to a doubling in value of the yen against the dollar within a 3-year period,[27] the Bank of Japan sought to ensure continuing economic growth by floating the economy on a sea of liquidity. Not only was the key discount rate sliced in half (from 5 percent to 2.5 percent) but funds were for all intents and purposes shoveled at the banks through the traditional

---

Investors from Dubai are behind the June purchase of the General Motors Building in New York City for $2.8 billion. The Abu Dhabi Investment council's sovereign wealth fund bought a 90% stake in the landmark Chrysler Building. General Electric's plastics division is gone, and its famed appliance unit could soon be in the hands of China's Haier or Korea's LG. Chrysler is hoping to hook up with India's Tata Motors or Italy's Fiat. Switzerland's Roche Holding is offering about $44 billion to acquire the 44% of the biotechnology outfit Genentech that it doesn't own. ... Unlike the 1980s panic about the Japanese buying up American landmarks like Rockefeller Center, the response of the financial establishment has been to welcome the latest rush of foreign investment (Israely and Boston, 2008, 49–50).

[27] This would have been a keen factor in promoting investment in developed economies whether it was the purchase of established firms or the scooping up of other assets. The exchange rate effect is rather simple. Assume a purchasing firm would be required to put up 10 percent of the sales price in order to arrange financing for the rest. The same number of yen that had doubled in value against the dollar would buy, as a down payment, the purchase of a much larger asset or more assets than had previously been possible.

mechanism of "window guidance."[28] Other than losing funds, the next worse thing a bank can do with its financial resources is to let them lie idle. Given that Japanese banks at that time earned most of their income from lending, finding borrowers became exigent. But suitable borrowers were not so readily available. Highly successful firms like Toyota could easily fund their expansion through retained earnings. Reliable corporate borrowers, even when pressed could not absorb the quantity of loans banks were eager to make. Therefore, less suitable and more risky targets soon caught their attention.

The key area here was the real estate market where loans seemed based on future asset inflation rather than the feasibility of any given project. Golf courses,[29] theme parks, and resorts sprang up as commercial and residential real estate prices predictably climbed. The more outrageous the project, the more banks seemed able to earn. A herd-like mentality ensured that no financial institution would hold back, given what appeared to be easy profits available to all who were willing to lend to each and every applicant. Given their domestic success, as asset prices did consistently climb, the natural next step was to extend this fool-proof formula overseas. Japanese banks had already branched out, operating in the financial capitals of the world. Overseas investment in the late 1980s became dominated by the financial and real estate sectors. Many in the financial world thought that given such easy access to what seemed to be bottomless funds, Japanese banks would roll over western competition much as their car manufacturers had done beginning with the 1970s.[30] The banks themselves seemed to buy this dubious analysis, seeing themselves as "Masters of the Universe" despite a clear lack of experience in the market into which they were now venturing. They

---

[28] This involved borrowing from the Bank of Japan according to a set formula. Though ostensibly optional, banks felt obliged to make full use of their assigned quota. For an interesting analysis of monetary policy and aims in this period, see Werner (2003, 2004).

[29] The enormous boom helped create a nation with 2,345 golf courses or one course for every 59 square miles.

[30] A widespread and subtle panic reflected a growing feeling that policy makers should be deeply concerned by this development.

> The second point I want to discuss is the obsession of the moment in financial services — namely, the success of the Japanese banks. ... what concerns

acted in the certainty that what had bought success domestically would also triumph in overseas ventures. Thus the domestic collapse of asset prices would have a parallel in the international market where Japanese investors had purchased commercial properties at inflated values.

> In most countries today, when banks lend money for corporate investment they pay close attention to the likely *cash flow* of a project. What banks want to know is whether a company will be able to pay the loan back out of a future stream of earnings. In Japan during the 1980s, however, the banks only ever cared about one thing: collateral, or the asset that a company could sell to repay a loan, if it ever faced a crunch. And the only collateral that mattered — at least in the eyes of bankers — was land. For by 1985, banks like LTCB [Long Term Credit Bank] had come to the conclusion that land was an almost fail-safe store of wealth; its value could only ever *increase* (Tett, 2003, p. 40).

With greater individual decision making at the firm level free of any clear constraints, overall Japanese FDI boomed.[31] Moreover, the initial trend toward overseas investment switching from developing to developed countries accelerated in this period between 1985 and 1993. Not only did the regional nature of the investment change, but so too

---

> policymakers here, however is the tremendous increase in Japanese bank penetration into the US banking market both in deposits and lending (to 10 percent of all US commercial and industrial loans) (Litan, 1990, p. 342).

[31] Though the economy grew more rapidly than comparable developed counterparts in the late 1980s, the amount of FDI grew even more rapidly with overseas investment not only complementing domestic activity but if anything magnifying the frenzy.

> In the first half of the 1980s, overseas investment increased briskly, in part to avoid automotive trade frictions with North America and Europe, to reach 412.2 billion by 1985 (around 1 percent of GDP). Even more rapid growth was experienced in the second half of the decade, likely reflecting booming economies at home and abroad and yen appreciation in the latter part of the decade; during the period 1986–89, nominal FDI outflows in dollars exceeded the cumulative overseas investment from all previous postwar years combined. By the late 1980s, Japan's FDI outflow had become the largest in the world, and a peak of $67.5 billion was reached in 1989 (around 2.5 percent of GDP) (Bayoumi and Lipworth, 1997, pp. 5–7).

This can best be seen in its cumulative effect when in a mere decade Japan had gone from playing a rather insignificant role in this area to being a force to be reckoned with and in the late

did the type.[32] Starting with the mid-1980s such investment was largely generated by the tertiary sector.

> Indeed, during the 1980s, the share of FDI outflows received by industrial countries rose to absorb over three fourths of the total, with the United States alone receiving close to one half, whereas the share received by developing countries (including Asia) declined from one half to around one quarter. Coincident with such a development was the spectacular growth in overseas investment in the tertiary sectors, including finance, insurance, transport and real estate, while the share of FDI in manufacturing and mining declined sharply (Bayoumi and Lipworth, 1997, p. 7).

To some degree, this transition period was something of an aberration since with the collapse of asset inflation domestically, FDI would also rapidly deflate. Moreover, it would shift back to more traditional regions, namely developing countries and in particular Asia, as well as toward more manufacturing opportunities. But this simply mirrored the constraints of a now floundering economy where firms looked toward a booming Asian region to pull them out of the mire left over from their "bubble" experience. What had shifted distinctly, however, was that Japanese firms in the overseas arena were capable of acting

---

eighties at least, feared.

> ... between 1982 and 1993, outbound Japanese FDI rose from 2.5 percent to 3 percent of domestic investment, translating into a significant net movement in productive capacity abroad. By 1993, the stock of outward Japanese FDI stood at $422.5 billion (Bayoumi and Lipworth, 1997, p. 5).

[32] The original motivation behind FDI provided the means for firms to ensure the reliability of raw materials and for those firms operating in declining industries to shift to more competitive overseas locations. With explicit trade barriers rising, protecting export markets also became a distinct and even leading component of such investment. During an era of seemingly unlimited funds, speculation would overwhelm both domestic and foreign investment activity. Fields such as real estate, insurance, and banking necessarily boomed.

> During the 1980s, the tertiary sectors, which during the 1970s had accounted for less than half of the total FDI outflow, gained a combined share of more than 70 percent. At the same time, the share received by the manufacturing sector declined to below one-fourth of total FDI from around one-third, and the share to primary products (mostly accounted for by mining), fell from around 10 percent of the total to about 2 percent (Bayoumi and Lipworth, 1997, p. 7, footnote 8).

much like firms from other developed countries. After slowly recovering and recouping from this era, FDI in the next century would be characterized by similar individual decision making that defined this boom period. However, with the lessons absorbed from previous mistakes, FDI would be determined much more carefully and conservatively. Issues of risk were once again part of the analysis.

> The post-bubble period has witnessed a partial reversal of the trends exhibited in the 1980s in both the regional and sectoral composition of Japanese FDI outflows. Regionally, the share of FDI to developing countries has risen to the early 1980s level, and the share received by Asia within this total has increased substantially, while FDI flows to industrial countries have declined, particularly that to the United States (Bayoumi and Lipworth, 1997, p. 7).

12.3 Not so Different After All: Recent Trends in Overseas Investment

> ...among US multinationals with affiliates in Canada, only 12 percent are of the purely horizontal type (i.e., they have negligible intrafirm flows of intermediate inputs) and only 19 percent are of the purely vertical type (i.e., they have negligible intrafirm flows of intermediate inputs in one direction only). The remaining 69 percent of the firms pursue more complex integration strategies (Helpman, 2006, p. 599).

The changes wrought in the domestic economy by the rather abrupt end to the good times fostered by asset inflation were certain to be reflected in overseas strategies by Japanese corporations. At home, the touchstone was consolidation as firms sought to resolve the excess capacity and debt-ridden balance sheets that were the natural hangover of the previous period. In matters of FDI it was largely back to the future for the remainder of the 1990s. Investment in developed countries slowed or even stagnated with the focus of what were now a smaller pool of funds turned toward the lesser developed countries of Asia and particularly toward China. These opportunities turned mostly on characteristically lower wages and the opportunity to sell in overseas markets. There was a clear shift away from the service sector and back toward manufacturing. These were of course some of the drivers of Japan's initial forays abroad. However this time, more emphasis was placed on selling back into the Japanese market. The impetus for this shift lay with individual Japanese firms rather than a collaborative effort between an assortment of firms and government agencies. This shift had much less to do with ensuring anything like a domestic low-risk middle-class economy and much more with the individual survival and advancement of the Japanese firms involved.[33] As expected, individual firms varied noticeably in the strategies adopted.[34] However, the overwhelming causes of this shift was an increasing need to cut costs in a sluggish economy and the booming growth of Asia, especially China, compared to the developed world. Like other firms, Japanese corporations shifted their attention to where opportunities lay.

> After 1995, the growth in the number of subsidiaries in DCs became nearly flat, and that more investments were then directed towards LDCs is due in part to the growth of interest in China. In our sample, there were 2443 subsidiaries in China as of the end of 1999, accounting for 21.7% of FDI in LDCs and 12.6% of the whole. This changing pattern in the choice of JFDI location corresponds closely with the changes in both the relative GDP growth in LDCs and DCs and the economic climate in Japan in this period (Makino, Beamish and Zhao, 2004, p. 379).

---

[33] The low-risk, middle-class society would be another casualty of the "bubble economy" as the Japanese labor force shifted to include many more part-time and temporary workers. This objective is today largely seen as dead, with political concern focused on the growing income disparity within the Japanese society. See Yamada (2006) for a summary of the problem as well as Honda (2005) for some implications of the rise of young temporary workers.

> The average number of non-permanent workers rose to 17.3 million by March 2007, government data show. That was 19 percent higher than five years earlier and more than 50 percent higher than a decade ago. … For decades, a majority of Japanese considered themselves middle class. As employment conditions change, economic inequalities are widening, although the gap between rich and poor is still much narrower than in the United States (Kubota, 2008, p. 1).

[34] The diversity of approaches which grew during the 1980s became particularly pronounced during this post-bubble period.

> Canon had among the highest R&D rates of all firms, and was the lowest of all major consumer electronic goods firms in terms of relative number of subsidiaries in LDCs versus DCs. In contrast, Hitachi had half of its subsidiaries in LDCs, rather than DCs (Makino, Beamish and Zhao, 2004, pp. 383–384).

One way to get some feel for the direction in which Japanese FDI is heading in this more independent era is to contrast the Japanese experience in China with that of the US. Since both have viewed this booming economy as a potential opportunity not to be ignored, it may prove instructive to note how the approaches have differed and whether such differences are fundamental or simply a product of specific constraints. It is quite easy to become misled by the apparent dissimilarities between the two. In broad terms, the approaches of each country's multinational corporations seemed driven by different necessities.

> In the 1970s, the FDI by Japanese MNEs focused predominantly on adjacent countries within their economic and strategic sphere of influence. Such FDI was mainly of a "natural resource seeking" and "vertically oriented efficiency seeking" kind. By contrast, most of the US FDI was concentrated in Canada and Europe, and was characterized as "market seeking" or "horizontally oriented efficiency seeking". These difference can be accounted for by the comparative economic institutional advantages and market opportunities of both investing and host countries. However, over the last 20 years, the Japanese MNE activity has changed its industrial and geographical profiles to place more emphasis on the European and North American markets as destinations for FDIs in the context of 'market' and 'horizontal efficiency'. By contrast, the US FDI has placed more emphasis on Asian markets as a "vertical efficiency" seeking. As a result, the regional distribution of both countries' FDI flows has been reversed in recent decades (Dunning, Kim and Lee, 2007, p. 29).

It is much simpler to say that in the 1970s the two countries and the firms based within them were operating at different developmental stages. The US had not, as of yet, been faced with the competitive onslaught from abroad that they were about to face. American multinationals sought instead to achieve economies of scale and scope by snatching opportunities in foreign markets. Resource-poor Japan was more concerned with ensuring the flow of natural resources and shifting out of lower to higher value added manufacturing as their domestic standard of living persistently rose. As Japanese multinationals became more competitive, they sought to spread subsidiary operations to developed countries while in reaction American multinationals resorted to lower wage investment opportunities in Asia to meet this competitive threat. However, the story described by Dunning, Kim and Lee (2007) extends only until 1996. Thus it largely limits the aftermath of two major events for both countries; the end of the "bubble economy" for Japan and the importance of the North American Free Trade Agreement for the US. When we in fact turn to the Chinese case we would expect to see more complex arrangements and motivations than those given previously. We would also expect that all multinationals in China share a common behavior of rooting out independently and aggressively any opportunity for reasonable gain.

Chinese exports have to a large extent been driven by overseas investment with such FDI defining the shift into goods that are at the value added, high-tech end of the spectrum. This is the type of technology transfer that often characterizes multinational investment. Without such FDI it could be expected that developing countries might under a given set of circumstances be condemned to pursue a comparative advantage limited to labor intensive goods.

> In 2004, they exported $339 billion, about 60% of China's exports. ... In the high-tech products category, foreign invested firms performed an even more important role. They produced about 88% of China's high-tech exports. ... Therefore, FDI not only boosted China's export growth, but also accelerated the transition of its exports from low value-added to high value-added products (Xing, 2007, p. 686).

At first glance, there would seem to be significant differences between the US and the Japanese approach to investing in China. Accumulated stocks of such investment by the US was only approximately half that of the Japanese. As Tables 12.1 and 12.2 illustrate, the differences in such sectors as transportation equipment and electrical goods are particularly striking (see Tables 12.1 and 12.2).

But it is not simply a matter of size. Japanese investors used China basically as an export base as opposed to the US strategy of focusing on the Chinese domestic market. In some sectors of the market, Japanese multinationals shipped almost all of their output back to their home base (see Fig. 12.5). The impetus for this approach was the need to remain competitive in a domestic market that had seen practically no wage growth over a long decade of sluggish economic activity and

Table 12.1 Cumulative Japanese FDI in China (in $US million)

Sectors	1984	1992	2004
Food	20.9	139.6	1,167.2
Textile	2.6	283.5	2,049.2
Chemical	14.0	108.4	1,731.6
Metal	3.0	103.2	1,900.2
Machinery	2.1	229.9	2,713.7
Electrical	2.7	657.4	5,316.9
Transport	1.2	55.6	4,137.3

Table 12.2 Cumulative US FDI in China (in $US million)

Sectors	1989	1992	2004
Food	10	69	593
Chemical	27	93	1,643
Metal	2	−3	149
Machinery	21	14	455
Electrical	10	13	493
Transport	NA	NA	1,832

Source: Xing, 2007, pp. 688, 690.

continued to face weak consumer demand. This pattern remained even after the resurgence in the Japanese economy which has now (starting in 2008) come to an end.

> Using China as an export platform is one of the major motivations that Japanese multinational enterprises have to invest in China. By investing in China, Japanese MNEs are able to strengthen their global competitiveness by combining China's low production costs together with their superior technology, brand recognition, and global distribution networks. According to a JETRO study (2003), 61.6% of Japanese firms operating in China exported at least 70% of their products. In 2001, Japanese affiliated manufacturers in China as a whole sold 65% of their products in overseas markets ... Another unique practice of Japanese affiliated manufacturers is their extensive involvement in "reverse imports," exporting their products back to Japan. ... on average, more than 50% of exports headed for Japan (Xing, 2007, p. 688).

Since the days of the 19th century, China has held a distinct fascination for American traders. Population numbers grabbed their

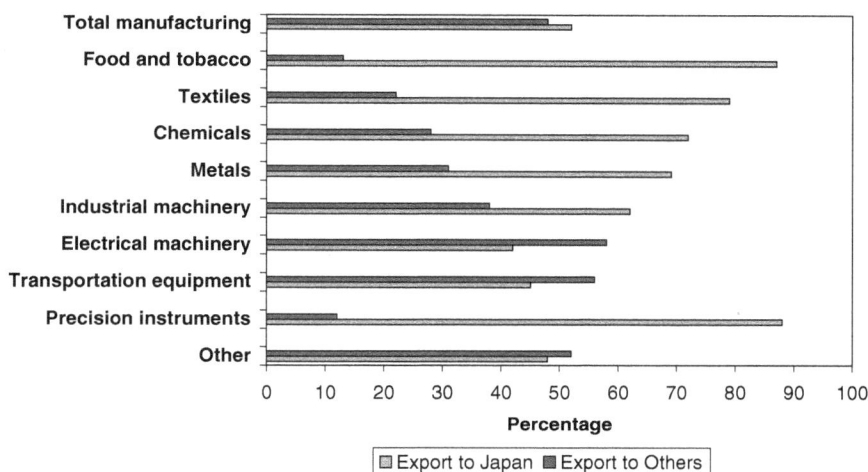

Source: Xing, 2007, p. 689

Fig. 12.5   Export destinations of Japanese affiliates in China 2003.

imagination. Selling just one bar of soap to each individual in China would make some wily entrepreneur's fortune. Much the same mindset seems to have propelled more recent US direct investment there.

> Moreover, unlike Japanese FDI, the US FDI is primarily domestic market oriented, and simply functions as a means of accessing the Chinese market rather than using it as an export platform. According to the Government Accountability Office, in 2003 the US affiliates in China sold about 75% of their products in China, and 25% in overseas markets. Of the total exports, only 7% were exported back to the US (Xing, 2007, p. 690).

What appears to be a defining difference between the two countries tends to dissipate when looked at from a wider lens. As previously explained, the shift by Japanese multinationals into the US in the 1970s and 1980s was largely an attempt to sustain and enlarge a key export market. The US did not serve as an export platform to any significant extent but instead investment was aimed at serving the North American market. Similarly, if US overseas investment were to be restricted to the Western Hemisphere it would tend to resemble that between Japan and China (see Figs. 12.6 and 12.7). The determining factor is geographic rather than any characteristic inherent in the nature of the individual corporate decision makers. Investment in one's backyard looks different from that done on the other side of the world. This pattern should become even more reinforced when and if transport costs rise.

> The study, published in May [2008] by the Canadian investment bank CIBC World markets, calculates that the recent surge in shipping costs is on average the equivalent of a 9 percent tariff on trade. "The cost of moving goods, not the cost of tariffs, is the largest barrier to global trade today," the report concluded, and as a result

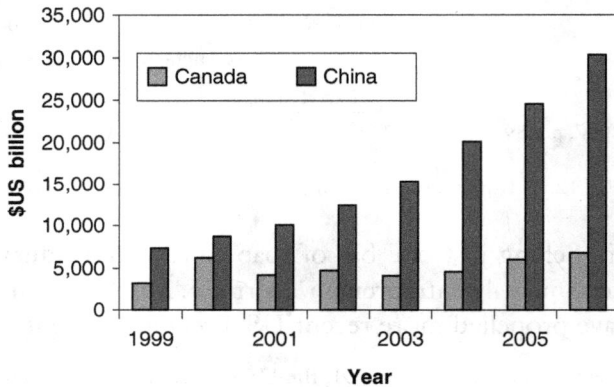

Fig. 12.6   Japan FDI positioning Canada and China.

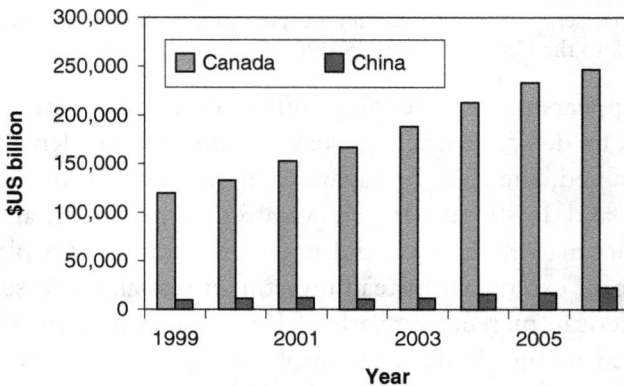

Fig. 12.7   US FDI positioning Canada and China.

"has effectively offset all the trade liberalization efforts of the last three decades" (Rohter, 2008, p. 2).

12.4 Convergence: Looking Exactly Unlike Each Other

Outward FDI is still not very large relative to the Japanese economy despite the rapid growth since the mid-1980s, so there is still scope for significant increases before it reaches the levels of other OECD countries. The outsourcing and relocation of production will particularly affect labor-intensive manufacturing operations, not least because of demographic factors. On the domestic scene, this will facilitate the necessary restructuring of the Japanese economy towards more advanced activities with higher value added (Blomström, Konan and Lipsey, 2000, p. 23) (see Figs. 12.8 and 12.9).

To estimate the future direction of Japanese FDI we clearly need to have some idea of future changes in the multinationals that make such decisions and the objectives they will pursue.[35] What seems clear is

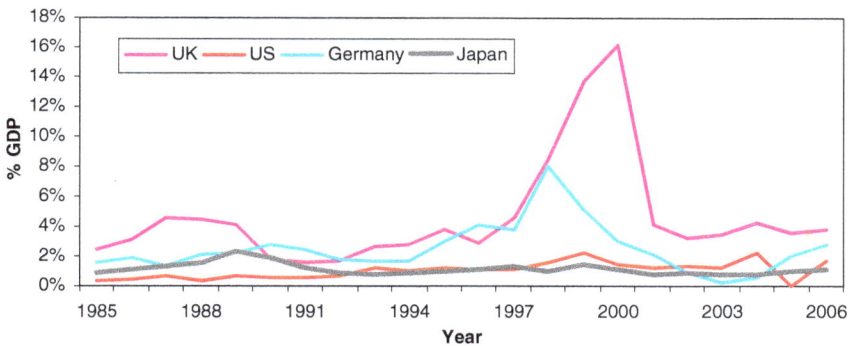

Source: OECD

Fig. 12.8   FDI as % GDP selecting countries.

---

[35] Seemingly, Japanese firms have discovered the limited scope for expanded investment in the domestic economy due to low returns. As a result, business saving has been increasing while comparable household saving is approaching the low figures characteristic of Anglo-American economies (see Fig. 12.11). Instead, cash flow has been employed to whittle down corporate debt (see Fig. 12.12).

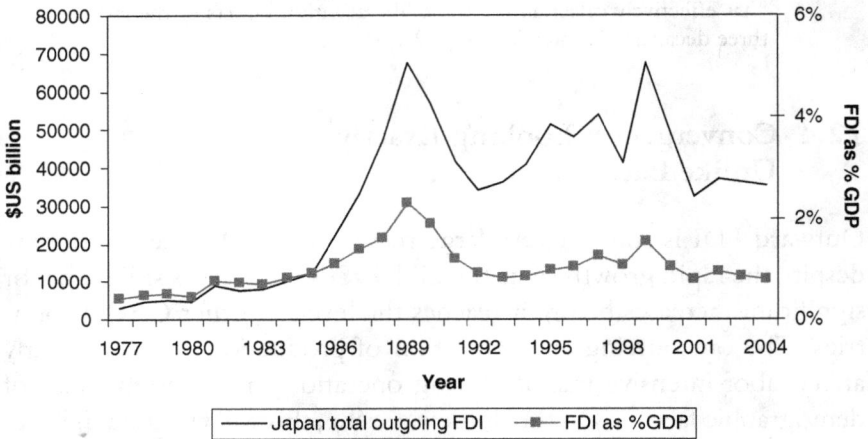

Source: UNCTAD; IMF

Fig. 12.9   Japan FDI in relation to GDP.

that each firm will consult its own particular interests and act ever more aggressively in what is an increasingly competitive global market. To what degree Japanese firms have actually changed in the last decade is still a matter of debate.

However, it is clear that these firms have more foreign ownership than ever before and fewer corporate cross-holdings.[36] Together, this is reflected in what seems to be a shift toward seeking higher profits domestically as well as in foreign subsidiaries.[37] Japanese firms have also shifted away from an inclination to place the domestic market first. Instead, they are moving toward a strategy of seizing opportunities wherever and wherever they might occur. Many corporate managers

---

[36]The change is striking. As of 1992, with the collapse of asset inflation, cross share holdings by Japanese corporations accounted for 42 percent of stock while foreign holdings consisted of only 6 percent of the total outstanding shares. Twelve years later in 2004 as the Japanese economy was crawling out of its decade of slow growth, cross share holdings were down to only 24 percent, while foreign owned shares now amounted to 22 percent. As Japanese corporations disentangled from the post-war *keiretsu* style web, foreign investors were largely scooping up the shares Japanese firms were shedding.

[37]The long history of over investment and falling returns by Japanese companies is well documented but there are now some grounds to think that this trend is turning around. When it does, return on Japanese FDI should accordingly rise as well.

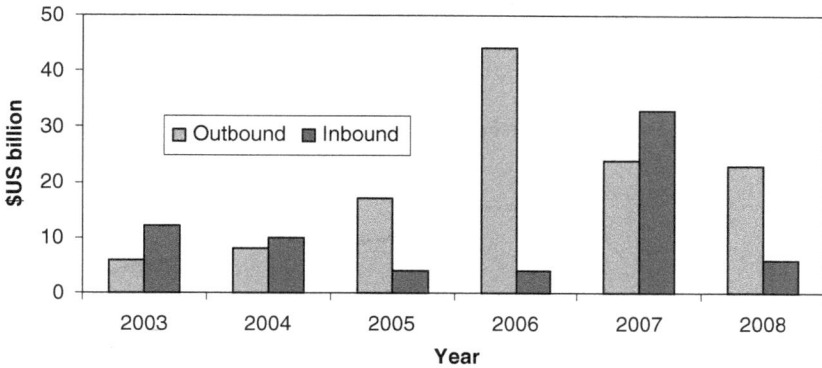

Source: Thomson Reuters data

Fig. 12.10   Japan M&A activity — cross border flows (2008 figures are for the year up to July).

now realize that given the constraints of the domestic market, growth needs to be led externally, specifically through mergers and acquisitions overseas (see Fig. 12.10).[38]

> Japanese companies are turning increasingly to overseas acquisitions to drive growth, buy technology and build market share, spurred by a stagnant domestic economy, shrinking population and largely unburdened by subprime credit damage. ... Already this year, outbound acquisitions from Japan total $24 billion according to Thompson Reuters data, nearly matching the haul for all of 2007 (Munroe and Emoto, 2008, p. 1).

> Looking at foreign direct investment, for example, US data show American companies' returns were the same in Japan as in the rest of the world. Using Japanese FDI data, Japanese returns abroad are lower than foreign returns in Japan. Looking at Japanese financial data from the MOF for large manufacturing companies, their returns were quite similar to the returns on Japan's foreign investments. ... The question that I had was why Japanese companies continued to invest at such a prodigious rate when returns kept falling lower and lower. The answer I think lies in corporate governance and bank-centered finance, where profits were not the objective of businesses or their lenders. That is all now changing and we should expect returns on investment to start rising. ... I have a chapter in my book *The Arc of Japan's Economic Development* (Routledge, at better book stores everywhere) devoted to this issue (Alexander, 2008, p. 1).

[38] Putting this in perspective, Japan is once again a major overseas investor (see Fig. 12.13).

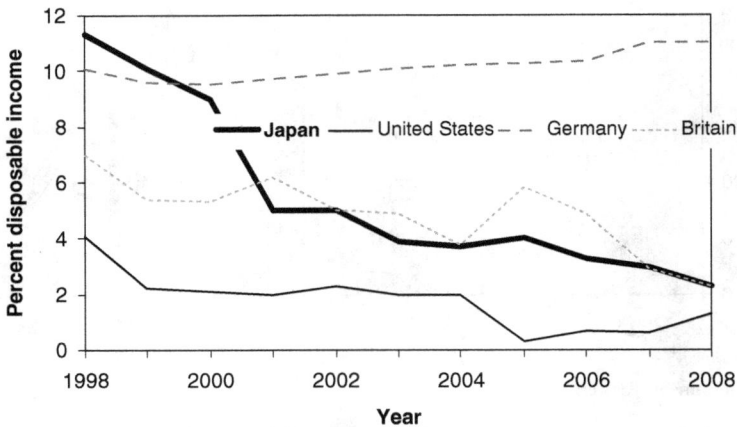

Fig. 12.11   Household savings in four countries.

One clear direction is in seeking out more mergers and acquisitions abroad. Poor judgment followed by a collapsing economy made Japanese corporations and financial institutions[39] extremely shy of repeating the mistakes made during their "cowboy" era. The moves now are more conservative and measured but this seems clearly the direction an increasing number of Japanese multinationals are taking. These include moves by pharmaceutical companies such as Takeda, Eisai, and Daiichi Sankyo; Kirin Beer (acquiring the Australian industry leader in dairy (Dairy Farmers and National Foods) and beverages (Lion Nathan)); and precision instrument maker Olympus (buying a British medical equipment business) (Iinuma, 2008, p. 8).

> Having come back from the brink so recently themselves, the Japanese bankers may well believe that they know how to spot a bargain. SMFG is attracted to Barclays, believing that it has reliable revenue from its British retail operations (and the Japanese bank hopes the two can co-operate in new areas, such as wealth-management in Asia). MUFJ has yet to make a big move, though

---

[39] Cashed up Japanese financial institutions are finding opportunities by grabbing bargain assets. In the aftermath of Lehman Brothers collapse, Nomura snatched the failed bank's Australian holdings. At the same time, Mitsubishi UFJ agreed to take a 21 percent share in Morgan Stanley for some $9 billion, Japan's number two bank, Sumitomo Mitsui was rumored to be interested in investing several hundred billion yen in Goldman Sachs.

Cash hoarding

Debt levels fall

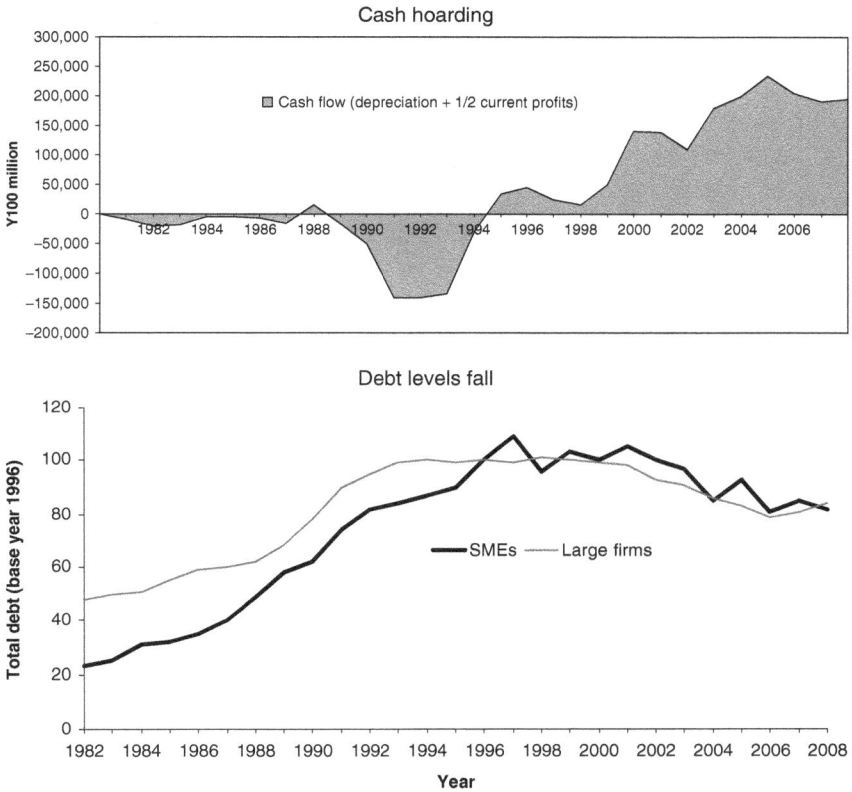

Source: Ministry of finance

Fig. 12.12   Business savings and debt reduction.

it is thought to be considering an acquisition. Of course the deals themselves, at around $1 billion apiece, are hardly more than a toe in the water. But it is just that conservatism that has recently worked to Japan's banks' advantage (*Economist*, 2008, p. 1).

There will always be minor differences between Japanese firms and Anglo-American ones, but there also will be striking difference between firms operating within the same market sector. Japanese firms may simply be more conservative and slower to move due in part to corporate structure and practices. American firms for instance seem more willing to divest themselves of divisions and businesses than their Japanese counterparts. The cause is often attributed to a greater reluctance

Inward and Outward Foreign Direct Investment
2008 (Calender Year)

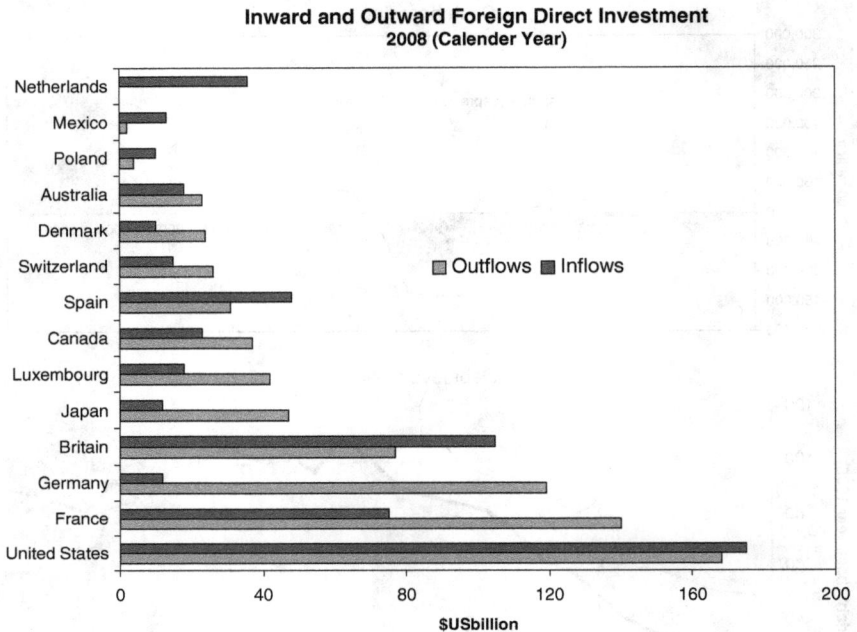

Source: OECD

Fig. 12.13   Foreign direct investment (first half of 2008).

to focus more exclusively on a limited number of promising sectors. Yet there may be some sense to this alternative strategy. Japanese firms are more concerned with continuing to earn quasi-rents from an established roster of brand name products by maintaining their existing good reputations among Japanese consumers. As a consequence, these corporations are eager to offshore the lower-tech aspects of production in order to remain price competitive while retaining the higher end of technological processes.

> And yet, despite all this, in April–June, Toshiba suffered a net loss of ¥11.6 billion ($107 million), its first quarterly loss in three years, largely because of failing semiconductor operations. Although 75% of the loss came from falling markets for chips for video games, the company says it will not cut back on its investment plans for those kinds of chips. It says it doesn't want to repeat its "error" of letting the Koreans out-invest it in DRAM chips. It remains to be seen

whether this will prove to be wisely farsighted or foolishly stubborn
(Iinuma, 2008, p. 8).

Japanese firms have changed not from any specific desire to imitate western strategies, but rather the constraints and incentives under which they operate have evolved over time. Their more active role in seeking out and creating individual opportunities is nothing remarkable. Rather, the environment in which they now operate has greatly altered, making such actions more imperative. Though Japanese firms will continue to be somewhat distinct in their overseas investment strategies and different from each other as well, in the realm of foreign direct investment it is the similarities rather than the differences that should most inform our analysis.

Appendix: Data Summary

Figure 12.1: GDP is calculated by expenditure approach, measured in national currency (millions). FDI figures are aggregated figures by industry, in submitted currency. Source: OECD.

Figure 12.2: Regional shares of Japanese foreign direct investment calculated as percentages of total sampled. Data based on Reports and Notifications, Gross. Disinvestment not included. Series discontinued 2004, data for 2005 and 2006 are based on international investment position, net. "Other LDC" is aggregate of Africa, Middle East, and non-Australasian Oceania. "Asia" includes ASEAN, East Asia, and Indian Sub-Continent. "Europe" is aggregate of data for Western and Eastern Europe. Source: JETRO for all data.

Figure 12.3: Industry shares of Japanese foreign direct investment calculated as percentages of total sampled. Services, trade, and other categories are as defined by source. Data based on Reports and Notifications, Gross. Disinvestment not included. Series discontinued 2004, data for 2005 and 2006 are based on international investment position, net. Source: JETRO for all data.

Figure 12.4: FDI data are for all outward flows, in $US at current prices (million). Source: UNCTAD.

Figure 12.6: FDI data are for position in host economy in $US current prices and market values. Source: OECD.

Figure 12.7: FDI data are for position in host economy in $US current prices and market values. Source: OECD.

Figure 12.8: FDI data are in submitted currency. Data for GDP by expenditure approach, in national currency at current prices (millions). Source: OECD.

Figure 12.9: FDI data for outward flows are in $US current prices in millions. Source UNCTAD. Data for GDP by expenditure approach are in $US current prices in millions. Source: International Financial Statistics (International Monetary Fund).

Figure 12.10: Figures for Merger and Acquisition activity are in $US billion at current prices. Figures for calendar year 2008 are partial to July 2008 only. Source: Thomson Reuters.

Figure 12.11: Figures include estimates for 2008. Source: OECD.

Figure 12.12: Figures for cash flow are in terms of 100 million yen at current prices. Debt levels are a comparative measure using 1996 as the suitable index year. Source for all figures: Ministry of Finance.

Figure 12.13: Figures compare national inflows and outflows for the first half of 2008. Source: OECD.

References

Alexander A. (2008) Robots: Over investment. *NBR Japan Forum.* May 28, 2008, japanforum@lists.nbr.org.

Aramaki K. (2006) Sequencing of capital account liberalization — Japan's Experiences and their implications for China. *East Asian Bureau of Economic Research: Finance Working Papers,* 669, 1–56.

Bailey D. (2003) Explaining Japan's kudoka: A case of government and strategic failure? *Asia Pacific Business Review,* 10(1), 1–20.

Bayoumi T, Lipworth G. (1997) Japanese foreign direct investment and regional trade. *IMF Working Paper.* WP/97/103, 1–35.

Befu H. (2001) *Hegemony of Homogeneity.* Trans Pacific Press, Melbourne.

Blomström M, Konan D, Lipsey R. (2000) FDI in the restructuring of the Japanese economy, *NBER Working Paper Series.* Working Paper 7693, 1–32.

Cowling K, Tomlinson PR. (2001) The problem of regional 'Hollowing Out' in Japan: Lessons for regional industrial policy. *Warwick Economic Research Papers,* 625, 1–26.

Delanghe H. (2005) Postwar Japanese cotton textile investment in Brazil, 1955–1980. *Enterprise and* Society, 6(1), 76–97.

Dower JW. (1999) *Embracing Defeat.* Norton, New York.

Drake TA, Caves RE. (1992) Changing determinants of Japanese foreign investment in the United States. *Journal of the Japanese and International Economies*, 6, 228–246.

Dunning JH, Kim ZK, Lee C-I. (2007) Restructuring the regional distribution of FDI: The case of Japanese and US FDI. *Japan and the World Economy*, 19, 26–47.

The Economist (2008) On the prowl again. *The Economist.com*, June 26, 1, http://www.economist.com/finance/PrinterFriendly.cfm?story_id=11637791, August 15, 2008.

Fallows J. (1989) Containing Japan. *The Atlantic Monthly*, May, 1–22.

Froot KA. (1991) Japanese foreign direct investment. *NBER Working Papers Series.* Working Paper No. 3737, 1–30.

Helpman E. (2006) Trade, FDI, and the organization of firms. *Journal of Economic Literature*, 44(September), 589–630.

Honda Y. (2005) Freeters: Young atypical workers in Japan. *Japan Labor Review*, 2(3), 5–25.

Iinuma Y. (2008) Disenchantment. *The Oriental Economist*, 76(8), 7–8.

Israely J, Boston W. (2008) The Great American Yard Sale. *Time Magazine*, August 25, 49–51.

Kojima K. (1973) A macroeconomic approach to foreign direct investment. *Hitotsubashi Journal of Economics*, 14(1), 1–20.

Kubota Y. (2008) Old Marxist novel revived by Japan's economic anxiety. *International Herald Tribune*. August 12, 2008, 1–2, http://www.iht.com/bin/ printfriendly.php?id=15204522, August 19, 2008.

Litan R. (1990) Commentary: U.S. Banking in an increasingly integrated and competitive world economy. *Journal of Financial Services Research*, 4(4), 341–344.

Makino S, Beamish PW, Zhao NB. (2004) The characteristics and performance of Japanese FDI in less developed and developed countries. *Journal of World Business*, 39, 377–392.

Munroe T, Emoto E. (2008) Shrinking market sends Japan Inc buying abroad. *Reuters*, July 3, 1–3, http://www.reuters.com/article/JapanInvestment08/ idUSHKG35293220080703?pageNumber=2, July 31, 2008.

Murakami Y. (1982) The age of new middle mass politics: The case of Japan. *Journal of Japanese Studies*, 8(1), 29–73.

Noguchi Y. (1998) The 1940 System: Japan under the wartime economy. *The American Economic Review — Papers and Proceedings*, 88(2), 404–407.

O'Brien PA. (1992) Industry structure as a competitive advantage: The History of Japan's post-war steel industry. *Business History Review*, 34(January), 128–159.

Ozawa T. (1979) International investment and industrial structure: New theoretical implications from the Japanese experience. *Oxford Economic Papers*, 31(1), 72–92.

Rohter L. (2008) Shipping Costs Start to "Crimp Globalization." *The New York Times*, August 3, 1–4, http://www.nytimes.com/2008/08/03/business/ worldbusiness, August 4, 2008.

Sheard P. (1989) The Japanese general trading company as an aspect of interfirm risk-sharing. *Journal of the Japanese and International Economies*, 3(3), 308–322.

Smith MC. (2005) *Tokyo Station*. Macmillan, London.

Tett G. (2003) *Saving the Sun*. HarperCollins, New York.

Werner RA. (2003) *Princes of The Yen*. Sharpe ME, Armonk, New York.

Werner RA. (2004) *The New Paradigm in Macroeconomics — Solving the Riddle of Japanese Macroeconomic Performance*. Palgrave Macmillan, Houndmills, Basingstoke.

Wilkens M. (1982) American–Japanese Direct Foreign Investment Relationships, 1930–1952. *Business History Review*, 56(4), 497–518.

Xing Y. (2007) Foreign direct investment and china's bilateral intra-industry trade with Japan and the US. *Journal of Asian Economics*, 18(4), 685–700.

Yamada M. (2006) In Search of a New Kind of Equality. *Japan Echo*, 33(6), 38–43.

Yoshino MY. (1974) The Multinational Spread of Japanese Manufacturing Investment since World War II. *Business History Review*, 48(3), 357–381.

Index

Brazilian market, 453
Bridge between democratic and
    communist Asia, 110
Bureaucracy, 4, 17, 36, 213, 304,
    375, 393, 402, 446
Bureaucratic sectionalism, 375
Car industry, 160, 411, 449
Central Government Reform Law of
    June 1998, 354
Chequebook diplomacy, 397
Chinese market, 66, 81, 426, 430,
    475
City banks, 418, 428, 455
Closed country, 385
Cold War alliance with US, 47
Comprehensive Development
    Framework, 329
Comprehensive National Security
    Ministerial Council, 146
Comprehensive Policy Assistance
    Survey, 340
Comprehensive security, 142, 146,
    147, 149, 152, 156–158,
    162, 165, 167–172, 360
Constitution, 3, 4, 16, 37, 70, 71,
    157, 166, 187, 196, 197,
    200, 202, 209, 211, 244,
    392, 397
Constitutional limits, 16, 142
Constraints, 8, 12, 13, 15–20, 25,
    26, 28–30, 33, 35, 36, 67,
    69, 70, 84, 86, 87, 91,
    96–98, 108, 134, 137, 142,
    143, 153, 166, 170, 193,
    194, 201, 206, 232, 239,
    248, 249, 265, 301, 302,
    322, 334, 349, 356, 368,
    370–376, 378, 381–383,
    397, 414, 443–445, 447,
    449, 450, 452, 454, 458,
    461, 466, 468, 469, 472,
    479, 483
Consumer electronics, 409, 455, 457
Convoy system, 306, 426
Corporate loyalty, 412
Dai-ichi Kangyo, 426

Defense Agency, 34, 35, 150, 151,
    202, 214, 220, 227, 235,
    237, 238
Democratic Socialist Party, 195
Deshima, 385
Diet, 72, 73, 77, 78, 90, 98, 125,
    126, 128, 195, 196, 204,
    207, 208, 333, 354, 397,
    400, 402, 410, 434, 436
Diplomacy, 1, 2, 47, 60, 91, 116,
    171, 185, 251, 285, 367
Diplomatic Bluebook, 40, 42, 127,
    146, 154, 155, 157, 206,
    278, 315, 373
Dirty industries, 456
Division of roles, 125
Domestic constraints, 16, 29, 170,
    206, 374
Domestic political stability, 91
Early Voluntary Sectoral
    Liberalization (EVSL), 313
East Asia Greater Co-Prosperity
    Sphere, 22
Economic bubble, 397
Economic miracle, 4, 9, 291
Economic strength, 7, 9, 10, 13, 15,
    17, 21, 23, 24, 26, 104, 122,
    125, 126, 129, 130, 134,
    145, 146, 155, 170, 171,
    181, 191, 202, 206, 265,
    292, 353
Edo, 386, 387
First oil shock, 69, 396, 414, 450,
    460
Fiscal Investment and Loan Program
    (FILP), 333, 334
Five principles, 196, 227, 235, 243
Fixed exchange rate, 130
Foreign economic policy, 4, 10, 14,
    18, 178
Foreign policy, 1, 4, 8, 9, 11–14,
    17–19, 26, 29, 30, 36, 39,
    40, 45, 46, 65, 71, 90, 96,
    105, 131, 147, 154, 164,
    185, 188, 192, 207, 211,
    219, 221, 281, 286, 302,